USDA

United States Department of Agriculture

I0096369

Tropical Nursery Manual

A Guide to Starting and Operating a Nursery for Native and Traditional Plants

Kim M. Wilkinson • Thomas D. Landis • Diane L. Haase
Brian F. Daley • R. Kasten Dumroese

EDITORS

Forest
Service

Agriculture
Handbook 732

April
2014

An Orchard Innovations Reprint Edition
November 2020
Printed in the United States of America

ISBN: 978-1-951682-50-7

Tropical Nursery Manual

A Guide to Starting and Operating a Nursery for Native and Traditional Plants

U.S. Department of Agriculture, Forest Service

Agriculture Handbook 732
April 2014

Edited by

Kim M. Wilkinson

Thomas D. Landis

Diane L. Haase

Brian F. Daley

R. Kasten Dumroese

The use of trade or firm names in this publication is for reader information and does not imply endorsement by the U.S. Department of Agriculture, Forest Service of any product or service.

Pesticides used improperly can be injurious to humans, animals, and plants. Follow the directions and heed all precautions on the labels. Store pesticides in original containers under lock and key—out of the reach of children and animals—and away from food and feed. Apply pesticides so that they do not endanger humans, livestock, crops, beneficial insects, fish, and wildlife. Do not apply pesticides when there is danger of drift, when honey bees or other pollinating insects are visiting plants, or in ways that may contaminate water or leave illegal residues. Avoid prolonged inhalation of pesticide sprays or dusts; wear protective clothing and equipment if specified on the container. If your hands become contaminated with a pesticide, do not eat or drink until you have washed. In case a pesticide is swallowed or gets in the eyes, follow the first-aid treatment given on the label, and get prompt medical attention. If a pesticide is spilled on your skin or clothing, remove clothing immediately and wash skin thoroughly. Do not clean spray equipment or dump excess spray material near ponds, streams, or wells. Because it is difficult to remove all traces of herbicides from equipment, do not use the same equipment for insecticides or fungicides that you use for herbicides. Dispose of empty pesticide containers promptly. Have them buried at a sanitary landfill dump, or crush and bury them in a level, isolated place.

NOTE: Some States have restrictions on the use of certain pesticides. Check your State and local regulations. Also, because registrations of pesticides are under constant review by the Federal Environmental Protection Agency, consult your county agricultural agent or State extension specialist to be sure the intended use is still registered.

Nomenclature for scientific names follows the U.S. Department of Agriculture, Natural Resources Conservation Service PLANTS (Plant List of Accepted Nomenclature, Taxonomy, and Symbols) database (2008). http://plants.usda.gov.

CONTENTS

CONTENTS (continued)

Developing Your Nursery

5. Propagation Environments 89
Douglass F. Jacobs, Thomas D. Landis, Tara Luna, and Diane L. Haase

6. Growing Media 101
Thomas D. Landis, Douglass F. Jacobs, Kim M. Wilkinson, and Tara Luna

7. Containers 123
Thomas D. Landis, Tara Luna, and R. Kasten Dumroese

CONTENTS (continued)

Plant Propagation

CONTENTS (continued)

CONTENTS (continued)

CONTENTS (continued)

About the Authors

Brian F. Daley is a forest ecologist in the U.S. Virgin Islands. He was the Agroforestry Research Specialist for the University of the Virgin Islands for 10 years. While he was at the university, he developed native tree propagation protocols and low-cost "gap-planting" methods using native plants to enrich degraded dry forests dominated by exotic plants. His research includes landcover change analysis of St. Croix using Landsat and focusing on the relationship between forests, agriculture, and development. He is currently a senior partner with Geographic Consulting, LLC, a natural resources management company with projects ranging from phytoremediation of contaminated industrial sites to sea turtle nesting research and writing legislation.

R. Kasten Dumroese is the U.S. Department of Agriculture (USDA), Forest Service National Nursery Specialist and a research plant physiologist in the Rocky Mountain Research Station. His background as a nursery manager and researcher shapes his philosophy that nursery production problems are simply "unsolved opportunities." His research focuses on collecting, growing, and outplanting native plants; removing bottlenecks to efficient plant production and quality; and correctly using native plants in response to climate change and to restore ecosystem function. In 2000, he initiated the *Native Plants Journal* and the Native Plant Network; this journal and searchable Internet database foster sharing of information about growing and planting native flora.

Diane L. Haase is the USDA Forest Service Western Nursery Specialist, providing technical expertise to nurseries in the 17 Western States and the Pacific islands. Through publications, presentations, conferences, workshops, and on-site visits, Diane assists nursery managers and other plant professionals in improving nursery growing practices, increasing seedling quality, and maximizing plant growth and survival after outplanting. She has published numerous scientific articles and technical papers and is a co-author of the book *Propagation of Pacific Northwest Native Plants*. In addition, she is the Editor for *Tree Planters' Notes*, a journal focused on nursery production and outplanting of trees, shrubs, and native plants for reforestation, conservation, and restoration.

Douglass F. Jacobs is the Fred M. van Eck Professor of Forest Biology in the Department of Forestry and Natural Resources at Purdue University. He is the Editor-in-Chief of *New Forests*, an international journal on the biology, biotechnology, and management of afforestation and reforestation. His research explores eco-physiological development of young trees in response to culture and environmental stresses. He teaches conceptual thinking and problemsolving skills relevant to the multifaceted, fluid decisionmaking process of operational management for nurseries and land managers. Having worked in Hawai'i for more than 10 years, he was closely involved in the formation of the Tropical Hardwood Tree Improvement and Regeneration Center.

David P. Janos is Professor and Cooper Fellow in the Department of Biology, University of Miami. His specialties are ecology, mycology, and tropical botany, and his research concerns the ecophysiology of mycorrhizae—mutualistic symbioses between fungi and the roots of vascular plants. The objective of his work is to understand the biology of mycorrhizae in natural ecosystems so that they can be exploited for human benefit in sustainable forest management, polycultural agriculture, and reforestation. As a former managing editor of the journal *Mycorrhiza*, he has worked extensively with the mycorrhizae of tropical tree seedlings in Costa Rica, Panama, and Australia.

Thomas D. Landis was the National Nursery Specialist for the USDA Forest Service; he taught a series of tropical nursery training sessions in Hawai'i, American Samoa, and Micronesia. In 2003, he invited Wilkinson, Luna, and Jacobs to participate in teaching a tropical nursery workshop that was so successful that it became the impetus for this book. Landis has authored many articles and books on nursery technology including *Forest Nursery Notes* and the *Container Tree Nursery Manual* series, which helped promote key nursery concepts including the target seedling and propagation protocols. After retiring, he has continued to work as a consultant specializing in writing and training projects concerning nurseries, reforestation, and restoration.

Tara Luna is a botanist and ecologist involved in the conservation and restoration of ecologically significant areas. She specializes in documenting plant species and plant community diversity on indigenous lands, including helping to locate, protect, and restore areas with rare and culturally significant species. She has worked with American Indian tribes in the Western United States and has also taught native plant nursery short courses in the tropical Pacific. She edited *Nursery Manual for Native Plants: A Guide for Tribal Nurseries* and has authored native plant propagation, conservation, and restoration publications for the *Native Plants Journal*, USDA Forest Service and Foreign Agriculture Service, and Montana Natural Heritage Program.

Kim M. Wilkinson is a social ecologist who works with ecological restoration and cultural renewal, helping bring back native and traditional plants, as well as human connections to them. She worked for 10 years in Hawai'i as the owner/operator of a nursery for native and traditional trees. She also focused on applying traditional Polynesian agroforestry practices to sustainable farm and forestry planning. She continues to work at the intersections of food security, ecosystem restoration, and human health. She has authored several books, including *Agroforestry Guides for Pacific Islands*; *Growing Koa: A Hawaiian Legacy Tree*; and *Other Voices, Other Ways, Better Practices: Bridging Local & Professional Environmental Knowledge*.

Acknowledgments

The U.S. Department of Agriculture (USDA), Forest Service funded this project. Primary funding was provided by State and Private Forestry, Cooperative Forestry, through the Virtual Center for Reforestation, Nurseries, and Genetics Resources (RNGR). The Rocky Mountain Research Station also supported this effort.

Jim Marin provided graphic design and layout with unfailing skill, patience, and attention to detail. Richard Zabel, Western Forestry and Conservation Association, through an agreement with the RNGR team, was instrumental in developing this manual.

J.B. Friday, College of Tropical Agriculture and Human Resources, University of Hawai'i generously shared his expertise, insights, and many excellent photographs. Jill Wagner of Future Forests Nursery, Hawai'i, contributed photographs and her expertise on nursery management and seed saving. Craig Elevitch of Agroforestry Net, Hawai'i, provided photographs and his expertise in traditional trees, agroforestry, and nursery development. Ray D. Rodríguez Colón, Fideicomiso de Conservación de Puerto Rico, graciously hosted visits to his country's nurseries and gave insightful input. Dania Rivera Ocasio, University of Puerto Rico, facilitated nursery visits. Michael Morgan of the University of the Virgin Islands made many thoughtful contributions. Vital review, fact-checking, or information was provided by: Robert L. James, USDA Forest Service (retired); Mike Amaranthus, Mycorrhizal Applications, Inc.; Jim Trappe, Oregon State University; RNGR team members George Hernández, Ron Overton, and Jeremiah R. Pinto; and Margie V. Cushing Falanruw, Institute of Pacific Islands Forestry, Yap Institute of Natural Science. Krystal Beley provided consultation on photograph use and caption clarity. We thank Katie Friday, USDA Forest Service Institute of Pacific Islands Forestry for contributing photographs and information and assisting with the tropical nursery training session that first brought our authoring team together.

We are grateful to the many individuals across the tropical nursery community and other professionals who helped create this publication: **American Samoa:** Aitasi Sameli, Endangered Plant Program; Forestry staff, American Samoa Community College; **Guam:** David Limtiaco, USDA Forest Service; Guam Forestry staff; **Hawai'i:** Rick Barboza, Hui Kū Maoli Ola Native Plant Nursery; Mike Donoho, Pu'u Wa'awa'a Forest Reserve; John L. Edson, Hawai'i Reforestation Nursery; Jack Jeffrey Photography; Baron Horiuchi and his nursery staff, U.S. Department of the Interior (DOI), U.S. Fish & Wildlife Service Hakalau Forest National Wildlife Refuge; Joy Hosokawa, DOI National Park Service Volcanoes National Park; Mark and K.B. Kimball, Holualoa Tree Farm; Elliott Parsons, Pu'u Wa'awa'a Forest Reserve; Ethan Romanchak, Native Nursery; Matt Schriman, Hui Kū Maoli Ola Native Plant Nursery; Jacob Witcraft and his nursery staff, Kamuela State Tree Nursery; Aileen Yeh, Po Wai U Nursery; Jim Ferrell, Mitiku Habte, Harold Keyser, and James Leary (University of Hawai'i); Patty Moriyasu (Volcano Rare Plant Facility); **Idaho:** J. Chris Hoag, USDA Natural Resources Conservation Service; **Mississippi:** J.A. Vozzo, USDA Forest Service Southern Research Station (retired); **New York:** Kenneth Mudge, Cornell University; **Oregon:** Bruce McDonald and Timber Press, Inc.; David Steinfeld, USDA Forest Service Pacific Northwest Region; **Palau:** Palau Forestry staff; **Puerto Rico:** Alberto Areces, Parque Dona Ines; Christian Torres Santana, USDA Forest Service International Institute of Tropical Forestry; **U.S. Virgin Islands:** Jovan Augustin, Geographic Consulting, Errol Chichester, Virgin Islands Department of Agriculture; Christina Gasperi, Art Farm; Veronica Gordon, Virgin Islands Department of Agriculture; David Hamada, St. George Village Botanical Garden; Cynthia Holmes, Cruzan Gardens; Dean Yanez (Geographic Consulting, LLC); Vanessa Forbes, Dexter Hipolit, and Paulino "Papo" Perez (University of the Virgin Islands); **Yap:** Staffs at Yap Forestry, USDA Forest Service Institute of Pacific Islands Forestry, Yap Institute of Natural Science. We also thank the many individuals who were photographed working in the nursery, planting in the field, or attending a training session.

We are grateful to the teachers, mentors, and plant propagators from earlier times, whose names we may not know but who protected and passed down knowledge of the native and traditional plants we enjoy today.

Introduction

Who Is This Handbook For?

This handbook was written for anyone endeavoring to start and operate a nursery for native and traditional plants in the tropics. Because the tropics cover a vast area of the world, however, the scope of the handbook is geared toward readers in the U.S. affiliated tropics. Specifically, the U.S. affiliated tropics are a diverse area spanning two oceans and half the globe, including the nations of the Federated States of Micronesia, the Republic of Palau, and the Republic of the Marshall Islands, as well as the Territory of Guam, the Commonwealth of the Northern Mariana Islands, the Territory of American Samoa, the Commonwealth of Puerto Rico, the U.S. Virgin Islands, and the State of Hawai'i, southern California, Texas, and the southern part of Florida (see map on following page). Areas with similar conditions may also be served. This handbook is not a species-by-species account, though propagation protocols for many tropical species are available on the Native Plant Network (http://www.nativeplantnetwork.org).

The chapters in this handbook discuss aspects of nursery management, providing an overview of the factors to consider when planning or upgrading a nursery. Key concepts and processes are presented, based on proven techniques, practices, and the best science available at the time of this writing. An understanding of some of these concepts and principles will make it easier to operate a nursery successfully, to serve clients, and to meet project objectives in the field.

At the same time, every nursery is unique. Local conditions and ingenuity, combined with these basic principles, will shape the best practices for any given nursery. Information in this handbook is meant to provide an empowering overview of concepts and principles. Each reader is free to adapt, adopt, or disregard this information, as appropriate to their situation.

> *The goal of this handbook is to provide practical, user-friendly, science-based, and locally adaptable information about how to start, operate, or upgrade a nursery for native and traditional plants in the tropics.*

What's in This Handbook?

A nursery is a web of interrelated factors, and every aspect of the nursery will affect everything else. Therefore, this handbook covers topics from initial nursery founding and planning through crop production, outplanting, and ongoing learning. The important roles tropical nurseries play in ecological restoration and human well-being (Chapter 1) are discussed before going into the details of nursery site selection and planning (Chapter 2). Then, the focus shifts to what species and stocktypes the nursery will provide to best serve different projects and objectives (Chapter 3). The practicalities of planning crops, scheduling production activities, and developing ways to grow new crops is discussed (Chapter 4). Crop growth relies on good design of propagation environments (Chapter 5) and other infrastructure, including choices of growing media (Chapter 6) and appropriate containers (Chapter 7). Plant propagation includes collecting, processing, and storing seeds (Chapter 8), germinating and sowing seeds (Chapter 9), and vegetative propagation (Chapter 10). Plant care includes water quality and irrigation management (Chapter 11), plant nutrition (Chapter 12), working with beneficial organisms (Chapter 13), and holistic prevention and management of pests and diseases (Chapter 14). As crops get closer to being ready for the field, nursery management continues with hardening (Chapter 15), care in harvesting and shipping of nursery crops (Chapter 16), and finally, outplanting onto field sites and monitoring the results (Chapter 17).

All these activities combine to produce the best quality plants with the best chance to survive and flourish on outplanting sites. It is important, however, not to become so focused on production that other key aspects of nursery planning and management are neglected. Equally important is time building relationships with customers, the community, nursery staff, and other colleagues. These activities include training and education for nursery staff and outreach and education to clients and the public (Chapter 18). Overseeing nursery operations pulls many of the previous topics together as the nursery gains momentum in its operations (Chapter 19). Running a nursery is a continuous learning process and in-house research, trials, and feedback systems help improve plant productivity to expand on successes and learn from failures over time

(Chapter 20). Best efforts in each of these areas of tropical nursery management serve ecological, cultural, and economic goals to protect and restore native and traditional ecosystems and agroecosystems.

We hope you find this handbook to be a useful reference for your nursery and restoration work in the tropics.

This handbook emphasizes principles and processes for successful nursery operations that can be adapted as appropriate to each nursery's context.

Tropical Forests of the United States and Affiliated Islands

Adapted from USDA Forest Service, State and Private Forestry (2007) and Arbor Day Foundation (2006).

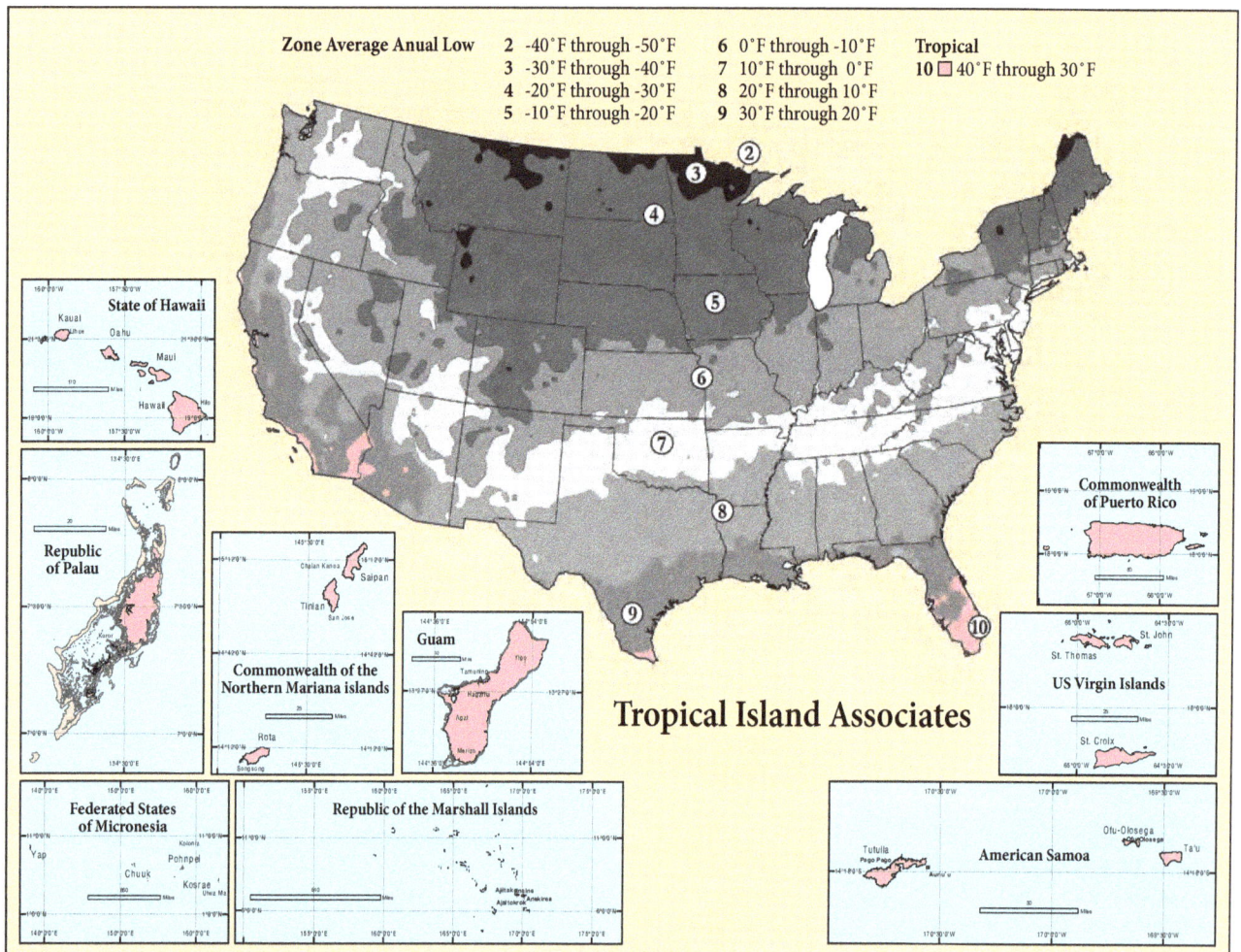

Zone Average Anual Low		
2 -40°F through -50°F	6 0°F through -10°F	Tropical
3 -30°F through -40°F	7 10°F through 0°F	10 ☐ 40°F through 30°F
4 -20°F through -30°F	8 20°F through 10°F	
5 -10°F through -20°F	9 30°F through 20°F	

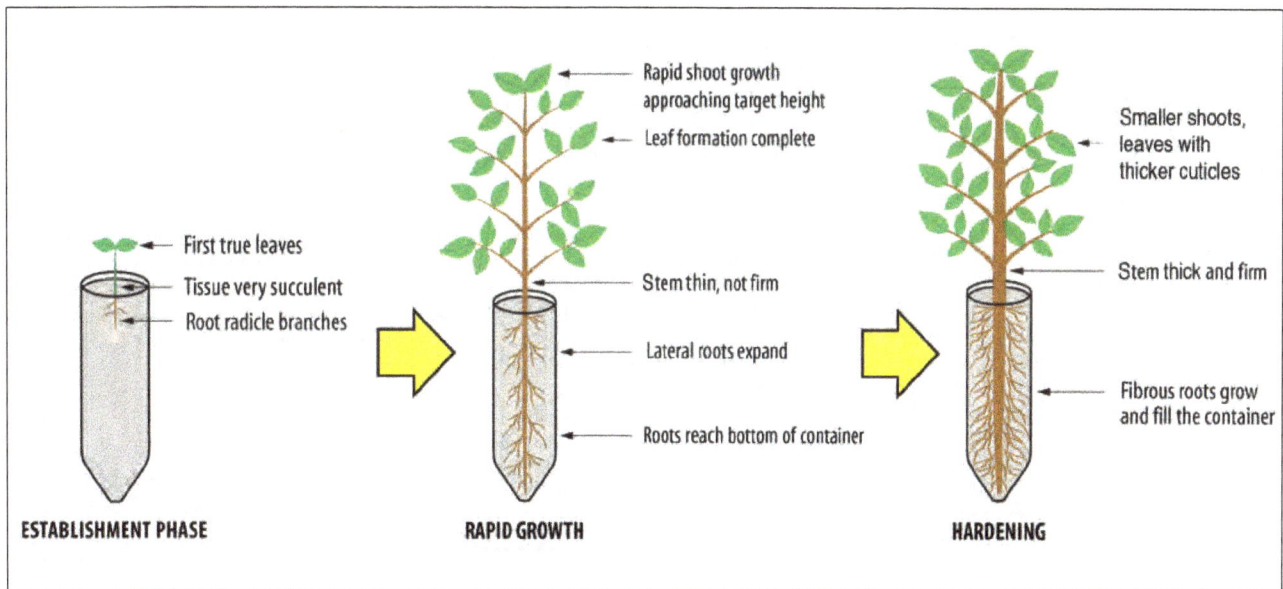

The development of most nursery crops can be divided into three phases: establishment, rapid growth, and hardening. Adapted from Dumroese and others (2008) by Jim Marin.

References

Arbor Day Foundation. 2006. Hardiness zone map. http://www.arborday.org/media/zones.cfm. (October 2011).

Dumroese, R.K.; Luna, T.; Landis, T.D. 2008. Nursery manual for native plants: volume 1, a guide for tribal nurseries. Agriculture Handbook 730. Washington, DC: U.S. Department of Agriculture, Forest Service. 302 p.

U.S. Department of Agriculture, Forest Service, State and Private Forestry, Program Redesign Committee. 2007. Tropical forests of the United States: applying U.S. Department of Agriculture, State and Private Forestry programs. http://www.hawaiistateassessment.info/library/tropicalforests-of-the-United-States-Final60607.pdf. (November 2011).

Why Start a Tropical Nursery for Native and Traditional Plants?

Kim M. Wilkinson and Brian F. Daley

1

Tropical ecosystems and agroecosystems are vital, life-giving landscapes and are home to diverse plants, animals, and people in a range of climatic, geologic, cultural, and environmental contexts. These systems provide services, such as cleaning air, improving water quality, stabilizing soil, and regulating the climate. The landscapes offer essential products including timber, food, fibers, and medicines.

During the past few centuries, waves of change have swept through tropical landscapes. These changes include obliterated native forests, drained wetlands, and decimated agroforests and indigenous management practices. Agricultural and industrial land uses, tourism, urbanization, climate change, and the introduction of problematic new plants, animals, pests, and pathogens have caused high rates of extinction (Carter and others 2001). Today, people are working to protect and regenerate tropical ecosystems and agroecosystems (Robotham and others 2004). Key tasks in revitalizing these systems are planting, protecting, and perpetuating native and traditional species, and sowing awareness of these plants among people. This is the work of the tropical nursery manager.

Nurseries in the tropics range in size from a single owner-operator growing a few plants for neighbors, to community organizations, universities, or cultural groups growing plants for certain goals, to large commercial nurseries, to governments founding native plant programs for their region. Without regard to scale, tropical nurseries are a key link in ecological restoration, sustainable agriculture, and cultural renewal (figure 1.1) by providing native and traditional plants.

Facing Page: *Nursery on Pohnpei, Federated States of Micronesia. Photo by Ronald Overton.*

Figure 1.1—*Nurseries in the tropics come in many shapes and sizes to serve diverse needs. Shown here are native tree seedlings in a nursery in Guam (A), a backyard nursery in Mexico (B), and a commercial nursery in Puerto Rico (C). Photo A by J.B. Friday, photo B by Thomas D. Landis, and photo C by Ronald Overton.*

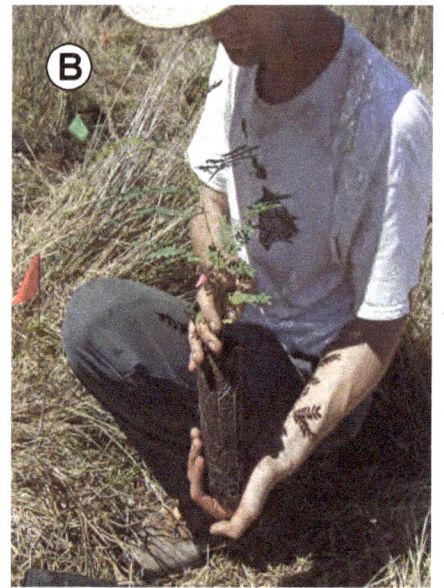

Figure 1.2—*Nurseries play a key role in ecological restoration, cultural renewal, economic resilience, and sustainable agriculture by providing native and traditional plants. Nursery-grown plants are often used for planting native species in the U.S. Virgin Islands (A) and Hawai'i (B). Photo A by Brian F. Daley, and photo B by J.B. Friday.*

Examples of these links include—

- **Ecosystem Restoration and Biodiversity Protection**—Jump-starting or accelerating succession on disturbed sites; enriching species-poor secondary forests with rare or later successional species; partnering with farmers and agroforestry practitioners to facilitate tropical forest recovery; bringing native plants for native pollinators and wildlife into agricultural areas, urban landscapes, and backyard gardens; propagating threatened and endangered plants for their conservation and reintroduction to forests; and the full-scale restoration of native plant communities in conservation areas.

- **Sustainable Agriculture and Economic Resilience**—Enhancing farmer livelihoods and community food security with agroforestry practices; rediscovering

diverse native and traditional species for timber, crafts, fibers, foods, and other uses; diversifying monoculture fields with traditional species of trees, shrubs, and vines; using native and traditional plants in conservation plantings, such as windbreaks, urban street trees, and erosion control installations.

- **Learning and Cultural Renewal**—Rekindling locally adapted practices and plant technologies; cultivating culturally significant plants in the forest understory for nontimber forest products; replacing exotic ornamentals with local species in landscapes; starting gardens of traditional species in schoolyards; revitalizing and sustaining human connections with local plants and ecosystems (figure 1.2).

The Environmental and Social Context in the U.S. Affiliated Tropical Islands

One of the greatest challenges of nursery management is choosing how to focus your efforts to be of most benefit to the land and the local people. Understanding your context requires integrating a "bird's-eye view" and a "worm's-eye view." A quick "bird's-eye view" of the context in the U.S. Affiliated Tropical Islands is shown in table 1.1; you are the only one who can describe your unique local context (the "worm's-eye view").

The U.S. Affiliated Tropical Islands house an immense diversity of native ecosystems, including mangrove swamps, wetlands, riparian areas, rainforests, dry forests, submontane forests, cloud forests, and more (table 1.2). These ecosystems are home to many unique, endemic plants found nowhere else on earth and are considered biodiversity hotspots of local and global significance in relatively small areas (figure 1.3). The health of the terrestrial areas affects diverse marine systems including estuaries, salt ponds, and coral reefs. These systems provide resources for a tremen-dous range of marine animals and critical breeding grounds for migratory and residential birds. The rich and unique biological diversity of these islands is an international heritage.

Islands are particularly susceptible to environmental changes and disturbances. The small populations of endemic plants and animals that evolved in isolation are unable to change locations or rapidly adapt when large changes occur. Changes facing island ecosystems include habitat destruction because of human development (urban expansion, agriculture, industrial use, and recreational use) and loss of habitat because of introductions of exotic invasive species (plants, animals, and diseases). Islands are extremely vulnerable to temperature shifts, altered or increased storm regimes, floods, and droughts associated with climate change. On islands, many native plants and animals are endangered; the islands are in an extinction crisis, experiencing the highest extinction rates anywhere in the United States (Carter and others 2001).

Throughout the tropics, native forests were cleared and converted to agriculture and then abandoned, leading to widespread creation of secondary forests. In the Caribbean, where land area is limited and human population density is

Table 1.1—*Characteristics of U.S.-Affiliated Tropical Islands. Adapted from USDA FS SPF Program Redesign Committee (2007), Carter and others (2001), U.S. Census Bureau (2014a, 2014b), and Brandeis and Oswalt (2007).*

Name	Status with United States	Geologic description	Total area (acres)	Forested area (acres)	Estimated human population (2010)
Commonwealth of Puerto Rico	Territory	One volcanic main island composed of uplifted sedimentary rocks and several smaller islands	2,199,901	710,156	3,721,208
U.S. Virgin Islands	Territory	Three volcanic main islands (St. Croix, St. John, and St. Thomas) composed of uplifted sedimentary rocks and several smaller islands and cays	85,587	52,477	106,267
Hawaiian Islands	State	Eight volcanic islands (Kaua'i, O'ahu, Moloka'i, Lana'i, Maui, Kaho'olawe, Ni'ihau, and Hawai'i) and several atolls	4,110,720	1,490,000	1,360,301
American Samoa	Territory	Five volcanic islands and two coral atolls (Ofu, Ta'u, Swains Island, Tutuila, Olosega, Rose Island, and Aunu'u)	49,280	28,686	55,467
Commonwealth of the Northern Mariana Islands	Territory	14 volcanic islands	113,280	40,000	53,517
Republic of the Marshall Islands	FAS*	5 low-lying volcanic islands and 29 coral atolls (each made up of many islets)	44,800	Not mapped	65,859
Republic of Palau	FAS*	Several hundred volcanic islands and a few coral atolls (eight islands inhabited)	114,560	77,241	20,879
Federated States of Micronesia	FAS*	607 small islands consisting of volcanic islands and coral atolls	149,804	76,527	107,154
Guam	Territory	One volcanic island composed of uplifted sedimentary rocks	135,680	65,005	159,434

* Freely Associated State in a Compact of Free Association with the United States.

Table 1.2—*Some ecosystems in the U.S.-Affiliated Tropical Islands, present or historically present. Adapted from US OTA (1987).*

	Puerto Rico	U.S. Virgin Islands	American Samoa	Hawai'i*	Guam	Northern Marianas	Marshalls	Palau	Federated States of Micronesia			
									Kosrae	Pohnpei	Yap	Truk
Cloud forest	✔	✔	✔	✔	✔	✔			✔	✔		
Submontane rainforest	✔		✔	✔					✔	✔		✔
Lowland rainforest	✔		✔	✔	✔	✔		✔	✔	✔	✔	✔
Riverine and swamp forest	✔		✔	✔	✔	✔		✔	✔	✔	✔	✔
Subtropical moist/ seasonal forest	✔	✔		✔								
Subtropical dry forest	✔	✔		✔								
Scrub	✔	✔	✔	✔	✔	✔	✔	✔	✔	✔	✔	✔
Wetlands	✔	✔	✔	✔	✔	✔	✔	✔	✔	✔	✔	✔
Mangrove forest	✔	✔	✔		✔	✔	✔	✔	✔	✔	✔	✔
Atoll/beach forest and scrub	✔	✔	✔	✔	✔	✔	✔	✔	✔	✔	✔	✔
Lagoons/shallow bottoms	✔	✔	✔	✔	✔	✔	✔	✔	✔	✔	✔	✔

* Hawai'i also has subalpine and alpine ecosystems.

high, secondary forests on old agricultural land are already the most important and rapidly expanding forest cover type (Lugo and Helmer 2004). Secondary forests have novel species compositions, lower native species diversity, and higher influence of exotic species. In many areas in the Pacific Islands, secondary forests are composed exclusively of exotic species. Secondary forests will likely play an increasing role in conservation of forest biodiversity, especially in fragmented landscapes (Brown and Lugo 1990; Chazdon and others 2009).

Inextricably linked to these diverse ecosystems are diverse traditional cultures of the islands. A few examples include the Chamorro cultures of Guam and the Mariana Islands, the Samoan and Hawaiian cultures, the Boricua culture of Puerto Rico, and cultural groups who speak multiple languages and call the islands of the Federated States of Micronesia home (Carter and others 2001). Most of the islands have significant populations practicing traditional lifeways, including agricultural practices, hunting, fishing, gathering, and resource management. Agroforestry systems are, on some islands, a key forest type (figure 1.4). Traditional resource management in the islands espouses a ridge-to-reef perspective, the wisdom of which has lessons for watershed protection anywhere on earth (USDA FS SPF 2007).

Within the past few centuries, immigration and migration have added to the cultural diversity of the islands. Local culture is now infused with, for example, the influence of the Africans, Danish, French, and Spanish in the Caribbean; the Asians and Americans in Hawai'i; the Spanish in Guam; and countless others in other islands. Lifestyles in the islands range from densely populated urban areas to remote villages on outer islands (Carter and others 2001). Many islands have urban areas, agriculture, forest, and residential neighborhoods in close proximity to each other. Most of the islands currently experience a high level of dependency on mainland economies for food, energy, and other resources, but many also maintain a strong foundation and knowledge base of traditional subsistence agriculture and resource management.

Interconnections between social and ecological conditions are more evident to islanders than they are to people who live on large continents. Nurseries may provide native plants, traditional species, and other species to serve both humans and nature. Nurseries operate in urban, rural, and village settings, often integrating goals of economic resiliency, ecosystem protection and restoration, cultural renewal, and other community and ecosystem needs.

Why Grow Native Plants?

Native plants are the backbone of ecosystem function and integrity from soil nutrient cycling, clean water, and carbon sequestration to higher wildlife interactions. Individual species have evolved during the millennia to the

Figure 1.3—*The U.S.-Affiliated Tropical Islands house an immense diversity of ecosystems including mangrove swamps, wetlands, rainforests, dry forests, submontane forests, cloud forests, and more: mixed native and introduced forest on O'ahu (A), dryland forest on Hawai'i (B), coastal pandanus (screw pine) forest in Hawai'i (C), and Rock Islands of Palau (D). Photos A, B, and C by J.B. Friday, and photo D by Thomas D. Landis.*

Figure 1.4—*Diverse agroecosystems such as agroforests are important to environmental health and human livelihood in the tropics. Snow on Mauna Kea (14,000-ft [4,600-m] elevation) framed by palm trees and breadfruit growing at 700-ft (215-m) elevation on the Big Island of Hawai'i (A); an agroforest in Palau with betel nut palm (Areca catechu) overstory, bamboo for building materials, bananas and avocados for fruit, and taro for starch (B); mixed land use in the U.S. Virgin Island with residential, pasture, forest, and commercial areas in close proximity (C); and Coconut Island in Hawai'i (D). Most visitors to the tropics do not realize that many of the landscapes they enjoy include plant species humans introduced and cultivated for centuries in the area. Photos A, B, and D by J.B. Friday, and photo C by Brian F. Daley.*

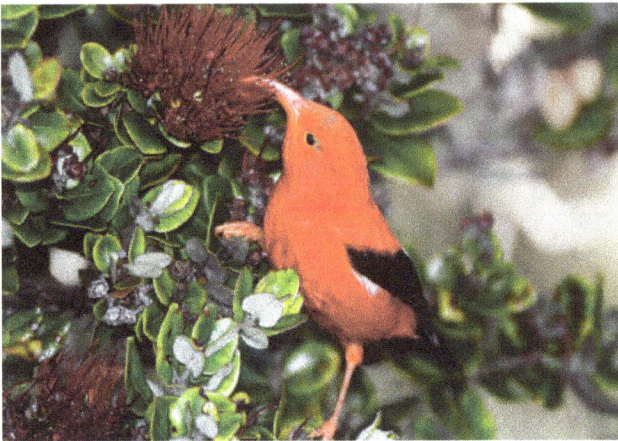

Figure 1.5—Deploying a diversity of locally adapted native plants helps support and regenerate ecosystems for local flora and fauna. Pictured is the ʻiʻiwi (Vestiaria coccinea) drinking nectar from an ʻōhiʻa lehua (Metrosideros polymorpha) blossom in Hawaiʻi. Photo ©Jack Jeffrey Photography.

climatic and edaphic conditions where they now grow in association with a myriad of other species. The resulting assemblage of plants and animals is what makes each ecosystem unique and contributes to people's sense of place. When species associations are disrupted, local extinctions can occur (figure 1.5), leading to declining ecosystem function or even to ecosystem collapse (Hawkins and others 2008, USDI BLM SOS 2011). Restoring durable, self-sustaining, and resilient ecosystems depends on native plants to (Erickson 2008, 2010)—

- Recover natural vegetative composition, structure, and successional patterns.
- Protect biodiversity and plant genetic resources.
- Provide habitat connectivity.
- Maintain plant and pollinator interactions.
- Support wildlife populations.
- Increase system resilience to disturbances and stressors.
- Provide desired goods, services, and benefits.
- Provide economic benefit to rural communities.

In this handbook, native plants are defined as locally adapted, genetically appropriate native plant materials. Although that sounds simple, it is not a straightforward definition (see next section). The issue of plant nativity is hotly discussed in some areas; and this handbook does not intend to solve these debates, only to provide a working definition. In general, making a list of native plants for a region or an island may not be sufficient information because it does not indicate local adaptedness. Many widely distributed native species have local populations adapted to local conditions including climate, soils, elevation, precipitation,

and environmental stresses, such as wind or drought. Local native plant materials, collected from the same or similar habitats as the outplanting site, have been shown to perform better than nonlocal sources. Using locally adapted seed sources is a key factor in ensuring the survival of native plants and of the native fauna that depend on these plants. In addition, deploying a diversity of locally adapted native plants creates communities and ecosystems that are more adaptable and resilient to climate change (Horning 2011, Erickson and others 2012). For some species, seed zones or transfer guidelines may have been defined (as discussed in Chapter 3, Defining the Target Plant), but establishment of seed zones is rare for most native tropical species. For most projects, growers must decide on a case-by-case basis what will be appropriate for their outplanting sites (Withrow-Robinson and Johnson 2006). The genetics guidelines provided in Chapter 8, Collecting, Processing, and Storing Seeds, detail essential elements of seed collection to ensure local adaptedness and genetic diversity.

Why Grow Traditional Plants?

This handbook recognizes that traditional plants are a sustainable and regenerative resource in the tropics, and that tropical nurseries work to serve those needs in addition to native plant conservation. Many people define "native" as those species present before any humans inhabited an area, but humans have resided in many parts of the tropics for millennia and have influenced the flora. Research is revealing that many tropical forests once thought to be undisturbed primary forests (such as in the Brazilian Amazon) are actually the result of ongoing human management and disturbances dating back, in some cases, for thousands of years (Berkes 1999) The first people to migrate to a new area brought many plants with them.

For example, in the Caribbean, Amerindians with cultural centers in Venezuela traveled by small boats northward, bringing with them important food crops, including trees such as the genip (*Melicoccus bijugatis*) and zapote (*Manilkara zapota*), which were then cherished for their fruit, much as they are today. Both species are now naturalized throughout the Caribbean Islands. When the first Polynesians arrived to the Hawaiian Islands, they found few edible native plants. The abundant agroecosystems of breadfruit, coconut, bananas, taro and other species that early Europeans thought to be native were in fact intentionally introduced species in Polynesian agroforestry systems. Islanders of the Pacific and Caribbean enjoyed a high level of food security and self-sufficiency before European contact (Thaman and others 2000). Their agroecosystems were built around a diverse base of native and introduced species (Elevitch and Wilkinson 2000). Many of these agroecosystems were displaced by colonial and later corporate entities, to convert land for development or to export crops such as sugar, coffee, or cattle. Today people are working to revitalize and reintroduce traditional species and agroecosystems for personal health and for economic, environmental, and political reasons (figure 1.6). For example, the U.S. Virgin Islands have seen a recent resurgence in Ital cooking that follows traditional Rastafarian practices of using locally grown herbs and vegetables without meat. Native Hawaiians are successfully overcoming nutrition-related disorders, such as obesity and diabetes, by reembracing traditional foods. The ancestral way of eating is cultivated in an interdisciplinary way involving cultural teachings and family support (Shintani and others 1994). On the islands, the general trend is toward locally grown foods in response to higher food prices, the desire to eat more organically and healthfully, to increase household food security, and to support food sovereignty movements. In the latter, local people claim the power to determine their own food systems as a basic human right, rather than allowing food systems to be controlled by global market forces (Whittman and others 2010). Growing traditional species in nurseries helps strengthen and renew sustainable agroecosystems (figure 1.7).

Helping to meet human needs using time-tested, traditional species also reduces pressure on more intact tropical ecosystems, without the risk of newly introduced and potentially invasive or noxious species. Traditional species can

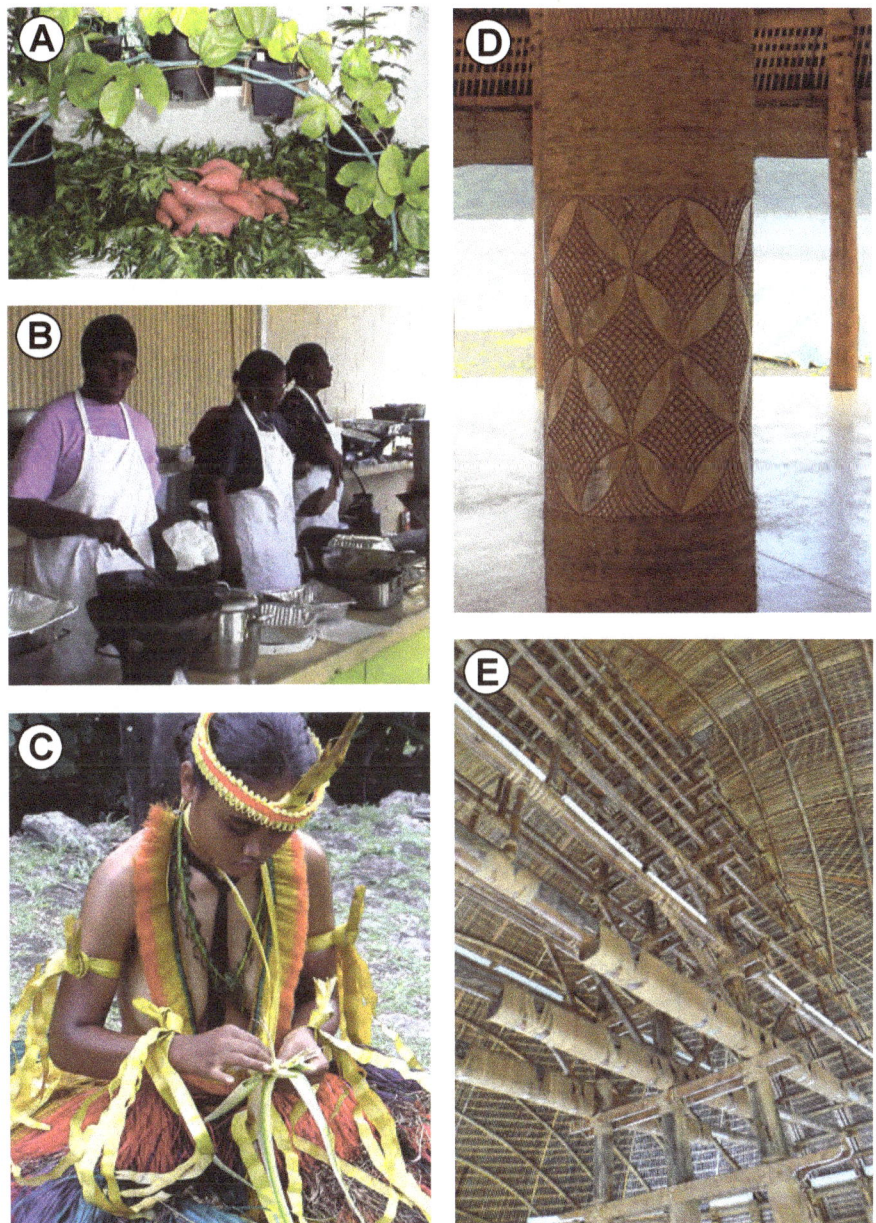

Figure 1.6—*Traditional plant species sustain lifeways and livelihoods in tropical areas, providing food security, building materials, medicines, crafts, and more: a display of crops from an agroforestry system in the U.S. Virgin Islands, including a native passion fruit vine, medicinal neem tree leaves (originally introduced from India), and sweet potatoes (A); these food plants are part of traditional cooking and food security in the U.S. Virgin Islands (B). Traditional species also provide material for economic livelihoods, such as weaving materials for this traditional basket weaver on Yap (C). Specific native trees are used for building traditional fales in American Samoa (D and E). Photos A and B by Brian F. Daley, photo C by Thomas D. Landis, and photos D and E by Diane L. Haase.*

Figure 1.7—Growing traditional species in nurseries helps strengthen and renew sustainable agroecosystems: taro paddy in Waipio Valley, Hawai'i (A), shade-grown coffee under native 'ōhi'a forest shade, Kona, Hawai'i (B). Photos by J.B. Friday.

also be an integral part of tropical forest restoration using what is known as an agro-successional restoration approach (Vieira and others 2009, Holl and Aide 2010). In this approach, agroforestry and other agroecological practices are employed as a transition phase for forest restoration. Farmers share in restoration efforts to improve soil, establish trees, and exclude weeds while meeting their own needs for food security and livelihood (Vieira and others 2009). In this handbook terms including "traditional," "culturally significant," and "culturally important" are used interchangeably to refer to these kinds of plant species; some gray areas exist as to which species are in this category. Some culturally significant species are also native species; some are introduced species. Of the introduced species, some arrived with the first peoples of a place; others came with later waves of settlement. Some were adopted after European contact. For example, enslaved Africans arrived by ship to the Caribbean during the centuries of European colonization. Although most of the enslaved traveled without personal possessions, they somehow smuggled items that were culturally and spiritually important, including tree seeds. The native African baobab tree (*Adansonia* species) arrived in the Caribbean this way. Today in the U.S. Virgin Islands, the giant baobab trees (figure 1.8) serve as a tangible connection between modern Virgin Islanders and the first people who arrived from Africa and planted these tree seeds. A traditional species may not be of indigenous use, but may still be culturally significant. As a nursery manager, you will need to consider your scope to determine what species are appropriate to prioritize and perpetuate based on your area's unique environmental and cultural context.

Of course it is unwise to introduce to an island any species that is harmful (invasive, noxious, or untested in the area). In most cases, intentionally introducing new species is also unnecessary, given the diversity of time-tested plants already present.

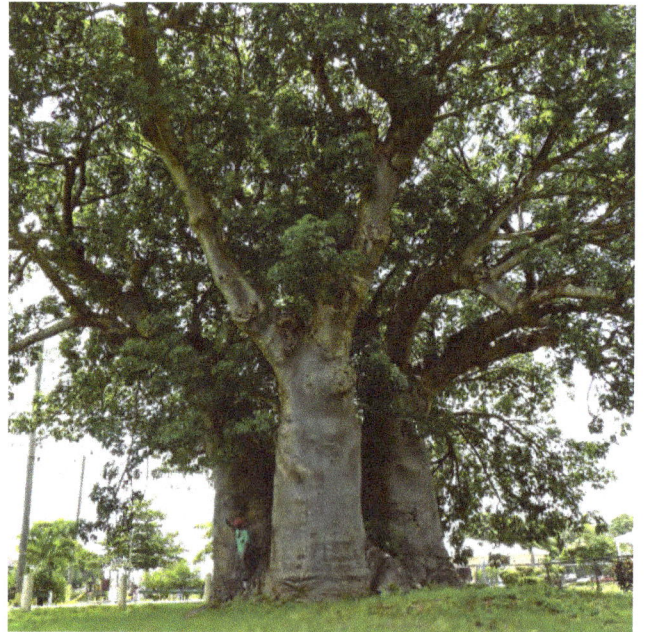

*Figure 1.8—Seeds of the baobab tree (*Adansonia digitata*) were first brought to the Caribbean by Africans, who somehow managed to carry viable tree seeds through the ordeal of enslavement and travel on slave ships, and who planted their seeds upon arrival. Today the baobab is a culturally important tree in the Caribbean, linking today's islanders with centuries of African heritage in the region. Photo by Brian F. Daley.*

Figure 1.9—Nurseries play a key role in conservation and restoration of species and ecosystems. This Department of Natural Resources nursery in Puerto Rico is growing threatened and endangered species. Photo by Ronald Overton.

The Role of Nurseries in Ecosystem Restoration and Cultural Renewal

Nurseries Provide Quality Plant Materials to Facilitate Sustainable and Regenerative Practices

The nursery environment is a place to germinate, grow, and protect locally adapted seedlings until they are healthy, strong, and large enough to meet the challenges of outplanting sites and achieve project goals (Evans 1996). The work nurseries do to produce high-quality native and traditional plants helps perpetuate these species (figure 1.9). Nursery-grown native plants overcome barriers to natural recolonization, such as weed competition, animal predation, and lack of a natural seed bank. Nursery-grown traditional species ensure heritage varieties, and culturally important characteristics are passed on to the next generation. Good nursery work makes successfully establishing native and traditional plants more effective, affordable, and more likely to happen, whether nursery clients are farmers, gardeners, restoration ecologists, community groups, or others. Quality plants can mean the difference between people believing it is too hard to plant native and traditional species, and having an attitude that they can do this (figure 1.10).

Nurseries Serve as a Cornerstone of Ecological Restoration

Without human disruption to their health, tropical ecosystems regenerate naturally after disturbances through the process of succession. Forests can be degraded or damaged by humans to the point where they require some help, however, and that is where nurseries come in. Often, the intensity, duration, or extent of the disturbance results in a lack of native propagules (seedlings, seed bank in the soil, and so on) on the site or within a distance that they will naturally disperse to revegetate the disturbed site (Holl and Aide 2010). In addition, limiting factors on the site, such as takeover by highly competitive weeds, low soil fertility, excessively compacted soil, or nonnative animals that eat seeds and young plants can arrest natural succession until these conditions are overcome (Vieira and others 2009). In these scenarios, the planting of nursery stock is a cornerstone of ecological work.

Figure 1.10—The work nurseries do to produce high-quality native and traditional plants helps break down barriers to planting and perpetuating these species. Good nursery work makes outplanting more effective and affordable for clients. Pictured: tree planters head out to plant native trees in Brazil (A) and Hawai'i (B). Photos by Douglass F. Jacobs.

Figure 1.11—Nurseries can be wonderful places for working and learning about plants (A) and passing on knowledge and values to the next generation (B). Photo A by Brian F. Daley, and photo B by Megan Parker.

Nursery plants may be used to (Holl and Aide 2010, Vieira and others 2009)—

- Jump-start succession (for example, planting trees to shade out aggressive weeds or improving soil with nitrogen-fixing pioneer native species).

- Stabilize highly disturbed areas and minimize further environmental damage, such as erosion.

- Enrich species-poor secondary forests or pioneered sites with rarer, more diverse, or later successional species.

- Serve as "islands" to act as dispersal points for propagules to adjacent land in need of restoration.

- Establish trees through an agro-successional approach.

- Complete full-scale restoration projects.

Nurseries Provide Livelihood and Learning Opportunities for People

Nurseries and nursery mangers are a bridge between the natural world and human needs. For example, perhaps an important cultural plant has become rare, and, because elders are unable to gather it, the children are not learning about this species and the local economy is no longer benefitting. The nursery can identify the species, learn how to propagate it, and help people to replant it, thus serving the local culture, economy, and ecology.

Some nurseries provide plants, employment, and knowledge to serve certain cultural groups, such as women, youth, or farmers. In many areas, nurseries tend to become centers

and gathering places for people to connect with each other and learn about native and traditional species (PRAP 1999) (figure 1.11).

One of the most rewarding objectives for growing and outplanting native and traditional plants is the education of young people. Some native plant nurseries are operated by schools with a primary objective of environmental education, and other nurseries simply make themselves available to school groups. Young children can learn the names and uses of native and culturally important plants, and older children can enjoy the art and science involved in growing and outplanting different species. Gaining familiarity with species is a useful gateway to a deeper understanding of traditional ecological knowledge and resource management.

Nurseries Are a Key Link in Biodiversity Conservation

Loss of tropical biodiversity is a cause for serious concern. High levels of endemism in relatively small spaces mean that local habitat destruction can put already vulnerable species at greater risk of extinction. Nursery work to propagate and increase rare species is essential for conservation and reintroduction of these species (Prance 2005).

The restoration of disturbed sites is vital to conservation success, but so is the establishment of seed banks, including nurseries as living seed banks, to serve future needs. Conventional seed banks can conserve only species having "orthodox" seeds that can be dried and placed in long-term storage. Most tropical species, however, have

Time-Lapse Glimpses of the Tarzan River Savanna Area of the Cotal Reserve, Guam

Dr. Margie Cushing Falanruw recalls her ancestral knowledge that became a basis for a vegetation strategy for southern Guam. She writes (2002 p. 11):

"In the 1950s and early 1960s, the savanna above and along the trail leading to upper Tarzan falls in Guam was a child-friendly wonderland of shrubs. Some, such as the weird *Geniostoma micranthum* and lovely shiny-leaved *Decaspermum fruticosum*, grew to heights of about 7 feet and formed a dense maze through which children and adults could walk. 'Abas duendes' *Gloichidion* bushes with bright red tip leaves produced little 'guavas for elves.' The bonsai-like *Myrtella bennigseniana*, and the pink-flowered *Melastoma malabathricum* grew lower than a child and were interspersed with lavender, *Spathoglottis* ground orchids, yellow flowered *Curculigo orchioides,* and blue flowered *Dianella* lilies. The 'miniature iba tree,' *Phylannthus saffordi*, was present along with the 'out of focus wolf paw plant' *Lycopodium cernuum*, which was used to decorate nativity scenes in those days. We made garlands of *Cassytha*, *Lygodium*, or *Gleichenia* vines to shield our heads from the sun, soothed our eyes with isotonic drops of liquid from *Scaevola taccada* berries, and sipped nectar from *Stachytarpheta* flowers. We learned to stop bleeding with crushed *Glochidion* leaves and to heal bruises and sprains with *lada Morinda* leaves warmed on a campfire. We walked through soft *Dianella* grass, enjoyed the scent of wild mint and the 'chewing gum smell' of methyl salicicate-laced *Polygalla* roots. We rested below gagu, the 'singing tree' *Casuarina equisetifolia* and listened to the 'sound of silence' as wind blew through its needle branches.

Most of these species were present in the 1970s when my flora and fauna class compiled a list of species in the area on July 18, 1970. By the 1980s however, the area was invaded by invasive *Pennisetum* grass, which may have increased its vulnerability to wildfires that were reported to have swept through the area. The burned area had been subsequently planted to *Acacia* trees. I no longer lived on Guam at that time. When I visited The Tarzan river area with my grandchildren on Saturday, August 27th, 2002, most of the savanna species were no longer as abundant and do not grow as tall nor luxuriant as they did before the area was invaded by *Pennisetum* and fire.

The Tarzan river area of the Cotal Reserve has refreshed five generations of my family, and I hope that it can be restored to its former state so that my great grandchildren and their children may also experience this remnant bit of old Guam."

Using that ancestral knowledge, the restoration strategy in table 1.3 was developed.

Table 1.3—Revegetation strategy. Adapted from Bell and others (2002).

Type of site	Problem	Restoration/stewardship objectives
Shaded fuelbreaks	Grass dominated watersheds are unbroken expanses that burn readily and at high intensity.	Compartmentalize contiguous fuels to reduce fire size and provide enhanced control opportunities. Establish shaded fuelbreaks of *Acacia* species in a strategically designed pattern to compartmentalize fuels.
Swordgrass grasslands	Swordgrass is highly flammable, fires tend to kill other vegetation and contribute to the spread of swordgrass.	Convert portions of swordgrass dominated grasslands to forests. Plant and maintain buffers of native trees. Underplant Acacia plantations with native trees. Plant nursery-grown natives *Callophyllum inophyllum, Intsia bijuga, Hibiscus tiliaceus, Neiosperma oppositifolia,* and *Pandanus tectorius* adjacent to existing ravine forests.
Native savanna shrub and ravine forest	Erosion of biodiversity as a result of fire, feral animals, and invasive species.	Protection and restoration. Weed out invasive plants, protect from fire. Assist or enhance regeneration of native trees, shrubs, and plants. Nursery propagation of native species to assist with natural regeneration of uncommon and rare species.

Figure 1.12—*Laulima: "Many hands working together." The newly minted sign for Hakalau Forest National Wildlife Refuge's Native Plant Nursery, Hawai'i. Photo by J.B. Friday.*

"recalcitrant" seeds, meaning they cannot be dried and stored over extended periods (Kettle and others 2011). Thus, successful restoration and conservation of tropical forests requires that nurseries propagate and maintain genetically diverse living banks of recalcitrant species (Kettle and others 2011, Merritt and Dixon 2011).

Growing plants in the nursery is far more efficient than attempting to establish seeds through direct seeding in the field. Nurseries make the most efficient use of limited seeds by ensuring that each one receives the necessary care and attention to survive and develop into a mature plant. Also, nursery propagation does not deplete naturally regenerating areas because it does not involve uprooting wildings to transplant.

Good nursery management supports genetic and sexual diversity to ensure conservation of plants and all the other life forms that depend on them, from pollinators to primates. Genetic diversity is also essential for future adaptability and resilience in the face of climate change. Protecting local biodiversity and ecosystem resilience also protects local cultural diversity and economic resilience.

Challenge and Opportunity

Much needs to be done to restore tropical forests, recharge aquifers, regenerate wetlands, revitalize local economies, rekindle traditional practices, reclaim wastelands, and renew human connections to nature. The challenges may seem overwhelming. It is fortunate that even the loftiest goals can be reached with practical, persistent, everyday work (figure 1.12). Starting and operating a nursery for native and traditional species is a vital, positive endeavor full of challenge and opportunity. Good nursery work contributes to species conservation, ecosystem resiliency, cultural diversity, enhanced human livelihoods, and greater health and productivity of the land.

References

Bell, F.; Falanruw, M.; Lawrence, B.; Limtiaco, D.; Nelson, D. 2002. Vegetation strategy for southern Guam. Draft (September 2002). Honolulu, HI: U.S. Department of Agriculture, Forest Service and Natural Resources Conservation Service; Government of Guam Division of Forestry.

Berkes, F. 1999. Sacred ecology: traditional knowledge and resource management. London: Taylor and Francis. 209 p.

Brandeis, T.; Oswalt, S. 2007. The status of the U.S. Virgin Island's forests 2004. Resource Bulletin SRS-122. Ashville, NC, U.S. Department of Agriculture, Forest Service, Southern Research Station. 62 p.

Brown, S.; Lugo, A. 1990. Tropical secondary forests. Journal of Tropical Ecology. 6: 1–32.

Carter, L.M.; Shea, E.; Hamnett, M.; Anderson, C; Dolcemascolo, G; Guard, C; Taylor, M.; Barnston, T; He, Y; Larsen, M.; Loope, L.; Malone, L.; Meehl, G. 2001. Potential consequences of climate variability and change for the U.S.-affiliated islands of the Pacific and Caribbean. In: The potential consequences of climate variability and change: foundation report. Report by the National Assessment Synthesis Team for the U.S. Global Change Research Program. Cambridge, United Kingdom: Cambridge University Press: 315–349. Chapter 11. http://www.usgcrp.gov/usgcrp/Library/nationalassessment/11Islands.pdf. (December 2011).

Chazdon, R.L.; Peres, C.; Dent, D.; Shell, D.; Lugo, A.E.; Lamb, D.; Stork, N.E., Miller, S.E. 2009. The potential for species conservation in tropical secondary forests. Conservation Biology. 23: 1406–1417.

Elevitch, C.R.; Wilkinson, K.M., eds. 2000. Agroforestry guides for Pacific Islands. Holualoa, HI: Permanent Agriculture Resources. http://www.agroforestry.net/afg/book.html. (December 2011).

Erickson, V.J. 2008. Developing native plant germplasm for national forests and grasslands in the Pacific Northwest. Native Plants Journal. 9: 255–266.

Erickson, V.J. 2010. Personal communication. Pendleton, OR. Geneticist/Native Plant Program Manager, U.S. Department of Agriculture, Forest Service, Pacific Northwest Region.

Erickson, V.J.; Aubry, C.; Berrang, P.; Blush, T.; Bower, A.; Crane, B.; DeSpain, T.; Gwaze, D.; Hamlin, J.; Horning, M.; Johnson, R.; Mahalovich, M.; Maldonado, M.; Sniezko, R.; St. Clair, B. 2012. Genetic resource management and climate change: genetic options for adapting national forests to climate change. Internal document. Washington, DC: U.S. Department of Agriculture, Forest Service. http://www.fs.usda.gov/Internet/FSE_DOCUMENTS/stelprdb5368468.pdf. (September 2012).

Evans, J. 1996. Plantation forestry in the Tropics. Oxford, United Kingdom: Clarendon Press. 403 p.

Falanruw, M. 2002. Appendix 3. Time-lapse glimpses of the Tarzan River savanna area of the Cotal Reserve. In: Bell, F.; Falanruw, M.; Lawrence, B.; Limtiaco, D.; Nelson, D. Vegetation strategy for southern Guam. Draft (September 2002). Honolulu, HI. U.S. Department of Agriculture, Forest Service and Natural Resources Conservation Service; Government of Guam Division of Forestry.

Hawkins, B.; Sharrock, S.; Havens, K. 2008. Plants and climate change: which future? Richmond, United Kingdom: Botanic Gardens Conservation International. 96 p.

Holl, K.D.; Aide, T.M. 2010. When and where to actively restore ecosystems? Forest Ecology and Management. 261(10): 1558–1563.

Horning, M. 2011. Personal communication. Bend, OR. Plant Geneticist, U.S. Department of Agriculture, Forest Service, Pacific Northwest Research Station.

Kettle, C.J.; Burslem, D.F.R.P.; Ghazoul, J. 2011. An unorthodox approach to forest restoration. Science. 333: 36.

Lugo, A.; Helmer, E. 2004. Emerging forests on abandoned land: Puerto Rico's new forests. Forest Ecology and Management. 190: 145–161.

Merritt, D.J.; Dixon, K.W. 2011. An unorthodox approach to forest restoration—response. Science 333: 36–37.

Pacific Regional Agricultural Programme [PRAP]. 1999. Pacific agroforestry: an information kit. Suva, Fiji Islands: Pacific Regional Agricultural Programme.

Prance, G. 2005. Foreword. In: Lilleeng-Rosenberger, K.E. Growing Hawai'i's native plants. Honolulu, HI: Mutual Publishing.

Robotham, M.P.; Mas, E.; Lawrence, J.H.; Eswaran, H. 2004. The Tropical Natural Resources Technology Consortium: working together for tropical conservation. In: Raine, S.R.; Biggs, A.J.W.; Menzies, N.W.; Freebairn, D.M.: Tolmie, P.E. eds. Conserving soil and water for society: sharing solutions. ISCO International Soil Conservation Organisation Conference, July 2004, Brisbane, Australia: ASSSI/IECA. http://www.ttc.nrcs.usda.gov/news/TTC_paper_ISCO.pdf. (June 2011).

Shintani, T.; Beckham, S.; O'Connor, H.K.; Hughes, C.; Sato, A. 1994. The Waianae diet program: a culturally sensitive, community-based obesity and clinical intervention program for the native Hawaiian population. Hawai'i Medical Journal. 53: 136–147.

Thaman, R.R.; Elevitch, C.R.; Wilkinson, K.M. 2000. Multipurpose trees for agroforestry in the Pacific Islands. Agroforestry guides for Pacific Islands #2. Holualoa, HI: Permanent Agriculture Resources. http://www.agroforestry.net/afg/book.html. (December 2011).

U.S. Census Bureau. 2014a. International Programs, International Database. Midyear population and density: Puerto Rico, USVI, American Samoa, Commonwealth of the Northern Mariana Islands, Republic of the Marshall Islands, Republic of Palau, Federated States of Micronesia, Guam. http://www.census.gov/population/international/data/idb/region.php (March 2014)

U.S. Census Bureau. 2014b. State & County QuickFacts: Hawai'i. Population 2010. http://quickfacts.census.gov/qfd/states/15000.html (March 2014)

U.S. Congress, Office of Technology Assessment [US OTA]. 1987. Integrated renewable resource management for U.S. insular areas. OTA-F-325. Washington, DC: U.S. Government Printing Office. http://www.princeton.edu/~ota/disk2/1987/8712/871201.pdf. (November 2011).

U.S. Department of Agriculture, Forest Service, State and Private Forestry [USDA FS SPF], Program Redesign Committee. 2007. Tropical forests of the United States: applying U.S. Department of Agriculture, State and Private Forestry programs. http://www.hawaiistateassessment.info/library/tropicalforests-of-the-United-States-Final60607.pdf. (November 2011).

U.S. Department of the Interior, Bureau of Land Management, Seeds of Success [USDI BLM SOS]. 2011. Seeds of success training, module 1: introduction and overview, seed collection for restoration and conservation. Native Plant Materials Development Program. Internal document. Washington, DC: U.S. Department of the Interior, Bureau of Land Management. http://www.nps.gov/plants/sos/. (January 2014).

Vieira, D.L.M.; Holl, K.D.; Peneireiro, F.M. 2009. Agro-successional restoration as a strategy to facilitate tropical forest recovery. Restoration Ecology. 17: 451–459.

Withrow-Robinson, B.; Johnson, R. 2006. Selecting native plant materials for restoration projects: insuring local adaptation and maintaining genetic diversity. Corvallis, OR: Oregon State University Extension Service. http://ir.library.oregonstate.edu/xmlui/bitstream/handle/1957/20385/em8885-e.pdf. (August 2006).

Wittman, H.; Desmarais, A.; Weibe, N., eds. 2010. Food sovereignty: reconnecting food, nature and community. Oakland, CA: Food First Books. 232 p.

Planning a Tropical Nursery

Kim M. Wilkinson and Thomas D. Landis

2

Every nursery is unique. Tropical nurseries operate in a vast range of environmental, social, and economic contexts. Each nursery has a unique design based on distinct needs, goals, and resources (figure 2.1). With so many diverse factors to consider, no standard blueprint for how to design a particular nursery exists. The best nursery design will be matched to your specific location, plants, community, and goals.

Although planning a nursery can seem like a somewhat complex process, the basic formula is to answer the questions of why, who, what, how, where, and when. Why start a nursery? Who will the nursery serve? What will the nursery grow? How will the plants be propagated and the nursery be managed? Where will the nursery be located? When will be best to carry out production tasks? This chapter is intended to guide you through the process of answering these questions for planning a native plant nursery.

Facing Page: *The best nursery design will be matched to your specific context and goals to meet the needs of your clients. Photo from American Samoa by Diane Haase.*

Figure 2.1—*Native plant nurseries have many unique characteristics, including growing a wide diversity of species. Photo by Tara Luna.*

The Importance of Planning

The startup phase of successful nurseries involves thoughtfulness, research, and careful planning. Too often this crucial planning phase is rushed or misdirected by preconceived ideas of how a nursery should look (such as, "all nurseries should have a big greenhouse") or what the nursery should do (such as, "we ought to grow seedlings of this species for reforestation"). Before making these types of decisions, it is important to do some strategic planning. The initial planning phase is an opportunity to step back and clarify the vision and goals of the nursery and to coordinate all components needed to reach these goals (figure 2.2). For example, the first idea may be to build a large structure, such as a greenhouse. Deeper exploration of the nursery's goals and the actual needs of the species to be grown, however, may reveal how to create a site-appropriate design of several different, smaller scale environments that are ultimately more economical, efficient, and effective for producing plants.

Planning is essential because each aspect of the nursery affects every other aspect. For example, consider the seemingly simple act of choosing what kind of container to use for growing plants. Containers come in many sizes and shapes (see Chapter 7, Containers) and will dictate the nursery layout and benches needed, what types of

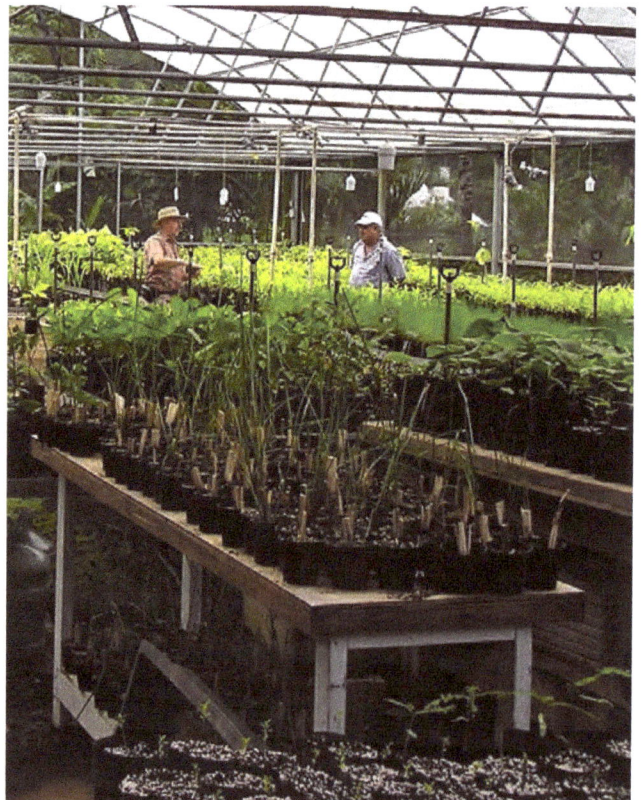

Figure 2.2—*Take time to visit other nurseries, talk with potential clients, and clarify your vision and goals before starting a nursery. Photo by Ronald Overton.*

growing media will be used, how seeds will be sown, how plants will be watered, how plants will be delivered, and so forth. Container type and size will also affect scheduling and production costs. It would be unwise to invest in containers without thinking these other factors through. Browsing through this handbook can be helpful before making any big decisions or purchases. The example with containers is only one illustration of the interconnectedness involved in planning a nursery. Both direct and indirect factors must be considered in nursery design (figure 2.3).

Defining the Nursery's Vision and Objectives

Most nurseries are founded on a vision how the landscape and community could be 10, 50, or 100 or more years from now as a result of efforts today. This vision will be a guiding force for the nursery's work.

Some of the vision process involves locating your "north star," the condition in the future that you may be inspired to work and move towards your whole life, but may not live to see. Visioning is the chance to dream big and may also include very personal aspects, such as how you would like your lifestyle, livelihood, and role in your community to be.

Any nursery founded to propagate native or culturally important plants must be aware of its vital role in protecting ecosystem health and diversity. Biodiversity is defined at three different levels (Wilson 1988, Landis and others 1993):

- Genetic level—the number of alleles or genotypes within a species.
- Species level—the number of species within a population and the number of these populations within a community or ecosystem.
- Ecosystem level—the number of communities and ecosystems in the world.

Nurseries play a key role in helping to preserve biodiversity at all three levels (figure 2.4). Mindfulness of appropriate local genetics and diversity allows for nursery work to be of enormous benefit for the environment, the community, and future generations of plants, animals, and people.

Determining Community Needs

Visions are translated into practical objectives through interactions with the local community and the local environment. The nursery founder may have a vision, for example, of seeing many kinds of people planting a wide

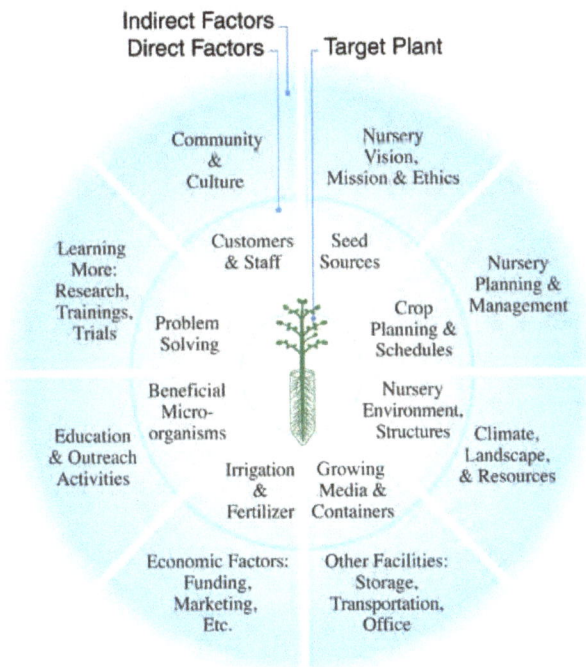

Figure 2.3—A nursery is a web of interrelated factors. Getting a good overview of direct and indirect factors for plant production in any situation will help design the best nursery to meet local needs. Illustration from Dumroese and others (2008).

Figure 2.4—Nurseries play a key role in helping to preserve biodiversity. For example, every time you collect seeds to propagate, you can help protect local species and genetic diversity. Photo by Douglass F. Jacobs.

diversity of native and culturally important plants provided by the nursery, while native animals from pollinators to birds and mammals also benefit. You can hold a broad vision for the future, while working practically within a scope that makes sense for the present. For example, an approach of—"if we grow it, they will plant it"—may result in wasted effort if the community has little desire or knowledge about how to use the nursery's plants. To help bridge the gap between a vision and practical objectives, start by asking questions such as—

- What is truly needed and wanted in our community?
- Who are the potential clients of our plant materials at this time?
- Who might be potential clients in the future (if we engage in outreach and education)?
- What are the needs and priorities of the potential clients?

Formal and informal avenues should be used to gather as much information as possible. Trade groups, guilds, elders, and instructors that work with plant products are often tremendous sources of information. Holding a gathering, discussing hopes for the future of the local environment and community, interviewing people, publishing an article in the local newspaper and asking for responses, or conducting formal market research can be useful in this phase. It is also imperative to understand the challenges people in the community face on diverse outplanting sites (figure 2.5). For example, if you plan to grow species to serve local farmers for their conservation practices (such as erosion control, windbreaks, or riparian buffers), make field visits to observe actual conditions on the farms.

This "end-user needs assessment" is key to helping a nursery determine not only what species to grow but also the container size (stocktype) clients might prefer. With culturally important plants, particularly those used for medicine and crafts, clients often have exacting specifications. It is essential to assess these expectations during the planning phase to ensure that the nursery will provide what clients actually need and want (figure 2.6). In addition, an assessment will help determine how long the existing demand is likely to last, which may indicate whether the nursery will be viable in the long term.

The nursery may also use its own vision to avoid being swept up into meeting the short-term demands of a changing market. For example, if public interest in planting a certain exotic ornamental species becomes high, a nursery might expect financial gain from meeting this demand. Would meeting that demand, however, help fulfill the vision of the nursery? Perhaps it would and perhaps not; deciding whether to meet a certain demand depends on the circumstances and the nursery's objectives.

Figure 2.5—*Understanding the challenges of your client's outplanting sites is important so you can grow the best plants for their needs. A farmer planting trees for forage on a dry site in East Timor (A); "badlands"—bauxite mining areas—on the main island of Palau where revegetation is very challenging (B); an abandoned pasture in St. Croix, U.S. Virgin Islands, infested with invasive coral vines (Antigonon leptopus) that smother other vegetation (C). Photo A by J.B. Friday, photo B by George Hernández, and photo C by Brian F. Daley.*

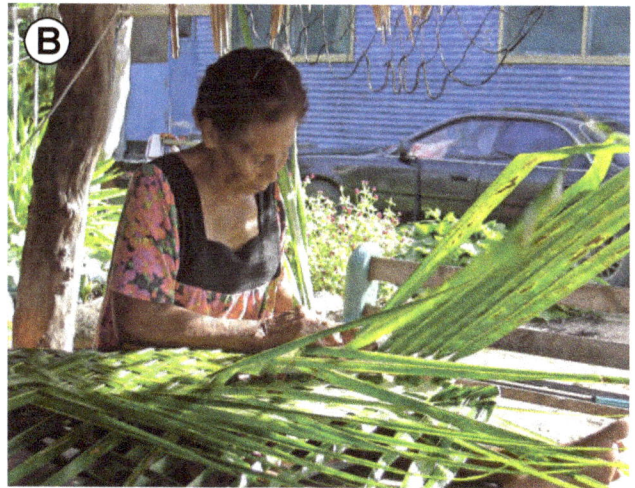

Figure 2.6—*The perpetuation of culturally important plant materials is a key objective for many tropical nurseries. The nursery must work with end-users in the community to ensure that the plants produced will meet cultural needs, such as Kava, an important medicinal and ceremonial plant of the Pacific Islands (A) or plants for traditional weaving on Yap (B). Photo A by Ronald Overton, and photo B by Megan Parker.*

Keep in mind that nursery-community communication goes both ways. Although the nursery must listen to the needs and wants of its community, it can also share its visions and goals by engaging in education and outreach to share information with clients and the community about the benefits and attributes of its plant materials. For example, if local farmers or landscapers believe only a certain ornamental plant works well as a boundary hedge, it may be because people are unaware of a native or traditional species that can be planted successfully for the same purpose, while providing other benefits. A good understanding of local ecology, environmental issues, history, soil types, and site needs for outplanting materials is important for effectively communicating with potential clients (figure 2.7).

Defining Target Plant Needs and Other Services

Successful nurseries provide healthy, high-quality, locally adapted plants that have high survival rates after outplanting. In addition, nurseries must provide the field-ready plants for outplanting when environmental conditions and the outplanting sites are optimal for survival. Nursery planning is critical for matching the plant materials produced with the needs and conditions of clients' outplanting sites to ensure that the plants can produce the materials or products (medicine, wood, food, and so on) that clients expect. (See Chapter 3, Defining the Target Plant, for more discussion about this topic.) These needs dictate the plant's target size, age, genetic source, container type, and management in the nursery.

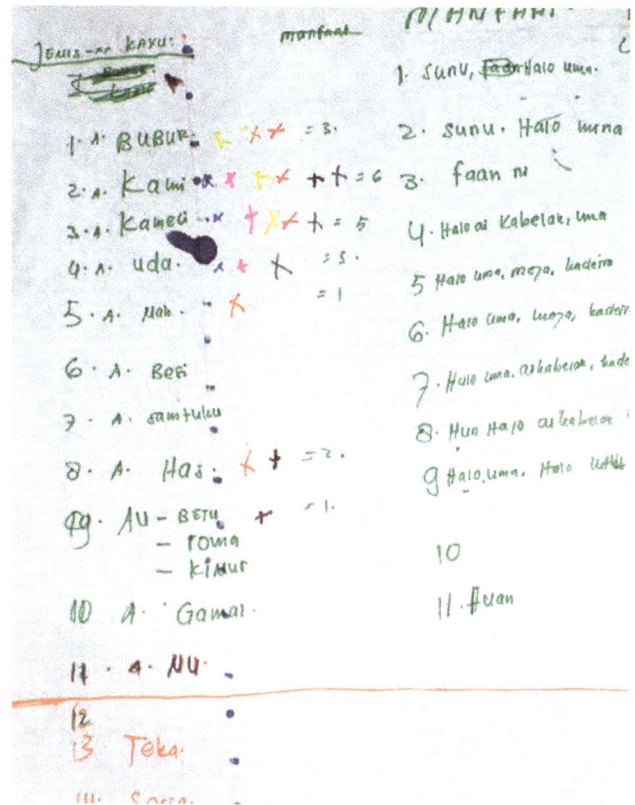

Figure 2.7—*Gathering information about the community needs helps clarify what the nursery could grow. Here, villagers in Baucau, Timor Leste, developed a list of local agroforestry species and their uses. Villagers used colored markers to vote on which trees they would like to plant. The most popular was candlenut, Aleurites moluccana, whose nuts could be sold locally and processed for food or oil. Ai kameli is sandalwood (Santalum album) and ai bubur is Eucalyptus alba, the local firewood. Note that the typical forestry trees, teak (Tectona grandis) and toon (Toona species), did not receive any votes. The language is Tetun. Photo by J.B. Friday.*

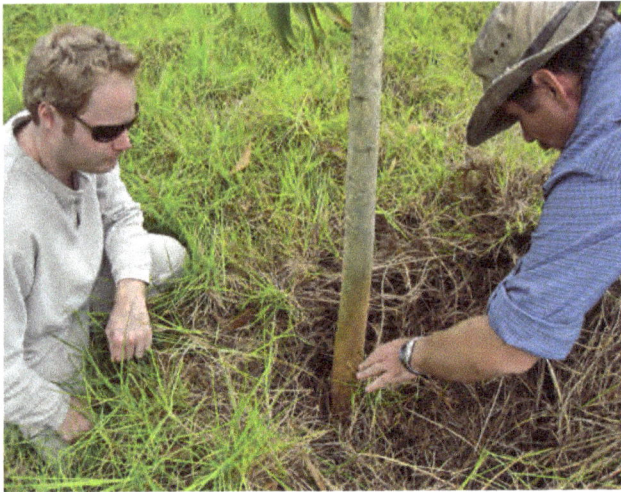

Figure 2.8—*Nurseries dedicate time and resources to cultivating relationships with clients, including visiting clients' sites months or years after the plants left the nursery, to see how the plants are doing. Photo by Douglass F. Jacobs.*

Some topics to consider when deciding what to grow include—

- The species the nursery might be capable of growing.
- Specific end-user requirements for each species (such as medicine, food, timber, habitat, soil stabilization, windbreak, and commercial products).
- The types of environments in which plants will be outplanted.
- The size and age of stock preferred.
- The season during which people prefer to plant (in the tropics, usually the beginning of the rainy season).
- The quantity of each species people may want to plant.
- The distance people are willing to travel to obtain the plant materials.

Another consideration is what species are most needed from an ecological standpoint. For example, in some tropical forests, rarer or later successional species needed to restore the diversity of the forest may not return without human help, and these species may be a higher priority for nursery work (Holl and Aide 2011).

The target plant requirements will differ among species and outplanting sites and will influence all aspects of nursery design: location, structures, container types, scheduling, management practices, propagule collection, and so forth. In addition to producing plants, many nurseries offer a range of services such as consultations and planting plans, seed selection and collection, testing of new propagation methods, plant delivery, and outplanting support (figure 2.8). Successful nurseries also dedicate time and resources

to community education, client communications, marketing, and establishing good relationships with farmers, natural resource managers, landscapers, and planners.

Assessing Resources and Costs

How will we start a nursery? How will the finances work? What resources and costs are involved? Is starting a nursery even feasible? Each of these questions is discussed in the following sections.

Starting With a Small Pilot Nursery

It is often wise to start with a small pilot nursery to better understand how to produce native plants and successfully manage a nursery in your conditions to meet your community's needs. A pilot phase is an opportunity to try out production on a smaller scale with less risk (figure 2.9). The design of the pilot nursery is essentially your "best educated guess" on what type of set-up would be optimal to produce plants, based on this handbook and your personal experiences. You can expect a large learning curve when developing methods for growing native and culturally important plants. High crop losses may occur during the first few seasons, and more losses may take place for the sake of experimentation (figure 2.10). A few seasons of growth and observation in a pilot nursery can preclude unnecessary expenditures, develop viable propagation strategies, and eliminate many of the unknowns regarding how to produce plants and manage the nursery, thereby providing enough detailed information to effectively plan a larger facility. A pilot nursery can also be invaluable in estimating costs and making a more accurate feasibility assessment when the time comes to expand.

Figure 2.9—*Starting with a smaller scale pilot phase reduces the number of unknown factors and risks and is a key part of developing a successful nursery. Photo by Thomas D. Landis.*

Figure 2.10—*The pilot phase is the time to test ideas and accept the fact that failures lead to better results. These growers tried to repurpose Styrofoam® cups as nursery containers. They found that, unlike proper root-training nursery containers, the round shape allowed roots to spiral, which could be a serious problem after outplanting. Photo by J.B. Friday.*

A small pilot nursery can help assess the following practices:

- How to take crops through all phases of development, from germination through hardening and distribution.
- How to develop realistic timelines and budgets for future production.
- How to plan infrastructure for production (and what infrastructure is truly necessary versus optional).
- Which growing media, container types, and propagation strategies are optimal for the plants.
- What labor and material costs are involved.
- What types of challenges may arise.
- How clients respond to the plants that were produced.
- How plants perform on different outplanting sites.
- What aspects of the nursery vision are feasible to carry out at this time.

The key is to start small, learn lessons along the way, and adjust your system accordingly. Keep in mind that no one who works with plants will ever feel as if they have learned everything they need to know; even very established nurseries are always learning more about how to grow and perpetuate plants, how to manage facilities and resources better, and how to improve relations with clients and the community. At some point, however, you will be confident that it is time to expand on the successes of the pilot nursery and continue development on a larger scale.

Assess Finances

Finances are an essential part of determining how a nursery will start and operate. Nurseries differ greatly in terms of their financial objectives. Some nurseries may be funded through grants or government programs while others are aligned with a particular project or organization. Some may have startup or pilot phase money, but are expected to be financially self-sufficient in the future. Private, for-profit nurseries must earn enough income from the sale of plants to at least pay for development, infrastructure, production costs, and staff time. Whatever the circumstances, finance is a key part of nursery planning. It determines—

- How much money can be invested in the nursery at the outset.
- If staff can be hired.
- In what timeframe the nursery can start to produce plants for sale.
- How many plants can be produced.
- What price can be charged for the plant materials.

Even if plants are to be distributed freely and not sold, it is still essential to know the cost to produce each kind of plant for planning, assessing feasibility, and ensuring the financial viability of the nursery. For a new nursery, predicting the cost of plants is complicated and depends on infrastructure, nursery size, staff skills, knowledge base, and many other factors. Nurseries that have gone through a pilot phase probably have a good grasp of the production costs. These costs can be revised to reflect production on a larger scale. Without a pilot phase, estimating costs before production is very difficult to do accurately, especially because high crop losses may be expected during the first few seasons while successful propagation methods are developed.

Visiting other nurseries to get an idea of similar production processes can be very helpful as resources and finances are assessed. Government nurseries are a great source of information because staff members usually share production details openly, and their production costs are public information. Visiting private nurseries is also useful in assessing all the stages that go into plant production, although they may be less open regarding financial and operational details. These production details can then be used to estimate costs in the planned nursery.

Estimate crop production costs by considering all phases of production, from collecting seeds to mixing growing media to delivering the plants (figure 2.11). To improve the accuracy of the estimated costs, consider the timeframe

Figure 2.11—*To accurately estimate the time and expenses required for growing plant materials in a nursery, examine all aspects of plant production, from collecting seeds to delivering plants. Photo by Thomas D. Landis.*

for growing the crop, the size of the stock, the labor and materials required, and the fact that some crop losses will take place during production. Remember to account for the following factors:

- Material production costs (for example growing media, water, fertilizer, seeds, pest control).

- Labor costs for production, maintenance, and delivery.

- Shipping costs and shipping time required for supplies and equipment (shipping can be costly and slow in remote areas and islands—order well in advance).

- Time and labor for customer relations (such as helping clients determine their target plant needs, answering e-mail messages or telephone calls, and visiting sites after outplanting).

- Inventory required (for example, the time, space, and materials each crop will require, such as nursery benches, containers, and trays).

- Structures (for example, protected germination area, shadehouse, and storage).

- Overhead costs (such as rent, insurance, water, utilities, and taxes).

- Time and labor for administration (bookkeeping, payroll, and staff relations).

- Time and funds for outreach, advertising, or educational programs.

It is wise to estimate a range of best-case (most economical) and worst-case production scenarios. After production is underway and actual costs are known, it is imperative to revisit the price structure of the plants to ensure that they are in line with actual costs. In some cases, the costs of producing plants on a larger scale will be lower per plant than during the smaller scale pilot phase. But it is also possible that costs related to rent, utilities, labor, and so on may be higher.

Assess Feasibility

After assessing resources and costs, it is time to evaluate whether starting the nursery is a realistic and achievable undertaking. Again, starting with a small pilot phase is a good way to determine the feasibility of starting a nursery. The feasibility assessment needs to include the species potentially available to grow, client needs, production costs, market price, and the nursery's site, goals, and capabilities. Will the emphasis be on growing plants from seeds or cuttings? How long does it take to grow these species to target specifications? What size plants need to be produced? Several scenarios need to be examined, including a variety of facility designs, sizes, and locations, so that the best conditions to meet projected needs are identified.

Other feasibility questions that need to be asked include, "Can the vision and objectives be fulfilled without starting a new nursery? Do alternatives exist?" Acting as a distributor instead of as a producer may be an economical alternative to starting a new nursery; this alternative has its benefits and drawbacks (table 2.1).

Selecting a Nursery Site

After the decision has been made to move beyond the pilot phase and develop a nursery, an appropriate nursery site must be selected. If possible, the pilot nursery can be located on the proposed permanent site to maximize familiarity with production and management on that site. Sometimes the nursery site is selected after the pilot phase, and this approach also has merit because you may be clearer about what you are looking for in a nursery site. Nursery site selection involves working with nature, rather than against it, for the most effective, efficient, and economical design (figure 2.12). The less the natural environment has to be modified to produce high-quality plants, the less expense the nursery will have to incur to create optimal crop conditions. Again, an understanding of the methods and costs associated with producing target plants along with the client-needs assessment will help in choosing a site. Careful observation of site conditions and an assessment of past and present climatic records are important. Even in cases where the site is already chosen, the process of site observation and inventory described here is helpful to understand the strengths and challenges of that site. Of course, no site is perfect.

Table 2.1—*The benefits and drawbacks of either starting a nursery or distributing plants from another supplier. Adapted from Landis and others (1994).*

Benefits	Drawbacks
Purchase plants	
• Time and capital available for other uses • No nursery staff needed • More long-term flexibility • Short-term or no commitment required	• No control over growing process • Less control over plant quality, genetics, and availability • Plants may not be adapted to local environment • Unique needs of local clients may not be met
Start own nursery	
• High control over growing practices (can choose organic methods, local resources, and so forth) • High control over quality, genetics, and availability of plants • Plants will be adapted to local environment • Can develop local expertise on plant growing and handling • Can use traditional or culturally appropriate methods if applicable • No reliance on others to provide plants • Create job opportunities	• Large initial investment, capital, and time • Long-term professional and economic commitment • Native plant markets are notorious for year-to-year fluctuations • Steep learning curve to gain proficiency in quality plant production and nursery management

Figure 2.12—*Good site assessment and an understanding of crop needs will help determine the best structures for a nursery. Shown here is nursery construction in American Samoa. Photo by Thomas D. Landis.*

Planning a Tropical Nursery

Critical nursery site selection factors include the following—

- Access to good-quality, affordable, and abundant water.
- Unobstructed solar access.
- Easily accessible flat area for delivery or processing of bulky, heavy material such as soil, sand, mulch, and fertilizer.
- Easy access and close proximity to staff.
- Adequate land area.
- Reliable energy supply (if water pumps, fans, or lights are used).
- Freedom from insurmountable ecological concerns (such as neighboring chemical pollution, unmanageable noxious weeds, and so on).
- Freedom from problematic political concerns (such as problematic zoning and historical land use issues).

Climatic and biological attributes top the list for importance in site selection. An abundance of good-quality, reliable, affordable water is the number one factor; water quality always needs to be tested when a site is being considered for nursery construction. See Chapter 11, Water Quality and Irrigation, for more information about this topic. Unobstructed solar access is also essential; plants need sun to grow. Access to electricity is important only if the nursery uses practices such as electric water pumps, fans to move air through the nursery, lights at night, or communication devices. At least one person needs to have quick access to the nursery in case of emergency; if the nursery site will be far away from human dwellings, it may be advisable to construct a caretaker residence on site. The amount of land selected for the nursery must be large enough for the production areas and any support buildings, and also allow for the efficient movement of any equipment and materials. In addition to immediate needs, potential nursery sites need to be evaluated on the basis of available space for possible expansion. Ecopolitical site selection factors, notably land use zoning and concerns about neighboring land uses that may involve herbicide, pesticide, or potential groundwater contamination are also important factors for determining suitable sites for nursery development.

Table 2.2—Decision matrix for evaluating potential container nursery sites. In this example, Site A received the highest score and is therefore considered the best choice for a nursery site. Adapted from Landis and others (1994).

Site selection criteria	Weight valuea	Site A		Site B		Site C	
		Rating	Weighted score	Rating	Weighted score	Rating	Weighted score
Critical Factors							
Good solar access	10	9	90	7	70	9	90
Water quality	9	9	81	7	63	4	36
Water quantity	8	10	80	8	64	9	72
Available energy	8	9	72	9	72	10	80
Adequate land area	7	8	56	8	56	10	70
Zoning restrictions	7	10	70	6	42	8	56
Pollution concerns	6	9	54	7	42	9	54
Secondary factors							
Microclimate	6	9	54	8	48	9	54
Topography	5	10	50	9	45	10	50
Labor supply	4	9	36	8	32	10	40
Accessibility	4	8	32	6	24	8	32
Shipping distances	3	9	27	7	21	10	30
Total score			702		579		664
Site suitability			#1		#3		#2

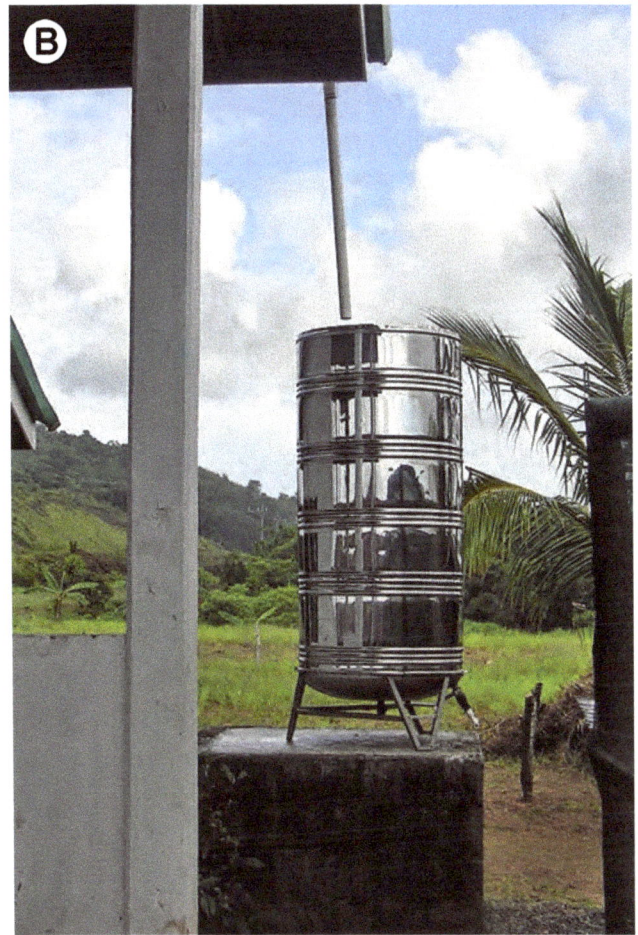

Figure 2.13—*Planning for local environmental conditions and for risk is essential during the process of nursery design. This nursery in Guam uses natural windbreaks to reduce water use and add protection to the nursery site (A); this nursery in Palau catches rainwater as a backup water supply (B). Photo A by Tara Luna, and photo B by George Hernández.*

Protected microclimate can make dramatic improvements in nursery productivity and reduce cost expenditures. A site with a climate sheltered from extremes such as high winds, storms, and severe temperature fluctuations is ideal. Gentle topography also makes nursery set-up and management much easier than hilly or steep terrain. Access to the nursery by staff and clients is also useful for economical nursery production. In areas at risk of high winds, making use of a natural windbreak (figure 2.13) or having the ability to quickly remove the plastic from the roof of a greenhouse may save a structure in a severe storm. A backup water supply ensures crop survival through periods of drought or uncertainty. Firebreaks or a site selected to minimize fire risks can preclude disaster.

Each potential nursery site will likely have good and bad attributes. A decision matrix (table 2.2) can be constructed by listing the potential nursery sites across the top and the significant site selection criteria down the side. The next step is to assign each site selection criterion an importance value on a scale from 1 to 10, with the most critical factors receiving the highest values and the less important ones receiving progressively lower values. Next, the suitability of each potential nursery location is evaluated and rated, again on a scale of 1 to 10, based on the information that has been gathered. The score for each cell in the matrix is then calculated by multiplying the weights for each site selection factor by the rating for each site. Finally, the weighted scores are totaled for each site, and, if the weights and rankings have been objectively assigned, then the potential nursery site with the highest total ranking should be the best choice. If all the potential sites are close in score, then the process needs to be repeated and careful attention paid to the relative values of each factor. The selection criteria can also be adapted or expanded to include other factors important to you. If the scores are still close, the sites are probably equally good.

Planning a Tropical Nursery

Figure 2.14—Good planning examines the flow of work and sets up effective workstations for efficient and enjoyable plant production during all phases of growth. Photo by Kim M. Wilkinson.

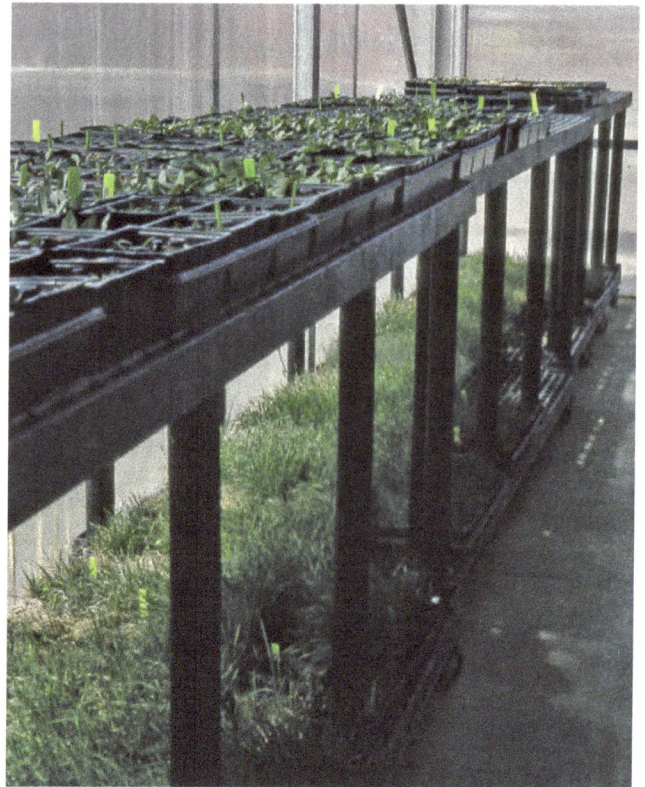

Figure 2.15—Good planning translates to making efficient use of resources and space. This small greenhouse saves water and labor by growing sedges and wetland grasses on benches beneath those for dryland forbs. Photo by Tara Luna.

Planning the Flow of Work

Good nursery planning takes place in time and in space (figure 2.14). Overall nursery planning examines the flow of work and materials through all seasons and phases of growth.

The requirements to produce target plants in time for the client's outplanting season guide all other aspects of nursery design. Good site selection and a sound knowledge of propagation methods are important for creating the most appropriate environments for the crop's needs. Rather than a single, large nursery structure or area, it is common to have a diversity of smaller areas and some structures tailored to meet the needs of the crops as they go through their development.

Although crop production is the core of nursery activities, it is only part of the whole picture. Preparation, cleanup, and storage must also be well planned. Where will seeds be cleaned, stored, treated, and tested? Where will containers be cleaned, sterilized, and stored? Where will clients be met? The flow of work through time and seasons and design to facilitate the movement of people and plants in an efficient and safe way is an essential component of nursery planning (figure 2.14).

Considering the nursery's local effect is also important. For example, consider not only where good-quality water will come from for irrigation, but also where the water could go after nursery use. The water may contain fertilizers and be a potential source of pollution, possibly creating problems and legal issues for the nursery. With good planning for flow over time, however, that same water may be used as a resource, directed to other crops (figure 2.15), or recycled. Thoughtful design minimizes the amount of water used, provides for the needs of plants, and deals with runoff appropriately, as discussed in Chapter 11, Water Quality and Irrigation. Consider as many elements as you can during the planning phase, and be prepared to adapt as new opportunities for efficiency present themselves after the nursery is operational.

Planning as an Ongoing Process

The initial planning phase is a crucial part of successful nursery development, but the planning process does not stop after the nursery is operational. The vision of the nursery needs to be revisited regularly. Set aside time to assess the nursery's progress in fulfilling its objectives, visualize new possibilities, and adapt to changing circumstances.

Figure 2.16—*Planning a nursery is an ongoing process that is aided by visiting other nurseries and continually learning more. Photo by Kim M. Wilkinson.*

Continually learning more through nursery visits, conferences, and field days will also help with ongoing planning and improvement (figure 2.16). Following up with clients and revisiting target plant specifications are also essential for planning for success. See Chapter 18, Working With People, and Chapter 19, Nursery Management, for more discussion about these topics.

References

Holl, K.D.; Aide, T.M. 2010. When and where to actively restore ecosystems? Forest Ecology and Management. 261(10): 1558–1563.

Landis, T.D.; Lippitt, L.A.; Evans, J.M. 1993. Biodiversity and ecosystem management: the role of forest and conservation nurseries. In: Landis, T.D., tech. coord. Proceedings, Western Forest Nursery Association, 14–18 September 1992—, Fallen Leaf Lake, CA. Gen. Tech. Rep. RM-221. Fort Collins, CO: U.S. Department of Agriculture, Forest Service, Rocky Mountain Forest and Range Experiment Station: 1–17.

Landis, T.D.; Tinus, R.W.; McDonald, S.E.; Barnett, J.P. 1994. The container tree manual: volume 1, nursery planning, development, and management. Agriculture Handbook 674. Washington, DC: U.S. Department of Agriculture, Forest Service. 188 p.

Wilson, E.O., ed. 1988. Biodiversity. Washington, DC: National Academies Press. 521 p.

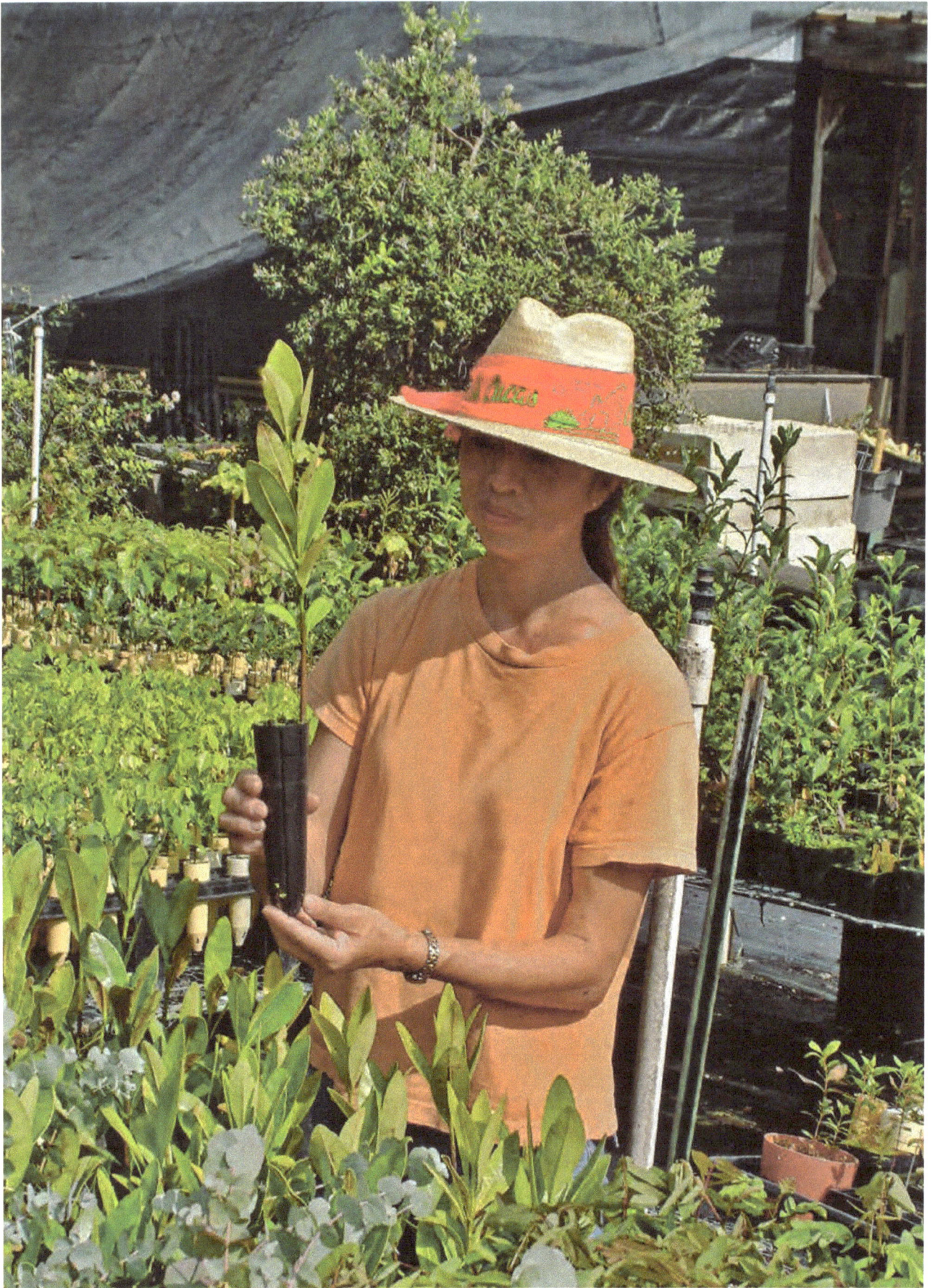

Defining the Target Plant

Thomas D. Landis and Kim M. Wilkinson

3

People planting native and traditional species in the tropics have diverse goals and face a multitude of challenges on their outplanting sites. Understanding these goals and challenges and the steps necessary to meet them is essential to outplanting success. The Target Plant Concept is used to define what plant materials to grow in the nursery to meet the needs on the outplanting sites and achieve project objectives. A "one-size-fits-all" approach to plant materials does not work well. Instead, plant materials must be matched to meet the challenges of the outplanting site. Establishing targets is critical; for a given species, the target plant destined for a harsh restoration site where care will be minimal after outplanting is very different from one that will be outplanted in a city park or hotel landscape where it will be pampered. Thus, the definition of the target plant depends on how it will be used—its "fitness for purpose" (Sutton 1980). This definition is the essence of the Target Plant Concept.

The Target Plant Concept was developed as a way to define the target plant, and it has two equally important components. The first component incorporates three simple approaches that provide the broad, fundamental basis necessary to successfully complete outplanting projects (figure 3.1). The second component is the step-by-step process of defining the target plant material. The nursery manager and client systematically answer eight sequential, but interrelated questions about the outplanting site and project goals to ultimately define the target plant material. The target plants are then produced, outplanted, and monitored; then the cycle repeats. An understanding of the Target Plant Concept is vital when starting a new nursery or upgrading an existing one and is also useful when working with customers. Let us examine the first of the two components in detail.

Facing Page: *The "target plant" is cultivated to meet the challenges of the outplanting site and the objectives of the project. Photo by J.B. Friday.*

Important Approaches for Implementing the Target Plant Concept

The first component of the Target Plant Concept incorporates three simple, often overlooked ideas that, when considered together, guide the broad approach for defining and selecting the target plant materials for a specific site.

Start at the Outplanting Site

With the Target Plant Concept, the nursery production process starts with the characteristics of the outplanting site. Land managers specify exactly what type of plant material would be best for their site conditions (figure 3.2). Understanding these needs, the nursery grows plant materials that are locally adapted, genetically appropriate, and the optimal size, age, and so on to survive and thrive on the outplanting site.

Forge a Nursery-Client Partnership

With the Target Plant Concept, the land manager and nursery manager work together to define the ideal type of plant for the project, the nursery grows the plants, and they are outplanted (figure 3.3). Based on performance after outplanting, the land manager and nursery manager may work together to revise target plant characteristics to improve survival and growth of future crops (figure 3.4). See Chapter 18, Working With People, for information on how to facilitate meaningful, mutually supportive dialogue after outplanting. Good communication between native plant customers and nursery managers builds partnerships and ensures the best possible plants for the project. This feedback also ensures that both nurseries and clients are learning and adapting, thereby improving successes over time.

The Target Plant Concept

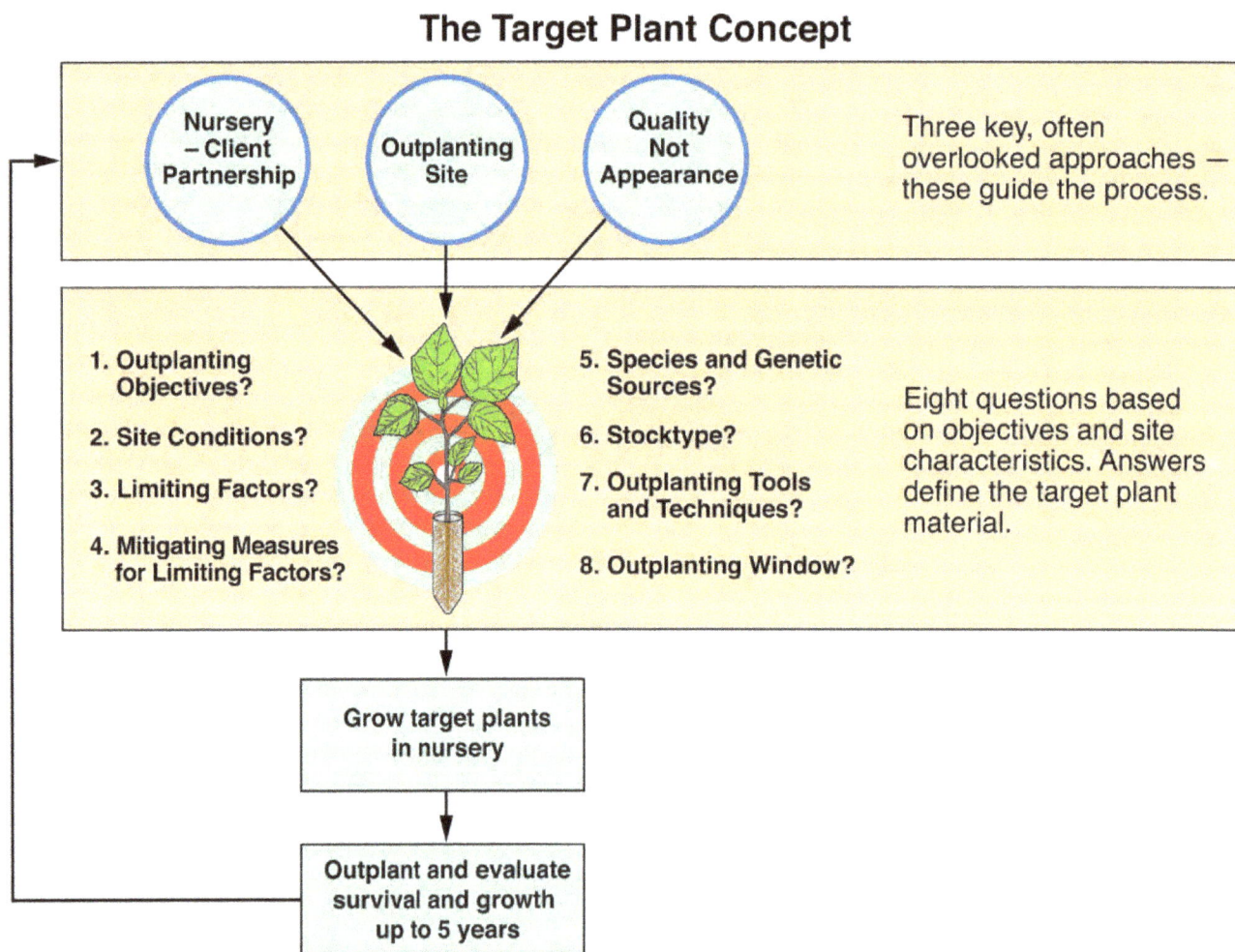

Figure 3.1—The Target Plant Concept starts with a partnership between the client and nursery manager that focuses on putting the best plant materials on specific project sites. The manager and client then answer eight questions about the project; their answers define the target plant material necessary to meet the objectives of that project. The nursery produces the plants. The client and manager subsequently reassess successes and failures and use that information to improve the next crop. Adapted from Landis (2011).

Figure 3.2—*Plant materials must be matched to meet the challenges of the outplanting sites and the goals of the projects they serve. A nursery in East Timor grows agroforestry species in polyethylene bags to serve village needs (A). The Palau Municipal Nursery grows native and culturally important seedlings in large pots for urban forestry projects (B). Future Forests Nursery in Hawai'i grows native trees and shrubs in several types of containers and growing environments for diverse restoration and farm forestry projects (C). Photo A by J.B. Friday, photo B by Katie Friday, and photo C by Jill Wagner.*

Figure 3.3—*Using the Target Plant Concept, nursery and land managers work together to specify what type of plant material would be best suited for the project. Shown is a native reforestation project in Guam, where target plants included native trees such as* Intsia bijuga *grown in large, 1-gallon root-training square containers (A). The native seedlings were planted using a mattock in soft clay soil (B). Photos by J.B. Friday.*

Figure 3.4—*Using the Target Plant Concept, the land owner and nursery manager work together to define the ideal type of plant for the project. Based on performance of the first crop, the managers make necessary changes to improve survival and growth. Here a nursery manager and land owner are standing in a 1-year-old mixed forest planting (foreground) and discussing performance of a 4-year-old planting (background) to make some decisions together about next year's target plants. Photo by Craig R. Elevitch.*

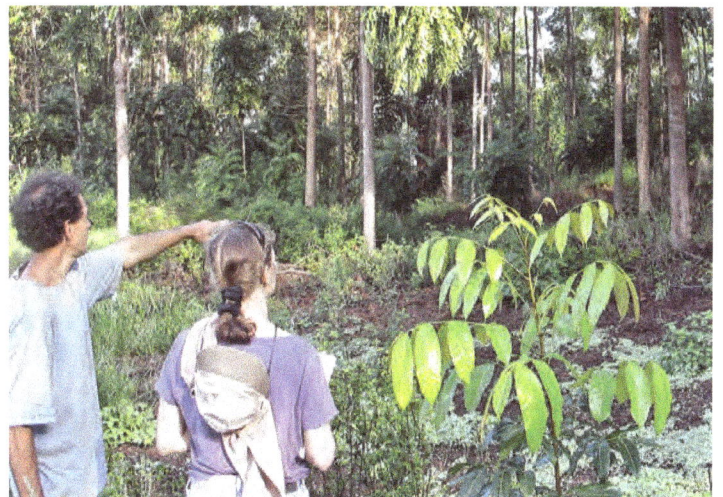

Defining the Target Plant

Emphasize Seedling Quality, Not Appearance

With the Target Plant Concept, plant quality is not determined by how good a plant looks as it sits in the nursery, but by outplanting performance. A beautiful crop of plants in the nursery may perform miserably if the plants are inappropriate for conditions on the outplanting site. Without the Target Plant Concept, inexperienced clients may believe they can find cheap, all-purpose native plants that will thrive nearly anywhere. Using the Target Plant Concept, plants are grown in the nursery with the view of their fitness to thrive on the outplanting site and their ability to fulfill the project objectives.

The second component of the Target Plant Concept is the process of defining the target plant materials. The nursery manager and client use the characteristics of the outplanting site to systematically answer eight sequential, but interrelated questions (figure 3.1) to ultimately define the target plant material.

1. What Are the Outplanting Objectives?

Native and traditional plants are grown for a variety of reasons; these project objectives critically influence target plant characteristics (figure 3.5).

In the tropics, project objectives may include reforesting land that has been deforested; enriching sustainable agriculture with windbreaks or erosion control using native species; providing shade in pastures; producing timber or wood for crafts; rekindling traditional agroforestry practices; ensuring local supplies of cultural or medicinal plants; restoring degraded land; controlling invasive species; creating habitat for pollinators, birds, or wildlife; planting native trees in urban areas; protecting and producing traditional foods; conserving soil and water quality; educating young people; and developing small businesses. Some projects hold a combination of objectives.

Figure 3.5—Native and traditional plants are grown for a variety of project objectives, which critically influence target plant characteristics. Objectives may be production of teak for commercial timber in Samoa (A); regeneration of heritage species, such as breadfruit trees, for food security (B); perpetuation of native and traditional species to sustain traditional lifeways and craftspeople (C); and reforestation of sites overcome by invasive species, such as this swordgrass area on Guam (D). Photos by Thomas D. Landis.

See the following examples of how target plants are linked to project objectives:

- Commercial timber production is a common objective for planting trees. For this objective of producing saw logs, the target plant would be a commercially valuable tree species that has been genetically selected for fast growth, good form, or desirable wood quality.

- The target plant for a watershed restoration project to stop erosion, stabilize the stream bank, and ultimately restore a functional plant community could be riparian trees and shrubs with extensive root systems and thick stems to withstand flowing water.

- Projects restoring threatened or endangered native plant species require target plants that perpetuate the genetic diversity and unique adaptations of these imperiled local populations or may require target plants that can restore or create critical habitat for these ecologically important species.

- Projects to restore or enhance food security and food sovereignty might require target plants that are native foods and cultivars of traditional or heritage food plants and varieties. Target plants may also include species and genotypes that yield the most or best-quality fruits, nuts, or other food.

- Project objectives for a burned, eroding former sugarcane field might be to stop soil erosion, replace exotic weed species with native or other desirable plants, restore nutrient cycling, and build up organic matter for future productivity. Target plants for such a project might include a direct seeding of native grasses and forbs or possibly a noninvasive annual plant to first stabilize the soil, followed by an outplanting of native nitrogen-fixing trees and other species to out-compete the weeds and build fertility on the site. These actions can improve site conditions over time. Later, more diverse species can be planted.

- Renewing native and traditional species for crafts or other cultural uses is an objective for many projects. Target plants may include local cultural plant species to help protect wild plants from the stresses of over-collection and to make their collection and use more accessible to elders and young people.

- Some projects have the objective to reduce the effects of weeds or invasive species. The presence of invasive exotic plants is often a result of disturbances that create ideal conditions for these plants to thrive. Therefore, simply removing undesired species does not solve the problem. Instead, undesirable plants must be replaced with desired ones. For example, most invasive grasses

thrive in full sun, so the target plant to shade out the grass would need to be large enough to overtop the grass immediately after outplanting, and quickly form dense shade.

Sometimes project objectives are straightforward and target plants are easily defined. For complex, large, or specialized projects, such as Forest Stewardship, conservation, or habitat improvement, the assistance of a professional may be needed. This expertise helps define objectives and target plant material requirements for every species to be planted. Many restoration projects follow an approach that includes finding reference sites, considering succession, and creating measurable goals.

Selecting Reference Sites

"Reference sites" are natural or recovered areas that serve as models for desirable recovery of native plant communities (figure 3.6A). The comparison of the soils, climate, vegetation, and other characteristics of reference sites to the project site provides guidance about what species may be established and is essential for setting attainable, site-appropriate goals for restoration (Steinfeld and others 2007) (figure 3.6B). Often several reference sites of different ages and recovery stages are used for one project. Reference sites also show succession, which is how plant communities may change over time.

Planning for Succession

Land managers need to understand not only how a healthy 200-year-old forest looks, but also how a healthy recovering tropical forest looks 1, 3, or 5 years into its development. Understanding this recovery process is necessary because if native species can colonize and become established on a disturbance, the processes of succession (ecosystem development over time), including soil genesis and nutrient cycling, are initiated (figure 3.7). Effective revegetation of disturbed sites aims to initiate or accelerate processes of natural succession following disturbances. Native plants may be established on disturbed sites through seeding or planting (figure 3.8). Sometimes passive revegetation (natural colonization) of some species is possible where native seed banks are available and limiting factors are mitigated. If passive restoration is possible, nurseries may be involved in growing enrichment or later successional species that will not regenerate on the site naturally.

Translating Objectives into Measurable Goals

Some projects formally translate their objectives into measurable goals within specified time frames. These goals

Figure 3.6—*Reference sites provide guidance about setting attainable, site-appropriate goals for restoring the outplanting site, including which species to plant. Information about conditions on reference sites is compared with the conditions on the outplanting site. Measuring trees on a regenerating, 30-year-old stand of native forest after cattle were removed from a pasture (A); surveying a pasture where forest recovery is desired (B). Photo A by J.B. Friday, and photo B by Douglass F. Jacobs.*

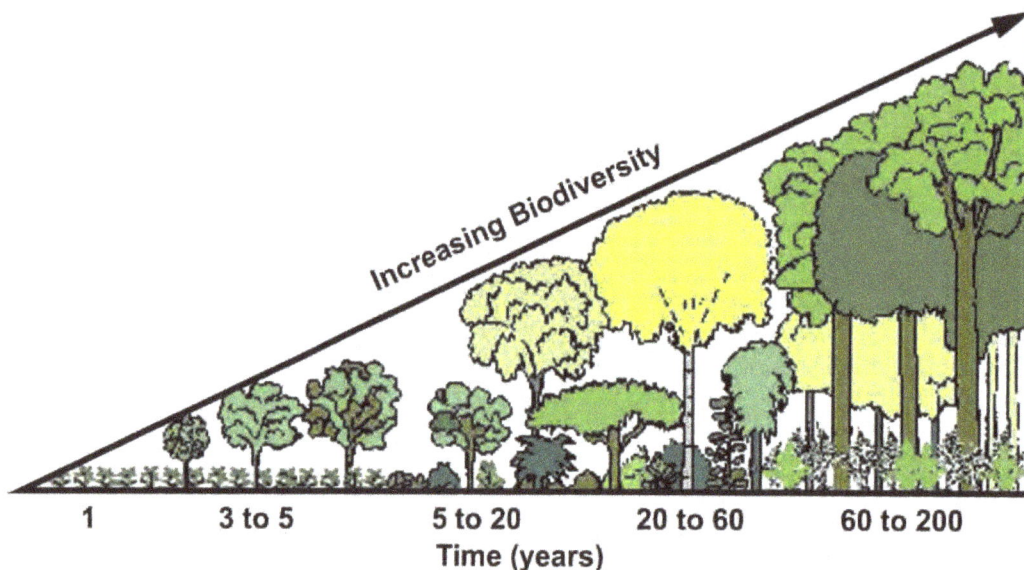

Figure 3.7—*Effective revegetation of disturbed sites aims to initiate or accelerate processes of natural succession following disturbances. Reference sites of different ages (5 years recovered, 20 years recovered, and so on) help to set reasonable timelines and appropriate species compositions for project development. Illustration adapted from Cerro Nara Rainforest Conservation (2010) by Jim Marin.*

are sometimes called success criteria or desired future conditions. For example, a reforestation project might set a goal of 400 living trees per acre 2 years after outplanting whereas a native plant project may have a goal of 75-percent vegetative ground cover of which 90 percent will be composed of perennial native species 1 year after outplanting. Production of food, craft materials, or timber might be stated in yields. Habitat restoration will define desired fauna moving into the planting area and will provide information about the plants themselves. Many restoration projects take place in stages. Short-term objectives might be to stabilize the soil and reinitiate natural succession, whereas longer term objectives include greater diversity and complexity. Monitoring is then planned to measure if these goals were achieved. See Chapter 17, Outplanting, for more information.

2. What Are the Conditions of the Outplanting Site?

Site evaluation is necessary for clients to determine their target plant requirements and achieve their goals. The information-gathering step may be informal, based on observation and spending time on the site. More complex projects often involve different tests and a systematic approach to determine site conditions. The most elaborate site assessments are usually carried out to meet regulatory requirements, such as a project requiring an environmental impact statement before it can proceed. For restoration of disturbed sites, the reference sites described previously are also surveyed to compare their conditions with those of the outplanting sites. At a minimum, basic land features need to be mapped and the site evaluated for basic information about soils, vegetation, climate, and site history.

Maps

Finding or creating a basic site map is an important step for projects of any scale. Topographic maps and aerial photos are especially useful and usually easy to find. Topographic maps indicate elevations, contour lines, waterways and water features, slopes, aspects, and human-made features including roads and settlements. Aerial photos can reveal features such as vegetation, access, structures, and surroundings and offer a snapshot of the conditions at one point in time. Special maps can be obtained as needed for more detailed information such as hydrology, soils, or forest cover.

Soils

The U.S. Department of Agriculture, Natural Resources Conservation Service (NRCS) and other organizations have soil surveys available for many areas; these surveys provide basic information on soil type and slope. In addition, a soil test can provide information on pH and nutrients (the client can contact the extension service to find out how to supply a soil sample to a testing facility). The client's personal observations are also a valuable addition. From these tests and observations, challenges such as issues with drainage, compaction, erosion, incorrect pH, depth to water table, and so on can be identified. For projects on large areas, a soil scientist may be called in to survey the site and provide a report, usually in combination with the NRCS or other data.

Vegetation

Vegetation information is obtained by observing and recording the site's existing vegetation. At its simplest, clients walk their site and list the vegetation they see, getting some help from a plant-savvy friend for species they cannot identify. Often, publications are available to

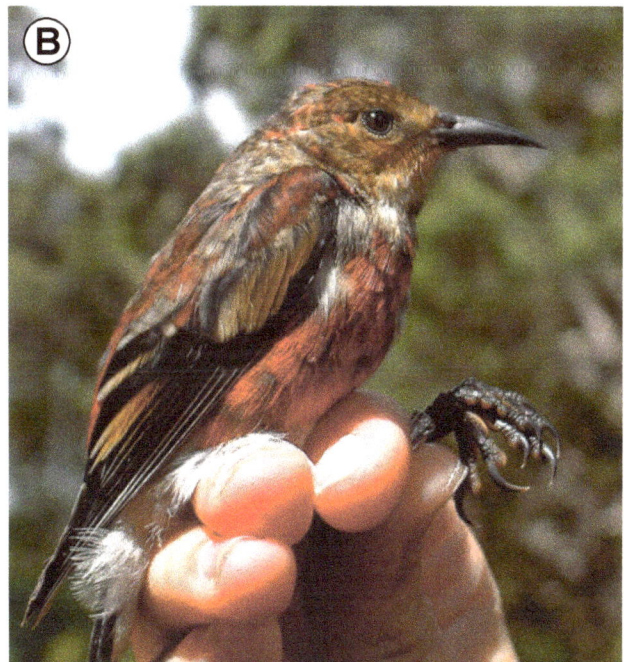

Figure 3.8—At Hakalau Forest National Wildlife Refuge, koa (Acacia koa) seedlings are outplanted in three parallel lines marching up the hill from the lower forest to the upper pastures (A). The goal is to establish corridors so that the forest birds can increase their range uphill. Scientists at the refuge monitor the health and population of the native forest birds, such as this 'Apapane (Himatione sanguinea) (B). Photos by J.B. Friday.

help identify plants and plant communities. More detail is reached when botanists survey the entire site and create a comprehensive list of species present, categorized as native, desired, or problematic, and sometimes further defined by successional phase.

When Global Positioning System (GPS) receivers are used for surveys, all the plant information collected is spatially explicit and mapping, analyzing, and sharing data becomes easier. Rapid Ecological Assessments are increasingly common and include vegetation mapping at various spatial scales. The advantage to this tool is that the data has a spatial component and the vegetation data is easily combined with soil and topography in a Geographic Information System (GIS).

Observing the vegetation also verifies and reveals additional characteristics of the site: dry areas, bogs, and areas subject to strong prevailing winds. Understanding the current vegetation is essential for site-appropriate actions later, including protecting and perpetuating native species already on the site.

Climate

Climate information can be obtained from national (for example, the National Oceanic and Atmospheric Administration) or regional weather service and charted back in some places for decades. At a minimum, clients need to understand the average rainfall and temperatures on their site and the fluctuations and patterns of these conditions throughout the year. For example, trends of when the rainy season normally starts and ends and the intensity of rain events are as important, if not more important, as only knowing the average annual rainfall.

Climate data is too broad to use on its own without also observing the microclimates on the site. Two sites situated only a few miles apart can experience dramatically different wind effects, rainfall, and temperatures (Mollison and Slay 1991). Onsite observation can help the client determine key climate information including aspect, winds, and moisture.

Aspect is whether a slope faces the sun (facing south above the equator or north below the equator) or away from the sun. Sun-facing slopes are warmer and drier; slopes facing away from the sun are cooler and wetter. Aspect is a major determinant of vegetation types on a site.

In most tropical areas, especially islands, storm winds and hurricanes may come from any direction, but prevailing winds are consistent and can be anticipated (Mollison and Slay 1991). Observing vegetation, especially trees bent or flagging in one direction, also indicates the direction of prevailing winds.

Figure 3.9—*Native tree growers and their partners consult aerial photographs and discuss elevation, exposure, and other site conditions in preparation for a forest restoration project in St. Croix, U.S. Virgin Islands. Photo by Brian F. Daley.*

Water and the way it moves through a site are important factors for microclimate. Salt spray, fog, and mist can influence site conditions. The site's proximity to the ocean will determine the extent of the moderating effects of the ocean. Water features such as ponds, lakes, springs, and streams also create microclimates that affect vegetation.

Site History

Site history can be as simple as asking the elder neighbors about the past uses and conditions of the site, or as elaborate as a full archeological survey (required for some projects). An intermediate option is going to the local library or to the Internet to find aerial and other photos of the site dating back over time (figure 3.9). Cadastral offices provide publically available information on zoning changes, construction, and ownership changes of parcels. Information from the soils, vegetation, and climate surveys can be used to understand site history including floods, landslides, fires, severe storms, and other events that took place in the past and may take place again.

3. What Factors on the Project Site Could Limit Success?

The information gathered answering question 2 is used to identify the environmental factors that are most limiting to plant survival and growth on the site and to specify which plant species and stocktype would be most appropriate (figure 3.10 and table 3.1). On most outplanting sites, newly planted plants must quickly establish root contact with the surrounding soil to obtain enough water to survive and grow. Water is often the most limiting factor, especially on sites with a pronounced dry season or low annual rainfall. Where populations of grazing and browsing animals are high, animals may be the

Table 3.1—*Comparison of different plant establishment methods. Adapted from Landis and others (1992).*

Characteristics	Transplanting wildlings	Outplanting nonrooted cuttings	Direct seeding	Outplanting nursery stock
Efficient use of seeds and cuttings	N/A*	No	No	Yes
Cost of establishment	High	Moderate	Low	Moderate
Ability to establish difficult species	Yes	No	No	Yes
Option of using specific genotypes	No	No	Yes	Yes
Precise scheduling of plant establishment	Yes	Yes	No	Yes
Control of stand composition and density	Yes	Yes	No	Yes
Matching stocktypes to site conditions	No	No	No	Yes
Depletion of adjacent plant stands	Yes	Yes	No	No

*N/A: Not applicable.

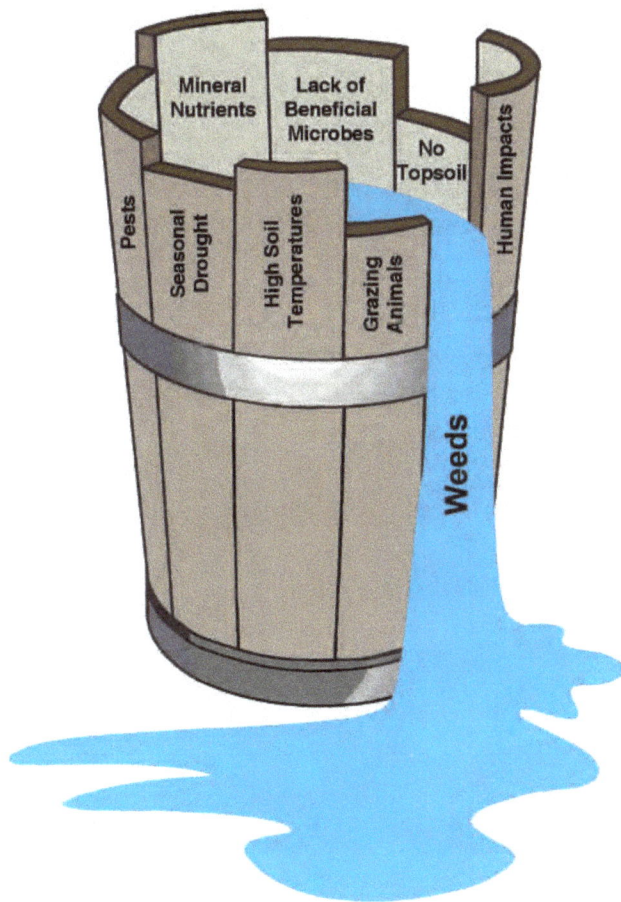

Figure 3.10—*Limiting factors to a given project site can be displayed as unequal boards of a barrel. Water can only be held to the level of the most limiting factor. Illustration by Jim Marin.*

most limiting factor because they will eat any plants you try to establish. If wildfire is a recurring disturbance on the site, then soil conditions are often severely altered and very specific measures, such as fire breaks are essential in the early years of the restoration project. Severe soil disturbances can also eliminate all soil microorganisms including mycorrhizal fungi. Therefore, plants destined for severely altered sites need to be inoculated with the appropriate symbionts before outplanting. (See Chapter 13, Beneficial Microorganisms, for a complete discussion on this topic.) Riparian restoration projects may require bioengineering structures to stabilize streambanks and retard soil erosion before the site can be planted (Hoag and Landis 2001). In desert areas, low soil moisture, hot temperatures, and high winds with sand blast may be listed as limiting factors. High winds, salt spray, weeds, soil fertility, seasonal flooding, insect pests, and land use challenges, such as people driving over restoration areas, are further examples of limiting factors.

Awareness of native plant needs and ecology (based on reference sites) is important to determine if the factors are truly limiting based on project objectives. For example, a site may not receive much rainfall, but if the goal is dryland ecosystem restoration and the dryland native species are adapted to that amount of rainfall, these plants will be able to thrive on the site.

4. How Will Limiting Factors Be Mitigated?

Mitigating measures are the steps the client will take to overcome any limiting factors on the site and achieve project

Figure 3.11—Target plants are cultivated with the limiting factors of the site in mind. "Badlands" on the main island of Palau are bauxite mining areas developed before World War II that are still not revegetating (A). Nursery site for native seedlings for restoration of the mined site (B). A native species, Calophyllum inophyllum, outplanted on the badlands (C). Photos by George Hernández.

objectives. Some mitigating measures can be defined by the client and included in his or her target plant requirements (figure 3.11); others must be carried out by the client on his or her site to establish plants successfully.

Nursery efforts to produce target plants will sometimes be the key to overcoming certain limiting factors on the site. For example, an absence of beneficial microorganisms on the site can be mitigated by inoculating plants with beneficial microorganisms in the nursery, as described in Chapter 13, Beneficial Microorganisms. Sometimes mitigating measures will be a combination of nursery efforts to produce target plant materials and client efforts on the site (figure 3.12). For example, sites with strong prevailing winds may call for target seedlings with sturdy, thick stems to withstand the winds; at the same time, the client may install wind barriers around the trees to help them get established, or windbreaks may be planted to protect the area in advance of other plantings.

Figure 3.12—Overcoming limiting factors to restore disturbed sites involves a combination of nursery and land manager efforts. On a site with tall grass, the land manager would take steps to control the grass competition, and the nursery may also grow trees tall enough to overtop the grass quickly. Photo by Douglass F. Jacobs.

For sites with browsing or grazing animals, species selection for less palatable species may be important, but the land manager must find ways to exclude these animals from newly planted areas or at least provide shelter for the plants as they establish (figure 3.13). Individual plants can be protected with netting or fencing or the entire project area may be fenced. In some areas, the presence of wild pigs or other animals may make restoration impossible, in which case, whole restoration areas may need to be fenced and managed to exclude problematic animals.

Limiting factors that cannot be mitigated through reasonable target plants and land manager efforts in the field require the client to revise project objectives to be appropriate and achievable on their project site.

5. What Species and Genetic Sources Will Meet Project Objectives?

Land managers decide what species they will plant based on project objectives, reference sites, project site conditions, and limiting factors as described previously (figure 3.14). The reference sites provide a natural model for determining appropriate species and plant community composition (what percent of which species, spaced how far apart) for the recovering site (figure 3.15).

In some cases, mitigation of limiting factors alone is sufficient to allow for natural regeneration (passive restoration)

Figure 3.13—*Goats eat anything—very few target plants could be cultivated to co-exist with goats. If goat browsing is a limiting factor, the land manager will need to exclude goats with fencing. Photo by Kim M. Wilkinson.*

of certain native and desirable plant species on the site. For example, on some upland sites in Hawai'i, simply removing grazing and browsing animals and scarifying the soil allows long-dormant koa seeds in the seed bank to sprout (figure 3.16). In these cases, the nursery work may focus on those species that do not regenerate naturally. On many disturbed sites, however, no amount of mitigation will lead to adequate natural regeneration of native or desired species, and in these cases, the nursery will be involved in propagating these species for reintroduction by planting.

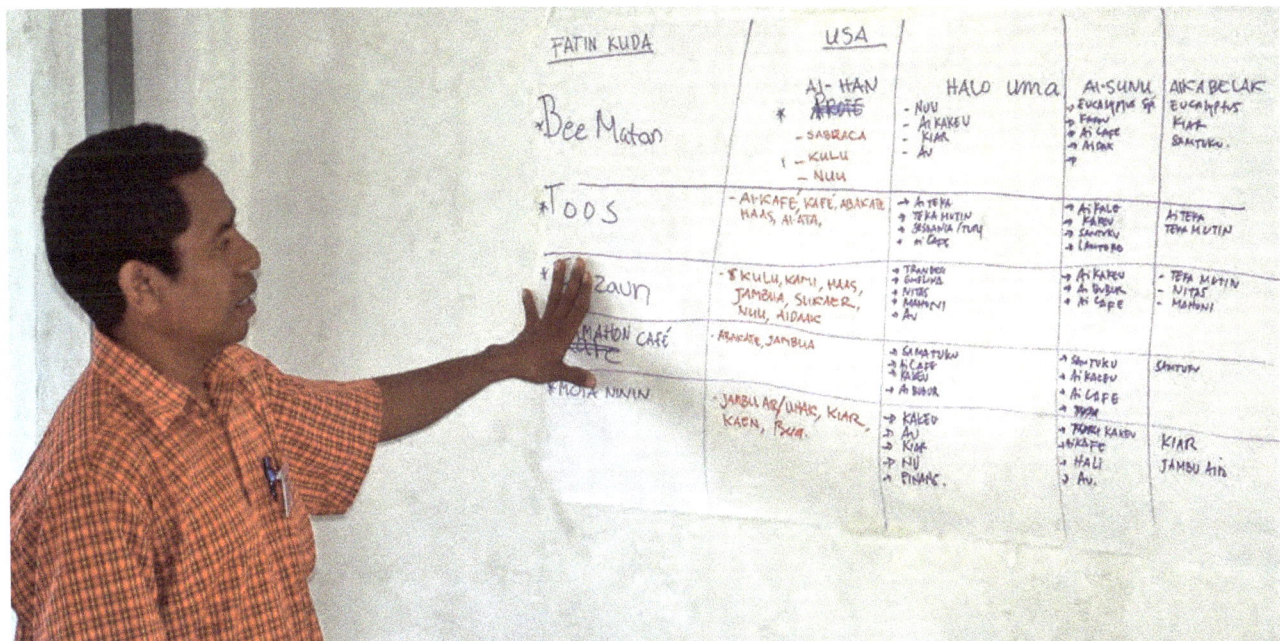

Figure 3.14.—*A forester in East Timor develops a tree selection chart for different planting sites (along the left) and different uses (across the top). Planting sites include near springs and on farm fields. Uses include food, fallow improvement, firewood, and timber. Photo by J.B. Friday.*

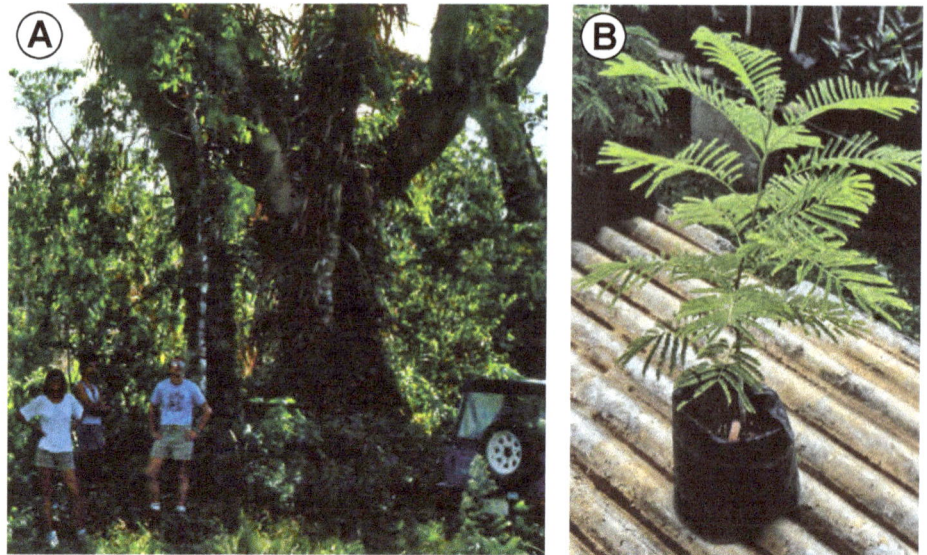

Figure 3.15—Reference sites and succession processes guide which species to plant. One of the few endangered Serianthes nelsonii *trees surviving on Rota (A). Because natural regeneration is not enough to sustain populations, nurseries on Rota produce* Serianthes nelsonii *seedlings (B). Photos by Thomas D. Landis.*

Of course, most nurseries have the occasional call from a person who asks, "What should I plant?" It is not surprising that some potential clients expect the nursery to tell them what to plant. Using the Target Plant Concept, the client and the nursery work together to determine what plant species are appropriate to plant for a given site.

Genetic Sources

In addition to proper species selection, three factors concerning genetics need to be considered when collecting plant materials: local adaptation, genetic diversity, and sexual diversity. See Chapter 8, Collecting, Processing, and Storing Seeds, for additional information.

Local Adaptation

Plants are genetically adapted to local environmental conditions and, for that reason, plant materials should always be collected within the same area where the plants will be outplanted. "Seed zone," "seed source," and "seed lot" are terms used to identify seed collections. A seed zone is a geographic area that has relatively similar climate and soil type (figure 3.17). For some native species, seed zones or transfer guidelines have been defined by geneticists to help land managers choose appropriate seed sources. For most tropical native species, such work has yet to be completed, so growers are advised to use sources from the same geographic area, environmental conditions, and elevation in which the nursery stock is to be outplanted.

Figure 3.16—In some cases, some species may be able to regenerate naturally if limiting factors are removed. This photo shows natural regeneration of Acacia koa *on an upland site after grazing cattle and horses were excluded. Photo by Douglass F. Jacobs.*

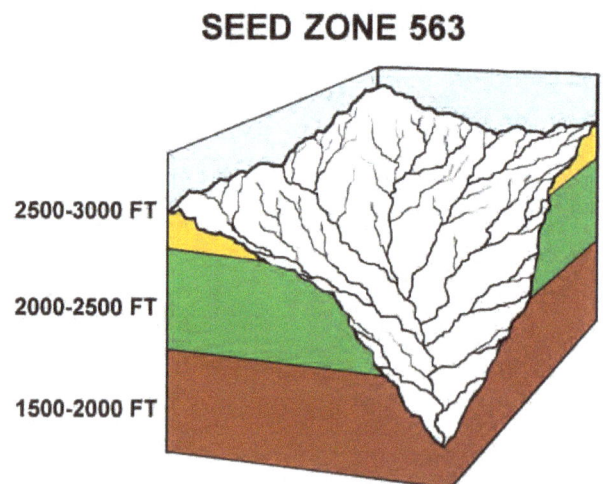

SEED ZONE 563

2500-3000 FT

2000-2500 FT

1500-2000 FT

Figure 3.17—Seed zones have been developed for some species to provide guidelines for collecting seed from the same geographic area and elevation zone. Where no seed zones have been defined, do your best to collect plant materials from the same geographic area, environmental conditions, and elevation in which the nursery stock is to be outplanted. Adapted from St. Clair and Johnson (2004).

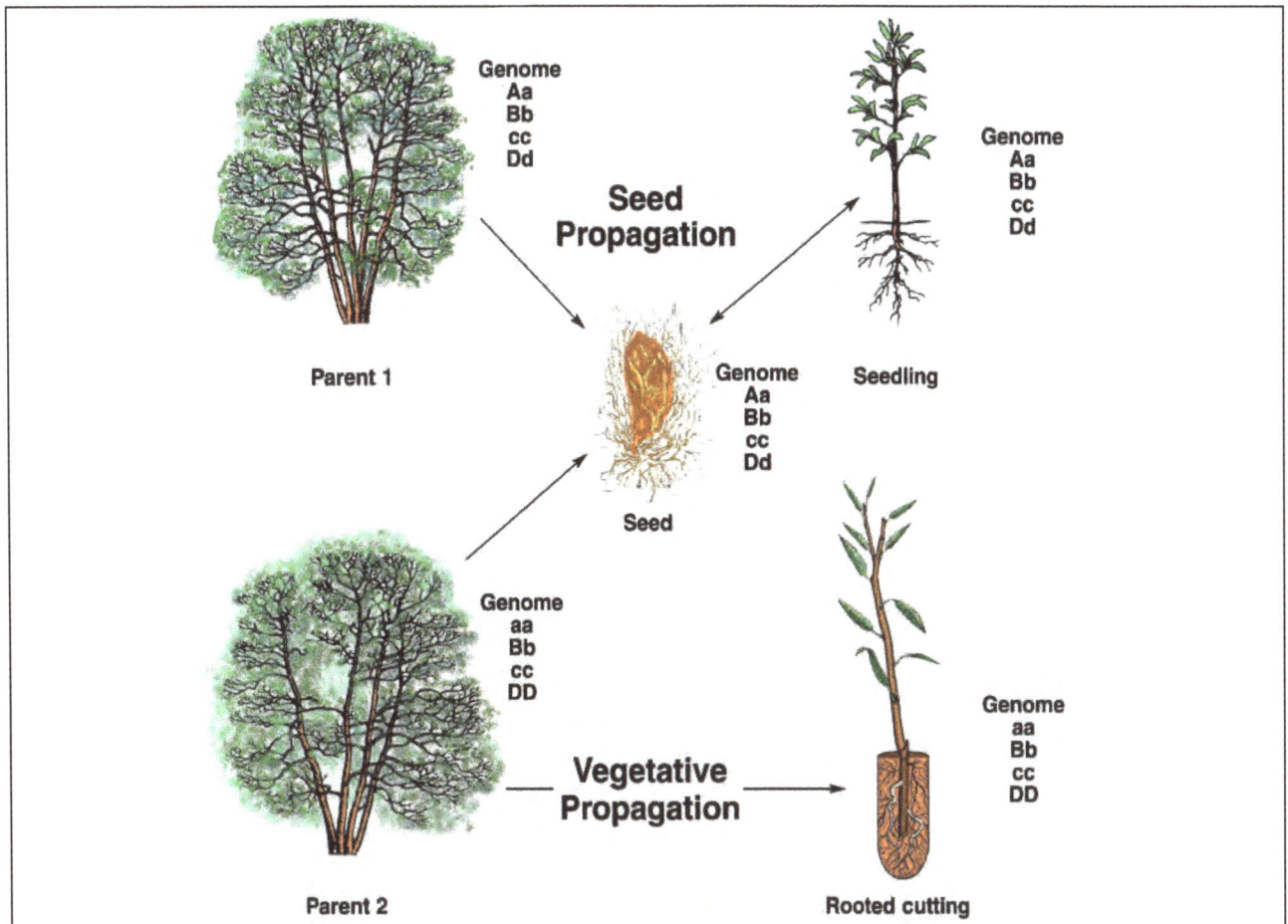

Figure 3.18—*When collecting seed or cuttings from plants, genetic and sexual diversity must be considered. Adapted from Landis and others (2003).*

Local adaptation can affect outplanting survival and growth in many ways, including growth rate and environmental tolerances. For example, in temperate areas, commercial conifers grown from seeds or cuttings collected from higher latitudes or elevations will grow slower but tend to be more cold tolerant than those collected from lower elevations or more southerly latitudes (St. Clair and Johnson 2003). Many tropical islands have a pronounced "wet side" and "dry side." Conventional wisdom and research (Ares and others 2000) indicates to refrain from moving plant materials from the wet side of an island to the dry side, or vice-versa. In addition to rainfall tolerances, local adaptation issues may be important for other site conditions such as soil types.

In some cases, local adaptation may be essential for long-term viability and habitat value of restoration plantings. For example, local pollinators are often adapted to the flower sizes and shapes of their locally adapted food plants (Kramer 2007). If a site is restored with the same species, but not the appropriate local adaptation of that species, local pollinators may not be able to pollinate them, leading to a project that cannot perpetuate itself.

Genetic and Sexual Diversity

Target plant materials should attempt to represent all the genetic and sexual diversity present on the reference sites (figure 3.18). To maximize genetic diversity, seeds or cuttings need to be collected from as many plants as possible. Guinan (1993) provides an excellent discussion of all factors involved in preserving biodiversity when collecting plant materials and suggests collecting from 50 to 100 donor plants.

Dioecious species are challenging because they have male and female plants. Therefore, all vegetatively propagated dioecious plants will be the same sex as their parent, which can be particularly important on sites where a male population is geographically separated from a female population. In such cases, plant material collectors may not realize they have collected only one sex, leading to a single sex being outplanted on a project site. The resulting lack of seed production would compromise project objectives and future natural regeneration. Therefore, when collecting cuttings from dioecious species, care must be taken to ensure that male and female

Figure 3.19—Pandanus tectorius, *an example of a dioecious plant of Polynesia. Photo by J.B. Friday.*

Figure 3.20—*Plant materials must be sourced from parents that possess the desired attributes, especially in the case of medicinal or food plants.* Piper methysticum *(kava) is an important ceremonial and medicinal plant for many Pacific Island cultures, and different cultivars have different properties and concentrations of active compounds (A). The essential food plants* Colocasia esculenta *(taro) and* Musa *species (banana) have diverse heritage cultivars with a wide range of properties and tastes (B). Photos by Thomas D. Landis.*

plants are equally represented. Dioecious species include cycads (Cycadaceae, Stangeriaceae, and Zamiaceae families), mulberries (*Morus* species), pandanus (*Pandanus tectorius*) (figure 3.19), kukui nut (*Aleurites moluccana*), and the rare Caribbean "yellow prickle" (*Zanthoxylum* species). Rooted cuttings or other vegetatively propagated stocktypes need to be labeled by sex so that males and females can be outplanted in a mixed pattern to promote seed production.

Additional Considerations About Source

To meet project objectives, other selection factors may be considered when defining the appropriate propagule sources. In special cases, seeds must be collected from parents that possess desired attributes. For example, if a native or traditional species is being grown for timber or craft use, seeds need to be collected from trees showing the desired form or wood characteristics. Plants grown for traditional medicinal purposes must meet the end user's exacting requirements for quality and potency of the source plants (figure 3.20). When applicable, these other source considerations are in addition to, not instead of, the three factors of local adaptedness, genetic diversity, and sexual diversity. For traditional species, the genetic situation needs to be considered on a case-by-case basis; sometimes perpetuating heritage varieties is the goal and sometimes improving the genetic diversity will be the goal.

6. What Types of Plant Materials (Stocktypes) Are Best Suited to the Project Site and Objectives?

Common plant materials include traditional nursery stocktypes, such as container seedlings, bareroot seedlings, and rooted cuttings, as well as wildings, rootstock, nonrooted cuttings, and seeds (table 3.2). Appropriate stocktypes for a project are determined by considering limiting factors, species, and genetics. The characteristics of a particular species will help determine if direct seeding, nursery propagation, or other methods are the more appropriate strategy (Steinfeld and others 2007). Many options can be considered; some options are summarized in table 3.1. Native plant nurseries can provide a wide variety of plant materials that will meet the needs of any reforestation or restoration project (table 3.2).

Table 3.2—Many different types of native plant materials can be provided by nurseries.

Plant materials	Examples	Advantages	Disadvantages
Seeds	Grasses, forbs	• Small and easy to outplant • Seeds of some native plants can be stored for long periods • Plants develop natural root structure • Maintain genetic diversity	• Some species do not produce seeds regularly • Many tropical seeds do not store well • Direct seeding more inefficient use of seeds than nursery plants
Bareroot plants	Coconut, mahogany, cedrela	• Less expensive to produce in nursery than container plants • Easier to transport • Roots have not been restricted by containers	• Take longer to produce • Roots dry out easily • Often lower survival and slower growth especially on drier sites
Container plants	All species	• Well-established root systems means less transplant shock • Available in a variety of sizes • Can be planted all year long • Large stocktypes provide "instant" plants on site	• More expensive to propagate • More difficult to transport, especially larger stocktypes
Root stock	Yams, kava, breadfruit, bananas	• Easy to store and transport • Excellent survival after outplanting	• Only works with certain species
Nonrooted cuttings	Erithrina, Gliricidia, gumbo-limbo, Guazuma ulmifolia	• Ideal for live stakes • Can be efficiently and economically produced in nursery stooling beds	• Only works with species that root easily • Best for mesic environments
Layer cuttings	Citrus, breadfruit	• Do not have to rely on seed crops • Ideal for maintaining same genotype	• Requires healthy mother plant • Only works with species that root easily
Rooted cuttings	Many species	• Do not have to rely on seed crops • Ideal for maintaining same genotype • Stooling blocks can be developed for large multiyear projects	• Must be handled carefully during transportation and outplanting

Seeds

Seeds are often easy to handle, store, and outplant, but the effectiveness of seeding directly on the project site varies with species, harshness of the site, project objectives, and project timeframe. Directly broadcasting seeds offers three principal advantages: (1) seeds can be inexpensive compared with other plant materials, (2) spreading seeds is relatively easy, and (3) seedlings from broadcast seeds develop a natural root system and occur in a more random (that is, "natural") pattern.

Many drawbacks exist as well. Even when the correct species and origin are located, seeds are (1) often difficult to obtain or are very expensive; (2) not produced in adequate numbers every year; (3) sometimes require specialized cleaning and processing; and (4) difficult to store. In addition, predation by birds and rodents, competition from weed species, and unpredictable weather often reduce establishment success (Bean and others 2004). Finally, with direct seeding, it is difficult to control species composition and plant spacing over the project area (Landis and others 1992).

Direct seeding is usually most successful for grasses, forbs, and some woody shrubs. Seeding with native grass species after wildfires is often used to stabilize soils and prevent erosion. Some trees may be established through direct seeding, particularly those with large seeds. In California, the direct seeding of acorns to establish native oaks has been quite successful (Landis and others 1992). Sowing seeds directly in the field may result in poor germination and survival. Therefore, direct seeding is recommended only for species in which efficient use of seeds is not necessary.

Bareroot Plants

Bareroot plants are started from seeds or cuttings, are grown in the ground or in raised beds, and are harvested without soil around their roots (figure 3.21). Because they require a considerable amount of high-quality soil and often take longer to reach shippable size, fewer species of native plants are grown for conservation and restoration as bareroot stock than are grown for commercially important objectives, such as timber production. Tropical soils are challenging to work with, so bareroot plants are usually produced in raised beds with a mix of growing media (for example, sand mixed with compost) on a drip irrigation line. One serious drawback is bareroot stock needs more postharvest care than container stock. Bareroot is suitable only for plants with root systems that

Figure 3.21—Bareroot coconut plants (A) are grown in fields and are harvested and shipped with no soil surrounding the roots. Tropical soils are challenging to work with, so bareroot plants are usually produced in raised beds (B). Photos by Thomas D. Landis.

can tolerate more disturbance and handling than species that need their root systems kept in contact with soil during harvest, shipping, and outplanting.

Container Plants

Container plants are the stocktype of choice for many tropical nurseries. Container propagation is best when small amounts of many different native plants are desired. Another advantage is that container stock is more tolerant and durable during handling, shipping, and outplanting (figure 3.22). Trees and shrubs are typically established

Figure 3.22—Container plants (left) and bareroot plants (right) have different morphological characteristics. Container plants come in many types and sizes but all form their roots into a plug resulting in less disturbance to the root system during harvest and outplant. Illustration from Dumroese and others (2008).

using container stock rather than by direct seeding for two reasons. First, obtaining seeds from most tree and shrub species is expensive and time consuming; in many years, seeds can be difficult to find. Second, shrub and tree seeds germinate and grow into seedlings at a slower rate than grass and forb species, giving them a disadvantage on sites where grasses and forbs are present. Outplanting shrubs and trees as plants gives them a competitive advantage over grasses and forbs because the plants have access to full sun and roots are often longer and better developed, allowing access to deeper soil moisture. In general, grass and forb species are seldom established from container plants because of the high cost. Exceptions are when grass or forb seeds are rare or hard to collect or propagate; if species are difficult to establish from seeds on disturbed sites; or when the project requires restoring threatened or sensitive species (Steinfeld and others 2007).

Container seedlings can range in size from tiny liners and plugs to large pots containing many gallons of growing medium. Because containers come in many sizes and shapes (figure 3.23), they can be matched to the project objectives and site conditions. When ordering container plants, age, stem diameter, height, root size, and depth are usually specified, in addition to species and seed source. See Chapter 7, Containers, for more information.

The distinguishing feature of container seedlings is that, because the roots are restricted, they bind growing media into a cohesive "plug" (figure 3.23) making outplanting easier, especially on harsh sites.

Wildings

Plants are typically grown in a nursery. For some projects, however, plants are salvaged from areas, such as development sites or roadsides, before planned disturbances. Salvaged plants (sometimes called wildings) can be an important component of protecting native plant diversity. Sometimes salvaged plants are simply relocated quickly from one area to another. At other times, plants may be transplanted into a nursery, cared for, and outplanted at a later time (Steinfeld and others 2007).

Nonrooted Cuttings

Long "pole" cuttings are a common type of nonrooted cutting used extensively in the tropics as live fence posts. Sometimes called "quick sticks," these nonrooted stakes of easy-to-root species, such as *Gliricidia sepium*, *Erythrina* species, or *Bursera simaruba*, are cut from the major branches or stems of trees. They are inserted into the ground with a minimum of 1 ft (30 cm) of the cutting in contact with the soil (ideally more). Pole cuttings are usually at least 4.0 ft (1.2 m) long and at least a 2-in (5-cm) diameter. Sometimes pole cuttings are used in riparian restoration projects (Hoag and Landis 2001). For this application, cuttings are often 6.0 ft (1.8 m) or more in length and up to 8- to 12-in (20- to 30-cm) in diameter so that they can be inserted deep enough such that the

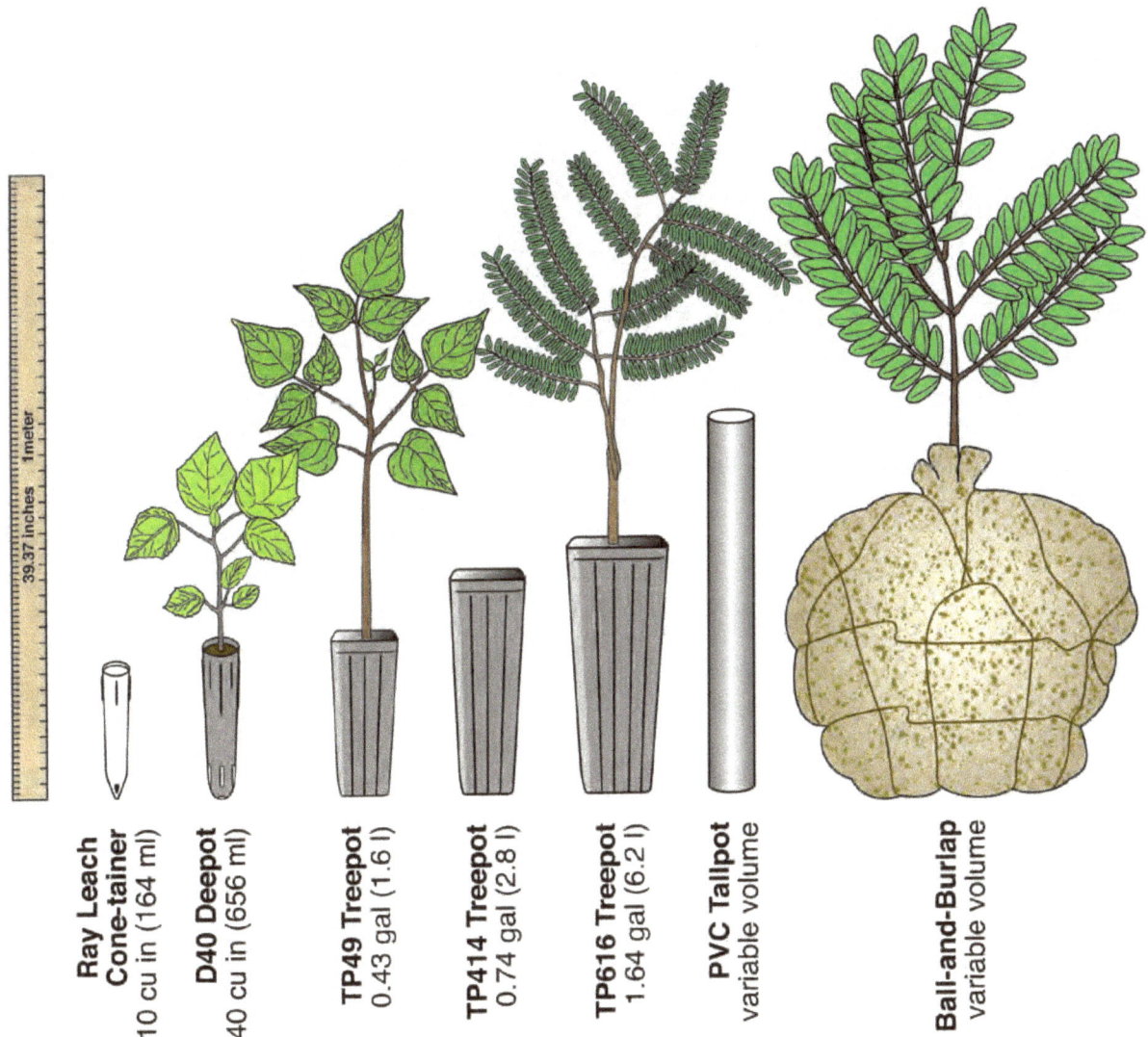

Figure 3.23—Nursery stock can be grown in many sizes and shapes. Consider the advantages and drawbacks of different options when defining the target plant materials for a project. Illustration adapted from Steinfeld and others (2007) by Jim Marin.

Defining the Target Plant

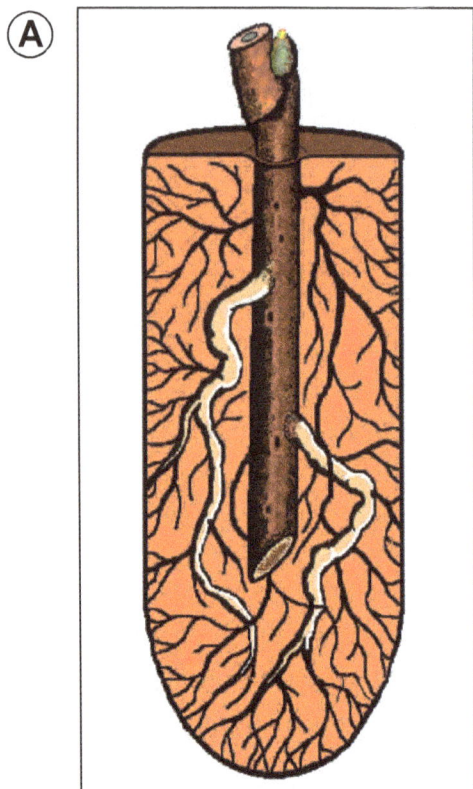

Figure 3.24—Rooted cuttings use a shorter section of stem with a bud (A). Cuttings quickly grow into large plants under nursery culture (B). Illustration A from Dumroese and others (2008), and photo B by Thomas D. Landis.

butt ends remain in contact with the water table. Pole cuttings are very effective in stabilizing stream or riverbanks because they resist erosion. When large numbers of poles are required, they can be grown in stooling beds in nurseries to avoid the negative effect of collecting from wild "donor" plants.

Rooted Cuttings

It is more effective to root cuttings of most woody species in a nursery before outplanting them on the project site. A 2- to 4-in (5- to 10-cm) stem section can be used (figure 3.24), but it needs to have a healthy bud near the top (Dumroese and others 2003). Some species, such as sweet potato (*Ipomoea batatas*), can be propagated from nonrooted vine cuttings, but may be easier to establish in the nursery if they are first allowed to root a little in water or a planting media before transplanting into containers. See Chapter 10, Vegetative Propagation, for more information about collecting and culturing rooted cuttings.

Rootstock

Rootstock refers to specialized roots, such as bulbs and corms, and to modified underground stems, such as rhizomes and tubers (figure 3.25). Rootstock can be

Figure 3.25—Rootstock can be used to establish some grasses, sedges, forbs, and wetland plants that cannot be direct seeded or outplanted as seedlings. Photo by Thomas D. Landis.

used for the vegetative propagation of certain grasses, wetland plants, food plants, and even some trees. Examples of species propagated from rootstock include yams (*Diosorea* species), kava (*Piper methysticum*), and breadfruit (*Artocarpus* species). Bananas and plantains (*Musa* species) are often propagated from their corms or root structures.

7. What Are the Best Outplanting Tools and Techniques?

Each outplanting site has different climatic and soil conditions, so outplanting tools and techniques must be matched accordingly. Nursery managers must know in advance which planting tools will be used so they can develop proper plant material specifications, especially root length and volume or cutting length and diameter.

No single tool or technique will work well under all site conditions. For example, plants with narrow, long root systems may not be the appropriate root shape and size if deep, narrow holes are impossible to dig efficiently on the site because of rocky or muddy conditions. It is important to ensure that the planting holes are large and deep enough so that the seedlings can be planted properly.

Hand tools such as shovels (figure 3.26), pick mattocks, planting hoes ("hoedads"), and planting bars are very popular for outplanting native plants. Plants grown in deeper "tall pots" used in many restoration projects may require specialized outplanting equipment. Nursery managers must work closely with clients to make certain that their target plants can be properly outplanted in the soil conditions on the project site. A more complete discussion of outplanting tools and techniques is in Chapter 17, Outplanting.

Figure 3.26—The type of outplanting tool to be used is critical to defining the size and shape of the target plant. Photo by Thomas D. Landis.

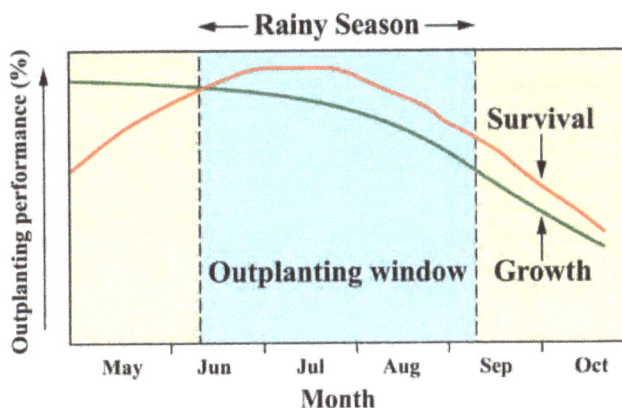

Figure 3.27—The outplanting window is the period of time in which site conditions are the most favorable for plant survival and growth. The window will vary among geographical locations. For sites with a pronounced dry season, the outplanting window occurs at the onset of the rainy season. Illustration adapted by from South and Mexal (1984) by Jim Marin.

8. What Is the Best Time for Outplanting?

Each site has an optimal time when chances for plant survival and growth are greatest—the "outplanting window." The outplanting window is usually defined by looking at the climate and historical information from Question 2 and the limiting factors described in Question 3. For example, in some tropical areas, soil moisture is the main limiting factor. In these cases, the outplanting window is at the onset of the rainy season when soil moisture is increasing and evapotranspirational losses are low (figure 3.27) Areas without a dry season may have other limiting factors, such as heavy rainfall and flooding, that define outplanting windows differently. The specific dates of outplanting windows will change with latitude and elevation.

In producing target plants for a project, the nursery must work backwards from the project's outplanting window to schedule propagation. This approach ensures the plants will be ready at the beginning of the outplanting window, as described in Chapter 4, Crop Planning: Propagation Protocols, Schedules, and Records.

Learning and Adapting: Field Testing the Target Plant

Starting small and expanding on successes is a basic principle of effective project management (Mollison and Slay 1991). If land managers are able to take a season or more to test out some plant materials and strategies before committing on a large scale, they can learn important lessons and ultimately increase their successes. At the start of any planting project, the land manager and the nursery manager need to agree on certain morphological and physiological specifications based on answers to the eight questions that define a target plant. This prototype target plant is grown in the nursery, and its suitability is then verified by outplanting trials that monitor survival and growth.

Monitoring survival and growth during the first few months after outplanting is critical because problems can show up soon after planting. Problems with seedling quality, poor planting, or exposure to drought conditions result in plants gradually losing vigor and perhaps dying. Therefore, plots must be monitored during the first month or two after outplanting and again at the end of the first year for initial survival. Subsequent checks after 3- and 5-year periods will give a good indication of plant growth rates. This performance information is then used to give valuable feedback to the nursery manager who can work with the client to refine the target plant specifications for the next crop (figure 3.1).

The strategy of starting small is not always possible. Some projects are urgent and require full planting as soon as possible. Clients with projects that must be planted all at once will not be able to benefit from the learning opportunities generated by the target plant feedback cycle. In such cases, the best available information and experience is used to define the target plants to immediately serve the client's needs. When the project is complete, however, the nursery and other people involved can still learn from the outcomes and apply the lessons to future projects of a similar nature.

References

Ares, A.; Fownes, J.H.; Sun, W. 2000. Genetic differentiation of intrinsic water-use efficiency in the Hawaiian native *Acacia koa*. International Journal of Plant Sciences. 161(2): 909–915.

Bean, T.M.; Smith, S.E.; Karpiscak, M.M. 2004. Intensive revegetation in Arizona's hot desert: the advantages of container stock. Native Plants Journal. 5: 173–180.

Cerro Nara Rainforest Conservation. 2010. Analog forestry employed in Cerro Nara. Central West Coast, Costa Rica: Pro-Nara. http://www.cerronara.org/. (August 2010).

Dumroese, R.K.; Wenny, D.L.; Morrison, S.L. 2003. A technique for using small cuttings to grow poplars and willows in containers. Native Plants Journal. 4: 137–139.

Dumroese, R.K.; Luna, T.; Landis, T.D. 2008 Nursery manual for native plants: volume 1, a guide for tribal nurseries. Agriculture Handbook 730. Washington, DC: U.S. Department of Agriculture, Forest Service. 302 p.

Hoag, J.C.; Landis, T.D. 2001. Riparian zone restoration: field requirements and nursery opportunities. Native Plants Journal. 2: 30–35.

Kramer, A.T. 2007. Successful restoration of plant communities: why pollinators matter. Lecture at the Chicago Botanic Garden. http://www.chicagobotanic.org/downloads/staff/kramer/Kramer_071907DonorTalk.pdf. (August 2010)

Landis, T.D.; Dreesen, D.R.; Dumroese, R.K. 2003. Sex and the single *Salix*: considerations for riparian restoration. Native Plants Journal. 4: 110–117.

Landis, T.D.; Lippitt, L.A.; Evans, J.M. 1992. Biodiversity and ecosystem management: the role of forest and conservation nurseries. In: Landis, T.D., ed. Proceedings, Western Forest Nursery Association. Gen. Tech. Rep. RM-221. Fort. Collins, CO: U.S. Department of Agriculture, Forest Service, Rocky Mountain Forest and Range Experiment Station: 1–17.

Landis, T. D. 2011. The Target Plant concept - a history and brief overview. In: Riley, L.E., Haase, D.L. and Pinto, J.R. tech coords. National Proceedings: Forest and Conservation Nursery Associations – 2010. Proceedings RMRS-P-65. Fort Collins, CO: US Department of Agriculture, Forest Service, Rocky Mountain Research Station, Proceedings. 61-66.

Mollison, B.; Slay, R.M. 1991. Introduction to permaculture. Tyalgum, Australia: Tagari Publications. 198 p.

South, D.B.; Mexal, J.G. 1984. Growing the "best" seedling for reforestation success. Forestry Department Series 12. Auburn, AL: Auburn University. 11 p.

St. Clair, B.; Johnson, R. 2003. The structure of genetic variation and implications for the management of seed and planting stock. In: Riley, L.E.; Dumroese, R.K.; Landis, T.D., tech. coords. National proceedings: forest and conservation nursery associations—2003. Proceedings RMRS-P-33. Ogden, UT: U.S. Department of Agriculture, Forest Service, Rocky Mountain Research Station: 64–71.

Steinfeld, D.E.; Riley, S.A.; Wilkinson, K.M.; Landis, T.D.; Riley, L.E. 2007. Roadside revegetation: an integrated approach to establishing native plants. Vancouver, WA: Western Federal Lands Highway Division.

Sutton, R. 1980. Evaluation of stock after planting. New Zealand Journal of Forestry Science 10: 297-299.

Additional Reading

Guinon, M. 1993. Promoting gene conservation through seed and plant procurement. In: Landis, T.D., tech. coord. Proceedings, Western Forest Nursery Association. Gen. Tech. Rep.. RM-221. Ft. Collins, CO: U.S. Department of Agriculture, Forest Service, Rocky Mountain Forest and Range Experiment Station: 38–46.

Jeffrey, J.; Horiuchi, B. 2003. Tree planting at Hakalau National Wildlife Refuge—the right tool for the right stocktype. Native Plants Journal. 4: 30–31.

Landis, T.D.; Dumroese, R.K.; Haase, D.L. 2010. The container tree nursery manual. volume 7: seedling processing, storage, and outplanting. Agriculture Handbook 674. Washington, DC: U.S. Department of Agriculture, Forest Service. 188 p.

Millar, C.I.; Stephenson, N.L.; Stephens, S.L. 2007. Climate change and forests of the future: managing in the face of uncertainty. Ecological Applications. 17(8): 2145–2151.

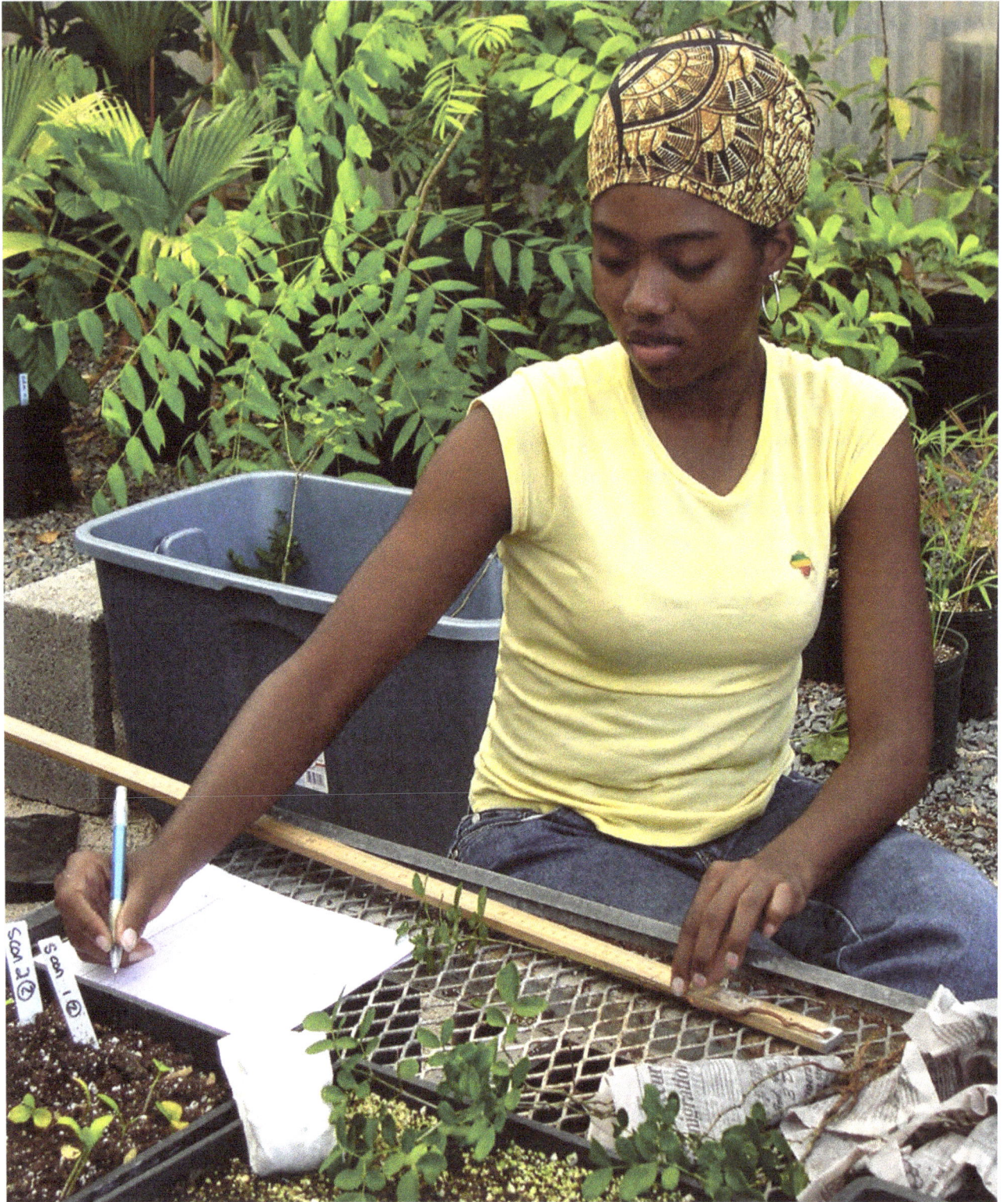

Crop Planning: Propagation Protocols, Schedules, and Records

Kim M. Wilkinson and Douglass F. Jacobs

4

A successful nursery provides healthy, high-quality plant materials ready to plant when clients need them. For areas with a pronounced dry season, clients usually need plants at the beginning of the rainy season. For areas with adequate rainfall all year or that can be irrigated, the outplanting date may be anytime. In addition to being ready on time, plants must also be of the correct species, quantity, genetic source, size, age, and container type, as defined by target plant requirements described in Chapter 3, Defining the Target Plant (figure 4.1). To ensure that plants germinate, grow, remain healthy, and become hardy to survive outside the nursery, all the plant's environmental and nutritional requirements must be met while they are in the nursery. These requirements change as the plants develop. The planning and scheduling to meet these requirements is called nursery crop planning. Crop planning coordinates time, resources, labor, and space to produce a healthy crop of plants on time. Throughout this chapter, the following example of how target plant requirements work with nursery crop planning is used.

> *In March, a retired cattle rancher calls your native plant nursery. To leave a legacy for her grandchildren, she wants to plant 500 koa trees (*Acacia koa, *an endemic species important in many Hawaiian forests) on a former cattle pasture now fenced and free of cows. Her property is at 2,000-ft [610-m] elevation on the leeward side of the Big Island of Hawai'i. The area has been in pasture for more than a century. She had the soils analyzed, and they are typical from a nutrient standpoint. She wants easy-to-plant trees. Although the rainy season starts in mid-November, she plans to plant with help from her son, daughter-in-law, and two grandchildren during the holiday, so her ideal delivery date is December 15. She plans to remove the grass from the planting areas and then plant the seedlings using a mattock and shovel.*

With these details, you can now begin to work with the client to establish target plant requirements for her koa seedlings (figure 4.1).

Facing Page: *Crop planning organizes schedules, resources, labor, and space to produce a healthy crop of plants on schedule. Victoria Henry records some information on a crop in the Agroforestry Research Greenhouse at the University of the Virgin Islands, Agriculture Experiment Station in St. Croix. Photo by Brian F. Daley.*

Figure 4.1—*Crop planning begins with defining specifications of the "target plants" the nursery will produce, as described in Chapter 3, Defining the Target Plant. Adapted from Landis (2011) by Jim Marin.*

1. Outplanting Objectives
2. Site Conditions
3. Limiting Factors
4. Mitigating Measures for Limiting Factors
5. Species and Genetic Sources
6. Stocktype
7. Outplanting Tools and Techniques
8. Outplanting Window

1. **Objective**—Native reforestation/legacy planting with locally adapted *Acacia koa*.

2. **Site Evaluation**—Client's soil analysis is unremarkable; she has looked at existing vegetation (pasture grasses, weeds) and realizes control is needed; she examined climate data for the area, especially historical trends of when the rainy season starts and ends, and the average rainfall.

3. **Limiting Factors on Outplanting Site**—Likely shortage of viable population of appropriate beneficial local microorganisms (*Rhizobium* bacteria and mycorrhizal fungi); competing grass and weeds; minor risk of a cow or horse eating the young trees.

4. **Mitigating Measures for Limiting Factors**—Seedlings will be inoculated with *Rhizobium* bacteria and mycorrhizal fungi in the nursery. Client will remove competing grass and weeds before planting; advise her to mulch around trees and diligently continue to control weeds. Client has fenced site to minimize risk of a cow or horse getting in and eating the seedlings and will keep secure.

5. **Genetic Considerations**—Seeds sourced according to transfer guidelines from forestry department for locally adapted, genetically appropriate koa for this site. In this case, seeds will be collected (by permission) from a nearby koa forest at a similar elevation: minimum 50 parent trees of good form.

6. **Type of Plant Materials**—500 *Acacia koa* seedlings from genetic sources listed previously. Containers: Ray Leach "Stubby" cells; Size: 15 cm height, 3.5 mm stem diameter; Roots: firm and nodulating with *Rhizobium*, inoculated with mycorrhizal fungi (AMF). Seedlings will be watered thoroughly while still in their containers immediately before they are outplanted.

7. **Outplanting Tool or Technique**—Seedlings will be outplanted with a mattock and shovel. After outplanting, seedlings will be mulched with a biodegradable weed barrier topped with macadamia nut husk mulch, being careful not to let the mulch touch the stems. Trees will be flagged with a bamboo stake and bright flagging for ease of monitoring and maintenance.

8. **Timing of Installation/Outplanting Window**—This area's rainy season usually begins in November, but labor will not be available until December. Target date for seedling delivery is December 15.

For complex, large, or specialized projects, the assistance of a professional planner is usually needed to assess the site and create a plan, including appropriate species selection and determination of the other target plant needs for each species to be planted. Examples of more specialized plans include projects that warrant a Forest Stewardship Plan, a Conservation Plan, a Habitat Restoration Plan, Farm Plans (such as the U.S. Department of Agriculture, Natural Resources Conservation Service might do for soil conservation or riparian areas) and others. If your client requires this level of assistance, steer him or her to the appropriate agency or professional and invite the client to place an order when the plan is ready. See Chapter 18, Working With People, for more information on client education and project planning.

Based on the client's target plant requirements, including the agreed-upon delivery date, the nursery manager can now schedule crop production (figure 4.2). Crop production generally includes these activities:

- Developing and refining propagation protocols for the species so that requirements are met during germination, establishment, rapid growth, and hardening.

- Developing growing schedules for the crop based on the crop's three growth phases (establishment, rapid growth, and hardening) and the distinct requirements for each phase.

- Developing facilities schedules to ensure that space, labor, equipment, and supplies to support the crop (and the other crops being grown simultaneously) during all growth stages are available.

- Keeping written records, including a daily log and plant development record, so that any shortcomings can be corrected and successes can be replicated in future crops.

Developing Propagation Protocols

A propagation protocol describes all the steps necessary to grow a species under local conditions, from the collection of seeds or cuttings all the way through shipping the plants to the client. It is meant to be a reliable, repeatable guide to producing and scheduling a crop of that species. It will also help you coordinate the production of all crops being grown simultaneously in the nursery.

A protocol is ideally comprehensive, systematic, and detailed, much like a cookbook recipe. Protocols with the most detailed information make it easier to plan and schedule the next crop. The example protocol in table 4.1 shows the type of information usually included. The exact schedule and performance of any species will vary greatly depending on the unique conditions of the nursery and on other variables, such as seed sources and weather patterns so protocols may need to be adjusted accordingly to produce the best plants.

After protocols are developed, they are refined with each crop, leading to dramatic improvements in nursery efficiency and effectiveness from season to season. Propagation protocols serve as an essential guide for planning and scheduling each crop.

A protocol typically describes the following aspects and characteristics:

- Species name and ecotype.
- Time necessary to grow to target plant specifications.
- Target plant specifications (for example, height, root system, and stem diameter).
- Propagule sources, characteristics, collection, and processing.
- Preplanting propagule treatments.
- Growing area preparation.
- Management for, and length of, establishment, rapid growth, and hardening phases.
- Harvesting and shipping practices.
- Outplanting window and planting technique(s).

Draft a Protocol

The protocol is developed using firsthand experiences and outside sources of information. If little to nothing is known about the species, the process of drafting a protocol can help you organize what is known and take an educated guess at how to proceed with growing a particular species. Start by systematically searching relevant literature published by trade journals, native plant societies, and botanical gardens. An excellent source of propagation protocols, continually updated by growers and free of charge, is online at

the Native Plant Network (http://www.nativeplantnetwork.org) (Landis and Dumroese 2000; 2002). If specific information on the desired species is unavailable, try to find another species within the same genera or even a related species grown in similar climatic zones, to see if any information may be applicable. Next, gather information from observations of how the plant grows in nature. This information may be observed first hand in the field and by asking local people who are familiar with the plant. Although collectors of plant materials for cultural uses may have never propagated the species,

Figure 4.2—*The diversity of species grown in native plant nurseries (A) calls for detailed crop planning and scheduling to ensure that high-quality plants (B) are delivered to clients when they need them. Photo A by Diane L. Haase, and photo B by Douglass F. Jacobs.*

they are likely to know the plant's life cycle such as when and how seeds are dispersed. Finally, seek advice from other nursery managers. Although some managers of private nurseries may be disinclined to share their propagation methods, government nurseries and botanical gardens are often excellent sources of information.

Based on the information gathered, the first draft is the best-informed guess of what will be required to grow a species in your nursery the first time. The plants themselves will prove the protocol right or wrong as they grow. Nursery records, including the daily log and plant development record described later in this chapter, will enable a comparison between projected development and actual growth.

Test and Adjust Protocols

Refine the protocol with site-specific information from your nursery after the production of each crop. Do not be discouraged if a protocol drafted from background research or another nursery's experience does not produce the same results; the goal is to adjust the protocol to reflect your nursery conditions. Year-to-year variations in weather or unforeseen operational changes often keep crops from growing exactly as projected. Allow room for flexibility and make adjustments based on observed factors. You may want to tinker with growing media ingredients, seed germination methods, irrigation practices, and so on. Keeping records is key. Sometimes new information and discoveries will significantly improve

Table 4.1—An example protocol for Acacia koa, *adapted from Wilkinson and Elevitch (2003; 2004).*

Family scientific name	Fabaceae
Family common name	Legume
Scientific name	*Acacia koa* Gray
Common name	Koa
General distribution	Native to six major Hawaiian Islands: Hawai'i, Moloka'i, Maui, Lana'i, O'ahu, and Kaua'i. Original range: 300–7,000 ft (90–2,134 m). Today, most thriving koa trees are found between 3,000 and 6,000 ft (915 and 1,830 m) elevation. Introduced pests and diseases limit their presence below 2,000 ft.
Propagation goal	Plants (tree seedlings)
Propagation method	Seed
Product type	Container: 115 ml Ray Leach "Stubby" Cell
Time to grow	16 to 18 weeks
Target specifications	Seeds from locally adapted, genetically appropriate source matched to outplanting site; seedlings approx. 15 cm tall; diameter 3.5 mm; and roots firm and nodulating with *Rhizobium*.
Propagule collection	Genetic quality is crucial; source must be carefully matched with the outplanting site before seeds are collected. Diversity is also important to withstand diseases; collect at least 50 mother trees, throughout the canopy. Pods are about 6 in (15 cm) long and 1 to 1.5 in (2 to 4 cm) wide, with 6 to 12 seeds per pod. Pods are ready to pick when brown, and when opened the seeds inside are deep brown and full (not green, flat, or small). Seeds can also be collected from the ground. In some populations, koa seeds can be collected any time of year, in other populations August to October (end of dry season) is best time to collect.
Propagule processing	Pods are dried in the sun until they can be opened easily. Seeds are extracted by hand or by threshing. Once out of the pods, seeds are dried more as necessary (ideal moisture content 6 to 8%). Dried seeds can be stored in an airtight container away from direct sunlight. Properly dried seeds can store for 12 to 24 months at room temperature, many years longer in cooler conditions.
Seeds/kg	Seed size is highly variable, a kilo of processed seed can contain between 5,000 and 15,000 seeds (2,500 to 7,500 seeds/lb).
Purity	100%.
Germination	70 to 90% (can be lower depending on weather conditions during ripening).
Pre-sowing treatments	Scarification is required. Mechanical scarification (nicking with a nail clippers on the side opposite the point of attachment to the pod) is used for small lots. Hot water treatment (195 °F, 90 °C) in a volume ratio of at least 5 parts water to 1 part seeds for 1 to 3 minutes. In either case, scarified seeds are soaked overnight to allow water to penetrate into the seed. Seeds germinate in 2 to 7 days.
Growing area	If possible, some cover (greenhouse or temporary cover) is ideal for the first 2 weeks after germination to protect sprouts from seed-eating birds and rodents and from hard rains. Thereafter, uncovered growing areas work well.

Table 4.1 *(continued)*

Growing medium	Most well-drained media work fine. One example media is 50% peat moss, 25% perlite, 25% vermiculite, amended with compost, dolomite lime, gypsum, and triple super phosphate. Media should also be inoculated mycorrhizal fungi, local strains if available. Seedlings will be inoculated with *Rhizobium* at 2 weeks.
Establishment phase	Scarified seeds will germinate in 2 to 7 days. They may be direct seeded after scarification (1 seed/cell) or, for less viable seedlots, seeds (sown on paper towels or in beds) are transplanted into tube containers that have been pre-filled with medium (1 seed/cell) as soon as the root begins growing from the seed. Cover with growing medium shallowly (about 1/4 inch or 0.6 cm deep), followed by a thin mulch layer such as #2 poultry grit. Water with a fine-headed sprayer to keep moist, but not wet. Full sun is best. Daily water is usually necessary, by hand or with an automated system. Protect from bird and rodent predators who are attracted to the sprouts. At 2 weeks of age, inoculate with *Rhizobium* using a slurry made from native nodules collected from seed source areas.
Length of establishment phase	2 to 3 weeks
Rapid growth phase	Seedlings are watered daily, usually in the morning. Especially hot, dry days may necessitate a second watering in the early afternoon. (Late afternoon and evening watering is not recommended, as it facilitates pest problems, such as sooty molds.) The media should not be allowed to dry out. After about 4 weeks, check to ensure *Rhizobium* inoculation was effective. After about 6 weeks, seedlings may be double-spaced in the Ray Leach trays (from 98 trees per tray to 49 trees per tray) to ensure each seedling receives full sunlight and good air movement to facilitate strong stem development. At the period, depending on seed lot, about 5 to 10% of the seedlings will be apparent poor performers, and these should be culled. Remaining seedlings are monitored for pests, but pests are generally not problematic in the nursery. If any weeds enter the media, they should be removed. No fertilizer application as necessary if seedlings were inoculated with *Rhizobium* and mycorrhizal fungi. No pruning.
Rapid growth phase	7 to 10 weeks
Hardening phase	Seedlings should never be allowed to dry out, but watering frequency is reduced to introduce seedlings to temporary, moderate water stress. If the outplanting site is an especially windy area, "brush" seedlings gently using a length of PVC pipe to improve stem strength. Seedlings remain outside, exposed to full sunlight, not fertilized.
Length of hardening phase	6 weeks
Harvesting, storage, and shipping	When seedlings have reached target size, they may be delivered to the planting site. Water thoroughly before shipping and just before outplanting. They are not extracted from their container until the moment they are planted, as keeping them in the container is necessary to protect the roots and the viability of the *Rhizobium* nodules. Seedlings may be stood up in buckets, cardboard boxes, or delivered in their trays. Seedlings must be protected from wind and excessive heat during transport, but refrigeration is not recommended. Empty containers and trays may be returned after the planting is complete.
Outplanting and cultivation comments	Planting areas must be fenced to exclude any grazing animals, and competitive vegetation must be removed. At planting, seedlings should be carefully removed from their container and planted at the correct depth, so the ground is even with the root collar. Soil should be firmed around the tree, muddied in with water if possible. A weed barrier/mulch around the tree (but not touching the trunk) can aid establishment.
Citations	Wilkinson, K.M.; Elevitch, C.R. 2004. Propagation protocol for production of container *Acacia koa* Gray plants; permanent agriculture resources, Holualoa, Hawai'i. In: Native Plant Network. URL: http://www.nativeplantnetwork.org (September 2013). Moscow, ID: University of Idaho, College of Natural Resources, Forest Research Nursery.

production methods (see Chapter 20, Discovering Ways to Improve Nursery Practices and Plant Quality) and will be added to the protocol. As the protocol is updated, the nursery develops an increasingly accurate and helpful guide for how to grow each species.

Developing Growing Schedules

With the propagation protocol in hand, it is time to develop a growing schedule that covers all phases of crop production and the time necessary to complete each step. When the timing for nursery crops is understood, appropriate dates for sowing seeds or striking cuttings can be calculated by counting backwards from the desired outplanting date. Knowing when propagules can be collected and how long the species will take to produce enables the nursery to work with clients' schedules. For example, koa requires 18 weeks to grow, including time for preparing seeds for sowing. So, if plants are needed for outplanting on December 15, seeds must be ready for sowing by August 11. The total time required for the production of each crop will vary by species, container size, season, and nursery environment. Genetics and the variability of seedlots may also cause variations in crop scheduling even for the same species. Less well-known or more temperamental species require the nursery manager to build a safety margin of 2 to 4 weeks into the schedule in case of problems with germination or growth. The growing schedule focuses on these steps as plants move through the nursery: propagule collection, cleaning, and treating; the three phases of plant growth (establishment, rapid growth, and hardening); and storage and shipping. Although other chapters cover these topics in detail, in this chapter, they will be discussed in general terms as they relate to scheduling.

Propagule Collection, Processing, and Treatment

Collection

Most often, nurseries growing native and culturally important plants cannot obtain their seeds or cuttings from a central supplier or mail-order catalog. Therefore, key questions are where, when, and how to collect seeds or cuttings. The where is usually answered by the location of the outplanting sites: locally adapted, genetically appropriate materials should be collected from the same or similar areas as the outplanting site (figure 4.3A). For some native species, usually commercially important trees, recommendations for appropriate sources or seed zones may be available, as mentioned in Chapter 3, Defining the Target Plant. For most other native species, the nursery will have to do

its best to research, define, and obtain locally adapted and genetically appropriate propagules for its client's site. The when question is answered by the plants living in the collection sites: when does this species, in the appropriate collection site(s), produce seeds? (Or for vegetative propagation, when is the best time to collect cuttings?) For some species, it may be possible to collect throughout the year. For other species, a narrow window may be all that is available, and if this window is missed, orders will have to wait until the following year. Seeds of some species may store well for many years, enabling the nursery to develop collections to keep on hand. Finally, how to collect may be determined based on published literature, local knowledge, and experience. To provide plants when the client needs them, the nursery manager has to account for the time needed to obtain the propagules and grow the plants.

Processing

Propagules need to be processed immediately after collection. For most seeds, processing helps ensure that the

Figure 4.3—*Nursery crop planning includes scheduling propagule collection (A), processing, and seed treatments (B) to produce target plants by the delivery date. Photo A by J.B. Friday, and photo B by Craig R. Elevitch.*

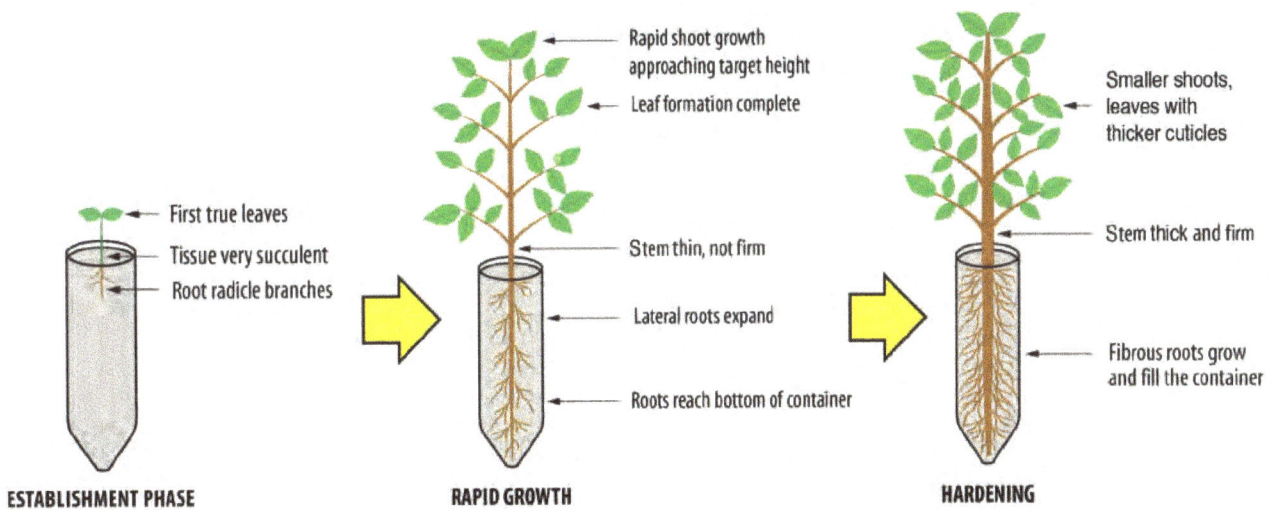

Figure 4.4—*Understanding the growth phases that crops go through is essential to crop planning. The development of most nursery crops can be divided into three phases: establishment, rapid growth, and hardening. Adapted from Dumroese and others (2008) by Jim Marin.*

seeds stay dormant until they are needed. Depending on the species, seeds may need to be processed in one or more of the following ways: extraction from pods or fruits, washing, winnowing, sorting, grading, and drying. Some seeds do not store and must be sown when they are fresh. Cuttings may need to be dried, soaked, placed in rooting beds, or other treatments. Processing requirements and the time and space needed to complete them need to be considered as part of the schedule.

Treatment

Seeds of native species, and sometimes seedlots of the same species, vary widely in dormancy, so seed treatments need to be scheduled properly. Similarly, the optimum time to harvest cuttings varies among native species. Scheduling when to treat propagules is important for planning a target sowing or cutting establishment date for the crop (figure 4.3B).

Crop Growth Phases

Because a tiny germinant has different needs than a large plant that is nearly ready for outplanting, understanding the growth phases of crops is essential to nursery planning. The development of most nursery crops can be divided into three phases: establishment, rapid growth, and hardening (figures 4.4, 4.5). Plants in each phase have distinct requirements for light, water, nursery space, and the types of attention and labor necessary to keep them healthy. The nursery manager's objectives for the crop are also different at each phase. Table 4.2 summarizes some typical aspects of each of the three phases.

Establishment

For plants grown from seeds, the establishment phase is defined as the time from the sowing of the seeds through the germination, emergence, and development of the first true leaves or primary needles (figure 4.6A). For plants grown from cuttings, the establishment phase extends from placing cuttings into containers through the initial development of roots and shoots. This phase is of critical importance because mistakes can prevent or delay emergence or rooting. For seeds, some species require light to germinate and need to be surface sown while seeds

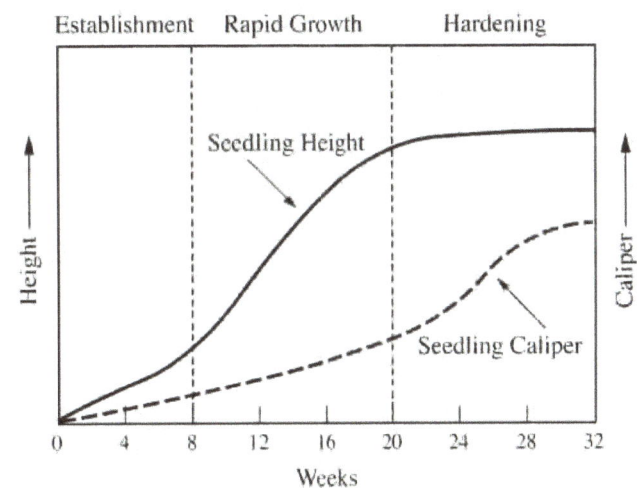

Figure 4.5—*Changes in seedling morphology during the three growth phases. Growth is relatively slow during the establishment phase. Most shoot growth occurs during the rapid growth phase, which ends when target height specifications are met. During hardening, roots continue to grow, resulting in an increase in seedling stem diameter (caliper).*

Table 4.2—*The three general phases of crop development for seedlings. After the three phases of crop development are understood for a species, the growing and facilities schedules can be developed to meet crop needs during each phase. Adapted from Landis and others (1998).*

Phase	Establishment	Rapid growth	Hardening
Definition	From germination through emergence and formation of true leaves.	From emergence of true leaves to when seedling approaches target size. Rapid increase in size, particularly in terminal shoot.	Energy diverted from shoot to root growth; seedling reaches target height and stem diameter; seedling is conditioned to endure stress.
Duration	Typically 14 to 21 days for germination; 4 to 8 weeks for early growth.	Varies widely, typically about 10 to 20 weeks.	Varies widely, normally from 4 to 12 weeks.
Objectives	• Fill containers efficiently • Maximize uniform germination • Maximize survival • Minimize damping-off	• Minimize stress • Encourage shoot growth • Maintain environmental factors near optimum levels • Monitor as seedling approaches target height and roots fully occupy container	• Slow shoot growth • Encourage root and stem diameter growth • Acclimate to outplanting environment • Condition to endure stress • Fortify for survival after outplanting
Special needs	• Protect from weather and pests • Keep temperature warm • Irrigate to keep soil "moist, but not wet" • No or low fertilizer	• Protect from stress • Monitor sun exposure • Irrigate appropriately • Fertilize properly	• Induce moderate moisture stress • Progressively expose to sun equivalent to outplanting conditions (full sun or partial shade) • Expose to ambient temperatures and humidity • Provide good air flow/wind • Reduce fertilization rates and change mineral nutrient ratios
Labor	• Monitor germination • Introduce beneficial microorganisms • Thin • Resow and transplant if necessary • Scout for pests and diseases	• Monitor environment • Modify crop density to encourage good development • Adjust culture to avoid excessive shoot height • Scout for pests and diseases	• Monitor crops and environment carefully; see Chapter 14, Problem Prevention and Holistic Pest Management, and Chapter 19, Nursery Management, for details • Deliver crops to clients in a timely fashion to avoid problems with holdover stock • Scout for pests and diseases

of other species may be covered with mulch. For cuttings, some species need rooting hormones applied at the proper rates and timing. The establishment phase typically lasts 4 to 8 weeks, although species slow to germinate from seeds or root from cuttings may take 1 year or more. The main goal of this phase is to maximize survival with uniform germination and establishment of the plants.

Rapid Growth

During the rapid growth phase, plant shoots increase dramatically in size, often approaching target size (figures 4.6 B and C). Plants need to be somewhat protected dur-ing this phase to encourage rapid (but not excessive) shoot growth and minimize stress.

Hardening

Although it is relatively easy to grow a seedling to target size, the tricky part is the hardening phase. During hardening, energy is diverted from shoot growth to root growth (figures 4.6 D, 4.6 E). Hardened plants are conditioned to endure the stresses of shipping, handling, and outplanting and fortified so that they have the energy and nutritional reserves to survive and grow after outplanting. If the hardening phase is too short and plants do not

Figure 4.6—Shown is koa (Acacia koa) at different growth phases: germination and establishment (A), establishment phase 2 weeks after germination (B), early rapid growth phase (C), late rapid growth phase (D), hardening phase in outdoor area (E), and target plant ready to ship to client (F). Photos by Douglass F. Jacobs.

have time to reach the appropriate physiological condition, plants may still have the correct physical size, but survival and growth after outplanting are compromised. Therefore, good crop planning ensures adequate hardening before on-time delivery to the client. See Chapter 15, Hardening, for more discussion on this topic.

Harvesting and Shipping

After plants are hardened, prompt outplanting is essential to ensure that they can take full advantage of their hardened condition. Proper crop scheduling ensures that a crop goes through the three phases of growth and that healthy plants are ready for shipping (figure 4.6 F) and outplanting on the agreed-upon delivery date. See Chapter 16, Harvesting and Shipping, for more discussion on this topic.

Problems With Holdover Stock

A common problem is the failure of clients to pick up plants on schedule. This problem can be avoided by good scheduling practices and frequent communication with clients, especially by providing periodic updates to advise them when seedlings will be ready. In some cases, having penalties, such as storage fees, in the contract for late pickups may also encourage clients to pick up their plants in a timely fashion. When communicating with clients, emphasize upfront that prompt outplanting is in everyone's best interest, not only for the nursery and the health of the plants, but also for the success of the client's project. See Chapter 19, Nursery Management, for more information about contracts and communicating with clients.

If the schedule to outplant after hardening is not met, problems can develop. When plants are held too long in the nursery, the root system becomes woody and loses its ability to take up water and nutrients (figure 4.7A). Structural problems may also occur; roots may spiral (figure 4.7B) and, instead of expanding outward and downward into the soil after outplanting, girdle the plant or cause it to be unstable in high winds. Shoot growth may resume and negatively affect the root-to-shoot ratio (figure 4.7C), and the plant loses its resistance to stress. Making a growing schedule as shown in table 4.3 is very helpful to provide plants on time; neither ready too early or too late.

Developing Facilities Schedules

Ensuring that the nursery facilities and resources required to meet plant needs through the growing cycle are available at the appropriate times is the goal of facilities scheduling. The space, labor, equipment, and supplies required for each crop during the different stages of propagation must be planned.

Except for nurseries with elaborate climate control systems, crops are often moved from one structure to another as they progress through the three development phases. See Chapter 5, Propagation Environments, for additional information. Using the koa example, crops are protected in a special germination area during the establishment phase and then moved to an outdoor growth area for rapid growth and hardening (table 4.4). Needs differ for various crops and nurseries; for example, another species might have seeds in trays on benches, then be moved to containers in a shade house, and finally transplanted to large pots in full sun for hardening. The amount of space the crop will require varies by growth phase: emerging seedlings may take up little room, but plants take up much more space after they have been transplanted into larger containers or spaced more widely as they grow larger. Although the example in table 4.4 does not go into such detail, the facilities schedule should include calculations for how much space each crop will use, how many hours of labor will be needed, and the quantities of materials (such as growing media) required during crop production.

A good facilities plan considers crop layout, that is, what crops and stocktypes go where in the nursery. This layout is planned to effectively provide appropriate growing requirements (temperatures, sunlight) and other cultural requirements (frequency of fertilization, watering, or other treatments) for all the crops grown each season. Fast-growing species with similar growing and cultural requirements usually can be grouped together in one area, and moderate and slower growing species can be grouped together in another area of the nursery. This grouping method allows for species with similar requirements and growth rates to be treated effectively and efficiently. Likewise, the flow of plants out of a protected area to an outdoor nursery needs to be taken into consideration so that plants that finish in the same timeframe can be moved out and a new crop, if scheduled, can be planned for the available empty space.

Facilities scheduling is indispensable in determining how resources within a nursery can be best distributed to maximize production and minimize conflicts associated with overlapping needs (figure 4.8). The facilities schedule (table 4.4) may be combined with or posted side by side with the growing schedule (table 4.3) and the staff needs to have easy reference to it.

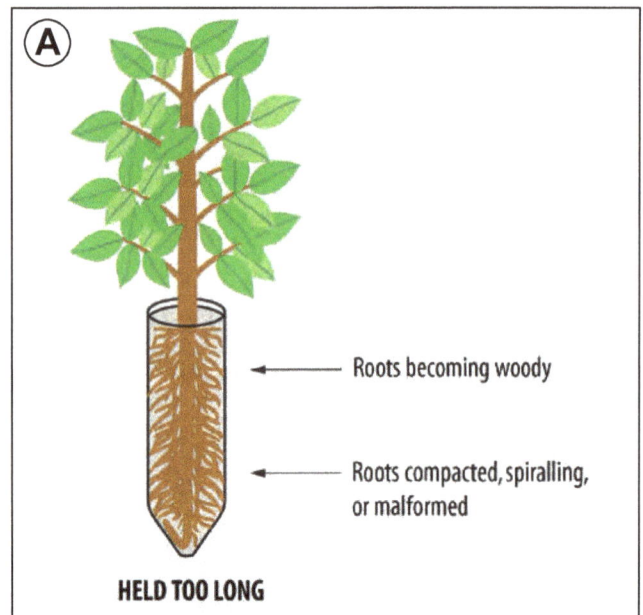

Roots becoming woody

Roots compacted, spiralling, or malformed

HELD TOO LONG

Figure 4.7—Crops that are held too long (holdover stock) will not be properly conditioned to endure the stresses of transportation and outplanting (A). The root systems spiral and the plants become rootbound, such as this māmane (Sophora chrysophylla) (B). The shoots grow too tall for their roots to support and become top heavy (C). Illustration A from Dumroese and others (2008) by Jim Marin, photo B by J.B. Friday, and photo C by Thomas D. Landis.

Table 4.3—*This example crop schedule shows the necessary steps in each crop development phase and the time required to complete each. This schedule should be posted in the nursery so that staff can track the crop's development and understand what cultural practices are required. If appropriate, the schedule can also be shown to clients to help them fully understand the time required to produce their crop.*

Activity	Seed collection and processing	Seed treatments	Establishment phase	Rapid growth phase	Hardening phase
Duration	2 days	2 days	3 weeks	10 weeks	6 weeks
Dates	Scope July 15; collect Aug. 1; process Aug. 2	Aug. 3 to scarify; Aug. 4 to sow	Aug. 4 to Aug. 25	Aug. 26 to Nov. 3	Nov. 3 to Dec. 14
Propagation environment	Field-collection sites	Indoors	Germinant area protected from slugs, birds, rodents, rain, etc.	Main outdoor growth area and full sun	Main outdoor growth area and full sun
Fertilization	None	None	In growing media: triple super phosphate, dolomite lime, gypsum, and mycorrhizal fungi; inoculate at 2 weeks with *Rhizobium*	None	None
Irrigation	None	None	Daily gentle hand watering to keep moist	Once daily by hand to saturation	Gradual reduction
Target size at end of phase	600 viable seeds plus extras to store for future orders	600 germinants	Not applicable (they will usually be about 1 to 2 in (2 to 5 cm) tall, but no target is set)	Approx. 10- to 12-cm height, 2.5- to 3-mm root-collar diameter	15 cm tall, stem diameter 3.5 mm; Roots: firm with *Rhizobium* nodules
Actions	Field collection of pods. Extract, dry and clean seeds at nursery	Mechanical scarification; soak overnight in clean water	Make potting media; sow seeds; inoculate seedlings with *Rhizobium* at 2 weeks of age	Pest management; check nodulation with *Rhizobium*; space double in trays; cull poor performers	If to be outplanted in windy areas, "brush" daily to simulate wind and improve stem strength

Scheduling Multiple Crops

Most native plant nurseries must deliver a suite of diverse species on a single shipping date to meet client needs. Therefore, the growing and facilities schedules are essential to coordinate production of multiple crops of different species. The schedules must reflect the growth rates (time required to grow the crop) of each species. For example, without proper scheduling, the faster growing species may become overgrown before the delivery date or the slower growing species may not be ready in time. Therefore, slow-growing species need to be sown earlier than fast-growing species so they will all be ready to plant at the correct time.

In the example in figure 4.8, the nursery is growing six species that need to be ready for the same outplanting date in December. To meet the target outplanting, koa needs to be sown in August, as they take about 18 weeks to grow, but if a client also wanted native sandalwood trees in 1-gallon pots at the same time as the koa, nursery work would need to begin 1 year in advance to bring this slower growing species through

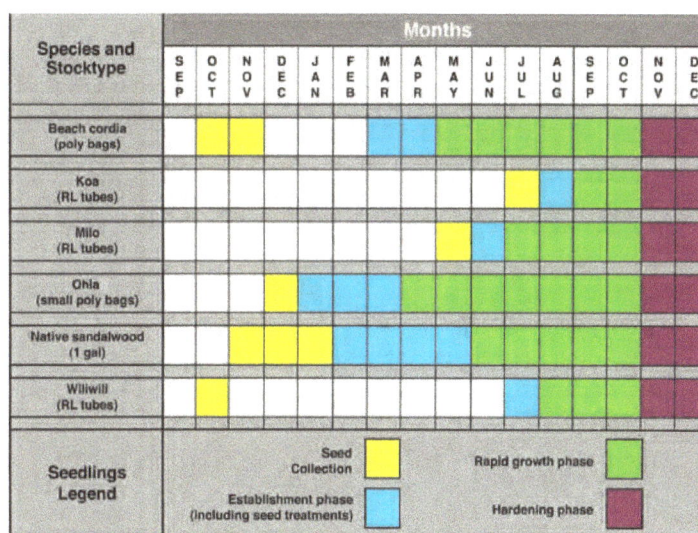

Figure 4.8—*In this hypothetical schedule from Wilkinson and Elevitch (2004), six Hawaiian species must be ready at the same time in December. Different stock types and species require more or less time to grow in the nursery, depending on many factors. Please note this schedule is hypothetical only—timing will vary by location, species, and seed sources. Illustration by Jim Marin.*

all the phases of development. Some species may be fast growing, such as the native wili-wili, but seed collection sites may be seasonal and require more advanced notice to collect. (Please note: these examples are hypothetical—timing, especially of the seed collection, will vary by location and species.)

Keeping Written Records Makes Planning Easier

Propagation protocols, growing schedules, and facilities schedules can all be improved each season by keeping good records. It is important to keep records of how to replicate each crop. How long did it take to produce the crop? What materials were purchased? How was the crop fertilized, watered, and managed during each growth phase? What did we learn that will help us next time we grow this species?

Propagation protocols should be revised on a seasonal or annual basis, becoming more accurate each year, which then improves the usefulness of the crop and facilities schedules.

The best way to improve the accuracy of your protocols is to keep two kinds of written records:

1. The daily log is a journal that notes nursery conditions, activities, and management practices on a daily basis. In other words, what was done?

2. Regular plant growth records describe the development of each crop. In other words, how did the crop respond to particular management practices?

The daily log and plant development records interrelate with the propagation protocols (figure 4.9).

Daily Log

A daily log is a key record that provides a history of nursery management, problem-solving, and crop development (figure 4.10). A daily log example is in table 4.5, and appendix 4.B includes a blank daily log form that a small nursery might use. Make it a habit to at least jot down something each day. Large nurseries may keep more complicated daily

Table 4.4. An example of a facilities schedule for Acacia koa.

Activity	Seed collection and processing	Seed treatments	Establishment phase	Rapid growth phase	Hardening phase
Length	2 days	2 days	3 weeks	10 weeks	6 weeks
Dates	Scope July 15; collect Aug. 1; process Aug. 2	Aug. 3 to scarify; Aug. 4 to sow	Aug. 4 to Aug. 25	Aug. 26 to Nov. 3	Nov. 3 to Dec. 14
Labor	Two staff members to scout out collection site in July (1/2 day). Two staff members to go to collection site on Aug. 1 and collect (1 full day per person). Two staff members to dry, process, and clean seeds on Aug. 2 (a few hours intermittently throughout day as pods dry).	One staff member to hand-scarify seeds late in day on Aug. 3, and put them in water to soak overnight.	Make growing media; fill containers; sow seeds; hand water daily; monitor germination; protect from slugs, birds, and rodents. Collect *Rhizobium* nodules and inoculate seedlings on Aug. 18. Update client on progress.	Move to outdoor growth area, irrigate, monitor growth, double-space in trays as seedlings grow larger, and manage weeds/pests. Update client as end of phase nears. If overstock seedlings will be available, offer them to the client or look for another home for them.	Monitor growth; monitor and gradually reduce irrigation; brush to encourage stem diameter. Keep in regular touch with client. Schedule pick-up day and time.
Facility/ space needed	Permissions and/or permits to collect at collection site(s). Sunny, level area at nursery to lay out pods for drying.	Indoors (home or nursery office).	Benches in germinant area (protected).	Benches in main outdoor growth area.	Benches in main outdoor growth area.
Materials needed	For collection: vehicle, pole pruner, pruning ladder, collection bags, maps, and written collection permissions. For processing: tarp and seed storage containers.	Seeds, nail clippers, a clean container, and clean water for soaking the seeds.	Scarified seeds, containers and trays, growing media and amendments, mycorrhizal inoculant, fine-headed sprayer and hose for irrigation, blender and nodules to make *Rhizobium* inoculant (on Aug. 18).	Extra trays for double-spacing seedlings, irrigation supplies.	PVC pipe or bamboo pole for brushing, irrigation supplies, boxes or buckets for transport unless plants will be transported in trays.

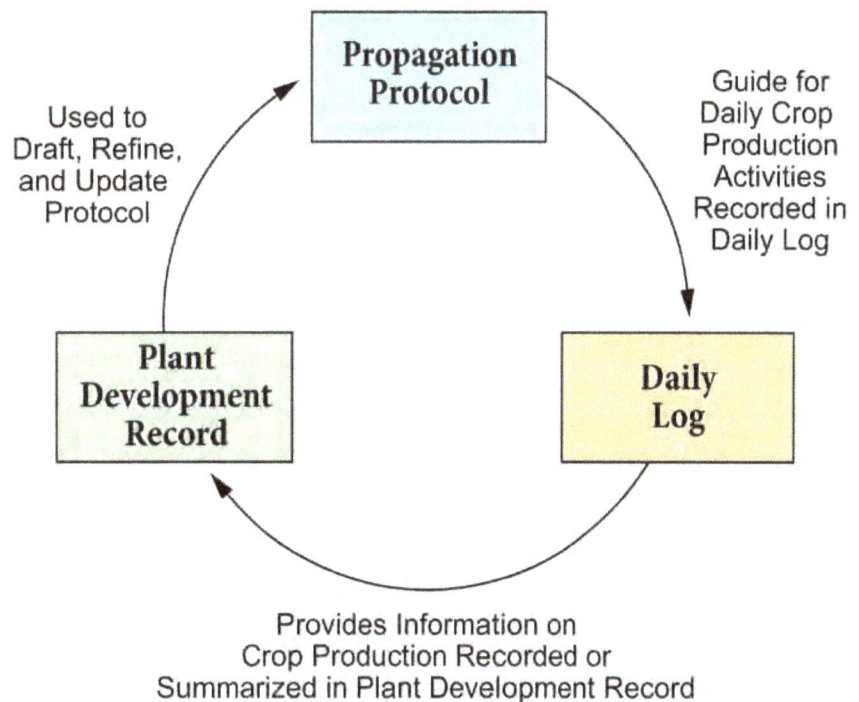

Figure 4.9—The three basic crop records and how they relate. Use a protocol to plan and schedule daily activities. Record activities in the daily log. The log helps with the collection of information about the development of each crop. This information is recorded in the plant development record. The protocol is then refined and expanded based on this new information, which will improve production practices the next time the crop is grown. Illustration from Dumroese and others (2008) by Jim Marin.

records and may have separate logs for irrigation, fertilization, and the like. Tailor the daily log to suit your nursery. What is recorded in the daily log about management practices, environmental conditions, and general crop performance will become an invaluable resource for many years to come.

Plant Development Record

Keeping a simple plant development record (or register) for each crop is a great way to build a foundation for accurate, site- and species-specific protocols. Some growers choose to record a large amount of detail in their daily log and then later summarize information about each crop into a plant development record. Others jot notes into a plant development record for each crop on a regular basis; weekly, monthly, or when the crop is entering a new stage in its development.

A plant development record notes what is happening with a crop of plants from crop initiation through delivery. At a minimum, you can simply put a couple of fresh sheets of paper in a three-ring binder, make a tab with the species name and date for that crop, and jot down notes on a regular basis as the crop progresses. One way to make it easier to keep track of this valuable information is to use a form such as the one provided in appendix 4.C or by entering information into a computer. An example Plant Development Record is in table 4.6.

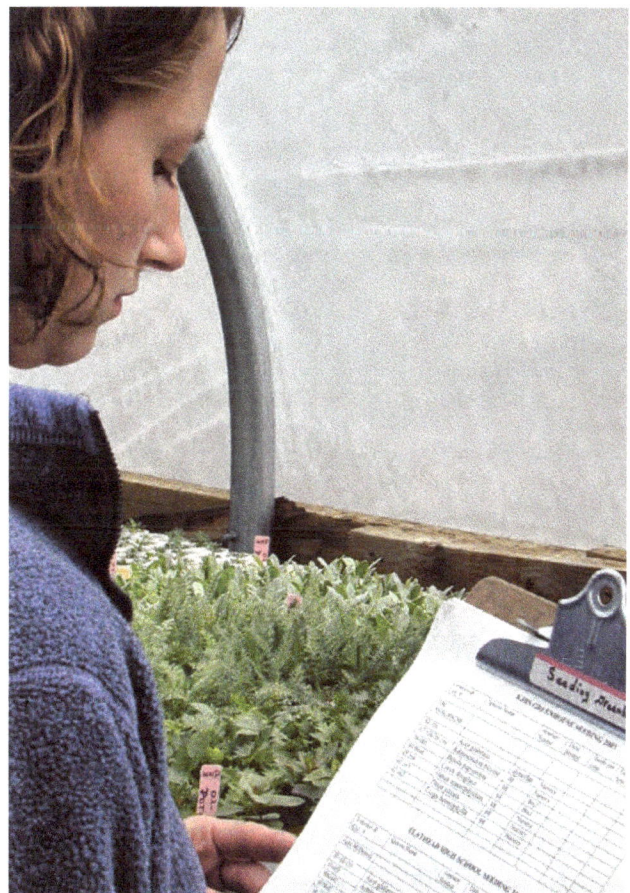

Figure 4.10—Jot down a few notes every day about what was done and what happened with the crop. These records become invaluable resources when adjusting protocols and fine-tuning crop and facilities schedules. Photo by Tara Luna.

Table 4.5—*An example of a daily log.*

Daily log	
Date	April 4, 2015
Environmental conditions in growing areas (light, temperature, and humidity)	Outdoor growing area: 65 °F min; 78 °F max
Sunrise/Sunset times	Sunrise: 5:40 a.m. Sunset: 6:55 p.m.
Moon phase	Full moon.
Other weather notes (cloud cover, and so on)	Partly cloudy, no rain today.
What water did plants receive? (irrigation type and frequency or precipitation)	First thing in the morning, automatic overhead watering for 1 hour on most plants in main rapid-growth outdoor area. Hand-watered benches 1- to 6-in outdoor growing area. Handwatered germination area with fine-headed sprayer in morning.
Today's activities (note how many person-hours per activity) (fertilization, pest management, transplanting, packing and shipping, making potting media, moving crops from one structure to another, treating or sowing seeds, and so on)	Growing media and filled trays for the new order for 300 seedlings, 2 hours total. Handwatered the germinant area and hardening areas, 1 hour. Fixed the small leak (noticed yesterday) in the main water line, 1 hour. Answered e-mail correspondence, 1 hour. Fertilized the beach cordia, sandalwood, and ʻōhiʻa with 200 parts per million (ppm) Peter's 20-20-20 (40 ppm nitrogen), 1 hour. Checked on status of milo germinants, 30 minutes. Weed control around perimeter of outdoor growing area, 1 hour.
Growth phase status (make notes when a crop moves from one phase to another)	The milo seedlings sown earlier this month are germinating well. I better make space in the rapid growth area because I will be able to move them in a couple weeks. The sandalwood seedlings that are to be outplanted this December are all transplanted and starting the rapid growth phase.
Purchases (what supplies or equipment were purchased and their cost)	Bought a new coupling for fixing the irrigation line plus an extra one to have on hand in case of another leak: $10.87. Bought potting media materials for upcoming order: $28.45.
Orders (what plant materials were delivered and payments made)	Next week is the pickup of 250 sandalwood seedlings for the high school's graduating class to plant as a class gift to the community forest. The seedlings are ready; I just have to keep the slugs at bay.
General crop/nursery observations	Things look good in general.
Questions or concerns	There seem to be lots of slugs out… I would like to explore some other organic slug control options… maybe I will call around and see if anyone I know has had success with that copper barrier stuff and what the cost might be. I need to follow up with the Smiths to see if they are ready to confirm koa seedling order for November planting—if so I need to give them their contract, collect a deposit, and get planting so we can be ready when the rainy season starts.

Table 4.6—*An example of a plant development record for an* Acacia koa *crop.*

Plant development record (Koa crop for Waimea Ranch due Dec. 15)	
Species name	*Acacia koa*
Propagule source	Collection site ABDA, at 2,000 ft (610 m) elevation on the leeward side of the Big Island of Hawaiʻi from 55 parent trees of good form.
Date(s) of propagule collection	July 15 and Aug. 1
Establishment	
Type and length of propagule treatment (for example, scarified, stratified)	Hand scarified then soaked in water overnight.
Date of propagule establishment	Aug. 2 to 3
Growing media and tray or container type used	Direct sown in Ray Leach Stubby cells; growing media consisting of 50% peat, 25% perlite, and 25% vermiculite with amendments and mycorrhizal fungi.
Germination notes (including date begins and ends, percent germination)	Fairly uniform germination of about 92% from Aug. 5 to 12.
Cutting notes (for example, special conditions, hormone treatments)	N/A*
Date transplanted (if not direct sown)	N/A*
Container type and growing media for transplanting	N/A*
Microorganisms used?	Mycorrhizal fungi inoculant in media; inoculated with *Rhizobium* on Aug. 20, 2014
Misting/Irrigation (type and frequency)	Daily hand-watering
Fertilization type, rate, and frequency, if any	N/A
Environmental conditions for crop (light, temperature, humidity)	Under plastic cover of screened-in greenhouse during establishment so birds and rodents do not eat the seeds.
Horticultural treatments (for example, cultivation practices)	N/A*
Date establishment phase completed	Aug. 26
Notes (resowing or thinning activities, problems, or challenges)	N/A*
Rapid growth	
Time after sowing and sticking to enter rapid growth phase	3 weeks (seeds scarified Aug. 1 and moved to rapid growth area Aug. 25)
Plant size at start of phase (height)	About 5 cm tall
Irrigation (type and frequency; for example daily, every other day, etc.)	Daily hand-watering
Fertilization type, rate, and frequency	N/A*
Environmental conditions for crop (light, temperature, and humidity)	Moved to full sun Aug. 27
Horticultural treatments (for example, spacing, cultivation practices)	Spaced out 50% on Sep. 9
Date rapid growth phase completed	Nov. 3, 2014
Notes (development, vigor, and health, challenges or problems)	Culled about 5% that were not growing quickly before beginning hardening phase on Nov. 3.

Table 4.6—*Continued*

Hardening	
Plant size at start of phase (height and stem diameter)	Average about 10- to 12-cm height, 2.5- to 3.0-mm stem diameter on Nov. 3
Irrigation (type and frequency; for example, daily, every other day, etc.)	Approximately every other day hand-watering or as needed (very hot days will water daily)
Fertilization type, rate, and frequency, if any	N/A*
Environmental conditions for crop (light, temperature, and humidity)	Full sun, ambient temperature
Horticultural treatments (for example, spacing, cultivation practices)	Some weeding. Weather has been windy; no need to brush.
Plant size at end of phase (height and stem diameter)	15-cm tall; 3.5-mm stem diameter
Date hardening phase completed	Dec. 10—ready to go
Date plants delivered	Dec. 15
Notes (vigor and health, challenges or problems)	
Other notes	
Notes on performance of crop after outplanting	Follow up by phone call scheduled for Jan. 5. Client is using a mattock and shovel to plant.

*N/A: Not applicable

Figure 4.11—*Proper planning ensures that the needs of the nursery, the plants, and the clients are met in a timely fashion. Photo by Douglass F. Jacobs.*

Keep a separate plant development record for each crop grown, even if it is just a small trial of a few plants or even if the species has been grown before. Any intended improvements, trials, or experiments done with a species (such as increasing ventilation in the nursery area or switching to a new kind of fertilizer) can also be recorded in a plant development record. When these records are reviewed, the information enables nursery managers to determine if intended improvements actually had a positive effect on plant health and growth compared with what was normally done (figure 4.11). More information on trials, or experiments is provided in Chapter 20, Discovering Ways to Improve Nursery Practices and Plant Quality.

References

Dumroese, R.K.; Luna, T.; Landis, T.D. 2008. Nursery manual for native plants: volume 1, a guide for tribal nurseries. Agriculture Handbook 730. Washington, DC: U.S. Department of Agriculture, Forest Service. 302 p.

Landis, T.D.; Tinus, R.W.; Barnett, J.P. 1998. The container tree nursery manual: volume 6, seedling propagation. Agriculture Handbook 674. Washington, DC: U.S. Department of Agriculture, Forest Service. 166 p.

Landis, T.D.; Dumroese, R.K. 2000. Propagation protocols on the Native Plant Network. Native Plants Journal. 1: 112–114.

Landis, T.D.; Dumroese, R.K. 2002. The Native Plant Network: an on-line source of propagation information. International Plant Propagators' Society, Combined Proceedings. 51: 261–264.

Landis, T. D. 2011. The Target Plant concept - a history and brief overview. In: Riley, L.E., Haase, D.L. and Pinto, J.R.tech coords. National Proceedings: Forest and Conservation Nursery Associations – 2010. Proceedings RMRS-P-65. Fort Collins, CO: US Department of Agriculture, Forest Service, Rocky Mountain Research Station, Proceedings. 61-66.

Wilkinson, K.M.; Elevitch, C.R. 2003. Growing koa: a Hawaiian legacy tree. Holualoa, HI: Permanent Agriculture Resources.

Wilkinson, K.M.; Elevitch, C.R. 2004. Propagation protocol for production of container *Acacia koa* Gray plants: permanent agriculture resources, Holualoa, Hawai'i. In: Native Plant Network. Moscow, ID: University of Idaho, College of Natural Resources, Forest Research Nursery. http://www.nativeplantnetwork.org. (September 2009).

Wilkinson, K.M.; Elevitch, C.R. 2004. Propagation protocols for production of container *Cordia subcordata*, *Thespesia populnea*, *Santalum freycinetianum*, *Metrosideros polymorpha*, and *Erythrina sandwicensis* species. In: Native Plant N etwork. Moscow, ID: University of Idaho, College of Natural Resources, Forest Research Nursery. http://www.nativeplantnetwork.org. (September 2009).

Additional Reading

Evans, J. 1992. Forest nurseries. In: Plantation forestry in the tropics: tree planting for industrial, social, environmental, and agroforestry purposes. Second edition. New York: Oxford University Press. Chapter 10.

Jacobs, D.F.; Wilkinson, K.M. 2008. Planning crops and developing propagation protocols. In: Dumroese, R.K.; Luna, T.; Landis, T.D., eds. 2008. Nursery manual for native plants: a guide for tribal nurseries. Agriculture Handbook 730. Washington, DC: U.S. Department of Agriculture, Forest Service. 302 p

Wescom, R.W. 1999. Nursery production scheduling. In: Wescom, R.W. 1999. Nursery Manual for Atoll Environments. RAS/97/330 Working Paper No. 9. U.S. Department of Agriculture, Natural Resources Conservation Service: 12–14. Chapter 5.

Appendix 4A—A sample propagation protocol form

Propagation protocol	
Family scientific name	
Family common name	
Scientific name	
Common name	
General distribution	
Propagation goal	
Propagation method	
Product type	
Time to grow	
Target specifications	
Propagule collection	
Propagule processing	
Seeds/kg	
Purity	
Germination	
Pre-sowing treatments	
Growing area	
Growing medium	
Establishment phase	
Duration of establishment phase	
Rapid growth phase	
Duration of rapid growth phase	
Hardening phase	
Duration of hardening phase	
Harvesting, storage, and shipping	
Outplanting and cultivation comments	
Citations	

Appendix 4B—*A sample daily log form*

Daily log	
Date	
Environmental conditions in growing areas (light, temperature, humidity, etc.)	
Sunrise/Sunset times	
Moon phase	
Other weather notes (cloud cover, etc.)	
What water did plants receive? (irrigation type and frequency or precipitation)	
Today's activities (note how many person-hours per activity) (fertilization, pest management, transplanting, packing and shipping, making growing media, moving crops from one structure to another, treating or sowing seeds, and so on)	
Growth phase status (make notes when a crop moves from one phase to another)	
Purchases (what supplies or equipment were purchased and their cost)	
Orders (what plant materials were delivered and payments made)	
General crop/nursery observations	
Questions or concerns	

Plant development record	
Species name	
Propagule source	
Date(s) of propagule collection	
Establishment	
Type and length of propagule treatment (for example, scarified, stratified)	
Date of propagule establishment	
Growing media and tray or container type used	
Germination notes (including date begins and ends, percent germination)	
Cutting notes (for example, special conditions, hormone treatments)	
Date transplanted (if not direct sown)	
Container type and growing media for transplanting	
Microorganisms used?	
Misting/irrigation (type and frequency)	
Fertilization type, rate, and frequency, if any	
Environmental conditions for crop (light, temperature, humidity)	
Horticultural treatments (for example, cultivation practices)	
Date establishment phase completed	
Notes (resowing or thinning activities, problems or challenges)	

Rapid growth	
Time after sowing and sticking to enter rapid growth phase	
Plant size at start of phase (height)	
Container type and growing medium	
Irrigation (type and frequency; for example, daily, every other day, etc.)	
Fertilization type, rate, and frequency	
Environmental conditions for crop (light, temperature, and humidity)	
Horticultural treatments (for example, spacing, cultivation practices)	
Date rapid growth phase completed	
Notes (development, vigor and health, challenges or problems)	
Hardening	
Plant size at start of phase (height and stem diameter)	
Irrigation (type and frequency; for example, daily, every other day, etc.)	
Fertilization type, rate, and frequency, if any	
Environmental conditions for crop (light, temperature, and humidity)	
Horticultural treatments (for example, spacing, cultivation practices)	
Plant size at end of phase (height and stem diameter)	
Date hardening phase completed	
Date plants delivered	
Notes (vigor and health, challenges or problems)	
Other notes	
Notes on performance of crop after outplanting	

Propagation Environments

Douglass F. Jacobs, Thomas D. Landis, Tara Luna, and Diane L. Haase

5

Many environmental factors influence growth and production of nursery plants. The primary processes affected by environmental factors are photosynthesis and transpiration. Photosynthesis is the means by which light energy from the sun is converted into chemical energy in the presence of chlorophyll, the green pigment in leaves. During photosynthesis, sugars are produced from carbon dioxide from the air and water from the soil while oxygen is released back into the air (figure 5.1). Photosynthesis is a "leaky" process because, to allow the intake of carbon dioxide, water vapor is lost through pores, or stomata, on the leaf surfaces. This water loss is called transpiration. To maximize the photosynthesis necessary for plant growth, growers must reduce the factors that limit photosynthesis or increase the factors that promote photosynthesis.

Photosynthesis, and therefore growth, can be limited by factors associated with the growing medium, other organisms, or the atmosphere (figure 5.2). Limiting factors related to growing media include water and mineral nutrients and are discussed in detail in Chapter 6, Growing Media, Chapter 11, Water Quality and Irrigation, and Chapter 12, Plant Nutrition and Fertilization. Photosynthesis can be limited by the absence of beneficial organisms or by the presence of harmful organisms; these instances are discussed in Chapter 13, Beneficial Microorganisms, and Chapter 14, Problem Prevention and Holistic Pest Management. Atmospheric factors that affect photosynthesis include light, temperature, relative humidity, and carbon dioxide levels. Propagation structures, or environments, are any area that is modified to encourage the growth of nursery plants by controlling these atmospheric factors during all phases of growth in the nursery. Understanding different types of propagation structures and how they work is critical whether designing a new nursery facility or modifying an existing one.

Tropical nursery facilities differ not only in their complexity but also in their biological and economical aspects. Propagation environments can be as simple as a garden plot where water and fertilizer are applied, or as complex as high-tech greenhouses that also modify all atmospheric factors. Although modifying atmospheric factors can also influence the growing media and occurrence of other organisms, our focus in this chapter is primarily on modifying atmospheric factors (light, temperature, and relative humidity) through a variety of propagation environments.

Facing Page: *Propagation environments modify atmospheric factors such as light and temperature. In this nursery, removable palm thatch provides shade for young seedlings but allows full sun to reach maturing plants. Photo by Thomas D. Landis.*

Matching Propagation Environments to the Site

The best possible propagation environment is designed for a specific nursery site (Landis 1994). Whether building a new nursery or modifying an existing one, it is critical to analyze the limiting factors on the site. The value of such an analysis can be clearly demonstrated on the Big Island of Hawai'i. One of the Hawai'i Volcanoes National Park Service nurseries is located near sea level where the most limiting site factors are intense sunlight and seasonal high winds. This situation requires a strong structure to withstand wind loads and a shadecloth to minimize heat buildup. Moving up slope to the town of Volcano at 3,700 ft (1,130 m), the climate is milder year round than at the coast and the limiting factors are low sunlight with heavy rains, so a structure with a clear covering to maximize light transmission while protecting the crop from heavy rains would be ideal. Moving to an even higher elevation (7,000 ft [2130 m]), the limiting factor at Hakalau National Wildlife Refuge nursery is cold, with nighttime temperatures that can dip to freezing any time of the year. Thus, it is necessary to have an enclosed structure to protect the crops. As expected, the costs of nursery development increase with greater control of the propagation environment. A nursery that is well matched to its environment, however, will be much less expensive to operate than a poorly designed one.

The Challenge of Growing Many Species and Stocktypes

Tropical nurseries grow an increasing diversity of native plant species. Often, these diverse crops must be started on various dates, so, at any one time, a nursery might have everything from germinating seeds to large plants. Although some species are grown from seeds, others in the same nursery might have to be grown from rooted cuttings. So, a good native plant nursery should be designed with various propagation environments in which plants of similar requirements and growth stages can be grown. For example, a controlled environment such as a greenhouse or other sheltered area can provide ideal conditions for germinating seeds and establishing young seedlings in containers. After young seedlings are established, they could be moved to a shadehouse or open compound to continue their growth. During hardening, the crops can be acclimated to the ambient environment in the same shadehouse or open compound.

Figure 5.1—Two important processes occur in the leaves of green plants. In photosynthesis, sunlight triggers a chemical reaction in which water from the soil and carbon dioxide from the air are converted to sugars and oxygen, which are released back to the atmosphere. During the process, water vapor is lost from the leaves in a process known as transpiration. Illustration from Dumroese and others (2008).

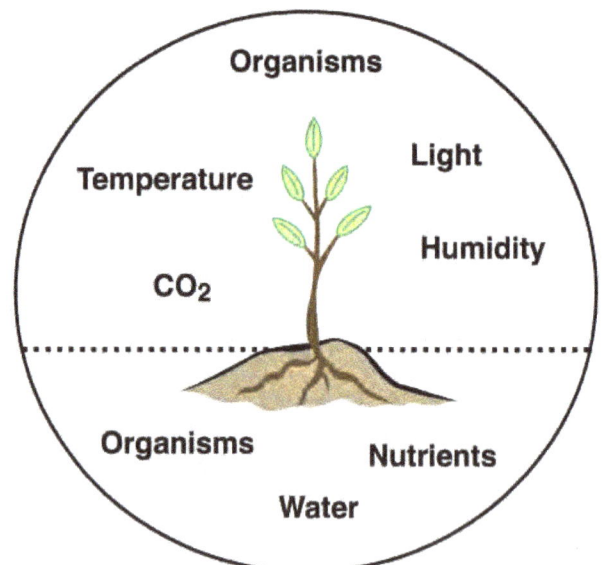

Figure 5.2—It is useful to think of the nursery environment in terms of factors that might be limiting to plant growth. Limiting factors in the soil include water and mineral nutrients whereas, temperature, light, carbon dioxide, and humidity can be limiting factors in the atmosphere. Other organisms can either be beneficial or detrimental. Illustration from Dumroese and others 2008.

Tropical Nursery Manual

Figure 5.3—Open compounds, like Waimea State Tree Nursery on the Big Island of Hawai'i, are common in tropical climates and often used for hardening crops grown in greenhouses or other structures (A). Open compounds often have irrigation and are fenced as seen at this Republic of Palau Forestry Department nursery (B). Photo A by Thomas D. Landis, and photo B by Tara Luna.

Minimally Controlled Propagation Environments

A minimally controlled environment is the simplest and least expensive of all types of propagation environments. The most common type is an open growing compound. It consists of an area where plants are exposed to full sunlight and is usually nothing more than an irrigation system and a surrounding fence.

Open Growing Compounds

Open growing compounds are popular in tropical climates (figure 5.3). Nurseries use open compounds for plant propagation and for areas to expose crops previously grown inside structures to ambient conditions during hardening. Plants can be grown on elevated platforms, benches, or pallets to improve air pruning of the roots, or directly on a layer of gravel (to provide drainage) that is covered with landscape fabric (to control weeds). Irrigation is provided by sprinklers for smaller containers or driplines for larger ones; plants obtain nutrients from controlled-release fertilizers that are incorporated into the growing media. The compound needs to be fenced to minimize animal damage, and, in windy areas, a shelterbelt of trees around the compound can protect from desiccation and improve irrigation coverage.

Wetland Ponds

Artificial ponds are another type of minimally controlled environment. They are used for growing riparian and wet-land plants and are especially good for propagating sedges and rushes. They can also be used to provide specific habitats for certain wetland plants, such as for mangroves adapted to saline coastal habitats. Wetland ponds can be aboveground reservoirs, such as children's wading pools or cattle troughs, or they can be constructed with pond liners either in an excavated area or at ground level using a raised perimeter (figure 5.4). These simple propagation environments use growing media amended with controlled-release fertilizer and require only periodic flood irrigation. Some islands, like Hawai'i and American Samoa, have freshwater wetland species that can be grown as container plants with freshwater flood irrigation.

Figure 5.4—Wetland ponds can be constructed in the outdoor nursery for growing wetland species. On a smaller scale, plastic tubs can be used instead. Photo by Thomas D. Landis.

Semicontrolled Propagation Environments

Another category of propagation environments is called "semicontrolled" because only a few of the limiting factors in the ambient environment are modified. Semicontrolled environments consist of a wide variety of growing structures ranging from simple cold frames to shadehouses.

Cold Frames

Cold frames are low-to-the-ground structures consisting of a wood or metal frame with a transparent covering. As their name suggests, they have no heating source except for the sun. Cold frames are the most inexpensive propagation structure and are easy to build and maintain. Because conditions inside can stay relatively warm and moist, cold frames can be used for seed germination or rooting cut-

Figure 5.5—*Cold frames are an inexpensive alternative to a greenhouse. Cold frames should be placed in a sheltered location for additional protection (A). Coverings may be removed (B) or held open to manage humidity and heat levels (C). Photos by Tara Luna.*

tings. They can also be used to protect seedlings and cuttings from heavy rains and wind.

The ideal location for a cold frame is an area with a slight slope to ensure good drainage. A sheltered spot against the wall of a building or greenhouse provides additional protection (figures 5.5A). Some nurseries sink the floor of the cold frame 6 to 12 in (15 to 30 cm) into the ground to use the earth for insulation. Other nurseries make their cold frames lightweight enough to be portable so they can move them from one section of the nursery to another.

It is relatively easy to build a cold frame. Frames are usually made of wood such as mahogany that will resist decay; the new recycled plastic lumber also works well. Never use creosote-treated wood or wood treated with pentachlorophenol because these substances are toxic to plants. The cold frame needs to be built so that it is weather-tight and so the top can be opened partially or fully to allow for various levels of ventilation, watering, and the easy removal of plants (figure 5.5B, 5.5C). The cover must be able, however, to be attached securely to the frame to resist wind gusts. Heavy plastic film is an inexpensive covering but usually lasts only a single season. Hard plastic or polycarbonate panels are more durable and will last for several years. Cold frame kits may also be purchased and are easily assembled; some kits even contain automatic ventilation equipment.

Cold frames can be labor-intensive because they need to be opened and closed daily to manage temperature and humidity levels. A thermometer that can be conveniently read without opening the cover is mandatory. In a cold frame, plants grow best at 65 to 85 °F (18 to 29 °C). If air temperature goes above 85 °F (29 °C), the top must be opened to allow ventilation. In the tropics, cold frames usually need to have shadecloth suspended above them to help moderate temperatures.

Hoop Houses and Polyethylene Tunnels

Hoop houses and polyethylene ("poly") tunnels are versatile, inexpensive propagation environments. They are usually constructed of semicircular frames of polyvinyl chloride (PVC) or metal pipe covered with a single layer of heavy polyethylene and are typically quite long (figure 5.6). Some hoop houses have end walls made of solid material such as water-resistant plywood. The cover on hoop houses is changed or removed during the growing season to provide a different growing environment, eliminating the need to move the crop from one structure to another. In general, during the rainy season, a clear plastic

Figure 5.6—Hoop houses can be used for a variety of propagation environments by changing or removing the coverings. Photo by Douglass F. Jacobs.

cover is used during seed germination and seedling establishment. The plastic cover protects the young germinants and seedlings from heavy rains and can be pulled back as needed to provide adequate ventilation. As the dry season approaches and the seedlings are established, the plastic cover can be removed and replaced with shadecloth. Sometimes, a series of shadecloths, each with a lesser amount of shade, are used to gradually expose crops to full sun. During hardening, the shadecloth is completely removed to expose the plants to the ambient environment.

Shadehouses

Shadehouses are the most permanent of semicontrolled propagation environments and serve several uses. In the tropics, shadehouses are commonly used to propagate plants under conditions of intense sunlight (figure 5.7A). Less permanent shadehouses consist of a metal pipe frame covered with shadecloth and allow for rapid take down when tropical storms threaten. When used for growing, shadehouses can be equipped with sprinkler irrigation and fertilizer injectors (figure 5.7B). When the shade is installed on the sides of the structure, shadehouses are very effective at protecting crops from wind and therefore help to reduce transpiration. Shadehouses can also be built with local materials (figure 5.7C).

Fully Controlled Propagation Environments

Fully controlled environments are propagation structures in which all or most of the limiting environmental factors are controlled. Examples include growth chambers (high-cost option used almost exclusively for research) and greenhouses. Tropical nurseries with large forestry and restoration programs often make use of greenhouses. Fully controlled environments have the advantage of year-round production in nearly any climate. In addition, most crops can be grown faster and have more uniform quality than those grown in propagation environments with less control. These benefits must be weighed against the higher costs of construction and operation. The more complicated a structure is, the more problems that can develop. This concept is particularly true in the remote locations of many tropical nurseries, where electrical power outages can be common and it is difficult, time-consuming, and expensive to obtain specialized parts and repair services. Some good references that provide more detail about greenhouse design include Aldrich and Bartok (1989), Bartok (2000), and Landis and others (1994).

Figure 5.7—Shadehouses are semicontrolled environments that are used for protecting plants from intense sunlight, rain, or wind (A). They can be constructed of wood frames with lath or metal frames with shadecloth and are equipped with irrigation systems that can also apply liquid fertilizer (B). In addition, shade can be created with locally available materials (C). Photos by Tara Luna.

Greenhouse Engineering Considerations

All greenhouses are transparent structures that allow natural sunlight to be converted into heat (figure 5.8A). At the same time, greenhouses are poorly insulated and require specialized cooling and ventilation systems to regulate temperatures. Keeping a greenhouse cool during sunny days requires carefully engineered ventilation systems. It is important to understand that greenhouse construction requires specialized skills (figures 5.8B, 5.8C). In developed areas, greenhouses may be regulated by municipal building codes and zoning, which is another good reason to work with a professional contractor before buying and constructing a greenhouse.

Design Loads

The load on a greenhouse includes dead loads (the weight of the structure), live loads (caused by building use), and weather-related loads (wind). Live loads include people working on the structure and the weight of equipment, such as irrigation systems, fans, lighting systems, and even hanging plants.

Foundations, Floors, and Drainage

The foundation connects the greenhouse to the ground and counteracts the design load forces. Inexpensive floors can consist of gravel covered with landscape cloth, but the ground beneath the floor must drain water freely to prevent standing water and safety issues. Nursery crops require frequent irrigation and, depending on the irrigation system, much of this water may end up on the floor. Drain tiles might be needed to ensure that the greenhouse floor will not become a swamp. Full floors can be engineered with drains so that all water and fertilizer runoff can be contained on site; runoff containment is a legal requirement in many places. It may be necessary to design the greenhouse so that all wastewater drains into a pond or constructed wetland to prevent contamination of water sources; these ponds or wetlands can sometimes be used for other purposes, such as growing wetland plants as described previously in this chapter.

If wheeled equipment will be used to move plants, concrete walkways between the benches are necessary. Note that black asphalt heats up rapidly and becomes soft, so concrete is a better, but more expensive, option. Full concrete floors will eliminate many pest problems, especially algae, moss, and liverworts that thrive in the humid nursery environment.

Figure 5.8—*Greenhouses, like this one in American Samoa, are the most sophisticated propagation environments (A). Workers with specialized skills are needed from the initial surveying (B) to the final construction (C). Photo A by Thomas D. Landis, and photos B and C by Ronald Overton.*

Framing Materials

Ideal framing supports the greenhouse covering with minimal shading and heat loss while allowing ease of access and handling. Framing materials include galvanized steel, aluminum (lightweight but expensive), and treated wood.

Greenhouse Kits

The heating and cooling systems of fully controlled greenhouses must be carefully engineered to match both the size of the structure and the ambient environment. Be aware that inexpensive greenhouse kits often have vents or fans that are too small for the size of the greenhouse. Kit greenhouses were designed for some "average" environment and will probably have to be modified to handle the limiting environmental factors on your site. Before purchasing a greenhouse kit, it is a good idea to hire an experienced consultant, speak with a knowledgeable company representative, and discuss designs with other growers or professionals.

Greenhouse Coverings

A wide variety of greenhouse coverings are available and the selection of a particular type is usually based on cost, type of structure, and the environmental conditions at the nursery site (figure 5.9).

Polyethylene tarps are relatively cheap but require replacement every 2 to 4 years depending on the grade of plastic. Double layers of polyethylene sheeting that are inflated with a fan are stronger and provide better insulation longer than a single layer. The two layers are attached to the framing with wooden furring strips or specially designed fasteners. This process is relatively simple so many growers change their own coverings. Because they are so well insulated and airtight, polyethylene greenhouses require good ventilation to prevent condensation.

Polycarbonate ("polycarb") panels, the most popular permanent greenhouse covering, have about 90 percent of the light transmission properties of glass. Polycarb is strong and durable but is one of the more expensive coverings.

These panels are the most common greenhouse coverings, and a more detailed description of costs and engineering and operational considerations is available in Landis and others (1994).

Controlling Greenhouse Temperatures

One of the most challenging aspects of a greenhouse is controlling temperature. Sunlight is converted into heat that can become lethal to plants. A sophisticated control system that can maintain a designated temperature through a series of heating and cooling stages is a necessary and wise invest-

Figure 5.9—Greenhouses are covered with transparent coverings such as plastic sheeting or hard plastic panels to maximize the amount of sunlight reaching the crop. Photo by Brian F. Daley.

ment to minimize energy costs. Vents and fans are used to keep air moving inside the greenhouse and exhaust heat from the structure. In dry, windy environments, wet walls use the power of evaporation to cool incoming air. Growers can also use short bursts of their irrigation system for cooling. Automatic sensing instruments are available that can be connected with cooling equipment to trigger a cooling cycle for the greenhouse. Mechanical thermostats provide the best and most economical form of temperature control and can be used to activate motorized vents and fans within a greenhouse.

Specialized Rooting Propagation Environments

The most common type of vegetative propagation is the rooting of cuttings. Often, this form of propagation requires a specialized environment known as a rooting chamber that creates specific conditions to stimulate root initiation and development. Because cuttings do not have a root system (figure 5.10A), rooting chambers must provide frequent misting to maintain high humidity to minimize transpiration. Root formation is stimulated by warm temperatures and moderate light levels; these conditions maintain a high level of photosynthesis. Therefore, many rooting chambers are enclosed with polyethylene coverings that, in addition to maintaining high humidity, keep the area warm. If the chambers are outside, the covering further protects cuttings from rain and drying winds. For more information on rooting cuttings, see Chapter 10, Vegetative Propagation.

Enclosed Rooting Chambers

Because it is easy to construct and very economical, a simple enclosed rooting chamber is essentially the same

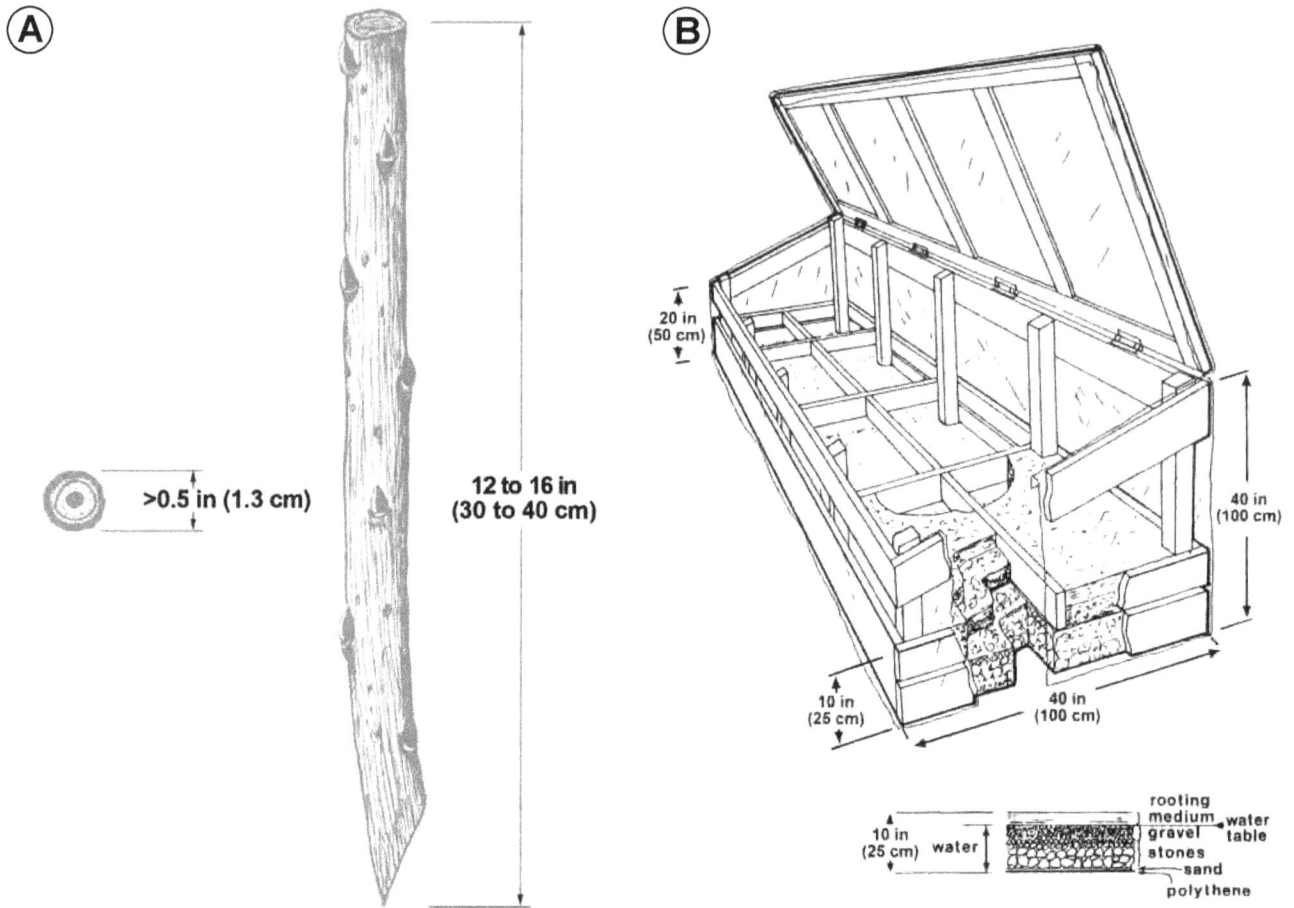

Figure 5.10—Rooting cuttings require a specialized propagation environment because cuttings lack a root system (A). The "poly propagator" is the most simple and inexpensive rooting chamber (B). Illustrations by R.H.F. Wilson from Longman 1993.

as the cold frame discussed earlier. They are commonly used in tropical nurseries throughout the world because they do not require electricity. Enclosed rooting chambers rely on manual operation so they require diligent daily inspection to regulate humidity and air temperatures, and the rooting medium must be watered as needed. They typically have shadecloth suspended above them to moderate temperatures, but, if heat or humidity becomes excessive, enclosed chambers need to be opened for ventilation. One design is known as a "poly propagator" because it is covered with polyethylene plastic sheeting and is a simple and inexpensive design (figure 5.10B).

Intermittent-Mist Rooting Systems

These rooting propagation environments are either enclosed or open. Rooting cuttings is much easier in these environments because intermittent-mist rooting chambers have a high degree of environmental control (figure 5.11A). Clock timers (figure 5.11B) control the timing and duration of misting from specialized nozzles (figure 5.11C). Frequent misting maintains high humidity that

reduces water loss from the cuttings, and evaporation of the small droplets moderates air and leaf temperature.

Mist systems require high water pressure that is supplied through PVC pipes. Mist timing is controlled by two time clocks that open and close a magnetic solenoid valve in the water line linked to the nozzles. One clock turns the system on during the day and off at night and the other controls the timing and duration of the mists. Because the aperture of the mist nozzles is so small, a cartridge filter needs to be installed in the water line after a gate valve.

Because of the proximity of water and electricity, all employees need to receive safety training. All wiring used for mist propagation must be grounded and must adhere to local building codes. Electrical outlets and components must be enclosed in waterproof coverings. The high humidity encourages the growth of algae and mosses, so the mist propagation system needs to be cleaned regularly. Mist systems require water that is low in dissolved salts; "hard" water may result in whitish deposits that can plug mist nozzles. See Chapter 11, Water Quality and Irrigation, for more information.

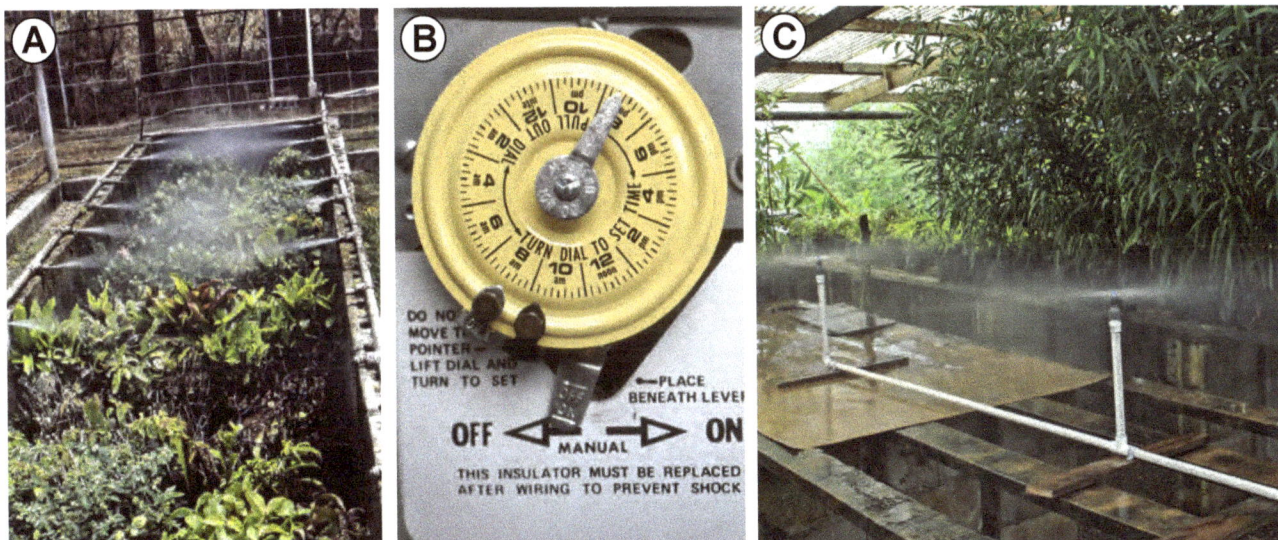

Figure 5.11—Intermittent-mist systems are easily controlled environments (A). Programmable timers control the timing and duration (B) of specialized mist nozzles (C), which keep humidity levels high, reduce transpiration, and provide cooling. Photos A and C by Tara Luna, and photo B by Thomas D. Landis.

Modifying Light and Temperature in Propagation Environments

As mentioned earlier, light is necessary for photosynthesis, which provides energy for plant growth. For light-loving species, more light results in more growth (figure 5.12A), but greenhouse light levels are often too intense to grow some species of tropical plants (table 5.1). As a result, growers apply shadecloths to lessen light intensity and the resultant heat (figures 5.12B, 5.12C). Shadecloths are

Table 5.1—Shade requirements of a variety of tropical plant species.

Scientific name	Light requirement
Acacia species	Sun
Pandanus species	Sun
Scaevola species	Sun
Bobea species	Partial shade
Bonamia menziesii	Partial shade
Pritchardia species	Partial shade
Cyathea, Cibotium species	Shade
Cyrtandra species	Shade
Elaeocarpus bifidus	Shade

rated by the amount of shade they produce, ranging from 30 to 80 percent. Black has been the traditional color because it is relatively inexpensive, but now shadecloth comes in white, green, and reflective metal. Because black absorbs sunlight and converts it into heat that can be conducted into the propagation structure (figure 5.12D), black shadecloth should never be installed directly on the covering of any propagation structure, but instead needs to be suspended above it to facilitate air movement. Although more expensive than black shadecloth, white or aluminized shade fabrics are better for tropical environments and will do a much better job of cooling the propagation environment while still keeping light levels high. Applying a series of shadecloths, each with a lesser amount of shade, over a period of time is a good way to gradually harden nursery stock and prepare it for outside conditions.

Monitoring Temperatures

Thermometers that record the maximum and minimum temperatures during the day are simple and economical instruments (figure 5.13A) that can help growers monitor subtle microclimates within any propagation environment. New devices, such as self-contained, programmable temperature sensors, are revolutionizing the ways in which temperature can be monitored in nurseries (figures 5.13B, 5.13C). Many of these sensors are small enough to be placed within a container or storage box and can record temperatures (between -40 and 185 °F [-40 and 85 °C]) for more than 10 years. Because these single-chip recording devices can be submersed in water and are resistant to dirt and impact, they can be used to monitor temperatures under

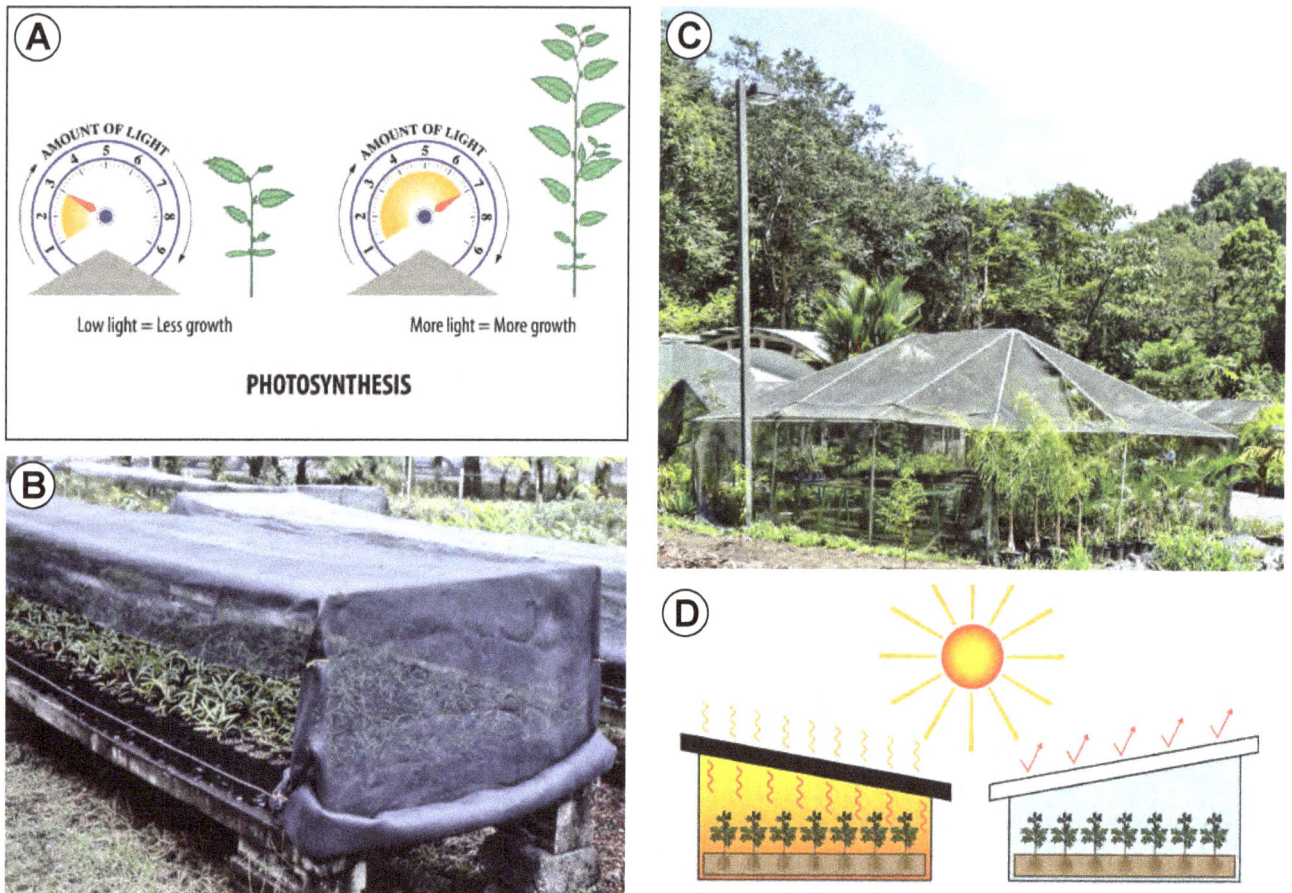

Figure 5.12—*Sunlight provides the energy necessary for plant growth (A) but is converted to heat inside propagation structures. Shadecloth reduces light intensity and cools the environment in small enclosures (B) and larger shadehouses (C). Compared with white or reflective shadecloth, black shadecloth can absorb heat and radiate it into the propagation environment (D). Illustration A from Dumroese and others (2008), photo B by Tara Luna, photo C by Brian F. Daley, and illustration D by Jim Marin.*

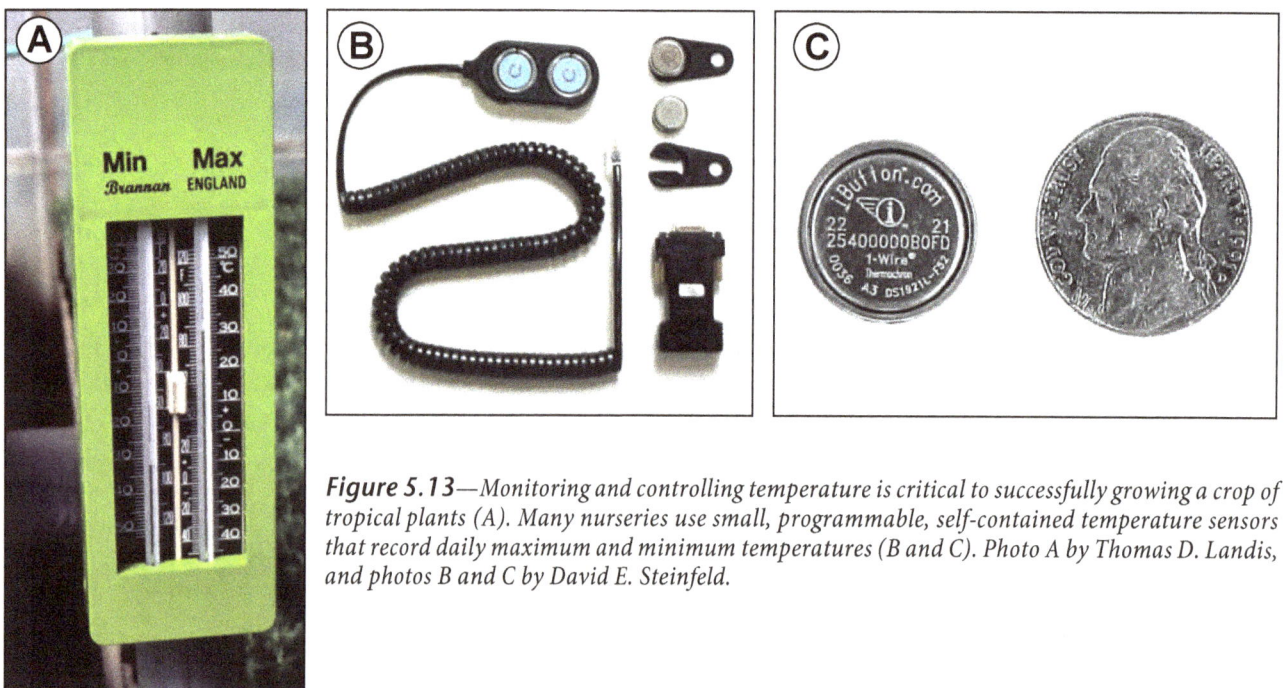

Figure 5.13—*Monitoring and controlling temperature is critical to successfully growing a crop of tropical plants (A). Many nurseries use small, programmable, self-contained temperature sensors that record daily maximum and minimum temperatures (B and C). Photo A by Thomas D. Landis, and photos B and C by David E. Steinfeld.*

most nursery conditions. The data recorded on the sensors must be downloaded to a computer and can then be easily placed into a spreadsheet. The small size of the sensor can also be a drawback; it is easy to misplace. Attach a strip of colorful flagging to indicate where the sensors are located and write any necessary information on the flagging with a permanent marker.

Equipment Maintenance

Even if you purchase the most reliable "automatic" environmental control equipment, it must be monitored and maintained. The hot and humid tropical nursery environment is particularly hard on equipment, and especially so in coastal areas where equipment may also be exposed to salt. Regular maintenance ensures longevity, reduces costly repairs, and may help avoid disasters.

Routine maintenance of all greenhouse and nursery operation equipment should be a top priority. Someone who is mechanically inclined should be given the responsibility for equipment maintenance. Equipment records should be included in the nursery's daily logbook. See Chapter 4, Crop Planning: Propagation Protocols, Schedules, and Records, and Chapter 19, Nursery Management, for more details. These log books will be invaluable when solving problems, budgeting, and developing maintenance plans. A system of "promise cards" specifies when servicing needs to be done and can be incorporated into the nursery computer system. Keep a supply of spare parts on hand, especially parts that may not be readily available or may take a long time to receive. It is a good idea to have a spare cooling fan motor on standby and a handy supply of hardware items such as washers, screws, and bolts. Familiarize all employees on the operation of all equipment so that problems can be detected early. The instruction manuals for all equipment need to be kept and easy to find.

References

Aldrich, R.A.; Bartok, J.W., Jr. 1989. Greenhouse engineering. NRAES-33. Ithaca, NY: Cornell University, Northeast Regional Agricultural Engineering Service. 203 p.

Bartok, J.W., Jr. 2000. Greenhouse for homeowners and gardeners. NRAES-137. Ithaca, NY: Cornell University, Northeast Regional Agricultural Engineering Service. 200 p.

Dumroese, R.K.; Luna, T.; Landis, T.D. 2008. Nursery manual for native plants: volume 1, a guide for tribal nurseries. Agriculture Handbook 730. Washington, DC: U.S. Department of Agriculture, Forest Service. 302 p.

Landis, T.D. 1994. Using "limiting factors" to design and manage propagation environments. International Plant Propagators' Society, Combined Proceedings. 43: 213–218.

Landis, T.D.; Tinus, R.W.; McDonald, S.E.; Barnett, J.P. 1994. The container tree nursery manual: volume 1, nursery planning, development, and management. Agriculture Handbook 674. Washington, DC: U.S. Department of Agriculture, Forest Service. 188 p.

Longman, K.A. 1993. Tropical trees: propagation and planting manuals: volume 1, rooting cuttings of tropical trees. London, United Kingdom: Commonwealth Science Council. 137 p.

Additional Reading

Clements, S.E.; Dominy, S.W.J. 1990. Costs of growing containerized seedlings using different schedules at Kingsclear, New Brunswick. Northern Journal of Applied Forestry. 7: 73–76.

Landis, T.D.; Tinus, R.W.; McDonald, S.E.; Barnett, J.P. 1992. The container tree nursery manual: volume 3, atmospheric environment. Agriculture Handbook 674. Washington, DC: U.S. Department of Agriculture, Forest Service. 145 p.

Growing Media

6

Thomas D. Landis, Douglass F. Jacobs, Kim M. Wilkinson, and Tara Luna

A growing medium can be defined as a substance through which plant roots grow and extract water and nutrients. Selecting a good growing medium is fundamental to good nursery management and is the foundation of a healthy root system.

Growing media for use in container nurseries is available in two basic forms: soil based and organic based. Compared with soil based media that has field soil as a major component, organic based media (a base of organic materials that may be compost, peat, coconut coir, or other organic materials, mixed with inorganic ingredients) promotes better root development. In temperate areas, nurseries can choose from a wide range of commercial products for their growing media, including peat moss, vermiculite, and perlite, and premixed blends of these ingredients. Most nurseries in the tropics, however, do not have easy and affordable access to these materials, and even nurseries in temperate areas are seeking to replace some of these ingredients with more local and sustainable materials. In the tropics, growers often create their own media using locally available ingredients.

A favorable growing medium consists of two or more ingredients. Growers must be familiar with the positive and negative characteristics of the various ingredients and how they will affect plant growth when creating a suitable growing medium, or even when purchasing a commercial one. This chapter describes the uses, functions, and properties of growing media ingredients. From this information, you can experiment with available materials and find the best combination(s) for your nursery.

Facing Page: *Many tropical nurseries create their own growing media with a mix of local materials. Photo by Douglass F. Jacobs.*

Functions of Growing Media

A growing medium serves four functions (figure 6.1).

1. Physical Support

The growing medium must be porous yet provide physical support. Young plants are fragile and must remain upright so that they can photosynthesize and grow. With larger nursery stock in individual containers, a growing medium must be heavy enough to hold the plant upright against the wind. Bulk density is the responsible factor and will be discussed in the next section.

2. Aeration

Plant roots need a steady supply of oxygen to convert the photosynthate from the leaves into energy so that the roots can grow and take up water and mineral nutrients. The byproduct of this respiration is carbon dioxide that must be dispersed into the atmosphere to prevent the buildup of toxic concentrations within the root zone. This gas exchange occurs in the large pores (macropores) or air spaces in the growing medium. Because nursery plants grow rapidly, they need a medium with good porosity—a characteristic termed "aeration" that will be discussed in more detail in the next section.

3. Water Supply

Nursery plants use a tremendous amount of water for growth and development, and this water supply must be provided by the growing medium. Growing media are formulated so that they can hold water in the small pores (micropores) between their particles. Many growing media contain a high percentage of organic matter such as peat moss and compost because these materials have internal spaces that can hold water like a sponge. Therefore, growing media must have adequate porosity to absorb and store the large amounts of water needed by the growing plant.

4. Supply of Mineral Nutrients

Most of the essential mineral nutrients that nursery plants need for rapid growth must be obtained through the roots from the growing medium. Most mineral nutrients are electrically charged ions. Positively charged ions (cations) include ammonium nitrogen (NH_4^+), potassium (K^+), calcium (Ca^{+2}), and magnesium (Mg^{+2}). These cations are attracted to negatively charged sites on growing medium particles up to the point when the roots extract the cations. The capacity of a growing medium to adsorb these cations is referred to as cation exchange capacity (CEC), and this important characteristic is discussed in the next section. Different media components vary considerably in their CEC, but peat moss, vermiculite, and compost have a high CEC value, which explains their popularity in growing media.

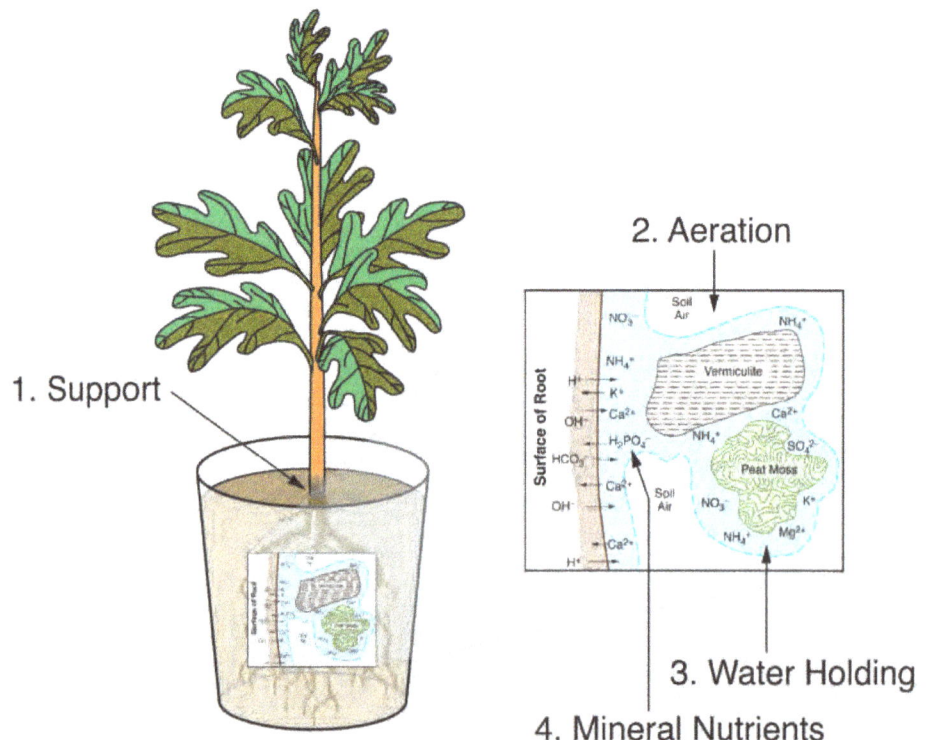

Figure 6.1—*Primary functions of growing media include the capacity to hold water and nutrients for root uptake, providing adequate root aeration, and ensuring structural support to the plant. Illustration from Dumroese and others (2008).*

Physical Properties of Growing Media

Water-Holding Capacity

Micropores absorb water and hold it against the pull of gravity until plants can use it (figure 6.2). The water-holding capacity of a medium is defined as the percentage of total pore space that remains filled with water after gravity drainage. A good growing medium has a high water-holding capacity but also contains enough macropores to allow excess water to drain away and prevent waterlogging. Water-holding capacity varies by the types and sizes of the growing medium ingredients. For example, a peat moss particle will hold much more water than a similarly sized piece of pumice. The degree of compaction is also extremely important. When growing medium particles are damaged during mixing or compacted when the containers are filled, the percentage of macropores is severely reduced. Overmixed or compacted media will hold too much water and roots will suffocate. Finally, the height of the container affects the water-holding capacity; a certain amount of water will always remain in the bottom of the container (figure 6.2). When filled with the same medium, short containers will have a higher percentage of waterlogging than taller ones (see Chapter 7, Containers).

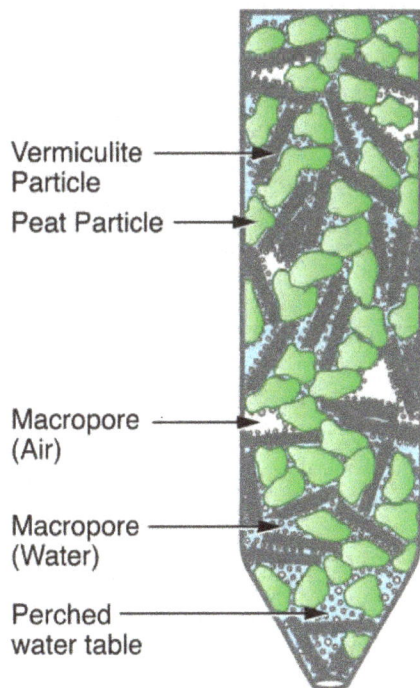

Figure 6.2—A good growing medium contains micropores that hold water and macropores that allow for air exchange. All containers also have a perched water table in the bottom (see also Figure 7.2). Adapted from Landis and others (1989).

Aeration

The percentage of pore space that remains filled with air after excess water has drained away is known as aeration. As we have already discussed, oxygen for good healthy roots is supplied through the larger macropores (figure 6.2), which also allow the carbon dioxide from respiration to dissipate. A good growing medium, especially for rooting cuttings, contains a high percentage of macropores.

Porosity

The total porosity of a growing medium is the sum of the space in the macropores and micropores; plants need both. A growing medium composed primarily of large particles will have more aeration and less water-holding capacity than a medium of smaller particles, which will have less aeration and more water-holding capacity (figure 6.3). Either of these media would restrict plant growth. Plants growing in a medium with all large particles would dry out too quickly, and those growing in a medium with all small particles would suffer from waterlogging. For a single-component medium, the ideal particle range to promote both water-holding capacity and aeration is about 0.03 to 0.24 in (0.8 to 6 mm). In actual practice, however, a good growing medium will contain a mixture of ingredients with different particle sizes and characteristics.

Bulk Density

Media bulk density is the weight per volume and varies with the inherent bulk density of its ingredients and how much they are compressed. An ideal growing medium is lightweight enough to facilitate handling and shipping while still having enough weight to provide physical support. For a given container type and growing medium, excessive bulk density indicates compaction. Bulk density and porosity are inversely related; when bulk density increases, porosity decreases. Even a very porous growing medium can be ruined if it is compressed when the containers are filled.

Chemical Properties of Growing Media

Fertility

Rapidly growing young plants use up the stored nutrients in their seeds soon after emergence. Thereafter, plants must rely on the growing medium to meet their increasing demands for mineral nutrients. As described in Chapter 12, Plant Nutrition and Fertilization, many container nursery managers prefer media with inherently low fertility (for example, peat-vermiculite) to discourage damping-off during the establishment phase and add soluble fertilizers to media throughout the remainder of the growing season. If fertilizers are difficult to obtain or cost prohibitive, organic amendments such as manure or compost can be included in the growing medium. Some plants grow better under low fertilization; in addition, beneficial microorganisms, such as mycorrhizal fungi, sometimes require low fertility

to become established on plant roots. See Chapter 13, Beneficial Microorganisms, for more discussion on this topic.

pH

The pH of growing medium is a measure of its relative acidity or alkalinity. pH values range from 0 to 14; those below 7 are acidic and those above 7 are alkaline. Most native plants tend to grow best at pH levels between 5.5 and 6.5, although some species are tolerant of higher or lower pH levels. The main effect of pH on plant growth is its control on nutrient availability (figure 6.4). For example, phosphorus availability drops at extreme pH values because phosphorus binds with iron and aluminum at low pH levels and with calcium at high pH levels. The availability of micronutrients, such as iron, is even more affected by pH. Iron chlorosis, caused by high pH, is one of the most common nutrient deficiencies of nursery stock. Exceptionally

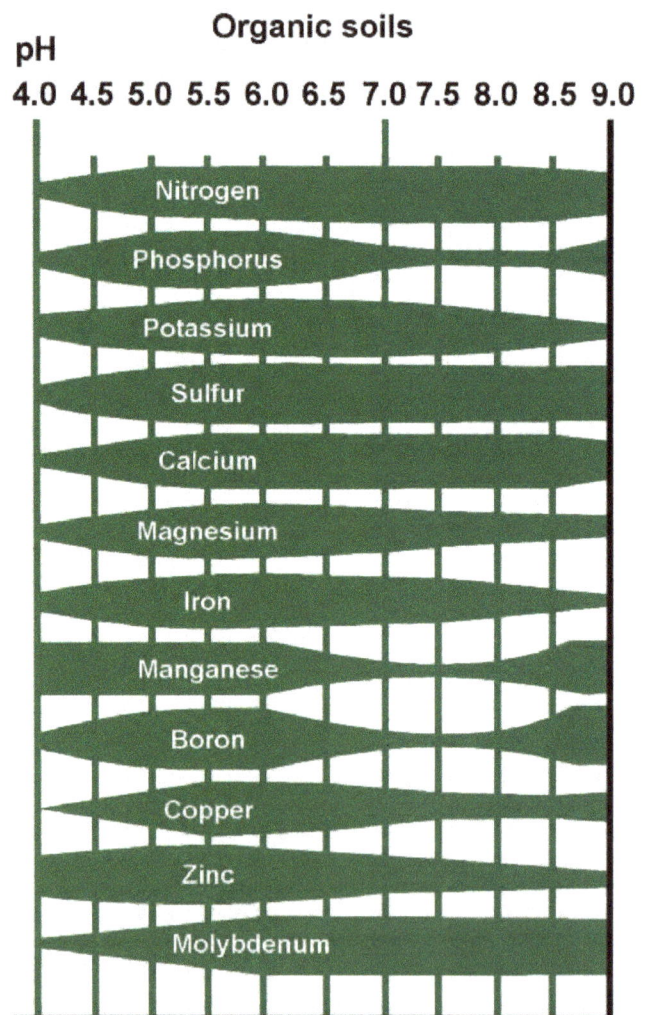

Figure 6.3—These two containers each contain growing media with either large (left) or small (right) particle sizes (A). The corresponding balloons show the relative amounts of air being held, and the glasses show the relative amounts of water being held. When particle sizes are too small, such as this example of a high-clay growing medium, then root development is inhibited (B). Illustration A by Jim Marin, and photo B by J.B. Friday.

Figure 6.4—The availability of all mineral nutrients is affected by the pH of the growing medium. In organic-based growing media, maximum availability occurs between 5.5 and 5.6. Illustration adapted from Bunt (1988) by Jim Marin.

high or low pH levels also affect the abundance of pathogens and beneficial microorganisms. For example, low pH can predispose young plants to damping-off fungi.

Cation Exchange Capacity (CEC)

CEC refers to the ability of a growing medium to hold positively charged ions. Because most growing media are inherently infertile, CEC is a very important consideration. In the growing medium, plant roots exchange excess charged ions for charged nutrient ions (figure 6.1), and then these nutrients are transported to the foliage, where they are used for growth and development. Because the CEC of a growing medium reflects its nutrient storage capacity, it provides an indication of how often fertilization will be required. Because nutrient leaching occurs during irrigation, container nurseries prefer a growing medium with a very high CEC.

Biological Properties of Growing Media

Growing media may contain pathogenic bacteria or fungi. Growing media ingredients that may contain pathogens can be treated with sterilization or pasteurization before use, as described later in this chapter. Organic-based growing media are preferred in nurseries because they are generally pest free. Although peat moss is not technically sterile, it does not contain pathogens or weed seeds when obtained from reliable sources. Vermiculite and perlite are rendered completely sterile during manufacturing, when they are exposed to temperatures as high as 1,832 °F (1,000 °C). Well-prepared composts are generally pest free because sustained, elevated temperatures during composting kill most pathogens. Another benefit of composting is that beneficial microorganisms increase in the final stages of the process. Composted bark of some tree species, for example, contains microbes that suppress common fungal pathogens and nematodes. These suppressive effects depend on the parent material and composting time (Castillo 2004).

Growing Media Ingredients

Once the functions and characteristics of growing media ingredients are understood (table 6.1), an effective and affordable growing media can be developed. Many tropical nurseries mix growing media themselves. Some purchase premixed commercial brands. Some may mix their own media for larger containers, but purchase sterile media for germinants. A typical growing medium is a composite of

Table 6.1—*Different chemical and physical properties of some common materials used to create growing media. Soils are covered separately because they are a combination of both organic and inorganic components, and are extremely variable. Adapted from Buamscha and Altland (2005), Johnson (1968), Lovelace and Kuczmarski (1994), and Newman (2007).*

Component	Bulk density	Porosity:water	Porosity: air	pH	Cation exchange capacity
Organic ingredients					
Sphagnum peat moss	Very low	Very high	High	3 to 4	Very high
Bark	Low	Low	Very high	3 to 6	High
Coir	Low	High	High	6 to 7	Low
Sawdust	Low	High	Moderate	3 to 6	Low
Rice hulls	Low	Low	Moderate	5 to 6	Low
Compost	Variable	Variable	Variable	6 to 8	High
Inorganic ingredients					
Vermiculite	Very low	Very high	High	6 to 8	High
Perlite	Very low	High	High	6 to 8	Very low
Sand	Very high	Moderate	Very low	Variable	Low
Pumice	Low	Low	High	6 to 8	Low
Field soil					
Field soil	Variable	Variable	Variable	Variable	Variable

Why Field Soil Is a Poor Growing Medium

Although it may seem intuitive that potting up nursery plants in containers filled with local field soil would work well, it is not the case. Placing soil in a container results in growing conditions that are completely different from those of unrestricted field soil. These conditions are unfavorable to healthy root growth and plant development in the nursery. In fact, field surveys of tropical and sub-tropical areas of Africa, Asia, and Latin America showed unexpectedly poor field growth of seedlings after outplanting, and correlated this problem with poor root development because of using soil-based media in nurseries (Miller and Jones 1995). The recommended alternative is to replace soil-based media whenever possible with an organic-based, or "artificial" growing media consisting of ingredients such as compost, peat, or coconut coir (Miller and Jones 1995). If soil must be used, it should be only a small percentage of the mix, amended with other ingredients to overcome some of the problems listed in the following sections.

Restricted Volume

Unlike in field conditions, nursery plants will have access to a very limited amount of soil. This limited rooting volume provides seedlings with only small reserves of available water and nutrients and the amount of these resources can change quickly. Because plants will only have a limited area in which to grow their roots, this medium needs to be the best possible material.

Imbalance of Soil Microorganisms

Native soils contain a myriad of microorganisms: some are beneficial and some are pathogenic. These organisms exist in a natural balance in field soils, but when these soils are placed in the nursery growing environments, this delicate balance is upset and problems can develop. Frequent irrigation and fertilization in nurseries favors the development of pathogenic organisms, such as damping-off fungi. Well-processed, organic ingredients, especially composts, often discourage these harmful organisms.

Problems With Water and Air

Clay and silty soils have very small particle sizes and are therefore dense, heavy, and have few air spaces, making it difficult for water to drain freely out of the bottom of the container. Tropical soils tend to be rich in clay and low in organic material and are susceptible to compaction through routine handling and watering in the nursery. Heavy soils also accumulate at the bottom of containers, creating airless places inhospitable for root growth. In addition, some soil-based media shrink when dry and swell when wet, damaging plant roots.

Problems With Nutrition

In containers, native soils do not provide the quantities and ranges of nutrients needed for rapid plant growth and often immobilize certain nutrients (Landis 1995). Clays adsorb some nutrients so strongly that they become largely unavailable for plant uptake, while sandy soils hold nutrients poorly and lose most nutrients through leaching.

Variability and Weeds

Soils are naturally variable, so it is difficult to maintain the same quality from container to container, crop to crop, and year to year—making consistent crop production very difficult. In addition, soil also contains weed seeds, which compete for nutrients and water with the plants sharing their container and compel the grower to spend more labor on weeding.

Sustainability Concerns

Ecological sustainability must also be considered. Harvesting topsoil is actually a mining operation that uses up a limited resource that took thousands of years to develop. For example, in Mexico, millions of square meters of soil are mined each year for use in tree nurseries, leaving behind many acres of depleted areas where plants cannot grow well (Wightman 1999).

Because of these problems with field soil, growing media for tropical nurseries will ideally be based upon organic ingredients, such as composts, bark, rice hulls, or other materials, not field soil. If a medium containing soil must be used, it should contain 10 to 30 percent soil at most, amended with organic ingredients to promote aeration and drainage while maintaining water-holding abilities (Landis 1995). More detail on how to use organic materials to create growing media, and how to incorporate some soil in growing mixes if necessary, is described later in this chapter.

Figure 6.5—Common organic ingredients of growing media include Sphagnum *peat moss (A), compost (B), composted tree bark (C), coconut coir (D), and sawdust (E). Photos A and E by Thomas D. Landis, photo B by George Hernández, and photos C and D by Tara Luna.*

two or three ingredients selected to provide certain physical, chemical, or biological properties. Mixtures of organic and inorganic ingredients are popular because these materials have opposite, yet complementary, properties (table 6.1).

Organic Ingredients

Common organic ingredients include compost, coconut coir, peat moss, bark, rice hulls, sawdust or any other appropriate, locally available material. These materials are lightweight, have high water-holding capacity and CEC, and some contain minor amounts of mineral nutrients. Some of these organic ingredients require screening or composting of local raw materials before use. The nursery may choose to do the processing, or a local supplier may specialize in the composting or processing local materials to sell to the nursery at a reasonable cost.

Peat Moss

Sphagnum peat moss is currently the most common organic component of growing media in temperate zone nurseries (figure 6.5A). Although types of peat moss may appear similar, they can have very different physical and chemical properties. The horticultural properties of *Sphagnum* peat moss (table 6.1) and the fact that it has uniform quality make it the only peat moss choice for plant nurseries that use peat moss. Most peat moss comes from Canada, some comes from New Zealand, and the one known tropical source is Indonesia (Miller and Jones 1995). Therefore it is expensive and problematic to import

peat for most tropical nurseries. In addition, extraction and transportation of peat moss on a large scale is a sustainability concern, and even temperate nurseries are considering alternatives. For tropical areas where peat moss is reasonably affordable and available, some nurseries use it in limited amounts for germinant mixes or for learning to grow unfamiliar native species. Some nurseries may use peat as a transition component, comparing peat's properties to local materials such as composts or coir to develop local alternatives for growing media while moving forward with plant production.

Compost

Because of the risks of using soils and the expense of importing peat moss, many tropical nurseries prefer organic compost as a green alternative to peat moss (figure 6.5B). For example, in Florida, a variety of native plants grown in biosolid yard waste compost were as large or larger than those grown in a peat-based growing medium (Wilson and Stoffella 2006). Composts are an excellent sustainable organic component for any growing medium and significantly enhance the medium's physical and chemical characteristics by improving water retention, aeration porosity, and fertility. Some composts have also been found to suppress seedborne and soilborne pathogens. Compost quality can vary considerably between different source materials and even from batch to batch so growers need to always test new materials before general use.

Composting is the physical and chemical decomposition of organic materials caused by the digestive activities

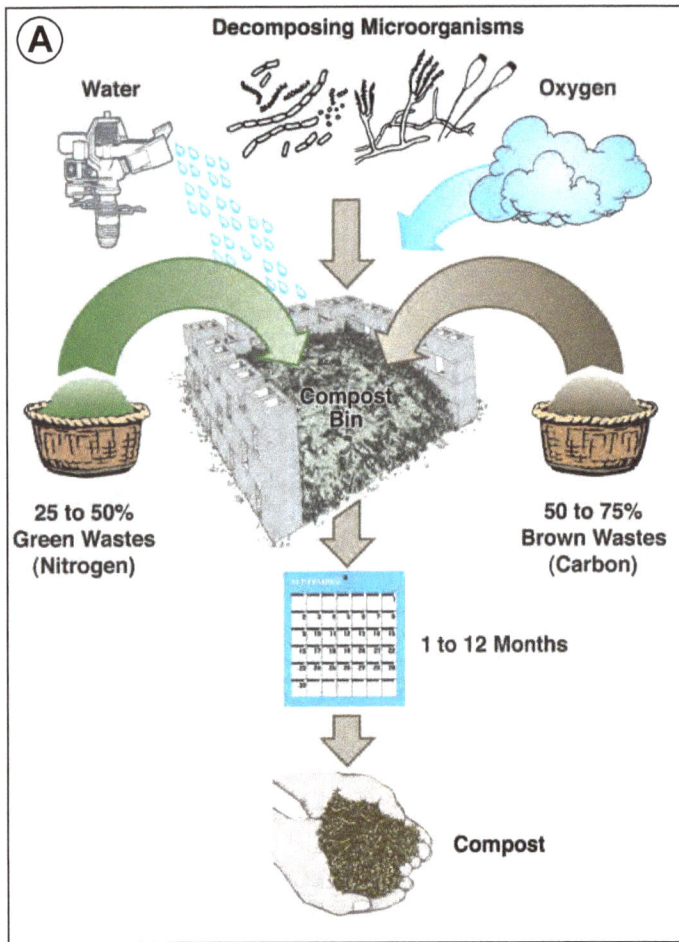

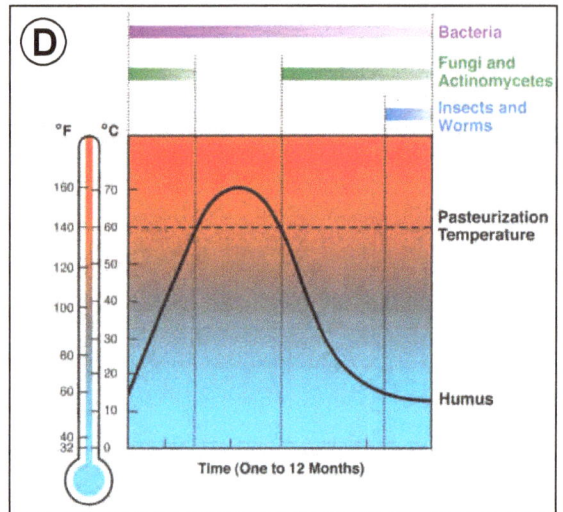

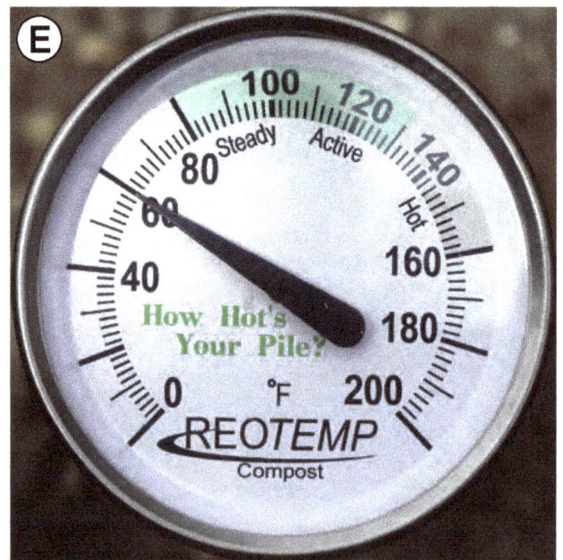

Figure 6.6 —*Creating good compost takes 1 to 12 months and requires the proper mix of organic materials and an ideal environment for the microorganisms that decompose the materials (A). Frequent mixing to foster good aeration is critical and can be done by hand (B) or using equipment (C). Compost goes through a typical temperature curve because of a succession of different microorganisms (D), so the process should be monitored with a long-stemmed thermometer (E). Illustrations A, B, and D from Dumroese and others (2008), photo C by Ronald Overton, and photo E by Thomas D. Landis.*

of insects, fungi, and bacteria (figure 6.6A). Raw materials for compost include any plant wastes such as vegetable or fruit scraps, leaves, weeds, or byproducts, such as cacao pods, coffee pulp, sugarcane bagasse, orchard prunings, and rice hulls; aquatic wastes such as aquatic weeds (such as the noxious weed water hyacinth) or fish parts from fish processing; animal wastes such as manures, feathers, and bedding; and wood wastes such as bark or sawdust. Sometimes these products are considered waste materials and are burned or disposed of at a cost to the producer—composting turns them into a valuable resource. Organic nursery wastes may also be recycled through composting, including used growing media and culled seedlings. Sustainability and renewability of the compost source is important to consider. For example, seaweeds were once considered a good compost material, until people began to understand the importance of seaweeds to fish breeding and the damage that comes from depleting wild seaweed during fish-breeding season. Some nurseries grow part of their own compost ingredients using nitrogen-fixing trees or fast-growing plants such as comfrey, which can be cut back year after year. Growers anywhere should be able to find a sustainable source of organic matter that can be composted and used as a growing media component.

Composted tree bark from a wide variety of species has been successfully used as a growing media component (figure 6.5C), especially for larger volume containers. In the Southern United States, composted pine bark has become a standard ingredient in growing media for horticultural nurseries (Landis and Morgan 2009). The size of bark particles is important, and particle size can be controlled by hammer milling and screening (Gordon 2004). Obtaining bark of consistent quality can be a problem. Composting bark with supplemental nitrogen fertilizer supplies the nitrogen that microorganisms require during decomposition and helps lower the carbon-to-nitrogen (C:N) ratio.

Creating consistent-quality compost year after year is a challenging goal (Miller and Jones 1995). A nursery may choose to make its own compost or contract this work to a local processor. Ideally, compost is made from a mixture of organic materials. All material should be chopped, shredded, or cut into small pieces (0.5 to 2 in [1 to 5 cm]) to encourage faster decomposition and a more uniform final product. The most common method of making compost is to place organic materials in piles and allow them to decompose. The piles need to be mixed periodically to maintain adequate aeration and moisture needs to be maintained at about 50 percent with the feel of a damp sponge (figures 6.6B, 6.6C). Temperatures in the piles change over time as microbial decomposition progresses (figure 6.6D). Within the first few days, temperatures rise to 100 to 120 °F

(38 to 49 °C) as the smaller and easily biodegradable materials decompose. Next, temperatures rise to 130 to 150 °F (54 to 65 °C) as more materials decay. A peak temperature of about 160 °F (71 °C) needs to be maintained for several days to kill weed seeds and fungal pathogens. Finally, temperatures fall to around 105 °F (40 °C) and lower during the "curing" stage. The process can be monitored with a thermometer (figure 6.6E). Mature compost can be produced in 2 to 4 months in the humid tropics. It is important to note that the finished compost will only be about 40 percent by volume of the original fresh material. Often, growers have

Figure 6.7—*The maturity of commercial or homemade compost needs to be checked before use in growing media; in mature compost, original components are no longer visible and the material is dark and crumbly (A). Earthworms and soil insects are often visible in mature compost (B). Photo A by Tara Luna, and photo B by Thomas D. Landis.*

two or more compost piles in varying stages of decomposition to have a continually available supply. For detailed guidelines on making compost, see Wightman (1999), Martin and Gershuny (1992), and Castillo (2004).

Mature compost should not produce an unpleasant odor or heat before incorporating into a growing medium. The compost should be dark in color and have a rich, earthy smell (figure 6.7A). The texture should be friable and crumbly; the original organic materials should not be recognizable. Earthworms and soil insects can live in mature composts and can be a sign that the compost is complete and ready to use (figure 6.7B). To determine if compost is ready, place two moist handfuls in a plastic bag, seal it, and leave in a dark, cool place. After 24 hours, open the bag: the compost is not ready if it feels hot or smells like manure or ammonia. Finished composts should be sifted through a screen similar to that used for field soil before use. Compost can be tested by sending to a soil lab, testing with a "bioassay," and testing with an EC meter as described in the section on testing growing media.

C:N is a good indicator of whether nitrogen will be limiting or excessive (Landis and Morgan 2009). The higher C:N is, the higher the risk of nitrogen being unavailable to plants. The carbon in easily decomposed compounds, such as sugars and cellulose, are quickly used as an energy source by soil microorganisms, which also need nitrogen for growth and reproduction. Because this nitrogen is stored in their cells, it is unavailable for plant uptake. As carbon sources become depleted, the high populations of soil microorganisms gradually die and nitrogen is released for plant growth. When C:N is greater than 15:1, available nitrogen is immobilized. When C:N is below 15:1, however, nitrogen becomes available for plant uptake. Some composts have C:N as low as 10:1, indicating they are such a ready source of available nitrogen that they are considered fertilizers. Wood wastes, such as sawdust, have very high C:N (400:1 to 1,300:1). These materials are often composted with manure or supplemented with fertilizer to supply the needed nitrogen. The C:N of tree bark can be considerably lower than sawdust (70:1 to 500:1), and has become a preferred material for horticultural composts.

Coconut Coir

A byproduct of processing coconut husks is known as coir dust, coco peat, or simply coir. This material has proven to be an excellent organic component for container growing media and is readily available in some tropical locales (figure 6.5D). Coconut coir has many desirable qualities: high water-holding capacity; excellent drainage; absence of weeds and pathogens; physical resiliency (withstands compression of baling better than *Sphagnum* peat); slow decomposition; easy wettability; and acceptable levels of pH, cation exchange capacity, and electrical conductivity.

Coir is very similar to peat in appearance and structure, and, like peat, physical and chemical properties of coir can vary widely from source to source (Evans and others 1996; Noguera and others 2000). Coir is low in nitrogen, calcium, and magnesium but can be relatively high in phosphorus and potassium (Noguera and others 2000).

Excess salinity and phenolic compounds in coir can be a problem in areas with inadequate quality control (Ma and Nichols 2004). In addition, some coir sources have reportedly contained chlorides at levels toxic to many plants. Thus, it is very important that salts and other compounds are thoroughly leached with fresh water before shipment and use. Compared with Asia, little coir production occurs in tropical America, and, currently, supplies of coir are limited in some areas. Nurseries must locate a quality, consistent source and then add coir to media on a trial basis first, testing effects on a species-by-species basis.

Sawdust

Raw sawdust, with its high C:N, can negatively affect nutrient availability, especially nitrogen but its properties can be improved with composting (figure 6.5E; Miller and Jones 1995). Also, because of inherent differences in chemical properties between different woods, the suitability of sawdust as an organic growing media component is extremely variable. Some species produce sawdust with phytotoxic effects. Only consider using sawdust from sawmills because other wood residues, such as from treated boards, may contain preservatives or harmful chemicals. Sawdust from coastal sawmills can contain high levels of salts, so all potential sources need to be tested before general use in the nursery.

Rice Hulls

Rice hulls are the sheaths of rice grains, a waste product of rice processing (Landis and Morgan 2009). Rice hulls or husks have been used as a component of potting medium with locally obtained peat for many years in Indonesia (Miller and Jones 1995). Several nurseries have used composted, screened, and hammer-milled rice hulls in place of composted bark (Landis and Morgan 2009).

Other Possible Organic Ingredients

Nearly any other organic material that is locally available has the potential to be an important addition to nursery growing media. Composted material takes longer to produce, but has a more reliable texture and nutrient content than raw material. For example, composted manure from livestock

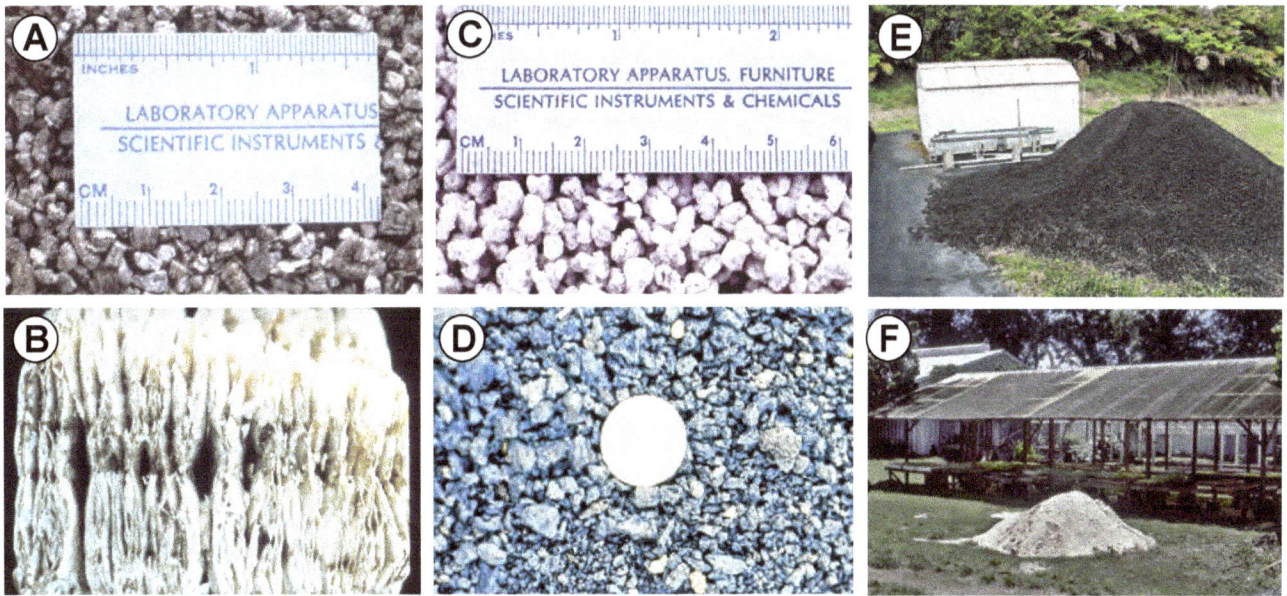

Figure 6.8—Common inorganic ingredients of growing media. Horticultural vermiculite particles (A) look like accordions (B) because of their expanded structure of parallel plates that allow vermiculite to absorb water and dissolved mineral nutrients like a sponge. Perlite particles have a closed-cell structure that prevents water absorption and improves aeration and drainage (C). The particles of pumice (D) and cinders (E) also improve aeration. Sand is also used as an inorganic component but may affect pH (F). Photos A, B, C, and D by Thomas D. Landis, and photos E and F by Tara Luna.

pens and other organic waste from agricultural operations are excellent candidates and are frequently available for free if you can haul them. All "homemade" materials will take effort to process and fine-tune to create a consistent product. The final product will be worth the effort because you will be developing your own specialized growing media with low-cost local ingredients that do not have to be shipped.

Inorganic Ingredients

Inorganic materials are added to growing media to produce and maintain a structural system of macropores that improves aeration and drainage (Mastalerz 1977). Many inorganic ingredients have a very low CEC and provide a chemically inert base for the growing medium. Inorganic materials with high bulk densities provide stability to large, freestanding containers. Several materials are routinely used as inorganic ingredients in growing media in native plant nurseries, including gravel, sand, vermiculite, perlite, pumice, and polystyrene beads.

Vermiculite

Vermiculite is a common component (figure 6.8A) and is a hydrated aluminum-iron-magnesium silicate material that has an accordion-like structure (figure 6.8B). Vermiculite has a very low bulk density and an extremely high water-holding capacity, approximately five times its weight. This material also has a neutral pH, a high CEC (table 6.1), and contains small amounts of potassium and magnesium. Vermiculite is

produced in four grades based on particle size, which determines the relative proportion of aeration and water-holding porosity. Grades 2 and 3 are most commonly used in growing media; grade 2 is preferred when more aeration porosity is desired, whereas grade 3 produces more water-holding capacity. A 1:1 mixture of peat moss and coarse vermiculite is a common growing medium mix in many temperate nurseries.

Perlite

Perlite is a siliceous material of volcanic origin (figure 6.8C). Perlite particles have a unique closed-cell structure so that water adheres only to their surface; they do not absorb water as peat moss or vermiculite do. Therefore, growing media containing perlite are well drained and lightweight. Perlite is also rigid and does not compress easily, which promotes good porosity. Because of the high temperatures at which it is processed, perlite is completely sterile. It is essentially infertile, has a minimal CEC, and has a neutral pH (table 6.1). Perlite is typically included to increase aeration, and commercial mixes contain no more than 10 to 30 percent perlite. Perlite grades are not standardized, but grades 6, 8, or "propagation grade" are normally used in growing media. Perlite grades often contain a range of particle sizes, depending on the sieve sizes used during manufacturing. One safety concern is that perlite can contain considerable amounts of very fine dust that causes eye and lung irritation during mixing. Wetting the material while mixing and wearing dust masks and goggles can reduce this risk.

Pumice and Cinder (Scoria)

Pumice (figure 6.8D) is a type of volcanic rock consisting of mostly silicon dioxide and aluminum oxide with small amounts of iron, calcium, magnesium, and sodium. The porous nature of pumice particles improves aeration porosity but also retains water within the pores. Pumice is the most durable of the inorganic ingredients and so resists compaction. Cinder (often called scoria) is another type of volcanic rock and a common growing media component in volcanic areas such as Hawai'i, where growers may sift the cinder rocks to obtain the desired sizes for their containers (figure 6.8E).

Sand

Sand is one of the most readily available materials and is relatively inexpensive. The composition of sand varies widely. When considering if local sand is a suitable component, the type of sand and sand particle sizes must be considered. For example, some silty river sands with small particle size can have a serious negative effect on growing media by making them excessively heavy and not contributing to improved aeration or drainage.

Nurseries with access to siliceous (granite or schist derived) sands may be able to use local sand as an inorganic component. Sands derived from calcareous sources (such as coral or limestone) (figure 6.8F) are high in calcium carbonate ($CaCO_3$), however, and can have dangerously high pH values. Growers can test sands by adding a drop of dilute acid or even strong vinegar—a fizzing reaction indicates the presence of $CaCO_3$. It is better not to use coral-based soils or sands if at all possible but, if necessary, add lots of organic matter to help buffer the effects. Some plants grown in your nursery may be adapted to local calcareous soil conditions and may not suffer from the increased pH if the sand is used sparingly.

Sand is used to increase porosity, but small sand particles can lodge in existing pore spaces and reduce aeration and drainage. In general, sizes of 0.002 to 0.010 in (0.05 to 0.25 mm) are too small and will block drainage holes and reduce aeration (Wilkerson 2011). Larger (medium to course) particles are more suited to increase porosity. The general recommendation is to wash sand (flushing out salt content if present) and sterilize or pasteurize it before incorporating it in the growing medium (Miller and Jones 1995). These techniques are described later in the chapter. Perhaps the more serious drawback of using sand in growing media is its weight, which causes problems with handling and increases the cost of shipping (Gordon 2004).

Polystyrene Beads or Flakes

Polystyrene is more commonly known by its trademarked name Styrofoam™. Beads or flakes of polystyrene are a processing byproduct. Polystyrene increases aeration and drainage, decreases bulk density, and is highly resistant to decomposition (Wilkerson 2011). New polystyrene is unlikely to be a locally available material and many people are phasing out the use of polystyrene for sustainability concerns. It may be possible to recycle polystyrene and use pieces in growing media although it is not biodegradable and is often considered undesirable to outplant on project sites.

Developing a Growing Medium

It is likely that as many recipes exist for growing media as the number of nurseries; there are no global recommendations (Jaenicke 1999). Every nursery manager needs to be able to experiment and find suitable, local, affordable ingredients to create good growing media. Three general types of growing media are used in container nurseries (table 6.2):

1. **Seed Propagation Media.** For germinating seeds or establishing germinants (sprouting seeds), the medium must be sterile and have a finer texture to maintain high moisture around the germinating seeds.

2. **Rooting Cuttings Media.** Cuttings are rooted with frequent misting, so the growing medium must be very porous to prevent waterlogging and allow good aeration necessary for root formation.

3. **Transplant Media.** When smaller seedlings or rooted cuttings are transplanted into larger containers, the growing medium is typically coarser.

Because of the diverse characteristics of various growing media ingredients, a growing medium can be formulated with nearly any desired property. The physical, chemical, and biological properties of each growing medium strongly interact with nursery cultural practices, however, particularly irrigation, fertilization, and the type of container. When considering a new growing medium, first test it on a small scale with several different species and evaluate its suitability before making a major change to the whole crop. Information about testing is provided at the end of this chapter, and more details about proper ways to test are in Chapter 20, Discovering Ways to Improve Nursery Practices and Plant Quality.

Purchasing a Commercial Mix

A variety of commercial mixes are available that feature combinations of organic and inorganic ingredients described previously. To appeal to a wider market, many brands contain a wide variety of additional amendments including fertilizers, wetting agents, hydrophilic gels, and

Table 6.2—*Example growing media for different nursery uses. The ideal growing medium will vary among nurseries, environments, and plant species.*

Media type	Properties	Examples of media (by volume)	Reference
Seed propagation	Maintains uniform moisture around germinating seeds (not too wet or too dry); no fertilizer; free from pests and diseases.	• 3 parts perlite to 1 part coarse vermiculite (for beach plants) • 4 parts perlite to 1 part peat • 3 parts small rinsed cinders to 1 part peat and 1 part perlite	Lilleeng-Rosenberger (2005)
		• Fine, washed quartz sand [0.02 to 0.04 in (0.5 to 1 mm)] (100% sand will need frequent watering)	Jaenicke (1999)
Rooting cuttings	Porous to prevent waterlogging and to allow good aeration for root formation; provide support for cuttings; free from diseases and weed seeds.	• 3 parts perlite to 1 part vermiculite • 3 parts small rinsed cinders to 1 part peat and 1 part perlite • 100% rinsed small cinder (but needs frequent misting)	Lilleeng-Rosenberger (2005)
		• 100% washed quartz sand (2 mm)	Jaenicke (1999)
		• 1 part grit or fine gravel to 1 part washed sand to 1 part aged sawdust • 1 part grit or fine gravel to 1 part aged sawdust	Longman (1998)
Transplant	Coarser; heavy enough to keep plants upright; may contain some nutrients; free from diseases and weed seeds.	• 1 part peat and 1 part vermiculite • 2 parts cinder or perlite to 1 part well-decayed compost and 1 part peat	Lilleeng-Rosenberger (2005)
		• 1 part coarse sand, 2 parts coconut coir, 1 part topsoil/duff • 2 parts bagasse to 1 part rice hulls and 1 part alluvial soil • 1 part well-composed grasses to 1 part rice hulls or pumice • 3 parts composed bark to 1 part sand and 1 part shale	Miller and Jones (1995)
		• 2 parts well-decayed compost to 2 parts sand and 1 part clay soil	Wightman (1999)
		• 3 parts coir to one part compost • 30% composted rice hulls, 50% pine bark, and 20% sand	Lovelace (2011)

even beneficial microorganisms. Many amendments are formulated for crops other than tropical nursery plants and may do more harm than good. In particular, hydrogels can cause growing media to retain too much water and actually decrease aeration porosity when expanded. Always check the label to be sure of exactly what is in the mix.

Creating a Custom Mix

Many tropical plant growers prefer to mix their own custom growing media (figure 6.9). In addition to saving money, custom mixing is particularly useful in small nurseries where separate mixes are needed to meet propagation requirements of different species. A very porous and well-drained medium, for example, might be needed for plants from very dry habitats, but a second type is needed for coastal plants, and a third is needed for wetland species.

Standard commercial ingredients, such as peat and vermiculite, can be bought in bulk (by the pallet or container load to islands) to reduce costs. These ingredients have been used worldwide and may provide good, basic media ingredients during nursery start-up phases. Because of the steep learning curve with growing tropical plants and running a nursery, some managers may choose to import expensive but well-researched ingredients until they identify a consistent supply of local equivalents. Others may use small amounts of imported ingredients for seed propagation or cutting propagation, but use local ingredients for transplants.

Figure 6.9—Many growers prefer to mix their own species-specific media using different ingredients (A). Growing media including local sand and compost mixed with some imported ingredients is used and sold at the native tree nursery at Reserva Natural, Cañón de San Cristóbal, Barranquitas, Puerto Rico (B). Photo A by Tara Luna, and photo B by Brian F. Daley.

Use of Field Soil

The use of field soil is not recommended for growing nursery plants. Circumstances may require, however, that some nurseries include some field soil in their media while more affordable and sustainable alternatives are being developed, so soil-based media is discussed here.

When selecting soil, use dark topsoil that has a high percentage of organic matter; lighter sandy loams are better than heavy clays. After collection, sift the soil through a 0.5 in (12 mm) screen to remove debris and large objects such

as rocks (figure 6.10). When using field soils, heat pasteurization (described later in this chapter) can eliminate fungal pathogens, insect pests, nematodes, and weeds.

Soil-based mixes are safest for transplant media when transplanting into larger containers, such as polybags or 1 gallon pots. The properties of soil-based mixes make them unsuitable for smaller containers, and the risk of disease makes them unsuitable in media for germinating seeds or rooting cuttings. Soil should comprise no more than 10 to 20 percent of the transplant media by volume although some nurseries use up to 30 percent. The remaining ingredients, for example, bark, sawdust, and pumice, promote drainage and aeration while maintaining a high water-holding capacity (Landis 1995).

Use of Amendments

An amendment is a supplemental material that contributes less than 10 percent of the mixture, whereas an ingredient usually constitutes a larger percentage. A variety of materials may be added to growing media during the mixing process, including fertilizers, lime, surfactants, hydrogels, and mycorrhizal inoculum. Many of these materials may not be

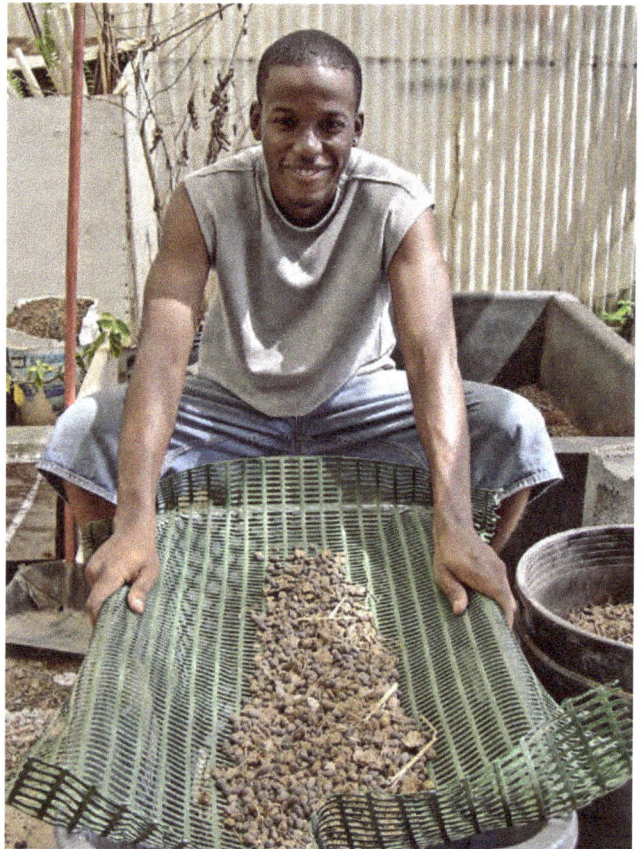

Figure 6.10—If field soil must be used as an ingredient, it needs to be screened for debris and other large particles before use. Photo by Brian F. Daley.

desirable, however, and, in fact, may be detrimental to plant growth because they are formulated for other crops. If the decision is made to use amendments, uniform incorporation is important because plant roots have access to only a limited volume of growing media in the relatively small containers used in tropical plant nurseries. Uneven mixing of incorporated fertilizers is one of the major factors causing uneven growth in container nursery stock (Whitcomb 2003). If you decide to use any amendments, test them first on a small scale, using the techniques described in Chapter 20, Discovering Ways To Improve Nursery Practices and Plant Quality.

Dolomitic Limestone. Called "lime" in horticulture, it has traditionally been added to growing media to raise the pH and supply calcium for plant nutrition. Better ways of supplying calcium exist, so we do not recommend limestone amendments unless the nursery is growing plants that require a neutral or alkaline pH.

Starter Fertilizers. Some commercial media contain a small "starter dose" of soluble granular fertilizer. If fertigation (irrigation water containing liquid fertilizer) is not possible, then starter fertilizer may be a good idea to ensure that young, developing plants have quick access to mineral nutrients. Because fertilizer is a salt, incorporating larger quantities of soluble fertilizer is never recommended because of the high potential for salt toxicity.

Controlled-Release Fertilizers. Commercial growing media and custom mixes often include controlled-release fertilizers. It is important to know the fertilizer formulation and release rate. See Chapter 12, Plant Nutrition and Fertilization, for more discussion about these fertilizers. Keep in mind that, when used in warm, tropical climates, controlled-release fertilizers will have much faster release rates than indicated on the label, which are targeted to temperate areas.

Surfactants. These chemical amendments, also known as "wetting agents," break down the surface tension of water and increase the wettability of hydrophobic organic materials such as peat moss and pine bark. Some surfactants have been shown to adversely affect plant growth. Before using surfactants, be certain that a problem really exists and can potentially be solved by using the product. Ask other nurseries about their experiences with surfactants and perform small tests before using them operationally.

Hydrophilic Gels ("hydrogels") are cross-linked polymers that absorb many times their own weight in water. They have been proposed as additives to increase the water-holding capacity of growing media. Several brands of growing media contain hydrogels, but no empirical evidence shows they improve plant growth. Because nursery crops are regularly irrigated, the use of hydrogels is rarely justified.

Mycorrhizal Inoculum. One method of inoculating native plants with beneficial mycorrhizal fungi is to incorporate inoculum into the growing medium at the time of mixing. As with all amendments, this practice needs to be tested first before adopting it on a large scale. See Chapter 13, Beneficial Microorganisms, for more discussion on this topic.

Rock Phosphate. Rock phosphate may be added to increase phosphorous availability. Excessive phosphorus, however, may hinder development of mycorrhizae and also interfere with the absorption of other mineral nutrients (Wilkerson 2011).

Other Amendments. Some growers add small amounts of other amendments to their mixes, such as worm castings, bone meal, kelp, guano, humic acid, compost tea, and others. Consider any amendment carefully as to what it will accomplish, if it is necessary, and if it may do more harm than good.

Treatment of Growing Media Ingredients

Some growing media ingredients may need to be treated before mixing to reduce potential damage to plants. These treatments may include removing salts, killing unwanted organisms, and sifting.

Flushing Out Salts

Flushing out salts may be necessary for materials such as coir, sand, sawdust from mills near the ocean, and composts with excessive soluble salt levels. Leaching with fresh water can effectively lower soluble salts below damaging levels (Carrion and others 2006, Landis and Morgan 2009). Because of its low salinity, rainwater is ideal for this process but any fresh water source will work if enough is applied. Check the electrical conductivity (EC) of the leachate from the ingredients or composts to verify that the salts have been removed (as described in the following section on testing growing media).

Pasteurizing Ingredients

Sterilization refers to the complete elimination of all living organisms whereas pasteurization targets pathogenic fungi and bacteria. For growing plants, completely sterile growing media is not desirable because many beneficial microorganisms normally found in growing media can actually be antagonistic to pathogens. Some commercial growing media are pasteurized to prevent the introduction of pests, weeds, and diseases into the nursery. If concerned, contact the supplier to find out if their media has been treated. If you mix your own media, common inorganic ingredients, such as vermiculite and perlite, are inherently sterile; organic ingredients are suspect. The heat from the

Figure 6.11—*For nurseries making their own media, pasteurization with steam (A) or wood heat (B) is simple, effective, and can be accomplished with portable equipment. Electric soil sterilizers can heat the soil long enough to eliminate most weed seeds and pathogens (C). Photos A and B by Thomas D. Landis, and photo C by J.B. Friday.*

composting process will kill pathogens and other pests in composts, but when using field soil, growers need to seriously consider pasteurization.

Heat pasteurization is the most common way of treating growing media. Several heat sources can be used for pasteurizing growing media: moist heat from steam, aerated steam, or boiling water; dry heat from flame, electric pasteurizers, or microwave ovens; and solar heat. Ingredients and media are pasteurized commercially with large, expensive equipment, but smaller pasteurizing equipment is available for nurseries (figures 6.11A, 6.11C) and some nurseries have developed their own pasteurization process using fire or solar heat (figure 6.11B). A practical technique would be to enclose small batches of media spread thin (no more than 6 in [15 cm] deep) under black plastic tarps on an inclined table or on top of a tarp to expose it to maximum sunlight. Long-stemmed thermometers can be used to penetrate the tarp in several locations to ensure that temperatures stay in the recommended range of 140 to 177 °F (60 to 80 °C) for 30 minutes. After treatment, the material can be dumped off the table or tarp into a clean wheelbarrow or mixing area, cooled, and used in the growing medium.

Regardless of the heating method, it is important to maintain the entire mass of growing medium at a uniform temperature that exceeds the thermal mortality threshold of the various nursery pests. Pests may vary in their inability to tolerate high temperatures (figure 6.12), but most can

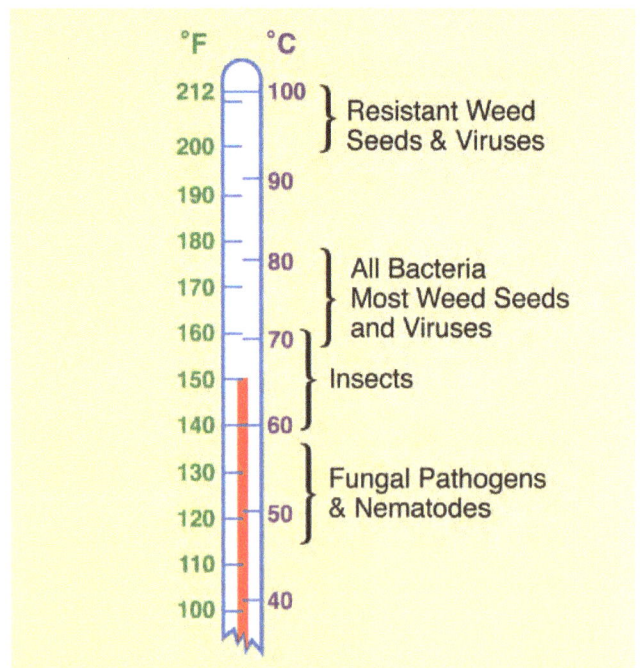

Figure 6.12—*Necessary temperatures for heat pasteurization vary depending on the target pest. Temperatures need to be held for 30 minutes in the target range to be effective on that pest. Illustration adapted from Baker (1957) by Jim Marin.*

Tropical Nursery Manual

Figure 6.13—Screening growing medium ingredients may be necessary to achieve the desired particle size. Photo by Thomas D. Landis.

be eliminated by heating the growing medium to 140 to 177 °F (60 to 80 °C) for at least 30 minutes. Excessively high temperatures can eliminate beneficial soil organisms and produce toxic chemical compounds.

Sifting or Screening Ingredients

Some ingredients, such as soil, sand, and cinder, may require screening or sifting to achieve the desired particle size (figure 6.13). Excessively small or fine particles can clog container drainage holes and reduce aeration whereas excessively large particles can interfere with container filling, root development, and plant extraction. It may be necessary to sift twice, once with a small mesh to eliminate material larger than desired, and a second time with a larger mesh to remove material smaller than desired.

Mixing Growing Media

Whitcomb (2003) emphasized that improper media mixing is one of the major causes of variation in container plant quality. Mixing should be performed by diligent, experienced workers who will faithfully monitor the growing media quality. Creating a uniformly mixed growing medium that has not been compacted, contaminated, or compromised is the challenge and the goal.

Small batches of growing media ingredients can be mixed by hand. Measure out the ingredients by volume and mix together in a wheelbarrow or bucket (figure 6.14A). Workers can mix larger batches on any clean, hard surface using hand shovels. Pile the ingredients on top of one another and broadcast any amendments over the pile. Then work around the edge of the pile with a large scoop shovel, taking one shovel full of material at a time and turning it over onto the top of the pile (figure 6.14B). Make sure that all parts of the pile are mixed by gradually moving the location of the pile

Figure 6.14—Nurseries that mix their own media can do so by hand (A) or by using the moving pile technique (B). To reduce labor, a cement mixer (C) can also be used but care must be taken to avoid overmixing and resultant damage to particle size and structure. Photo A by Diane L. Haase, and photos B and C by Thomas D. Landis.

to one side. Some organic ingredients repel water when dry, so frequently misting the pile with water at regular intervals during mixing improves water absorption. Continue this procedure until samples from the pile appear to be well mixed. Do not compress or compact the mixture.

Managers of nurseries that regularly require larger quantities of custom growing media should consider purchasing a mixer. A cement mixer (figure 6.14C) works well as long as care is taken to avoid excessive mixing, which breaks down the size and texture of ingredients. Fragile materials, such as vermiculite and peat moss, are particularly vulnerable to overmixing, which can easily happen when mixers are run too long, are overfilled, or if the ingredients are too wet. Over-mixed media compacts easily during container filling, which leads to reduced aeration and waterlogging.

Safety Considerations

Workers need to follow certain precautions when handling growing media or its ingredients, including the time spent filling containers. Dust is the most common concern, so work areas need to be well ventilated and workers need to wear protective dust masks and safety glasses (figure 6.15). Misting the growing media and work areas with water reduces dust.

Perlite dust is of particular concern because of potential for silicosis, an inflammation that occurs over time when dust that contains silica is inhaled into the lungs. Based on medical studies, however, no relationship exists between handling perlite and the development of silicosis (Schundler Company 2002). The use of commercial vermiculite horticulture products presents no significant asbestos exposure risk to commercial greenhouse or home horticulture users (Chatfield 2001). Nonetheless, dust is irritating and common sense dictates that proper safety precautions be taken.

Workers with cuts or abrasions on their hands need to be especially careful handling *Sphagnum* peat moss because of sporotrichosis, which is a condition caused by a fungal pathogen sometimes found in peat moss and other organic materials. The spores of this fungus can invade cuts on the hands or arms of workers or can even be inhaled (Padhye 1995). Preventative measures include the following—

- Store peat moss and peat-based growing media under dry conditions.
- Ventilate work areas well.
- Wear gloves, dust masks, and long-sleeved shirts to protect hands and arms.

Figure 6.15—*When mixing growing media or filling containers, nursery workers need to wear dust masks and safety glasses. Photo by J. Chris Hoag.*

- Thoroughly wash arms and other exposed parts of the body with soap and water to reduce the risk of infection.
- Treat any injury that breaks the skin with a disinfectant, such as tincture of iodine.
- Regularly sweep and wash work areas.

Testing Growing Media

As each nursery develops its own growing media based on local ingredients, issues can arise because of variability in materials. Homemade materials, particularly composts, may vary in their quality despite best efforts to achieve a consistent product year after year. Purchased materials can also be variable on occasion depending on source and quality control procedures.

To preclude surprises, test compost and mixed growing media well in advance of use. It is also recommended to test and record the results of growing media batches that worked well, to compare them to new or experimental batches (Grubinger 2007), and to develop and refine suitable alternative mixes with similar favorable properties.

Plant Bioassay Test

One easy and effective test is known as a plant bioassay (Grubinger 2007). Simply put a sample of the growing medium in the containers that will be used in the nursery, sow an abundantly available, fast-growing species into the medium, and observe how the planting performs over a few weeks. Some growers like to use more sensitive, slower growing crops to test their mixes. It is also a good idea to test a few seeds of other plant species intended for the mix in addition to the bioassay seeds. Do the seeds germinate as expected? As they grow, is damping-off observed? Are pest problems, such as gnats or maggots, emerging? Is the medium stable, not becoming compacted or waterlogged over time? If the results are not good, growers will be glad they tested the mix with readily available seeds instead of with rare native plant seeds. If the mix works, it is ready to try in the nursery.

Testing With an Electrical Conductivity (EC) Meter

The salinity (salt level) of the growing medium is a key parameter affecting the development and health of plant roots. Salts may come from growing media ingredients, irrigation water, and from added fertilizers. Measuring EC is a way to measure the amount of nutrients and salts present to ensure they are in the appropriate ranges for the species grown. Excessively high salt levels can damage or even kill succulent young plants.

The best growers routinely measure the EC of their growing media ingredients, their growing media before and during a crop cycle, their fertilizer applications to ensure correct dosages, and their water quality. Some types of EC meters can only be used with aqueous solutions and so are ideal for measuring irrigation water and fertilizer solutions but are not ideal for growing media (for more details on proper technique with these meters, see Landis and Dumroese 2006). Direct sensor models are small handheld devices and have probes small enough to be inserted directly into growing media (figure 6.16). The advantage of the direct sensor procedure is that readings can be taken quickly and nondestructively. To ensure the probe has good contact with the growing medium, always test at the same media moisture content. The recommendation is to monitor about 1 hour after irrigation or fertigation. Direct sensor testing works best with small containers; readings in larger containers can vary significantly so a couple of readings should be taken and averaged. Always take readings at a standard depth. If the probe is inserted into a medium containing controlled-release fertilizers and the tip of the probe gets close to or punctures a prill, the EC reading might be extremely high,

Figure 6.16—*Growing media salinity can be measured using an EC meter. Photo by J.B. Friday.*

requiring a second insertion of the probe into a different area. Regardless of the type of EC meter used, it needs to be calibrated frequently to ensure correct readings.

Three things make using EC data challenging. First, EC can be measured in a variety of units, so pick a unit and stick with it. Conversions for the most common EC units are available in Landis and Dumroese (2006). Second, native plants vary considerably in their tolerance to salinity; a plant growing on the beach may have a much greater tolerance for high salt levels than a plant growing far inland or at higher elevations. Third, little information is available on the EC tolerances of many native plants. These challenges make providing an acceptable range for EC difficult, but start with general guidelines (table 6.3).

Regularly record EC values throughout each crop production cycle, especially during the Establishment Phase, and compare those with the quality of the final plants (see Chapter 4, Crop Planning: Propagation Protocols, Schedules, and Records). Often, it can be the change in EC values that is more important. For example, if during the course of 1 month, the crop growth is declining at the same time the EC values are dropping, this pattern indicates insufficient nutrients are available and fertilization needs to be increased. Conversely, if growth is declining and EC values are increasing dramatically, this pattern could indicate salt toxicity that can be remedied by reducing the fertilizer rates and leaching the medium with clear water. Collecting EC data for a couple of years will help any nursery manager hone in on the proper levels for their particular nursery and crops. More information about EC meters and water quality is in table 11.1 of Chapter 11, Water Quality and Irrigation.

Table 6.3—*Electrical Conductivity (EC) guidelines for artificial growing media. Adapted from Timmer and Parton (1982).*

EC range (µS/cm)	Salinity rating
0 to 1,200	Low
1,200 to 2,500	Normal
2,500 to 3,000	High
3,000 to 4,000	Excessive
Greater than 4,000	Lethal

µS/cm= microSiemens per centimeter

Sending Growing Media to a Soil-Testing Laboratory

For more formal testing, growing media samples can be sent to a soil-testing laboratory (private, local extension office, or land-grant university) for testing. A measurement of pH, soluble salts (electrical conductivity), and nutrients should be requested (Grubinger 2007). Results can vary among laboratories depending on their procedures, so it is best to stick with one lab for testing from year to year, provided that the data appears accurate and consistent.

Obtaining test results from laboratories may take a few days to several weeks, and bioassay results always take several weeks. Laboratory staff can help with interpretation of results. Results may indicate that the growing medium requires modification and further testing before it can be used. Therefore, start the testing well in advance of when the medium is needed. Changing to a new growing medium will also require adjusting irrigation, fertilization, and other cultural procedures, so other trials and experiments might be valuable (see Chapter 20, Discovering Ways to Improve Nursery Practices and Plant Quality).

References

Baker, K.F. 1957. The U.C. system for producing healthy container-grown plants through the use of clean soil, clean stock, and sanitation. University of California, Division of Agricultural Sciences, Manual 23. Berkeley, CA: University of California. 332 p.

Buamscha, G.; Altland, J. 2005. Pumice and the Oregon nursery industry. Digger. 49(6): 18-27.

Bunt, A.C. 1988. Media and mixes for container grown plants. London, United Kingdom: Unwin Hyman. 309 p.

Carrion, C.; Abad, M.; Fornes, F.; Noguera, V.; Maquieira, A.; Puchades, R. 2006. Leaching of composts from agricultural wastes to prepare nursery potting media. Acta Horticulturae. 697: 117–124.

Castillo, J.V. 2004. Inoculating composted pine bark with beneficial organisms to make a disease suppressive compost for container production in Mexican forest nurseries. Native Plants Journal. 5(2): 181–185.

Chatfield, E.J. 2001. Review of sampling and analysis of consumer garden products that contain vermiculite. Hampshire, United Kingdom: The Vermiculite Association. http://www.vermiculite.org/pdf/review-EPA744R00010.pdf. (February 2006).

Dumroese, R.K.; Luna, T.; Landis, T.D. 2008. Nursery manual for native plants: volume 1, a guide for tribal nurseries. Agriculture Handbook 730. Washington, DC: U.S. Department of Agriculture, Forest Service. 302 p.

Evans, M.R.; Konduru, S.; Stamps, R.H. 1996. Source variation in physical and chemical properties of coconut coir dust. HortScience. 31: 965–967.

Gordon, I. 2004. Potting media constituents. International Plant Propagators' Society, Combined Proceedings. 54: 78–84.

Grubinger, V. 2007. Potting mixes for organic growers. Brattleboro, VT: University of Vermont Extension. http://www.uvm.edu/vtvegandberry/factsheets/pottingmix.html. (August 2011).

Jaenicke, H. 1999. Good tree nursery practices: practical guidelines for research nurseries. International Centre for Research in Agroforestry. Nairobi, Kenya: Majestic Printing Works. 93 p.

Johnson, P. 1968. Horticultural and agricultural uses of sawdust and soil amendments. National City, CA: Paul Johnson. 46 p.

Landis, T.D. 1995. Improving polybag culture for sustainable nurseries. Forest Nursery Notes. (July 1995): 6–7.

Landis, T.D.; Dumroese, R.K. 2006. Monitoring electrical conductivity in soils and growing media. Forest Nursery Notes. (Summer 2006): 6-10.

Landis, T.D.; Morgan, N. 2009. Growing media alternatives for forest and native plant nurseries. In: Dumroese, R.K.; Riley, L.E., tech. coords. National proceedings: forest and conservation nursery associations—2008. Proc. RMRS-p.58. Fort Collins, CO: U.S. Department of Agriculture, Forest Service, Rocky Mountain Research Station: 26–31.

Lilleeng-Rosenberger, K. 2005. Growing Hawaii's native plants. Honolulu, HI; Mutual Publishing.

Longman, K.A. 1998. Growing good tropical trees for planting: volume 3, tropical trees, propagation and planting manuals. Edinburgh, United Kingdom: Commonwealth Science Council.

Lovelace, W. 2011. Personal communication (with Thomas D. Landis). Elsberry, MO. President and CEO, Forest Keeling Nursery, Inc.

Lovelace, W.; Kuczmarski, D. 1994. The use of composted rice hulls in rooting and potting media. International Plant Propagators' Society, Combined Proceedings. 42: 449–450.

Ma, Y.; Nichols, D. 2004. Phytotoxicity and detoxification of fresh coir dust and coconut shell. Communications in Soil Science and Plant Analysis. 35:205-218.

Martin, D.L.; Gershuny, G. 1992. The Rodale book of composting. Emmaus, PA: Rodale Press. 278 p.

Mastalerz, J.W. 1977. The greenhouse environment. New York: John Wiley & Sons. 629 p.

Miller, J.H.; Jones, N. 1995. Organic and compost-based growing media for tree seedling nurseries. World Bank Tech. Pap. No. 264, Forestry Series. Washington, DC: The World Bank. 75 p.

Newman, J. 2007. Core facts about coir. Greenhouse Management and Production. 27(2): 57.

Noguera, P.; Abad, M.; Noguers, V.; Puchades, R.; Maquieira, A. 2000. Coconut coir waste: a new and environmentally friendly peat substitute. Acta Horticulture. 517: 279–286.

Padhye, A.A. 1995. *Sporotrichosis*—an occupational mycosis. In: Landis, T.D.; Cregg, B., tech. coords. National proceedings, forest and conservation nursery associations. Gen. Tech. Rep. PNW-GTR–365. Portland, OR: U.S. Department of Agriculture, Forest Service, Pacific Northwest Research Station: 1–7.

Schundler Company. 2002. Perlite health issues: studies and effects. Edison, New Jersey: The Schundler Company http://www.schundler.com/perlitehealth.htm. (February 2002).

Timmer, V.R.; Parton, W.J. 1982. Monitoring nutrient status of containerized seedlings. In: Proceedings, Ontario Ministry of Natural Resources Nurseryman's Meeting, 1982 June, Thunder Bay, ON. Toronto, ON, Canada: Ontario Ministry of Natural Resources: 48–58.

Whitcomb, C.E. 2003. Plant production in containers II. Stillwater, OK: Lacebark Publications, 1,129 p.

Wightman, K.E. 1999. Good tree nursery practices: practical guidelines for community nurseries. International Centre for Research in Agroforestry. Nairobi, Kenya: Majestic Printing Works. 93 p.

Wilkerson, D. 2011. Texas greenhouse management handbook. College Station, TX: Texas A&M University, Texas Cooperative Extension, Extension Horticulture. http://aggie-horticulture.tamu.edu/greenhouse/nursery/guides/green/index.html. (August 2011).

Wilson, S.B.; Stoffella, P.J. 2006. Using compost for container production of ornamental wetland and flatwood species native to Florida. Native Plants Journal. 7: 293–300.

Additional Reading

Hundly, L. 2006. How to make compost: a composting guide. Dallas, TX: compostguide.com http://www.compostguide.com. (February 2006).

Kuepper, G.; Everett, K. 2010. Potting mixes for certified organic production. Horticultural Technical Note. Butte, MT; The National Center for Appropriate Technology (NCAT) Sustainable Agriculture Project. https://attra.ncat.org/attra-pub/viewhtml.php?id=47. (August 2011).

Landis, T.D.; Tinus, R.W.; McDonald, S.E.; Barnett, J.P. 1989. The container tree nursery manual: volume 5, nursery pests and mycorrhizae. Agriculture Handbook 674. Washington, DC: U.S. Department of Agriculture, Forest Service. 171 p.

Landis, T.D.; Tinus, R.W.; McDonald, S.E.; Barnett, J.P. 1990. The container tree nursery manual: volume 2, containers and growing media. Agriculture Handbook 674. Washington, DC: U.S. Department of Agriculture, Forest Service. 88 p.

Swanson, B.T. 1989. Critical physical properties of container media. American Nurseryman. 169 (11): 59–63.

Wilson, S.B.; Mecca, L.K.; Stoffella, P.J.; Graetz, D.A. 2004. Using compost for container production of ornamental hammock species native to Florida. Native Plants Journal. 4: 186–195.

Containers

Thomas D. Landis, Tara Luna, and R. Kasten Dumroese

7

A nursery container could be anything that holds growing media, drains, allows for healthy root development, does not disintegrate before outplanting, and allows for an intact, healthy root system to be removed with a minimum of disturbance to the plant. Understanding how container properties affect plant health and growth, as well as nursery operations, will help growers choose the best containers for their needs. Container type and dimensions affect root development, amount of water and mineral nutrients available for plant growth, nursery layout, bench size, production scheduling, and plant transportation method. After a container is selected, it can be expensive and time consuming to change to another type.

Most nurseries grow a wide variety of species and therefore several different containers are required (figure 7.1A). Container choice for a particular plant species depends on root system morphology, target plant criteria (see Chapter 3, Defining the Target Plant), and economics. In general, the following points hold true regarding container type:

- Plants that develop shallow, fibrous root systems, as most forbs do, grow better in shorter containers (figure 7.1B).

- Plants with long taproots, such as many kinds of trees, grow better in taller containers (figure 7.1C).

- Plants with multiple, thick, fleshy roots, and species with thick, fleshy rhizomes grow better in wide containers (figure 7.1D).

Facing Page: *Nurseries growing a wide variety of species use many different container types. Photo of Po'o Wai U Nursery on the Big Island of Hawai'i by Diane L. Haase.*

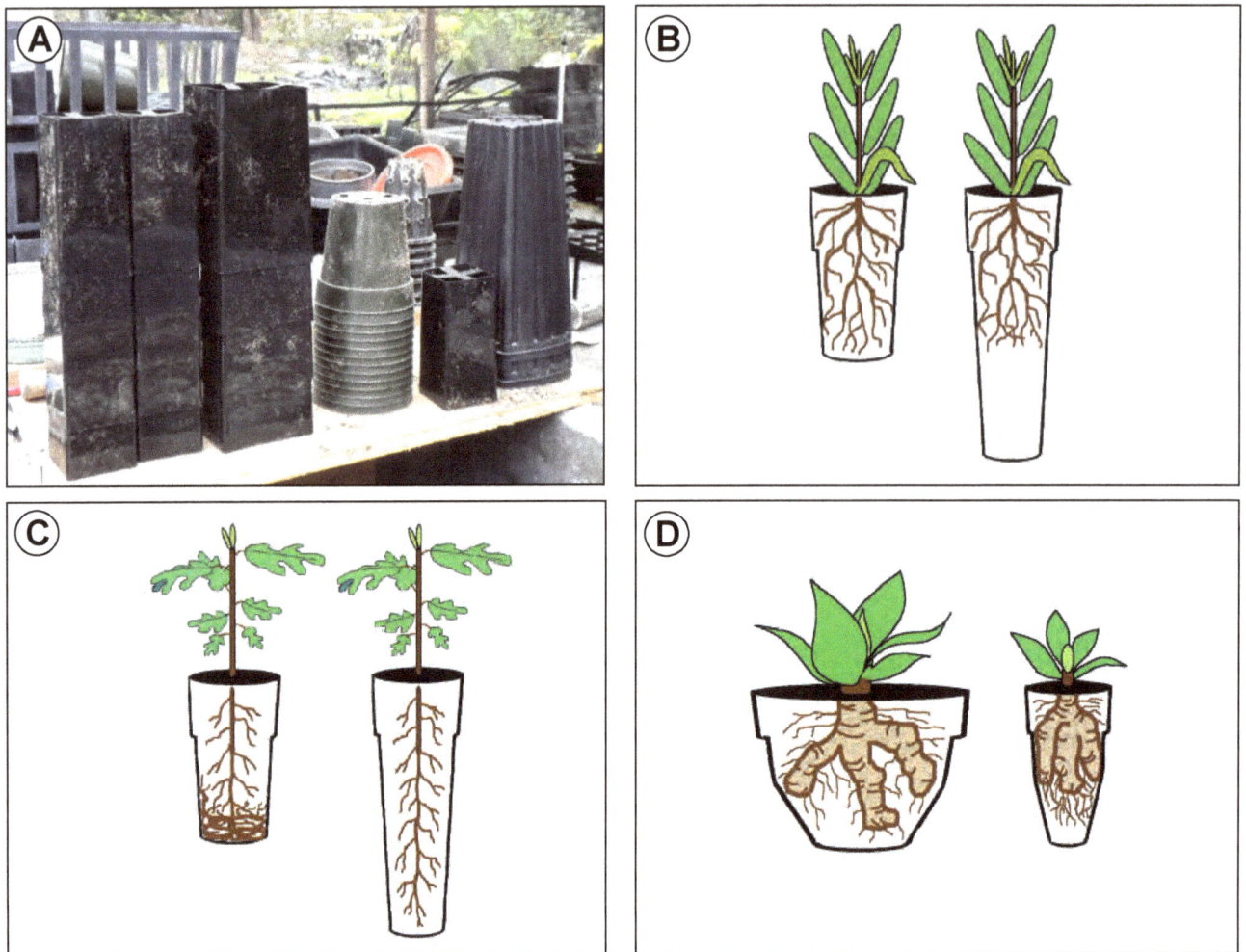

Figure 7.1—*Nurseries use a variety of containers to produce different species and stocktypes (A). Some plants, including most forbs, grow best in shorter containers (B) whereas taprooted species do better in taller ones (C) and fleshy-rooted plants should be grown in short wide containers (D). Photo A by Diane L. Haase, and illustrations B, C, and D adapted from Dumroese and others (2008).*

In the ornamental trade, large individual containers are called "pots" or "cans," but they are simply called "containers" in native plant nurseries. An inexpensive alternative to the plastic pot is the "bag" or polybag, which has the same general purpose and function. Plants grown in small-volume containers are often referred to as "plugs." Plug seedlings are usually grown in individual containers called "cells" or "cavities" that are aggregated into "blocks," "trays," or "racks." Often, many plants will be germinated in a tray, transferred to a small pot, and later transplanted to a larger container. Making the right container choices at the right time is an important task for a nursery manager. This chapter describes some of the key biological and operational considerations necessary for choosing appropriate container types.

Container Characteristics Affecting Plant Development

Volume

The volume of a container dictates how large a plant can be grown in it. Optimum container size is related to the species, target plant size, growing density, length of the growing season, and growing medium used. For example, to grow large woody plants for an outplanting site with vegetative competition, a nursery would choose large-volume containers with low growing densities. This method creates taller plants, with larger stem diameters, which have been shown to survive and grow better under these conditions.

In all nurseries, container size is an economic decision because production costs are a function of how many plants can be grown in a given space in a given time. Larger containers occupy more growing space and take longer to produce a firm root plug. Therefore, plants in larger containers are more expensive to produce, store, ship, and out-plant. The benefits, however, may outweigh the costs if the outplanting objectives are more successfully satisfied.

Height

Container height is important because it determines the depth of the root plug, which may be a consideration on dry outplanting sites. Many clients want their plants to have a deep root system that can stay in contact with soil moisture throughout the growing season. Height is also important because it determines the proportion of freely draining growing medium within the container. When water is applied to a container filled with growing medium, gravity percolates it downward until it reaches the bottom and runs out of the drain holes in the bottom of the container. There, it stops because of its attraction for the growing medium, creating a saturated zone that always exists at the bottom of any container. Container height and the type of growing medium control the depth of this saturated layer. With the same growing medium, the depth of the saturation zone is always proportionally greater in shorter containers (figure 7.2). For example, a 4-in (10-cm) tall container will have the same depth of saturation as a 10-in (25-cm) tall container, but the 4-in-tall container will have a smaller percentage of freely drained medium.

Diameter

Container diameter is important in relation to the type of species being grown. Broad-leaved trees, shrubs, and herbaceous plants need a larger container diameter so that irrigation water applied from above can penetrate the dense foliage and reach the medium. Diameter also affects growing density in the nursery.

Shape

Containers are available in a variety of shapes and most are tapered from top to bottom. Most containers are round but some are square and maximize the growing space used in the greenhouse. Container shape is important as it relates to the type of outplanting tools used and the type of root system of the species grown.

Plant Density

The distance between plants is another important factor to consider. Spacing affects the amount of light, water, and nutrients that are available to individual plants (figure 7.3A). In general, plants grown at closer spacing grow taller and have smaller stem diameters than those grown further apart (figure 7.3B). Plant leaf size greatly affects growing density. Broad-leaved species should be grown only at fairly low densities, whereas smaller leaved and needle-leaved species can be grown at higher densities. Container spacing will affect height, stem straightness, stem diameter, and bushiness. Container spacing also affects nursery cultural practices, especially irrigation. Trays holding individual containers provide some flexibility in spacing because, as

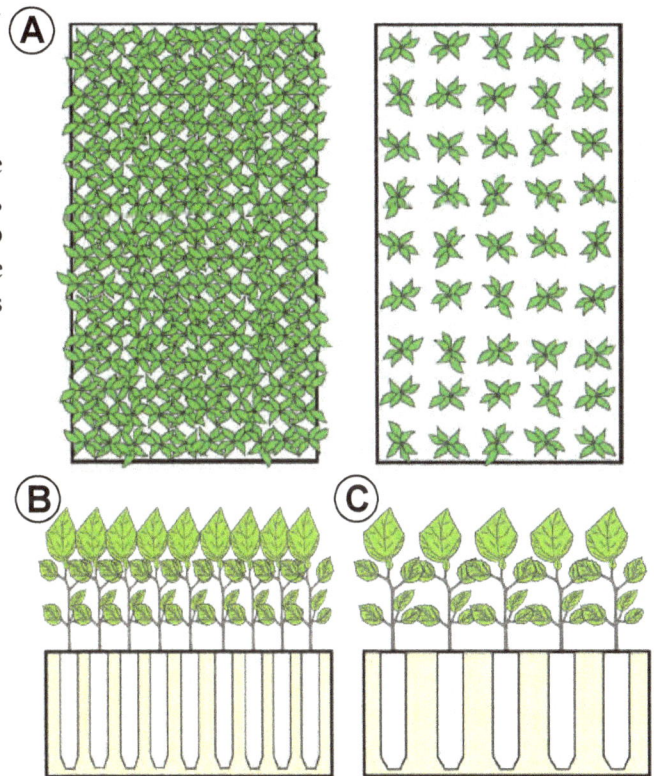

Figure 7.3—Next to volume, spacing is the most important characteristic in container choice (A). Plants grown too close together become tall and spindly and have less stem diameter (B). Trays with removable containers are popular because they allow flexibility in spacing between plants(C). Adapted from Dumroese and others (2008).

Figure 7.2—A saturated layer of growing medium always exists in the bottom of containers. With the same growing medium, the proportion of saturated media is greater for shorter containers. Adapted from Landis and others (1989).

Table 7.1—*Effects of container density.*

High density	Low density
Plants will be taller and have smaller stem diameters	Plants will be shorter and have larger stem diameters
Difficult to irrigate and fertilize with overhead sprinklers because water and liquid fertilizers need to penetrate dense patches of foliage	Easier to irrigate and fertilize with overhead sprinklers
Greater likelihood of foliar diseases due to poor air circulation between plants	Easier to irrigate and fertilize with overhead sprinklers
Cooler medium temperature	Better air circulation between seedlings; less disease problems
Foliage in lower crown will die because of shading	Plants have fuller crowns because more light reaches lower foliage
Greater number of plants can be grown in an area requiring less space and sometimes lower costs.	Fewer plants can be grown in a given area of the nursery

the plants grow, one-half of the containers can be moved to another tray, thereby allowing greater space between plants (figure 7.3.C). Some of the other effects of plant growing densities are shown in table 7.1.

Drainage Holes

Containers must have a bottom hole or holes large enough to promote good drainage and encourage "air pruning." Roots stop growing when they reach an air layer under the container. Some containers feature a bottom rail to create this air layer (figure 7.4A), whereas flat-bottomed containers must be placed on specially designed benches (figures 7.4B, 7.4C) or on a bed of coarse gravel. The drainage hole must also be small enough to prevent excessive loss of growing medium during the container-filling process. The correct drainage hole size is related to the type of medium you use; different types of containers work better with certain media types. Sandy mixes, for example, are more likely to fall out of large holes while media rich in fibrous organic material tend to hold together.

Root Pruning

Spiraling and other types of root deformation have been one of the biggest challenges for container growers, and nursery customers have concerns about potential problems with root-binding after outplanting (figure 7.5A). Research shows that rootbound seedlings are more likely to perform poorly or even blow over after outplanting. In addition to holes on the bottom of the container for air root pruning, many containers have vertical ribs within the container to force the roots to grow downward.

Figure 7.4—*Some block containers are designed to promote air pruning (A). Other containers must be placed on mesh-topped benches (B) or be supported (C) to create an effective air space underneath. Photo A by Thomas D. Landis, and photos B and C by Diane L. Haase.*

Figure 7.5—*Plants with aggressive roots often exhibit spiraling and other deformities after outplanting. If rootbound, roots often do not grow out beyond the original plug (A). Containers coated with copper will chemically prune roots (B), and other containers are available with lateral slits to reduce spiraling and encourage air pruning and on the side of the plug (C, D). Illustrations A, B, and C adapted from Dumroese and others (2008), and photo D by Thomas D. Landis.*

Inappropriate Containers and Growing Media

In an effort to save the cost of purchasing trees from the local nursery, an engineering firm decided to produce its own large mahogany trees for roadside planting projects. Because 55-gal drums were available in large quantities, they were cut in half and filled with local soil. Young mahogany seedlings were planted in the drums and watered regularly for nearly 3 years. The trees grew to be 15 to 20 ft (5 to 6.5 m) tall and were deemed to be the perfect size for the project (figure 7.6). The soil used was rich in clay and the containers did not have sufficient drainage holes, however, causing the root systems to be severely stunted. Even worse, the drums and clay made the trees too heavy to be transported easily. In the struggle to transport them and to remove them from the containers, the trees were damaged. In the end, transport costs tripled and one-third of the trees had to be replaced. Poor planning and improper containers turned this money-saving idea into a very costly project.

Figure 7.6—*Inappropriate containers and growing media can lead to serious problems, as with these mahogany trees in soil-filled 55-gallon drums. Photo by Brian F. Daley.*

Chemical pruning involves coating the interior container walls with chemicals that inhibit root growth (figure 7.5B), such as cupric carbonate or copper oxychloride. Copper-coated containers are available commercially (such as the Copperblock™). Some nurseries apply the chemical by spraying or dipping the containers. It can even be applied to polybags to greatly improve plant quality and outplanting performance, as described under the section on polybags. Fabrics treated with Spin-Out™ or similar copper coating can be placed as a groundcover under containers to prevent rooting into the ground. Copper toxicity has not been shown to be a problem for most native species, and the leaching of copper into the environment has been shown to be minimal.

Several companies have developed containers that feature air slits on their sides to control root deformation by air pruning (figures 7.5C, 7.5D). In the same manner as plant roots air prune when they reach the bottom drainage hole, they also stop growing and form suberized tips when they reach the lateral slits in sideslit containers. Using these containers (such as the RootMaker®) requires managing for (1) roots that sometimes bridge between containers and (2) seedlings in sideslit containers that dry out much faster than those in containers with solid walls.

Root Temperature

Color and insulating properties of the container affect medium temperature, which directly affects root growth. Black containers can quickly reach lethal temperatures in full sun whereas white ones are more reflective and less likely to have heat buildup. In hot, sunny climates, a grower should use containers in white or other light-reflecting colors to protect against root injury (figure 7.7). Another option is to use white plastic, Styrofoam™, or other insulating material around the outside perimeter of the containers.

Economic and Operational Factors Affecting Container Choice

Cost and Availability

Associated expenses for various container types, such as shipping and storage costs, must be considered in addition to purchase price. Nursery managers in the tropics often face high shipping costs and long shipping times. Long-term availability must also be considered to ensure that ample supplies of the container can be secured in the foreseeable future. The environmental costs must also be considered and a number of new alternative container types are becoming available, made with recycled or green materials (Nambuthiri and others 2013).

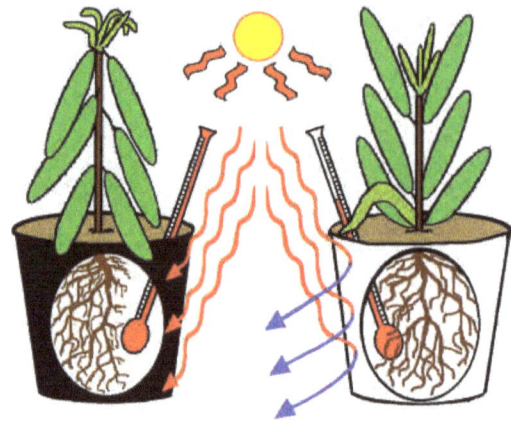

Figure 7.7—Container color is a consideration, especially when containers are exposed to direct sunlight. Roots in white containers stay cooler than those in black ones. Adapted from Dumroese and others (2008).

Durability and Reusability

Containers must be durable enough to maintain structural integrity and contain root growth during the nursery period. Containers made out of rolled newspaper have gained popularity amongst gardeners; however, these containers disintegrate too quickly to be suitable for growing plants on a nursery scale. The intense heat and ultraviolet rays in container nurseries can cause even some types of plastics to become brittle and break, although many container plastics now contain ultraviolet (UV) inhibitors. Some containers are designed to be used only once, whereas others can be reused for 10 or more crop rotations. Reusability must be considered in the container cost analysis because the cost of reusable containers can be amortized over their life span after adjusting for the cost of handling, cleaning, and sterilizing of the containers between crops (discussed later in this chapter).

Refundable Deposits for Containers and Trays

Containers are expensive, and most are made of plastic—a nonrenewable, petroleum-based product. Although alternative containers made from renewable resources are being developed (Chappell and Knox 2012, Nambuthiri and others 2013), many of these have not yet been adequately tested in tropical nurseries. Reusing containers is important to save money and resources and to protect the environment from waste. Charging a refundable container deposit (similar to bottle deposits for beverage containers) encourages clients to return containers to the nursery for reuse. Used containers need to be washed and sterilized after they are returned to the nursery.

Ease of Handling

Containers must be moved several times during crop production, so handling can be a major concern from logistic and safety standpoints. Collapsible or stackable containers, such as Zipset™ Plant Bands or Spencer-Lemaire Rootrainers™, have lower shipping and storage costs; they must, however, be assembled before filling and sowing and thus require additional handling. The size and filled weight of a container will affect ease of handling. Containers must be sturdy enough to withstand repeated handling.

Large containers are increasing in popularity, but they become very heavy when saturated with water. Weight must also be considered for shipping and field planting. It is easier for a tree planter to carry and plant hundreds of trees if the seedlings are small. With large containers, the outplanting may go slower, but survival and ability to outcompete other vegetation will likely be greater. If containers will be shipped or trucked to the outplanting site, then the type of shipping and storage system must be considered during container selection. If seedlings are to remain in the container, then some sort of shipping box must be used to protect them. Pros and cons exist with every method, and it is up to you to know the needs of your plants, clients, and site conditions for outplanting to choose the best option, as discussed in Chapter 3, Defining the Target Plant.

Ability to Cull, Consolidate, and Space

One advantage of tray containers with interchangeable cells is that cells can be removed from the tray and replaced. This advantage is particularly useful during thinning, when empty cells can be replaced with cells containing a germinant, and during roguing, when diseased or otherwise undesirable plants can be replaced with cells containing healthy ones. Plants of the same size can be consolidated and grown under separate irrigation or fertilizer programs. This consolidation can save a considerable amount of growing space in the nursery. This practice is particularly valuable with seeds that germinate slowly or unevenly, and so exchangeable cells are very popular in tropical nurseries. Another unique advantage is that cells can be spaced farther apart by leaving empty slots; this practice is ideal for larger leaved plants and also for promoting good air circulation later in the season when foliar diseases can become a problem.

Holdover Stock

Some nurseries will hold onto their stock without transplanting in an effort to reduce costs and save growing space, hoping that the stock will be outplanted next year. This practice, however, can result in the root system becoming too rootbound to grow well after outplanting (figure 7.8),

Figure 7.8—*Many tropical plants have aggressive roots and cannot be held over from one growing season to the next or they will become dangerously rootbound. Photo by Thomas D. Landis.*

as discussed in Chapter 4, Crop Planning: Propagation Protocols, Schedules, and Records, and Chapter 15, Hardening. If nursery stock must be held over, then the nursery needs to keep a supply of larger containers so the plants can be transplanted to keep the root systems healthy and to maintain good shoot-to-root balance.

Types of Containers

Many types of containers are available, and each has its advantages and disadvantages. It is a good idea to try new containers for each species on a small scale before buying large quantities. Several containers types are used in container plant nurseries and can vary considerably in size (table 7.2).

One-Time-Use Containers

One of the first major distinctions in container types is whether they will be used once or whether they can be cleaned and used again. Some one-time-use containers, such as Jiffy® products, can be outplanted directly whereas others, such as Zipset™ Plant Bands, are removed and discarded at the time of outplanting. The idea of growing a plant in a container that can be transplanted or outplanted directly into the field is attractive, and many designs have been tried. Most of these early attempts failed because the

> *"Seedlings produced in a nursery in Indonesia using root trainers and a peat-based growing media cost about 20 percent more than seedlings produced in a neighboring nursery using polybags and topsoil. But reduced transport costs to the field and better seedling survival and growth eliminated this difference completely."* (Jaenicke 1999: 27)

Table 7.2—*Volumes and dimensions of containers used in native plant nurseries. Adapted from Stuewe and Sons, Inc. (2013), and other sources.*

Container brand or type	Volume in3 (ml)	Depth in (cm)	Top diameter in (cm)
One-time-use containers			
Jiffy® pellets	0.6 to 21.4 (10 to 350)	1.2 to 5.9 (3 to 15)	0.8 to 2.2 (2.0 to 5.6)
Jiffy® pots	4.4 to 137.7 (72 to 2,257)	1.9 to 5.9 (4.9 to 15.0)	2.0 to 6.5 (5.1 to 16.5)
Zipset™ plant bands	6 to 42 (98 to 688)	4 to 14 (10 to 36)	1.5 to 3 (3.8 to 7.6)
Single free-standing containers			
RootMaker® singles	6.0 to 13.25 (172 to 1,125)	6.0 to 11.3 (15.3 to 28.7)	6.0 to 13.3 (15.3 to 33.8)
Polybags	90 to 930 (1,474 to 15,240)	4 to 8 (10 to 20)	6 to 8 (5 to 20)
Treepots™	101 to 1,848 (1,655 to 30,280)	9.5 to 24.0 (24 to 60)	3.8 to 11.0 (10 to 28)
Round pots	90 to 4,500 (1,474 to 73,740)	6 to 18 (15 to 45)	6 to 14 (15 to 35)
Containers with exchangeable cell held in a tray or rack			
Ray Leach Cone-tainer™ cells	3 to 10 (49 to 164)	4.75 to 8.25 (12 to 21)	1.0 to 1.5 (2.5 to 3.8)
Deepots™	13 to 60 (210 to 983)	3 to 14 (7.6 to 36)	2 to 2.5 (5 to 6.4)
Book or sleeve containers			
Rootrainers™	3.3 to 67 (55 to 1,100)	4.25 to 10.0 (10.8 to 25.4)	1.0 x 1.0 to 3.0 x 2.5 (2.5 x 2.5 to 3.0 x 2.5)
Rectangular blocks composed of cavities or cells			
Styroblock™ and Copperblock™	0.5 to 195.3 (8 to 3,200)	2 to 7 (5.1 to 17.9)	0.6 to 6.2 (1.4 to 15.8)
Ropak® Multi-Pots™	3.5 to 6.0 (57 to 98)	3.5 to 4.75 (9 to 12)	1.25 to 1.5 (3.2 to 3.8)
IPL Rigi-Pots™	0.3 to 21.3 (5 to 350)	1.7 to 5.5 (4.4 to 14.0)	0.55 x 0.55 to 2.3 x 2.3 (1.4 x 1.4 to 5.9 x 5.9)
Hiko™ Trays	0.8 to 32.3 (913 to 530)	1.9 to 7.9 (4.9 to 20.0)	1.0 to 1.3 (2.5 to 3.3)
Miniplug trays			
"Groove Tube" System™	1.4 to 11.7 (23 to 192)	2.50 to 5.25 (6.4 to 13.3)	1.13 to 2.25 (2.9 to 5.7)
RootMaker® propagation trays	1.6 to 6.0 (26 to 172)	2.0 to 4.0 (5.1 to 10.2)	6.0 to 13.3 (15.3 to 33.8)

Figure 7.9—Jiffy® pellets are composed of dry compressed peat surrounded by mesh and expand when watered. Smaller pellets are used to start germinants and can be transplanted into larger Jiffy® containers or other containers. Photo by Don Willis.

Figure 7.10—Zipset™ Plant Bands are inexpensive containers that can be shipped directly to the field. Photo courtesy of Stuewe and Sons, Inc.

Figure 7.11—Recyclable containers like these constructed of paper fiber are ecologically friendly but do not hold up well in wet, humid climates such as greenhouses. Photo by Tara Luna.

container material broke down in the nursery before the plants were ready or they failed to decompose after outplanting. Still, new products are continually being introduced and are attractive to ecologically minded growers (Nambuthiri and others 2013; Chappell and Knox 2012).

Jiffy® Pellets and Pots

Jiffy® products consist of dry, compressed peat growing media inside a soft-walled, meshed bag and come in a variety of sizes (figure 7.9). When sown and irrigated, the pellet expands into a cylindrical plug surrounded by mesh that encourages air pruning all around the plug. Pellets are supported in hard plastic trays, so individual pellets can be consolidated to ensure full occupancy. Irrigation schedules must be adjusted (frequency increased) because of greater permeability of the container wall. Some root growth occurs between the pellets, so they must be vertically pruned

before harvesting. Jiffy® Forestry Pellets are popular in forest nurseries in the Northeastern United States and Eastern Canada, where they are outplanted directly into the field. Smaller Jiffy® pellets are used for starting plants that are then transplanted into larger Jiffy® sizes or other containers. This system works well for species that germinate very slowly or over a long period of time.

Zipset™ Plant Bands

Zipset™ Plant Bands are square, one-use containers composed of bleached cardboard containers that are assembled in a hard plastic tray (figure 7.10). Zipset™ Plant Bands maintain their integrity in the nursery but biodegrade after 9 to 18 months. Some tropical nurseries prefer Zipset™ Plant Bands because they protect the root plug during storage and shipping.

Other Natural Fiber Containers

Containers made of fiber, such as coir or compressed paper, come in a variety of sizes (figure 7.11) and are popular with gardeners for vegetable seedlings. The roots can develop without the potential deformity problems of solid-walled containers, and natural fiber pots can be transplanted or outplanted with minimal root disturbance or transplant shock. When they are outplanted, roots penetrate the container as it breaks down. These containers have a few problems, however, when used in tropical nurseries. They may break down too quickly in warm, humid climates to be suitable for growing native plants. They tend to become coated

Figure 7.12—The RootMaker®, which was the first to feature side-slit air pruning, is available as a single, free-standing container or in aggregate blocks. Photo by Tara Luna.

with algae over time, which makes them slippery to handle and nearly impossible to store, so they present challenges for shipping and handling. If a nursery is growing some fast-growing species that will not need to be transported very far before outplanting, natural fiber containers may be a suitable option. Natural fiber pots need to be tested before use to ensure they will not break down or become coated with algae too quickly for the growing cycle of the species propagated in them.

Single, Free-Standing Containers

Several types of single-cell containers are being used to grow native plants for specific conditions.

RootMaker® Containers

These unique containers have staggered walls and a staggered bottom that prevent root circling and direct roots toward the holes in the walls and the bottom of the container. The containers were among the first to use side "air slits" to air prune plant roots (figure 7.12) and are available in many sizes of single containers that are either square or round. Smaller volume RootMaker® cavities are joined together in blocks.

Polybags and Polytubes

Bags made of black polyethylene (poly) plastic sheeting are the most commonly used nursery containers in the world because they are inexpensive and easy to ship and store (figure 7.13A). It is unfortunate but polybags generally produce seedlings with poorly formed root systems that spiral around the sides and the bottoms of the smooth-walled con-

Figure 7.13—Polybags are inexpensive containers (A) but can result in problems with seedling quality. Root spiraling is often serious, but polytubes in trays (B and C) and with copper-coating (D, on the right) can solve that problem. Photos A, B, and C by Tara Luna, and photo D by R. Kasten Dumroese.

tainers. This problem worsens when seedlings are held over and not outplanted or transplanted at the proper time.

In cases in which converting to hard plastic containers would be operationally or financially impractical, ways exist to improve container production using polybags. Some of these cultural modifications include (Landis 1995)—

- Managing container seedlings as a perishable commodity with a limited "shelf life." This concept is particularly critical in tropical nurseries where seedlings grow year round. If seedlings cannot be outplanted when their roots fill the container, then they must be transplanted into a larger container. Holding over polybag seedlings is not an option.

- Using polytube containers (a polybag open at both ends, sometimes called a polysleeve) instead of polybags (figure 7.13B). These containers can usually be obtained from the same supplier as polybags or cut from a continuous roll with no bottom (Jaenicke 1999). Poly tubes eliminate much of the root spiraling. Poly tubes will hold growing media if they are properly filled and placed on elevated screen-bottomed trays to promote air pruning of roots (figure 7.13C).

- Using copper-coated polytubes or polybags. Plants grown in copper polybags produce a much finer, fibrous root system that is well distributed throughout the containers (figure 7.13D), but availability can be a problem.

- Switching from soil-based to "artificial" or organic-based growing media (composts, bark, or other materials instead of soil). See Chapter 6, Growing Media, for more information.

- Carefully transplanting germinants or direct-seeding into the polybag or polytube containers to avoid root deformations from improper transplanting of newly emerged seedlings.

Treepots™

These large-volume containers are constructed of flexible hard plastic and are good for growing trees and woody shrubs. Many sizes are available that are either square or round (figure 7.14A); square shapes increase space and irrigation efficiency in the growing area. Treepots™ feature vertical ribs on the inside wall to prevent root spiraling, are reusable, and store easily because they can be nested when empty. The depth of their root plug helps plants access soil water on dry sites and, for riparian restoration, provides stability against water erosion. Because of their large height-to-diameter ratios, Treepots™ require a support rack for growing and shipping (figure 7.14B), which can be made with fencing or other materials.

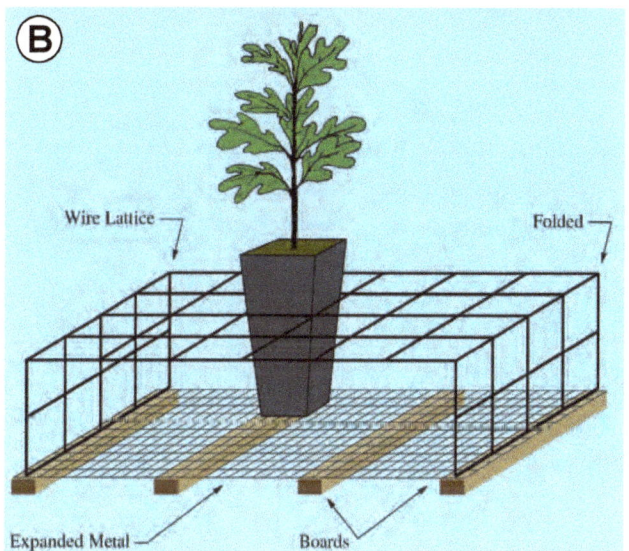

Figure 7.14—Treepots™ are popular native plant containers because of their deep root systems (A), but they need to be held in a rack system (B). Photo A by Thomas D. Landis, and illustration B from Dumroese and others (2008).

Round Pots

Round black plastic pots are available in many sizes from numerous manufacturers; one encouraging feature is that some brands are recyclable (figure 7.15A). Round pots are used in some tropical nurseries, especially for landscaping applications (figure 7.15B). Round pots are very durable and so can be reused for many years; because they can be nested when empty, they use little storage space. Most designs have a ridged lip that makes the pots easier to move and handle when they are wet. Root deformation has been a serious problem with these containers, although some are now available with internal ribs or copper coating to prevent root spiraling.

Figure 7.15—*Some standard round plastic containers or "cans" are now recyclable (A), and are sometimes used to grow native plants for ornamental landscaping (B). Photo A by Thomas D. Landis, and photo B by Diane L. Haase.*

Figure 7.16—*Ray Leach Cone-tainer™ cells are one of the most popular container types for growing native plants (A) because they can be consolidated and spaced in the racks (B). Photos by Diane L. Haase.*

Exchangeable Cells Held in a Tray or Rack

The major advantage of growing plants in individual cell containers supported in a hard plastic rack or tray is that the individual cells are interchangeable allowing for consolidation and spacing as described earlier. Racks are designed to create enough air space underneath to promote good air pruning. Plastic cells can be reused for several growing seasons.

Ray Leach Cone-tainer™ Cells

One of the oldest container designs on the market, the Ray Leach Cone-tainer™ cells are still popular with native plant growers. In this system, individual soft, flexible plastic cells are supported in a durable hard plastic tray (figure 7.16). Trays are partially vented to encourage air circulation between cells and have a life expectancy of 8 to 10 years. Cells come in three types of plastic: recycled, low density, and low density with UV stabilizers. All have anti-spiral ribs and a center bottom drainage hole with three or four side-drain holes on the tapered end.

Deepots™

These single cells are constructed of thick plastic and held in hard plastic racks (figure 7.17). Available in several sizes, they have internal vertical ribs for root control and supports on the bottom of each container provide stability. Racks hold the containers together but do not create an air space underneath, so Deepots™ must be grown on wire mesh or well-drained gravel to facilitate air pruning of the roots. Due to their large volume and depth, Deepots™ are popular with native plant nurseries growing woody shrubs and trees.

Figure 7.17—Deepots™ come in large sizes and are popular for growing native shrubs and trees. Photo by Diane L. Haase.

Book or Sleeve Containers: Spencer-Lemaire Rootrainers™

These unique "book" containers are composed of flexible plastic cells that are hinged at the bottom, allowing the growing media and root system to be examined during the entire growing season when the books are open (figure 7.18A). The books are held together in plastic or wire trays or "baskets" to form blocks of cells (figure 7.18B). As the name implies, Rootrainers™ have an internal rib system to guide plant roots to the drainage hole and to prevent spiraling. One real advantage of using the books is that they nest easily and can be shipped inexpensively; the nesting feature also makes for efficient storage. The plastic is less durable than other container types, but the books can be reused if handled properly.

Block Containers Made Up of Many Cavities or Cells

Styroblock™ and Copperblock™

Styroblock™ containers are the most popular type of container used in forest nurseries in the Western United States and are available in a wide range of cavity sizes and densities (figure 7.19), although outside block dimensions are standard to conform to equipment handling. This container has also been used for growing native grasses, woody shrubs, and trees. The insulation value of Styrofoam™ protects tender roots from temperature extremes and the white color reflects sunlight,

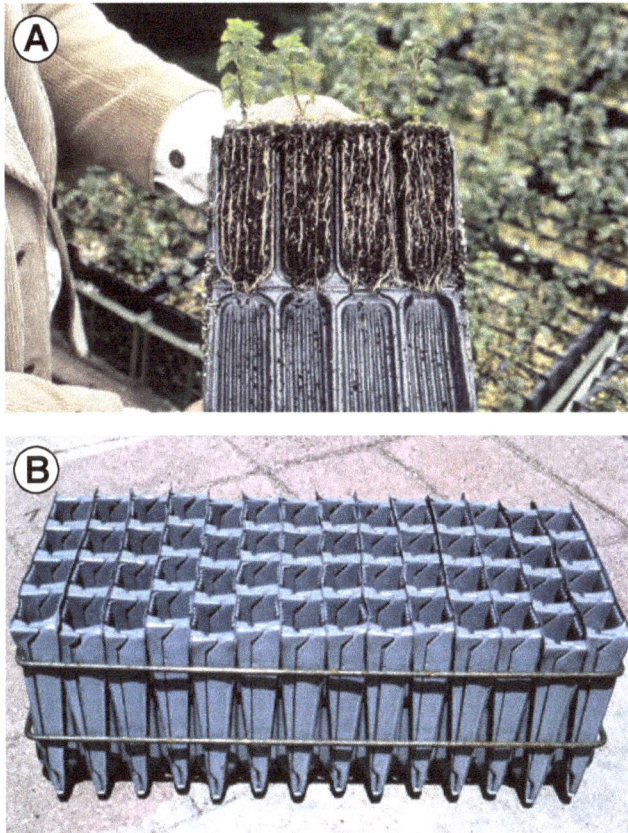

Figure 7.18—Spencer-Lemaire Rootrainers™ are designed to allow easy inspection of growing media and the root plug (A). The hinged soft plastic sheets are assembled and placed into hard plastic trays or wire "baskets" to form blocks (B). In addition, these containers encourage good root formation along the length of the plug (left) compared with spiraled roots formed in the bottom of a polybag (right) (C). Photos A and B by Thomas D. Landis, and photo C by J.B. Friday.

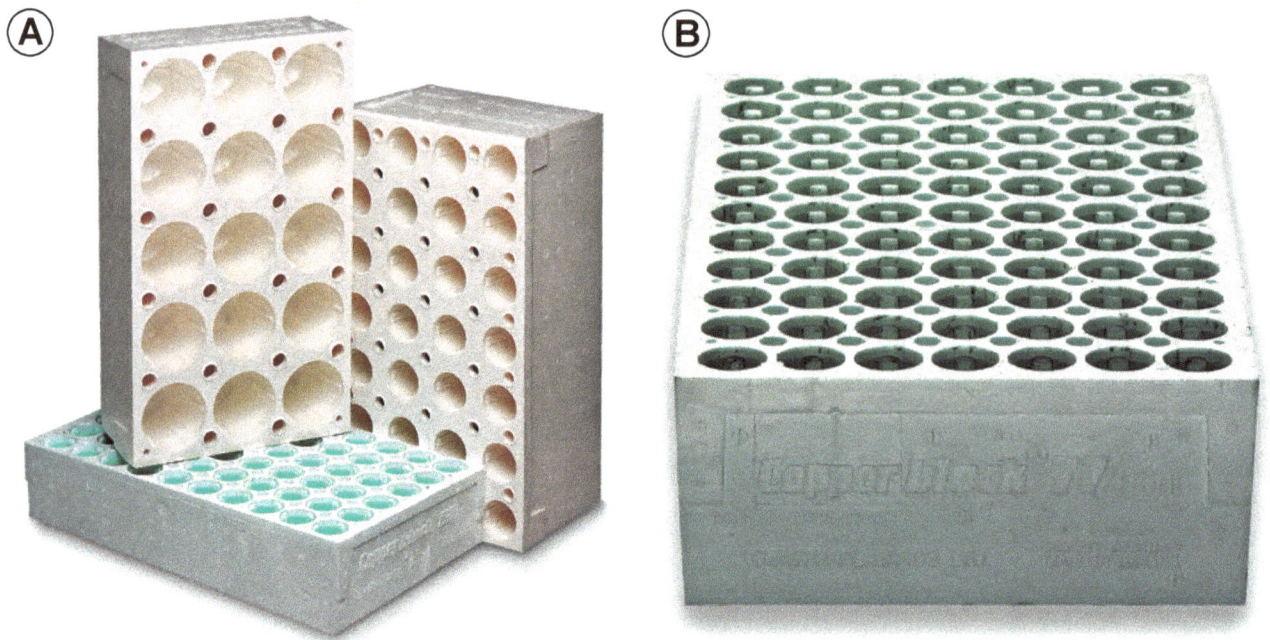

Figure 7.19—A wide assortment of Styroblock™ containers is available (A). The cavity walls of Copperblock™ containers are coated with copper, which causes chemical root pruning of species with aggressive roots systems (B). Styroblock™ and Copperblock™ containers have been used to grow a variety of native plants. Photo A courtesy of Stuewe and Sons, Inc., and photo B by Thomas D. Landis.

keeping the growing medium cool. Styroblock™ containers are relatively lightweight yet durable, tolerate handling, and can be reused for 3 to 5 years or more. One major drawback is that plants cannot be separated and consolidated so empty cavities and cull seedlings reduce space use efficiency. Species with aggressive roots may penetrate the inside walls of the cavities (especially in older containers reused for several crops), making the plugs difficult to remove. The Copperblock™ container is identical to the Styroblock™ except that it is one of the few commercially available containers with copper-lined cavity walls to promote root pruning.

Hardwall Plastic Blocks

Hardwall plastic blocks are available in a variety of cavity sizes and shapes and outside block dimensions (table 7.2). Extremely durable, these containers have a life expectancy of more than 10 years. The thick plastic is impervious to root growth.

Ropak® Multi-Pots are white in color, available in square and round cavity shapes, and have been used to grow a wide variety of species (figure. 7.20A). Because they are so durable, they are popular in mechanized nurseries and have been used to grow herbaceous and woody species. Cavity walls have vertical ribs to prevent root spiraling. IPL® Rigi-Pots™ are usually black, but other colors

can be obtained in large orders. They are available in a variety of block dimensions and cavity sizes and shapes including sideslit models to encourage air pruning of roots (figure 7.20B). The Hiko™ Tray System features a variety of block and cavity sizes and shapes (table 7.2). All cavities have vertical root training ribs and sideslits (figure 7.20C). "The Groove Tube" Growing System™ features grooves in the side walls and large drainage holes to promote root development (figure 7.20D).

Miniplug Trays

Miniplug containers are used to start young seedlings that are transplanted into larger containers after establishment (figure 7.21). They are particularly useful for species with very small seeds that make precise seeding difficult. Multiple germinants can be thinned and plugs transplanted to larger containers. In these situations, the use of miniplug trays is much more space and labor efficient than direct seeding into larger cells. They require constant attention, however, because they dry out quickly. If miniplug trays are used, they may need to be irrigated several times a day or watered with automatic mist or subirrigation to keep them from drying out.

Seeds may also be started in trays, as discussed in Chapter 9, Seed Germination and Sowing Options.

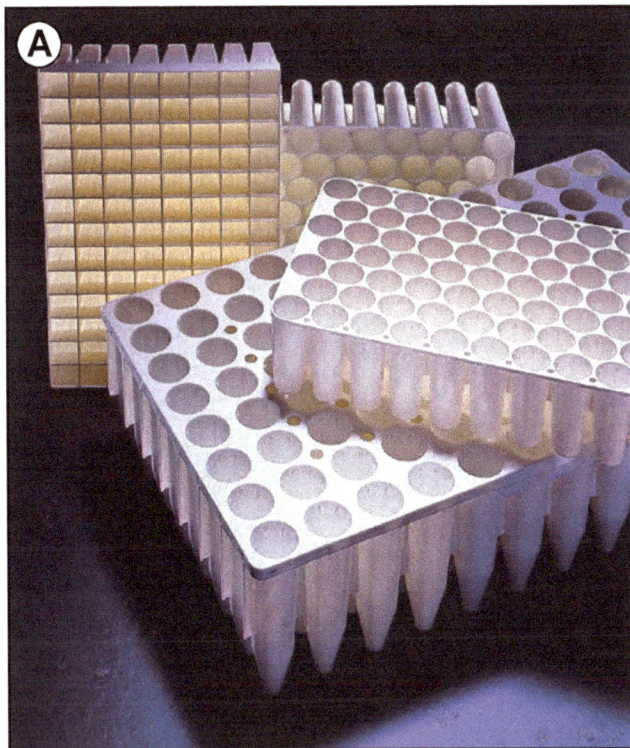

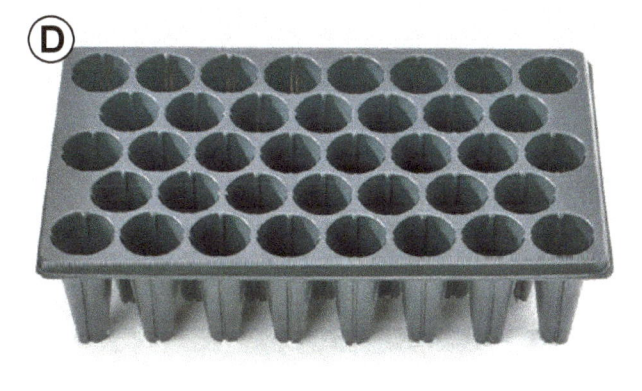

Figure 7.20—Hardwall plastic blocks are extremely durable containers made by several manufacturers. Ropak® Multi-Pots (A), IPL® Rigi-Pots (B), the Hiko™ Tray System (C), and the "Groove Tube" Growing System™(D). Photos A, C, and D courtesy of Stuewe and Sons, Inc., and photo B by Thomas D. Landis.

Figure 7.21—Miniplug containers are used to grow small seedlings that are transplanted into larger containers. Photo by Tara Luna.

Cleaning Reusable Containers

Most nursery containers are reusable. Charging a deposit (for example 10 cents per cell, refundable if returned within 30 days of plant delivery) or otherwise encouraging clients to return containers saves money and resources. Reusable containers usually have some residual growing medium or pieces of roots that could contain pathogenic fungi. Seedling roots sometimes grow into the pores of containers with rough-textured walls, such as Styroblock™ containers, and remain after the seedling plug has been extracted (figure 7.22A). Liverworts, moss, and algae also grow on containers and are very difficult to remove from reusable containers. Used containers should be washed first to remove old growing media and other debris. If available, a pressure washer is excellent for this purpose. Otherwise, a regular hose, or a soak in a garbage can followed by a rinse with a hose, works too.

Next, the containers should be sterilized. Because many tropical nurseries choose not to use pesticides and chemical disinfectants, hot-water dips are the most safe, environmentally friendly, and effective way to kill fungi and other pests in used containers. Most pathogens and weed seeds are killed when containers are held at 158 to 176 °F (40 to 60 °C) for more than 3 minutes (figure 7.22B). A good rule of thumb is to use a soaking temperature of 165 to 185 °F (75 to 85 °C) for 30 to 90 seconds for Styrofoam™ containers; 15 to 30 seconds is probably sufficient for hard plastic containers (Dumroese and others 2002). Soaking Styrofoam™ at hotter temperatures can cause the material to distort. Commercial units are available, but many nurseries have built homemade container dipping systems that hold the containers under hot water in a dip tank.

Other options for sterilizing containers and nursery tools include using household bleach or alcohol. These chemicals are phytotoxic to plants and should never be used on or near seedlings. For bleach, use regular household bleach (5.25-percent sodium hypochlorite concentration), diluted 1 part bleach to 9 parts water. Dip or soak the containers and tools in this bleach solution; then rinse them well before using. If the diluted bleach is stored in a covered container, such as a garbage can with a good lid, the solution may be used again, as long as it has not lost its strength. Wood, grain, or rubbing alcohol (70 to 100 percent) may also be used to sterilize containers and tools. Alcohol is used full strength. Dip or soak the containers and tools in the alcohol, but do not rinse them. Allow the containers and tools to dry in the air before using them.

References

Baker, K.F. 1957. The U.C. system for producing healthy container-grown plants through the use of clean soil, clean stock, and sanitation. University of California, Division of Agricultural Sciences, Manual 23. Berkeley, CA: University of California. 332 p.

Chappell, M.; Knox, G.W. 2012. Alternatives to petroleum-based containers for the nursery industry. Bulletin 1407. Athens, GA: University of Georgia, Cooperative Extension. 4 p. http://www.caes.uga.edu/applications/publications/files/pdf/B%201407_1.PDF. (March 2013).

Dumroese, R.K.; James, R.L.; Wenny, D.L. 2002. Hot water and copper coatings in reused containers decrease inoculum of *Fusarium* and *Cylindrocarpon* and increase Douglas-fir seedling growth. HortScience. 37(6): 943–947.

Dumroese, R.K.; Luna, T.; Landis, T.D. 2008. Nursery manual for native plants: volume 1, a guide for tribal nurseries. Agriculture Handbook 730. Washington, DC: U.S. Department of Agriculture, Forest Service. 302 p.

Jaenicke, H. 1999. Good tree nursery practices: practical guidelines for research nurseries. International Centre for Research in Agroforestry. Nairobi, Kenya: Majestic Printing Works. 93 p.

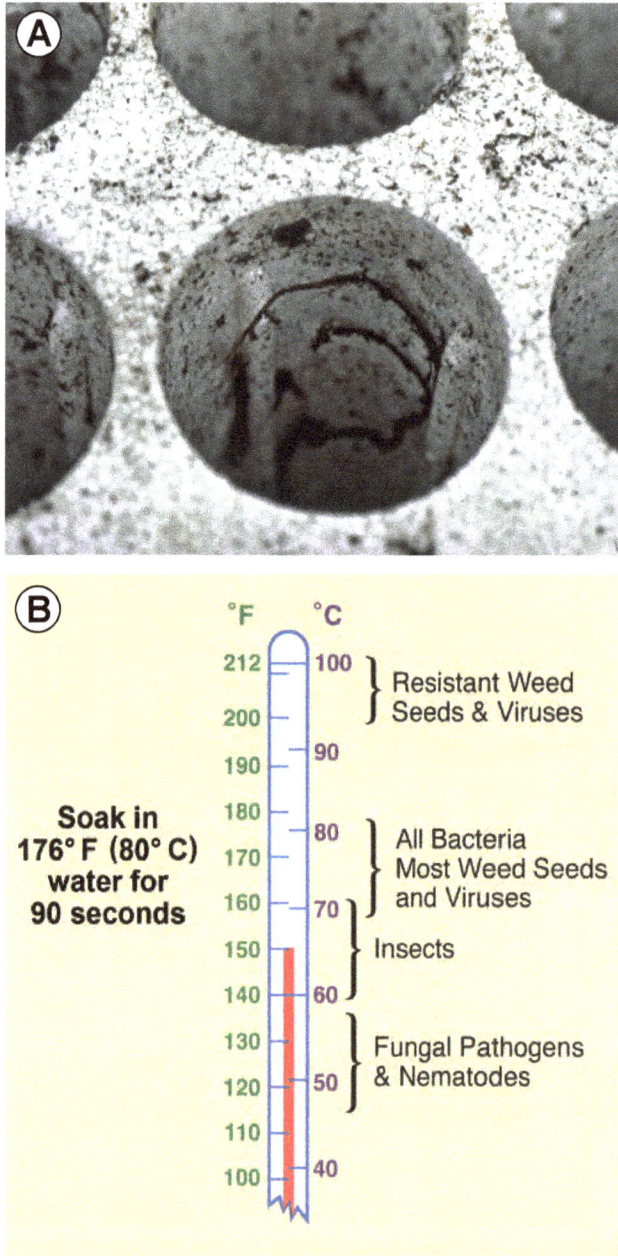

Figure 7.22—*Used containers should be washed and sterilized before reusing (A), because residual growing media and seedling roots can contain disease organisms. Submersion in water of 165 to 185 °F (75 to 85 °C) for 30 to 90 seconds has been shown to be adequate for all types of containers (B). Photo A by Thomas D. Landis, and illustration B adapted from Baker (1957) by Jim Marin.*

Landis, T.D. 1995. Improving polybag culture for sustainable nurseries. Forest Nursery Notes (July 1995): 6–7.

Nambuthiri, S.; Schnelle, R.; Fulcher, A.; Geneve, R.; Koeser, A.; Verlinden, S.; Conneway, R. 2013. Alternative containers for a sustainable greenhouse and nursery crop production. Hort-Fact—6000. Lexington, KY: University of Kentucky Cooperative Extension Service, Horticulture Department. http://www.uky.edu/Ag/Horticulture/alternativecontainers.pdf. (March 2013).

Stuewe & Sons, Inc. 2013. Tree seedling nursery container catalog. http://www.stuewe.com. (February 2013).

Additional Reading

Dumroese, R.K.; Wenny, D.L. 1997. An assessment of ponderosa pine seedlings grown in copper-coated polybags. Tree Planters' Notes. 48(3): 60–64.

Landis, T.D.; Tinus, R.W.; MacDonald, S.E.; Barnett, J.P. 1990. The container tree nursery manual: volume 2, containers and growing media. Agriculture Handbook 674. Washington, DC: U.S. Department of Agriculture, Forest Service. 88 p.

Collecting, Processing, and Storing Seeds

Tara Luna and Kim M. Wilkinson

8

Nurseries that work to strengthen and expand the presence of tropical native species are concerned about fostering diverse, strong, and well-adapted populations. For many tropical plants, however, the natural diversity of wild populations has been depleted. Habitat loss has reduced the range and sheer numbers of plants. For plants with commercial value, unsustainable harvesting practices may have reduced the numbers of plants with desirable characteristics while leaving behind inferior plants. The process of depleting a population of the best genetic properties so that future populations are weaker than the original populations is called genetic degradation. Seed collection for plant propagation is an opportunity to reverse trends of genetic degradation and species loss. Nurseries have a key role in conserving the gene pool of native plants. This chapter covers some important principles for genetic diversity and seed source selection; it also includes practical procedures for collecting, processing, and storing seeds.

Facing Page: *Seeds are removed from fruit and cleaned on screens in a shaded outdoor location at the nursery of Reserva Natural, Cañón de San Cristóbal, Barranquitas, Puerto Rico. Photo by Brian F. Daley.*

Understanding Genetic Diversity and Seed Collection Ethics

Before creating a strategy for collecting native plant seeds, it is important to understand some key points regarding genetics and collection ethics. Seed collection strategies must protect genetic diversity for the future both at the collection sites and in the places where the offspring will be planted. On the outplanting sites, good seed collection practices ensure that inbreeding will not become a problem (Withrow-Robinson and Johnson 2006) and that plant populations will be genetically viable to survive and adapt to new stresses. For restoration and conservation projects, maintaining genetic diversity is a key part of project objectives and of the target plant requirements (see Chapter 3, Defining the Target Plant).

Collecting Locally Adapted Native Seeds

It is critical to identify suitable seed collection sites. As much as possible, collect seeds from a habitat similar in elevation, aspect, and soils to that of the outplanting site to ensure local genetic adaptation. In some parts of the world, plant geneticists have defined "seed zones" for native species to show practitioners where locally adapted seed sources can be found for different restoration project locations. It is rare to find these recommendations for native tropical species, however, so collectors just have to do their best. Working with locally adapted plant sources is important not only for the survival and health of the plants, but also for the native birds, insects, and animals that depend on the plants (figure 8.1).

In addition, it is important to be sure the population you plan to collect seed from is of wild origin, not planted by people (BLM/SOS 2011). For example, do not collect seeds of native species that were planted as street trees, in landscaping, or as part of a restoration planting after a disturbance, because the genetic diversity and origin is uncertain. (This guideline does not apply to nonnative cultural and traditional species; although diversity is still important, these plants may be selected cultivars.) More details about choosing a seed collection location are addressed later in this chapter.

Use Collection Methods That Ensure Genetic Diversity

Because reproductive strategies vary by species, no standard collecting procedure exists that will ensure genetic integrity for all species. The Seeds of Success seed-collecting program (part of the Native Plant Materials Development Program, led by the U.S. Bureau of Land Management) has developed a useful general protocol, which is used by many Federal agencies and partners for seed bank collections. Key seed collection practices for ensuring genetic diversity are summarized in table 8.1.

Figure 8.1—*To maximize genetic diversity, observe flowering throughout the season so early, middle, and late bloomers are represented. Different flowering and dispersal times may interact with different pollinators. Photo by Brian F. Daley.*

Why Collect Seed From More Than 50 Individual Plants?
(adapted from BLM/SOS 2011)

Research shows that seed collection from more than 50 individuals results in the greatest proportion of alleles (genetic codes specifying certain traits) present in the field population, while still being practical. Some studies show that at least one copy of 95 percent of the alleles occurring in the population at frequencies of greater than 0.05 can be achieved by sampling from—

1. 30 randomly chosen individuals in a fully outbreeding sexual species, or

2. 59 randomly chosen individuals in a self-fertilizing species.

The reproductive biology of many tropical species has not been studied, and to capture rarer alleles would require an increased sample size. Therefore, collectors are advised to sample from a single population with individuals of the target species in excess of 50 individuals, and to look for populations with larger numbers of plants.

Table 8.1—Seed collection techniques to safeguard genetic diversity of native species. Adapted from USDI BLM/SOS (2011).

Seed collection method	Rationale
Assess the target population and confirm that a sufficient number of individual plants (more than 50) have seeds at natural dispersal stage.	Ensure that adequate genetic diversity can be sampled from the population and that the seeds are likely to be at maximum possible viability and longevity.
Monitor seed maturation and assess insect damage and empty seeds throughout the population before making the seed collection. Carefully examine a small, representative sample of seeds using a cut test and for smaller seeds, a hand lens.	Estimate the frequency of empty or damaged seeds and confirm that the majority of seeds are mature and fully formed. (Seed development can vary within and between populations of the same species.)
Collect seed from more than 50 individuals.	Maximize the genetic diversity present within a collection of seeds. To gather the greatest proportion of alleles (genetic codes specifying certain traits) present in the field population as possible.
Collect from distant individuals to reduce the chance of collecting only close relatives. Collect equally and randomly across the population, maintaining a record of the number of individuals sampled.	Capture the widest possible genetic diversity from the plant population and to avoid only a few genotypes being propagated.
For trees, collect seeds or fruits equally from all parts of the crown—top, sides, and bottom. Gather from individual trees at least 150 ft (50 m) distant from each other (Dawson and Were 1997).	Ensure genetic diversity in tree seed, as these parts of the tree may have been pollinated at different times from different pollinators. Distance recommendation is to avoid collecting from closely related individuals (Dawson and Were 1997).
Return to the site to collect seeds from a population throughout its dispersal season. Collections taken from the same population during a single collecting season may be combined into one collection; do not mix collections between locations or years. Note multiple dates of collections on the seed label.	Maximize genetic diversity in the collection, capturing early, middle, and late bloomers. (These different dispersal times may also interact with different pollinators.)
Collect no more than 20% of the viable seed available at the time of collection.	Ensure that the sampled population is not over collected and is maintainable, so seeds that are needed for natural dispersal or for local fauna will remain available.
Clearly label all bags (inside and out) with the species, date collected, location of collection, and name of collector.	Ensure that each collection is properly identified so seeds can be used appropriately in restoration efforts.

Communicate About Seed Collection

When planning a seed collection strategy, some of these following communications will need to take place:

- In all cases, be sure to obtain landowner permission to collect seeds.

- Before collection, be absolutely certain of the species identification. If in doubt, collect a specimen and get help making a positive identification.

- If any other seed collectors are found using the site, cooperate with them to share the collection work and ensure that the genetic conservation practices described in this chapter are followed.

- Use great care in labeling seed sources and make sure that you, and the people who work with you, do not accidentally mix seeds with those from another plant collection area. Outbreeding depression resulting from the mixing of genotypes can potentially harm the population, resulting in the reduction of fitness and adaptive variation.

- For rare plant propagation, contact the appropriate organization in your area to obtain a collection permit in advance. These programs have jurisdiction over rare species and are responsible for monitoring and protecting the rare plant populations. The guidelines given in this chapter do not apply to threatened and endangered species; check with the appropriate organization to find the correct guidelines for each species in that category.

Figure 8.2—Cones of gymnosperms can be fleshy or woody at maturity, as seen in Cycas (A) and Pinus (B) which release winged seeds (B, C). Gymnosperm seeds are composed of the embryo, the nutritive tissue, and the seed coat (D). Photos A, B, and C by Thomas D. Landis, and illustration D from Dumroese and others (1998).

Protecting the Seed Collection Site

Collection strategies need to be planned to minimize negative effects on the site. Collectors should follow the following steps:

- Avoid soil disturbance and plant damage while collecting seeds.

- Be sure not to overharvest seeds, leaving too few behind for natural regeneration and wildlife needs.

- Avoid collecting from weed-infested areas and do not transport weeds into pristine habitats and rare plant localities.

- If possible, allow collection sites to rest for at least two growing seasons between collections. Keep in mind that longer rest periods may be needed for some species and locations.

Understanding Flowers and Seeds

The tropics support the highest degree of species diversity in the world. It has been estimated that more than 50,000 woody tree and shrub species are in this region. This diversity is also expressed in a wide range of flowers and fruits. Seed collectors and growers need to be able to distinguish fruits and seeds of species that they are collecting to ensure collection of the right structure at the right stage of development.

Plants are classified according to whether they produce spores or seeds. Spore-bearing plants such as ferns produce clusters of spores on the undersides of leaves that may or may not be covered with a papery covering. Spores can be collected like seeds just before they disperse, but they require special growing conditions to develop into plants. Seed-bearing plants are classified into two groups based on their flower types: gymnosperms and angiosperms.

Gymnosperms

Gymnosperms do not bear true flowers and are considered more primitive than angiosperms. Instead, gymnosperms bear male and female cones on the same tree. Male cones typically develop on the tips of branches and fall off after pollen is shed. Female cones enlarge and become more visible following pollination and fertilization, and seeds are borne naked on the mature scales. Gymnosperm cones can be dehiscent, indehiscent, or fleshy. Cones that are fleshy (such as *Cycas*) or surrounded by a fleshy aril (such as *Torreya*) resemble berries and are handled and processed in the same way (figure 8.2A). Dehiscent cones have scales that open at maturity to release the seeds (figure 8.2B) whereas indehiscent cones rely on animals to pry them open and disperse the seeds. In both dehiscent and indehiscent cones the seeds are usually winged (figure 8.2C). Fleshy cones resemble berries and their seeds lack wings. Gymnosperm seeds are composed of the embryo, the nutritive tissue, and the seed coat (figure 8.2D).

Angiosperms

Angiosperms bear true flowers, and seeds are enclosed in an ovary that develops and surrounds the seeds after fertilization. Pollen is transferred from anthers (male reproductive structure) to the stigma surmounting the pistil (female reproductive structure). Following pollination and fertilization, the ovary enlarges into a fruit that contains one to many seeds. The fruit protects the seeds, provides them with nutrition during development, and helps with the dispersal of mature seeds. The seed is a ripened ovule consisting of a seed coat, the nutritive tissue (endosperm), and the embryo (figure 8.3). Embryo size varies widely among species.

Most angiosperms have perfect (bisexual) flowers, meaning they contain both the male and female reproductive structures in the same flower (figure 8.4A). Perfect flowers can be showy or very small and inconspicuous. Some species such as *Swietenia* and *Ricinus* have imperfect flowers, meaning that separate male and female flowers are borne in single sex flower clusters on the same plant (figures 8.4B, 8.4C). Some species are dioecious, such as *Dondonea*, which means that individual plants are either male or female (figures 8.4D, 8.4E). Thus, often only the female plants will bear fruits and seeds (figure 8.4F).

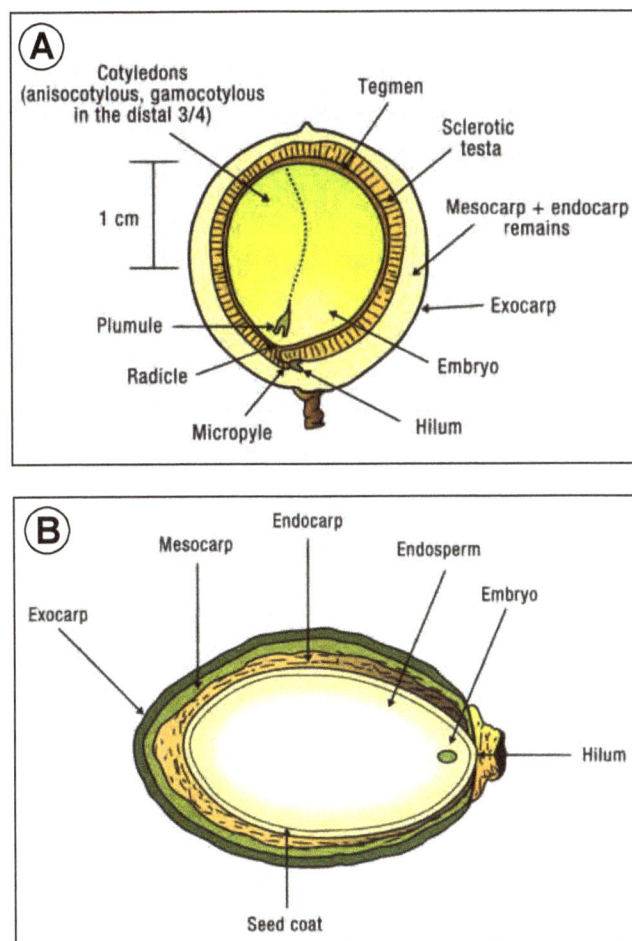

Figure 8.3—*Angiosperm fruits and seeds vary greatly among species;* Calophyllum *(A)* and Minquartia *(B). In some species, the embryo is not visible to the naked eye. Illustrations from* Vozzo (2002).

Because of the wide variety of flower types, resulting fruits also vary tremendously. Dry, dehiscent fruits are those that are woody or papery and split open at maturity. Some examples include capsules (figures 8.5A, 8.5B), some legumes or pods (figure 8.5C), and follicles (figure 8.5D). Dry, indehiscent fruits are those in which both the fruit and seed form an integrated part of the dispersal unit and do not split open at maturity. The thin shells that surround the seeds of these species are fused with the outer layer of the fruit and are dispersed as single units that resemble a seed and often have winged appendages. Examples of dry indehiscent fruits include achenes (figure 8.6A), schizocarps (figure 8.6B), nuts (figure 8.6C), and samaras (figure 8.6D). Some pods and capsules do not open at maturity and are basically handled as indehiscent fruits (figure 8.6E). Fleshy fruits are those where the tissue of the ovary is strongly differentiated. The pericarp is the part of a fruit formed by ripening of the ovary wall. It is organized into three layers: the skin (exocarp), the typically fleshy middle (mesocarp), and the membranous or stony inner layer (endocarp). These layers may become skin-like and leathery, fleshy, or stringy during development. Fleshy fruits such as berries, drupes, and pomes are indehiscent. Berries contain a fleshy pericarp with many seeds (figure 8.7A) while drupes have a tough stony endocarp (known as the stone or pit) that encloses only one seed (figure 8.7B). Furthermore, some fruits are known as aggregate fruits, as seen in *Ficus*, *Annona*, and *Morinda*, which grow in a cluster of multiple fruits developed from a single flower and bear one seed each (figure 8.7C).

Seed Longevity

Concerning longevity, seeds can generally be classified into four groups: viviparous, recalcitrant, intermediate, and orthodox. Viviparous seeds are those that germinate before they are dispersed from the plant. The most common examples are some species of mangroves such as *Avicennia* and *Rhizophora* (figure 8.8A) and some tropical legumes (figure 8.8B).

Recalcitrant seeds only retain viability for a few days, weeks, or months. Most tree species from the humid tropics, where rainfall is distributed on a relatively even basis throughout the year, have recalcitrant seeds (Vozzo 2002). In general, large-seeded species that drop moist from perennial plants in moist habitats are most likely recalcitrant (Hong and Ellis 1996) (figure 8.8C). Recalcitrant species are usually sown in the nursery immediately after collection.

Intermediate seeds are those that can withstand some degree of desiccation and storage at low temperatures, but they cannot tolerate freezing. Papaya has been stored suc-

Figure 8.4—*Examples of flowers: Perfect bisexual flower of Hawaiian kokia (Kokia drynarioides) (A). Imperfect male (B) and female (C) flowers can occur on the same monoecious plant, as with* Artocarpus *species; imperfect dioecious flowers borne on separate plants of* Dodonaea viscosa: *male flowers (D), female flowers (E), mature seed capsules on a female plant (F). Photo A by Tara Luna, photos B, C, D, and E by Gerald D. Carr, and photo F by C.H. Lamoureux, courtesy of Gerald D. Carr.*

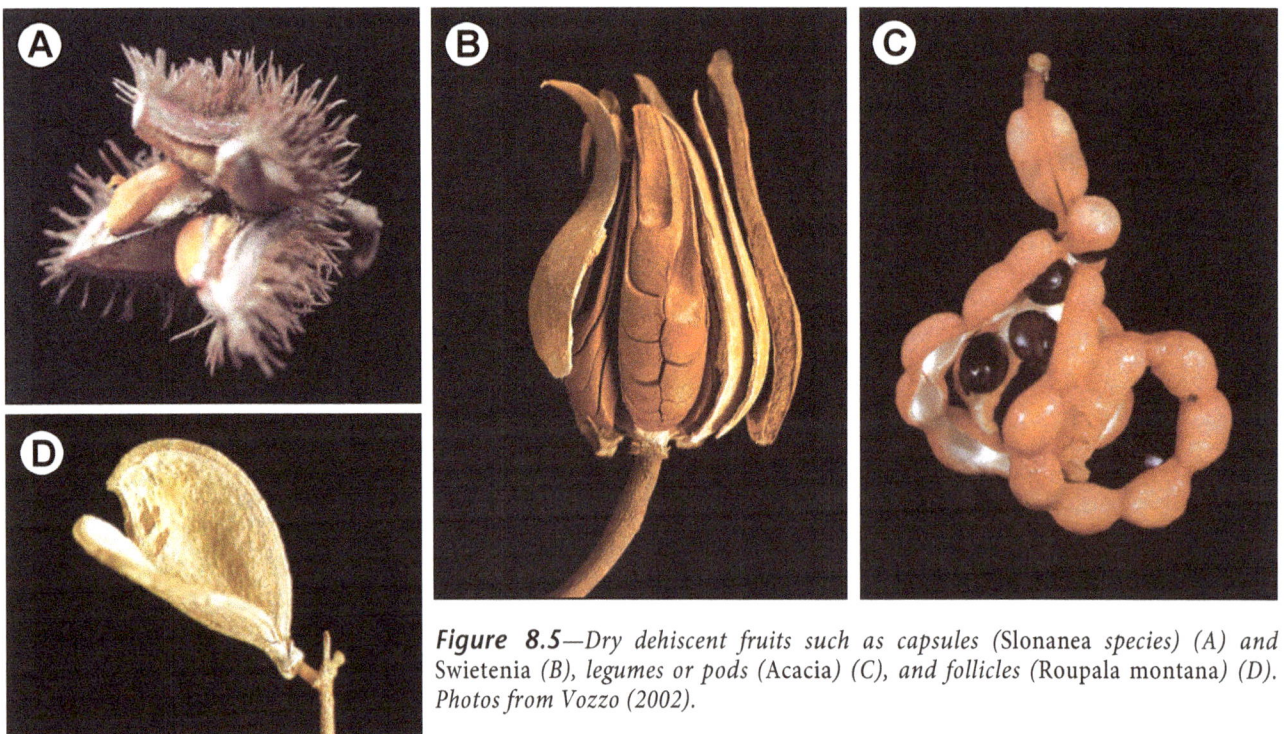

Figure 8.5—*Dry dehiscent fruits such as capsules (Slonanea species) (A) and Swietenia (B), legumes or pods (Acacia) (C), and follicles (Roupala montana) (D). Photos from Vozzo (2002).*

Figure 8.6—Dry indehiscent fruits—such as achenes (Asteraceae) (A), schizocarps (Hura crepitans) (B), nuts (Quercus) (C), and samaras (Terminalia) (D)—are actually a single unit where the fruit wall is fused to the seed. Some pods containing free seeds can also be indehiscent, while others are late dehiscent (Dipteryx) (E). Photos A and C by Tara Luna, and photos B, D, and E from Vozzo (2002).

Figure 8.7—Berries contain numerous seeds per fruit (A) (Myrica species), while drupes usually contain one seed surrounded by a stony pit (B) (Citharexylum spinosum). Noni (Morinda citrifolia) is an example of an aggregate fruit (C). Photo A from Vozzo (2002), photo B by Brian F. Daley, and photo C by Thomas D. Landis.

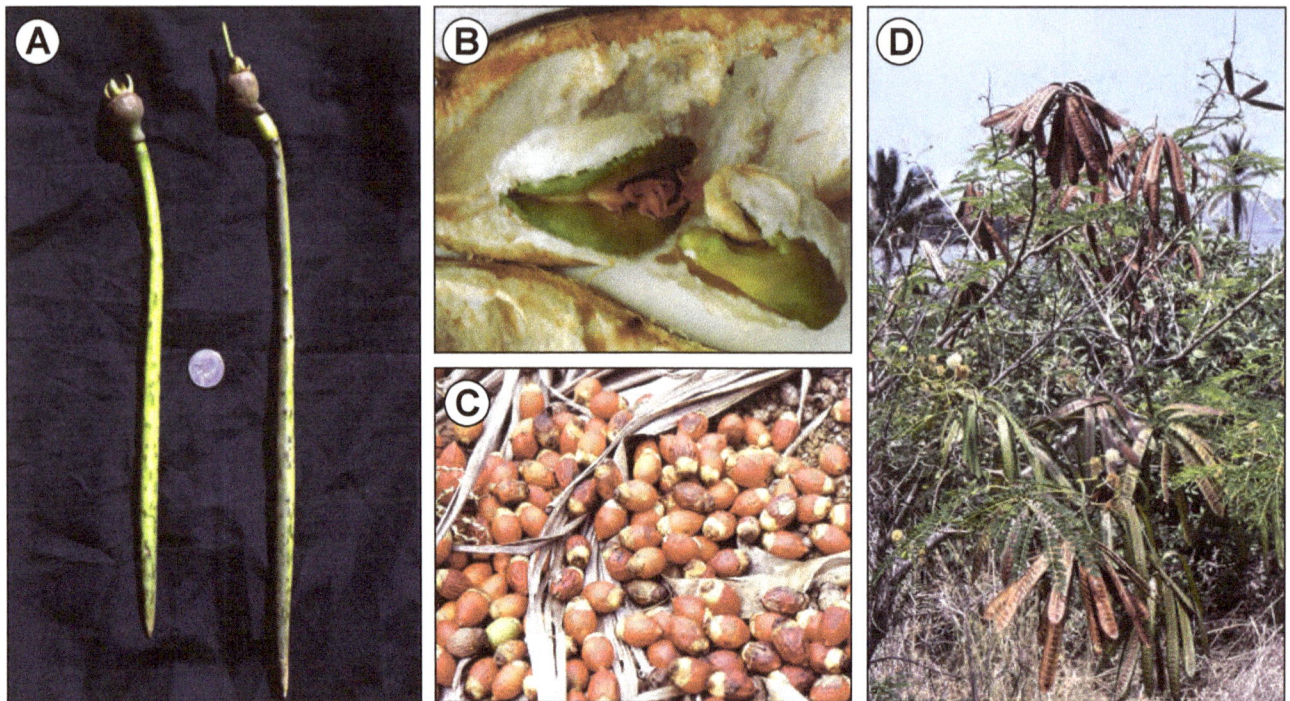

Figure 8.8—*Viviparous seeds germinate and develop into a propagule before they disperse as seen in some mangroves (A), or while still enclosed in the fruit in some tropical legumes (B). Recalcitrant seeds, like palms (C), need to be collected before they germinate or lose their viability. Orthodox seeds, such as* Leucaena *species (D), typically have hard seed coats. Photo A by Thomas D. Landis, photo B from Vozzo (2002), and photos C and D by Tara Luna.*

cessfully under conditions of 50-percent relative humidity with seeds dried to 10-percent moisture content for 6 years without affecting viability (Vozzo 2002). Other species that have shown intermediate storage behavior include neem, cinnamon, citrus, and coffee.

Orthodox seeds store easily for long periods of time because they tolerate desiccation. Tropical species that occur in areas of strong wet-dry seasonal cycles or semiarid environments along the coast often have orthodox seeds (figure 8.8D). In general, dry, hard seed coats and small seeds from dry, dehiscent fruits are most likely to be orthodox.

Collecting Seeds

Effective native seed collection involves a number of steps to ensure quality seeds are collected at the right stage. Proper seed collection requires the following practices:

- Locate populations of desired species before or during flowering.
- Investigate the viability of seeds after dispersal or maturation on a species-by-species basis.
- Monitor potential sites directly after flowering when fruits are becoming visible.
- Record the dates of flower, fruit, and cone formation. Cones are often a 2-year crop, so you can assess cone crop the year before collection.

- Observe carefully the weather patterns during pollination, fruit formation, and maturation.
- Visit the site frequently to monitor the development and quality of the seed crop.
- Use collection dates from previous years to predict target collection dates and other information.
- Use a cutting test of a few sample seeds to determine maturity before collection.
- Collect seeds during dry weather, if possible.

Selecting Locally Adapted, Genetically Diverse Seed Sources

The genetics discussion at the beginning of this chapter detailed essential elements of seed collection to ensure local adaptedness and genetic diversity. These elements include collecting from a minimum of 50 individuals; collecting from distant individuals to reduce the risk of collecting only close relatives; collecting equally and randomly across the population; and collecting throughout the seed dispersal season (BLM/SOS 2011) (figures 8.9A, 8.9B). Choosing a seed collection site is crucial to ensuring that locally adapted, genetically appropriate materials are planted. Within each species are genetic variations. Local populations of native plants have adapted to local climate, soils, elevation, precipitation, environmental stresses such as wind or drought, and other site conditions. Local native plant materials, collected from the same or similar habitats as the outplanting site, have been shown to perform better than nonlocal sources. Because seed zones have not been defined for most native tropical species, seed collectors must decide on a case-by-case basis what makes sense, considering climate, soil type, elevation, and other site conditions (Withrow-Robinson and Johnson 2006). Collectors should collect seeds from plants with high vigor and health. Collecting seeds from, and propagating, locally adapted plant sources improves not only survival and growth of the plants on the outplanting site, but also is important for the survival of native fauna, from insects to birds, that depend on these plants.

Selecting for Desired Characteristics

Tropical nurseries collect seeds for diverse clients and projects. Nursery-grown plants can be planted for many reasons: traditional uses, ornamental plantings, agroforestry, habitat restoration, silviculture, or a combination of these uses. Plants within a population can vary dramatically in their characteristics, such as the qualities, properties, and productivity of their fruit, wood, or medicinal products. For some projects, seed collectors may want to select for certain desired characteristics. Some of the desired characteristics (especially medicinal properties) may be difficult for seed collectors to discern. If in doubt, collectors can ask for help from end-users and clients to choose parent plants with preferred properties.

Seed selection may be for disease resistance. Depending on the disease vector, some plants showing obvious pest or disease problems may pass on that susceptibility to their offspring. Thriving local plants are excellent candidates as parents.

For plants with food, wood, fiber, or other uses, high productivity in terms of abundant fruit, nuts, foliage, or fast growth rate is often desired. Many native tropical species only produce large seed crops periodically. Heavy seed crops are often followed by light seed crops the following year. The interval between heavy seed bearing years is referred to as

Figure 8.9—*Good tree seed collection practices to maximize genetic diversity include collecting from individuals at least 150 feet (50 m) apart, collecting throughout the seed dispersal season, and collecting from throughout the canopy. Tools including pole pruners, ladders (A) and even equipment such as forklifts (B) are useful to help access the desired diversity. In addition to protecting genetic diversity, seed collection may involve selecting for certain desirable traits, such as the "canoe koa": straight-boled, healthy, large trees (C). Photo A by Thomas D. Landis, photo B by Clark Allred, and photo C by Craig R. Elevitch.*

periodicity. Depending on the goals of the project, collecting seeds across different periods may be advisable. For example, when restoring pollinator habitat or food for birds, continuity of supply even in sparse years is important.

For woody plants, growth form is also a key characteristic. For example, trees may range in form from small, multistemmed, shrubby individuals to large, straight-stemmed individuals. Depending on the preferred characteristics for the project needs, seed collectors can gather seeds from parents with the desired form. For example, in Hawai'i, the renaissance of traditional Hawaiian canoe culture has regenerated interest in the koa tree, a species that can range from shrubby and branchy to tall and straight in form. "Canoe koa," which are straight-boled, tall trees good for canoe making, are sought for some koa reforestation projects (figure 8.9C).

Choosing Quality Over Quantity When Collecting Seeds

Seed collecting is definitely an area where "quality over quantity" needs to be the standard to avoid perpetuating undesirable characteristics and eroding genetic diversity of the species. For example, sometimes plants produce high volumes of seed when they are stressed, diseased, or injured but those seeds may not be of high quality. Also, for tree seeds, it is much easier to collect from short, seedy, shrubby individuals than from tall, straight trees but collecting only from those easiest to reach results in less genetic diversity. For all plants, it is faster to collect from only a few individuals than to follow the recommendation to take small amounts from 50 or more individuals, but collecting with the goal of gathering the most seeds in the least amount of time is not an effective strategy. If working with contractors or nursery staff to collect seeds, it is recommended to pay collectors by the hour instead of by the pound, so that proper guidelines that ensure seed quality and protect genetic diversity are followed. The long-term ecological viability and future contribution of a planting is at stake.

Species Phenology

Monitoring species phenology (development throughout the season including flowering, fruiting and producing, and dropping leaves) is an important part of seed collection. Any observations may also provide clues on how to germinate the seeds. Good field experience has no substitute.

Be sure to record time and dates of flowering for each species. Flowering is easily observed in species with showy flowers but requires more attention for wind-pollinated species such as *Podocarpus* and *Terminalia*. Over time, recognizing the flowering sequence of the local flora enables staff to simplify the seed collection schedule by keying it to the flowering period of a few index species. Most developing fruits become visible only a few weeks after flowering and pollination. As you become familiar with the phenology of the species and local site conditions, you will be able to develop a seed collection schedule that is specific for your area.

Each species has its own flower and fruit arrangement, pollination strategy, and mode of seed dispersal. Some species will flower and fruit over an extended period of time while others will flower and fruit only once during a growing season. Different types of flower arrangements will have different blooming sequences. In tropical areas with a strong wet-dry seasonal cycle, most species will flower and fruit during defined periods. In tropical areas with an even distribution of rainfall, many species will flower and fruit irregularly throughout the year. These species produce several distinct fruit crops in 1 year within individual plants. For broad genetic representation, you will need to collect fruits from all periods of seed availability.

Fruits of many tropical species are available only for a short time after maturation. Some fleshy fruits can be picked before full maturation and ripened at the nursery without affecting seed viability. Other species will fail to ripen after they are detached from the tree. Collectors will also need to know how long the seeds of a species will remain viable on the ground. Collecting seeds from the ground needs to be timed correctly because a delay can result in loss of seed viability.

Often, a range of fruit maturity stages exists within a single plant. For example, some species have a flower stalk with a prolonged period of flowering and many different stages of fruit development. The seed collector will need to selectively harvest only the fully mature fruits and make repeated visits back to the collection site.

Be aware of the dispersal strategy of the species before attempting to collect seeds. Tropical fruits have developed many highly specialized strategies that aid in seed protection and seed dispersal away from the parent plant. Many species are dispersed by animals, including bats, monkeys, birds, and ants for which the fleshy fruits are food sources. Collectors need to time their collection before the fruit is consumed; in some cases, it may be necessary to bag or cage fruits to obtain seeds. Remember seed collection ethics and be sure to leave enough food for the native animals when collecting seeds.

Wind dispersal is very common for many tropical species. Seeds and fruits can have air-filled cavities, hairlike coverings, and various kinds of wings or parachutes (figure 8.10). Collectors need to time collection before seed dispersal and before windy days.

Some species such as *Cassia* and *Mimosa* disperse by force upon maturation. In these cases, you may need to bag the

Figure 8.10—Species that are wind dispersed must be collected as soon as they are mature. Shown: Heliocarpus appendiculatus. *Photo from of Vozzo (2002).*

developing fruits with cloth to capture the seeds (figure 8.11). Use a fine mesh cloth with a weave that allows light transmission but is small enough to prevent the seeds from falling through the cloth. Tie the bags over developing seed stalks so seeds will be captured when they are dispersed by force.

Factors Affecting Seed Formation and Collection Timing

Environmental conditions can be either beneficial or detrimental to flowering and seed development. For example, drought and high temperatures may promote flowering, but prolonged moisture stress may cause plants to abort developing fruits and seeds or to have poor seed viability. Perform a cutting test on seeds directly before collection, as described in the following section.

Elevation, latitude, and aspect affect seed maturation because it is temperature dependent. Populations found on open, sun-facing slopes (south-facing north of the equator, north-facing south of the equator) will mature sooner than those on protected, shade-facing slopes. Low-elevation populations usually mature first, and seed collectors can follow seed maturity up slope with increasing elevation. Collectors should use favorable microenvironments to their advantage. For example, populations growing in full sunlight tend to produce more seeds than those that are heavily shaded. Plants growing on moist and nutrient rich soils will produce more and healthier seeds. Sites intensely browsed by livestock are poor choices for seed collection because animals often consume the current season's growth, which limits flowering and seed production. Wildlife can quickly eliminate a maturing seed crop, and collectors may need to bag

or cage developing fruits. Certain insects and fungi may also consume seeds. Fruits or seeds that have small exit holes, are discolored, or are misshapen must be avoided.

Ensuring That Seeds Are Healthy

The easiest way to ensure that seeds are healthy and ready for harvest is to use a cut test. A cut test allows you to inspect for mature, abnormal, infested, or empty seeds. Several seeds from several individuals within the population need to be examined. The two essential tools are a hand lens and a safety razor, knife, or scalpel for cutting. With care, cut the fruit or seed along its longest axis. Inspect the seeds for their internal coloring, how completely the internal tissue fills the seed coat cavity, and for the presence of an embryo. Depending on species, the embryo may completely fill the cavity or be tiny and embedded in the endosperm. (A microscope may be needed for examining very small-seeded species.) If the seed coat is soft and the contents are watery and soft, the seed is immature. If the seed coat is hard and the contents are firm and light tan to white in color, the seed

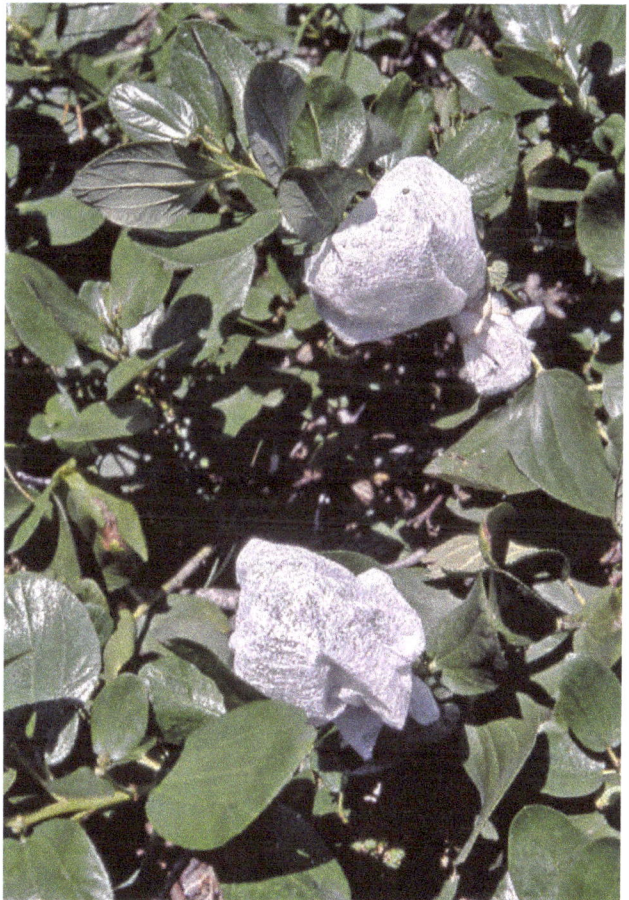

Figure 8.11—Seeds that disseminate by force with explosive capsules are best collected by tying mesh bags over the developing fruits. Photo by Tara Luna.

is approaching maturity or is fully mature. Some species can be collected just before maturity if the entire inflorescence is cut and the seeds are allowed to cure properly before cleaning. In general, the optimum time for seed collection is when fruits are splitting open at the top.

Seed Collection Methods

The choice of seed collection method depends on the species to be collected. Some general collection methods include hand picking or hand stripping, collecting by hand from the ground after seeds have fallen, cutting fruit clusters, raking or shaking branches over a canvas tarp, bagging or caging developing fruits or cones, and tying canvas tarps between large woody plants. The following tools and supplies are useful when collecting seeds from natural stands:

- Labels, permanent markers, pencils, and seed collection forms to attach to bags.
- Scissors, pruning shears, and extendible pruning poles, or safety and tree climbing gear for taller trees.
- Hand lens to examine seeds to ensure they are full.
- Safety razor blades or sharp pocketknife for the cutting test of seeds and to examine fruits.
- Large paper bags for dry fruits.
- White plastic bags for fleshy fruits.
- Canvas tarps for collecting fruits from the ground.
- Hand gloves.
- Wooden trays for collecting seeds of low-growing plants.
- A storage box or cooler to keep collections from being overheated during transport.
- Binoculars for spotting fruits in taller trees.
- Fine mesh bags, cages, fine mesh cloth, and rubber bands for species with rapid dispersal.

Purchasing Seeds From a Reputable Source

Collecting yourself or contracting seed collection according to your specifications is the best way to ensure you get locally adapted, genetically diverse sources. Sometimes, however, you may need to buy seeds. If purchasing from a seed supplier without overseeing collection practices, it is best to ask what sources the company has available, rather than asking for a particular source—unscrupulous suppliers may claim to have exactly what you want. If you cannot locate a suitable source of seeds for purchase, it is best to collect your own. If your seed suppliers are willing

and able to collect to your specifications, have them follow the guidelines provided in this chapter.

Purchased seeds must be of a high quality and free of weeds. When purchasing seeds, obtain and keep a certificate of the seed analysis for each seedlot. The seed analysis must have the scientific name of the species, cultivated variety (if applicable), origin of the seeds, an estimate of viability, the percentage of pure live seeds (PLS—discussed in the following section under Seed Testing), and the percentage of other crop seeds, weed seeds, and inert material. Purchase only seeds with high PLS values and very low percentages of weed seeds and other inert materials. It is often a good idea to ask about where the seeds were collected and to determine what weeds may be present in the seedlot.

Processing Seeds

The way in which seeds and fruits are handled during collection, temporary storage, postharvest handling, and cleaning can directly affect seed quality, viability, and storage life. Proper processing of fruits and seeds begins the moment the fruit or seed is removed from the parent plant. Proper processing includes short-term handling from the field back to the nursery, temporary storage at the nursery, and prompt and proper seed extraction if necessary. This step is followed by prompt and proper planting in the nursery (recalcitrant and orthodox seeds) or preparation for long-term storage (orthodox seeds).

In general, it is best to transport material from the field to the nursery as quickly as possible, avoiding exposure to direct sun, high temperatures, and physical abuse. Dry fruits, seeds, and cones can be left inside their paper collection bags for short durations. Placing plastic bags filled with fleshy fruits inside coolers will help prevent them from fermenting and being damaged by subsequent high temperatures.

Seed cleaning is necessary before sowing or long-term storage. In some cases, seeds will germinate slowly, or not at all, if they are not removed from the fruits.

Most tropical nurseries deal with small seedlots. Seed cleaning and processing can be laborious and time consuming, and specialized cleaning equipment can be expensive. A variety of inexpensive, low-tech methods and devices are easy to use, readily available, and work very well with a variety of fruit types. Some are described in the following sections. Whichever method of cleaning you choose, the seed cleaning area of the nursery needs to be well ventilated. Some fruits can cause allergic reactions, and fine dust can irritate skin, eyes, and lungs. It is important to wear gloves and dust masks during cleaning and to wash your hands afterward.

Recalcitrant Seeds

Recalcitrant seeds cannot withstand drying below a critical moisture level, so they are usually sown immediately after processing. During temporary storage before sowing, seeds must be kept fully hydrated by keeping them in trays under moist burlap or in plastic bags filled with moistened sand or peat moss in a shaded area with relatively cool temperatures. Relative humidity needs to be maintained at 80 to 90 percent.

Many species with recalcitrant seeds can be collected quite cleanly and are sown immediately without further cleaning. Others need additional cleaning that is typically accomplished by flotation in water. Immediately after collection, seeds are placed in a bucket of water. In general, the viable seeds sink whereas the nonviable seeds, trash, and debris float. As a side benefit, the soaking helps keep the seeds hydrated until they are sown. If seeds or fruits are collected from very dry ground, viable seeds may also temporarily float—a longer soak duration, perhaps even overnight, may be necessary to allow enough time for good seeds and fruits to hydrate and sink. Do a cut test to fine-tune this procedure.

Dry Fruits and Cones With Intermediate or Orthodox Seeds

After they arrive at the nursery, small quantities of dry fruits and cones can be dried in paper bags or envelopes as long as the contents are loose. Large quantities must be dried immediately by spreading the material evenly on a tarp or drying rack. A drying rack consisting of a simple wooden frame with multiple screens can be constructed at low cost and will make efficient use of space in a seed-drying room or greenhouse (figure 8.12). Drying racks can be made with mesh screens having fine holes that allow air movement but prevent seed loss. Different mesh screens will be necessary for different seed sizes. The materials will need to be turned several times per day to prevent it from becoming too hot, drying unevenly, or becoming moldy. Dry, dehiscent fruits, should also be covered with a fine mesh cloth as well to prevent the loss of seeds after fruits open. Good air movement, low relative humidity, and temperatures between 65 to 80 °F (18 to 27 °C) promote even drying and eliminate moisture buildup that can cause mold and damaging temperature. A ventilated greenhouse or storage shed works well for this purpose. Temperature control is very important; use a shade cloth to keep temperatures from rising too high. Avoid rewetting dry fruits after collection. Also, make sure to exclude animals from your seed-drying area.

Separating seeds from dry, dehiscent fruits is usually easy because the fruits split open at maturity. Shaking the fruit inside paper bags so that the seeds fall out will readily separate small lots of seeds and the woody capsules can then be removed from the bag. Modified kitchen blenders with rubber-coated blades are very useful for cleaning small lots of dry fruits (Thomas 2003). The ideal amount of dry fruit material to place in a blender varies with its size, but one-fourth to one-third of storage capacity of the blender works well (Scianna 2004).

Screening is the easiest way to separate extracted seeds from debris such as dry leaves, wings, and small pieces of dried fruits. Screens can be constructed of hardware cloth and wooden frames. Commercial screens are also available in a range of sizes (figure 8.13A). At least two screen sizes

Figure 8.12—Orthodox seeds require protection from wind during drying (A) and good ventilation to prevent mold development during post harvest handling and drying (B and C). Photos by Thomas D. Landis.

Figure 8.13—*Screens are used to separate large debris and fine chaff from the seeds and are available commercially in a wide range of screen holes sizes to compliment any species (A). Seeds of many species are very small and require fine screens or sieves for cleaning (B). Photo A by Tara Luna, and photo B by Thomas D. Landis.*

are needed. The top screen has openings large enough to allow the fruits and seeds to pass through, and the bottom screen has smaller openings that allow fine chaff, but not the seeds, to pass through. By placing the collected material on the top screen and shaking, most of the debris can be removed. When separating other small-seeded plants, such as sedges, rushes, and other tropical herbaceous species, you will need screens with very fine mesh or kitchen sieves to properly separate seeds from other debris (figure 8.13B).

If you are cleaning large, tough, leathery pods, you may need pliers, hammers, vices, or screwdrivers. Seeds that are contained in tough woody capsules can be extracted by heating the capsules in ovens or exposing them to fire in a portable barbecue grill. The heat treatment causes the pods to become brittle, which aids in the extraction of the seeds using hand tools. When using fire or heat and hand tools, be certain to not damage the seeds. By simply immersing them in water to separate fine chaff and other impurities, species with hard seed coats can be cleaned.

Conifer cones, after the scales open, can be placed in sack and shaken by hand or tumbled in a wire cage to dislodge seeds from the cone scales. Serotinous cones, such as those found on some tropical pines, require exposure to heat before the scales open. Cones need to be exposed to 170° F (77° C) temperatures by placing the cones in ovens for a period of a few minutes to a few hours or by dipping them in hot water for a few minutes. If an oven is used, cones will need to be checked frequently during drying and removed when most have opened enough to allow the extraction of seeds. If the cones are dipped in hot water, the combination of heat and drying after the soak needs to be sufficient to open them. Most tropical conifer seeds are dewinged before sowing, which can be done by filling a burlap or cloth sack one-fourth full, tying or folding it

shut, and gently kneading the seeds by squeezing and rubbing from outside the sack for a few minutes to detach the wings (figure 8.14). Repeat the screening process again with a mesh size that retains seeds but allows the smallest debris to pass through (Dumroese and others 1998). This method can be used on other winged tropical seeds as long as it does not damage the seeds. In cases where damage is a possibility, seeds are not dewinged and are planted as an intact unit.

The final step is fanning or winnowing, which separates detached wings, hollow seeds, and seed-sized impurities from good seeds (figure 8.15). When seeds are poured slowly in front of a small electric fan, they separate according to weight

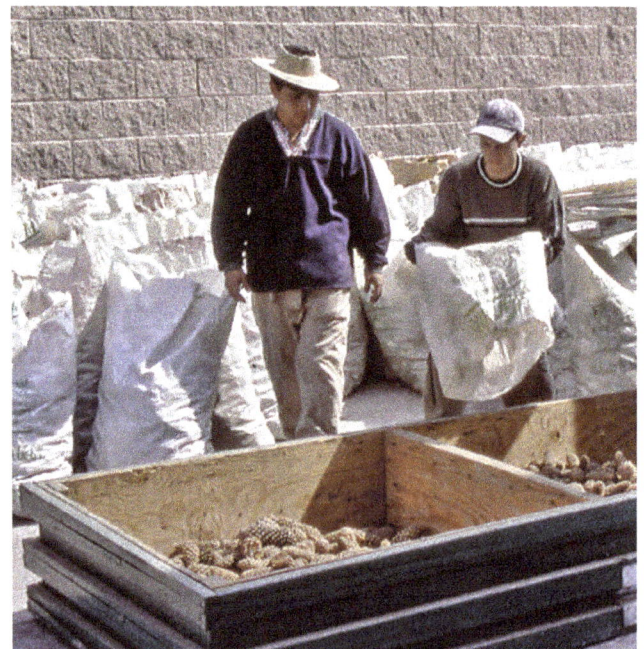

Figure 8.14—*Conifer seeds are dewinged before sowing by gently kneading them in a cloth or burlap sack. Photo by Thomas D. Landis.*

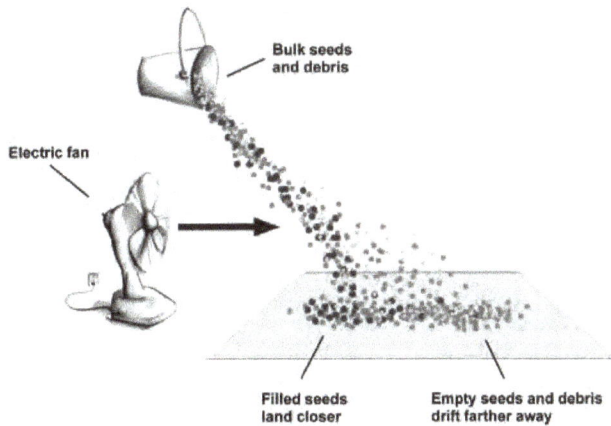

Figure 8.15—Use a small fan to winnow empty seeds and wings from filled seeds. The heavier filled seeds will land closer to the fan while lighter, empty seeds will land farther away. Illustration from Dumroese and others (1998).

from the base of the fan. Most heavy, sound seeds will come to rest near the base of the fan while hollow seeds, wings, and lighter impurities will tend to blow farther away. Moving from the fan outward, periodically collect a small sample of seeds and cut them in half to check for soundness, determining where the hollow seeds are and discarding them. All species will probably require several successive separations to obtain a desired degree of seed purity. A good target for most species is 90 percent or more sound seeds (Dumroese and others 1998).

Fleshy Fruits and Cones

Fleshy fruits and cones are very susceptible to fermentation, mummification, excessive heating, or microbial infestation, all of which can damage seeds. On the other hand, it is important not to let the fruits dry out because it can make cleaning them much more difficult. The best procedure is to temporarily store fleshy fruits in white plastic bags in a cool place or refrigerator until the seeds can be processed.

Seeds in fleshy fruits need to be processed shortly after collection. The first step in cleaning is to soak fleshy fruits in water to soften the pulp. The soak may need to last a few hours to a few days, depending on the species, and the water needs to be changed every few hours. After the pulp is soft, flesh can be removed by hand squeezing or mashing using a wooden block, rolling pin, or other device. The flesh can also be removed by wet screening, which involves hand-rubbing the fruits against screens using a steady stream of water to eliminate the pulp (figure 8.16). This method is used for most large fleshy tropical fruits. Another useful tool that can be used for small lots of fleshy fruits is the common kitchen blender or food processor with modified blades. Modified kitchen blenders can be used for small lots of

fleshy and dry fruits after the impeller blades are coated with rubberized plastic coating (the material used to coat hand-tool handles) to prevent damage to the seeds (figure 8.17) (Thomas 2003). Run them for about 1 minute to produce a puree of fruit and seeds. The puree should be placed in a bucket and water added slowly and continually resulting in most of the debris floating off and leaving clean seeds at the bottom of the bucket (Truscott 2004). Small, hobby-size rock tumblers (figure 8.18) are also useful for cleaning small fleshy fruits or removing barbs or other appendages from seeds and fruits. Wet tumbling uses pea gravel or crushed stones and water in a

Figure 8.16—Easily clean fleshy fruits by using a simple mesh cloth and running water to remove pulp from seeds (A). Ripe fruit from coco plum or icaco (Chrysobalanus icaco), a coastal shrub native to Puerto Rico and the U.S. Virgin Islands, has the stringy flesh removed, leaving cleaned seeds ready for storage (B). Photo A by Thomas D. Landis, and photo B by Brian F. Daley.

Figure 8.17—*Modifying kitchen blender blades by using rubber coating allows the grower to clean small lots of dry and fleshy fruits without damaging the seeds. Photo by R. Kasten Dumroese.*

Figure 8.18—*A small hobby-size rock tumbler can be used to clean dry fruits with hard-to-remove appendages or fleshy fruits. Photos by Tara Luna.*

rubber-lined tumbler vessel. Add only enough water to make a slurry from the gravel and fruit. The tumbler can be run overnight and checked the following day. After a course of tumbling, the contents are dumped into a sieve and the pulp or debris is washed off, leaving clean seeds (Dreesen 2004).

If fleshy fruits of species with dormant seeds are being cleaned, they need to be washed with water to remove any remaining pulp and dried for several days before storage.

Seed Testing

After seeds are cleaned, it is a good idea to determine their quality by testing seed viability, seed germination, or both. Seed viability tests estimate the potential for seeds to germinate and grow, whereas seed germination tests measure the actual germination percentage and rate. For seeds you are purchasing or selling commercially, you may also want to know the percentage of pure live seeds (PLS.)

Seed Viability Tests

Cutting tests, described previously, are the simplest seed viability tests and are usually performed during seed collection and often just before treating seeds for sowing. Cutting tests should also be performed on seedlots that have been stored for a long time to visually assess their condition. Cutting tests can reveal whether or not the seed is healthy, but really cannot determine anything about the potential for germination. A better test is the tetrazolium (TZ) test, a biochemical method in which seed viability is determined by a color change that occurs when particular seed enzymes react with a solution of triphenyltetrazolium chloride. Living tissue changes to red, while nonliving tissue remains uncolored (figure 8.19). The reaction takes place both with dormant and nondormant seeds, and results can be obtained within a couple of hours. Although the TZ test is easy to do, interpretation of results requires experience. For this reason,

some larger nurseries or nurseries that also sell seeds send seed samples to seed analysts that have the necessary laboratory equipment and experience for testing. A third test is an excised embryo test. Embryos are carefully removed from seeds and allowed to grow independent of the seed tissue. Seeds often must be soaked for several days to remove hard seed coats, and excision of the embryo is an exacting procedure that normally requires the aid of a microscope. As when doing TZ testing, most nurseries send their seed samples to seed analysts for excised embryo testing.

Germination Tests

A seed germination test determines both germination rate and total germination percentage, and is used to determine sowing rates so seeds are used efficiently (figure 8.20). The germination rate indicates how promptly seeds germinate, whereas germination percentage indicates what proportion of the seeds eventually germinate. Germination tests are used to determine how many seeds to sow per container and how long you can expect seeds will continue to germinate after sowing. See Chapter 9, Seed Germination and Sowing Options, for details about sowing rates and methods.

Figure 8.19—*Tetrazolium (TZ) tests stain living tissue red and can be used to estimate seed viability of a seedlot. Shown in this figure (left to right): dead embryo, damaged embryo, and healthy seed. From Stein and others (1986).*

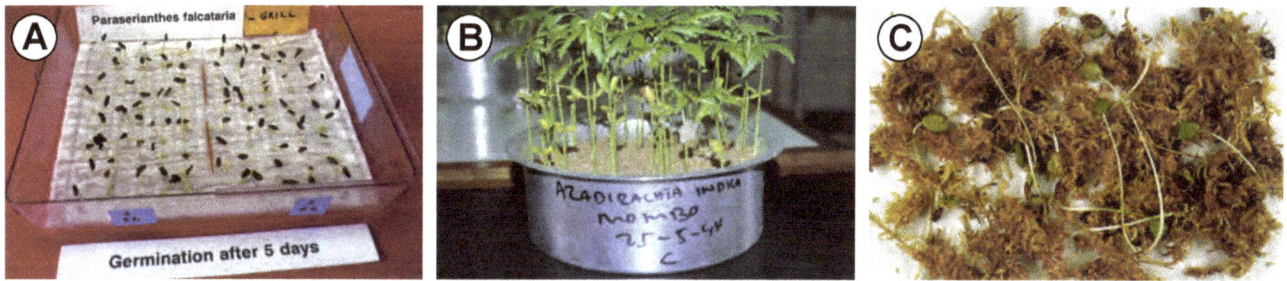

Figure 8.20—*Paper towels (A), sterile sand (B), and* Sphagnum *(C) are suitable substrates for germination testing. Photos from Vozzo (2002).*

If the species being tested has some type of seed dormancy, an appropriate treatment to remove dormancy will be needed before the germination test. Many nurseries will test dormant seedlots before and after the dormancy treatment to check its effectiveness. Actual germination in the nursery may vary greatly because of the inherent variability of germination in most plant species and differences in the environmental conditions during testing and growing at the nursery.

Use the following steps to conduct a germination test:

- Select an area in the greenhouse or office that can be kept clean.

- Line the bottom of plastic trays, Petri dishes, or similar containers with paper towels. For large-seeded species, line the bottom with moist sterile sand (bake sand in the oven at 212 °F [100 °C] for at least 1 hour to sterilize it) or unmilled *Sphagnum* moss.

- Moisten the paper towels or other substrate with distilled water.

- Remove equally sized seed samples from each container of the same seedlot, or, if only one container exists from the seedlot, remove the seeds from different portions of the container. Mix these samples together to form a representative sample (figure 8.21).

- From the sample, make 4 replicates of 100 seeds and spread each replicate onto the moist substrate in a container. The containers may be covered to reduce evaporation from the substrate.

- Use distilled water to remoisten the substrate as necessary, but never allow standing water to remain in the container.

- Place the containers under optimum germination conditions—ideally those in which light, temperature, and humidity can be controlled. Conditions similar to the nursery will yield more meaningful results.

- Count the number of germinants on a daily or weekly basis for up to 4 weeks on herbaceous species and up to 3 months on woody species. Uniformity of germination timing may be advantageous, but be sure you do not exclude healthy seeds that simply germinate more slowly from the genetic pool for that species.

Percentage of Pure Live Seed

The percentage of pure live seed (PLS) is a seed quality index that can be calculated during seed testing (figure 8.22). When seeds are bought or sold, it is important to know the seeds have high PLS values and very low percentages of weed seeds and other inert materials. It is often a

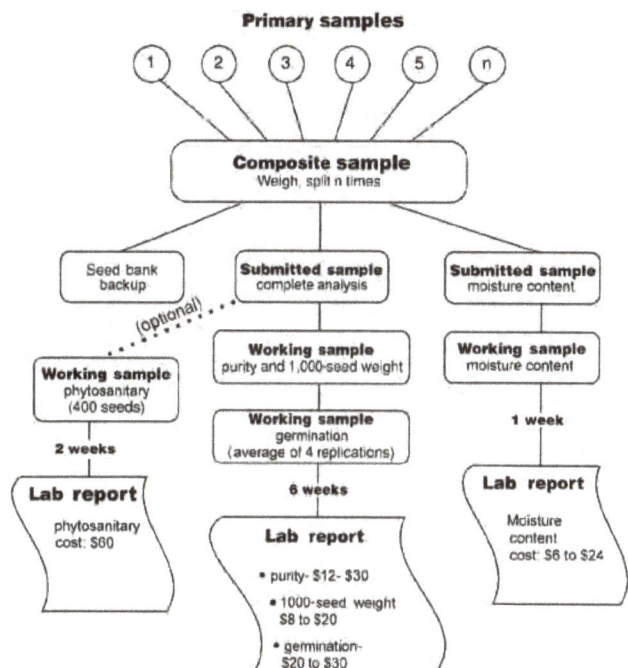

Figure 8.21—*Test seeds by collecting primary samples from an entire seedlot to make up a composite sample. The composite sample is further divided into samples tested at the nursery or submitted to a seed laboratory for testing. Illustration from Dumroese and others (2008).*

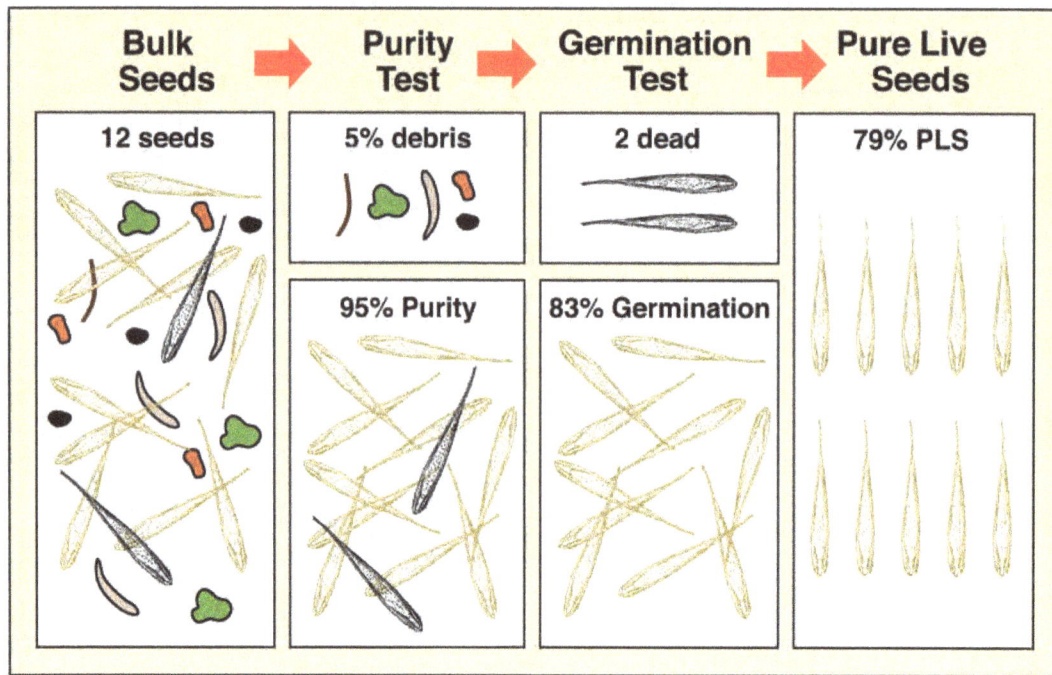

Figure 8.22—*Pure live seeds (PLS) is the percentage of the bulk seed weight that is composed of viable seeds. In this example, results of a purity test show 95 percent of the bulk weight is composed of seeds. The subsequent germination test indicates that 83 percent of the seeds germinated. Multiplying percentage purity by percentage germination yields 79 percent PLS. Illustration from Steinfeld and others (2007).*

good idea to ask about where the seed was collected and to determine what weeds may be present in the seedlot.

Storing Seeds

It can be quite beneficial to store seeds, especially for those species that yield seeds irregularly or to take advantage of a bumper crop of seeds. In addition, long-term seed storage is an important conservation method for threatened and endangered species. For proper seed storage, seeds must be mature and free of mechanical injury. The viability of seeds after storage depends on their viability at harvest, how they were handled during processing before storage, and storage conditions. Even under the best conditions, seeds degrade—the degree of longevity varies by species.

Storage Methods for Recalcitrant Seeds

As previously discussed, recalcitrant seeds of tropical species only retain viability for a short time; they are usually stored only temporarily before sowing. Some nut-bearing species, however, can be stored for a few months as long as seeds retain high moisture content (35 to 50 percent) under high relative humidity with good ventilation at cool temperatures. Recalcitrant seeds need to have constant gas exchange, so they are usually stored in unsealed containers in plastic bags filled with moist peat

moss in a cool place, such as in the refrigerator. Ideal temperature for recalcitrant seed storage must be determined on a species-by-species basis.

Because recalcitrant-seeded species are numerous and ecologically important in the tropics, nursery propagation efforts play a key role in conserving and restoring tropical recalcitrant species (Kettle and others 2011).

Storage Methods for Intermediate and Orthodox Seeds

Intermediate seeds can be stored if the proper storage conditions are provided and seeds are dried to the appropriate level of seed moisture content. The ideal seed-moisture content and storage temperature varies among tropical species, however. In general, dried intermediate seeds cannot be stored below 50 °F (10 °C).

In nature, orthodox seeds of most tropical species occur in areas with a distinct wet-dry seasonal cycle, arid beach strands, savannahs, or high-elevation environments (as seen in Hawai'i). For example, under proper storage conditions, the viability of *Acacia koa* seeds remained high after 25 years in storage (Young 1993). Orthodox seeds can be found in many tropical species within several families (Asteraceae, Brassicaceae, Chenopodiaceae, Combretaceae, Cucurbitaceae, Fabaceae, Lamiaceae, Poaceae, Rosaceae, Solanaceae, and Pinaceae). Species that produce achenes, many seeded berries, dry pods, follicles or capsules containing small seeds, or urticles, siliques, caryopses, or schizocarps tend to produce orthodox seeds (Hong and Ellis 1996, Vozzo 2002). Regardless, growers need to test freshly harvested orthodox seeds before long-term storage to develop a baseline germination percent.

After the seeds are clean, air-dry them in shallow trays for 2 to 4 weeks before storage to reduce the moisture content. Stir them once a week or often enough to prevent uneven drying. Storing orthodox seeds requires low relative humidity, low seed-moisture content, and cool temperatures (figure 8.23A). A small change in seed-moisture content has a large effect on the storage life of seeds. With most orthodox species, the proper seed-moisture content for storage is 6 to 10 percent. Small seedlots can be stored in sealed jars with rubber gaskets on the lids or envelopes kept in a sealed, thick-walled plastic tub with an airtight lid (figure 8.23B). Heat-sealed plastic pouches used for food are effective and can be resealed as needed (figure 8.23C). An electronic moisture meter can be used to measure seed-moisture content and is available from several suppliers (figure 8.23D).

Three seed storage methods are used by small tropical nurseries: room temperature storage, refrigeration, and in some rare cases, freezing. If cooler or freezer storage is being used and long power outages could occur, consider using a backup power supply; short-term fluctuations are generally not a problem.

Although orthodox seeds can be stored at room temperature, they will deteriorate faster than those stored at low temperatures. Room temperature storage should only be used when seedlots are held for a short time. Seed moisture content during room storage needs to be at the low end of the range—6 to 8 percent. Seeds must be placed in airtight containers and stored in a room or area with low relative humidity. This storage method works best in the more arid portions of the tropics.

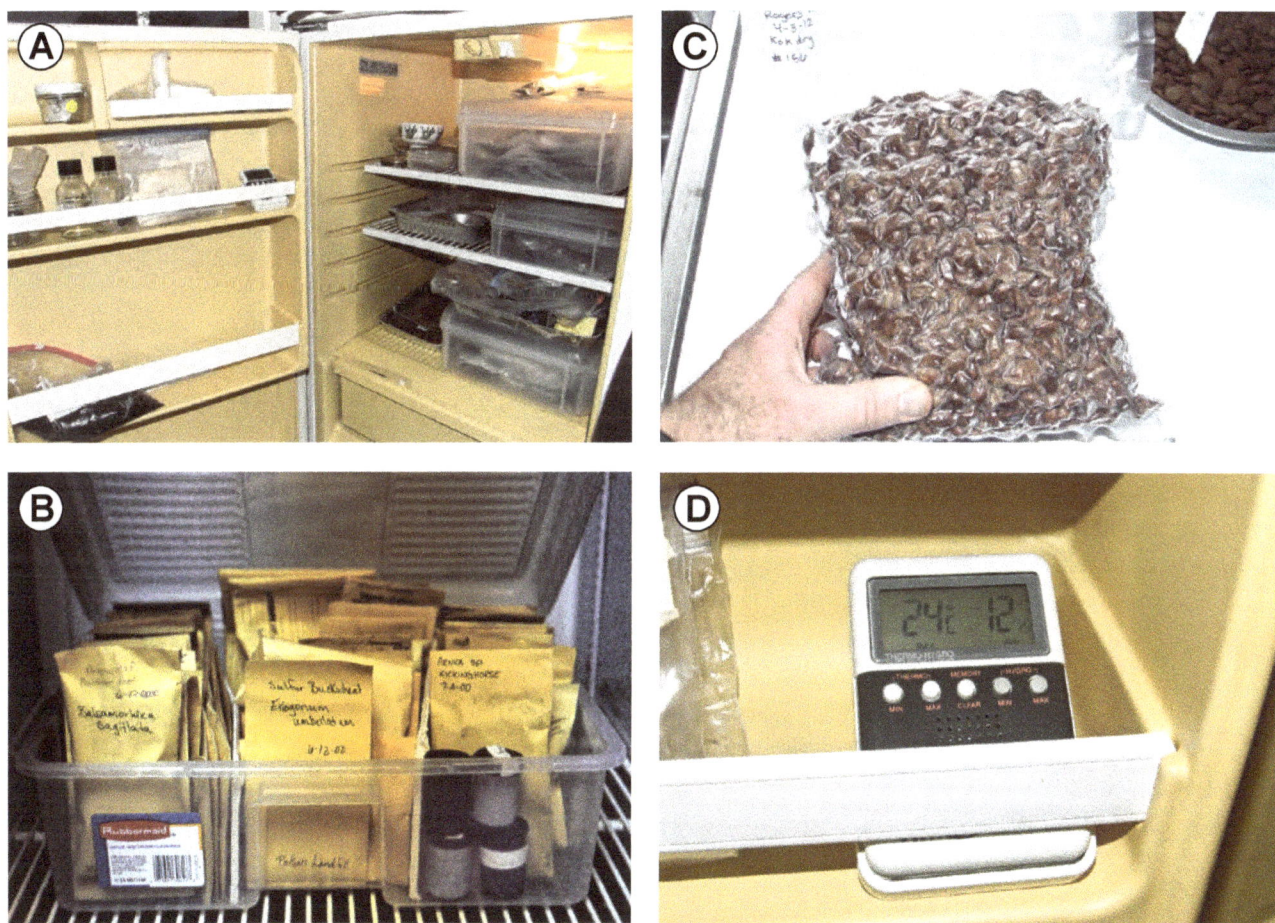

Figure 8.23—*Orthodox seeds need to be properly dried before storage and kept in moisture-proof containers under cool conditions with low humidity, such as in a refrigerator at the Hawai'i Island Seed Bank (A). Each seedlot should be labeled noting origin, date, and the viability percentage. Small lots can be stored in envelopes as long as they are kept in a moisture proof container (B) or in plastic pouches (C). An electronic meter measures temperature and moisture (D). Photos A, C, and D by J.B. Friday, courtesy of Jill Wagner and the Hawai'i Island Seed Bank, and photo B by Tara Luna.*

Orthodox seeds of many tropical species can be stored in a refrigerator at temperatures above freezing. Seeds need to be placed in an airtight container and kept at 38 to 41 °F (3 to 5 °C) in a self-defrosting refrigerator that maintains relative humidity between 10 to 40 percent. If the door is rarely opened, the humidity in a self-defrosting unit will maintain low relative humidity levels.

Very few tropical species will tolerate freezing—for those that do, dry seeds until the seed-moisture content is low and place them in airtight containers. When removing frozen seeds from the freezer, allow the container to reach room temperature before opening it. This practice prevents water condensation from forming on seeds.

Silica gels, available from hobby shops and florists, can be used to maintain low seed-moisture content with seeds that have been properly dried before storage. Silica gels have been used on short-lived native grass seeds placed into long-term storage to enhance longevity and should be tried with other short-lived seeds of native species (Dremann 2003). A general rule is to pour a teaspoon (about 5 ml) of silica gel into a paper envelope and place it with the seeds inside a tightly sealed jar for every 2 ounces (57 g) of seeds that need to be stored. The silica gel will remove water vapor and ensure that seeds remain at the proper storage moisture. To recharge them, the gels can be baked in an oven (150 °F [66 °C]) for 1 hour or so.

Sowing Seeds After Long-term Storage

In some cases, absorbing water too quickly may damage seeds of large-seeded species that have been dried to low-moisture levels. Therefore, when rehydrating these seeds, remove them from storage and spread them evenly in a sealed plastic tub. Place moistened paper towels in the tub so that the towels do not touch the seeds directly. Water vapor released from the towels will be slowly absorbed by the seeds; after a couple of days, the seeds will be able to handle water uptake without injury.

References

Dawson, I.; Were, J. 1997. Collecting germplasm from trees—some guidelines. Agroforestry Today. 9(2): 6–9.

Dremann, C. 2003. Observations on *Bromus carinatus* and *Elymus glaucus* seed storage and longevity. Native Plants Journal 4:61-64.

Dreesen, D. 2004. Tumbling for seed cleaning and conditioning. Native Plants Journal. 5: 52–54.

Dumroese, R.K.; Landis, T.D.; Wenny, D.L. 1998. Raising forest tree seedlings at home: simple methods for growing conifers of the Pacific Northwest from seeds. Moscow, ID: Idaho Forest, Wildlife and Range Experiment Station. 56 p.

Dumroese, R.K.; Luna, T.; Landis, T.D. 2008. Nursery manual for native plants: volume 1, a guide for tribal nurseries. Agriculture

---

Seeds Are a Link Between the Evolutionary Processes of the Past and the Potential for Future Adaptation
(Adapted from Flores 2002: 14–15)

"The genotype of a tree seed is the result of the evolutionary forces operating on the species for centuries. It is adapted to the present environmental conditions, but not to those of the future, especially when environmental conditions are being drastically modified by accelerated global change...The genetic combinations able to survive through environmental changes have intrinsic value.

Seed germination is influenced by the environmental conditions during seed development and maturation while on the parent tree. Day length, temperature, parental photothermic environment, light quality, and elevation are factors that significantly influence germination capacity. Additional factors include the inflorescence position on the parent tree, seed position in the fruit or infrutescence, and parent tree age during floral induction. These factors, plus others, explain the strong variation found in seed parameters (weight, color, water content, germinabilty) among seed groups and among seeds in the same group.

To most people, the concept of "seed" is deceptively simple. It is compared with a pill, isolated from the environmental effects, replicated many times, and capable of producing a plant. A seed is attached to a long and complex evolutionary and physiological history, however, and it is also conditioned to the variations of a long and complex future. The study of seeds has many facets and should not be limited to collection, storage, and sowing of this year's crop."

Handbook 730. Washington, DC: U.S. Department of Agriculture, Forest Service. 302 p.

Flores, E.M. 2002. Seed biology. In: Vozzo, J.A., ed. The tropical tree seed manual. Agriculture Handbook 721. Washington, DC: U.S. Department of Agriculture, Forest Service. 13–118.

Hong, T.D.; Ellis, R.H. 1996. A protocol to determine seed storage behavior. International Plant Genetic Resources Institute Tech. Bull. No. 1. Rome, Italy: International Plant Genetic Resources Institute.

Kettle, C.J.; Burslem, D.F.R.P.; Ghazoul, J. 2011. An unorthodox approach to forest restoration. Science. 333: 36.

Scianna, J.D. 2004. Blending dry seeds clean. Native Plants Journal. 5: 47–48.

Stein, W.I.; Danielson, R.: Shaw, N.; Wolff, S.; Gerdes, D. 1986. Users guide for seeds of western trees and shrubs. General Technical Report PNW-193. Corvallis, OR: U.S. Department of Agriculture, Pacific Northwest Station. 45 p.

Steinfeld, D.E.; Riley, S.A.; Wilkinson, K.M.; Landis, T.D.; Riley, L.E. 2007. Roadside revegetation: an integrated approach to establishing native plants. Technology Development Report FHWA-WFT/TD-07-005. Vancouver, WA: U.S. Department of Transportation, Federal Highway Administration. 413 p.

Thomas, D. 2003. Modifying blender blades for seed cleaning. Native Plants Journal. 4: 72–73.

Truscott, M. 2004. Cuisinart for cleaning elderberry (*Sambucus* sp. L. [Caprifoliaceae]). Native Plants Journal. 5: 46.

U.S. Department of the Interior, Bureau of Land Management, Seeds of Success[BLM/SOS]. 2011. Technical protocol for the collection, study, and conservation of seeds from native plant species for seeds of success. Native Plant Materials Development Program: 8–11. http://www.nps.gov/plants/sos/training/index.htm. (October 2011).

Vozzo, J.A., ed. 2002. The tropical tree seed manual. Agriculture Handbook 721. Washington, DC: U.S. Department of Agriculture, Forest Service. 899 p.

Withrow-Robinson, B.; Johnson, R. 2006. Selecting native plant materials for restoration projects: insuring local adaptation and maintaining genetic diversity. Corvalis, OR: Oregon State University Extension Service.

Young, Y. 1993. Seeds of the woody plants of North America. Portland, OR: Dioscorides Press. 407 p.

Additional Reading

Landis, T.D.; Tinus, R.W.; Barnett, J.P. 1999. The container tree nursery manual: volume 6, seedling propagation. Agriculture Handbook 674. Washington, DC: U.S. Department of Agriculture, Forest Service. 167 p.

Schmidt, L. 2000. Guide to handling of tropical and subtropical forest seed. Humlebaek, Denmark: Danida Forest Seed Centre. 511 p.

Seed Germination and Sowing Options

9

Tara Luna, Kim M. Wilkinson, and R. Kasten Dumroese

Seeds of many native species are challenging to germinate. One important thing a grower can do is to learn as much as possible about the life history, ecology, and habitat of the species he or she wishes to grow to understand the processes seeds from each target species go through in nature. Any observations will be valuable when trying to germinate and grow species that have little or no published information available. How seeds are handled, treated, and sown can affect the genetic diversity and the quality of the crop produced. Growers need to balance the desire for uniform crops and schedules with the need to protect the diverse characteristics within species. In this chapter, we discuss seed characteristics, treatments to improve or stimulate germination, and different types of sowing options for seeds.

Facing Page: *Hand-sowing. Photo by Tara Luna.*

Seed Characteristics

As discussed in Chapter 8, Collecting, Processing, and Storing Seeds (and shown in figure 8.8), tropical seeds can be divided into four categories related to their longevity and ability to be stored (Hong and Ellis 2002, Kettle and others 2011).

Viviparous: seeds that germinate before they are dispersed from the mother plant. The most common examples are some species of mangroves such as *Avicennia* and *Rhizophora* and some tropical legumes.

Recalcitrant: seeds that germinate soon after maturation and dispersal from the mother plant, and cannot be dried without losing viability. Most species from the wet, humid tropics have recalcitrant seeds because conditions in these environments are consistently favorable for germination and seedling establishment. Examples of common species with recalcitrant seeds include cacao, mango, longon, and jackfruit.

Intermediate: seeds that can germinate immediately but may also survive partial drying without losing viability. For example, papaya seeds that have been dried to 10-percent moisture content have been stored successfully under conditions of 50-percent relative humidity for 6 years without affecting viability (Vozzo 2002). Species that have shown intermediate storage behavior include neem, cinnamon, citrus, mahogany, and coffee.

Orthodox: seeds that can be dried without losing viability. These seeds are considered "dormant" and often require specific treatments to encourage germination. Dormant seeds will not germinate immediately upon maturation and dispersal from the mother plant even when ideal environmental conditions exist.

Before attempting to grow a plant, it is important to know the seed germination type because that helps determine the best seed treatments and sowing options for that seed. For orthodox seeds, knowing about the species helps you to provide the best conditions to dissipate, or "break," seed dormancy and achieve good rates of germination.

Dormancy in Orthodox Seeds

Dormancy is an adaptation that ensures seeds will germinate only when environmental conditions are favorable for survival. The conditions necessary to allow seeds to break dormancy and germinate can be highly variable among species, within a species, or among seed sources of the same species. This degree of variability is advantageous because seeds will germinate at different times over a period of days, weeks, months, or even years, ensuring that some offspring will be exposed to favorable environmental conditions for survival.

Tropical species inhabiting areas with a strong wet-dry seasonal cycle, arid or semiarid climates, or at high elevations subjected to cold temperatures often have dormant seeds. The degree of dormancy in these species can vary among and within seed lots, between seed crop years, and individuals. Examples of species with dormant seeds include acacias such as Hawai'i's native *Acacia koa*, and pines including the Caribbean's *Pinus caribaea*.

Dormancy may be caused by factors outside (external) or inside (internal) to the seeds. Some species have a combination of external and internal dormancy, a condition known as double dormancy. Knowing the type of seed dormancy is essential for successful propagation.

External Seed Dormancy

External seed dormancy may be physical, physical-physiological, chemical, or mechanical (Baskin and Baskin 1998, 2004). Seeds that have hard, thick seedcoats that physically prevent water or oxygen movement into seeds have physical dormancy. Physical dormancy is the most common seed dormancy type seen in the tropics. Species with external dormancy include many of the legumes (Fabaceae), mallows (Malvaceae), and other tropical species that are adapted to fire, or inhabit arid to semiarid island habitats or areas with pronounced wet-dry seasonal cycles. These seeds normally germinate over a period of several years. Depending on species and habitat, various environmental factors cause these seeds to become permeable over time or during a certain time of year. Seeds that require additional exposure to particular temperatures after they become permeable have physical-physiological dormancy.

The fruits that enclose the seeds cause other forms of external dormancy. Chemical dormancy describes fruits that contain high concentrations of germination inhibitors that prevent spontaneous germination of seeds. Mechanical dormancy describes tough, woody fruit walls that restrict seed germination and is best exemplified by the husks that surround coconuts (*Cocos nucifera*).

Internal Seed Dormancy

Internal dormancy may be morphological, physiological, or both (Baskin and Baskin 1998). Seeds with morphological dormancy have an underdeveloped embryo when dispersed from the mother plant. A period of after-ripening (usually warm and moist conditions) is needed for the embryo to fully mature before the seed is capable of germination. Tropical species that exhibit morphological dormancy are found in the Annonaceae, Dilleniaceae, Magnoliaceae, and Myristicaceae families and in many palm species. Seeds of this type may not germinate for several months to 1 year after sowing.

Physiological dormancy is found in some species in arid and semi-arid tropical environments. Seeds are permeable to water, but certain environmental conditions are necessary to modify the internal chemistry of the seed and thus enable germination. Usually a period of cold, moist conditions or holding seeds in dry storage overcomes physiological dormancy.

Seeds with morphological-physiological dormancy usually require a combination of warm and cold conditions, often over an extended period of time, before they are capable of germination.

Treatments To Overcome Seed Dormancy and Enhance Germination

A variety of seed treatments have been developed in response to the diversity of seed types grown in nurseries. Before treating seeds, be sure to consult available references to see what treatments have been used on that species; see the literature cited at the end of this chapter and the Native Plant Network (http://www.native plantnetwork.org). If no information is available, check references for closely related species. Any personal observations made on the species in the habitat may also provide some clues on how to germinate the seeds. In general, however, the process of treating seeds follows a fairly standard progression outlined in the following

Figure 9.2—Seeds that are not cleaned before treatment or sowing can easily mold or be susceptible to serious pathogens such as damping-off disease. Photo by Thomas D. Landis.

sections. Nondormant seeds are planted immediately after collection and cleaning. Intermediate seeds may be stored for several weeks or months in suitable conditions, and then cleaned, fully rehydrated, and sown. For dormant (orthodox) seeds, dormancy must be overcome using one or more of the methods described in this chapter before seeds can be rehydrated, enabling germination. It is essential to determine which type(s) of dormancy the seed has so you can do what is needed to overcome dormancy (figure 9.1). The nursery must determine whether seeds will need to be cleaned, scarified, soaked, stimulated, stratified, and treated in other ways before sowing on a species-by-species basis. The following sections describe the seed treatment options available.

Cleaning

Seed cleaning helps prevent diseases in the nursery. Cleaning seeds of bacterial and fungal infestation is especially necessary for species that easily mold (figure 9.2). Often, molding can be related to the most common disease seen in nurseries, damping-off. Seed cleaning is especially important in humid climates and for species that take a long time to germinate. Often, without cleaning, seeds can be lost to pathogens before they are planted in the nursery.

One of the best cleaning methods is to simply soak seeds in a stream of running water for 24 to 48 hours. The running water flushes bacterial and fungal spores from the seeds (James and Genz 1981). This treatment can also be used to satisfy the soaking requirement described in the next section.

Seeds can also be cleaned with several chemicals, some of which also act to stimulate germination. Bleach (5.25 percent sodium hypochlorite) is the most common chemical used. Depending on the species, bleach cleaning solutions range between one part bleach in eight parts water to two parts bleach in three parts water. With most species,

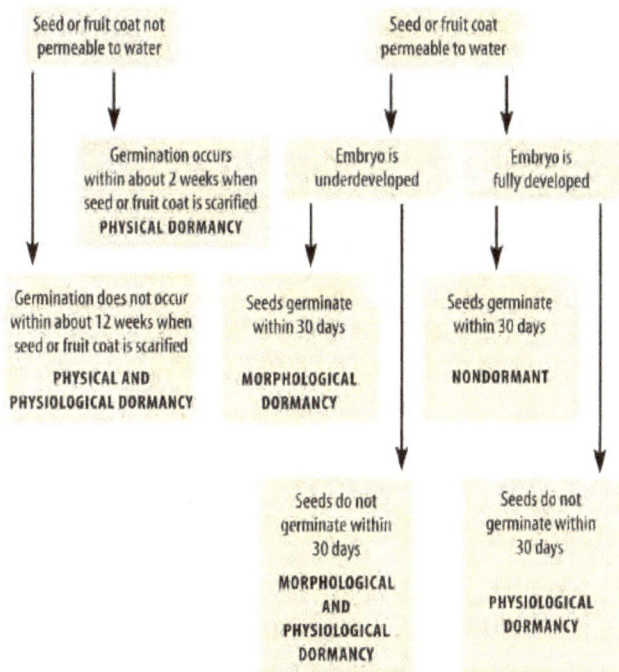

Figure 9.1—Key to dormancy types. Knowing the type of seed dormancy is essential to successful seed propagation. Illustration by Jim Marin.

treatment duration is 10 minutes or less. Species with very thin seed coats should not be cleaned with bleach. Hydrogen peroxide can be an effective cleanser and can sometimes enhance germination (Narimanov 2000). The usual treatment is one part peroxide in three parts water. Tropical species that benefit from hydrogen peroxide rinses include *Albizia* species and camphor tree seeds (Vozzo 2003).

Scarification

Seeds with external dormancy require scarification. Scarification is any method of disrupting an impermeable seed coat so that water and oxygen can enter the seeds. In nature, hard seed coats are cracked or softened by fire, extreme temperatures, digestive acids in the stomachs of animals, or by the abrasion of blowing sand. After the seed coat has been disrupted, oxygen and water pass into the seeds and germination can proceed.

Seeds can be scarified many ways. How well the method works depends on the species and the thickness of the seed coats. Whichever method is chosen, it is very important not to damage the endosperm, cotyledons, or embryo during the treatment. Taking time to learn seed anatomy of the

Figure 9.4—Hobby-size rock tumblers can be used to scarify seeds and avoid seed destruction that can occur with sulfuric acid or heat scarification. Photo by Tara Luna.

species is helpful. Trying several methods and recording the results will help determine the best method for that species and seed source.

Mechanical Scarification

Mechanical scarification includes filing or nicking seeds by hand and is most often used on large-seeded species such as *Acacia*, *Cassia*, and *Sesbania* (figure 9.3). Be sure to scarify on the side of the seed opposite the embryo. It is often done one seed at a time with a nail clipper. This method is time consuming and requires precision to adequately scarify the seed coat without damaging the internal portions of the seed. Sandpaper can be used on smaller seeded species such as sedges; placing seeds into a shallow wooden box and then rubbing them under a block of wood covered in sandpaper is the simplest technique. Often, however, the degree of scarification achieved with sandpaper can be variable.

Hobby-size rock tumblers can be used to process large batches of seed more quickly than manual mechanical scarification (figure 9.4). Dry tumbling involves placing seeds, a coarse carborundum grit (sold by rock tumbler dealers), and pea gravel in the tumbler and tumbling for several hours or several days. Wet tumbling includes the addition of water to the grit and pea gravel. A benefit of wet tumbling is that seeds are soaked in well-aerated water and chemical inhibitors may be leached from the seed.

Heat Scarification

Many species, especially those from fire-adapted ecosystems, respond to germination cues from heat. Using either wet or dry heat to scarify the seeds can simulate this response. Using wet heat is an effective method for many small-seeded species because it provides a rapid, uniform treatment that can be assessed within a few hours. Wet-

Figure 9.3—Mechanical scarification works well with large, easy-to-handle seeds. Great care is needed, however, so that the embryo or cotyledons are not damaged. Koa seed hand scarification (A), scarified lotus seeds (B). Photo A by Craig R. Elevitch, and photo B by Cardno JFNew Native Plant Nursery.

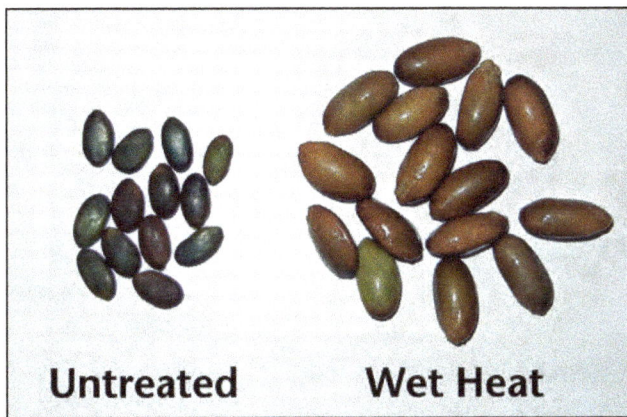

Figure 9.5—*Seeds that have been scarified by hot water are visibly larger than untreated seeds because the seed coat has been breached and seeds can then absorb water increasing their size. Photo by Greg Morgenson.*

heat treatments are effective for many tropical species including *Acacia, Cassia, Senna, Sesbania,* and *Tamarindus* (Vozzo 2002). Because the thickness of the seed coat may vary among sources, it is wise to dissect a few seeds and examine the thickness of their seed coats to help determine treatment duration. Seeds are added to boiling water for 5 to 10 seconds and then immediately transferred to a vat of cold water so that they cool quickly to prevent embryo damage. Seeds imbibe the cool water for 1 day and are then ready for sowing or for stratification (figure 9.5). Some species cannot tolerate excessively high temperatures, so you may want to heat the water to only 158 °F (70 °C) and monitor your results.

Dry heat is most commonly used on fire-adapted species. Seeds are placed in an oven at temperatures ranging from 175 to 250 °F (80 to 120 °C) from a few minutes to 1 hour, depending on the species. The seed coat cracks open in response to the heat. To avoid damaging seeds, this treatment needs to be monitored closely.

Chemical Scarification

Sulfuric acid is most commonly used on species with very thick seedcoats and with stony endocarps that surround the embryo (figure 9.6). It has been used on some species of *Acacia, Albizia, Cassia, Leucaena, Parkinsonia,* and *Terminalia* (Vozzo 2002). Treatment length varies with the species and often among seed sources, and it must be carefully monitored because seeds can be destroyed if the treatment is too long. A simple way to monitor the process is by removing seeds at regular intervals and cutting them with a sharp knife. When the seeds are still firm but can be cut fairly easily, the treatment is probably sufficient. Another way is to run a pilot test on a subsample of seeds. Again, remove some seeds periodically and evaluate how well they germinate. After the best

duration is known, the entire seedlot can be treated. Sulfuric acid is very dangerous to handle and requires special equipment, personal protective gear, and proper disposal after use. It should never be poured down sink drains. If acid is being diluted in water, the acid must be added to the water, never add water to acid—when water is added to acid, heat will be released, risking an explosion and other dangers. Some species have thick seed coats but can easily be damaged by sulfuric acid. Instead, citric acid or sodium or calcium hypochlorite baths with longer treatment durations may be used.

The safe use of sulfuric acid requires the following procedures:

- Treat seeds that are dry and at room temperature.
- Require workers to wear safety equipment, including face shield, goggles, thick rubber gloves, and full protective clothing.
- If diluting, add acid to water, never water to acid.
- Immerse seeds in an acid-resistant container, such as a glass, for the duration required.
- Stir seeds carefully in the acid bath; a glass rod works well.
- Immerse the container with seeds and acid in an ice bath to keep temperatures at a safe level for the embryos (this temperature depends on the species; many do not need this step).
- Remove seeds from the acid by slowly pouring the seed-acid solution into a larger volume of cool water, ideally one in which new, fresh water is continually being added.
- Stir seeds during water rinsing to ensure all surfaces are thoroughly rinsed clean.

Figure 9.6—*Seeds that have been treated with sulfuric acid. Photo by Nancy Shaw.*

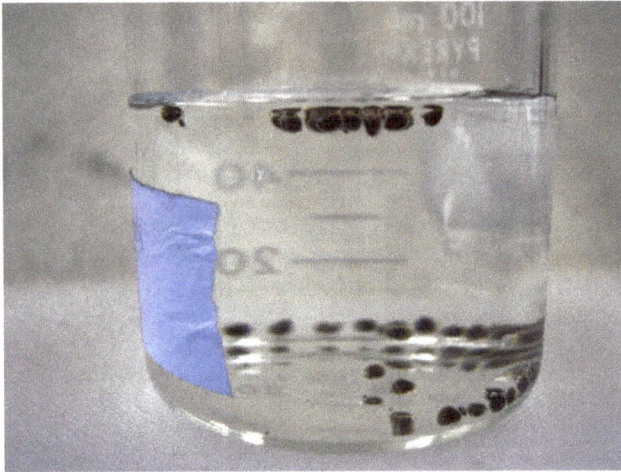

Figure 9.7—Many species of dormant seeds benefit from 1 to several days of water soaking before sowing to fully imbibe seeds and remove any chemical inhibitors within the seeds or on the seed coats. Photo by Brian F. Daley.

Soaking

After cleaning and scarification, seeds must have exposure to water and oxygen before germination can occur. The standard procedure is to soak seeds in water for 1 to several days until they are fully hydrated (figure 9.7). Hydration can be checked by taking a sample, allowing it to dry until the seed coat is still wet but dull, not glossy, and weighing it. When the weight no longer increases substantially with additional soaking time, the seeds have absorbed sufficient water. Scarified seeds will be more obvious; the seeds will enlarge drastically during the soak. Seeds that only had physical dormancy can be immediately planted. As mentioned previously, running water rinses are effective seed cleaning treatments that reduce the need for fungicides in nurseries (Dumroese and others 1990). Running water soaks also help to remove any chemical inhibitors present on or within the seeds. An aquarium pump can be used to agitate the seeds to improve the cleaning effect and keep the water well aerated. If seeds are not soaked with running water, change the water often (at least a couple of times each day).

Germination Stimulators

Several chemicals are known to increase seed germination. These chemicals are usually applied after seeds are fully hydrated. In general, only seeds with internal dormancy receive this treatment. Germination stimulators include gibberellic acid, ethylene, smoke, and potassium hydroxide.

Gibberellic Acid

Gibberellic acid is the most important plant hormone for the regulation of internal seed dormancy and is often used on seeds with complex internal dormancy and with those species having underdeveloped embryos. In some cases, it has been used to substitute for a warm, moist treatment and to hasten embryo after-ripening. Sandalwood is a species that has been successfully germinated using gibberellic acid. Gibberellic acid can be purchased from horticultural suppliers. Preferred concentrations vary, but most nurseries use 500 to 1,000 parts per million (ppm). High concentrations can cause seeds to germinate, but the resulting seedlings may be of poor quality. Therefore, it is best to experiment with low concentrations first. The following are some guidelines for treating seeds with gibberellic acid:

- Gibberellic acid takes a long time to dissolve. It may need constant stirring or you may want to prepare it the day before use.

- Store unused solution away from direct sunlight.

- Cut unbleached coffee filters into squares and fold them diagonally.

- Place gibberellic acid solution evenly into an ice cube tray.

- Place each folded coffee filter containing the seeds into the wells of the tray so that it wicks up the solution.

- After 24 hours, remove and either sow directly or place seeds into fresh coffee filters moistened with distilled water for stratification.

Ethylene

This gas occurs naturally in plants and is known to stimulate the germination of some species. Ethylene gas is released from ethephon, a commercially available product. Ethephon, used either alone or in combination with gibberellic acid, has enhanced the germination in doum palm (Mousa and others 1998) and may be used for other species inhabiting arid to semi-arid tropical and saline environments. It may inhibit germination in other species, so consult the literature and experiment before using operationally.

Smoke Treatments

Smoke stimulates germination in many fire-adapted species; for example, species from the California chaparral, longleaf pine communities in Florida, or species from fire-dependent ecosystems in Australia, South Africa, parts of South America, and the Mediterranean. Smoke especially stimulates seeds that have thin, permeable seed coats that allow entry of smoke into the seeds (Keeley and Fotheringham 1998). Seeds can be treated with smoke fumigation, a method in which smoke is piped into a specially constructed smoke tent containing seeds sown in trays (figure 9.8A),

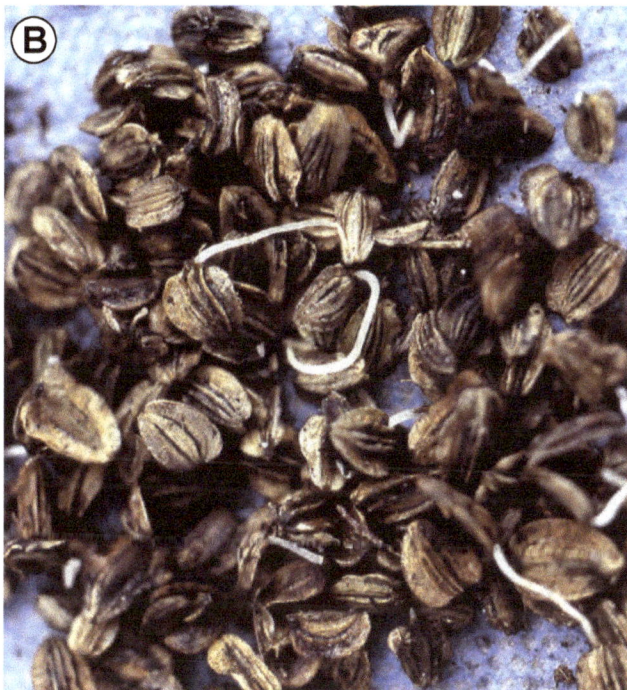

Figure 9.8—Smoke treatments have been used to overcome seed dormancy and enhance germination rates for many native species inhabiting fire-dependent ecosystems. A smoke tent for treating seeds (A). Smoke water-treated seeds of angelica (B). Photo A by Kingsley Dixon, and photo B by Tara Luna.

or with smoke water. Smoke water is an aqueous solution of smoke extract made by burning vegetation and piping the smoke through distilled water or allowing the smoke to infuse into a container of water. Seeds are then soaked in the treated water (figure 9.8B). Conversely, growers can experiment with commercially available smoke products such as liquid smoke or smoke-infused paper discs, or by adding ash to growing media.

Many variables, such as the material used for combustion, the combustion temperature, and the duration of exposure, will need to be determined on a species-by-species basis. Experiments performed by Keeley and Fotheringham (1998) found that the length of exposure to smoke was very important in some species; a 3-minute difference in exposure resulted in seed mortality. Some fire species did not germinate under heat or smoke treatments alone. With some species, seed burial for 1 year or stratification was required in addition to smoke exposure. All these factors can have an effect on germination and should be considered when determining whether to use smoke treatments. Success with this novel treatment will require trials, so good record keeping is critical.

Potassium Hydroxide Rinses

Potassium hydroxide has been used to stimulate germination in several native plant species. Optimum concentration varies from 5.3 to 7.6 Molar for 1 to 10 minutes depending on the species; longer soaks at higher concentrations were found to be detrimental (Gao and others 1998).

Other Stimulants

Potassium nitrate, thiourea, and kinetin have been used to stimulate germination in seeds, although the use of these compounds with tropical native plants is lacking. You may choose to experiment with these compounds on a limited basis with difficult-to-germinate seeds.

Temperature and Moisture Treatments

Many seeds with internal dormancy require a moist period at certain temperatures similar to what occurs in the natural habitat before they germinate and grow. Historically, stratification was a temperate zone practice of alternating layers of moist soil and seeds in barrels and allowing these "strata" to be exposed to winter temperatures. Nowadays, stratification is often used more generically to describe the combined use of moisture and any temperature to overcome seed dormancy. We use the term "stratification" to refer to only cold, moist treatments (rare to use in the tropics, but we cover it anyway for nurseries growing highland species). We use the term "warm, moist treatment" instead of "warm, moist stratification."

Some native species with double internal seed dormancy require a combination of a warm, moist treatment for a period of time followed by stratification. Some species or seedlots may require only a few days or weeks of stratification, while others may require several months. As a general rule, it is best to use the maximum recommended treatment. Also keep in mind that what works well at one nursery may not necessarily work well at another nursery because of differences in seed source, handling, processing, cleaning, and storage. An advantage to stratifying seeds of some species is that it can speed up germination and make it more uniform, which is desirable in a container nursery.

Warm, Moist Treatments

Warm, moist treatment enhances after-ripening of seeds with underdeveloped embryos. Warm, moist treated seeds are kept at temperatures of 72 to 86 °F (22 to 30 °C) for a period of time, usually in moist peat moss, sawdust, or other substrate. Although warm, moist treatments are not commonly used on tropical species, it can be considered for seeds with morphological or physiological seed dormancy.

Stratification

Stratification (cold, moist treatment) is used on seeds with internal dormancy from temperate areas, or high-elevation habitats in tropical regions. Some subtropical species may also benefit from a period of cool, moist stratification. In climates with four seasons, seeds sown in flats or containers in late summer or autumn and left outdoors during winter undergo "natural" stratification. This technique may be preferred if the species has double dormancy (requires both a warm, moist treatment or stratification), requires a very long stratification or requires low temperatures or fluctuating temperatures for a long period of time. Conversely, "artificial" stratification involves placing seeds under refrigeration at 34 to 38 °F (1 to 3 °C) for a period of time. Artificial stratification has several advantages: (1) it allows for a routine check of seeds to ensure they are moist and not moldy, (2) a large number of seeds can be stratified in a small space, and (3) seeds or seedlots that begin to germinate can be removed from the treatment and planted in the nursery as they become available. Artificial stratification is preferred over natural stratification unless the natural treatment provides higher rates of germination.

For artificial stratification of small seedlots and small seeds, seeds can be placed between sheets of moistened paper towels and inserted in an opened plastic bag or sown on a medium in flats with drainage holes. Paper towels need to be moist but not waterlogged, and seeds need to be evenly spread across the moist paper towel to help prevent molding (figure 9.9).

Another technique is "naked" stratification. Most conifer seeds, for example, are stratified in this manner (figure 9.10). Seeds are placed in mesh bags and then soaked in running water as described previously. After the seeds are hydrated, the bag is pulled from the soak, allowed to drip dry for 30 to 90 seconds, and then suspended in a plastic bag. Make sure the seeds are not in contact with standing water in the bag and hang the bags in the refrigerator. If naked seeds need a warm, moist treatment before stratification, it is easiest to first spread the seeds onto moistened paper towels enclosed in large plastic bags. After the warm treatment, the seeds can be returned to the mesh bags for stratification. One other hint: if a particular species or seedlot has a tendency to begin germinating during stratification, surface-dry the seed coats (seeds should be moist and dull, not shiny), and then put the seeds into the bag for refrigeration. The seeds need to still have enough moisture for chemical processes that dissipate dormancy to occur but not enough moisture to allow for germination.

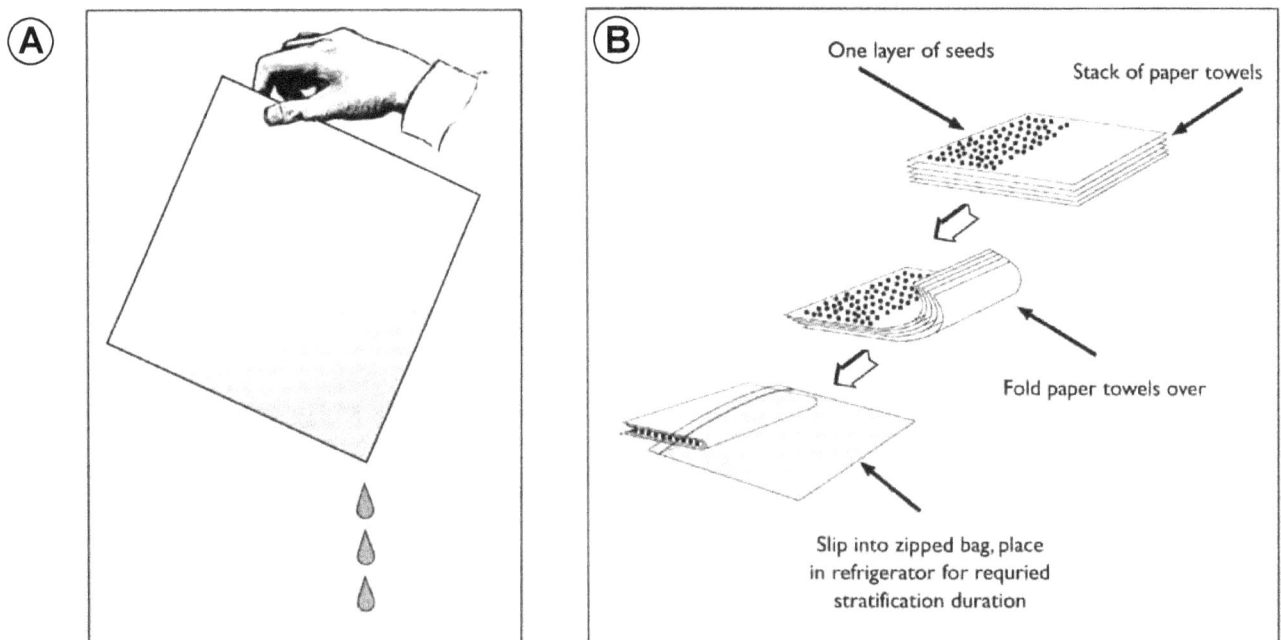

Figure 9.9—*Small seeds requiring only a few weeks of stratification can be stratified by moistening paper towels and holding by corner to let excess water drain away (A) or placing seeds onto moistened towels inserted into an unopened plastic zippered bag (B). Illustrations from Dumroese and others (1998).*

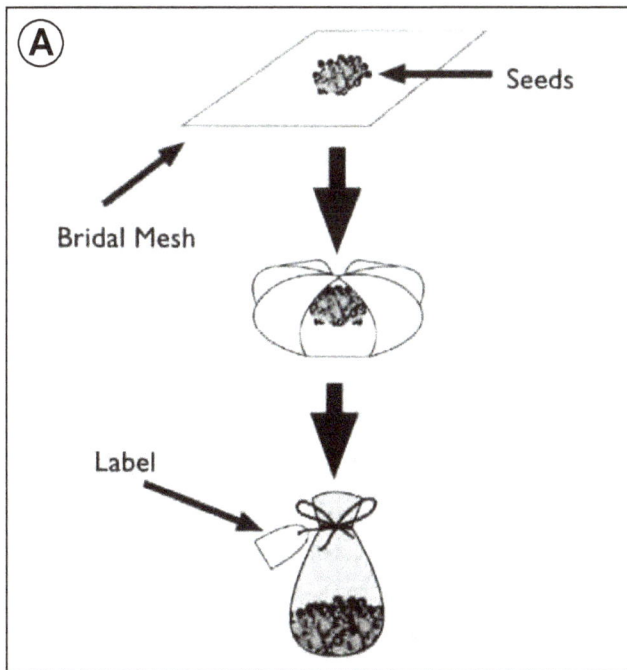

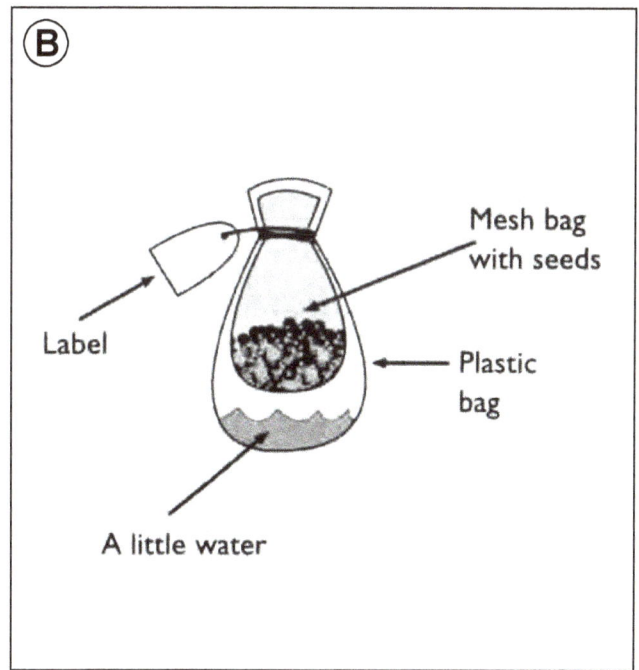

Figure 9.10—*Naked stratification: After soaking seeds in a mesh bag, allow the bag to drip dry for 1 minute and then suspend the mesh bag in a plastic bag (A). Hang the bag in the refrigerator. Make sure the seeds are not in constant contact with standing water in the plastic bag (B). Illustrations from Dumroese and others (1998).*

Many wetland and aquatic species can be treated with naked stratification in water. In general, these species can be easily stratified in Ziploc®-type bags filled with water. Insert a soda straw into the bag, ensuring that the end is sticking out of the bag, to allow some oxygen to reach the seeds. Then, seal the rest of the bag securely. Place under refrigeration if in need of a cold, moist stratification period.

Environmental Factors Influencing Germination

Four environmental factors affect germination: light, water, oxygen, and temperature. All plants have specific germination requirements based on ecological adaptations and the environmental cues that trigger germination for that species.

Light

Light quality and duration can influence germination. In nature, seeds of tropical pioneer species require high light levels associated with a canopy gap for germination and establishment, whereas shade tolerant species generally can germinate in very poor light or deep shade. Many small-seeded, tropical native species fall into this category. Thus, pioneer species, such as 'ōhi'a in Hawai'i, with very small dust-like seeds (figure 9.11), require light for germination and fail to germinate even if they are buried only 2 mm deep (Drake 1993). Therefore, these seeds need to be sown on the surface of the medium so they are exposed to light during germination. Other species are conditioned to germinate only if they are buried in the soil. Species requiring darkness to germinate are those that germinate readily under the deep shade of a closed forest canopy. Tropical trees and shrubs with medium to larger sized seeds often require darkness for maximum germination, but shade tolerant vines and herbaceous plants may have smaller seeds. Other species requiring darkness to germinate include some of the species that colonize sand dunes along coastlines.

Figure 9.11—*In general, small-seeded pioneer species such as 'ōhi'a require light to germinate and must not be buried. Photo by Tara Luna.*

Water and Oxygen

Water is also important for germination. Overwatering seeds during germination results in reduced levels of oxygen in the medium and promotes tissue breakdown and disease whereas underwatering delays or prevents germination. Therefore, seeds need to be kept evenly moist during germination. Although oxygen is needed for respiratory processes in germinating seeds, some aquatic species may require low oxygen levels for germination. For example, tropical floodplain forest or wetland species naturally germinate during periods of high water inundation and respond positively to low water oxygen levels (Kurbitzky and Ziburski 1994, Vozzo 2002).

Temperature

Temperature influences seed germination rate and percentage. Some germination patterns in response to temperature include seeds that require cool temperatures, tolerate cool temperatures, require warm temperatures, and (or) require alternating temperatures (Hartman and others 1997, Vozzo 2002). Species requiring cool temperatures generally germinate below 77 °F (25 °C), which coincides with high elevations in tropical or subtropical regions. Species that tolerate cool temperatures will germinate over a wide range of temperatures from 41 to 86 °F (5 to 30 °C). Many species will not germinate under excessively high temperatures. Most tropical species require warm temperatures and will only germinate if temperatures are above 70 °F (21 °C). In addition, some species germinate better when exposed to alternating temperatures. Alternating temperatures are particularly important with dormant, freshly harvested seeds. Many tropical tree species germinate to their highest percentages at alternating temperatures of 86/68 °F (30/20 °C) or are provided with at least 10 °F (5.6 °C) difference between the day and night time temperature. Some difficult-to-germinate tropical species may require even greater temperature fluctuations.

Seed Sowing Methods

Several sowing techniques have been used for native plants (table 9.1) and are described in the following sections. The process of sowing seeds for nursery production will vary with the species, type of seed, seed quality, and nursery environment.

Direct Sowing

Direct sowing is fast, easy, and economical because it minimizes seed handling and labor. It can be mechanized when done on a large scale. For direct sowing to be efficient, the seeds need to be easy to handle, abundant in supply, have simple dormancy treatments, and have a known high-germination rate (figure 9.12). If the direct sowing will be mechanized, seeds must also be uniform in size and shape.

The success of direct seeding depends on the accuracy of seed germination information. Growers must realize that actual seedling emergence may be different from the results of laboratory germination tests that are conducted under ideal environmental conditions. Nursery managers must adjust for this discrepancy based on their own operational experience. Growers should conduct a small germination test of each seedlot to determine the

Figure 9.12—Direct sowing works well for seeds that have little or no dormancy (or have been treated to overcome dormancy), are easy to handle and are in abundant supply (A). Simple tools like a film canister (B) or a folded envelope (C) can be used to accurately sow small seeds. Photo A by Douglass F. Jacobs, and photos B and C by Dawn Thomas.

Table 9.1—*Methods for sowing seeds. Adapted from Landis and others (1999).*

Propagation method	Good method for seeds with the following characteristics	Advantages	Disadvantages
Direct Sowing: Seeds are sown into containers	• Have a known high-percentage germination • Are inexpensive • Are in abundant supply • Have uniform, smooth shapes	• Fast and easy • Economical • Minimizes seed handling • Seeds are all sown at once	• Less efficient use of space, seeds, and/or growing medium • Causes of poor germination are difficult to track • May require thinning and/or consolidation and associated labor costs • Not good for large or irregularly shaped seeds
Planting Germinants: Seeds sprouting or germinating in trays or bags are sown into containers while roots are just beginning to emerge	• Are of unknown viability • Are valuable or rare • Have unknown germination requirements • Germinate during an extended period of time or during stratification	• Efficient use of seeds • Efficient use of nursery space • Can adjust for unknown seed quality or performance	• Labor intensive • May result in nonuniform crop development • Root deformation possible • Requires frequent, skilled monitoring
Transplanting emergents: Seeds are sown into flats or seedbeds for germination; once germinated and leaves appear, seedlings are transplanted to containers	• Are being tested but will not be transplanted to produce a crop • Do not respond well to other sowing methods • Have long or unknown dormancy • Good for trials to observe seed performance	• Useful with fibrous rooted species • Efficient use of seeds • Efficient use of nursery space • Can adjust for unknown seed quality or performance	• Not recommended for woody and/or taprooted species because of problems with transplant shock and or root deformation • Requires skilled labor
Miniplug transplants: Seeds are sown directly into small containers. After germination, they are transplanted into larger containers	• Are of unknown quality • Are valuable or rare • Have unknown germination requirements • Have very tiny seeds • Will be transplanted into large containers	• Efficient use of space • Uniform crop development • Low risk of transplant injury	• Requires two sets of containers • Timing is critical • Transplanting by hand is labor intensive

percentage of germination for each seedlot. Those percentages can then be used to determine the number of seeds to direct sow (see table 9.2). Follow these steps for successful direct sowing:

- Determine how many seeds must germinate to obtain the production target.
- Determine if seeds can be single-sown or will require multiple seeds to reach the production target (see following sections).
- Cleanse and treat seeds as necessary to break dormancy.
- Sow seeds, ideally centering the seeds in each container. Some seeds require a specific orientation for

optimal growth and development; if so, make sure seeds are sown in the correct orientation.

- Depending on the light requirements of the species, cover seeds with the correct amount of mulch.
- Gently water the seeds with a fine watering head to press them into the growing media.

Multiple-Seed Sowing and Thinning

Sowing more than one seed into each container with the expectation that at least one will germinate is the most common direct-sowing practice. The number of seeds to sow can be calculated based on the seeds'

Figure 9.13—*Calculating and testing germination rates help reduce costs and problems associated with thinning. Photo by Thomas D. Landis.*

expected germination percentage. Two to five seeds are typically sown per container. As a general rule, seeds with less than a 50-percent germination are not recommended for direct sowing because the high density of nonviable seeds in the container may cause disease problems, more containers will need to be thinned, and many plants will be wasted (figure 9.13). Table 9.2 provides general recommendations for the number of seeds to sow per container based on the germination percentage. At some point, adding more seeds per container does not really increase the number of containers with plants (table 9.3) but does drastically increase the number of containers with too many plants and the amount of seed wasted. Sometimes it may be better to single-sow a few containers than thin extra seedlings from many containers. For example, sowing a single seed per container of a seedlot with 85-percent germination yields 15 percent empty containers whereas sowing two seeds per container yields only 2 percent empty containers, but sowing the extra seed requires

Table 9.2—*For a given seed germination, increasing the number of seeds sown per container increases the number of filled containers. In general, a target of 90- to 95-percent filled containers is reasonable. Adapted from Dumroese and others (1998).*

Seed germination percentage	Seeds to sow per container	Percentage of containers with at least one seedling
90 +	1 to 2	90 to 100
80 to 89	2	96 to 99
70 to 79	2	91 to 96
60 to 69	3	94 to 97
50 to 59	4	94 to 97
40 to 49	5	92 to 97

Table 9.3—*A sowing example for a seedlot of* Acacia koa *having a 65-percent germination rate. Assuming 1,000 seedlings are desired, notice that adding more than three seeds per container really does not improve the number of containers with seedlings and wastes many seeds. Adapted from Dumroese and others (1998).*

Seeds sown per container	Empty containers (%)	Containers with at least one seedling (%)	Seed sown	Seedlings produced
1	35	65	1,000	650
2	12	88	2,000	880
3	4	96	3,000	960
4	1	99	4,000	990
5	0	100	5,000	1,000

thinning 72 percent of the containers. The nursery manager may have been better off, in terms of seed use efficiency and labor, to have simply oversown 10 percent more containers rather than pay for the labor to thin. Therefore, the amount of seeds to sow per container is a function of germination, seed availability, nursery space, thinning costs, and so on.

When more than one seedling germinates in the same container, seedlings compete for light, water, and nutrients. This competition results in lower initial growth rates and requires that seedlings be thinned (clipped, culled, or removed from the container). For this reason, thinning should be done as soon as possible after seedlings emerge. Thinning is a labor-intensive practice and it can damage remaining seedlings if done improperly. Train workers to thin plants carefully and to follow these guidelines:

- Thin germinants as soon as possible; the more developed the root system becomes, the more difficult it is to thin.

- Retain the strongest seedling closest to the center of the container. Thinning is an opportunity for selecting the healthiest seedling while removing inferior plants.

- Pull or cut extra plants. For species with a long, slender taproot at germination (such as pine seedlings), extra seedlings can be easily pulled before they develop secondary roots. For species with vigorous, fibrous root systems, cutting extra plants at the stem with sharp scissors or nipping them with fingernails may be better.

- Discard culled plants into compost or waste.

- Check the remaining seedling and correct any disruptions caused by the thinning process. (For example, if thinning disrupted the mulch, adjust it so the seedling has the best environment possible.)

Single-Seed Sowing

Sometimes, particularly when seeds are scarce or costly or are expected to have close to 100-percent germination, single seeds can be directly sown into containers. This practice ensures that every seed has the potential to become a plant and no thinning will be necessary. If a particular number of plants are required, then extra containers are planted, often referred to as "oversowing," to make up for any empty cells. The number of extra containers to sow can be calculated based on the percentage of germination. If a seedlot has only a 78-percent germination, for 100 plants, you must sow at least 28 extra containers (100 desired seedlings/0.78 success rate = 128 containers required). The number of oversown containers may need to be increased to account for seedling losses during the growing cycle.

Oversowing works best if the nursery has extra space and is using containers with individual, exchangeable cells because containers with live plants can be consolidated and the extra containers can be removed (see Chapter 7, Containers). Single sowing is efficient because no seeds are wasted and plants that do emerge are not subjected to competition or the stresses of thinning as they are with the multiple-sowing technique. Oversowing wastes potting materials and bench space, however, and consolidating the empty containers is labor-intensive.

Sowing Germinants

Germinant sowing ("sowing sprouts") is the practice of sowing seeds that are germinating (or sprouting) into the container when their young root emerges (figure 9.14). When done properly, germinant sowing ensures that one viable seed is placed in each container, thereby making efficient use of space and seeds. The resulting seedlings are often larger because they can begin to grow immediately without competition. This technique can be labor-intensive but results in minimal waste of materials and space. Sowing germinants works best for seeds that:

- Are from a rare or valuable seedlot.

- Have a low or unknown germination percentage.

- Are large or irregularly shaped.

- Germinate in stratification.

- Have deep dormancy and germinate over a long period of time.

- Rapidly produce a long root after germination (such as many desert and semidesert species).

Germinant sowing is a relatively simple process. Seeds are treated as necessary, then germinated in trays or bags.

Figure 9.14—*Germinants must be sown as soon as the radicle emerges from the seed coat. Photo by Tara Luna.*

Figure 9.15—*When planting germinants, seeds must be sown as soon as the radicle is visible and must be oriented correctly when planted. Incorrect orientation leads to severe root deformation in woody species (A, B). Photo A by Thomas D. Landis, and photo B by R. Kasten Dumroese.*

Seeds may be spread out between layers of moist paper towels or moist cardboard. Larger seeds are sometimes placed in plastic bags filled with a moist medium such as *Sphagnum* peat moss. Seeds are closely spaced, but far enough apart so that mold does not spread if it forms. Seeds are checked every few days. After seeds begin to germinate, they must be checked daily. Germinated seeds are removed daily and planted directly into growing medium in their containers. Larger seeds can be planted by hand; smaller seeds are often sown using tweezers.

Timing and root orientation are critical when sowing germinants. Seeds need to be sown into containers as soon as the root emerges. The embryonic root, often called a "radicle," needs to be short, ideally no longer than 0.4 in (1 cm). If the radicle becomes too long, it may be difficult to plant without causing root deformation (figure 9.15). Some growers like to prune the radicle of taprooted species before planting to ensure a more fibrous root system. No more than the very tip (up to 0.1 in [3 mm]) is trimmed with

Figure 9.16—*For transplanting emergents, seeds are hand-sown in trays that are usually filled with about 2 in (5 cm) of peat moss-vermiculite growing medium. To prevent root deformities, it is important the trays be deep enough that the roots will not touch the bottom before the emergents can be transplanted. Photo by Thomas D. Landis.*

clean scissors. The germinating seed is carefully placed in the container with the radicle extending downward. After the seeds are properly planted, the medium needs to be firmed around the root and the seed covered with mulch.

An advantage of planting germinants is that the germination process is more visible to the growers than when seeds are direct sown. Germination timing can be better monitored and the causes of germination problems are easier to track, but because seeds in trays or bags are very close together, a mold or pathogen can contaminate all the seeds if not properly monitored. Labor is required to routinely check for germination, skill is required to achieve proper planting orientation of the seeds, and planting must be done in a timely fashion. Because germinants may emerge over several weeks or longer for some species, crop development will be more variable and require special cultural treatments.

Transplanting Emergents

Transplanting emergents ("pricking out") is a practice for germinating seeds in a small area. Seeds are hand-sown in shallow trays that are usually filled with about 2 in (5 cm) of peat moss-vermiculite (or similar) growing medium (figure 9.16). Soon after the seeds germinate, they are "pricked out" of the tray and transplanted into a container. This technique is not recommended for woody plants and other taprooted species, because root problems often result.

Transplanting emergents works best when—

• Species have a fibrous root system that recovers well from transplanting (herbaceous forbs without a taproot, grasses, sedges, and rushes).

- Tests or trials are being used to observe seed treatments, germination timing or percentage, early growth rate or other early developmental issues.
- Seeds are too small or fragile to be sown by any other method.
- Seeds have very complex dormancy or germinate over an extended period of time.
- Limited nursery growing space makes direct seeding uneconomical.
- Timing to transplant emergents is scheduled promptly.

Some key disadvantages include the following—

- Disease potential is high in densely planted trays.
- Root orientation and timing is critical; root malformations and other problems can result if neglected.
- Transplanting is skill and labor intensive.

Training, care, good timing, and proper technique is required to prepare seedling trays, sow the seeds, and to transplant emergents properly. As with many other nursery functions, some trial and error occurs in finding the medium mixture and tray depth that works best for each species. Larger seeds are scattered by hand over the surface of the moistened medium, or place in indentations in the medium. Smaller seeds can be sown with a salt shaker with enlarged holes. Sown seeds are then covered with a light application of fine-textured mulch or medium, irrigated, and placed in a

Figure 9.17—*Root and shoot development at various stages after germination of the Caribbean coastal shrub,* Chrysobalanus icaco. *The large-seeded species is easily transplanted at these stages. Photo by Brian F. Daley.*

favorable environment for germination. Although the exact size or age to transplant the germinating seedlings varies by species, it is usually done at the primary leaf stage (after cotyledons emerge) and well before root systems reach the bottom of the seed tray (figure 9.17).

Emergents are carefully removed from the tray, usually by gently loosening the medium around them (figure 9.18A). A small hole is made in the medium of the container and the germinant is carefully transplanted, ensuring proper root orientation (figure 9.18B). Some species benefit from root pruning before transplanting. The potting medium is then firmed around the root and stem (figure 9.18C).

Figure 9.18—*Transplanting emergents works well for fibrous-rooted shrubs, forbs, and grasses. Great care must be taken to lift the emergent from the pricking out tray without damaging the roots (A) and to carefully and properly transplant it into the new container filled with moistened growing media (B, C). Photos by Tara Luna.*

When timed incorrectly or done improperly, especially on taprooted woody species, transplanting emergents can produce a "J-root" or kink in the seedling stem or root (figure 9.19). These malformations can cause mechanical weakness, poor growth in the nursery and later in the field, and mortality after outplanting. Therefore, unless no other sowing method works, transplanting emergents of woody plants is discouraged.

Transplanting Plugs

Small-volume containers, such as miniplugs (figure 9.20) or expanded peat pellets, in which seeds are direct sown (see Chapter 7, Containers) can be transplanted into a larger container after the seedlings are well established. Transplanting small plugs has a number of benefits. The small plug container preserves healthy root form because damage to roots during transplanting is eliminated. Planting small plugs also makes efficient use of growing space. Large numbers of small plugs can be started in a very small area and managed intensively during germination and early growth.

Plants in miniplug containers must have a firm enough root plug to hold the plug together and withstand the

Figure 9.20—Miniplugs are a viable option for growing seedlings that will later be transplanted to a larger container. Miniplugs work very well with species with very tiny seeds. Photo by Tara Luna.

Figure 9.19—Transplant emergents early to avoid root malformation. This palm seedling was permitted to get too large in the tray, causing the root to grow at a 90° angle. This root malformation will cause poor growth and performance later in the plant's life. Photo by Brian F. Daley.

transplanting process, but they must not have so many roots that they are rootbound or the roots may become deformed after transplanting. If peat pellets are used, too few roots are not a problem because the entire pellet can be transplanted. A hole large enough to accept the plug is made in the medium of the larger container, and the small plug-grown seedling is carefully inserted. Planters need to ensure that the roots go straight down and are not deformed during transplanting. The medium is gently firmed around the root system, mulch is applied, and the plant is watered.

Transplanting small plugs is labor intensive and requires skill. In some arid, windy areas, small plugs are not practical because they dry out too quickly between waterings. Before investing in small plugs on a large scale, a small trial is advised.

Seed Coverings (Mulch)

Regardless of the seed sowing method, a seed cover or "mulch" is recommended to create an optimal environment for germinating seeds. The only exception is for species that require light to germinate. Mulch is usually a light-colored, nonorganic material spread thinly over the seeds. Examples of mulches include granite grit (such as poultry grit) (figures 9.21A, 9.21B), pumice, perlite (figure 9.21C), coarse sand, or vermiculite (figure 9.21D). When properly applied, mulches—

• Create an ideal "moist but not saturated" environment around germinating seeds by making a break in the texture of the potting medium (water will not move from the medium into the mulch).

Figure 9.21—Seed mulches are important to hold the seeds in place and to moderate the surface temperature of the medium during germination. Common mulches include poultry grit (A, B) perlite (C), and vermiculite (D). Photos A and B by Craig R. Elevitch, and photos C and D by Thomas D. Landis.

- Keep seeds in place. This practice improves contact with the medium and minimizes the number of seeds washed out of the containers by irrigation or rainfall.

- Reflect heat when mulches are light colored, so seeds do not get too hot on bright, sunny days.

- Reduce the development of moss, algae, and liverworts (figure 9.22).

The recommended depth of the seed covering varies by species; a general rule is to cover the seed twice as deep as the seed is wide. If mulch is too shallow, seeds may float away in the irrigation water. If the mulch is too deep, small plants may not be able to emerge above it (figure 9.23).

Seeds requiring light need to be left uncovered. Very small seeds need to be left uncovered or barely covered with a fine-textured material such as fine-grade perlite or milled *Sphagnum* peat moss. Uncovered and barely covered seeds must be misted frequently to prevent them from drying out. After light-requiring and light-sensitive species have emerged and are well established, mulch can be applied to prevent moss and liverwort growth and to help keep the medium moist.

Figure 9.22—Mulches help to prevent the development of mosses and liverworts, which can compete with the seedling. Photo by Thomas D. Landis.

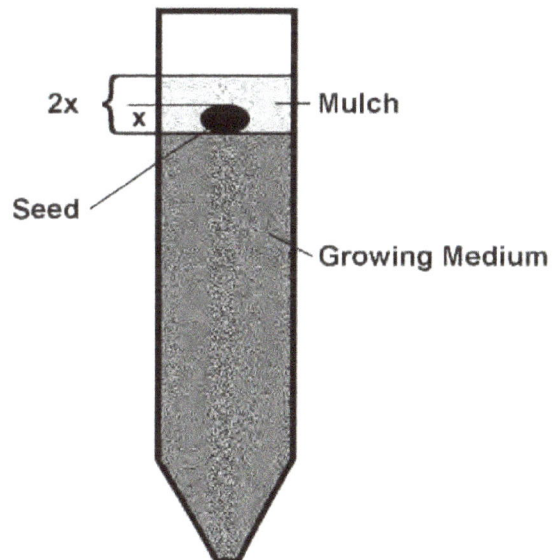

Figure 9.23—A general rule of thumb for covering seeds with mulch is to cover the seed twice as deep as the seed is wide. Species requiring light for germination should never be covered with mulch, although mulch can be added after germination to reduce the growth of moss, liverworts, and weeds. Illustration by Jim Marin.

Germinating Fern Spores

Ferns (figure 9.24) and fern allies (moonworts, mosses, and horsetails) differ from seed plants in that they produce spores instead of seeds. An understanding of the life cycle of ferns is essential for successful fern propagation in nurseries.

Ferns have two life stages—the gametophyte and the sporophyte—the latter being the spore-producing fern plant with which we are all familiar. The sporangia (spore-bearing structures) are variously placed on the lower surface of the leaves and occur in clusters known as sori. In many species, the sori are covered by specialized outgrowths of the leaf, known as the indusium, which lifts and shrivels when spores are ripe. A specialized layer of cells on the stalks of the spores, known as the annuli, contract and expand and the mature spores are disseminated with a catapult-like discharge.

Figure 9.24—*Native Hawaiian fern, a* Sadleria *species. Photo by J.B. Friday.*

After the spores disseminate, they germinate upon contact with a suitably moist substrate. Spore germination results in the gametophyte, which begins development as a small, pale-green, algae-like chain of cells known as the germ filament. Development continues into a flat, heart-shaped structure called the prothallus. Slender holdfasts, known as rhizoids, develop on the lower surface of the prothallus. The reproductive structures, the antheridia (male) and the archegonia (female), develop on the lower surface of the prothallus. Antheridia usually appear before the archegonia, mostly near the rhizoids. Archegonia appear near the notch of the prothallus.

Water must be present for the sperm to swim from the antheridia to the eggs in the archegonia. After fertilization, the young sporophyte receives its nutrients from the gametophyte via a foot-like structure. Further development is rapid and, after the sporophyte achieves a level of photosynthesis sufficient to maintain itself, the gametophyte disintegrates. The sporophyte completes the life cycle when it grows into a mature fern plant and produces spores.

Fern Propagation

When propagating ferns, maintaining a high level of sanitation during all phases of fern development is of the utmost importance. To collect fern spores, find fern fronds with ripe (dark brown, black, or gold) sori. Cut a piece off the frond. Lay each frond piece in a paper envelope, paper bag, or between two sheets of paper. Wait 24 to 48 hours for the spores to drop onto the paper, then collect (Lilleeng-Rosenberger 2005). Removal of nonspore material reduces the chances of contamination by fungi, algae, or bacteria during spore germination. Spores can be sterilized by adding them to a 2- to 5-percent bleach solution with a small drop of wetting agent, which prevents the spores from sticking together. Soak for a few seconds to 1 minute. Collect spores on filter paper and rinse with distilled water thoroughly for 2 minutes (Hoshizaki and Moran 2001).

Germinate spores using sterilized propagation flats that are at least 2 in (5.2 cm) deep with drainage holes. You can use peat cubes, peat pellets, or a sterilized clay brick placed within an airtight, clear plastic shoebox container. Any sterilized commercial growing mix without added fertilizers can also be used. Moisten the medium thoroughly with distilled water before sowing.

Spores can be sown by spraying them on the medium surface with an atomizer, or by delivering small amounts of spores through a syringe with distilled water. Another option is dip a cotton swab into an envelope filled with spores, and then apply the spores to the growing media using the cotton swab.

After sowing, irrigate with distilled water and cover immediately with a clear plastic lid to seal in moisture and to prevent fungal contamination. Place flats under 150- to 500-foot candles of light. If you are using artificial light (cool, white fluorescent), leave lights on for 8 to 24 hours per day. Optimum spore germination temperature is 68 to 86 °F (20 to 28 °C). Try to maintain a constant germination temperature to avoid excessive condensation in the sealed flats. Distilled water needs to be applied when the medium begins to dry slightly on the surface. Flats also need to be closely monitored for any fungal contamination. Spores germinate 10 to 20 days after sowing. If additional irrigation is needed, water only with distilled water delivered through a sterile mist bottle or by placing flats in trays filled with distilled water.

The presence of mold may require special treatments. Stop overhead watering. Make sure that water is not dripping excessively onto plants from condensation. Remove mold and at least 12 mm (0.5 in) of plant tissue and medium beyond the infected area. Apply a mild fungicide labeled for ferns if infection continues.

Shortly after spore germination, the thread-like germ filament can be seen with the aid of a microscope. In general, prothalli become visible 20 days after sowing. The prothalli continue to grow for up to 10 weeks before the reproductive structures, the antheridia and archegonia, become evident on the under surface of the prothallus. These structures can be seen with a microscope when sampling a few prothalli from a tray. After these structures appear, it is important to maintain a thin film of distilled water over the surface of the prothalli. It is very important to keep the germination surfaces evenly moist at all times.

The clear plastic lid is removed from the container when the antheridia have withered and disappeared, usually 4 weeks after their initial appearance. Flats are then transferred from under indoor lights to a shaded greenhouse. The young fern plants (sporophytes) with true leaves and a developing root system will appear sometime after fertilization; from a few weeks to a few months. They can then be transplanted into individual containers.

Try Different Sowing Techniques and Keep Detailed Records

Native plant growers often work with seeds of species that have not yet been propagated in nurseries. Little literature or experience is available to answer questions about seed dormancy-breaking requirements, environmental requirements, germination percentages, and other factors. Understanding the biology and ecology of tropical plants will provide important clues on how to overcome seed dormancy (if any) and provide the correct environmental conditions needed for germination.

It is important to develop a good recordkeeping system to refine and improve results over time and prevent the loss of valuable information. Keep details on the general information of the species, seedlot, seed treatments, and resulting germination. To improve propagation results, use these details to develop and refine propagation protocols, as described in Chapter 4, Crop Planning: Propagation Protocols, Schedules, and Records.

Figure 9.25—Small trials of seed germination and sowing options will help you discover the most effective approach for different species. Photo by Brian F. Daley.

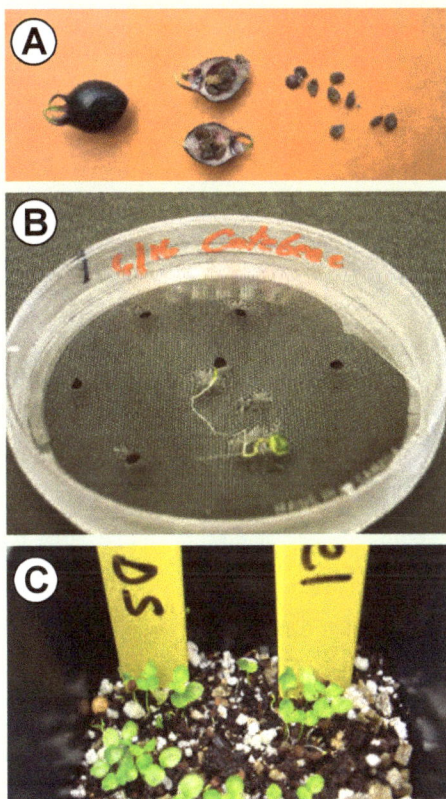

Figure 9.26—Seeds of Catesbaea melanocarpa *shown here with a fruit, a fruit in cross section, and with cleansed seeds (A) were evaluated in sterile dishes (B) to develop a successful germination protocol for this endangered species (C). Photos by Brian F. Daley.*

Trials To Develop a Successful Propagation Protocol for an Endangered Species

Catesbaea melanocarpa of Puerto Rico and the U.S. Virgin Islands is considered federally endangered throughout its range. The seeds (figure 9.26A) are small and challenging to work with.

A few individuals of *Catesbaea melanocarpa* were discovered in a pasture after a wildfire burned grass and underbrush that was obscuring them. With so few plants remaining and in danger of future fires, propagation by seed became a priority. After months of monitoring, a dozen or so ripe fruit were collected, each containing an average of eight small, flat seeds. The seeds were too small to be sown in traditional seed trays and monitored effectively. Due to their small size and scarcity, researchers at the University of the Virgin Islands decided to treat the seeds similar to the way they handle orchid seeds. Sterile dishes of sucrose rich agar (gel) were prepared and 6-8 seeds were placed in each of 10 dishes (figure 9.26B). This intensive germination method allowed for daily observations on every seed collected. Less than one-half of the seeds germinated, and later dissection revealed the nongerminated seeds were smaller than the germinated seed and did not have embryos. When the germinants produced adult leaves, the entire dish was transplanted into plant pots with a mix of ProMix (peat, perlite, and vermiculite blend) and coarse sand. More than 25 percent of the plants desiccated and died shortly after transplanting. The rest of the plants established, but grew slowly. Even with the addition of sand, the media seemed too coarse for the tiny plants.

Later in the season, more fruit were collected. The researchers now knew that one-half of the seeds were likely viable, but that the smaller, malformed seeds could be discarded because they do not have embryos. Researchers added vermiculite to the growing medium mix and sifted it through a screen. Seeds were sown directly into the new, fine medium and germinated in trays in the greenhouse with 80 percent success (figure 9.26C). The second set of seedlings grew more vigorously and did not suffer the transplant shock that killed plants in the first trial.

The first trial led to discoveries about the seeds' viability and identified problems with the growing medium and transplant shock. The second trial used this information and resulted in high germination rates and healthy seedlings of a federally endangered plant in the greenhouse.

Because growers have a number of options for sowing seeds, it is a good idea to do small trials of several of the methods described in this chapter (figure 9.25). See Chapter 20, Discovering Ways to Improve Nursery Practices and Plant Quality, for proper ways of conducting trials. Although several methods may "work"—that is, result in a viable plant produced—the question during the trials should be: Which method is optimal? Trials will help you decide how to answer this question yourself.

Larger Role of Nurseries in Conservation of Species

Each seed is a link between the evolutionary processes of the past and the potential for future adaptation (Flores 2002). While you clean, treat, and germinate seeds to grow your crops, be mindful how your actions affect that species genetic diversity and ability to adapt to the future. Do your best to maintain as much genetic diversity as possible within the species you propagate.

Nurseries are often involved in genetic selection beyond seed collection practices, intentionally or not. For example, production schedules may cause growers to favor faster germinating over slower germinating individuals of the same species, although the quality of the resulting plant would be similar. For some species, the earliest sprouters may be the healthiest. But in other cases, sprouting later may be an adaptive trait; one that could be selected out accidentally by nursery practices. Following up with plant performance in the field can reveal if, in fact, the slower germinating individuals grow well. If so, no reason exists to select these individuals out with nursery practices, and every reason to keep their traits in the gene pool. In this example, simply planting the slower sprouting individuals, as well as the fast ones, could protect diversity. This example is just one that shows how different steps in collecting, storing, germinating, and sowing seeds can affect subsequent plant genetics. The desire for uniform crop size and standardized schedule must be balanced with the need to protect and perpetuate species and genetic diversity.

Nurseries may also have an increasing role in the conservation of tropical species by helping protect and restore genetic diversity of recalcitrant species (species whose seeds do not store well). You are probably familiar with the concept of "seed banks"—seed storage facilities used as reserves to protect and restore species in case their habitats are threatened. Seed banks are also used for some traditional food crops that have become rare with conventional agriculture. Seed banks work well for orthodox species, whose seeds can store for many years and remain viable.

In tropical ecosystems, however, recalcitrant species are as numerous and as important as orthodox species. Because of this distinction, many tropical species cannot be "banked" in conventional seed banks. Instead, nurseries and seedling propagation efforts will play key roles in any efforts to conserve and restore tropical recalcitrant species (Kettle and others 2011).

References

Baskin, C.C.; Baskin, J.M. 1998. Seeds: ecology, biogeography and evolution in dormancy and germination. San Diego, CA: Academic Press. 666 p.

Baskin, C.C.; Baskin, J.M. 2004. Determining dormancy-breaking and germination requirements from the fewest numbers of seeds. In: Guerrant, E.O., Jr.; Havens, K.; Maunder, M., eds. Ex situ plant conservation: supporting species survival in the wild. Washington, DC: Island Press: 162–179.

Drake, D.R. 1993. Germination requirements of Metrosideros polymorpha, the dominant tree of Hawaiian lava flow and rainforests. Biotropica. 25: 461–467.

Dumroese, R.K.; Landis, T.D.; Wenny, D.L. 1998. Raising forest tree seedlings at home: simple methods for growing conifers of the Pacific Northwest from seeds. Contribution 860. Moscow, ID: Idaho Forest, Wildlife and Range Experiment Station. 56 p.

Dumroese, R.K.; Wenny, D.L.; Quick, K.E. 1990. Reducing pesticide use without reducing yield. Tree Planters' Notes. 41(4): 28–32.

Flores, E.M. 2002. Seed biology. In: Vozzo, J.A., ed. 2002. The tropical tree seed manual. Agriculture Handbook 721. Washington, DC: U.S. Department of Agriculture, Forest Service. 13–118. Chapter 1.

Gao, Y.P.; Zheng, G.H.; Gusta, L.V. 1998. Potassium hydroxide improves seed germination and emergence in five native plant species. HortScience. 33: 274-276.

Hartman, H.T.; Kester, D.E.; Davies, F.T.; Geneve, R.L. 1997. Plant propagation: principles and practices. 5th ed. Upper Saddle River, NJ: Prentice Hall Press. 770 p.

Hong, T.D.; Ellis, R.H. 2002. Storage. In: Vozzo, J.A., ed. 2002. The tropical tree seed manual. Agriculture Handbook 721. Washington, DC: U.S. Department of Agriculture, Forest Service. 13–118. Chapter 3.

Hoshizaki, B.J.; Moran, R.C. 2001. The fern growers manual. Portland, OR: Timber Press. 604 p.

James, R.L.; Genz, D. 1981. Ponderosa pine seed treatments: effects on seed germination and disease incidence. Report 81-16. Missoula, MT: U.S. Department of Agriculture, Forest Service, Northern Region, Forest Pest Management. 13 p.

Keeley, J.E.; Fotheringham, C.J. 1998. Smoke induced seed germination in California chaparral. Ecology. 79: 2320-2336.

Kettle, C.J.; Burslem, D.F.R.P.; Ghazoul, J. 2011. An unorthodox approach to forest restoration. Science. 333: 35.

Kurbitzky, K.; Ziburski, A. 1994. Seed dispersal in floodplain forests of Amazonia. Biotropica. 26: 30–43.

Landis, T.D.; Tinus, R.W.; Barnett, J.P. 1999. The container tree nursery manual: volume 6, seedling propagation. Agriculture Handbook 674. Washington, DC: U.S. Department of Agriculture, Forest Service. 166 p.

Lilleeng-Rosenberger, K. 2005. Growing Hawaii's Native Plants. Honolulu, HI; Mutual Publishing. 420 p.

Mousa, H.; Margolis, H.A.; Dubay, P.A.; Odongo, J. 1998. Factors affecting germination of doum palm (*Hyphaene thebaica* Mart.) from the semi-arid zone of Niger, West Africa. Forest Ecology and Management 104 (1-3): 27-41.

Narimanov, A.A. 2000. Presowing treatment of seeds with hydrogen peroxide promotes germination and development in plants. Biologia. 55: 425–428.

Vozzo, J.A., ed. 2002. The tropical tree seed manual. U.S. Department of Agriculture, Forest Service. Washington, DC: U.S. Government Printing Office. 899 p.

Additional Reading

Dreesen, D. 2004. Tumbling for seed cleaning and conditioning. Native Plants Journal. 5: 52–54.

Koebernik, J. 1971. Germination of palm seed. International Palm Society. 15: 134–137.

Landis, T.D. 2000. Where's there's smoke…there's germination? Native Plants Journal. 1: 25–29.

Schmidt, L. 2007. Tropical forest seed. Berlin, Germany: Springer-Verlag. 409 p.

Vegetative Propagation

Tara Luna and Diane L. Haase

10

Many desirable and ecologically important tropical plant species can be difficult or very time consuming to propagate by seeds. Thus, nursery growers may want to investigate how to propagate these species by vegetative propagation, which is accomplished by combining classic horticultural propagation techniques with an understanding of the ecological and reproductive characteristics of the species. Plants that inhabit tropical ecosystems often reproduce vegetatively (that is, asexually without seeds or spores). Vegetative propagation is commonly used with species that have short seed life, low seed viability, or complex seed dormancy. All new daughter plants that arise from vegetative propagation are genetically identical to the mother (donor) plant, and these resulting individuals are known as "clones" (figure 10.1).

Facing Page: *Vegetative propagation is the production of daughter plants from the stems, leaves, roots, or other portions of a single mother (donor) plant. Photo by Ronald Overton.*

Comparing Vegetative to Seed Propagation

The following situations favor vegetative propagation over seed propagation:

- Seed propagation is difficult or very time-consuming.
- Viable seeds are produced infrequently or in small quantities.
- Larger nursery stock is needed in a shorter period of time.
- An individual, unique plant needs to be propagated.
- A need exists to shorten time to flower for seed production.
- A uniform stocktype is needed.
- Specific genotypes are desired.
- Disease-free nursery stock is required.

Disadvantages of using vegetative propagation include—

- Greater production costs than seed propagation, usually because of increased labor.
- Reduced genetic diversity.
- Specialized propagation structures may be required, based on the time of year and the species to be propagated.

Depending on the plant species, vegetative propagation can be done with pieces of stems, leaves, roots, bulbs, corms, tubers, and rhizomes. The species, the type of vegetative material used, the time of year that material is collected, how it is handled and manipulated to induce rooting, and proper application of the correct environmental conditions all affect vegetative propagation.

Because vegetative propagation is more costly than growing seedlings, the production system must be efficient. A general rule of thumb is that at least 50 percent rooting must be obtained to produce cuttings economically. If rare species or individual plants are being propagated, however, costs may be less important.

Consider these methods to reduce production costs:

- Develop a smooth production line, from the collection of material to the final product.
- Train nursery staff how to properly collect, process, plant, and grow material.
- Build a dibble for making holes in the rooting medium.
- Keep good records to improve your results and to document production costs.

Figure 10.1—*Propagation of plumeria by cuttings produces genetically identical plants. Photo by Tara Luna.*

Cuttings

A cutting is the portion of a plant that is collected, treated, and planted to develop into a new intact plant complete with stems, leaves, and roots. Cuttings can be collected from mother plants in the wild, or special donor plants can be cultured in the nursery. Selection of mother plants must be done carefully; it is as important as the origin of seeds to ensure that nursery stock is well adapted to the outplanting environment. Collection of cuttings should follow the same ethical guidelines as collection of seeds to establish proper genetic diversity and sustainability of wild populations (see Chapter 8, Collecting, Processing, and Storing Seeds). In addition, the ability of cuttings to root is often clone-specific, so it is important to record the origin of cuttings and subsequent rooting success.

Striking is the process of placing the cutting into soil or a rooting substrate. Often, propagators will say that cuttings have been "struck" to indicate that the cuttings have been placed in the rooting substrate.

Shoot or Stem Cuttings

Shoot cuttings, also referred to as stem cuttings, are the most common type of cuttings and can be broadly placed

Figure 10.2—*Hardwood cuttings are collected during the dry season or when deciduous tropical species shed their leaves. Photo by Thomas D. Landis.*

into three categories depending on the stage of growth they are in when collected. Hardwood cuttings are made from the previous year's mature wood of trees and shrubs and are usually collected during the dry season in the tropics, when the leaves of deciduous species have dropped (figure 10.2). Semihardwood (greenwood) cuttings are collected towards the end of the active growth season when stem tissues have hardened and terminal buds have formed or just after a flush of growth has taken place and the wood is partially matured. Softwood cuttings are collected when stems and leaves are actively growing.

Hardwood Cuttings of Deciduous Species

Tropical deciduous hardwood stem cuttings are the easiest, least expensive type of cuttings because they are easy to prepare, are not as perishable as softwood or semihardwood cuttings, can be stored in coolers or shipped if necessary, and require little or no special equipment during rooting. They are sometimes struck directly on the outplanting site or brought back to the nursery to grow as bareroot or container stock.

If deciduous hardwood cuttings are struck directly on the outplanting site, they can be live stakes (12- to 16-in [30- to 40-cm] long), poles (12- to 16-ft [3.6- to 4.9-m] long), or branched cuttings (2- to 6-ft [0.6- to 1.8-m] long). These cuttings are collected during the dry season until the early onset of the rainy season and outplanted when the cutting is leafless and the soil at the outplanting site is wet. Live stakes and branched cuttings are usually driven

into the ground with a mallet and need to be planted deep enough to reach moisture in the soil profile with only three to four nodes (buds) above ground. Poles are much longer and are also driven deep enough so they can be in contact with the water table, but the aboveground stem is much longer. Hardwood pole cuttings of *Erythrina*, *Gliricidia*, and other species are commonly used this way for windbreaks, living fences, and restoration projects.

If hardwood cuttings are struck in the nursery, they can be straight, heel, or mallet cuttings (figure 10.3). Straight cuttings are made from straight hardwood stems and are the most common type for easy-to-root species. Heel cuttings are made from 2-year-old side shoots. To make a heel cutting, pull the side shoot away from the tip so that a section of older wood remains at the base of the cutting. Mallet cuttings include a cross-section of older stem at the base of the side shoot.

All hardwood stem cuttings have an inherent polarity and will produce shoots on the distal end (nearest the bud) and roots on the proximal end (nearest the main stem or root system). If planted upside down, the cutting will not root. When using straight or live stake deciduous cuttings, the tops and bottoms of the stems need to be distinguished. The absence of leaves can make it difficult to discern the top from the bottom, so it is useful to cut the bottoms diagonally and the tops straight across. The diagonal cut maximizes water uptake area at the base, and the straight cut minimizes the water loss area at the top.

Figure 10.3—Left to right: straight, heel and mallet cuttings. Straight cuttings are used on easy-to-root species, while mallet and heel cuttings are used on species that are more difficult to root. Photo by Tara Luna.

Hardwood Cuttings of Evergreen Species

Hardwood cuttings of broadleaf tropical evergreen and coniferous species are usually taken during the dry season or just after a new flush of growth during the growing season. Unlike deciduous hardwood cuttings, evergreen cuttings must be struck into a special rooting environment (see Chapter 5, Propagation Environments) as soon as possible because they cannot be stored for any length of time. Evergreens are best rooted in special rooting environments after being wounded or treated with rooting hormone (described in the following sections). Cuttings are usually 4 to 8 in (10 to 20 cm) long, with all leaves removed from the lower half. Green tips and side shoots also need to be removed. The large leaves of tropical broadleaf evergreen plants are usually cut in half to reduce water loss during rooting (figure 10.4). Straight, mallet, and heel cuttings are also used with evergreen species (figure 10.3).

Semihardwood Cuttings

Semihardwood (greenwood) stem cuttings are made from newer shoots of leafy broad-leaved evergreen plants and leafy deciduous species. Cuttings are taken just before the onset of the dry season, towards the end of the active growth season when stem tissues have hardened, or just after a flush of growth when the wood is partially matured. In many cases, the terminal bud has formed. Semihardwood cuttings are propagated in the same manner as evergreen hardwood cuttings.

Softwood Cuttings

Prepared from the new growth of deciduous or evergreen species, softwood cuttings generally root easier than other types of cuttings but require a special rooting environment and more attention to prevent desiccation. The best cutting material has some degree of flexibility but is mature enough to break when bent sharply (figure 10.5). Extremely fast-growing tender shoots are not desirable.

Herbaceous stem cuttings are softwood cuttings made from nonwoody plants. They are handled in the same way as softwood cuttings (figure 10.6). Many succulent tropical plant cuttings, including some cacti, are easily propagated in this manner; cuttings need to be allowed to develop callus for a week before inserting the cutting into rooting media. Succulent cuttings root readily without misting or high humidity.

Root Cuttings

Although not used as much as other types of cuttings, root cuttings can be made by dividing roots into individual segments containing dormant shoot buds capable of developing into new plants. Root cuttings are typically used on species that fail to root well from stem cuttings. Breadfruit (*Artocarpus* species) and noni (*Morinda citrifolia*) are commonly propagated from root cuttings (figure 10.7). Root sections are collected any time of the year in the tropics.

Figure 10.4—The leaves of some broadleaf evergreen cuttings are usually cut in half to reduce the amount of water loss during rooting. Photo by Thomas D. Landis.

Figure 10.5—Rooted softwood stem cuttings of hibiscus. Softwood stem cutting material has some degree of flexibility but is mature enough to break when bent sharply. Photo by Tara Luna.

Figure 10.6—Many herbaceous tropical species, such as āwikiwiki (Canavallia species) can easily be rooted from cuttings using the application of a rooting hormone and a mist environment or an enclosed poly propagator. Photo by Tara Luna.

Figure 10.7—Root cuttings, such as those sown here from breadfruit (Artocarpus species), can be used when stem cuttings do not root well. Photo by Thomas D. Landis.

Root cuttings are planted horizontally in planting beds or containers with the dormant leaf buds on the upper side. Some root cuttings are also planted vertically, but it is important to maintain the correct polarity. Root cuttings generally do not require a special rooting environment unless shoots are cut from the root piece and treated as a stem cutting.

Selecting Cuttings From Mother Plants

A variety of factors such as seasonal timing, juvenility, plagiotropism, species, and cutting size and quality can greatly influence the rooting success of cuttings. Collectors need to be aware of these factors and, with experience, will be able to discern the right type of cutting material to collect.

Some species can be readily propagated from cuttings collected in any season of the year, while others have very specific seasonal trends when they will form roots. For any given species, small experiments are required to determine the optimum time to take cuttings, which is related to the physiological condition of the donor plant at collection time rather than any given calendar date. Recordkeeping is important to improve rooting results from year to year.

All plants progress from a juvenile phase (incapable of producing flowers) to a mature or adult flowering phase. Different parts of the plant, however, can be at different stages of maturity at the same time. Sometimes the juvenile phase can be distinguished from the adult phase by differences in leaf shape or color or by the overall habit of the plant. Some broadleaf species, such as eucalyptus, have distinct juvenile leaves that differ from adult leaves. In conifers, juvenile wood is usually found on the lower portion of the tree crown and the adult, cone-bearing wood is located in the upper crown. In broadleaf plants, juvenile wood is found near the stem base or root crown and can be discerned as the long, nonflowering shoots (sucker shoots). Cuttings collected from this region of the plant root more easily than those from older, mature wood. In some cases, many difficult-to-root species will root only from stems collected from young seedlings. Hedging or coppicing is the practice of regularly cutting back donor plants to maintain juvenile wood and is an efficient means of generating many long, straight cuttings from a limited number of plants. Donor plants in natural stands can be selected for hedging on an annual basis if cuttings will be collected from the area for several years. Otherwise, mother plants can be held in the nursery and used as a source of cuttings as described in the next section.

Plagiotropism is the habit of a cutting to continue to grow in the direction it was growing on the donor plant. Plagiotropism can be strong or weak depending on species and on the original position of the cutting on the donor plant. Plumeria is an example of a tropical broadleaf genus with strong plagiotripism. Often, plants produced from cuttings from lateral shoots will maintain a lateral habit, whereas plants produced from terminal shoots will grow vertically. This tendency can create problems with the growth habit of the nursery stock and is more of a concern with conifers than broadleaf species (Landis and others 1999) (figure 10.8).

Figure 10.8—Plagiotropism is the effect of the position of the branch on the growth habit of the progeny, The terminal shoot on the juniper cutting on the right was collected from a lateral branch and still exhibits lateral growth tendency. Photo by Thomas D. Landis.

Cutting size varies from species to species and by cutting type and seasonal timing. Easily rooted plants can be collected as long poles for rooting or made into small microcuttings. Microcuttings consist of one bud and a small section of internode stem and are typically less than 2 in (5 cm) long (figure 10.9). Hardwood cuttings vary in length from 4 to 30 in (10 to 76 cm). At least two nodes are included in the cutting. The basal cut is made just below a node and the top cut is made above a node. If more than one cutting is being made from a stem, be certain that nursery workers maintain the correct polarity. The very tip portions of the shoot, which are usually low in carbohydrates, are usually discarded. Central and basal portions of the stem usually make the best cuttings, but exceptions exist. Good cutting wood has some stored carbohydrates that will supply the cutting with food reserves until roots form. Very thin or elongated shoots are not desirable. If cuttings are collected from natural stands, harvest from individuals that are growing in full sun to partial shade and avoid those in deep shade. Often, the ability of a cutting to produce new roots changes from the base of the cutting to the tip. Softwood stem cuttings are usually straight, 3 to 6 in (7.5 to 15 cm) long with two or more nodes. In general, softwood cuttings root better from terminal shoots. Semihardwood cuttings are usually 3 to 6 in (7.5 to 15 cm) long with leaves retained in the upper end. Semihardwood cuttings usually root best from lateral shoots.

Many tropical plant species are dioecious, meaning that male and female flowers are borne on separate plants (table 10.1). For example, Hawai'i has the highest degree of diocity in its native flora than anywhere in the world. In such cases, collectors may not realize they have collected cuttings of only one sex. Outplanting plants of only one sex onto the restoration site may compromise project objectives because seed production over the long term will be impossible. Therefore, be sure to collect both male and female cutting material (see Landis and others 2003).

Establishing Mother Plants at the Nursery

Some nursery managers find it advantageous to maintain donor stock plants at the nursery as a continual source of cutting material in a convenient location. Most broadleaf tree species will coppice (regenerate stems from cut stumps), which can provide new cuttings year after year. Maintaining stock plants at the nursery can be more efficient than collecting from wild populations, especially if the same ecotypes will be used for a long-term restoration project. The disadvantage to using mother plants grown at the nursery is that they require nursery space and must be intensively managed.

Mother plants are usually planted in field beds at the nursery or, in some cases, are kept in large containers. These areas are often referred to as "stooling beds"

Figure 10.9—Microcuttings are small stem cuttings with one or two nodes. Photo by Tara Luna.

Table 10.1—Tropical dioecious species.

Scientific name	Common name
Aleurites moluccana	Kukui nut
Broussaisia arguta	Kanawao
Cycas species	Cycad
Morus species	Mulberry
Pandanus tectorius	Podocarp
Piper methysticum	Kava
Pittosporum hosmeri	Ho`awa
Zanthoxylum flavum and *Z. thomasianum*	Yellow prickle

or "hedgerows." Mother plants must be clearly labeled as to species and origin. If mother plants are in field beds, an accurate map should be kept. Mother plants should be hedged on an annual basis to maintain wood juvenility, discourage thick shoots or dominant leaders, and encourage production of numerous straight shoots to use as cutting material. When hedging, it is important to leave enough leaves to keep the root system alive. Moderate shade will encourage shoot elongation, thereby resulting in longer internodes and more easily rooted cuttings (Longman 1993). Mother plants also need periodic watering and nutrients and should be kept free of weeds by mulching or other means.

Collecting, Transporting, and Storing Cuttings

Some basic equipment and supplies are necessary to efficiently collect cuttings and ensure their health until they are struck (figure 10.10). The following items are recommended:

- High-quality, sharp pruning shears and pruning poles for collecting from trees.
- Spray bottles filled with disinfectant (1 part bleach [5.25 percent sodium hypochlorite] in 10 parts water) to disinfect pruning shears.
- Permanent labels and marking pens for noting origin of collection.
- Large, white plastic bags with ties for bulk collections.
- Spray bottles filled with water to keep cuttings moist in the plastic bags after collection.
- Portable, insulated coolers for transport back to the nursery.
- Newspaper, moss, or other materials to moisten and wrap around cuttings.

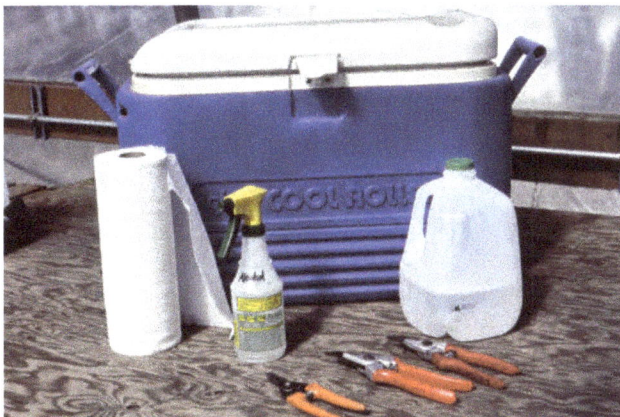

Figure 10.10—Equipment used to collect cuttings includes sharp tools, a cleaning agent for tools, and a cooler to keep cuttings from drying out during transport. Photo by Tara Luna.

When collecting and handling cuttings, it is important to—

- Collect only from healthy donor plants.
- Keep cuttings cool to avoid wilting and desiccation.
- Handle cuttings carefully so that tissues are not bruised.
- Make sure that some buds or leaves are present on stem cuttings.
- Collect from nonflowering shoots. In general, cuttings root better before or after flowering.
- Place cuttings in the same direction when bundling to avoid mix-ups with polarity.

Cuttings should be collected on cloudy, cool days or during the early morning. All cuttings should be handled with care. Cuttings need to be kept cool and shaded during collection and transport back to the nursery to avoid water loss and physical damage. Wrap cuttings loosely in moistened newspaper (or other moistened material to protect from desiccation), place them into white plastic bags, mist them, and label with origin information and the date. When collecting from mother plants, make a proper cut that facilitates healing of the mother plant. Take the cutting just above a node, ensuring that you do not leave a stub. Then trim the base of the cutting to just below the node where rooting is more likely to occur. Between collection sites, disinfect the pruning shears with the bleach solution to avoid spreading disease.

Deciduous hardwood cuttings can be wrapped in moist peat moss or burlap and stored in a shaded, dry environment with periodic moisture to prevent dessication. Cuttings can be stored for several days but generally no longer than 4 to 8 weeks. Inspect stored cuttings frequently to make certain that tissues are slightly moist and free from fungal diseases. Hardwood and softwood evergreen cuttings, deciduous softwood cuttings, and semihardwood cuttings should be struck in propagation beds the same day of collection and should never be stored for longer than 1 day.

Types of Rooting

The development of new roots on a shoot is known as "adventitious root formation" (figure 10.11A). Two types of roots occur depending on whether buds capable of producing new roots are present. Many tropical species have buds present and the resulting roots are termed "preformed" or "latent." In the nursery, cuttings of these species are usually struck directly into containers because they do not require a special rooting environment. This method is the easiest and most economical way to produce these species because no additional transplanting is needed.

Figure 10.11—*Adventitious roots of a cutting (A), callus and roots forming at the base of a cutting (B), adventitious root formation during a 6-week period (C). Photos by Tara Luna.*

If no buds are present, then the roots are termed "wound-induced" and new roots will form only in response to the wound caused by preparing the cutting. Species requiring wounding can vary considerably in their ability to form new roots. After a cutting is wounded, callus tissue forms at the base, primarily from the vascular tissue (figure 10.11B). In easy-to-root species, callus formation and root formation are independent processes that occur at the same time because of similar environmental triggers (figures 10.11B, 10.11C). In difficult-to-root species, adventitious roots arise from the callus mass. In some cases, excessive callus can hinder rooting and is a signal to use a lower concentration of rooting hormone. Often, excess callus needs to be scraped away and the cutting replaced in the rooting environment.

In general, all species with wound-induced roots must first be rooted in a special propagation environment with tightly controlled air and medium temperatures, high relative humidity, reduced light levels, and "moist, but not wet" medium (figure 10.12). See Chapter 5, Propagation Environments, for more details on propagation environments. Easy-to-root species are often struck directly into containers filled with regular growing medium and, after they are rooted in the special propagation environment, they are moved into the regular nursery. Hard-to-root species are often struck into trays or beds containing a special rooting medium and, after roots form, they are transplanted into containers to continue their growth.

Cutting Preparation

While preparing cuttings, it is important to keep the work area clean. Use sharp, well-maintained shears and knives to make clean cuts. Disinfect these tools often to reduce the possible spread of disease. Preparing cuttings standardizes their size and shape, promotes side shoots, and eliminates shoot tips that often die back. It is important to maintain polarity during this process, especially for deciduous hardwood cuttings. Cuttings that will require hormone treatment

to encourage rooting, such as those of hardwood narrowleaf evergreens or any softwood or semihardwood cuttings, should have one-third to one-half of the leaves and buds removed to reduce the amount of water loss from the cutting. Any flower buds also need to be removed. It is important, however, to retain some buds or leaves on the cutting so that the cutting can manufacture food during rooting.

Wounding Cuttings

Wounding, used on species that are difficult to root, increases rooting percentages and improves the quantity and quality of roots produced. Wounding exposes more cells to rooting hormone, encourages callus formation, and, in some cases, removes thick woody tissue that can be a barrier to root formation. Cuttings are commonly wounded by hand-stripping small lower stems and leaves to create wounded areas along the basal portion of the cutting, scraping the base of the stem with a small, sharp knife

Figure 10.12—*Semihardwood cuttings in a shadehouse at the University of the Virgin Islands, agroforestry facility are struck in trays of 100 percent perlite and misted every hour to ensure that no standing water exists, but the cuttings are always moist. The shadecloth around the PVC frame provides a shady, low-wind, high-moisture atmosphere for the cuttings while they produce roots. Rooted cutting are later transferred to small pots in the shadehouse for 2 to 3 weeks and later transferred to full sun. Photo by Brian F. Daley.*

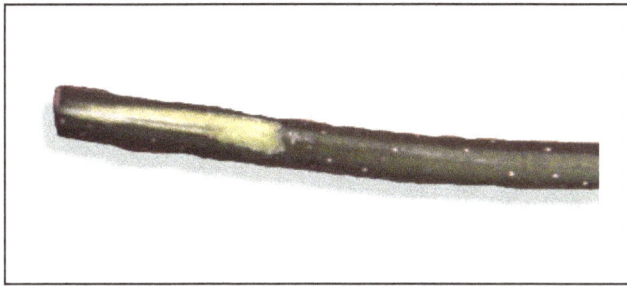

Figure 10.13—Wounding the lower end of a stem cutting increases rooting with difficult-to-root species. Photo by Tara Luna.

or potato peeler (figure 10.13), or slicing one or two long, shallow slivers (0.75 in to 1.25 in [2 to 3.2 cm] long) of tissue from the base of the stem, making sure to penetrate the cambium layer of the stem. Slicing requires precision and experience so that cuttings are not excessively damaged.

Rooting Hormones

Auxins are natural plant hormones that encourage root formation on cuttings and are available from natural and synthetic sources. In practice, auxins are commonly referred to as rooting hormones. Most cuttings are treated with synthetic hormones that are available in powder and liquid form, and some preparations may contain chemical fungicides (figure 10.14). Synthetic hormones can be purchased ready to use or can be mixed by growers to specific concentrations using ingredients purchased from horticultural suppliers. Indole-3-butyric acid (IBA) and naphthaleneacidic acid (NAA) are the most widely used synthetic auxins. Often, mixtures of IBA and NAA are more effective than either component alone. The effect of

rooting hormones varies widely between species and, in some cases, between genotypes. In general, rooting hormone powders are expressed as a percentage, while liquid solutions are expressed as parts per million (ppm).

It is generally easiest to purchase ready-to-use formulations. It is important to remember that all rooting hormones have a limited shelf life of 18 to 24 months. Therefore, when purchasing or mixing hormones—

- Record the date of purchase on the container.
- Order only what you plan to use within 18 to 24 months. Order smaller quantities more often to ensure that the rooting hormone remains effective.
- Keep containers sealed and refrigerated when not in use to preserve the activity of the rooting hormone.

Many growers prefer powders because several commercial products of varying strengths are available, they are easy to use, and large quantities of cuttings can be treated quickly. Powder must be applied uniformly to all cuttings; variable amounts of rooting powder adhere to the base of a cutting, which can affect rooting results (figure 10.15). The following precautions and special techniques are necessary when using powders:

- Wear gloves during application.
- Transfer enough hormone to a smaller container from the main stock container for use; never transfer unused hormone back to main stock container.
- Make sure the base of the cutting is moist so that the powder adheres; pressing cuttings lightly onto a moist sponge is a useful technique.

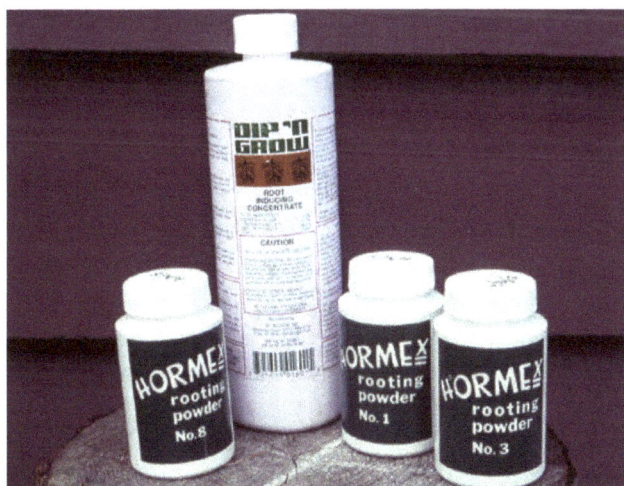

Figure 10.14—Advantages of rooting hormones are (1) increased rooting percentages if applied correctly at an effective concentration, (2) more rapid root initiation, (3) an increase in the total number and quality of roots, and (4) more uniform rooting. Photo by Tara Luna.

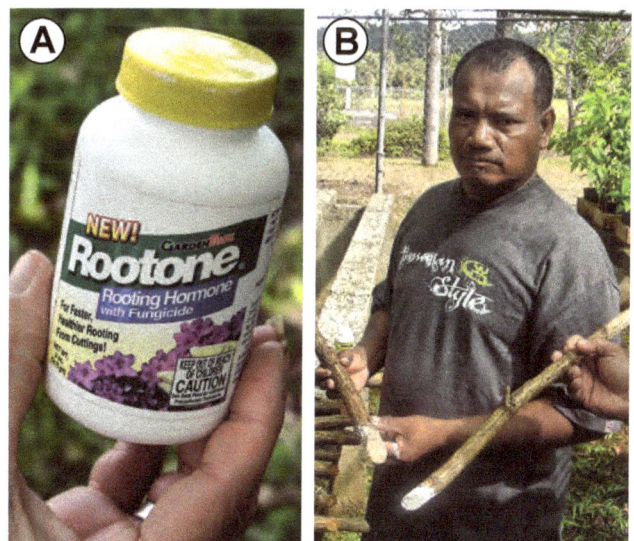

Figure 10.15—Many growers prefer powders to liquid hormones (A). Apply powder hormones evenly and consistently (B). Photo A by Thomas D. Landis, and photo B by George Hernández.

- Apply the hormone uniformly. Make sure cuttings are dipped into the powder to a depth of 0.2 to 0.4 in (5 to 10 mm). Make certain that cut surfaces and other wounds are also covered with rooting hormone.

- Remove excess powder by lightly tapping the cuttings on the side of the dish.

Liquid products are formulated with alcohol and often must be diluted with great care to create the desired strength. Some of the advantages of using solutions are the availability of a wide range of commercial preparations, specific concentrations can be formulated at the nursery, and they can be stored for longer periods under the right conditions. Some growers believe that liquid solutions are more accurate than powders regarding the amount of rooting hormone entering the stem tissue. The most common procedure for treating cuttings with liquid products is the quick-dip method in which the base of the cutting is dipped into the solution for 3 to 10 seconds. Whole bundles of cuttings can be treated at once (figure

Figure 10.16—*Using the liquid hormone "quick dip" method is preferred by many growers because bundles of cuttings can be treated at the same time with consistent uniformity of application. Photo by Tara Luna.*

10.16). An alternate method is to soak cuttings for a longer time in a more dilute hormone solution. When using liquid rooting hormones, it is important to—

- Wear gloves during mixing, preparation, and application.

- Make certain that the solution was precisely diluted to the correct concentration.

- Place the solution in a clean jar.

- Ensure that the treatment time is constant for a uniform application rate and to avoid damaging the plant tissue.

- Make certain that the basal ends are even to obtain uniform depth of dipping in the solution if bundles of cuttings are dipped.

- Allow the alcohol to evaporate from the stem of the cutting before striking cuttings into the propagation bed, a process that usually takes only a couple of minutes.

- Properly discard any remaining solution, because it is contaminated with plant material.

The optimum auxin rate for cuttings varies by plant species. A good starting rate is a 0.25-0.5 percent (2,500-5,000 ppm). With trial and error, this rate can be increased or decreased until optimum rooting occurs for a particular species. Longman (1993) listed rates of IBA for the following tropical species:

- 0.2 percent for *Triplochiton scleroxylon*, *Tripvochysia hondurensis*, and several other tropical tree species.

- A range of 0.05 to 0.4 percent for *Albizia guachapele*.

- 0.4 percent for *Cordia alliodora*.

- 1.0 percent for *Khaya ivorensis*.

Striking, Monitoring, and Growing Cuttings

Direct striking into containers is more efficient and therefore more economical than striking into a special rooting environment because the cuttings are handled only once and expensive transplanting is avoided. Easy-to-root hardwood cuttings, such as many *Erythrina* species, *Gliricidia sepium* (known locally as "quick stick" in much of the world), and mangrove propagules should always be direct struck (figure 10.17). Often, a dibble of the same diameter as the stem of the cutting is a useful tool for making openings in the medium into which the cutting can be struck. For striking several small cuttings, a template for the holes can be created by driving nails through a piece of plywood at the correct spacing and

Figure 10.17—Easy-to-root hardwood cuttings (A) or mangrove propagules (B) can be directly stuck into containers for rooting and is the most economical way of producing cuttings. Photo A by Tara Luna, and photo B by Thomas D. Landis.

depth. If using powdered rooting hormones, this practice of creating holes ahead of time will help keep the hormone from being brushed off. The following practices need to be encouraged when striking cuttings:

- Wear gloves if the cuttings were treated with rooting hormones.

- Maintain polarity (keep the correct end of the cutting up).

- When using stem cuttings, make certain that at least two nodes are below the surface of the rooting medium.

- If cuttings were wounded, make certain that wounded tissue is adequately covered with rooting hormone and is below the surface of the rooting medium.

- Strike cuttings firmly in the rooting medium. Make certain to avoid air pockets around the base of the stem.

- Try to strike cuttings within 1 to 2 days so that all the plants will have the same level of root development and thus can be hardened off properly before harvesting.

- Place labels before the first cutting and after the final cutting of a particular clone or batch of cuttings.

After cuttings are struck, maintain a clean rooting environment (figure 10.18); routinely inspect cuttings for proper temperature, humidity, and moisture levels and adjust as necessary. Check to ensure that all equipment (including bottom heat) is working properly.

Environmental Conditions for Direct Struck Cuttings

In general, easy-to-root hardwood cuttings directly struck into containers can be treated similar to seedlings.

Environmental Conditions in Special Rooting Environments

Achieving successful rooting requires attention to sanitation, relative humidity, temperature, light, rooting medium, and sometimes mycorrhizae and dilute fertilization. See Chapter 5, Propagation Environments, for information about equipment necessary to regulate humidity, temperature, and light.

Sanitation

Always keep the propagation environment as clean as possible. Strike cuttings into a sterilized rooting medium. Routinely inspect for and remove dead leaves or cuttings that could be a source of disease infection.

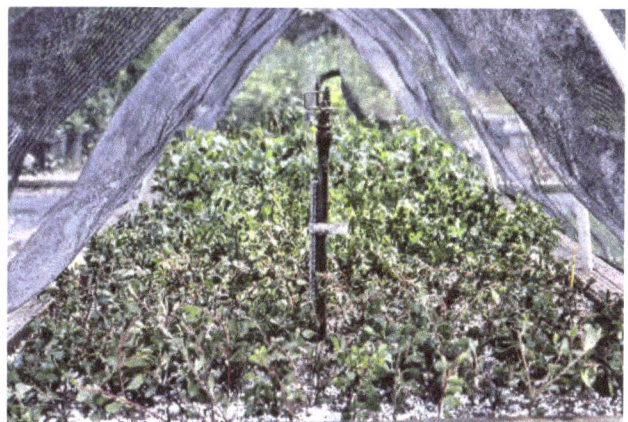

Figure 10.18—The propagation environment must be carefully maintained to ensure that the mist system, the timers that control the frequency of mist, and other equipment are working properly. Keeping the rooting environment as clean as possible during rooting is crucial for producing healthy plants. Photo by Tara Luna.

Humidity

Until the root system forms, high relative humidity must be maintained in the propagation environment to slow the rate of water loss from the cutting. Placing cuttings under an automatic misting or fogging system is often effective. Another method is to place the cuttings within a frame covered in clear or white polyethylene sheeting with a reserve of water below a moist rooting medium (Longman 1993). Cuttings in this "polypropagator" need to also be irrigated with a fine spray of water in late afternoon and early morning, especially when the weather is hot and dry. If possible, water temperature should not be significantly cooler or warmer than the rooting medium to avoid damaging the young roots from sudden changes in temperature. Achieving optimum humidity and medium moisture can be one of the most challenging aspects of successful propagation with cuttings. Too much moisture can encourage fungal pathogens and rotting, whereas too little moisture can result in lethal desiccation. Daily monitoring is important.

Light and Temperature

Providing light for photosynthesis is necessary so that cuttings can continue to manufacture food during rooting, but too much sunlight can cause high temperatures. Shadecloths of 30 to 50 percent shade cover are most effective to reduce air temperature while providing sufficient light. Shadecloth can also serve to reduce the effect of rain when propagating outdoors. The optimum air temperature for rooting cuttings is 68 to 80 °F (20 to 28 °C)—manage with shade so the air temperature does not exceed 91 °F (33 °C) maximum. Optimum temperatures of the rooting medium needs to be about 5 °F cooler [63 to 75 °F (17 to 24 °C)] than optimum air temperatures.

Rooting Medium

A good rooting medium provides aeration and moisture, physically supports the cuttings, and promotes the development of fibrous root systems. A pH of 5.5 to 6.5 is optimum for most plants, but acid-loving plants prefer 4.0 to 5.0. Some common components of rooting media generally include a combination of two or more of the following: large-grade perlite, pumice, *Sphagnum* peat moss, sawdust, sand, coir, grit, or fine bark chips. The ideal rooting medium drains freely and does not become waterlogged from misting. Different rooting media components are used depending on the species being propagated. Selection of the rooting medium components influences rooting percentages and the quality of roots produced. Using very fine-grade or very coarse-grade sands tends to discourage the development of secondary roots. Roots that do form tend to be brittle and break off during transplanting. See Chapter 6, Growing Media, for more details on developing a good growing medium.

Mycorrhizal Fungi

Some growers inoculate the rooting medium with mycorrhizal fungi or other symbiotic organisms, which has improved rooting results with some species (Scagel and others 2003). See Chapter 13, Beneficial Microorganisms, for more information on mycorrhizae.

Nutrient Mist

Some difficult-to-root cuttings may remain in a special rooting environment for a long period of time. Over time, nutrients can be leached from the leaves by the long exposure to overhead misting, resulting in yellowing of the leaves or leaf and needle drop. In these cases, the application of a dilute, complete foliar fertilizer through the mist line can improve cutting vigor and may aid in rooting. Because some species respond favorably to nutrient mist while others are adversely affected, you will need to do some preliminary trials before treating all the cuttings. Also, be aware that excessive nutrients can encourage unwanted growth of mosses and algae on the medium surface.

Transplanting Cuttings From Special Rooting Environments

A few weeks after striking cuttings into the rooting environment, they should be inspected for root development. Using a trowel, carefully dig well below the end of the cutting and excavate it to examine for rooting. When cuttings have developed adequate root systems, they need to be hardened for transplanting outside the rooting environment. See Chapter 15, Hardening, for more information. The goal is to condition stem and leaf tissues and promote secondary root development before transplanting. Following these guidelines can harden cuttings:

- Gradually reduce the misting frequency over a period of 3 to 4 weeks.
- Increase the frequency and duration of ventilation in enclosed propagation systems.
- Do not let the rooting medium dry out completely.

After cuttings have hardened, transplant them into containers and transfer them to the nursery for additional growth (figure 10.19). Because cuttings are more expensive to produce than seedlings, it is important to handle them

Figure 10.19—Cuttings can be transplanted into containers and moved to the nursery for hardening. Photo by Tara Luna.

carefully at this stage. It is essential to avoid root damage by following these guidelines:

- Examine each cutting to ensure it has a root system capable of sustaining the cutting after transplanting. Cuttings with only a few slender roots or very short roots need to remain in the propagation bed for further root development (figure 10.20A).

- Transplant only on cool, overcast days or during early morning hours to avoid transplant shock.

- Transplant cuttings in an area of the nursery protected from wind and sunlight.

- Prepare containers, medium, labels, and transplanting tools before transplanting cuttings.

- Moisten the growing medium before transplanting to prevent tender roots from drying out.

- Remove cuttings from the rooting medium carefully and remove only a few at a time so roots will not dry out. Loosely wrap a moist paper towel around the root systems until they are transplanted.

- Handle cuttings carefully by holding the cutting by the stem and by leaving any rooting medium still attached to the root mass. Do not shake medium off the root system.

- Partially fill the container with moistened medium before inserting the cutting. Then add additional moistened medium and gently firm the medium with fingers without breaking the roots (figure 10.20B).

- Do not transplant the cuttings too deep or too shallow.

After transplanting the cuttings, they need to be placed in a shadehouse or protected from full sun and wind for at least 2 weeks. When the cuttings appear to be well established, gradually increase the level of sunlight by moving them to a different area of the nursery or by exchanging the shadecloth for one with a more open weave. After a couple of weeks, move sun-requiring species into full sun. Cuttings need to be closely monitored for any sign of stress. Adequate sunlight is needed for new shoot growth and adequate accumulation of carbohydrates before outplanting.

Other Methods of Vegetative Propagation

Besides stems and roots, several other portions of mother plants can be used to vegetatively propagate new daughters, and stems can be used in ways other than the traditional rooted cuttings.

Layering

Layering is a technique by which adventitious roots are formed on a stem while still attached to the plant.

Figure 10.20—Cuttings need to have enough developed roots that can support the cutting after it is lifted and transplanted outside the mist chamber or polypropagator (A). Cuttings with under-developed roots need to be left in the propagation bed longer to develop an adequate root mass (B). Photos by Tara Luna.

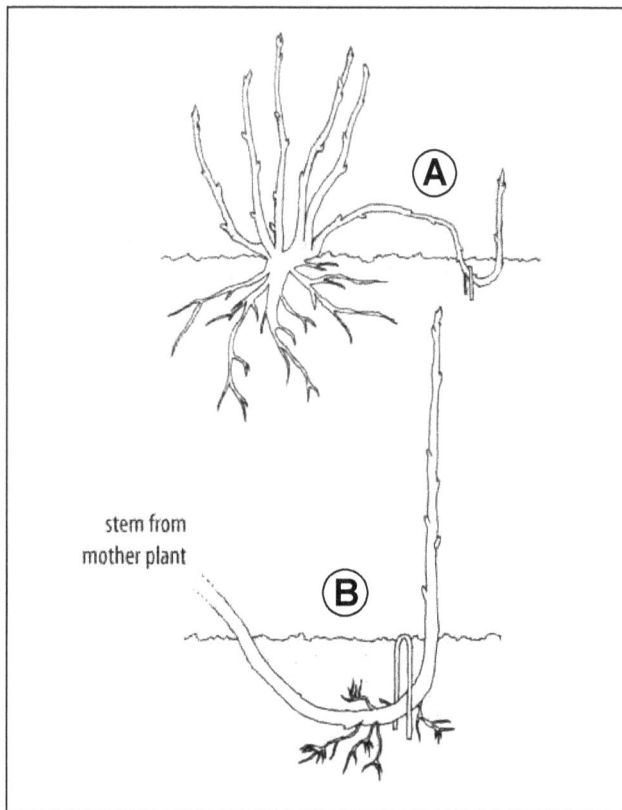

Figure 10.21—In simple layering, the stem from a mother plant is pinned down and covered with soil or an organic mulch (A). New plants can be severed after there is sufficient shoot and root development (B). Graphic courtesy of Bruce McDonald and Timber Press, Inc.

Layering often occurs naturally without the assistance of a propagator. It is mostly used on those species that fail to root from stem or root cuttings. Four types of layering are commonly used in tropical nurseries: simple, French, air, and mound. In addition, drop and stack are two other layering techniques that could be used.

Simple Layering

Simple layering is used on species that produce many shoots annually. Long, low-growing flexible shoots are pegged down 6 to 9 in (15 to 23 cm) from the shoot tip, forming a "U" (figure 10.21A). The bottom of the U stem is girdled with a sharp knife and is covered with soil, sawdust, or other organic mulch, leaving the tip exposed. After a sufficient root system is formed, the new plant can be severed from the donor plant (figure 10.21B).

French Layering

French layering is similar to simple layering but uses a long, single branch that is pegged down to the soil surface (figure 10.22A). After a period of time, the pegs are removed and the branch is laid into a trench and buried up to the tips of the shoots with well-aerated soil and sawdust or mulch (figure 10.22B). After burying repeatedly, each shoot along the stem will form roots by the second year (figure 10.22C) and can be severed from the mother plant (figure 10.22 D).

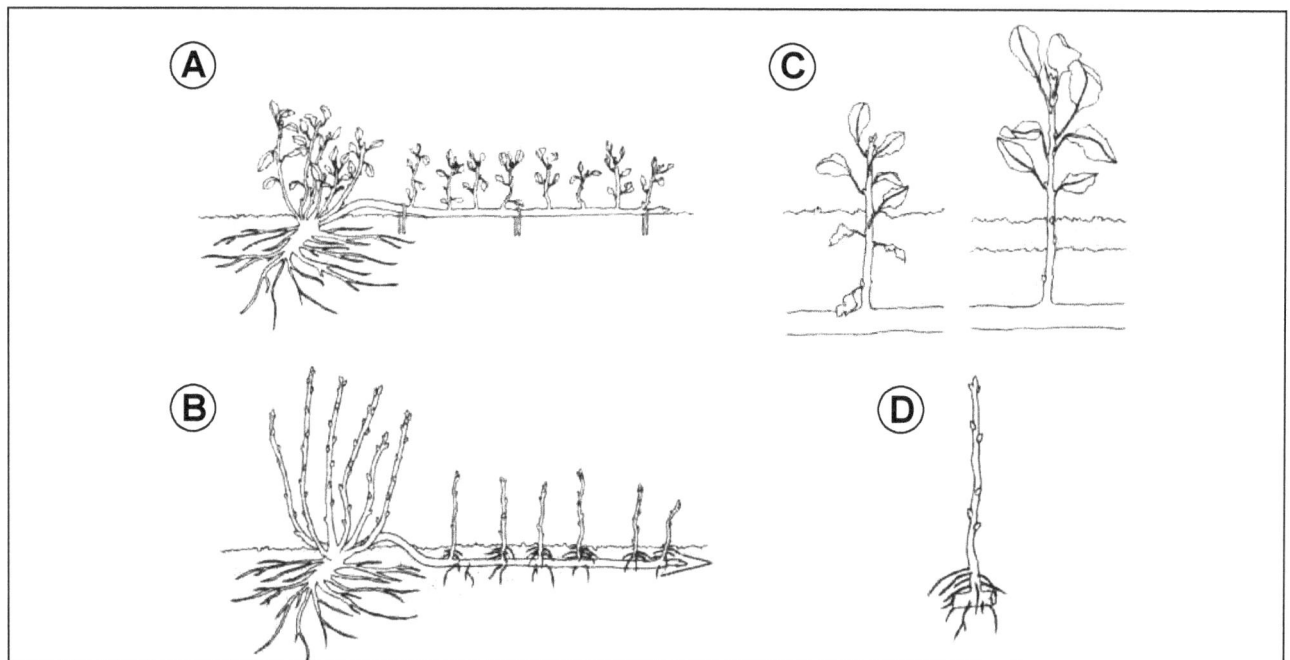

Figure 10.22—French layering consists of pegging a long branch to the soil surface and allowing for new shoots to develop (A). After a period of time, the branch is buried in a deeper trench to encourage root development on each new shoot (B). Repeated burying (C) results in sufficient root development for plants to be severed from the mother plant (D). Graphic courtesy of Bruce McDonald and Timber Press, Inc.

Tropical Nursery Manual

Figure 10.23—*After wounding the stem, an air layer is created by wrapping the area with peat moss (A), then enclosing this stem area in plastic wrap (B), and sealing the ends (C). After the layer has rooted (D), it can be severed from the stem and potted. Photos by Thomas D. Landis.*

Air Layering

Air layering is useful for producing a few plants of relatively large size. An advantage of air layering is that the rooted layer will be physiologically similar in age to the parent plant and will therefore flower and fruit sooner than a seedling or cutting. Air layering is used mostly on tropical fruit species, such as lychee, and to propagate rare and endangered tropical species. For optimum rooting, air layers are made on shoots produced during the previous season or during the mid- to late-active growing season on shoots from the current season's growth (figure 10.23). For woody plants, stems of pencil-size diameter or larger are best. An area directly below a node is chosen, normally about 1 ft (30 cm) from the tip. Leaves and twigs on the stem are removed 3 to 4 in (7 to 10 cm) above and below this point. Air layering techniques differ slightly depending on whether the species is a monocot or a dicot.

The following steps describe air layering of monocots:

- Make an upward 1.0- to 1.5-in (2- to 4-cm) cut about one-third through the stem.

- Hold the cut open with a toothpick or wooden matchstick.

- Surround the wound with moist, unmilled *Sphagnum* moss (about a handful) that has been soaked in water and squeezed to remove excess moisture.

- Wrap the moss with plastic and hold in place with twist ties or electrician's tape. No moss should extend beyond the ends of the plastic.

- Fasten each end of the plastic securely, to retain moisture and to prevent water from entering. If it will be exposed to the sun, the plastic needs to be shaded.

The following steps describe air layering of dicots:

- With a sharp knife, make two parallel cuts about 1 in (2.5 cm) apart around the stem and through the bark and cambium layer.

- Connect the two parallel cuts with one long cut.

- Remove the ring of bark, leaving the inner woody tissue exposed.

- Scrape the newly bared ring to remove the cambial tissue to prevent a bridge of callus tissue from forming.

- Application of a root-promoting substance to the exposed wound is sometimes beneficial.

- Wrap and cover using the same procedure as that described for monocots.

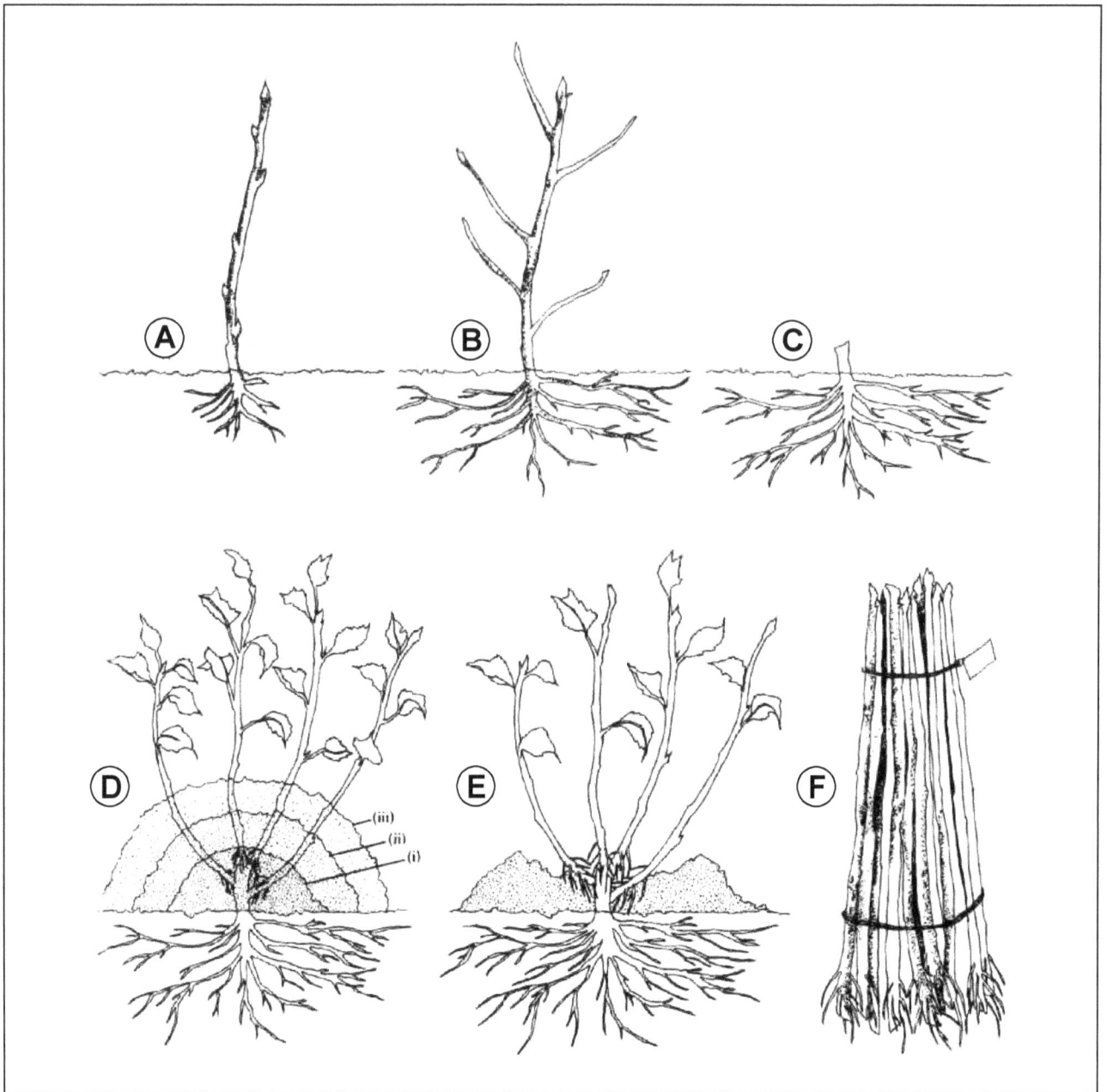

Figure 10.24—*Mound layering or stooling involves selecting a young stock plant (A, B) and cutting back its shoots (C). After new shoots develop, they are covered to one-half of their height with soil, sawdust, or other organic mulch; this procedure is repeated three times (D), encouraging root development on the new shoots (E). After 2 or 3 growing seasons, the well-rooted shoots are ready to plant as individuals (F). Graphic courtesy of Bruce McDonald and Timber Press, Inc.*

For both monocots and dicots, the stem is severed below the medium after the rooting medium is filled with roots (figure 10.23D). The layer is then potted and needs to be kept shaded with adequate moisture until the root system becomes more developed.

Mound Layering

Mound layering or stooling involves selecting a young stock plant (figures 10.24A, 10.24B) and cutting back shoots to 2 to 4 in (5 to 10 cm) above ground level (figure 10.24C). Numerous shoots develop in consecutive growing seasons and are covered to one-half of their height with soil, sawdust, or other organic mulch (figure 10.24D). This procedure is repeated three times as the shoots grow so that, by the end of the second or third growing season, the well-rooted shoots are unburied and are ready to plant as individuals (figures 10.24E, 10.24F).

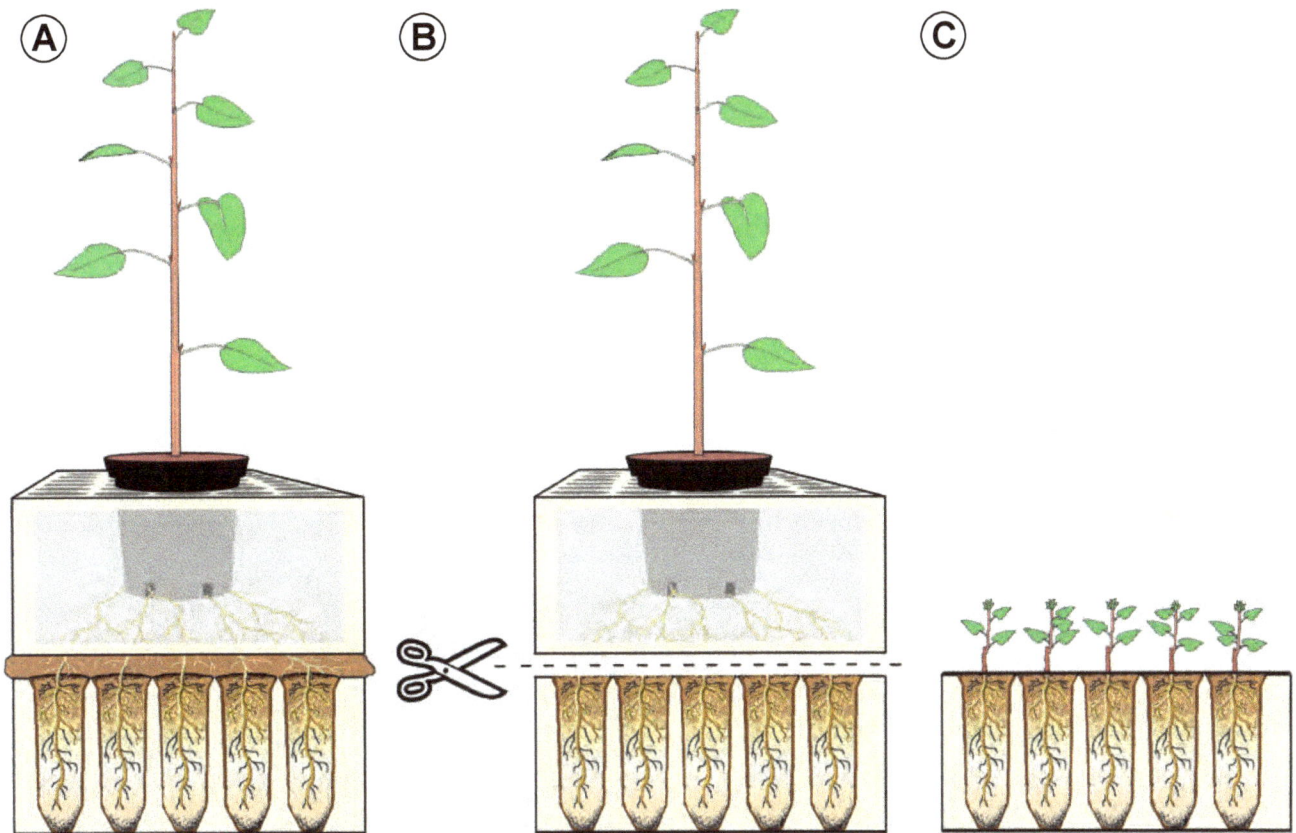

Figure 10.25—Roots from the mother plant grow downward through the cavities of stacked Styrofoam™ containers (A). The roots are then severed (B), after which they develop new shoots (C). Adapted from Landis and others (2006).

Drop Layering

Drop layering is very similar to mounding. Drop layering involves planting well-branched container plants deeply in the ground with only the tips of the branches exposed. New growth forms from the exposed branch tips, but the buried portions of the stems form roots along the stems.

Stacked Layering

Stacked layering is a new vegetative propagation method for rhizomatous species (Landis and others 2006). This technique takes advantage of the rapid and extensive root growth of seedlings and the fact that severed roots will form new shoots. In the spring, a stack of Styrofoam™ containers is created with a 1-gallon pot containing a seedling inserted in the top block. The lower Styrofoam™ containers are filled with growing medium with a thin layer of medium sandwiched between the blocks (figure 10.25A). After several months, the roots of the mother plant will have grown down through and colonized the cavities in the lower blocks. Running a sharp knife between the Styrofoam™ containers severs the roots, which then form new shoots (figure 10.25B). After a few months, the new plants can be transplanted into larger pots. Another set of filled Styrofoam™ containers can be situated below the block with the mother plant to start another propagation cycle.

Tuberous Roots, Tubers, Rhizomes, and Crown Division

Tuberous roots, tubers, and rhizomes are specialized plant structures that function in the storage of food, nutrients, and water. Many culturally important tropical species, which are not easily grown from seeds, have these structures.

Tuberous roots are swollen secondary roots. Separating each tuberous root that has a section of the crown bearing a shoot bud produces new plants. Cassava, yams, and sweet potatoes, that are widely cultivated throughout Polynesia, produce tuberous roots.

Tubers are swollen modified stems that serve as underground storage organs. One well-known common tuber is the white potato. "Eyes" in white potatoes are actually nodes containing buds. Propagation by tubers involves planting the entire tuber or dividing it into sections containing at least one eye or bud. Pia, taro, wapato, and elephant taro are examples of tropical species that produce tubers.

Rhizomes are specialized stems in which the main axis of the plant grows horizontally or vertically at or below the soil surface. Many native tropical species, such as native begonias, reproduce by rhizomes and are easily propagated into larger numbers from a few nursery plants by divisions. Rhizomes vary in length and size according to species. Rhizomes are cut into sections with each containing at least one shoot bud or active shoot; some roots are attached to the bottoms of the rhizomes and are planted into containers individually. Rhizomes can also be planted in nursery beds and used as a source for bareroot stock for planting or for cultural uses such as basketry.

Crown division is an important method for propagating many native herbaceous perennials that produce multiple offshoots from the crown. Crown divisions are usually done just before active growth and flowering. Plants are dug up and cut into sections with a sharp knife, each with a substantial portion of the root system, and transplanted individually.

Stolons, Runners, and Offsets

Stolons, runners, and offsets are specialized plant structures that facilitate propagation by layering. Stolons are modified stems that grow horizontally above the soil line and produce a mass of stems. Runners are specialized stems that arise from the crown of the plant and grow horizontally along the ground and produce a plantlet at one of the nodes. Raised beds planted with species with stolons or runners can be an endless source of propagation material, and plants can be dug and potted individually or transplanted as bareroot stock.

Plants with rosettes often reproduce by forming new shoots, called offsets, at the base of the main stem or in the leaf axils. Offsets are cut close to the main stem of the plant with a sharp knife. If well rooted, an offset can be potted individually. Plantain and banana are often propagated with offsets (figure 10.26). Sever the new shoots from the mother plant after they have developed their own root systems. Nonrooted offsets of some species may be removed and placed in a rooting medium. Some of these offsets must be cut off, while others may simply be lifted from the parent stem.

Grafting and Budding

Grafting is the art of connecting two pieces of living plant tissues, the scion and the rootstock, together in such a manner that they will unite and grow as one plant. Grafting is used primarily in the tropics for mango, citrus, other tropical fruits, and forest tree seed orchards. In Hawai'i, grafting has been used to propagate the highly endangered

Figure 10.26—Plantain and banana are often propagated with offsets. Photo by Ronald Overton.

species, *Kokia cookei* (figure 10.27). It is also used to repair or to top-work existing trees to change varieties, as well as to produce new plants.

The scion is a short piece of shoot including several shoot buds, which, when united with the rootstock, forms the upper portion of the plant. The rootstock is the lower portion of the graft, which develops into the root system. If grafting is done high in the tree, the rootstock includes the roots, main trunk, and scaffold branches. The rootstock may be a seedling, rooted cutting, or an older tree.

Budding is grafting using a scion with only a single bud attached to a piece of bark. It may or may not include a thin sliver of wood under the bark. Budding is the most commonly used technique for propagating new plants, but it is also used to top-work existing trees to a new variety.

The rootstock and the scion must be compatible for successful grafting. Compatibility is never a problem when grafting within a clone. Grafting between clones within a species is usually successful. Grafting between species in a genus is sometimes successful and is most often seen in the genus *Citrus*. Grafting between genera within a plant family is rarely done and the chances of success are slim. Grafting between plant families is impossible for woody plants.

In addition to compatibility, a number of factors exist that contribute to a successful graft or bud union. Vascular cambium of the scion must be placed and held in intimate contact with the vascular cambium of the rootstock. The grafting operation must be done at a time when both the rootstock and the scion are in the correct physiological stage. Immediately after grafting, all cut surfaces must be protected from desiccation. Breaking of the union between the scion and the rootstock will usually manifest failed grafts. Grafts can fail because the rootstock and scion are

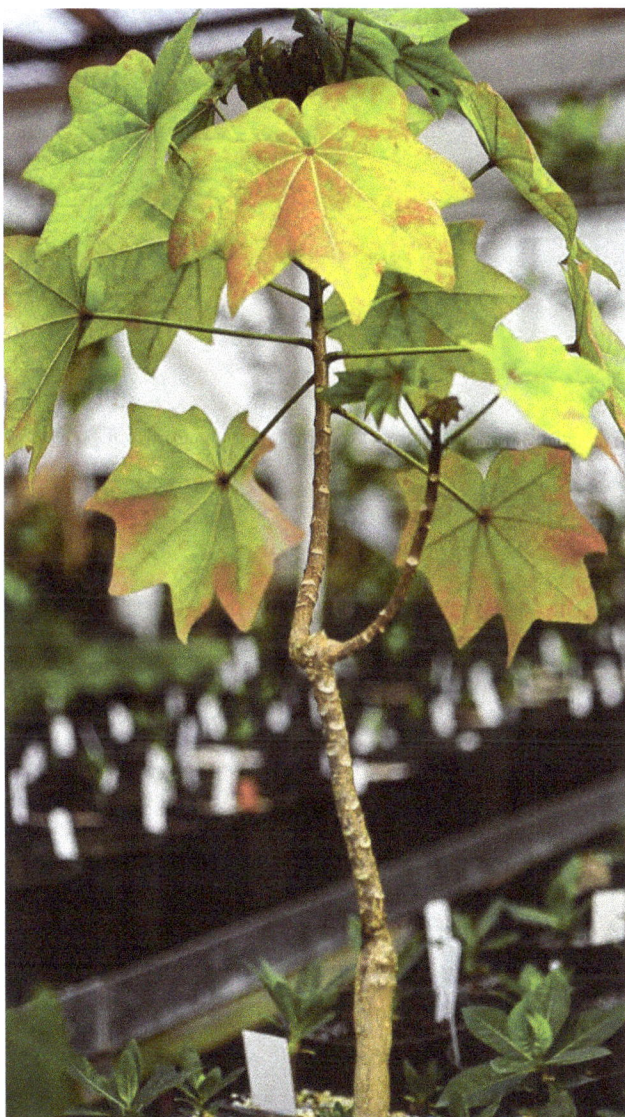

Figure 10.27—Grafting has been used to propagate highly endangered species in Hawai'i. Shown: Kokia cookei *scion grafted onto the rootstock of* Kokia drynarioides. *Photo by Tara Luna.*

not compatible, the rootstock and scion are not properly united, either the rootstock or the scion are not in the proper physiological state, or the grafted tissues dry out before the tissues grow together.

Some grafted species show excessive sap flow (bleeding) at certain times of the year. Excessive bleeding from the rootstock usually causes graft failure. Keeping recently performed grafts at 90 °F (32 °C) or lower with high humidity is essential. The graft union must also be protected from excessive drying or winds. In general, the more experienced the grafter, the better the success rate.

Grafting Tools

Sharp knives, sharpening stones, pruning shears, and saws are tools needed for grafting. These tools need to be kept very clean and only used for grafting. Knives need to be kept very sharp to minimize injury to the scion or rootstock. Dull knives strip and tear wood, leaving cuts that do not heal properly. Materials such as paraffin wax, budding rubber, and grafting tape can protect grafted tissues and seal cut surfaces of the graft. Aluminum foil wraps and plastic bags with twist ties are used in drier climates to protect the graft and provide a little extra humidity around the graft during union.

Collecting Scion Material

Budding is usually the preferred grafting method. For success, it is important to collect scion material with leaf buds and not flower buds. A small branch containing several buds suitable for grafting is called a bud stick. Bud sticks need to be collected when trees have well-developed buds. If buds have begun to swell or grow, the wood cannot be used successfully. Select parent trees of the desired variety that are disease free. Select straight, smooth bud sticks from 1-year-old wood that have 0.25- to 0.50-in (6- to 13-mm) diameters and contain at least three buds or nodes. The best bud sticks usually come from the inside canopy of the tree. Seal about 6 mm of the end of each bud stick with melted wax or grafting paint. When the seal is dry, tie the bud sticks into small bundles and surround each bundle with moist paper towels or moist wood shavings to prevent desiccation. Label each bundle. The bundles and wrapping material can be kept inside plastic bags. Keep the bundles as cool as possible and do not allow them to dry out.

Types of Budding

Chip budding works well and can be done whenever mature buds are available. Chip budding is widely used for citrus propagation. The cuts on the scion and the rootstock must be exactly the same. The first cut on the scion

Figure 10.28—Species like taro have been micropropagated to perpetuate certain clones and supply disease-free nursery stock. Photo by Tara Luna.

and the rootstock is made below a bud and downward at a 45-degree angle to a depth of about 0.12 in (3 mm). The second cut is started about the same distance above the bud and the knife is drawn downward to meet the first cut. If the bud scion happens to be narrower than the rootstock hole, line up one side of the bud scion tightly against the cut on the rootstock. The exact distances above and below the scion bud will depend on species. The entire graft needs to be wrapped with very thin (2-mil), clear polyethylene tape to prevent desiccation. If clear tape is unavailable, the graft can be wrapped with budding rubber and kept in a cool, shady location with high humidity. The key is to not let the bud dry out.

Slip budding is usually done during active growth. Like chip budding, mature buds must be available on the scion and the wood must have bark that will "slip." Bark that "slips" will easily peel in one uniform layer, without tearing, from the underlying wood. The appropriate time to do this step depends on the species and local climate. The first cut on the rootstock is horizontal. The second cut, about twice as long as the first, is vertical, originating near the midpoint of the horizontal cut. Where the cuts meet, gently use the knife to slightly flare open flaps of bark. On the scion, detach the leaf below the bud but retain some of the petiole. Make the first cut about 0.5 in (12 mm) below the bud and draw the knife upward just under the bark to a point about 0.25 in (6 mm) above the bud. Grasp the petiole and make a second cut horizontally across the bud stick so that it intersects with the first cut. The bud and its accompanying wood, termed a bud shield, is then inserted under the "flaps" on the rootstock, and slid down to ensure that the scion makes intimate contact with the rootstock. Use a budding rubber to hold the stem, flaps, and bud shield firmly together. Do not cover the bud.

Finishing the Graft

Grafted surfaces must be held tightly in place using a budding rubber or grafting tape. This wrap must either breakdown by weathering (as budding rubbers do) or must be removed in 2 to 3 weeks after the union has healed. If the material does not break down and is not removed, it will girdle the rootstock. After the union has healed, the portion of the rootstock above the graft must be cut away to force the scion bud to grow. Remove any unwanted sprouts as soon as they are visible. Unwanted sprouts can be easily rubbed off with fingers.

Micropropagation

Micropropagation is a process used to propagate plants using very specialized tissue culture techniques. Tissue culture is the procedure for maintaining and growing plant tissues and organs in an aseptic culture in which the environment, nutrient, and hormone levels are tightly controlled. A small piece of vegetative material called the explant is used to create a new, entire plant. Rare or greatly endangered tropical native species have been micropropagated to increase the number of individuals for restoration projects when other methods of propagation have been limiting or failed. Micropropagation has also been used as a method to offer plants in the nursery trade in order to preserve them from poaching and eventual extirpation from wild populations (figure 10.28). Micropropagation works well for some species and poorly for others. For some native plants, such as orchids, it is one of the only options for successful propagation. Most native plant nurseries do not have an elaborate tissue culture facility because of the high cost, although small-scale micropropagation can be done with minimal equipment in a clean room.

References

Landis, T.D.; Dreesen, D.R.; Dumroese, R.K. 2003. Sex and the single *Salix*: considerations for riparian restoration. Native Plants Journal. 4: 111–117.

Landis, T.D.; Dreesen, D.R.; Pinto, J.R.; Dumroese, R.K. 2006. Propagating native Salicaceae for riparian restoration on the Hopi Reservation in Arizona. Native Plants Journal. 7: 52–60.

Landis, T.D.; Tinus, R.W.; Barnett, J.P. 1999. The container tree nursery manual: volume 6, seedling propagation. Agriculture Handbook 674. Washington, DC: U.S. Department of Agriculture, Forest Service. 167 p.

Longman, K.A. 1993. Rooting cuttings of tropical trees: propagation and planting manuals, volume 1. London, United Kingdom: Commonwealth Science Council. 137 p.

Scagel, C.F.; Reddy, K.; Armstrong, J.M. 2003. Mycorrhizal fungi in rooting substrate influences the quantity and quality of roots on stem cuttings of hick's yew. HortTechnology. 13: 62–66.

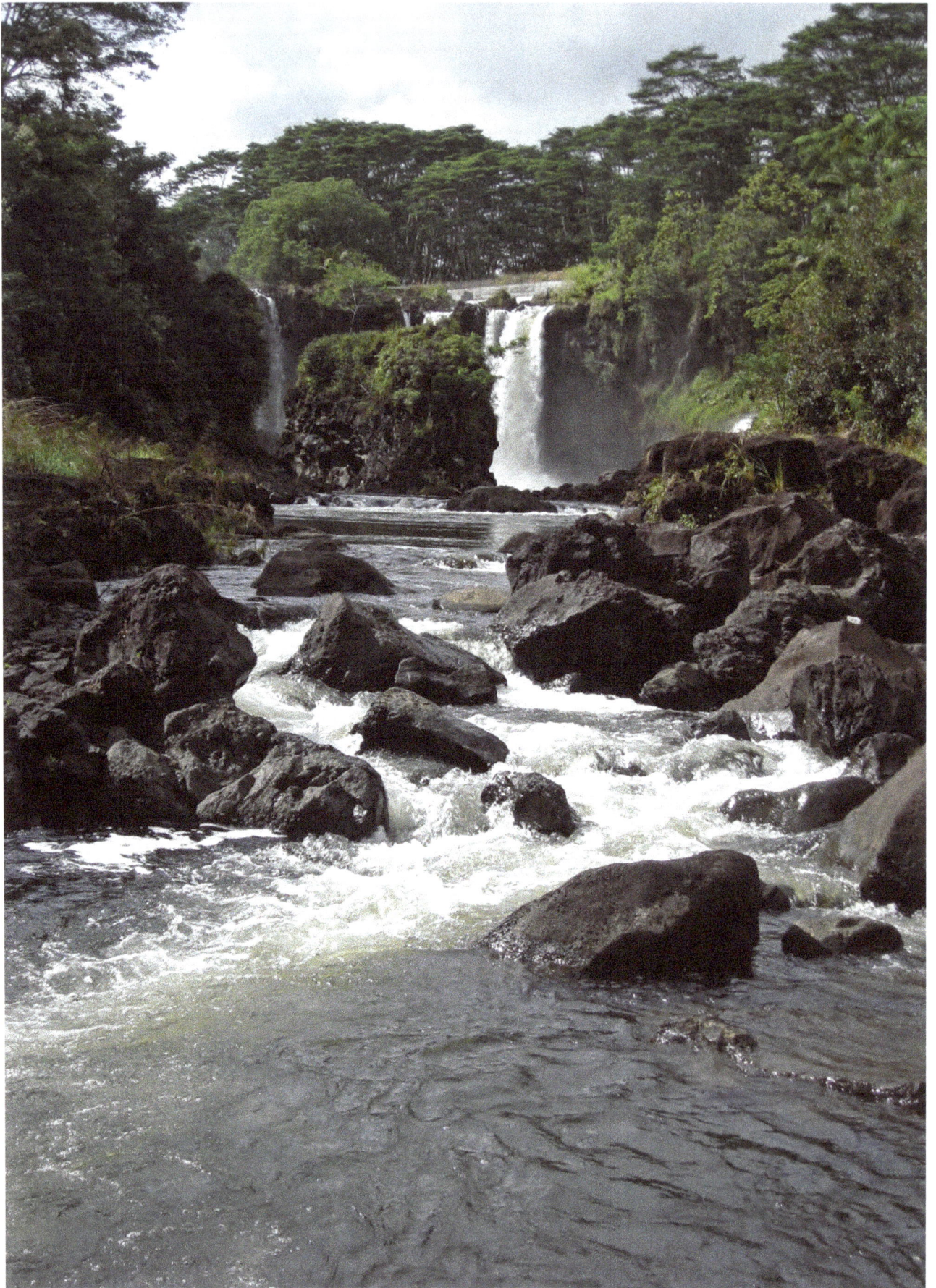

Water Quality and Irrigation

Thomas D. Landis and Kim M. Wilkinson

11

Water is the single most important biological factor affecting plant growth and health. Water is essential for nearly every plant process: photosynthesis, nutrient transport, and cell expansion and development. In fact, 80 to 90 percent of a seedling's weight is made up of water. Therefore, irrigation management is the most critical aspect of nursery operations (figure 11.1). In tropical nurseries, managing water depends on local climate. Finding and storing high-quality water is a challenge in dry climates, whereas controlling high humidity can be a problem in the humid tropics.

Determining how, when, and how much to irrigate is a crucial part of nursery planning and day-to-day operations. One missed irrigation can cause serious injury and even death to plants, especially during the establishment phase. Adequate watering is particularly important with container plants whose roots cannot access water beyond their container and therefore are entirely dependent on receiving enough water through irrigation. Excessive watering and humidity are also problematic; they are a major cause of root diseases and contribute to other problems with seedling growth.

Tropical nurseries typically grow a wide range of species with different water requirements. In addition, the distinct plant growth phases (establishment, rapid growth, and hardening) require different watering regimes. Designing an effective and efficient irrigation system is based on which types of irrigation practices and systems best serve plant needs at each developmental phase. The nursery might have various propagation areas and corresponding irrigation zones that provide for the changing needs of plants during all phases of growth. For example, the same nursery might have a mist chamber for the germination phase, a subirrigation system in the growing area, a selection of rare plants that receive daily hand watering, and some large plants under drip lines. The best design for any irrigation system will come from understanding the needs of the plants, the factors that affect water availability, and the details of how, when, and why to water.

Facing Page: *Water is a precious resource and the most important biological factor for plant health and growth. Pe'epe'e Falls, Wailuku River State Park, Hawai'i. Photo by Douglass F. Jacobs.*

Sources of Irrigation Water

Tropical plant nurseries can use water from several different sources, including rivers, ponds or reservoirs, rainwater, groundwater, and municipal sources. New nurseries need to evaluate the quantity, quality, and seasonal availability of all potential water sources. Surface water, such as rivers and streams, are typically dammed or diverted into ponds that have enough capacity to meet the water demands of the nursery. Groundwater can be pumped for nursery use, but generally the water is stored in a pond or reservoir. For either surface or groundwater, a hydrologic survey and analysis of local water rights needs to be conducted before nursery development. Surface water sources that have flowed through agricultural land need to be tested for waterborne pests or herbicides and may need to be treated. A wide variety of nursery pests have been detected in water supplies including fungi, nematodes, viruses, and bacteria (Zeng and others 2009). The water mold fungi (*Pythium* and *Phytophthora* species) are particularly destructive because they have a mobile stage.

Municipal water can be used for nursery purposes, but it may have been chemically treated with chlorine or fluoride. Low levels of chlorination guard against human pathogens, and studies have shown water with 2 ppm of free chlorine will not injure woody species (Cayanan and others 2008). Fluoride is added to some municipal drinking water at around 1 ppm to prevent cavities in children (Fawell and others 2006). Fluoride phytotoxicity has been documented for some nursery plants. Leaf damage to ti (*Cordyline fruticosa*) plants has been reported in a Hawaiian nursery, and the nursery recommends that irrigation water contain less than 0.25 ppm fluoride (Kaapuni Nursery 2011).

Rainwater is an attractive source of high-quality water for tropical nurseries if enough can be stored to supply all the needs. In high-rainfall areas, water can be collected from the roofs of buildings and then stored in tanks until needed. A special rainwater collection system is being used to supply water for irrigation at the native plant nursery

Figure 11.1—*A supply of good-quality water is one of the most critical requirements for a native plant nursery. Photo by Brian F. Daley.*

at Volcanoes National Park in Hawai'i (figure 11.2A). In these ground-level systems, the water must be pumped to generate enough pressure to run sprinklers in the nursery. In mountainous regions, rain water can be collected and stored in ponds or tanks above the nursery. Enough water pressure can be generated by the difference in elevation to run small microsprinklers or drip irrigation systems in a nursery. The water pressure can be calculated (figures 11.2B, 11.2C) or measured directly at the point of use in the nursery. A full discussion of all types of irrigation designs and calculations is available in Stetson and Mecham (2011).

Advantages of a Well-Designed Irrigation System

- Better plant quality and health
- Lower labor costs
- Improved crop uniformity and reliability
- Reduced runoff and waste of water

Attributes of Good Water Management

- Reliable source of water
- Efficient use of water
- Flexible approach tailored to the changing needs of the species grown and their development phases
- Responsible reuse, recycling, and management of any runoff water

---

Water Quality

Irrigation water quality is a critical factor in initial site selection and affects all phases of nursery management. Improving poor-quality irrigation water is expensive, often prohibitively so. Therefore, water quality needs to be a primary consideration during nursery site evaluation.

For irrigation purposes, water quality is determined by two factors:

- The types and concentrations of dissolved salts (total salinity and individual toxic ions).
- The presence of pests (pathogenic fungi, weed seeds, algae, and possible pesticide contamination).

Salts

For our purposes, a salt can be defined as a chemical compound that releases charged particles called ions when dissolved in water. Some salts are fertilizers that increase plant growth rates, while other salts can reduce growth or even cause injury or death. For example, sodium chloride (ordinary table salt) dissolves into harmful ions that can damage or even kill plant tissue.

An excess of dissolved salts in nursery irrigation water can clog nozzles (figure 11.3A), accumulate in growing media, and eventually harm plant tissue (figure 11.3B). The most characteristic symptom of high salinity is burn or scorch of leaf margins or tips (figure 11.3C). Symptoms can

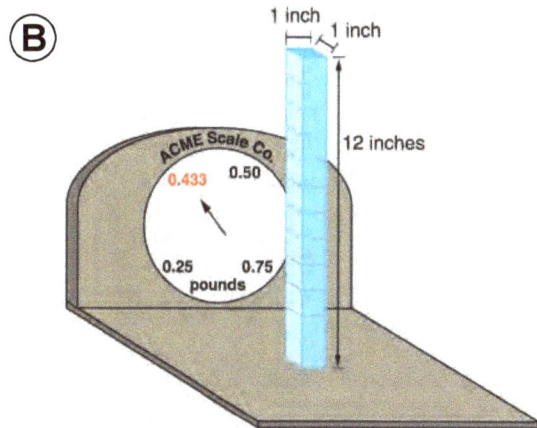

A 1-square-inch column of water weighs 0.433 pounds.

Therefore, the water pressure at the base of the column measures 0.433 pounds per square inch.

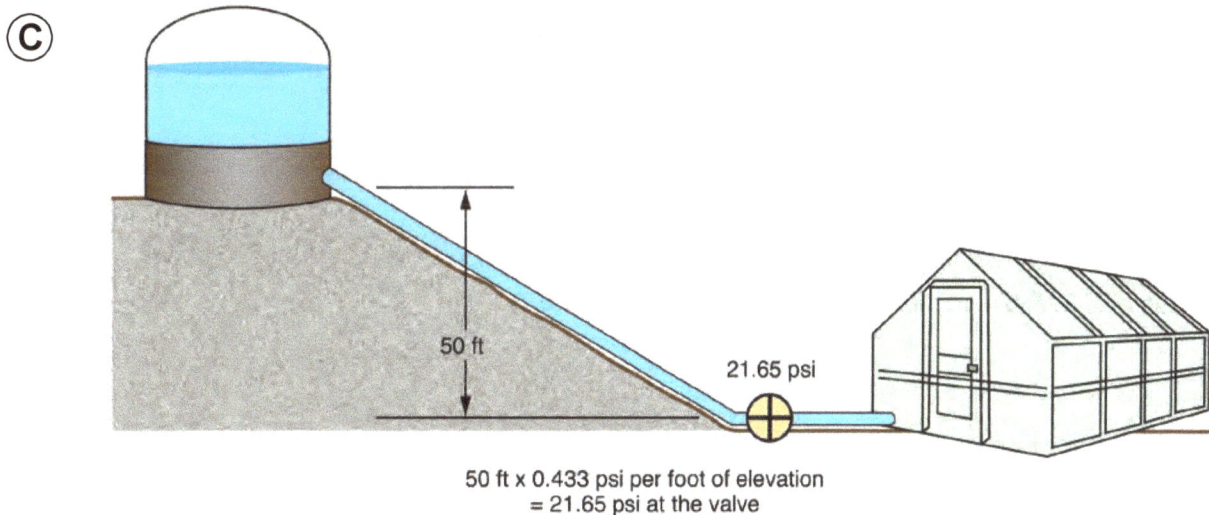

50 ft x 0.433 psi per foot of elevation
= 21.65 psi at the valve

Figure 11.2—*Rain collection systems are possible in high-rainfall climates (A). If the storage tanks are located at higher elevations, enough static pressure can be generated (B) to operate drip or microsprinkler systems in the nursery (C). Photo A by Thomas D. Landis, and illustrations B and C modified from Stetson and Mecham (2011) by Jim Marin. [Metric conversions: 1 in = 2.5 cm; 1 ft = 0.91 m; 1 psi = 0.007 MPa; 1 pound = 0.45 kg.]*

Figure 11.3—Agricultural water quality is determined by the level of soluble salts because they can build up on irrigation nozzles (A), accumulate in containers, usually around the drainage holes (B), and eventually "burn" seedling foliage (C). Photos by Thomas D. Landis.

vary with species but can include foliar tip burn, scorching or bluish color on leaves, stunting, patchy growth, and eventual mortality. The principal damage of high salinity is reduced growth rate, which usually develops before more visible symptoms become evident.

Other ways excess dissolved salts may affect nursery crops include the following—

- Water availability to the plant is reduced resulting in growth loss.
- Some ions (sodium, chloride, boron, and fluoride) are directly toxic to plants.
- Other ions (calcium) affect mineral nutrient availability.
- Other ions (bicarbonate or iron) cause salt crusts or staining.

An excess of dissolved salts in the water can be the result of a number of factors. The local climatic or geologic influences at the nursery's location are significant. In arid or semiarid climates where evapotranspiration exceeds precipitation, salts naturally accumulate in the soil, and ground water irrigation sources are often high in salt content. In coastal areas, saltwater intrusion can lower water quality. On Guam, the geology of the northern half of the island is formed from uplifted coral whereas the southern half is volcanic (Gingerich 2003). From a nursery standpoint, this distinction is that the groundwater in the north is very high in pH and calcium and in the south, the water is low in pH and dissolved salts. High fertilization rates or poor irrigation practices can also lead to salinity problems. Studies have shown that soluble salt levels double when the growing medium dries from 50- to 25-percent moisture content.

It is expensive to remove salts from irrigation water, so ideally the nursery needs to be established on a site where water salinity is within acceptable levels. Test results for salinity are traditionally expressed as electrical conductivity (EC); the higher the salt concentration, the higher the EC (table 11.1). The EC can be checked at the nursery using a conductivity meter or by sending water samples to a local laboratory. The most commonly used units in irrigation water quality are micromhos per centimeter (abbreviated as μmho/cm and pronounced "micro-mows") and the International System of Units of microsiemens per centimeter, which are equivalent. Microsiemens per centimeter (abbreviated as μS/cm) will be used as the standard EC unit in this handbook. General guidelines for salinity ranges are in table 11.1.

Irrigation water salinity tests need to be conducted before nursery establishment and retested periodically thereafter.

Table 11.1—Water-quality standards for nursery irrigation water. Adapted from Landis and others (1989) and Robbins 2011.

Quality index	Optimal	Unacceptable
pH	5.5 to 6.5	
Salinity (μS/cm)	0 to 500	>1,500
Sodium (ppm)	<50	>50
Chloride (ppm)	<70	>70
Boron (ppm)	<0.75	>0.75
Fluoride (ppm)	<1.00	>1.00**
Iron (ppm)	<1.00	>1.00

** Sensitive species may be damaged at lower levels

Table 11.2—*Water-quality test results from Micronesian Islands.*

Island	Electrical conductivity (µS/cm)	Quality rating (see table 11.1)
Guam (North)	840	Marginal
Guam (South)	150	Good
Saipan	1,860	Poor
Yap	185	Good
Palau	60	Good
Pohnpei (domestic)	125	Good
Pohnpei (rainwater)	16	Good

EC tests were conducted at native plant nurseries in some of the Micronesian islands and the results reflect local geology (table 11.2). As previously mentioned, the northern part of Guam is limestone and the EC is much higher than the volcanic soils in the southern part. The water in Saipan has very high EC readings because of limestone soils, and this marginal water quality can be seen in the nursery.

Water tests are particularly important in areas with high salinity because the addition of fertilizer could raise salinity to unacceptable levels (figure 11.4). In these cases, a nursery would need to be careful to use very dilute fertilizers, low-nutrient concentrations of organic fertilizers, or controlled-release fertilizers to keep salinity within acceptable ranges. See Chapter 12, Plant Nutrition and Fertilization, for details. Horticultural practices such as increasing the porosity of the growing medium and leaching more frequently when watering can also help alleviate the effects of saline water.

Pests

Tropical nurseries that use irrigation water from surface water sources such as ponds, lakes, or rivers may encounter problems with biotic pests; that is, weeds, pathogenic fungi, moss, algae, or liverworts. Surface water that originates from other nurseries or farmland is particularly likely to be contaminated with water-mold fungi, such as *Pythium* and *Phytophthora*, which cause damping-off. Recycled nursery irrigation water should also be suspect and needs to be analyzed. Many weed seeds and moss and algal spores are small enough to pass through the irrigation system and can cause real problems in nurseries. Chlorination and some specialized filtration systems may remove many disease and pest organisms from irrigation water, as discussed in the following section.

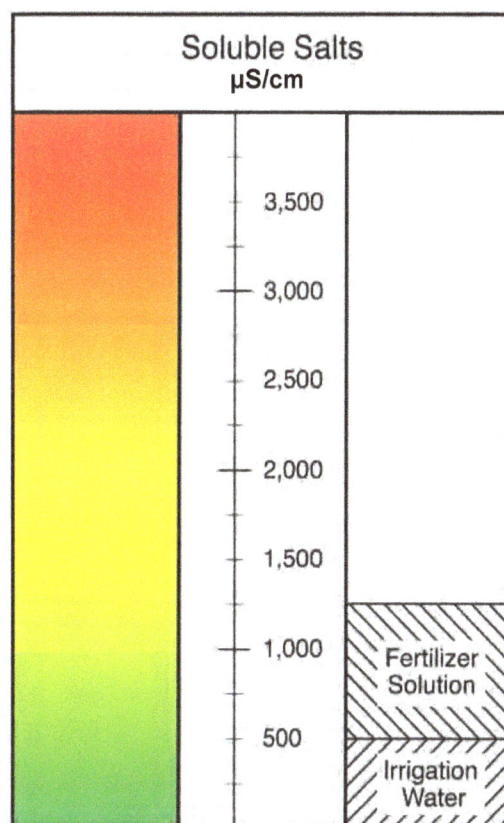

Figure 11.4—*When soluble fertilizers are injected into the irrigation system, salinity levels are cumulative. For example, a nursery with a base irrigation salinity of 500 µS/cm has good quality, but after soluble fertilizer is added, the total salinity can reach into the zone of caution. Illustration from Dumroese and others (2008).*

Irrigation water, especially in agricultural areas, may be contaminated with residual pesticides. Herbicides applied to adjacent cropland or to control aquatic weeds in reservoirs can affect ground water. Potential sources of irrigation water need to be tested for pesticide contamination when a nursery site is being evaluated.

Testing Water Quality

A water-quality test needs to be done before the nursery site selection is finalized to ensure adequate quality and quantity of water will be available before the nursery is established. A water-quality test can be repeated when the nursery is established and again at yearly intervals. A complete analysis of irrigation water quality consists of a salinity evaluation listing the concentrations of sodium, chloride, and boron, which are reported in parts per million (ppm). In addition to the individual ion concentrations, the analysis needs to include three standard water-quality indices: EC, toxic ion concentrations, and pH. Most labs have a standard irrigation water-quality test, which will cover all these concerns.

Irrigation water also needs to be tested for the presence of pathogenic fungi during the site selection process, and again if a problem is observed at a later date. Most plant pathology laboratories can conduct bioassays of irrigation water.

Testing for residual herbicides is also possible but can be expensive because of the sophisticated analytical procedures required. Because of the different chemical structures of various pesticides, a separate analysis for each suspected pesticide is usually required. Therefore, pesticide tests are generally considered only when a specific problem is suspected.

To collect an irrigation water sample, use a clean plastic bottle with a firm, watertight lid. A 16-fluid-ounce (475-ml) container is ideal for most water tests. To begin, let the water run for several minutes (figure 11.5), and then rinse the sample bottle well before collecting the sample. Label the sample bottle properly with a waterproof marker before sending it to the analytical laboratory. The sample needs to be sent away for testing as quickly as possible but can be stored under refrigeration for short periods, if necessary. Most laboratories charge $25 to $50 and will provide results within a few weeks.

Water Treatments

Establishing the nursery on a site with tested, good-quality water is the best way to preclude water-related problems. If existing water quality is poor, methods such as deionization and reverse osmosis can treat and improve irrigation water, but they are often prohibitively expensive and not feasible for most tropical plant nurseries. To correct or safeguard against minor problems with otherwise good-quality water, however, some treatments are low cost and highly effective for container nurseries.

Chlorination

Chlorination can be used to kill fungi, bacteria, algae, or liverworts introduced through the irrigation system (Zheng and others 2009). Studies have shown that *Pythium* and *Phytophthora* can be controlled with 2 ppm of free chlorine without injury to woody species (Cayanan and others 2008).

Filtration

Filtration is used to remove suspended or colloidal particles such as very fine sand or silt. Filtration prevents problems such as plugging or damaging irrigation or fertilization equipment. Filters also remove unwanted pests such as weed seeds or algae spores. Two types of filters are commonly used in nurseries: granular medium filters consist of beds of granular particles that trap suspended material in the pores between the particles and surface filters use a porous screen or mesh to strain the suspended material from the irrigation water. Granular medium filters can be used to remove fine sand or organic matter and are constructed so that they can be backflushed for cleaning. Surface filters include screens or cartridges of various mesh sizes to remove suspended material (figure 11.6A); screens must be physically removed and cleaned whereas cartridge filters are not reusable and must be regularly replaced. Jones (1983) recommends cartridge filters because they are easy to change. Backflushing screens or granular medium filters is not practical with many nursery irrigation systems.

Filters need to be installed at a location before the water passes through the nutrient injector to intercept sand particles that can cause excessive wear or plug valves (figure 11.6B). Handreck and Black (1984) recommend using filters small enough to remove particles

Figure 11.5—*Water quality needs to be tested before nursery establishment and then every few years to make certain that the quality has not changed. Photo by Brian F. Daley.*

Chlorination with Household Bleach To Treat Water for Pests

- Mix household bleach (5.25-percent sodium hypochlorite) at a rate of 2.4 ounces of bleach per 1,000 gal of water (18 ml per 1,000 L).

- This low dose (about 1 ppm chlorine) was not found to be phytotoxic to a wide range of plant species, and it has been successful in controlling moss and liverwort on noncrop surfaces.

greater than 5 microns in diameter, which will take care of most suspended materials (figure 11.6C). Specialized filtration systems, such as those manufactured by Millipore Corporation, can remove particles around 1 micron in diameter; such a system is therefore capable of removing some disease organisms and most suspended solids. More sophisticated filtration systems are relatively expensive and require frequent maintenance (Jones 1983).

Water Quantity

The amount of water necessary to produce a crop of container plants depends on many factors, such as climate, type of growing structures, type of irrigation system, growing medium, plant species, number of plants being grown, and container size. The amount of water to grow a crop will vary tremendously between humid and arid locations. Some examples of water use data from nurseries in the mainland United States are provided in table 11.3.

Remember that a nursery also needs water for operational requirements other than irrigating crops. Mixing growing media, cleaning containers, structures, and equipment, and providing for staff personal water needs all increase water use. Also, a nursery that starts small may choose to expand. Therefore, ensure that an abundance of water is available to meet present and future needs.

Even in cases in which the nursery has access to a steady, reliable, high-quality water source, a backup system is always a good idea in case of emergency. A prudent investment is a backup water storage tank containing sufficient water to meet the nursery's needs for at least 1 week (figure 11.7). Backup systems may be pumped into the normal irrigation system, but it is advantageous to locate the storage tank upslope so that water can be supplied by gravity in case of power failure.

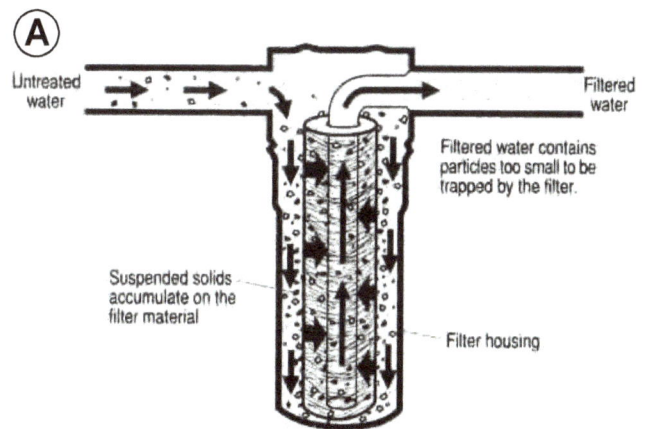

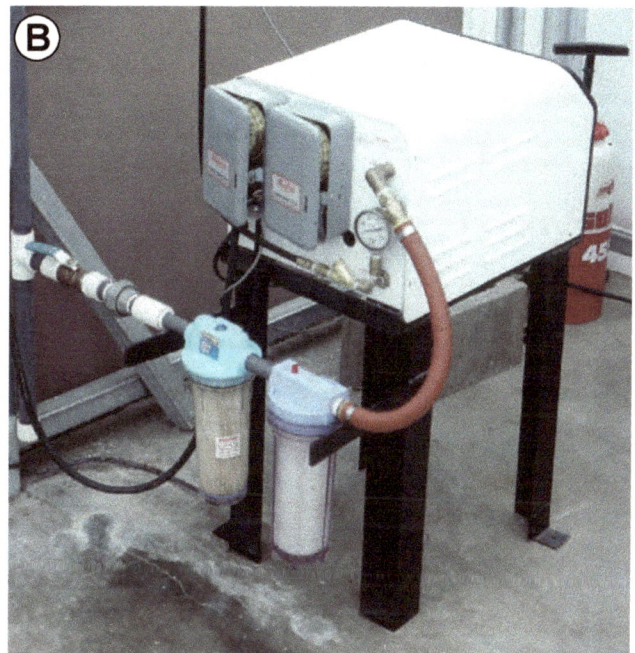

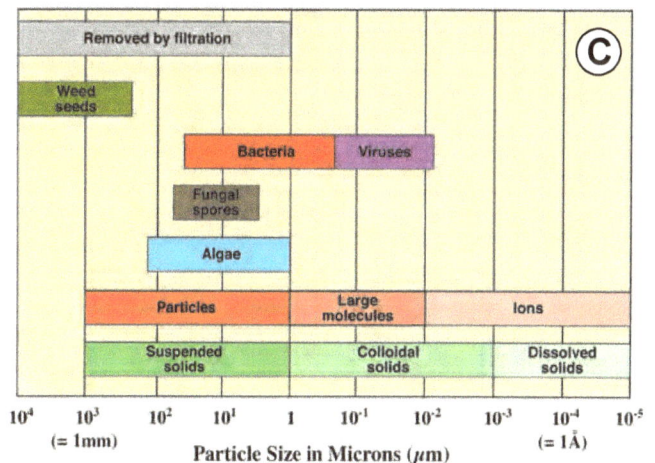

Figure 11.6—Cartridge filters (A) are an effective and inexpensive way to treat irrigation water: they need to be installed before the fertilizer injector (B) and can remove sand, silt, and fungal and algal spores (C). Illustration A from Dumroese and others (2008), photo B by Thomas D. Landis, and illustration C adapted from Tchobanoglous and Schroeder (1985) by Jim Marin.

Factors Affecting Water Availability to Plants

Plant water use is affected by environmental conditions such as humidity, temperature, season, and the amount of sunlight the plants receive. The growth phase of the crop will also affect the rate of evaporation and transpiration. During seedling germination and early emergence, evaporation is the primary cause of water loss (figure 11.8A). After the seedling's roots occupy the container, however, transpiration becomes the primary force for water loss (figure 11.8B).

The type of growing medium also influences water availability and use. Common components of artificial media behave very differently than soil. Peat moss and vermiculite have a high water-holding capacity, whereas perlite and pumice do not. Water infiltration and drainage are much higher with artificial media than with mineral soils. The average pore size of the growing medium is the most significant influence. All things being equal, a finer textured growing medium with a smaller average pore size holds more water than a coarser textured medium does (figure 11.9). See Chapter 6, Growing Media, for more details on this topic.

Container type, volume (table 11.3), and shape also affect water availability. Water in a container behaves differently than water in unconfined soil because it does not drain completely, resulting in a layer of saturated medium at the bottom (figure 11.8B). The height of this saturated medium is a function of the growing medium, but taller containers will have a smaller proportion of saturated medium than shorter ones (see Figure 7.2 in Chapter 7, Containers).

The small top opening of some containers in relation to their volume can make it difficult to get water into the containers with typical sprinkler irrigation, resulting in consid-

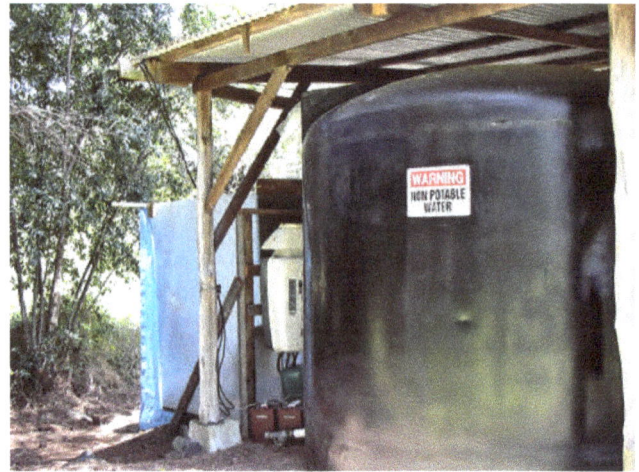

Figure 11.7—*A backup water storage tank containing sufficient water to meet the nursery's needs for at least 1 week is a prudent investment. Photo by Thomas D. Landis.*

erable variation in growing medium water content from one container to another. This distribution problem becomes even more critical when the plants become larger and their foliage begins to intercept water before it can reach the surface of the container. Subirrigation (described later in this chapter) and hand watering are sometimes used to overcome this problem. Because small containers have a correspondingly small volume of growing medium, they have limited moisture reserves and require frequent irrigation, especially in times of high evapotranspirational losses.

Determining How Much To Irrigate

When irrigating container nursery crops, it is important to apply enough water during each event to more than saturate the medium so that a small amount of leaching occurs. In other words, apply enough water so

Table 11.3—*Typical irrigation use in forest and conservation nurseries for a crop of 1,000 conifer seedlings on the mainland of the Western United States. Adapted from Dumroese and others (2008).*

Nursery and location	Container type and volume	Irrigation water use per week (gallons [liters])	
		Establishment phase	Rapid growth phase
University of Idaho, Moscow	Ray Leach Cone-tainer™ 4 in^3 (66 ml)	10 (38)	15 (57)
Mt. Sopris, Colorado	Ray Leach Cone-tainer™ 10 in^3 (172 ml)	15 (57)	50 (189)
University of Idaho, Moscow	Styroblock™ 20 in^3 (340 ml)	60 (227)	125 (473)

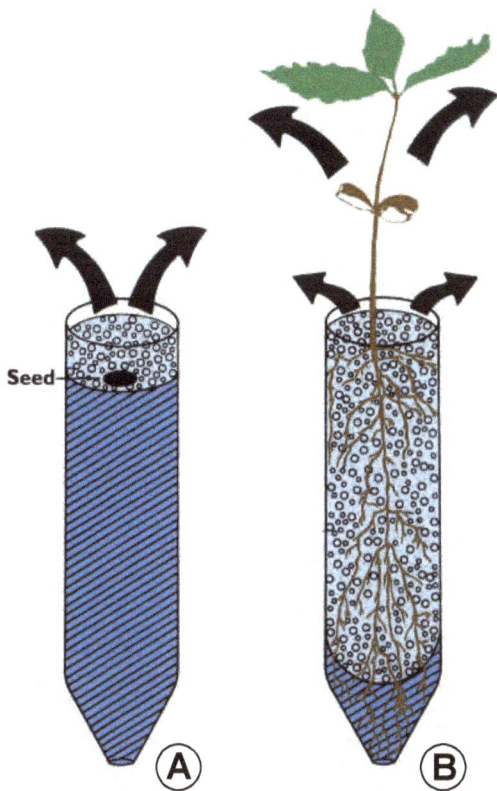

Figure 11.8—The amount and type of water use changes dramatically during the growing season. During the establishment phase, a relatively small amount of water is used by evaporation (A) but, when the seedling fully occupies the container during the rapid growth phase, a much greater amount is used for transpiration with relatively little lost to evaporation (B). Illustration adapted from Landis and others (1989).

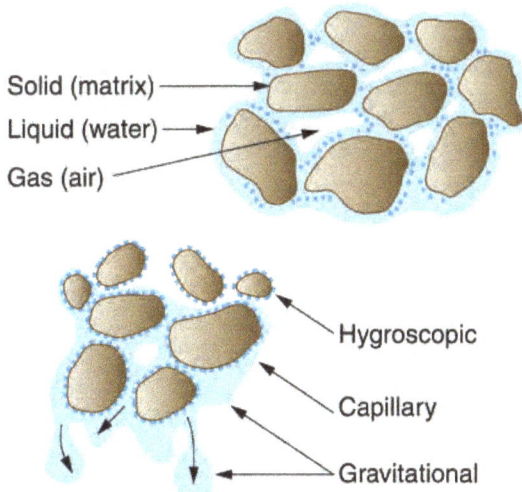

Figure 11.9—Water is held in the pores between particles by capillarity. For any growing medium, the larger the particles, the less water will be held. Plants can only use capillary water; gravitational water drains away, and hydroscopic water is held too tightly for plant use. Illustration from Dumroese and others (2008).

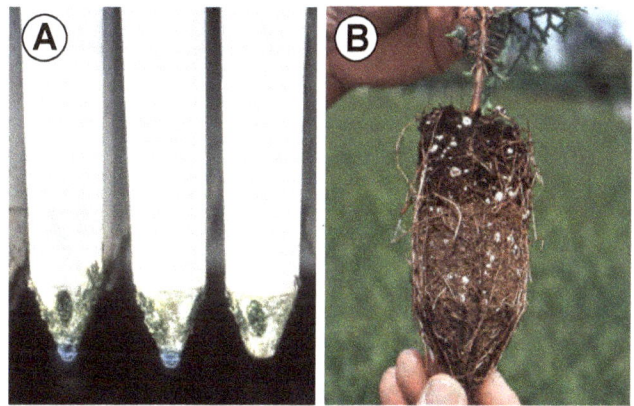

Figure 11.10—Apply enough water during irrigation to fully saturate the growing medium profile and permit some leaching out the bottom of the container. Some water will drip out of the bottom of each container if the plants were watered sufficiently (A). Insufficient irrigation will result in a dry layer within the growing medium (B). Photos by Thomas D. Landis.

that some drips out the bottom of the container (figure 11.10A), but not so much that water streams out the bottom. If the irrigation period is too short, the water will not reach the bottom of the container and a layer of dry growing medium underneath will exist (figure 11.10B). If the growing medium is not completely saturated after irrigation, the seedling will not develop roots in the dry medium at the bottom of the container, resulting in a poorly formed plug. In addition, fertilizer salts will accumulate in the medium and cause salinity damage or "fertilizer burn."

The general rule for sprinkler, overhead, hand-watering, or microirrigation is to apply approximately 10 percent more water than is needed to completely saturate the entire growing medium profile during irrigation. The best procedure to ensure that some water is dripping out of the bottom of the container during or immediately after irrigation is by direct inspection.

The amount of irrigation to apply varies during the growing season because of the stages of seedling development and the horticultural objectives of the nursery manager. As discussed in Chapter 4, Crop Planning: Propagation Protocols, Schedules, and Records, plants go through three phases of development: establishment, rapid growth, and hardening. Irrigation is an important strategy for managing plant growth and health as the crop moves through these phases.

Irrigating During the Establishment Phase

Immediately after the sown containers are placed in the growing area, the growing medium needs to be completely saturated. Thereafter, watering needs during establishment should be monitored carefully and tailored to the needs of the species. Some species require nearly continuous misting (figure 11.11) and may even benefit from a fog chamber. Other species require less water, but, nevertheless, inadequate or too-infrequent irrigations will cause the seeds to dry out, which will decrease germination success or even cause total crop loss. On the other hand, excessive irrigation may create overly wet conditions, promoting damping-off and decreasing germination.

To help determine the watering regime for a given species, consider the water availability in the plant's native habitat (such as rainforest, cloudforest, or dryland) at the time of year when this species usually germinates. Remember, until the seeds germinate and begin to grow, water loss is primarily from evaporation from the top of the container. Irrigation during this period, therefore, must be applied with the goal of replenishing the moisture in the thin surface layer of the medium. This practice is usually best accomplished by periodic misting or light irrigation with a very fine spray nozzle, which also protects germinating seeds from being moved or damaged by the force of the water. In some cases, if seeds are mulched, irrigation may not be necessary for the first week or so of the germination phase. Scratch through the surface of the mulch or grit to check the water status of the medium and ensure the medium is moist enough.

Irrigation can also be used to control the temperature around germinating seeds. High temperatures on the surface of the growing medium can injure germinants, particularly those covered by dark-colored mulches. If temperatures exceed 86 °F (30 °C), light misting will help keep germinants cool through evaporative cooling. This practice is sometimes called "water shading." When misting for cooling, do not

The key to irrigating during the establishment phase: keep the growing medium "moist, but not saturated."

add too much water to the medium, only enough to dissipate heat around the seedling. After plants develop thicker stems, they become more resistant to heat injury. Do not use water shading in nurseries with saline water because salts can build up in surface layers of the growing medium.

Irrigating During the Rapid-Growth Phase

After the seedling's roots have expanded throughout the container, the amount of water lost through transpiration increases greatly and so irrigations must be longer and more frequent. As seen in table 11.3, water usage can double or even triple during the rapid-growth phase. Each plant needs to be watered thoroughly (until some water drips out the bottom). Regular saturation is best for some species whereas others might benefit from periods of slight moisture stress between watering. No plants should ever be allowed to dry out completely (figure 11.12). Nursery managers need to be aware of the varying water requirements for different species and adjust irrigation practices accordingly. Grouping species together by their water requirements ("wet," "moderate," or "dry") makes this practice much easier.

During the rapid growth phase, the leaves of plants begin to form a tight canopy that causes a significant reduction in the amount of irrigation that can reach the growing medium surface if delivered from above. This "umbrella effect" is particularly serious with broadleaved species. Water will often drip through the foliage irregularly so that one container is fully saturated whereas the one right next to it may receive

Figure 11.11—During the establishment phase, watering needs to be tailored to the requirements of each species. For many species, mist nozzles in a special germination chamber generate a fine spray, which provides enough water for germination and also protects young germinants from heat injury. Overwatering must be avoided to prevent disease problems. Photo by Brian F. Daley.

very little water. To compensate for foliage interception, growers tend to irrigate more frequently and longer. This practice still results in uneven irrigation and wasted water, because the water runs off the leaves and onto the floor. The types of irrigation systems discussed later in this chapter will help address this issue for broadleaved species, particularly through subirrigation and hand watering practices.

The rapid growth phase is also the time when liquid fertilizers are most concentrated and water loss through transpiration is high, so growers must monitor for salt accumulation.

Irrigating During the Hardening Phase

Manipulating irrigation frequency is an effective way to initiate the hardening of plants before shipment and outplanting. Because seedling growth is so critically tied to moisture stress levels, growers can slow shoot growth and increase general resistance to stress by inducing moderate water stress. This "drought stressing" procedure consists of withholding irrigation for short periods of time until the plants can be seen to wilt or until some predetermined moisture stress is reached. After this stress treatment, the crop is returned to a maintenance irrigation schedule.

Implementing moisture stress, however, can be challenging with tropical plants because (1) hardiness is affected by other environmental conditions, (2) considerable variation in growing medium moisture content can exist among containers, and (3) if the growing medium is allowed to dry too far, it can become hydrophobic and difficult to rewet.

Water stressing must be done correctly and conscientiously, and there is no substitute for experience. Most of the water stress research has been done with commercial conifers, and good guidelines have been published for monitoring container weights (for example, Landis and others 1989). It is unfortunate that little is known about the response of most tropical native plants. Inducing moisture stress, therefore, can be risky if the plant's tolerance is unknown. Drought stressing simply does not work for some species and in some environments. Growers need to conduct their own trials of operational moisture stressing to determine the effect on their own species in their respective growing environments. Careful scheduling and communication with other nursery workers is essential (figure 11.13). Be sure to keep detailed records of how the crops respond.

In spite of these caveats, the induction of mild moisture stresses should be considered as a horticultural technique to manipulate seedling physiology and morphology. A further discussion of the hardening process, including moisture stress, is provided in Chapter 15, Hardening.

Figure 11.12—These seedlings are suffering from severe water stress because of improper irrigation. Seedlings use a lot of water during the rapid growth phase and frequent irrigation is needed to prevent growth loss. Photo by Thomas D. Landis.

Fertigation

Irrigation is critical to the proper application of fertilizers, especially when injecting liquid fertilizer solution into the irrigation system—a practice called "fertigation." Fertigation can be used with many different types of irrigation systems, from hand watering to automated sprinkler or drip systems. Fertilizer injectors range from simple, low-cost siphons for hand watering to sophisticated pumps for automated sprinklers. Because it can be designed to apply the proper mineral nutrients at the proper concentration and at the proper time, fertigation has several advantages over other types of fertilization. Remember that fertilizers are salts and that injecting liquid fertilizers adds to the base salinity level of the irrigation water. Frequent leaching with regular irrigation water ("clearwater flush") is needed to push excess salts out the bottom of the container. One of the first signs of a salinity problem is salt crust around the drainage holes (figure 11.3B). See Chapter 12, Plant Nutrition and Fertilization, for more information on fertigation and how it can be applied in tropical native plant nurseries.

Determining When to Irrigate

It is absolutely necessary to regularly monitor the moisture status of growing media. In small containers, the limited volume of moisture reserves means that critical moisture stresses can develop quickly.

Visual and tactile assessments are the most common method of monitoring irrigation effectiveness. Monitoring can also include formal or informal assessments of container weight. In addition, various tools such as tensiometers, electrometric instruments, balances, commercial moisture meters (figure 11.14), or pressure chambers can be used to monitor irrigation efficacy (Landis and others 1989). Any equipment-based method must also be supported by actual observation (visual and tactile) and the grower's experience.

Visual and Tactile Assessment of Growing Medium Moisture

Most nurseries successfully monitor irrigation efficacy based on the feel and appearance of the plants and the growing medium (figure 11.15A). The best technique is to observe the relative ease with which water can be squeezed from the medium and attempt to correlate this moisture condition with plant appearance and container weight (figure 11.15B). This process requires a lot of experience and is very subjective but can be very effective when used by a knowledgeable, experienced nursery manager.

Looking at the root systems or the growing media may involve damage to the plants that are examined, especially if they must be pulled from their containers. This practice may be necessary during the learning phase of growing a new crop. With time and experience, nondestructive indicators such as the appearance of the plant, the look and feel of the growing medium, and the weight of the containers will be practiced most of the time, and the need for destructive sampling will be reduced or eliminated.

Monitoring Container Weights

Monitoring container weight is one of the few objective, nondestructive, and repeatable techniques for monitoring irrigation in container nurseries. Container weight is also the best way to determine irrigation needs early in the

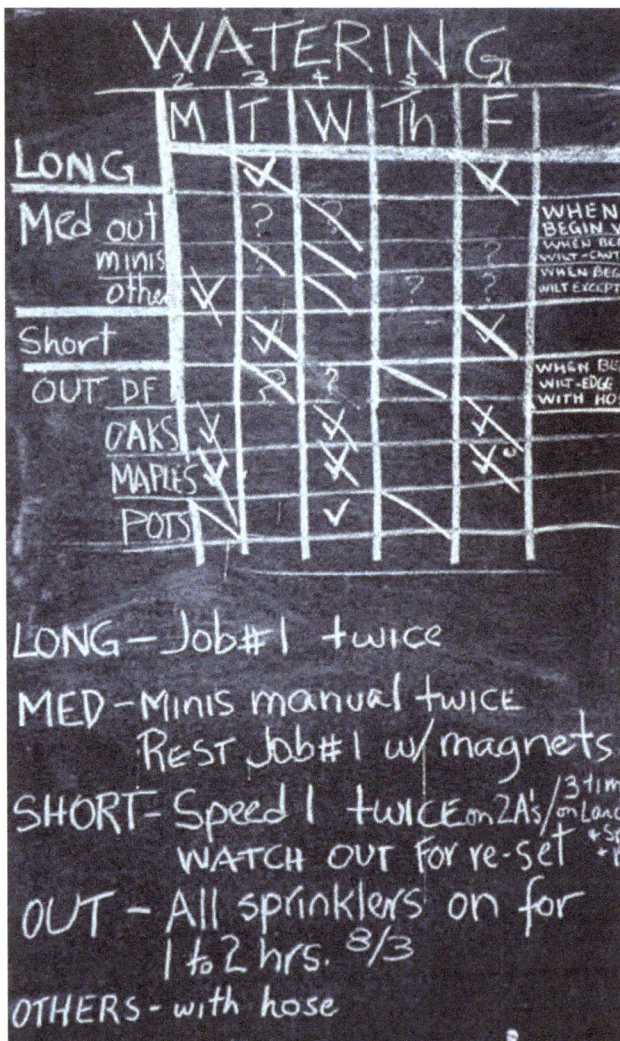

Figure 11.13—*Because so little is known about the response of most tropical plants to water stress, good scheduling, record-keeping, and communication are critical to determine plant needs. Photo by Thomas D. Landis.*

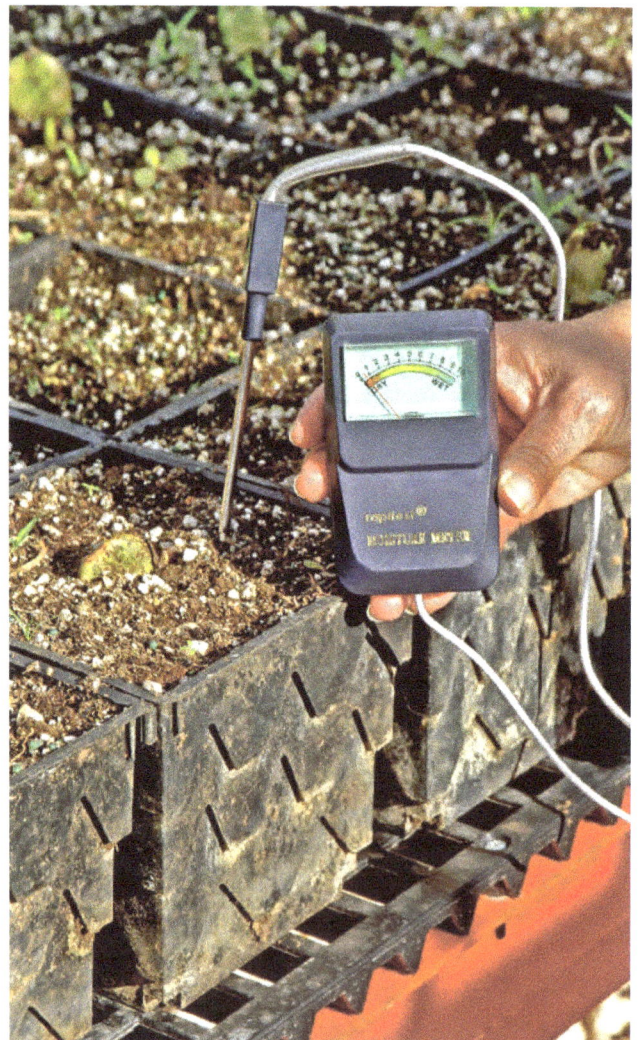

Figure 11.14—*Many types of tools can be used to help test and assess the effectiveness of water application, including this moisture meter. Visual and tactile assessments are more prevalent in tropical plant nurseries, however, and can be quite effective when carried out by trained staff. Photo by Thomas D. Landis.*

Figure 11.15—Growers can monitor the need for irrigation by careful observation of plant condition (A) so that water can be applied before plants are seriously wilted (B). Feeling the weight of containers can also be an effective way to determine when to irrigate (C). Monitoring container weights is a standard method to assess irrigation needs in container crops (D). Photos A, B, and C by Tara Luna, and photo D by Thomas D. Landis.

growing season before plants are large enough to show moisture stress or test in a pressure chamber. Container weight decreases between irrigations because the water in the growing medium is lost through evaporation and transpiration. When the container weight reaches some predetermined level, the crop is irrigated. With experience, workers can develop an intuitive sense of this level based on picking up a few randomly spaced trays (figure 11.15C). It can also be done objectively, weighing containers on a simple household scale (figure 11.15D).

The procedure is to completely saturate the growing media in a container or block of containers and let it drain—measured as the "wet weight." The container or block is then sown as usual, marked with a tag or flag stake, and placed out in the nursery. Then, once or twice per week during the growing season, this monitoring block is weighed and the weight is recorded as a percentage of the wet weight. A typical weight chart is shown in table 11.4 with the decision point on when to water at 85 percent of the wet weight during the rapid growth phase or 70 percent during the hardening phase. Decision points will vary between species because of the physiological response of different species to moisture stress.

```
┌─────────────────────────────────────────────┐
│       Visual and Tactile Clues for            │
│          Monitoring Irrigation                │
│                                               │
│  • Leaves should look and feel firm, not      │
│    wilted.                                     │
│                                               │
│  • Potting medium should be moist throughout  │
│    the plug; moisture should come out when    │
│    squeezed.                                   │
│                                               │
│  • Containers should feel relatively heavy    │
│    when lifted.                                │
│                                               │
│  • Immediately after watering, some water     │
│    will drip (but not stream) out of the      │
│    bottom of each container to indicate       │
│    plants were irrigated sufficiently.        │
└─────────────────────────────────────────────┘
```

Assessing Irrigation Distribution

Irrigation systems need to be checked every few months because nozzles or drippers can become plugged or wear down to the point that they are no longer operating properly. The evenness of overhead irrigation systems can be easily checked by running a simple "cup test," which involves measuring the irrigation water caught in a series of cups laid out on a regular grid system throughout the growing area (figure 11.16). Containers for cup tests should have circular openings that have narrow rims; the shape of the container below the opening is not important as long as the cups are stable and 2 to 4 in (5 to 10 cm) deep to hold water without any splashing out.

Simply distribute empty cups evenly throughout the nursery irrigation station and run the overhead irrigation as usual for a standard time period. Turn off the system and measure the depth of the water in the cups. If water depth is not relatively uniform among cups, check pressure in the line and also check for clogs or problems with individual nozzles.

Types of Irrigation Systems

The best method of applying irrigation water in tropical nurseries depends on the water requirements of the species being grown and on the size and complexity of the operation (table 11.5). Small nurseries and those growing a variety of species may prefer hand watering for irrigation. Large nurseries growing only a few species may use some sort of mechanical irrigation system. Most nurseries use a combination of several systems in different watering zones to fulfill their irrigation needs (figure 11.17).

With the exception of hand-watering, most irrigation systems can be hooked up to automatic controllers based on timers or container weight so that irrigation can be automatically applied. Controllers enable the nursery manager to preprogram periods of irrigation, thereby saving time and labor. The prudent grower, however, will never

Table 11.4—An example of a weekly irrigation-monitoring program using container weights. Adapted from Dumroese and others (2008).

	Mon	Tue	Wed	Thu	Fri	Sat	Sun
Wet weight	26.0	26.0	26.0	26.0	26.0	26.0	26.0
Actual weight	22.0	25.0	23.5	21.0	24.5	21.5	25.0
Wet weight (%)	85	96	90	81	94	83	96
Need to water?	Yes	No	No	Yes	No	Yes	No

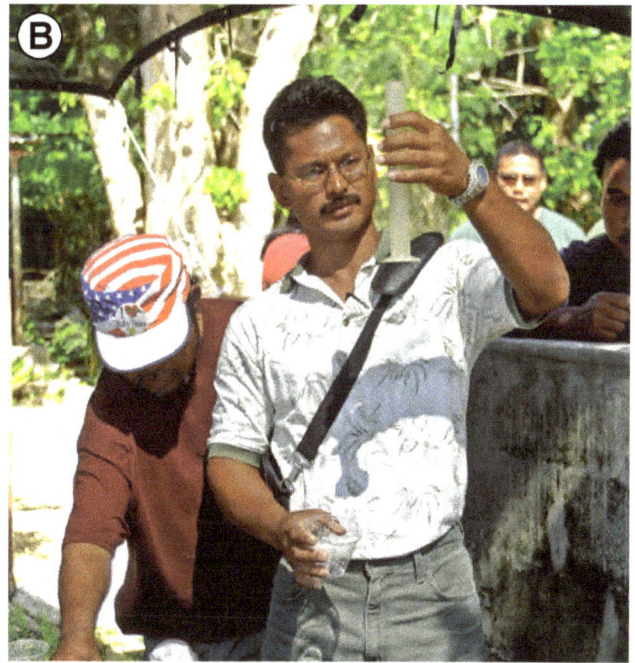

Figure 11.16—*Periodic checks of water distribution can easily be done with a "cup test" in which cups are arranged in a grid pattern (A). The depth of water in the cups is measured after a standard watering period (B). Photo A by Kim M. Wilkinson, and photo B by Thomas D. Landis.*

become completely reliant on automatic systems and will continue to directly monitor irrigation efficiency and its effect on plant growth on a regular basis.

Hand Watering

Hand watering is often the most practical irrigation strategy for small tropical plant nurseries, nurseries producing a wide diversity of species with radically different water requirements, or nurseries in the startup phase. Hand watering requires simple and inexpensive equipment; a hose, a couple of different nozzle types, and a long-handled spray wand are all that are absolutely necessary. The watering job will be more pleasant and efficient with a few additional small investments, such as overhead wires to guide the hoses and rubber boots for the staff (Biernbaum 1995). Although the task may appear easy, good technique and the application of the proper amount of water to diverse species of plants in different containers and at different growth stages is very challenging. Nursery managers need to ensure that irrigators have a conscientious attitude and are properly trained to work effectively with water application.

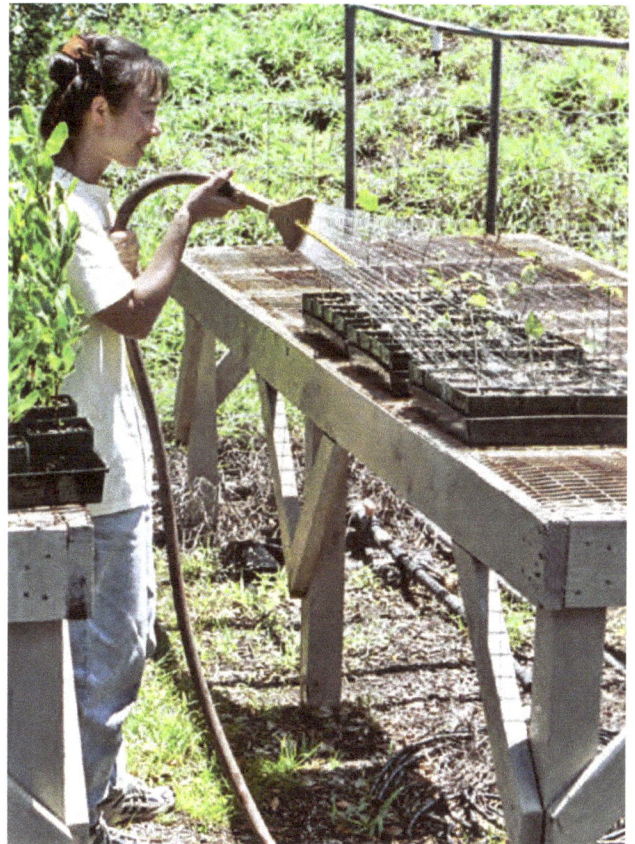

Figure 11.17—*Most native plant nurseries use a combination of irrigation types to meet the needs of diverse species. This growing area of a nursery has both overhead sprinklers and access to a hose for hand watering. Photo by Thomas D. Landis.*

Table 11.5—*Types of irrigation systems for container nurseries.*

Advantages	Disadvantages
Hand watering	
• Requires inexpensive equipment that is simple to install • Is flexible and can adjust for different species and container sizes • Irrigators have a daily connection to the crop and can scout out diseases or other potential problems • Allows water to be directed under plant foliage, reducing risk of diseases	• Is time consuming and labor intensive • Involves a daily responsibility including weekends and holidays • Requires skill, experience, and presence of mind to do properly • Presents a risk of washing out or compacting growing medium
Microirrigation	
• Water is delivered directly to the root zone of plants (not to foliage, where it may cause disease) • Use of water is very efficient; less than 10 percent of applied water is wasted • Delivery is uniform; an even amount of water is applied to each container • Infiltration rate is good (because of slow delivery). • The amount of leachate is low	• Designing the system and installing individual emitters for each plant is difficult and time consuming • It is not generally efficient to install for plants grown in containers smaller than 1 gallon in size • Each irrigation station must run a long time because of slow water delivery • Emitters can plug easily (water filtration and frequent irrigation system maintenance is required) • With drippers, it is difficult to verify water delivery visually; often, problems are not detected until it is too late
Sprinkler irrigation	
• Relatively simple and inexpensive to design and install • A variety of nozzle patterns and application rates are available • Water distribution patterns can be measured with a cup test	• Foliar interception makes overhead watering ineffective for large-leaved crops • Irrigation water can be wasted because of inefficient circular patterns • An increased risk of foliar diseases is possible from excessive water on leaves • For overhead sprinklers, nozzle drip from residual water in lines can harm germinants and young plants • For basal sprinklers, irrigation lines must run along the floor, creating obstacles for workers and equipment
Subirrigation	
• Although commercial products are available, subirrigation systems can be constructed from affordable, local materials • Foliage remains dry, reducing the risk of foliar diseases • Water use is efficient (up to 80 percent less water use than overhead watering systems) • Application among plants is uniform • Lower fertilizer rates are possible • Reduced leaching of mineral nutrients is possible • Drainage water can be captured for reuse or recycling • No splashing disrupts or displaces mulch, germinants, or medium • Provides the ability to irrigate different size containers and different age plants concurrently • Is efficient in terms of time and labor requirements following installation	• Overhead or hand watering may be required to ensure sufficient surface moisture until seeds germinate • It cannot be used with poor-quality water because salt buildup would occur • Less air pruning of roots occurs • Risk of spreading waterborne diseases is greater • High humidity within plant canopy is possible

Figure 11.18—Nursery plants on the outside of a bench or table always dry faster, especially in windy weather. Photo by Thomas D. Landis.

Good hand-watering practices include the following—

- Direct water to the base of the plants.
- Avoid spraying the foliage to conserve water and preclude foliar diseases.
- Angle the watering nozzle down (not sideways) and keep pressure low to avoid washing out seeds, medium, or mulch.
- Use an appropriate nozzle type and water volume for each crop: a very fine, gentle spray for young germinants and a larger volume nozzle for larger plants.

- Adjust the flow, volume, and pace of watering to irrigate efficiently without wasting water or compacting medium (Biernbaum 1995).
- Achieve uniformity of water distribution so all plants are well irrigated; account for microclimate differences in nursery. For example, plants on the outer edge of a bench or in direct sun will need more water (figure 11.18).
- Attend to the individual needs of each crop and its development phase so none are overwatered or underwatered; develop a feel for the watering needs of crops over time.

Microirrigation

For nurseries that grow plants in 1-gal (4-L) or larger containers, microirrigation can be a very efficient method for water delivery. Microirrigation usually involves polyethylene pipe fitted with microsprayers (sometimes called "spitters" or "spray stakes") (figure 11.19A), drippers inserted individually into each container (figure 11.19B), or smaller lateral tubing to reach all areas on the bench (figure 11.19C). Microsprayers are often preferred to drippers because they wet more surface area and distribute water more evenly throughout the container. It is also easier to visually verify the operation of a sprayer than a dripper. Filtration is a necessity for microirrigation systems to prevent emitters from clogging. Because of the slow infiltration rate of microirrigation systems, each irrigation station will need to run a long time to deliver adequate water to plants. Also, if containers are allowed to dry

Figure 11.19—Spray stakes are effective only for larger containers and work well because you can see them functioning and they have more even distribution (A). Drip emitters can also be used for larger containers (B, C). Illustration A from Dumroese and others (2008), photo B by Thomas D. Landis, and photo C by Brian F. Daley.

out, hand watering may be necessary to rewet the growing medium before drip irrigation will work.

Fixed Irrigation Systems

Overhead sprinkler systems are a common type of irrigation system and the kind that many people imagine when they think of irrigation. Many types of overhead irrigation systems exist, ranging from fixed sprinklers to moving boom systems.

Fixed Overhead Sprinklers

Fixed overhead sprinkler systems consist of a series of parallel irrigation lines, usually constructed of plastic polyvinyl chloride (PVC) pipe, with sprinklers spaced at uniform intervals to form a regular grid pattern. Overhead sprinklers apply water at a fairly rapid rate and will do an acceptable job if properly designed and maintained.

Several types of spray nozzles are used for fixed overhead irrigation systems. Spinner sprinklers, which have offset nozzles at the end of a rotating arm, spin in a circle when water pressure is applied (figure 11.20A). Stationary nozzles (figures 11.20B, 11.20C) have no moving parts but distribute water in a circular pattern; these nozzles also come in one-half and one-fourth of a circle patterns (figure 11.20D) so that full overlap coverage can be obtained by placing irrigation lines around the perimeter of the area to be irrigated. Mist nozzles are also sometimes installed on overhead irrigation lines and are primarily used during the germination period and for cooling and humidity control.

In general, the propagation environment is divided into irrigation "bays" or "zones" depending on the number of nozzles that the pump can operate at one time at the desired water pressure. Ideal operating pressures vary with the type of sprinkler, and specifications are available

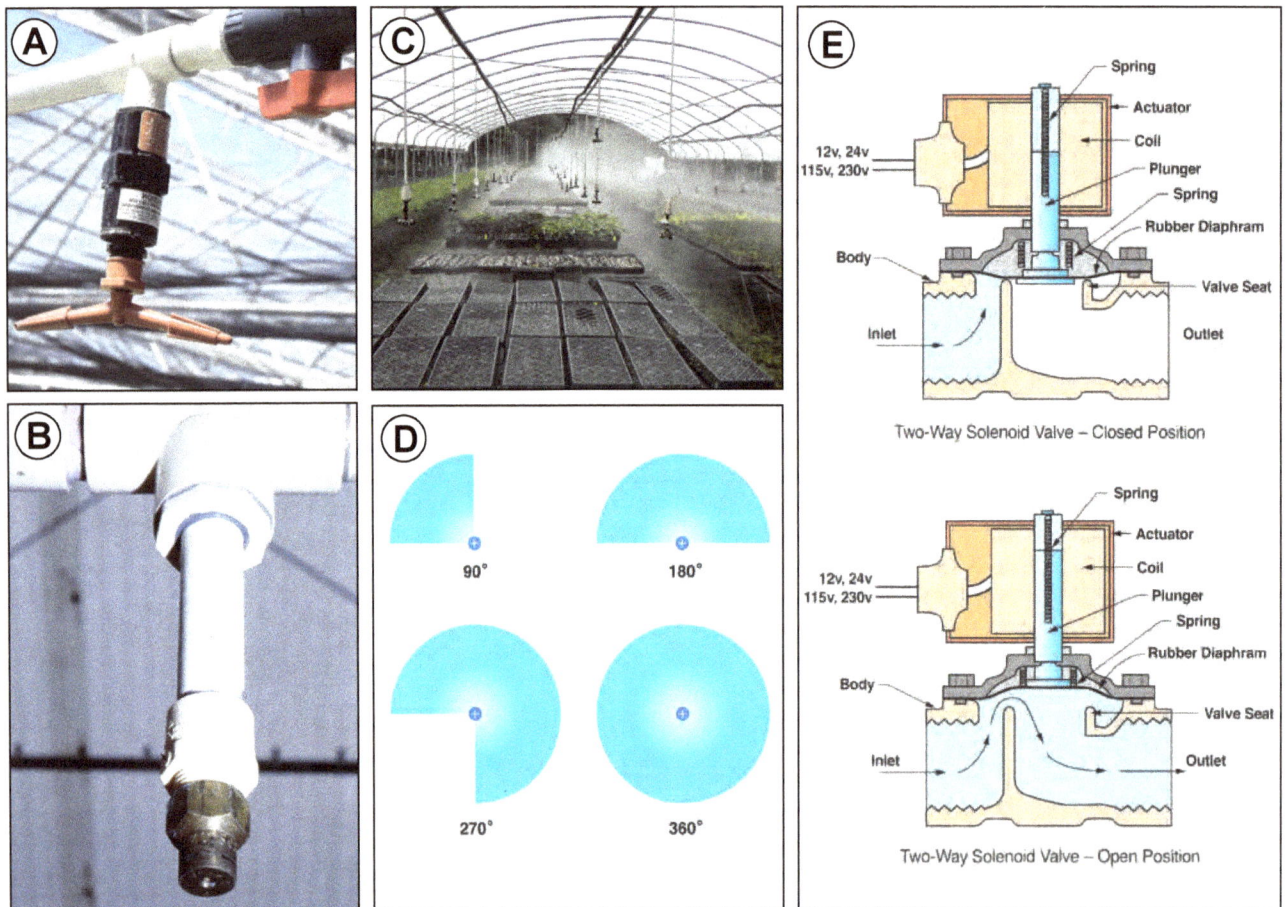

Figure 11.20—Either rotating spinners (A) or stationary nozzles (B) can be used with overhead (C) or basal sprinkler systems. In addition to the full-circle version, stationary nozzles are available in one-fourth, one-half, and three-fourths circle versions (D). Irrigation can be controlled with solenoid valves (E) connected to timers. Photos A and B by Thomas D. Landis, photo C by Diane L. Haase, illustration D by Jim Marin, and illustration E by John W. Bartok, Jr.

Figure 11.21—Fixed basal irrigation systems (A) are often used in outdoor growing areas. Rotating-impact sprinklers (B, C) are commonly used because of their greater coverage. Photo A by Brian F. Daley, and photos B and C by Thomas D. Landis.

from the manufacturer. A solenoid valve control (figure 11.20E) in each bay can be connected to an irrigation timer so that the duration and sequence of irrigation can be programmed. The size of each irrigation bay can be designed to accommodate plants with differing water requirements within a larger growing structure. When designing a new irrigation system, it is a good idea to obtain the help of an irrigation specialist to ensure that the system has balanced coverage and water pressure.

Fixed Basal Sprinklers

Basal irrigation systems are commonly used in large outdoor growing or holding areas (figures 11.21A, 11.21B). They are similar to overhead systems in design and operation in that they use a regular grid of permanent or movable irrigation lines with regularly spaced sprinklers. Both stationary sprinklers and rotating-impact nozzles (figures 11.21B, 11.21C) are commonly used. These sprinklers rotate slowly because of the impact of a spring-loaded arm that moves in and out of the nozzle stream. Rotating-impact sprinklers are available from several manufacturers in a variety of nozzle sizes and coverage capabilities. Because the water pressure out of the nozzle jet drives the impact arm, the water distribution pattern of these sprinklers is particularly dependent on proper water pressure. One advantage of basal irrigation systems is that impact sprinklers have relatively large coverage areas, which means fewer nozzles and less irrigation pipe are required.

Designing and Monitoring Fixed Sprinkler Systems

The efficiency and uniformity of an irrigation system is a function of five factors: (1) nozzle design, (2) size of the nozzle orifice, (3) water pressure and application rate at the nozzle, (4) spacing and pattern of the nozzles, and (5) amount of wind. Few operational procedures can improve a poorly designed system. Therefore, it is important to consult an irrigation engineer during the planning stages. Basic engineering considerations, such as friction loss in pipes or fittings and the effect of water pressure on sprinkler function, must be incorporated into the irrigation system design.

The size of the sprinkler nozzle and its resultant coverage pattern can be determined by consulting the performance specifications provided by the sprinkler manufacturer. Nursery managers need to select a nozzle size that is coarse enough to penetrate the plant's foliage and minimize wind drift but not large enough to create splash problems. Most stationary sprinklers throw water in a circular distribution pattern (figure 11.22A), so irrigation systems need to be designed to provide adequate overlap between sprinklers (figure 11.22B). This consideration is especially important in shadehouses or outdoor growing areas where wind drift can be a problem. Too often, sprinklers are spaced at greater intervals in a cost-saving effort, but this practice is false economy considering the profound effect of water and injected nutrients on plant growth.

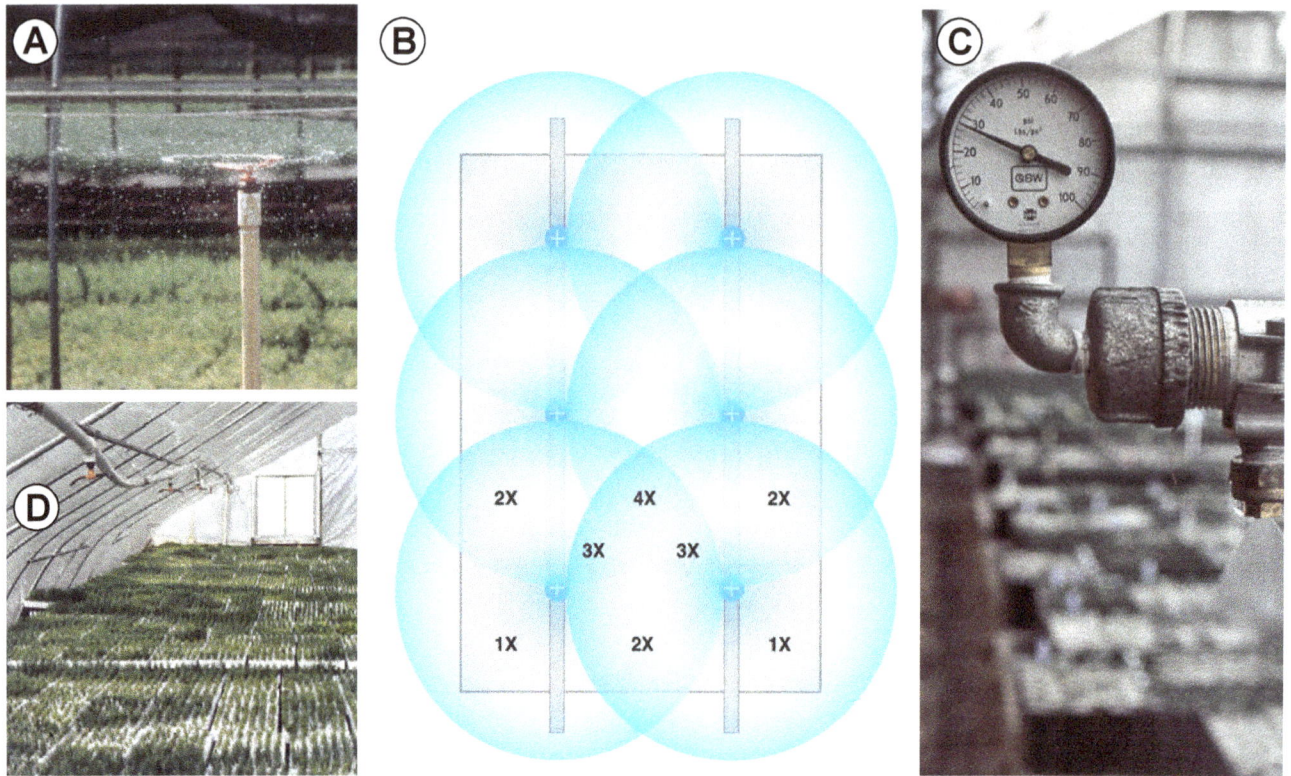

Figure 11.22—Because sprinklers produce a circular irrigation pattern (A), proper spacing is critical to produce enough overlap (B). Check the water pressure of irrigation systems annually to ensure efficient nozzle operation (C) before irrigation problems become apparent (D). Photos A, C, and D by Thomas D. Landis, and illustration B by Jim Marin.

Because water pressure has such an effect on sprinkler function and efficiency, it needs to be monitored regularly with a gauge permanently mounted near the nozzles (figure 11.22C) or with a pressure gauge equipped with a pitot tube directly from the sprinkler nozzle orifice. The pressure needs to be checked at several different nozzles including the nozzle farthest from the pump. The importance of regular water pressure checks cannot be overemphasized because many factors can cause a change in nozzle pressure. When water pressure is either too high or too low, it can cause erratic stripe or doughnut-shaped distribution patterns (figure 11.22D). Performance specifications for sprinklers at standard water pressures can be obtained from the manufacturer.

Moveable Boom Irrigation Systems

The most expensive but efficient type of overhead sprinkler irrigation is the moveable boom (figure 11.23A), which applies water in a linear pattern (figure 11.23B). Moveable booms are generally considered too expensive for smaller plant nurseries but need to be considered if appropriate to your scale. For more information, see Landis and others (1989).

Subirrigation

Overhead irrigation systems have often been the choice of container nurseries because the systems are relatively cheap and easy to install. The inherent inefficiency of overhead systems, however, becomes a very serious problem with many tropical species, especially those with broad leaves. Wide leaves combined with the close spacing of plants in a nursery create a canopy that intercepts most of the water applied through overhead irrigation systems, reducing water use efficiency and creating variable water distribution among plants (figures 11.24A, 11.24B). These problems can be precluded by subirrigation systems, which offer a promising alternative for tropical plant nurseries (Schmal and others 2011).

Subirrigation is a relatively new irrigation option but has been successfully used to grow many native plants, from forbs (Pinto and others 2008) to trees (Dumroese and others 2006, Davis and others 2008). Studies taking place with native tropical trees and other native species are demonstrating that subirrigated plants can grow as well as plants irrigated with overhead irrigation systems, but with less water use, less water wasted, and less run-

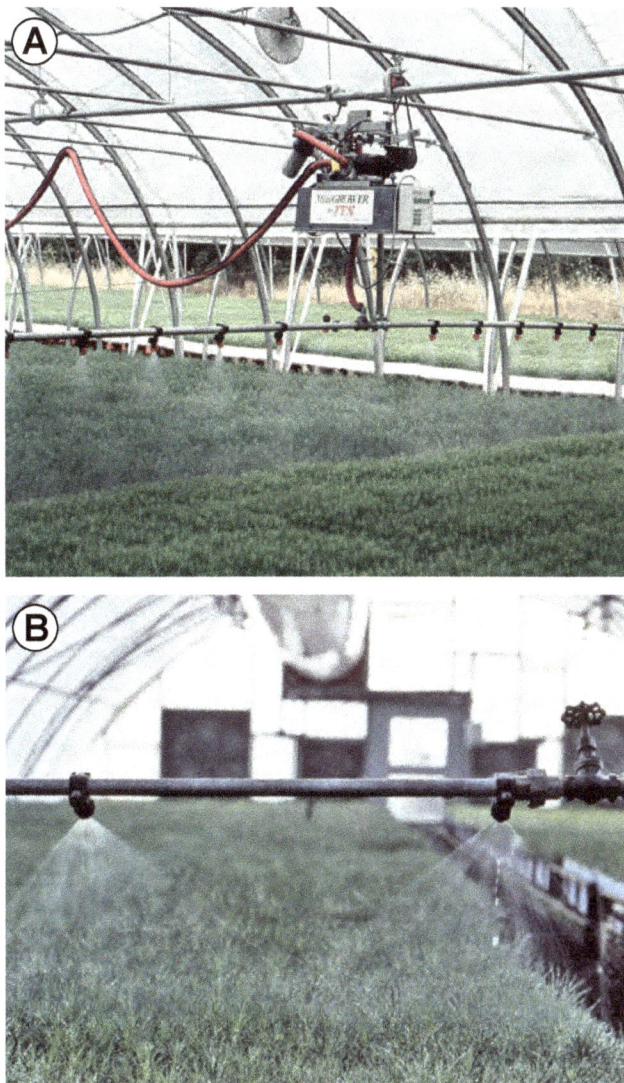

Figure 11.23—*Moveable boom irrigation systems (A) apply water in a very efficient linear pattern (B) but may be considered too expensive for many tropical nurseries. Photos by Thomas D. Landis.*

off of nitrogen fertilizers (Dumroese and others 2007). In subirrigation systems, the bottoms of containers are temporarily immersed in water on a periodic basis (for example, for several minutes once a day). The water is then drained away, leaving the growing medium thoroughly wet while the leaves remain dry.

Subirrigation systems rely on capillary action to move water up through the growing medium against gravity. Capillarity is the result of the attraction of water molecules for each other and other surfaces. After the subirrigation tray is flooded, water will move up through the growing medium in the containers (figure 11.24C). The height to which water will move will depend on the characteristics of the container and the growing medium. The

smaller the pores between the growing medium particles, the higher the water will move.

Several different subirrigation systems have been developed. Some, such as capillary beds and mats, will not work with the narrow-bottomed containers often used in tropical nurseries. With ebb-and-flow (or ebb-and-flood) subirrigation systems, containers sit in enclosures mounted on benches or on the floor. The enclosure may be a bench (figures 11.24D, 11.24E) or tray (figure 11.24 F) designed for subirrigation or may be constructed from pond liner material surrounded by a raised border of wood or masonry. Another type of subirrigation is the flooded floor type, where special concrete flooring is flooded and then water is drained. In trough subirrigation systems, enclosures are mounted on benches at a slight slope, and water is flowed through the enclosures. The drained water can be captured in a holding tank and reused on the crops or directed to landscaping, stooling beds, or other parts of the nursery, or drained to the ground (use caution with this step to ensure fertilizer salts do not affect groundwater quality). If water is recycled, be sure to monitor water quality periodically to avoid possible problems with accumulated salts or disease transfer.

Subirrigation systems are ideal for many topical native plants. Although prefabricated subirrigation systems are available commercially, nurseries on a limited budget may consider designing their own systems using available materials. For example, systems can be made out of concrete blocks and pond liner or out of prefabricated drainable plastic ponds, even plastic "kiddie pools" (figure 11.24 G) (Schmal and others 2007). (Note: Some materials, such as galvanized metal, are inappropriate because of zinc toxicity.)

Some important design considerations exist for subirrigation systems. The drainage holes at the bottom of the containers must have good contact with the water for the water to enter the container. Subirrigation may be less effective during the establishment phase, when growing medium in the upper portions of containers needs to be moist to promote germination and early growth; therefore, supplemental hand watering or sprinkler irrigation may be necessary initially. Air root pruning may be reduced with subirrigation, resulting in a need for hand pruning; making this system inadvisable for use with plants that are very sensitive to root pruning.

Figure 11.24—*Overhead irrigation is ineffective for broadleaved plants because so much water is intercepted by the foliage, called "the umbrella effect" (A), which can begin even when seedlings are young (B). Subirrigation works because water is drawn upward into the containers by capillarity (C). Subirrigation has been used effectively in a number of tropical nurseries and can be accomplished via benches (D, E), trays (F) or other enclosures (G). Illustrations A and C from Dumroese and others (2008), photos B, D, and E by Thomas D. Landis, and photos F and G by Diane L. Haase*

Water Conservation and Managing Nursery Wastewater

Depending on the efficiency of the irrigation system, nursery runoff and wastewater may be important factors to consider. Overhead sprinkler irrigation is less efficient than a boom system. Microirrigation or subirrigation systems are much more efficient but are impractical for some types of containers and plants.

The problem of poor irrigation efficiency involves more than simply wasted water, although that alone is a concern both environmentally and economically. In addition, many container nurseries apply some or all of their fertilizer and pesticides through the irrigation system. Liquid fertilizer is usually applied in excess of the actual amount needed to saturate the growing medium and to leach excess salts. Most pesticides are applied in a water-based carrier. Some of these chemicals inevitably end up in the nursery's wastewater runoff.

Until recently, it was thought that the soil beneath the nursery filtered out or decomposed fertilizer salts and pesticides, but this belief has been refuted. Leaching tests in conifer nurseries have shown that excess fertilizer nutrients and pesticides leach downward and may contaminate groundwater. Maximizing the efficiency of irrigation systems and implementing water conservation strategies (table 11.6, figure 11.25) is the most effective way to reduce runoff.

The direct recycling of used nursery water is generally not done except in subirrigation systems. Otherwise, on a small scale, the expense of water treatment and the risks of reintroducing excess salts or pests make the practice unpopular. Recycle systems for nursery runoff water may be economically viable in very water-limited areas, however. Less high-tech options for water reuse can make use of an impermeable nursery floor (such as pond liner) to collect water runoff from the nursery. This water can be stored in a pond or tank or run directly to other crops. Crops that are more tolerant of salts, such as rushes, may benefit from using runoff water, and these crops will even clean and filter the water. Nurseries growing aquatic or semiaquatic plants may be able to direct runoff to these plants and thereby increase the water-use efficiency of the nursery operation. Crops in the field, such as seed orchards, wetland crops, surrounding landscaping, or banana, palm, or tree crops, can all benefit from being irrigated with nursery runoff water. If the crops are located downhill from the nursery itself, the system can be gravity fed. Otherwise, a pump will be necessary to apply the water to the crops.

Table 11.6—Nurseries can incorporate a variety of horticultural practices to use irrigation water effectively and efficiently.

Nursery practice	Conservation effect
Mulches (figure 11.25A)	Reduces evaporation from the surface of the growing medium; the larger the container, the greater the savings
Windbreaks (chapter 2, figure 2.13A)	Reduces water loss and seedling stress because of wind
Remove cull plants and minimize space between containers, including aisles	Reduces unnecessary use of water and resultant runoff
Shadecloth and shadehouses (figure 11.25B)	Reduces water use for species that do not require full sunlight
Catch runoff and recycle water for use on landscaping and other crops	Saves considerable amounts of water and reduce fertilizer use
Treat runoff water via filtration or bioswales	Reduces contaminants in recycled water

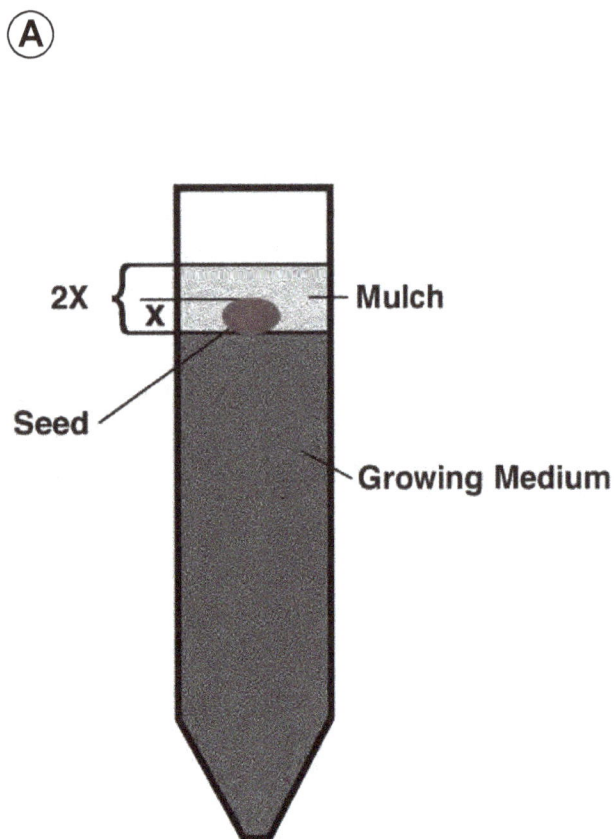

Figure 11.25—*Water can be conserved by many practices, such as covering sown containers with a mulch (A); reducing transpiration and evaporation water loss with shade (B); and insulating crop areas, such as with straw bale insulation around the perimeter of the growing area (C). Illustration A from Dumroese and others (2008), photo B by Thomas D. Landis, and photo C by Tara Luna.*

References

Biernbaum, J. 1995. How to hand water. Greenhouse Grower. 13(14): 39, 24, 44.

Cayanan, D.F.; Zheng, Y.; Zhang, P.; Graham, T. 2008. Sensitivity of five container-grown nursery species to chlorine in overhead irrigation water. HortScience. 43: 1882–1887.

Davis, A.S.; Jacobs, D.F.; Overton, R.P.; Dumroese, R.K. 2008. Influence of irrigation method and container type on growth of *Quercus rubra* seedlings and media electrical conductivity. Native Plants Journal. 9: 4–12.

Dumroese, R.K.; Jacobs, D.F.; Davis, A.S.; Pinto, J.R.; Landis, T.D. 2007. An introduction to subirrigation in forest and conservation nurseries and some preliminary results of demonstrations. In: Riley, L.E.; Dumroese, R.K.; Landis, T.D., eds. national proceedings: forest and conservation nursery associations—2006. Proceedings RMRS-P-50. Fort Collins, CO: U.S. Department of Agriculture, Forest Service, Rocky Mountain Research Station: 20–26.

Dumroese, R.K.; Pinto, J.R.; Jacobs, D.F.; Davis, A.S.; Horiuchi, B. 2006. Subirrigation reduces water use, nitrogen loss, and moss growth in a container nursery. Native Plants Journal. 7(3): 253–261.

Dumroese, R.K.; Luna, T.; Landis, T.D. 2008. Nursery manual for native plants: volume 1, a guide for tribal nurseries. Agriculture Handbook 730. Washington, DC: U.S. Department of Agriculture, Forest Service. 302 p.

Fawell, J.; Bailey, K.; Chilton, J.; Dahi, E.; Fewtrell, L.; Magara, Y. 2006. Fluoride in drinking water. World Health Organization. London, United Kingdom: International Water Association (IWA) Publishing. 134 p.

Gingerich, S.B. 2003. Hydrologic resources of Guam. Water-Resources Investigation Report 03-4126. Honolulu, HI: U.S. Department of the Interior, Geological Survey. 3 p.

Handreck, K.A.; Black, N.D. 1984. Growing media for ornamental plants and turf. Kensington, Australia: New South Wales University Press. 401 p.

Jones, J.B., Jr. 1983. A guide for the hydroponic and soilless culture grower. Portland, OR: Timber Press. 124 p.

Kaapuni Nursery. 2011. *Cordyline terminalis* 'Ti' plant. Kapahi, Kaua'i, HI: Kaapuni Nursery. http://www.kaapuninursery.com/Nursery.html. (December 2011).

Landis, T.D.; Tinus, R.W.; McDonald, S.E.; Barnett, J.P. 1989. The container tree nursery manual: volume 4, seedling nutrition and irrigation. Agriculture Handbook 674. Washington, DC: U.S. Department of Agriculture, Forest Service. 119 p.

Pinto, J.R.; Chandler, R.; Dumroese, R.K. 2008. Growth, nitrogen use efficiency, and leachate comparison of subirrigated and overhead irrigated pale purple coneflower seedlings. HortScience. 43: 897–901.

Robbins, J. 2011. Irrigation water for greenhouses and nurseries. Publication FSA6061. Little Rock, AR: University of Arkansas, Horticulture Department. 6 p.

Schmal, J.L.; Wollery, P.O.; Sloan, J.P.; Clark, D.F. 2007. A low-tech, inexpensive subirrigation system for production of broadleaved species in large containers. Native Plants Journal. 8: 267–269.

Schmal, J.L.; Dumroese, R.K.; Davis, A.S.; Pinto, J.R.; Jacobs, D.F. 2011. Subirrigation for production of native plants in nurseries – concepts, current knowledge, and implementation. Native Plants Journal. 12:81-93.

Stetson, L.E.; Mecham, B.Q. 2011. Irrigation. 6th ed. Falls Church, VA: Irrigation Association. 1,089 p.

Tchobanoglous, G.; Schroeder, E.D. 1985. Water quality: characteristics, modeling, modification. Melo Park, CA: Addison-Wesley Publishing Co. 768 p.

Zheng, Y.; Cayanan, D.F.; Dixon, M. 2009. Control of pathogens in irrigation water using chlorine without injury to plants. International Plant Propagators' Society, Combined Proceedings. 58: 248–249.

Plant Nutrition and Fertilization

Douglass F. Jacobs and Thomas D. Landis

12

Plants require adequate quantities of mineral nutrients in the proper balance for basic physiological processes, such as photosynthesis, and to promote rapid growth and development. Without a good supply of mineral nutrients, growth is slowed and plant vigor reduced. Young plants rapidly deplete mineral nutrients stored within their seeds, and cuttings have limited nutrient reserves. Therefore, nursery plants must rely on root uptake of nutrients from the growing medium. When nutrients are supplied in proper amounts and at the proper time, nursery plants can achieve optimum growth rates.

This chapter describes the importance of nutrition to plant growth development and details typical fertilization practices for producing plants in tropical nurseries.

Facing Page: *Topdressing native sandalwood (*Santalum *species) seedlings with controlled-release fertilizer at Waimea State Tree Nursery in Hawai'i. Photo by Douglass F. Jacobs.*

Basic Principles of Plant Nutrition

A common misconception is that fertilizer is "plant food" (figure 12.1A), but the basic nutrition of plants is very different from that of animals. Using the green chlorophyll in their leaves, plants make their own food in the form of carbohydrates from sunlight, water, and carbon dioxide in a process called photosynthesis (figure 12.1B). These carbohydrates provide the plant energy, and when combined with mineral nutrients absorbed from the soil or growing medium, carbohydrates are used to synthesize proteins and other compounds necessary for basic metabolism and growth.

Thirteen mineral nutrients are considered essential to plant growth and development and are divided into macronutrients and micronutrients based on the amounts found in plant tissue (table 12.1). Some mineral nutrients have a structural function. For example, nitrogen is an integral part of plant proteins, and nitrogen and magnesium are structural components of chlorophyll molecules needed for photosynthesis (figure 12.2). Understanding these basic functions has practical applications because a deficiency of either nutrient causes plants to be chlorotic (that is, yellowish in color). Other mineral nutrients have no structural role, but potassium, for example, is functionally important in causing the stomata in leaves to open and close.

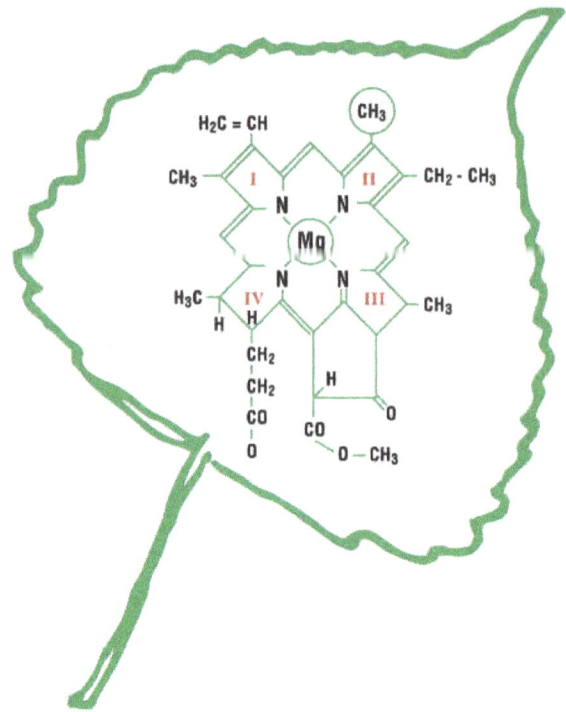

Figure 12.2—*Mineral nutrients such as nitrogen and magnesium are important components of chlorophyll molecules that give leaves their green color and are essential for photosynthesis. Illustration from Dumroese and others (2008).*

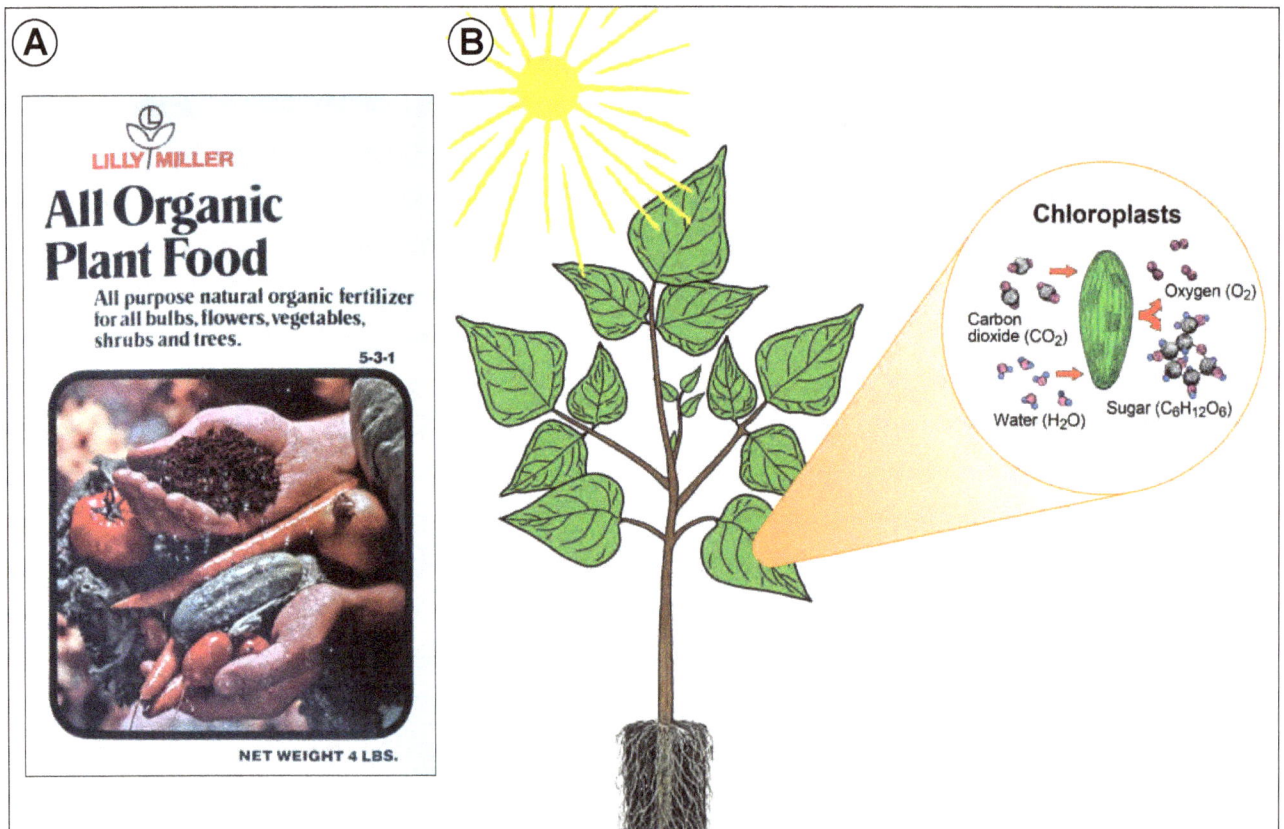

Figure 12.1—*Although some fertilizers are advertised as "plant food" (A), plants actually create their own food through the process of photosynthesis in their green leaves (B). Photo A by Thomas D. Landis, and illustration B by from Dumroese and others (2008).*

Table 12.1—*The 13 essential plant nutrients (divided into macronutrients and micronutrients). Nitrogen, phosphorus, and potassium are the most common fertilizer elements.*

Name (symbol)	Percent of plant tissue (oven dry weight)	Structural functions	Physiological functions	Deficiency symptoms (general)
Macronutrients				
Nitrogen (N)	1.5	Component of chlorophyll, amino acids, proteins, and nucleic acids	Vital to all physiological processes through roles in enzyme systems.	Old leaves turn yellow (chlorosis), plant growth stunted; small leaves. Differs from iron chlorosis because older foliage is affected first.
Phosphorus (P)	0.2	Component of cell walls and nucleic acids	Energy storage and release, functioning of cell membranes, regulates enzyme and cell buffering.	Some plants show purpling, but stunting is most common.
Potassium (K)	1.0	None	Osmotic adjustment. Important in maintaining cell turgor, phloem transport, cell growth.	Necrosis of leaf margins, stunting.
Calcium (Ca)	0.5	Component of cell walls	Facilitates cell division, stabilizes cell membranes, inhibits fungal infections and toxins.	Disintegration of cell walls, inhibition of meristems and especially root tips, increased susceptibility to fungal attack.
Magnesium (Mg)	0.2	Component of chlorophyll	Regulates cellular pH and ionic balance, energy transfer, enzyme stabilization.	Interveinal chlorosis or yellowing of needle tips, symptoms may occur in patches.
Sulfur (S)	0.1	Maintain protein structure, component of vitamins, and coenzyme A	Amino acids formation, protein synthesis, ion transport across membranes.	Light green foliage leading to chlorosis, often visible on younger foliage, stunting.
Micronutrients				
Iron (Fe)	0.01	Critical to manufacture of chlorophyll	Catalyst to several enzymes systems, especially for photosynthesis.	Chlorosis of newer foliage; in severe cases leaves turn whitish.
Manganese (Mn)	0.005	Structural component of ribosomes	Critical to Hill Reaction in photosynthesis, carbohydrate and nucleic acid synthesis, and lipid metabolism.	Chlorosis similar to iron deficiency except severe cases lead to necrosis.
Zinc (Zn)	0.002	Component of several enzymes	Enzyme catalyst for carbohydrate metabolism, protein synthesis, and auxin production.	Reduced internode elongation ("rosetting") and stunted foliage ("littleleaf"). Chlorosis or bronzing of younger leaves.
Copper (Cu)	0.0006	Constituent of proteins and enzymes	Photosynthetic functioning; phenol, carbohydrate, and nitrogen metabolism.	Chlorosis, tip dieback, twisted, needle tips.
Molybdenum (Mo)	0.00001	Component of several enzyme systems, notably for nitrogen uptake	Essential for reducing nitrate ions to ammonium after uptake; critical for nodule function in legumes.	Chlorosis and necrosis of leaf tissue.
Boron (B)	0.002	None	Involved in cell division and elongation, lignification of cell walls, synthesis of amino acids and proteins.	Distortion and discoloration of shoot and root tips, short shoot internodes producing a bushy or rosette appearance.
Chloride (Cl)	0.01	None	Osmosis and ion balance within cells; photosynthetic oxygen evolution.	Rare. Wilting of leaf margins and restriction of root elongation.

An important nutrition concept is Liebig's Law of the Minimum, which states that plant growth is controlled by the mineral nutrient in shortest supply. See Chapter 5, Propagation Environments, for more discussion about limiting factors. A good way to visualize the concept of limiting factors is a wooden bucket with staves of different lengths. If water is poured into the bucket, it can be filled only to the height of the shortest stave—the limiting factor. Nitrogen is nearly always limiting to plant growth in nature, which is the reason why nitrogen fertilizer is frequently applied in nurseries (figure 12.3).

Just as important as the absolute quantities of nutrients available to plants is the balance of nutrients. The proper nutrient balance is relatively consistent among plant species and can be expressed as Ingestad's Ratios. Healthy plant tissue contains approximately 100 parts of nitrogen to 50 parts of phosphorus, to 15 parts of potassium, to 5 parts of magnesium, to 5 parts of sulfur. On a practical basis, most tropical plant nurseries use complete fertilizers that contain a balance of all mineral nutrients.

Mineral nutrients are absorbed by root hairs as two types of ions: cations and anions. Cations have an electrically positive charge, while anions are negatively charged. Particles of soil, compost, and artificial growing medium are also charged, so nutrient ions attach to sites with an opposite charge. Roots typically release a cation (often H^+) or an an ion (for instance, HCO_3^-) when taking up a nutrient ion of the same charge from the soil or growing medium (figure 12.4). See Chapter 6, Growing Media, for more information on this topic. Fertilizers applied in the nursery break down into soluble nutrient ions, which are then taken up by plant roots.

Sources of Mineral Nutrients

Plants produced in container nurseries may acquire nutrients from several different sources, including the growing medium, irrigation water, beneficial microorganisms, and fertilizers. Many tropical nurseries use artificial growing media that are essentially infertile, which enables growers to apply the right type of fertilizer, in the right amount, and at the right time. Levels of mineral nutrients in a commercial growing medium are generally very low, which is why they are often amended with a "starter dose" of fertilizer. Native soils and composts contain higher nutrient concentrations than commercial growing media but rarely enough for the fast growth rate and nutrient balance desired in nurseries. If soil or other homemade growing media will be used, a soil test can be done to determine which nutrients are lacking (see the section on testing in the following paragraphs).

Figure 12.3—*The concept of limiting factors can be illustrated by a wooden bucket that can be filled with water only to the shortest stave. In this example, nitrogen (N) is the most limiting, which is typical in nurseries. Illustration from Dumroese and others (2008).*

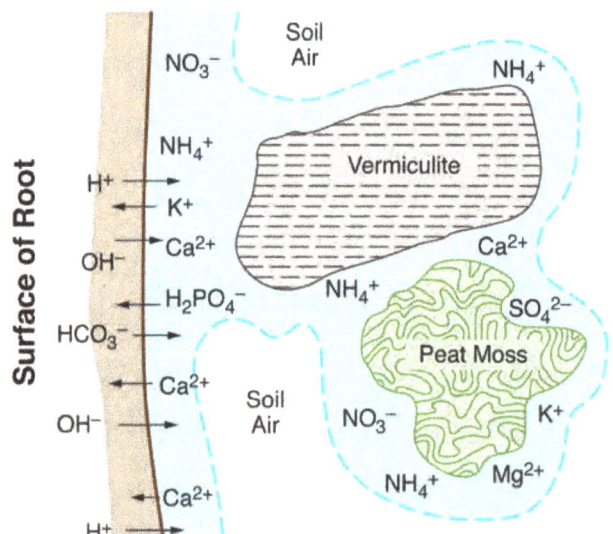

Figure 12.4—*Nutrient cations and anions are extracted by plant roots through an exchange process with soil, compost, or artificial growing media. Illustration from Dumroese and others (2008).*

Another potential source of mineral nutrients in nurseries is irrigation water. "Hard water" often contains enough calcium and magnesium for good plant growth. Sulfur is another nutrient often found in water sources. Beneficial microorganisms may provide an important source of nitrogen for some species, such as legumes, as detailed in Chapter 13, Beneficial Microorganisms.

To achieve the desired plant growth and health, fertilizers are the most common source of mineral nutrients in tropical plant nurseries. Growers need to have a good understanding of types of fertilizers and how and when to apply them. Many different types of fertilizers are used in tropical plant nurseries and vary according to their source materials, nutrient quantities, and mechanisms of nutrient delivery. The two main fertilizer categories are organic (figure 12.5A) and synthetic (figure 12.5B).

All commercial fertilizers are required by law to show the ratio of nitrogen to phosphorus to potassium (actually the oxides of phosphorus and potassium; $N:P_2O_5:K_2O$) and the complete nutrient analysis on the label (figure 12.5C). Some fertilizers contain only one mineral nutrient whereas others contain several. Examples of single-nutrient fertilizers include ammonium nitrate (34-0-0) or concentrated superphosphate (0-45-0). Fertilizers may be blended or reacted to supply two or more essential nutrients. An example of a blended fertilizer is a 12-10-8, which was formed by adding triple superphosphate (0-46-0), potassium magnesium sulfate (0-0-22), and ammonium nitrate (34-0-0). An example of a multiple-nutrient fertilizer is potassium nitrate (13-0-44).

Some tropical plant nurseries prefer organic fertilizers because they are less likely to burn crops if too much is applied and have lower risk of water pollution. If inoculating with beneficial microorganisms, organic fertilizers are generally preferred. The main drawbacks of organic fertilizers are that they are more expensive, and their lower nutrient content and solubility result in slower plant growth. Most of the research in tropical plant nurseries has

Figure 12.5—*The two main types of commercial fertilizers are organic (A), and synthetic (B). All fertilizers must show the nitrogen-phosphorus-potassium ratio on the label, and most also give a complete listing of mineral nutrients (C). Photos by Thomas D. Landis.*

been done with synthetic fertilizers because they are inexpensive, readily soluble, and quickly taken up by crops. Synthetic fertilizers are popular with growers because they stimulate the rapid growth rates desired in nursery culture.

Organic Fertilizers

Until the early 20th century, nearly all fertilizers used in agriculture, including nurseries, were organic. The shortage of Chilean nitrate, a major source of organic nitrogen, led to development of the Haber-Bosch Process, which converts the abundant nitrogen gas in our atmosphere into ammonia. This ammonia can then be chemically converted into a vast array of synthetic fertilizers. After the Second World War, these synthetic, ammonia-based fertilizers became cheap and readily available, and use of organic fertilizers dropped from 91 percent in the early 1900s to 3 percent by the 1950s. In recent decades, however, organic farming has seen a resurgence because of changes in public values. In tropical areas, concern about the environmental and economic implications of manufacturing, transporting, and using synthetic fertilizers is rising. In response to this increasing demand, a wide variety of organic fertilizers have been developed, and many have potential in tropical plant nurseries.

Defining organic fertilizers can be a complicated and confusing subject, and much of this confusion comes from terminology. For our purposes, organic fertilizers can be defined as materials that are naturally occurring and have not been synthesized, and we recognize two general categories: animal or plant wastes and natural minerals (figure 12.6).

Animal or Plant Wastes

These materials are what most people consider to be organic fertilizers and can be applied to crops directly or developed into a wide variety of other processed fertilizers. One of the attractions of these types of organic fertilizers is they are renewable and widely available.

Unprocessed Organics

This category is by far the largest and most complicated because nearly any type of animal or plant waste can be used as a fertilizer, including animal manure, sewage sludge, and peat moss. In tropical areas, guano is an excellent organic fertilizer and consists of the accumulated excrement of seabirds or bats. Guano has high levels of phosphorus and nitrogen and does not have any noticeable odor. One of the largest mining operations occurred on the small South Pacific island of Nauru where centuries of deposition by seabirds created vast reserves of mineralized guano.

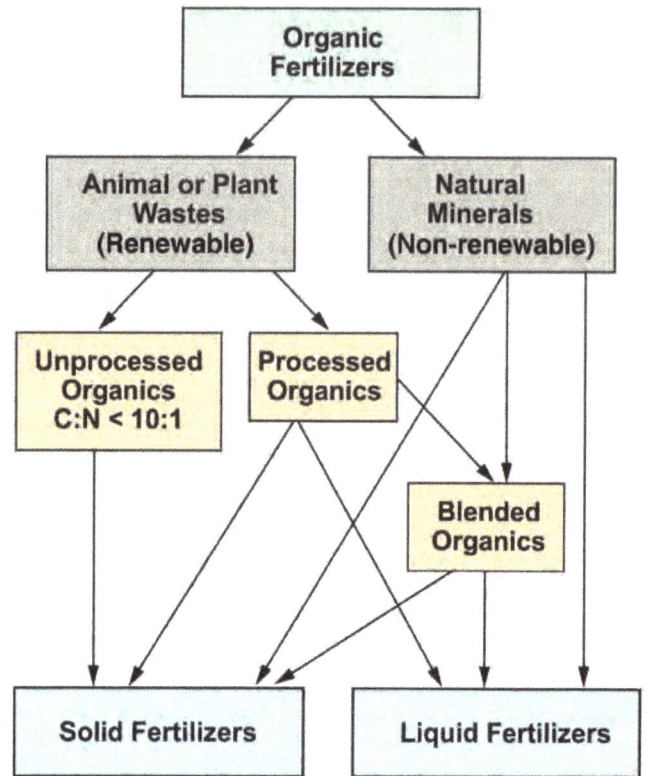

Figure 12.6—*The terminology of organic fertilizers is complicated, but various types can be illustrated in this flow chart from Landis and Dumroese (2011).*

The best criterion for determining which types of unprocessed organic matter are suitable fertilizers is the carbon-to-nitrogen (C:N) ratio. Organic materials with a C:N less than 10:1 are considered to be fertilizers. Unprocessed organics can be challenging to use because of their high potential for water pollution.

Processed Organics

This category includes any organic material that has been processed in some manner before being used as a solid or liquid fertilizer, and includes composts, blood meal, bone meal, and materials such as feather meal and kelp extracts (table 12.2). Manure is a good source of nutrients but will always need to be composted first so it will not damage plants or pollute water. One way to test if the manure is composted enough to use as fertilizer is to place a few handfuls into a plastic bag and seal it for 24 hours; if the material does not smell bad or give off heat at the end of the test period, it is ready to use; otherwise, it will need further composting. Nearly any organic waste matter can be composted and the composting process has been well documented. See Chapter 6, Growing Media, for more information on composting. Many new processed organic fertilizers are now available from horticultural supply sources.

Table 12.2—*Percentages of nitrogen, phosphorus, and potassium supplied by a variety of organic materials. Adapted from Diver and others (2008).*

Organic fertilizers	N	P	K
Bat guano (fresh)	10	3	1
Bat guano (old)	2	8	0
Blood meal	10	0	0
Bone meal (steamed)	1	11	0
Cottonseed meal	6	2	1
Eggshells	1.2	0.4	0.1
Fish emulsion	4	1	1
Fish meal	5	3	3
Greensand	0	0	7
Hoof and horn meal	12	2	0
Kelp meal	1.5	0.5	2.5
Soybean meal	7.0	0.5	2.3
Worm castings	0.5	0.5	0.3
Manure			
Cow	2	2.3	2.4
Horse	1.7	0.7	1.8
Pig	2	1.8	1.8
Sheep	4	1.4	3.5
Poultry	4	4	2

N = Nitrogen, P = Phosphorus, K = Potassium

Anyone considering the use of processed organic fertilizers needs to test them first to decide if a need exists for composting, determine proper application rates, and identify potential nutrient toxicities or deficiencies. It is also wise to initiate small-scale tests with any new fertilizer product to avoid possible problems and determine plant growth rates.

Natural Mineral Fertilizers

This second major category of organic fertilizers includes minerals and other materials that come directly from the earth (figure 12.6). Minerals like sodium nitrate are commonly used in many blended organic fertilizers because they are soluble and have a high nutrient content. Like all types of mining, however, obtaining natural minerals is an extractive process and nonrenewable in the long term.

Rock Phosphate

Natural deposits of fluoroapatite are the raw material of most phosphate fertilizers and are currently mined in North Africa, the former Soviet Union, and in Florida, Idaho, Montana, Utah, and Tennessee. The raw ore contains 14- to 35-percent phosphate (P_2O_5) and is processed by grinding and washing into a fine granular fertilizer. Rock phosphate is very insoluble in water and makes an effective slow-release granular fertilizer. Because of its low solubility, rock phosphate has been recommended as an ideal phosphorus fertilizer to encourage mycorrhizal development.

Sodium Nitrate

This salt ($NaNO_3$) is commonly known as Chilean or Peruvian saltpeter because of the large caliche mineral deposits found in both countries. Although this fertilizer has been used in organic farming for many years, several organic certifying agencies have concluded that mined mineral fertilizers conflict with basic organic principles. For example, the USDA National Organic Program currently restricts use of sodium nitrate to less than 20 percent of total annual applied nitrogen and requires that growers phase out its use over time.

Magnesium Sulfate

This mineral ($MgSO_4$) comprises Epsom salts or Kieserite. Although more widely used for medicinal purposes, magnesium sulfate is a very soluble source of magnesium and sulfur and has been used in the formulation of liquid fertilizers for container tree nursery crops.

Sul-Po-Mag

Technically known as sulfate of potash-magnesia or langbeinite, this salt is mined from marine evaporite deposits and is a common component in many blended organic fertilizers. It was originally discovered in Germany and contains soluble nutrients in the following ratio: 22-percent potassium, 22-percent sulfur, and 11-percent magnesium. Another common trade name is K-Mag Natural, an ideal product for supplying potassium and sulfur without any accompanying nitrogen.

Blended Organic Fertilizers

This category of organic fertilizers includes a wide variety of products containing a mixture of processed organic plant or animal wastes supplemented with natural minerals (figure 12.7). It is easy to identify blended organic fertilizers by checking the ingredients on their labels.

Solid Organic Fertilizers

Powdered or granular fertilizers can be derived from unprocessed organics, processed organics, natural minerals, or blended organics (figure 12.6). Solid organic fertilizers have not been widely used in forest or native plant nurseries. Biosol® (6-1-3) is a solid organic fertilizer that is supplemented with Sul-Po-Mag, however, and has potential for nursery use.

Liquid Organic Fertilizers

This category of organic fertilizers can be derived from processed organics, natural minerals, or blended organics (figures 12.5A, 12.6). Ingredients might include fertilizers such as fish waste, soybean meal, kelp, recycled foodstuffs, bat guano, sulfate of potash, feather meal, blood meal, steamed bone meal, or any number of ingredients. Many products are targeted to specific crops but others are for more general use. Some liquid organic fertilizers contain suspended material and must be filtered or continually agitated during fertigation to prevent the material from plugging nozzles.

Synthetic Fertilizers

The most important synthetic fertilizers are made using the Haber-Bosch process in which atmospheric nitrogen is converted into ammonia under high temperature and pressure. Having been called the most important invention of the 20th century, this industrial process produces 500 million tons of artificial fertilizer per year. Synthetic fertilizers are popular because they are relatively inexpensive, readily available, and have high nutrient content compared with organic products. In populated tropical areas, synthetic fertilizers can be found at garden supply shops and through horticultural dealers, but inaccessibility and transport costs may be a limitation in remote areas. In the humid tropics, storage of synthetic fertilizers becomes a challenge because they readily absorb moisture from the air.

Synthetic fertilizers can be divided into two classes: (1) soluble products that release nutrients quickly when dissolved in water and (2) slow-release or controlled-release fertilizers that release nutrients slowly over time. Both types have their advantages and disadvantages, which need to be considered before deciding upon a fertilization system (table 12.3). Other types of granular fertilizers that are used on lawns or in agriculture are not recommended for tropical plant nurseries.

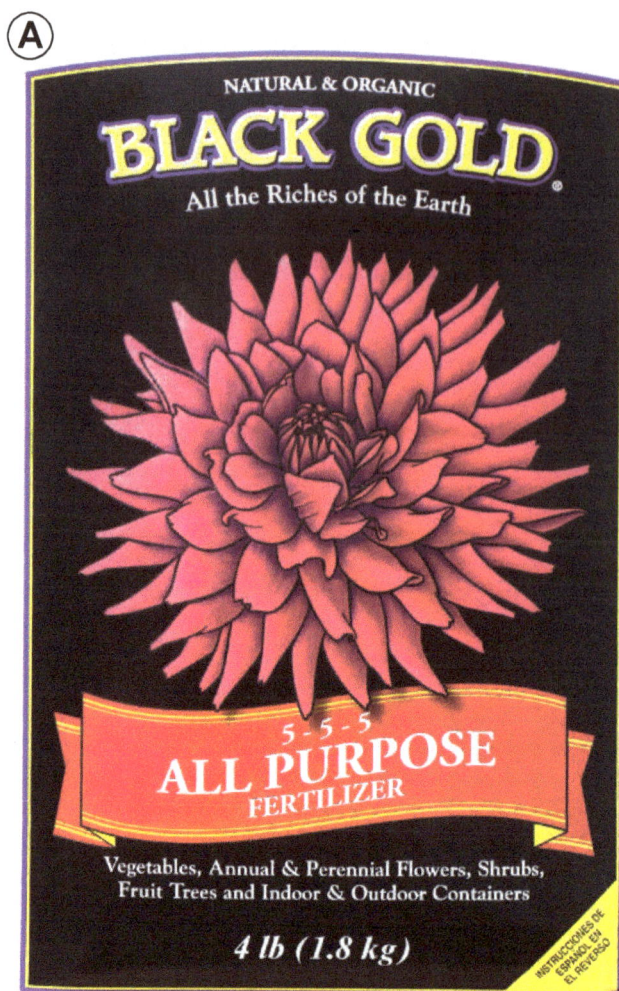

Figure 12.7—*Blended organic fertilizers (A) contain processed organic materials and natural minerals, such as sulfate of potash (B). Photos by Thomas D. Landis.*

Table 12.3—Comparison of advantages and disadvantages of two major types of synthetic fertilizers used in tropical plant nurseries.

Factor	Soluble fertilizer	Controlled-release fertilizer
Nutrient release rate	Very fast	Much slower—dependent on type and thickness of coating, as well as temperature and moisture
Number of applications	Multiple—must be applied at regular intervals	Usually once per season, but additional top-dressing is an option
Uniformity of application	Good, but dependent on irrigation coverage	Can be variable if incorporated, resulting in uneven growth
Adjusting nutrient rates and ratios	Easy and quick	Difficult
Nutrient uptake efficiency	Poorer	Better
Leaching and pollution potential	Higher	Lower
Potential for fertilizer burn (salt toxicity)	Low if applied properly	Low, unless prills damaged during incorporation or following high temperatures
Product cost	Lower	Higher
Application costs	Higher	Lower

Soluble Fertilizers

Soluble synthetic fertilizers come in either granules or water-soluble crystals (figure 12.8A). Soluble fertilizers are typically injected into the irrigation system, a process known as fertigation (see the discussion in the following section). Their popularity stems from the fact that the application rates can be easily calculated, distribution is as uniform as the irrigation system, and, if properly formulated and applied, the chance of fertilizer burn is very low (table 12.3). Because they are immediately soluble, the nutrients in these fertilizers are quickly available for plant uptake and it is easy to adjust nutrient levels and ratios, which gives the grower great control of plant growth rates. When growing a variety of plant species in the same area, it is necessary to separate them based on relative growth rates so that different fertilizer mixes can be applied. The major drawback to using soluble fertilizers is their relatively low nutrient uptake efficiency and subsequent high leaching rate. Because they are soluble, some nutrients that are not used by plants or are held on the cation exchange sites of the growing medium, leach out with each irrigation. Fixed overhead irrigation systems apply fertilizer solution to the aisles as well as to the plants, so all these nutrients run off and can cause pollution.

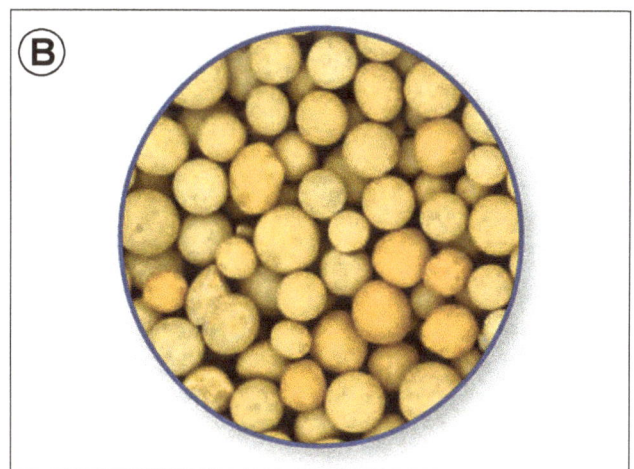

Figure 12.8—The two major types of synthetic fertilizers used in native plant nurseries are soluble crystals that dissolve completely in water (A), and polymer-coated controlled-release fertilizers, which are soluble fertilizers inside a thin plastic shell. These "prills" come in a variety of sizes, nutrient formulations, and release rates (B). Photo A by Thomas D. Landis, and photo B by Douglass F. Jacobs.

Special types of water-soluble fertilizers are sometimes applied to stimulate uptake through the foliage ("foliar feeding"). Although this method seems to be a good way to fertilize, remember that all leaves are covered with a water-repelling cuticle, so foliar uptake is very inefficient. More nutrient uptake actually occurs through the roots as a result of the fertilizer solution washing down into the soil or growing medium rather than through the foliage itself. Special care must be taken to prevent salt damage to foliage, so we do not recommend foliar feeding for smaller nurseries.

Controlled-Release Fertilizers

Coated fertilizers consist of a water-soluble fertilizer core covered with a less-soluble barrier, which affects the nutrient release rate. The most common coatings for controlled-release fertilizers (CRF) are sulfur or a polymer material. The major advantage of CRFs is that the gradual nutrient release results in higher nutrient uptake efficiency and less pollution potential (table 12.3). Often, CRF needs to be applied only once. Using CRF enables growers to supply nutrients for an extended duration without the specialized equipment needed to apply water-soluble fertilizers. Popular brands of polymer-coated fertilizers include Osmocote®, Nutricote®, and Polyon®, which have a variety of formulations for different plant species and growing cycles. Some release rates are so slow that they can provide an added benefit after outplanting.

Polymer-coated CRFs are widely used in tropical plant nurseries. The round, polymer-coated "prills" (figure 12.8B) have a more uniform nutrient release than sulfur-coated products. In addition, the prills can be formulated to contain both macronutrients and micronutrients (table 12.4), whereas sulfur-coated products generally supply only nitrogen.

Nutrient release from polymer-coated CRF is a multistep process. During the first irrigation, water vapor is absorbed through microscopic pores in the coating. This process creates an osmotic pressure gradient within the prill, causing the flexible polymer coating to expand. This expansion enlarges the tiny pores and allows the mineral nutrients to be gradually released into the soil or growing medium (figure 12.9). Besides water, temperature is the primary factor affecting the speed of this process. Nutrient release generally increases with increasing temperature. In warm, tropical climates, growers can expect CRFs to release more quickly than indicated on the label. The manufacturer adjusts the release rates of polymer-coated products by altering the thickness and nature of the polymer material, and longevities vary from about 3 to 18 months.

Table 12.4—*Nutrient analysis of 15-9-12 Osmocote® Plus controlled-release fertilizer. Adapted from Everris Company (2012).*

Nutrient	Percentage
Macronutrients	
Nitrogen (7% ammonium; 8% nitrate)	15
Phosphorus (P_2O_5)	9
Potassium (K_2O)	12
Calcium	0
Magnesium	1.3
Sulfur	5.6
Micronutrients	
Iron (0.09% soluble, 0.01% chelated)	0.46
Manganese	0.06
Zinc	0.05
Copper	0.05
Boron	0.02
Molybdenum	0.02

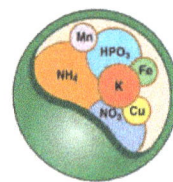

CRF Release Rate Varies With:
(1) Coating Type & Thickness
(2) Water
(3) Increasing Temperature

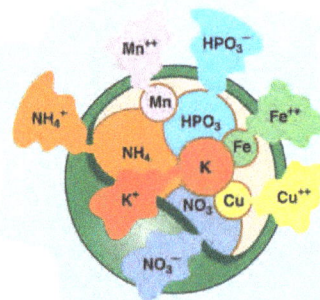

Figure 12.9—*Nutrient release from polymer-coated fertilizers occurs after water vapor is absorbed through the prill membrane, creating an osmotic pressure gradient that expands the pores within the coating and allows fertilizer nutrients to pass through to the growing medium. Illustration from Dumroese and others (2008).*

Other types of CRFs are nitrogen-reaction products, such as ureaform and IBDU Micro Grade Fertilizer. These fertilizers are created through a chemical reaction of water-soluble nitrogen compounds, which results in a more complex molecular structure with very limited water solubility. The rate of nutrient release of ureaform is controlled by many factors, including soil temperature, moisture, pH, and aeration, while IBDU becomes available primarily through hydrolysis. These materials are rarely used in tropical native plant container production but are sometimes applied at outplanting.

Comparison of Organic Versus Synthetic Fertilizers

Because of the variability involved, it is difficult to compare organic and synthetic fertilizers but some generalizations can be made (table 12.5).

Mineral Nutrient Analysis

Nearly all organic fertilizers have relatively low mineral nutrient analyses. The nitrogen percentage is rarely above 15 percent and more typically in the range of 5 to 10 percent (figure 12.7B). Higher analysis products are usually supplemented with natural minerals such as sodium nitrate. Organic fertilizers often contain all 13 mineral nutrients. Synthetic fertilizers can be specially formulated to contain only a few macronutrients or a range of all mineral nutrients.

Table 12.5—*Comparison of organic and synthetic fertilizers.*

Factor	Organic	Synthetic
Mineral nutrient analysis	Low	High
Range of mineral nutrients	All	One to many
Nutrient release rate	Slower	Faster
Compatibility with beneficial microorganisms	Yes	At low levels
Cost	More	Less
Handling	Bulkier	More concentrated
Ecological sustainability	Yes	No
Water pollution risk	Low	High
Other benefits	Improves soil texture and encourages soil microbes	Better for research

Nutrient Release Rate

One of the major differences between organic and synthetic fertilizers is how fast their nutrients become available to plants. Soluble synthetic fertilizers are formulated as salts and are readily available, whereas a range of release rates exist for synthetic CRF, depending on coating thickness. Unprocessed organic fertilizers must first be broken down into smaller particles by soil microorganisms and then converted to a soluble form. Even processed organics contain a large percentage of insoluble nitrogen that must undergo microbial decomposition before being available for plant uptake. Liquid organic fertilizers have the benefit of being already in solution, or at least, in aqueous suspension.

Compatibility With Beneficial Microorganisms

Perhaps one of the most underappreciated benefits of organic fertilizers is that they promote the growth of beneficial soil microorganisms, including mycorrhizal fungi and nitrogen-fixing bacteria because nutrients are released slowly and the organic component improves soil conditions. Research has shown that high levels of soluble synthetic fertilizers, especially nitrogen and phosphorus, can inhibit the establishment and development of mycorrhizal fungi. This is particularly evident in the soilless growing media of container seedlings where applications of soluble, synthetic fertilizers are common.

Cost

A comparison of fertilizer costs is difficult because each fertilizer contains different percentages of nutrients and values must be compared on a per-weight or per-volume basis. Although they can be more expensive strictly on a per nutrient basis, both processed and unprocessed commercial organic fertilizers provide many other benefits that are hard to valuate, including adding organic matter and stimulating soil microorganisms (table 12.5). Synthetic fertilizers also have hidden costs, such as the carbon emissions during their manufacture and the ecological effects of increased potential for water pollution. For tropical growers, the potential to reduce transport costs by sourcing local commercial or homemade organic fertilizers may be attractive. In the final analysis, fertilizers represent only a very small percentage of the cost of producing nursery stock, so price may not be a deciding factor on the type of fertilizer to use.

Handling and Application

Because of their bulkiness and low nutrient analysis, unprocessed organic fertilizers are more expensive to ship, store, and apply compared with synthetic fertilizers. Conversely, synthetic fertilizers are more uniform in quality, have a high nutrient analysis per unit weight, and are much easier to apply to crops.

Ecological Sustainability and Water Pollution

One of the real benefits of organic fertilizers is that they are kinder to the environment and many can be obtained from recycled materials. Not only can nurseries recycle their cull seedlings, weeds, and other organic materials through composting, but they can also serve to recycle leaves, yard clippings, and other such organic wastes from the local community that would otherwise go to landfills (Morgenson 1994).

Nutrients in organic fertilizers are much less susceptible to leaching than those in synthetic fertilizers. Both processed and unprocessed organic fertilizers release their nutrients slowly and in a form that remains in the soil profile. Synthetic fertilizers, especially soluble formulations, often release their nutrients much faster than plants can use them, with the excess nutrients potentially polluting surface or ground water.

Fertilizer Application Rates and Methods

Fertilizer application rates depend on the growing environment and other cultural factors such as container volume, type of growing media, and irrigation frequency. In particular, the size of the growth container has a profound effect on the best application rate and timing. Very small containers require lower rates applied frequently whereas larger containers can tolerate high application rates applied less frequentlyFor most fertilizer products, manufacturers provided general recommended application rates for container nursery plants on package labels. In addition, experimentation, consultation with other growers and development of propagation protocols (see Chapter 4, Crop Planning: Propagation Protocols, Schedules, and Records) will help refine fertilizer application rates for tropical native plant species.

Fertigation for Applying Soluble Fertilizers

Some tropical plant nurseries apply soluble fertilizers through their irrigation systems, a process known as fertigation. The best fertigation method varies depending on the type of irrigation and the size and sophistication of the nursery. The simplest method is to mix soluble fertilizers and water in a watering container or use a hose injector, and water plants by hand. This method can be tedious and time consuming, however, when fertigating a large quantity of plants. On the other hand, this method may be appropriate for smaller nurseries growing many different species with different fertilizer needs.

Fertilizer injectors are a much more precise way to apply soluble fertilizers, especially when growing large numbers of plants with the same fertilizer requirements. The simplest injectors are called siphon mixers (figure 12.10A) and the Hozon™ and EZ-FLO® are common brands and range in cost from $20 to $200. Siphon injectors are attached to the water faucet and have a piece of rubber tubing inserted into a concentrated fertilizer solution (figure 12.10B). When an irrigation hose is attached to the other end and the water is turned on, the flow through the hose causes suction that pulls the fertilizer solution up and mixes it with the water at a fixed ratio. For example, the Hozon™ injects 1 part of soluble fertilizer to 16 parts of water, which is a 1:16 injection ratio. Note that this injector requires a water pressure of at least 30 pounds per square inch (lb/in^2 [psi]) (0.207 MPa) to work properly whereas the EZ-FLO® functions at water pressures as low as 5 psi (0.034 MPa).

More complicated, but more accurate, fertilizer injectors cost from around $300 to more than $3,000. For example, the Dosatron® is a water pump type of injector that installs directly into the irrigation line and pumps the fertilizer solution into the irrigation pipe at a range of injection ratios (figure 12.10C). Among the most technologically advanced fertigation systems is the automated hydraulic boom, which provides very consistent and uniform coverage of water and fertilizer to the crop. The relatively high price of irrigation booms, however, makes them cost prohibitive for most tropical plant nurseries. Any injector must be calibrated after it is installed to verify the fertilizer injection ratio and then must be checked monthly to ensure that it is still working properly.

Some nutrients, notably calcium and magnesium, are very insoluble in water and can even cause solubility problems in concentrated fertilizer solutions. If they are not present naturally in the irrigation water, calcium and magnesium must be supplied in a separate fertilizer solution or in a dolomitic limestone amendment to the growing medium.

> *Caution: Every fertilizer injector must be installed with a backflow preventer to eliminate the possibility that soluble fertilizer could be sucked back into the water line and contaminate drinking water.*

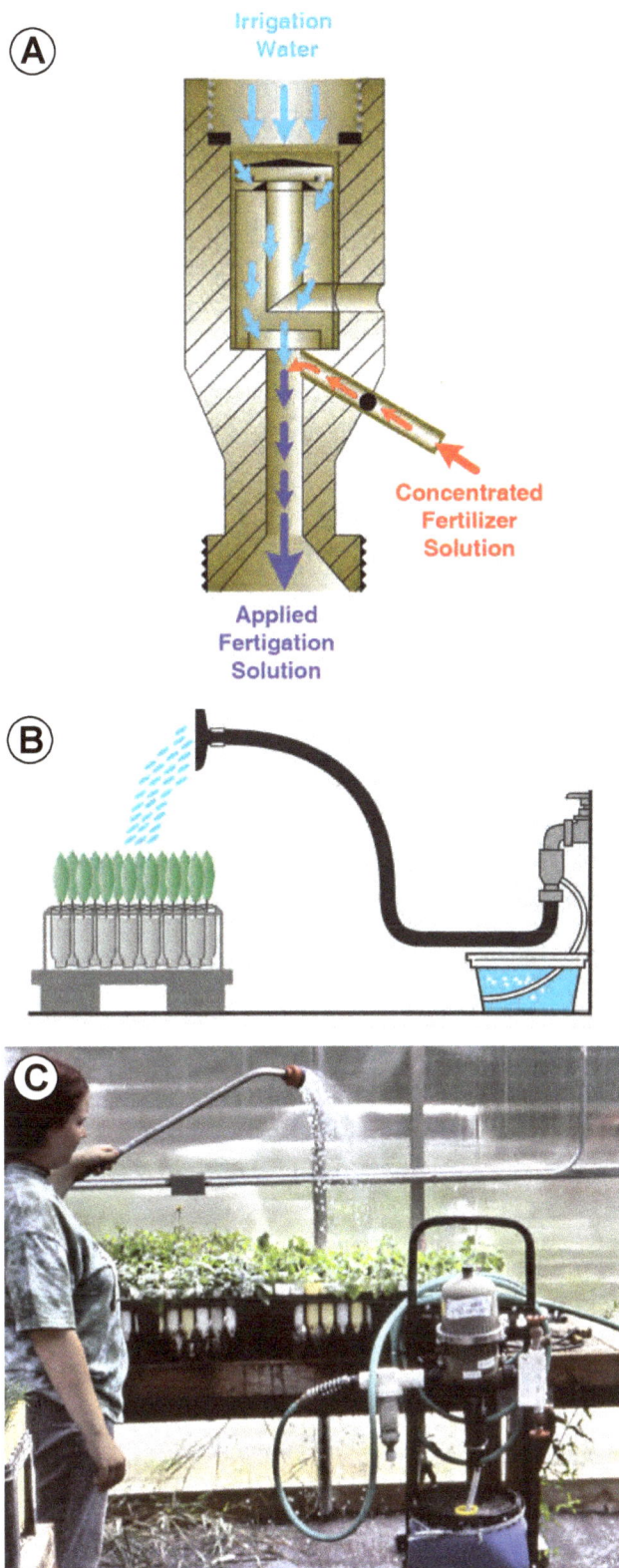

Figure 12.10—*Soluble fertilizers can be mixed with water and applied to the crop, a process called "fertigation." A siphon injector (A) sucks up concentrated fertilizer solution, mixes it with irrigation water, and the fertigation solution is then applied with a hose (B) or other irrigation system. The Dosatron® injector (C) allows for more precise control of injection ratios. Illustrations A and B courtesy of Hummert™ International, and photo C by Tara Luna.*

Applying Controlled-Release Fertilizers

CRF can be topdressed (sprinkled into the top of the container), if care is taken to ensure that each container or cell receives an equal number of prills (figure 12.11A, table 12.6). A special drop-type application wand can be used to topdress larger (>1 gal [4 L]) containers because a measured dose of fertilizer can be applied to the base of each plant. This method avoids the potential of fertilizer granules being lodged in foliage and burning it as soon as the crop is watered.

Another option for applying CRF is to incorporate it into the growing medium (figure 12.11B, table 12.6). If growers mix the growing medium on site, CRF can be incorporated but special care must be taken to ensure uniform distribution (figure 12.11C) and to prevent damage to the prill coating. If the coating is fractured, then the soluble fertilizer releases immediately, causing severe salt injury. Nurseries can purchase growing media with CRF that have already been evenly incorporated with special, commercial mixing equipment. Purchased medium

Table 12.6—*Manufacturer's recommendations for applying 15-9-12 Osmocote® Plus controlled-release fertilizer. Adapted from Everris Company (2012).*

Temperature		Longevity (months)
°F	°C	
60	15	4 to 5
70	21	3 to 4
80	26	2 to 3
90	32	1 to 2

Units	Incorporation rates		
	Low	Medium	High
lbs per yd³	3.0	8.0	12.0
kg per m³	1.8	4.7	7.1
g per L	1.8	4.7	7.1

Topdressing (grams per container)			
Container volume	Low	Medium	High
1 qt (946 cm³)	2	4	6
1 gal (4,546 cm³)	6	17	26
5 gal (22,730 cm³)	26	70	105

needs to be handled carefully and not stored for long because much of the nutrients can be released because of prill breakage or high temperatures.

Growers can use the general recommendations provided by manufacturers if they classify their crops by relative nutrient uses: low, medium, or high (table 12.6). Of course, these applications rates should be used conservatively until their effect on individual plant growth and performance can be evaluated. Because CRF nutrient release is so affected by temperature, growers need to be cautious about using CRF label recommendations. Manufacturers base their release rates on an average temperature of about 70 °F (21 °C), and those release rates increase by about 25 percent for every 9 °F (5 °C) increase in temperature (table 12.6). As with all nursery practices, growers should always initiate small scale trials before adopting any new fertilizer treatment.

Applying Organic Fertilizers

Composts could be incorporated into growing media but they must be fully mature to prevent fertilizer burn. One of the challenges of using liquid organic fertilizers is how to achieve the high soluble nitrogen levels necessary for rapid growth rates. High-quality nursery crops can be grown with organic fertilizers but, because their nutrient analysis is relatively low (figure 12.7B), production schedules may have to be adjusted.

Determining When to Fertilize

Because artificial growing media such as peat-vermiculite media are inherently infertile, fertilization should begin as soon as the seedlings or cuttings become established. Some brands of growing media contain a starter dose of fertilizer, however, so be sure and check the label. Homemade soil mixes that have been amended with compost or other organic fertilizers may not need fertilization right away but observe plant growth and establish small trials to be certain.

In nurseries, plant growth rates can be controlled by fertilization levels, especially nitrogen. As plants take up more nutrients, their growth rate increases rapidly until it reaches the critical point. After this point, adding more fertilizer does not increase plant growth but can be used

Figure 12.11—*Controlled-release fertilizers can be applied directly to containers ("topdressing") if care is taken to achieve uniform application (A). Incorporating controlled-release fertilizers when the growing medium is mixed (B) helps to achieve even distribution of prills in small containers (C). Photo A by Brian F. Daley, photo B by Diane L. Haase, and photo C by Tara Luna.*

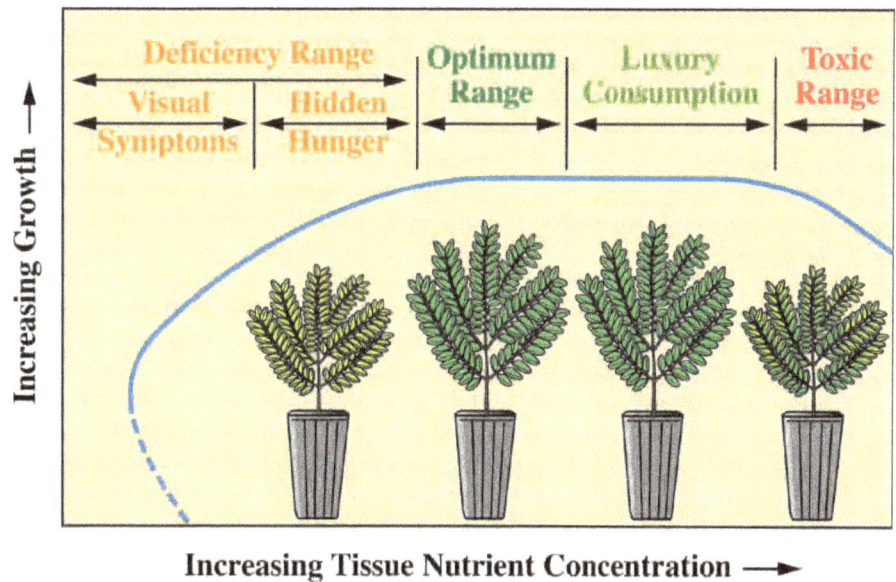

Figure 12.12—Fertilization is one of the most effective ways to increase plant growth, which follows a characteristic pattern. As nutrient content increases in plant tissue, growth increases and deficiency symptoms are abated but fertilization beyond the optimum range is not always beneficial. Illustration by Jim Marin.

to "load" nursery stock with extra nutrients for use after outplanting. Beyond a certain point, however, excessive fertilization can cause a decline in plant growth and eventually results in toxicity (figure 12.12).

Some tropical plant species require very little fertilizer while others must be "pushed" with nitrogen to achieve good growth rates and reach target specifications. Small-seeded species expend their stored nutrients soon after germination whereas those with large seeds contain greater nutrient reserves and do not need to be fertilized right away. Excess fertilization early in the growing season can be detrimental to legumes and other natives, which must establish nitrogen-fixing bacteria or mycorrhizal fungi on their root systems before outplanting. Experience in growing a particular species is the best course of action to develop species-specific fertilizer prescriptions.

Tropical native plant growers should never wait for their crops to show deficiency symptoms before fertilizing. Plant growth rate will slow down before visible symptoms appear. Even after fertilization, it can take weeks before growth will resume following a deficient condition. Evaluating symptoms of nutrient deficiencies based on foliar characteristics can be challenging even for experts because different nutrient deficiencies have similar characteristic symptoms and considerable variation in these symptoms may occur among species. In addition, typical foliar symptoms, such as chlorosis, could be caused by something other than nutrient stress, such as heat damage or root disease. The position of the symptomatic foliage can be somewhat diagnostic. For instance, nitrogen is very mobile within the plant and will be translocated to new foliage when nitrogen is limiting. Therefore, nitrogen deficient plants show yellowing in the older rather than the newer foliage (figure 12.13A). Conversely, iron is very immobile in plants, so deficiency symptoms first appear in newer rather than older foliage (figure 12.13B). Keep in mind that excessive fertilization can cause toxicity symptoms (figure 12.13C). So,

Figure 12.13—Nutrient deficiency symptoms such as chlorosis (yellowing) are common but can be caused by several different nutrients. Nitrogen chlorosis is seen first in older foliage (A), whereas iron chlorosis occurs in newer needles or leaves (B). Excessive fertilization can cause toxicity symptoms, such as necrosis along the leaf margin caused by boron toxicity (C). Photo A from Erdmann and others (1979), and photos B and C by Thomas D. Landis.

the take-home message is: foliar symptoms can be an indicator of nutrient (or other) problems but should never be used as the sole guide to fertilization. Crop monitoring and testing, experience, and knowledge about the growth phases are the best guides for determining fertilizer timing and rates.

Fertilization During Plant Growth Phases

Growers need to be aware of the different nutrient requirements during each growth phase and adjust fertilizer prescriptions accordingly (table 12.7). These adjustments are particularly important for nitrogen (especially the ammonium form of nitrogen), which tends to be a primary driver of plant growth and development (figure 12.14).

Establishment Phase

Fertilization needs to begin as soon as plants have emerged and have become established. Small plants are very succulent, however, and are particularly vulnerable to root damage from high salt concentrations. In addition, high nitrogen has been shown to increase the risk for damping-off fungi and other pest problems. Therefore, we recommend fertilizing with a low to moderate level of nitrogen (25 to 75 ppm) during this period.

Rapid Growth Phase

This phase is the period when plants attain most of their shoot development, and high levels of nitrogen (100

Table 12.7—Examples of fertilization regimes adjusted for plant growth phases.

Growth phase	Nitrogen	Phosphorus	Potassium
Establishment	Medium	High	Low
Rapid growth	High	Medium	Medium
Hardening	Low	Low	High

to 150 ppm) tend to accelerate this growth. In addition to nitrogen, fertilizers need to include adequate levels of all the other mineral nutrients. Growers must closely monitor plant growth and development during the rapid growth phase, however, to ensure that shoots do not become excessively large or top heavy.

Hardening Phase

The objective of the hardening phase is to prepare plants for the stresses of shipping and outplanting by slowing shoot growth while simultaneously promoting stem and root growth. See Chapter 15, Hardening, for a complete description of this topic. High nitrogen levels stimulate plant growth, so reducing the amount of nitrogen (25 to 50 ppm) helps them to begin hardening. A lower ratio of nitrogen to that of phosphorus and potassium typically is helpful (table 12.7). In addition, changing to fertilizers containing the nitrate form of nitrogen (as opposed to ammonium) is helpful because nitrate-nitrogen does not promote shoot growth. Calcium nitrate is an ideal fertilizer for hardening because it provides the only soluble form of calcium, which has the added benefit of helping to promote strong cell wall development. It is important to distinguish granular calcium nitrate from liquid calcium ammonium nitrate, which does contain ammonium. A good rule of thumb for many tropical plants is that hardening should begin when shoots have reached 75 to 80 percent of the target size. Plants take a few weeks to respond to this change in fertilization and will continue to grow after nitrogen fertilization has been reduced. Leaching the growing medium with several irrigations of plain water is a good way to make certain that all excess nitrogen is eliminated from the growing medium.

Monitoring and Testing

We recommend monitoring the electrical conductivity (EC) of fertilizer solutions and performing chemical analysis of plant foliage to determine if fertilization is sufficient, to prevent problems from developing, and to diagnose any deficiencies or toxicities if they do develop.

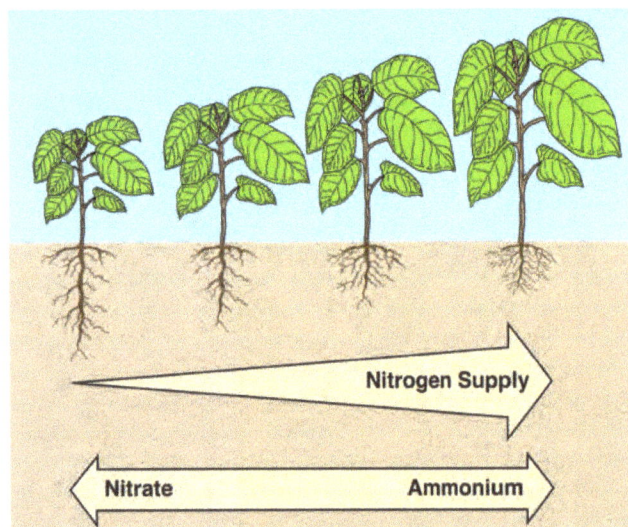

Figure 12.14—Because nitrogen is so critical to seedling physiology, nitrogen fertilization can be used to control the shoot-to-root ratio. It is also used to speed up or slow down plant growth. Fertilizers with the nitrate form of nitrogen are recommended during the hardening phase to slow shoot growth while stimulating roots; ammonium nitrogen is recommended during rapid growth. Illustration adapted from Dumroese and others (2008).

EC Testing

Because all fertilizers are taken up as electrically charged ions, the ability of a water solution to conduct electricity is an indication of how much fertilizer is present. Growers who fertigate need to periodically check the EC of the applied fertigation water and the growing medium solution. Measuring the EC of fertigation water as it is applied to the crop can confirm that the fertilizer solution has been correctly calculated and that the injector is functioning.

Simple handheld EC meters (figure 12.15) are fairly inexpensive and are very useful for monitoring fertigation. The EC reading indicates the total amount of fertilizer salts and natural salts present in the water source. Normal readings in applied fertigation should range from 0.75 to 2.0 uS/cm. Measuring the EC of water leached from containers can also help pinpoint problems of improper leaching and salt buildup within the growing medium. Measuring the EC of the solution in the growing medium, however, provides the best estimate of how much fertilizer is available to plant roots. The typical range of acceptable EC values in the growing medium for most tropical plant species is about 1.2 to 2.5 uS/cm. If the EC is more than 2.5, it is a good idea to leach out the salts with clean irrigation water. See Chapter 11, Water Quality and Irrigation, for more information about EC measurements, guidelines, and units.

Foliar Testing

The best way to monitor plant nutrition and responses to fertilization is to test plant foliage for an exact measurement of nutrients that the plant has acquired. By examining tissue nutrient concentrations and simultaneously monitoring plant growth, it is possible to identify if and when specific nutrients are deficient or excessive/toxic (figure 12.12). Little published information is available for ideal mineral nutrient levels in tropical nursery plants so we recommend small trials to develop guidelines for your own species. Foliar samples must be collected in a systematic manner and sent to a reputable laboratory for processing (recommendations may be available through local extension agents). The analyzed nutrient concentration values are then compared with some known set of adequate nutrient values to determine which specific elements are deficient (table 12.8). The cost to analyze these samples is relatively inexpensive considering the potential improvement in crop quality that may result from having data to guide fertilizer regimes.

Growth Trials

Small growth trials are another good way to monitor plant nutrition and fertilization needs. These trials are especially informative for tropical plant species because so little published information is available. Detailed

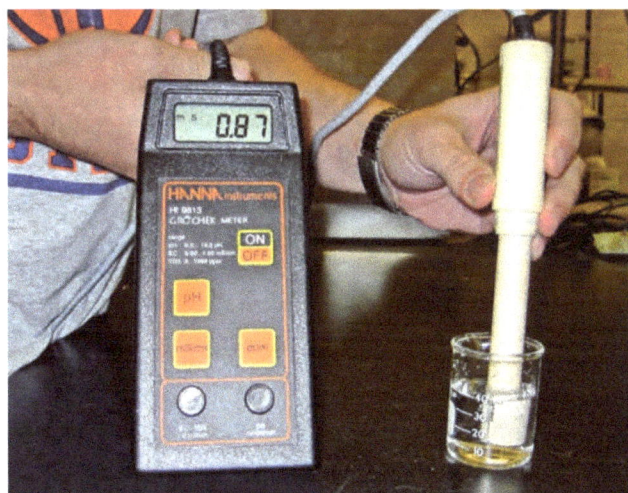

Figure 12.15—*An electrical conductivity meter used to estimate fertilizer salt concentrations in irrigation water, fertigation water, or saturated media extract. Photo by Douglass F. Jacobs.*

Table 12.8—*Estimated ranges of foliar nutrient levels for healthy tropical plants (based on data compiled by Drechsel and Zech [1991] on field-grown, broad-leaved, tropical tree species). Nutrient ranges can vary greatly among species. Nursery trials are recommended to determine the best ranges for specific species.*

Nutrient	Range of foliar levels in healthy plants
Macronutrients	(%)
Nitrogen	1.5 to 3.5
Phosphorus	0.10 to 0.25
Potassium	0.60 to 1.8
Calcium	0.50 to 2.5
Magnesium	0.15 to 0.50
Sulfur	0.10 to 0.30
Micronutrients	ppm (parts per million)
Iron	50 to 250
Manganese	35 to 250
Zinc	10 to 40
Copper	5 to 20
Boron	15 to 50
Molybdenum	0.10 to 1.0

documentation of growing conditions, fertilizer inputs, and resulting plant response can help to formulate future fertilizer prescriptions for a specific species within a nursery. See Chapter 20, Discovering Ways to Improve Nursery Practices and Plant Quality, for more information on how to make these discoveries through trials and experiments.

Reducing the Environmental Effects of Fertilization

Regardless of the method of fertilizer application or the type of fertilizer used, runoff of excess fertilizers is a major environmental concern. Nutrient ions, notably nitrate and phosphate, leach easily from container nurseries, and can pollute groundwater or adjacent streams. Many areas have laws and regulations limiting runoff and groundwater nitrate levels. Growers need to choose types of fertilizers and schedule their applications to minimize potential pollution concerns. Because nitrate and phosphate are so soluble in water, growers need to irrigate only when necessary and apply only enough water so that only small amounts drain out the bottom of the containers. This approach also makes sense from an economic standpoint, because the desire is to have most of the applied fertilizer taken up by crop plants rather than lost in runoff.

Reducing, eliminating, and managing environmental effects of fertilization in the nursery include these practices:

1. Apply fertilizer as part of a designed nutrient and irrigation program. The goal is never to push plants as quickly as possible through all phases of growth; instead, crops should be cultured to produce balanced, healthy plants for the best results after outplanting.

2. Consider using slow-release and controlled-release fertilizers in addition to, or instead of, highly soluble liquid fertilizers.

3. Select organic fertilizers that have less leaching potential.

4. Explore options to recycle or reuse irrigation water, including subirrigation systems or catchment ponds where runoff can be collected, treated, and reused.

5. Learn about water conservation and responsible management and reuse of runoff water, as discussed in Chapter 11, Water Quality and Irrigation.

A combination of these steps as appropriate for your nursery will help to minimize nutrient leaching and reduce the effects of fertilization on the environment.

References

Diver, S.; Greer, L.; Adam, K.L. 2008. Sustainable small-scale nursery production. Butte, MT: National Center for Appropriate Technology (NCAT) Sustainable Agriculture Project. https://attra.ncat.org/attra-pub/summaries/summary.php?pub=60. (November 2011).

Drechsel, P.; Zech, W. 1991. Foliar nutrient levels of broad-leaved tropical trees: a tabular review. Plant and Soil. 131: 29–46.

Dumroese, R.K.; Luna, T.; Landis, T.D. 2008. Nursery manual for native plants: volume 1, a guide for tribal nurseries. Agriculture Handbook 730. Washington, DC: U.S. Department of Agriculture, Forest Service. 302 p.

Everris Company. 2012. Coated fertilizers. The Netherlands: Everris International, B.V. http://everris.us.com/plant-nutrition/coated-fertilizers. (March 2012).

Landis, T.D.; Dumroese, R.K. 2011. Using organic fertilizers in forest and native plant nurseries. Forest Nursery Notes. 31(2): 9–18.

Morgenson, G. 1994. Using municipal organic wastes at Lincoln-Oakes nurseries. In: Landis, T.D., comp. proceedings of the northeastern and intermountain forest and conservation nursery association meeting. Gen. Tech. Rep. RM-GTR-243. Fort Collins, CO: U.S. Department of Agriculture, Forest Service, Rocky Mountain Forest and Range Experiment Station. 65–67.

Additional Reading

Amaranthus, M.A. 2011. What are mycorrhizae? Grants Pass, OR: Mycorrhizal Applications Inc. http://www.mycorrhizae.com/. (14 May 2011).

California Plant Health Association. 2002. Western fertilizer handbook. 9th ed. Danville, IL: Interstate Publishers. 356 p.

Card, A.; Whiting, D.; Wilson, C.; Reeder, J. 2009. Organic fertilizers. Fort Collins, CO: Colorado State University Extension, Colorado Master Gardener Program. CMG Garden Notes #234. 8 p. http://www.cmg.colostate.edu. (May 2011).

Chaney, D.E.; Drinkwater, L.E.; Pettygrove, G.C. 1992. Organic soil amendments and fertilizers. Pub. No. 21505. Oakland, CA: University of California, Agriculture and Natural Resources. 35 p.

Claassen, V.P.; Carey, J.L. 2007. Comparison of slow-release nitrogen yield from organic soil amendments and chemical fertilizers and implications for regeneration of disturbed sites. Land Degradation & Development. 18: 119–132.

Gaskell, M.; Smith, R. 2007. Nitrogen sources for organic vegetable crops. HortTechnology. 17: 431–441.

Hartz, T.K.; Smith, R.; Gaskell, M. 2010. Nitrogen availability from liquid organic fertilizers. HortTechnology. 20: 169–172.

Landis, T.D. 2011. Understanding and applying the carbon-to-nitrogen ratio in nurseries. Forest Nursery Notes. 31(1): 10–15.

Landis, T.D.; Campbell, S.; Zensen, F. 1992. Agricultural pollution of surface water and groundwater in forest nurseries. In: Landis, T.D., tech. coord. Proceedings, Intermountain Forest Nursery Association, 1991. Gen. Tech. Rep. RM-GTR-211. Fort Collins, CO: U.S. Department of Agriculture, Forest Service, Rocky Mountain Forest and Range Experiment Station. 1–15.

Landis, T.D.; Khadduri, N. 2008. Composting applications in forest and conservation nurseries. Forest Nursery Notes. 28(2): 9–18.

Landis, T.D.; Tinus, R.W.; McDonald, S.E.; Barnett, J.P. 1989. The container tree nursery manual: volume 4, seedling nutrition and irrigation. Agriculture Handbook 674. Washington, DC: U.S. Department of Agriculture, Forest Service. 119 p.

Meister Media. 2011. The Haber-Bosch Process. Washington, DC: Meister Media Worldwide. http://www.fertilizer101.org/. (8 November 2011).

Moral, R.; Paredes, C.; Bustamante, M.A.; Marhuenda-Egea, F.; Bernal, M.P. 2009. Utilisation of manure composts by high-value crops: safety and environmental challenges. Bioresource Technology. 100: 5454–5460.

The Scotts Company. 2006. Scotts fertilizer tech sheet. http://www.scottsprohort.com/products/fertilizers/osmocote_plus.cfm. (January 2006).

Rose, R.; Haase, D.L.; Boyer, D. 1995. Organic matter management in forest nurseries: theory and practice. Corvallis, OR: Oregon State University, Nursery Technology Cooperative. 65 p.

Roy, R.N.; Finck, A.; Blair, G.J.; Tandon, H.L.S. 2006. Plant nutrition for food security: a guide for integrated nutrient management. FAO Fertilizer and Plant Nutrition Bulletin 16. Rome, Italy: Food and Agriculture Organization of the United Nations. 366 p. ftp://ftp.fao.org/docrep/fao/009/a0443e/a0443e.pdf. (April 2011).

Sharpley, A.N.; Chapra, S.C.; Wedepohl, R.; Sims, J.T.; Daniels, T.C.; Reddy, K.R. 1994. Managing agricultural phosphorus for the protection of surface waters: issues and options. Journal of Environmental Quality. 23: 437–451.

Vaario, L.; Tervonen, A.; Haukioja, K.; Haukioja, M.; Pennanen, T.; Timonen, S. 2009. The effect of nursery substrate and fertilization on the growth and ectomycorrhizal status of containerized and outplanted seedlings of Picea abies. Canadian Journal of Forest Research. 39: 64–75.

Wikipedia. 2011a. Guano. http://en.wikipedia.org/wiki/Guano. (April 2011).

Wikipedia. 2011b. Sodium nitrate. http://en.wikipedia.org/wiki/Sodium_nitrate. (April 2011).

Beneficial Microorganisms

Kim M. Wilkinson and David P. Janos

13

The web of life depends on microorganisms, a vast network of small, unseen allies that permeate the soil, water, and air of our planet. Many kinds of microorganisms existed for billions of years before any plants or animals came into being. Microorganisms created the atmosphere, turned bare rock and lava into soil, helped plants colonize land, and remain vital to the survival of plants, animals, and people today.

For people who work with plants, the greatest interest in microorganisms is in the complex living communities that are part of the soil. One gram (the weight of a small paperclip) of healthy soil can contain between 1 and 10 billion microorganisms. The living component of soil has a central role in ecosystem and plant health. Communities of bacteria, fungi, algae, protozoa, and other microorganisms make nutrients available to plants, create water and air channels, maintain soil structure, counterbalance pathogen populations, and recycle nutrients from organic matter that enable plants to grow.

This chapter focuses on two of the most important beneficial microorganisms for nurseries: nitrogen-fixing bacteria (rhizobia, the generic term for species in the genera *Rhizobium* and *Bradyrhizobium*)(figure 13.1) and mycorrhizal fungi (figure 13.2) that form mutually beneficial partnerships with their plant hosts. Scientists call this "mutualistic symbiosis." In this manual, these beneficial microorganisms are called "microsymbionts." Partnerships between beneficial microorganisms and plants are essential to plant health, as well as to healthy ecosystems and agro-ecosystems.

Facing Page: *The nitrogen-fixing bacteria rhizobia (*Bradyrhizobium*) form nodules on roots of legumes—in this case, on a native* Acacia koa *seedling in Hawai'i. Photo by J.B. Friday.*

In natural ecosystems, the root systems of most plants have microbial partnerships that enable them to survive and grow even in harsh conditions. In fact, microbial partnerships played a key role in enabling plants to first colonize land as they evolved out of the sea. Without microsymbiont partners, plants remain stunted and often die. These failures are frequently attributed to poor nursery stock when the real problem was the lack of the proper microsymbionts. In the nursery, microsymbionts can be introduced by "inoculating" the root systems of plants with the appropriate beneficial microorganisms to form effective partnerships.

Mutualistic Symbiosis

Symbiosis technically refers to two or more organisms living intimately interconnected. As a scientific term, symbiosis can be mutualistic (both organisms benefit), parasitic (one organism benefits and the other is harmed), or commensal (one benefits, the other is unaffected). In popular usage, however, "symbiosis" is considered synonymous with "mutualistic symbiosis" —both organisms benefit. In this chapter, we employ the popular usage to refer to nitrogen-fixing bacteria and mycorrhizal fungi as "microsymbionts"—microorganisms that form a mutually beneficial partnership with their plant hosts.

Figure 13.1—Nitrogen-fixing bacteria include rhizobia, which form relationships with plants in the legume family. Pictured are native rhizobia nodules on the roots of the native Hawaiian forest tree koa (Acacia koa). Photo by J.B. Friday.

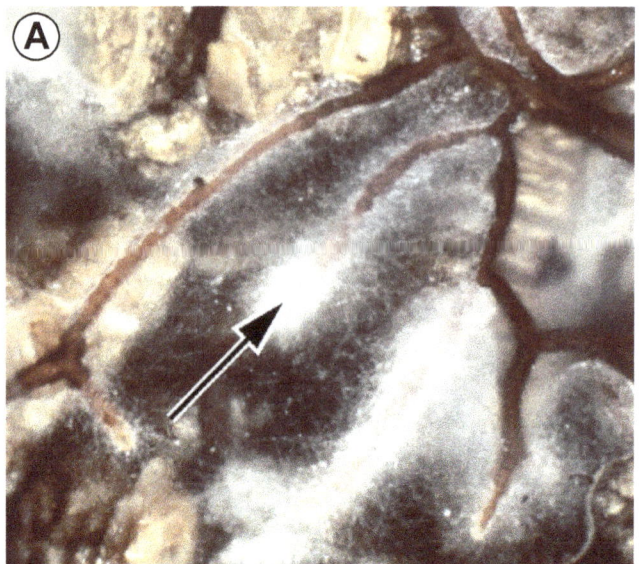

Figure 13.2—"Myco" means "fungus" and "rhiza" means "root;" the word "mycorrhizae" means "fungus-roots." Mycorrhizal root tip (arrow) on a pine tree root (the white filaments are the fungus extending beyond the root) (A). Dichotomously branched, ectomycorrhizal roots of Pinus elliottii in Florida; the finest rootlets are entirely ensheathed by white fungus filaments (B). Arbuscule of an arbuscular mycorrhizal fungus (C) that serves as a nutrient exchange site between the host plant and the fungus. Photo A by Thomas D. Landis, photo B by Tania Wyss, and photo C by Mark C. Brundrett.

The Importance of Beneficial Microorganisms in the Nursery

In natural ecosystems, the root systems of many plants have microbial partnerships with mycorrhizal fungi and, if applicable, with nitrogen-fixing bacteria. In the nursery, where plants have easy access to water and fertilizer, the benefits of these partnerships may not be apparent and their absence may go unnoticed. But in the field, plants need every advantage. Plants that have been inoculated in the nursery will be outplanted with microbial partnerships in place and often are better able to survive in the field. Noninoculated plants, however, must "fend for themselves" and establish microbial partnerships in the field. Many plantings take place on deforested or degraded land where native microsymbiont populations may be low or nonviable (figure 13.3).

Figure 13.3—*Microsymbionts often do not survive in the soil without their host plants. Native microsymbiont populations may be low on degraded sites, such as this formerly forested pasture in Hawai'i (A) and this test bauxite surface mine in southwestern Costa Rica—when the aluminum-rich topsoil was removed from the mine, most mycorrhizal fungi were removed with it (B.) Photo A by J.B. Friday, and photo B by David P. Janos.*

Figure 13.4—*Plants with established microsymbiont partnerships often have a better chance of survival after outplanting. This photo shows a palm species,* Bactris gasipaes; *the plant on the right has a mycorrhizal partnership in place and the same age plant on the left does not. Photo by David P. Janos.*

Inoculating plants in the nursery is an opportunity to introduce select microsymbionts (figure 13.4). Similar to using seeds from specific seed sources, the nursery manager can match plants with optimal microsymbionts for specific site conditions. The presence of microsymbionts is often an important target plant characteristic.

Using microsymbionts in the nursery has the following benefits:

- Reduced environmental effects and fertilizer use in the nursery.
- Improved plant health and vigor.
- Improved resistance to disease.
- Better performance on outplanting sites.

Although this manual is for tropical nurseries, some tropical regions have montane habitats and species, and so a broad range of plant species and microsymbionts are mentioned in this chapter. Not all species and microsymbiont partners are present in a given region, so it is important to check about native species needs before using microsymbionts.

Nitrogen-Fixing Bacteria

Nitrogen is one of the most important nutrients for plant growth. Nitrogen (N_2) is abundant in the Earth's atmosphere, but the N_2 gas must be converted to either nitrate (NO_3^-) or ammonium (NH_4^+) ions before most plants can use it. In nature, nitrogen-fixing bacteria convert ("fix") N_2 from the air into a form usable to plants. When the growing roots of a plant capable of forming a partnership with rhizobia come in contact with a compatible strain of nitrogen-fixing bacteria in soil or growing media, the rhizobia bacteria will enter ("infect") the roots. Nodules then form on the plant's roots where the contact occurred. The bacteria live and multiply

in the nodules on the host's root system, providing nitrogen from the atmosphere to their plant host (figure 13.5). Each nodule contains millions of the bacteria that convert atmospheric nitrogen.

Although plants that form a partnership with nitrogen-fixing bacteria are sometimes called "nitrogen-fixing plants" or "nitrogen-fixing trees," the plant itself is unable to obtain atmospheric nitrogen. Through the mutalistic symbiotic partnership, the bacteria give nitrogen accumulated from the atmosphere to the plant, and in exchange, the bacteria get energy in the form of carbohydrates from the plant (Singleton and others 1990). When the host plant sheds leaves,

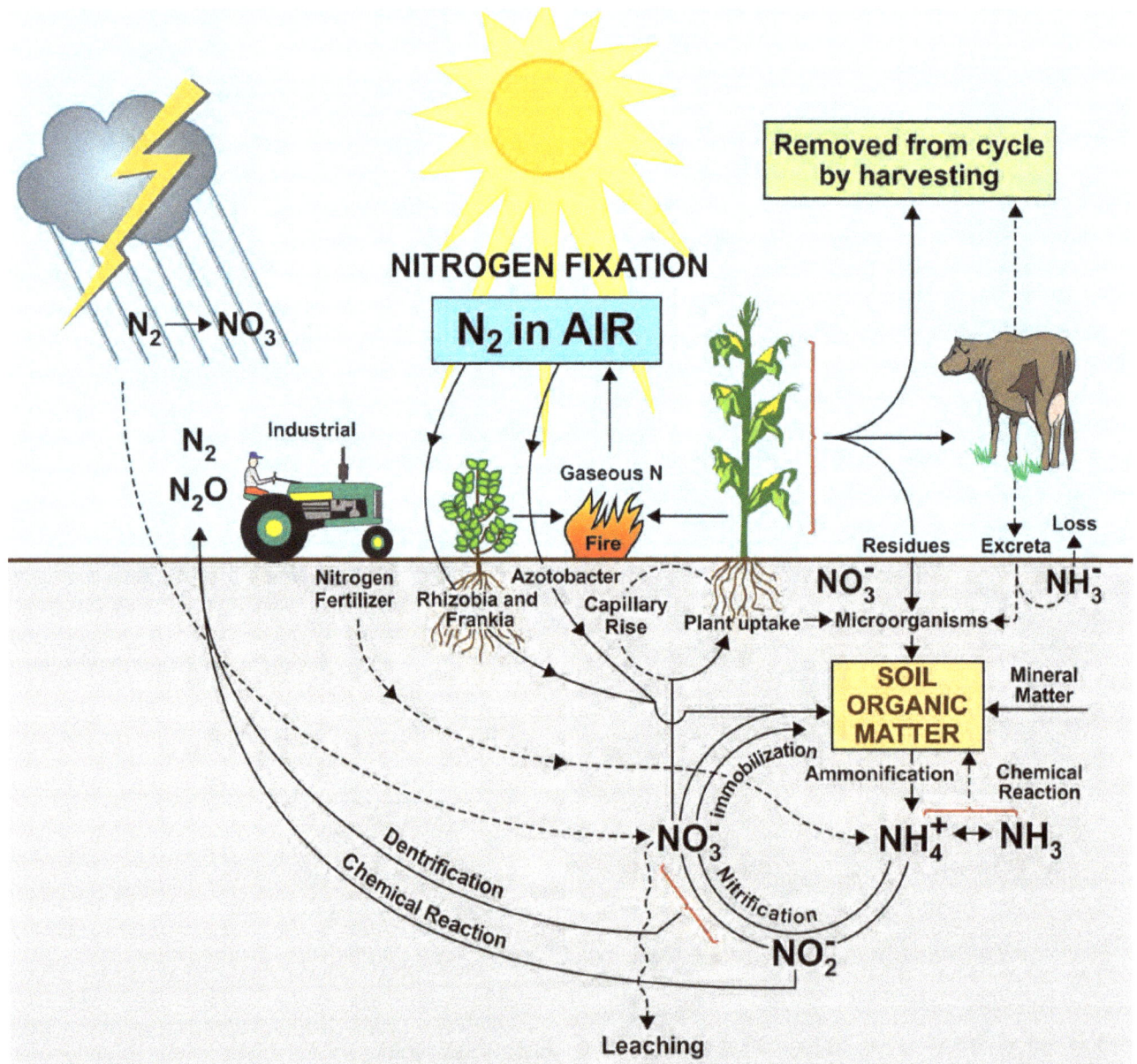

Figure 13.5—*The Nitrogen Cycle. All nitrogen in plants originates as an atmospheric gas, which is fixed by microorganisms (such as rhizobia and Frankia), fixed by humans in fertilizers by an energy-intensive industrial process, or to a very minor extent fixed by lightning or volcanism. The dashed lines in the diagram represent minor pathways; the solid lines represent major pathways. Adapted from Brown and Johnson (1996) by Jim Marin.*

Figure 13.6—*Because nitrogen-fixing species improve soil fertility on degraded lands, they are widely used for restoration and sustainable agriculture. Examples of native Hawaiian legume species that form relationships with nitrogen-fixing rhizobia bacteria include* Caesalpinia kavaiensis *(Uhiuhi) (A) and* Sophora chrysophylla *(māmane)(B). Other nitrogen-fixing species are known throughout much of the tropics, such as* Samanea *(C),* Gliricidia *(D), and* Sesbania *(E) species. Some nitrogen-fixing trees are considered weeds outside their native range, such as* Leucaena *species (F). Photos A through E by J.B. Friday, and photo F by Tara Luna.*

dics back, or dics, the nitrogen stored in the plant's tissues is cycled throughout the ecosystem. The process of nitrogen fixation provides the major source of nitrogen fertility in tropical ecosystems (figure 13.5).

In the early 20th century, human beings also learned to convert atmospheric nitrogen gas into fertilizers through an energy-intensive industrial process called the Haber-Bosch process. The process requires a source of hydrogen gas to react with nitrogen from the air under heat and high pressure. The most common sources for the hydrogen are fossil fuels, and additional energy is expended to power the reaction. Growers who use synthetic nitrogen fertilizers such as ammonium nitrate and urea are using products generated by this process. In contrast to industrial/synthetic nitrogen fixation, biological nitrogen fixation by bacteria associated with green plants is powered by the sun, and thereby is renewable and effectively inexhaustible.

Nitrogen-fixing trees and plants are usually outplanted to help restore fertility, nutrient cycling, and organic matter to the ecosystem. Soils at the outplanting site, however, may not contain a viable strain of bacteria to form an effective partnership with the plant. Inoculating plants in the nursery ensures that an effective partnership is formed to enhance plant survival and growth and to accelerate rehabilitation of degraded land. Unlike mycorrhizal fungi, which affect most trees and plants, only a fraction of plants can form partnerships with nitrogen-fixing bacteria; however, nitrogen-fixing plants play a vital role in nutrient cycling.

Two types of nitrogen-fixing bacteria form symbiotic partnerships with plants: rhizobia (consisting of several genera) and the genus *Frankia*. Rhizobia nodulate many (but not all) members of the legume family (Fabaceae, sometimes called Leguminosae) (figure 13.6). The legume family is made up of three subfamilies (Mimosoideae, Caesalpinioideae, and Papilionoideae [Faboideae]). Rhizobia also nodulate species of the genus Parasponia in the elm family (Ulmaceae). *Frankia* are a genus of filamentous bacteria (in a group called "actinomycetes" because of their somewhat fungus-like appearance) that form partnerships with about 200 different plant species distributed across eight families (figure 13.7). The species affected by *Frankia* are called "actinorhizal" plants (table 13.1).

Figure 13.7—Non-leguminous species that form relationships with nitrogen-fixing Frankia *bacteria include* Casuarina *species. Photo by J.B. Friday.*

Benefits of Inoculating With Nitrogen-Fixing Bacteria

Applications of inoculant for nitrogen-fixing bacteria can have some direct benefits in the nursery. If an effective partnership is formed, most of the plant's requirements for nitrogen will be met, thereby reducing or eliminating the need to apply nitrogen fertilizer and decreasing the nursery's need to manage pollution from fertilizer runoff.

In the field, however, is where the benefits of the partnership are most apparent. Nitrogen-fixing trees and plants sent from the nursery with their root systems already nodulated have faster early growth than plants that were not inoculated. Nursery inoculation can reduce costs in establishment and maintenance. The benefit from a few dollars' worth of inoculant applied in the nursery not only offsets the need for purchased nitrogen fertilizer but is also much cheaper than replacing a tree that dies from nitrogen deficiency. Also, instead of providing spurts of fertilizers in the field (which may benefit surrounding weeds as well as the desired plant), the natural nitrogen fixation process provides a steady supply of nitrogen for the plant's growth. Faster early field growth can lead to faster canopy closure, which in turn shades the soil and understory, reduces weed management expenses, and leads to faster restoration of the natural nutrient cycling and fertility role of nitrogen-fixing species in the ecosystem.

Inoculating in the nursery ensures both the effectiveness and the timeliness of the nitrogen-fixing partnership. Noninoculated plants may eventually form a partnership in the field with a *Frankia* or rhizobia strain if some of the bacteria are present on the outplanting site. This partnership does not guarantee, however, that the plant will benefit. Some

Table 13.1—Plants that form partnerships with nitrogen-fixing bacteria. Adapted from NFTA (1989) and Wall (2000).

Bacteria	Plant family	Subfamily (notes)	Examples (genus)
Rhizobia	Legume (Fabaceae)	Caesalpinioideae (about 1,900 species; about 23% fix nitrogen)	*Cassia* and *Senna*
		Mimosoideae (about 2,800 species; about 90% fix nitrogen)	*Enterolobium, Leucaena, Pithecellobium, Acacia, Albizia, Prosopis,* and *Mimosa*
		Papilionoideae (about 12,300 species; about 97% fix nitrogen)	*Sesbania, Cajanus, Erythrina, Gliricidia,* and *Robinia*
Frankia	Birch (Betulaceae)		*Alnus*
	She-oak (Casuarinaceae)		*Casuarina, Allocasuarina,* and *Gymnostoma*
	Coriariaceae		*Coriaria*
	Datiscaceae		*Datisca*
	Buckthorn (Rhamnaceae)		*Ceanothus* and *Rhamnus*
	Myrtle (Myricaceae)		*Myrica, Comptonia,* and *Myrtus*
	Oleaster (Elaeagnaceae)		*Elaeagnus* and *Hippophae*
	Rose (Rosaceae)		*Cercocarpus, Chamaebatia, Cowania, Purshia,* and *Chamaebatiaria*

Figure 13.8—*Some legumes can nodulate with a broad range of rhizobia strains, but not all strains are equally effective at fixing nitrogen. These tropical legume seedlings were inoculated with different rhizobia strains. Some partnerships were very effective (a green, thriving plant such as the one labeled 18b indicates that adequate nitrogen is being fixed at a low cost to the host plant) and others were not (a plant such as 4b is a little green, but not thriving and a plant such as 8b has no green). Careful selection of microsymbiont partners is important to ensure a productive partnership. Photo by Harold Keyser.*

plants will nodulate with a broad range of rhizobia strains, and not all strains are equally effective at fixing nitrogen (Keyser 2002). Some strains are very effective and productive, supplying plenty of nitrogen at a low cost to the host plant. Other strains are not productive, requiring a great deal of energy from the host plant with little return of nitrogen (figure 13.8). In other words, partnerships can range from mutually beneficial to parasitic (Evans 2002, Schmidt 2007, Baker and others 2009). Selecting microsymbionts that form healthy, productive partnerships is believed to warrant as much mindfulness as selecting seed sources (Schmidt 2007). In addition to source, time is also a factor for noninoculated plants after outplanting. It can take months or even years for effective partnerships to form if microsymbiont populations in the soil are low or inactive. Until the partnership forms, the plants are dependent on inputs of nitrogen fertilizers or the nitrogen available in the soil. Without fertilizer on poor sites, noninoculated plants will grow very slowly, and sometimes are outcompeted by weeds.

Acquiring Inoculants for Nitrogen-Fixing Bacteria

Inoculants are live nitrogen-fixing bacteria cultures that are applied to seeds or young plants, imparting the beneficial bacteria to the plant's root system. Inoculants for nitrogen-fixing bacteria tend to be very specialized. In other words, they are not "one size fits all." Care must be

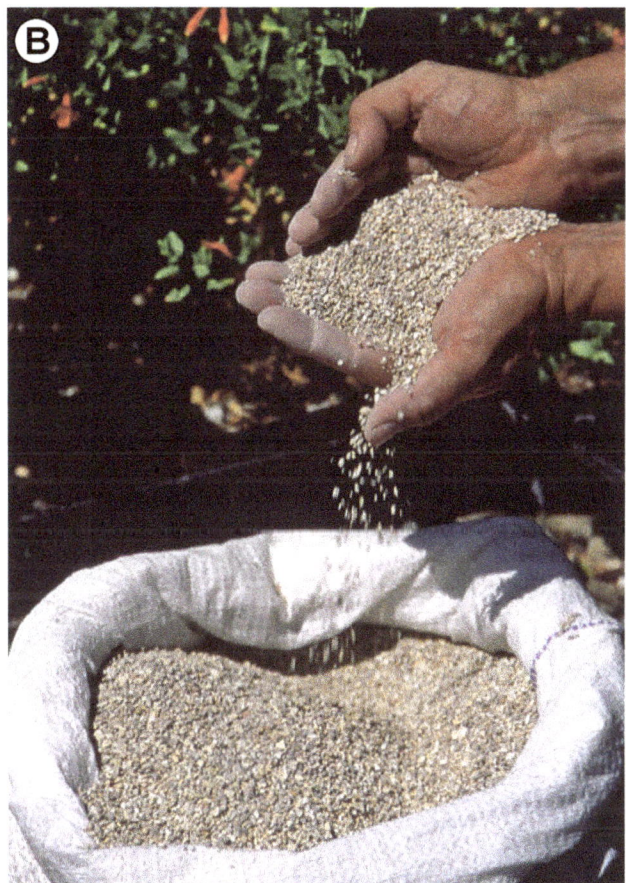

Figure 13.9—*Nitrogen-fixing bacteria are commercially available as pure-culture inoculant (A), often in a carrier (B). Photo A by Tara Luna, and photo B by Mike Evans.*

taken to select appropriate and effective nitrogen-fixing partners for specific plant species. Two forms of inoculant can be used for nitrogen-fixing plants in the nursery: pure-culture inoculant is purchased from commercial suppliers, seed banks, or sometimes, universities (figure 13.9) and homemade (often called "crude") inoculant is made from nodules collected from the roots of healthy nitrogen-fixing plants of the same species to be inoculated (figure 13.10). Whichever form is used, care should be taken when handling nitrogen-fixing bacteria inoculants because they are very perishable. These soil bacteria live underground in moist, dark conditions with relatively stable, cool temperatures. Similar conditions need to be maintained to ensure the viability of inoculant during storage, handling, and application.

Using Pure-Culture Inoculant

Pure-culture inoculants of nitrogen-fixing bacteria usually come in small packets of finely ground peat moss. Some manufactured inoculants contain select strains that have been tested for forming optimally productive partnerships with their host species. Select-strain inoculants should be considered if they can be obtained; these inoculants contain optimal partners for the host species to which they are matched, providing a good supply of nitrogen at a low cost to the plant. Superior strains can yield significant differences in the productivity and growth rate of the host plant; in some cases, they yield more than 40 percent better growth (Schmidt 2000). Not all manufactured inoculants are selected and matched to native species, however, so be sure to check the source. If a match cannot be found,

use the crude inoculant method instead. Manufactured products usually come with application instructions; these directions need to be followed. In general, about 3.5 oz (100 g) of cultured inoculant is sufficient to inoculate up to 3,000 plants, usually exceeding the recommended 100,000 bacteria per plant. Because they contain living cultures of bacteria, these inoculants are perishable and need to be kept in cool, dark conditions, such as inside a refrigerator.

Peat-based inoculants are added to chlorine-free water to create a slurry. (If the nursery's water supply is chlorinated, allowing a bucket of water to stand uncovered for 24 hours is a good way to let the chlorine evaporate.) A blender or electric mixer is recommended to blend the inoculant with water to ensure the bacteria are evenly mixed in the solution. If a blender is not available, a whisk can be used. After plants begin to nodulate, nodules from their roots can serve as the basis for making crude inoculant to use on future crops. This way, inoculant need be purchased only once for each plant species and can thereafter be perpetuated in the nursery.

Preparing Crude Inoculant

Nodules, the small root structures that house the bacteria, are used to make crude inoculant. Nodules can be col-

Figure 13.10—*To make crude rhizobia inoculant, pick nodules off healthy plants in the nursery (A) or in the field. Make sure the nodules are active (indicated by a pink to red color inside)(B). Then, blend the nodules collected from root systems (C) in clean, chlorine-free water (D) and immediately water onto 2-week-old seedlings (E). Photos by Craig R. Elevitch, courtesy of Wilkinson and Elevitch 2003.*

lected from the roots of nursery stock that were previously inoculated with cultured, select inoculant, or nodules can be collected from healthy, established host plants. For rhizobia, a brown, pink, or red color inside is usually a good indicator that the millions of bacteria in the nodule are actively fixing nitrogen. For *Frankia*, desirable nodules will be white or yellow inside. Grey or green nodules should be avoided, because they likely are inactive.

To make crude inoculant, choose healthy, vigorous plants of the same species as the plants to be inoculated. Dig shallowly around the base of the nodulated plant to expose some of its root system. Young roots often contain the most active nodules. Search for nodules with the proper color and pick them off cleanly (figures 13.10A, 13.10B). Collect nodules from several healthy plants of the same species to ensure diversity (figure 13.10C). Put the nodules in a plastic bag or container and place them in a cooler for protection from direct sunlight and heat. As soon as possible after collection (within a few hours), put the nodules in a blender with clean, chlorine-free water (figure 13.10D). About 50 to 100 nodules blended in about 1 qt (1 L) of water are enough to inoculate about 500 plants. This solution is a homemade liquid inoculant, ready to apply in the same way as cultured inoculant (figure 13.10E).

Applying Inoculant

Inoculant for nitrogen-fixing bacteria is commonly applied when seedlings are emerging, usually within 2 weeks of sowing, or just after cuttings have formed roots. This helps ensure successful nodulation and maximizes the benefits of using inoculants. The liquefied inoculant, made from either nodules or cultured inoculant as per the instructions in the previous sections, is then watered into the growing media or soil in which seedlings are growing (figure 13.10E).

Verifying the Nitrogen-Fixing Partnership

After 2 to 6 weeks, the noticeable signs in the following list should appear and are indications that the plant has formed a symbiotic partnership with nitrogen-fixing bacteria:

- Plants begin to grow well and are deep green despite the absence of added nitrogen fertilizer (figure 13.11A).

- Root systems give off a faint but distinctive ammonia-like scent.

- Nodules are visible on the root system.

- When a nodule is broken open, its inside is pink, red, or brown (for rhizobia) (figure 13.11B), or yellow or white (for *Frankia*).

Figure 13.11—*The 6-week-old native* Acacia koa *seedlings (right) were inoculated with rhizobia at 2 weeks of age; the seedlings on the left were not inoculated (A). Nodules from an* Acacia koa *seedling showing pink inside, signifying nitrogen is being fixed (B). Photo A by Craig R. Elevitch, and photo B by J.B. Friday.*

Management Considerations

As with any nursery practice, becoming familiar with the application and management of nitrogen-fixing microsymbionts is a learning process. Several factors are of primary concern to the nursery manager when using inoculants for nitrogen-fixing bacteria:

- **Timing**—Ensure the inoculant is applied when seedlings have just emerged or when cuttings have formed new roots to ensure successful nodulation and maximize the benefits of using inoculants.

- **Fertilization and Micronutrients**—The use of nitrogen-fixing bacterial inoculant requires some adjustments in fertilization. Excessive nitrogen fertilizer will inhibit formation of the partnership. If an optimal partnership is formed, the application of nitrogen may be eliminated from nitrogen-fixing plants and they may need to be isolated from nonnitrogen-fixing species to implement this change in fertilization.

Some nutrients, including calcium, potassium, molybdenum, and iron, are necessary to facilitate nodulation. These nutrients need to be incorporated into the growing medium. Phosphorus is also necessary for nodulation, supplied from the growing medium or, better yet, through mycorrhizal partnerships.

- **Water Quality**—Excessive chlorine in water is detrimental to rhizobia and *Frankia*. The water supply may need to be tested and a chlorine filter obtained if excessive chlorine is a problem in the water supply. As an alternative, chlorine will evaporate if clean water is left to stand uncovered in a container for 24 hours before use.

- **Sourcing Inoculants**—Locating appropriate sources of viable inoculants (either cultured or obtained as nodules) matched to native species may require some research and time but benefits of successful inoculation are well worth the effort.

- **Client Education**—Make sure nursery clients and people outplanting the plants understand the nitrogen-fixing bacteria so they appreciate the presence of nodules and are careful not to expose root systems to full sun. Also, educate clients so they know that only some species of plants can form this partnership—otherwise some might think all species can fix nitrogen.

- **Outplanting Site Considerations**—After nodules form, rhizobia are enclosed and usually less affected by soil conditions such as pH or aluminum toxicity than are other beneficial microorganisms such as mycorrhizal fungi. In very harsh outplanting conditions (such as extremely low pH in some rehabilitation sites), however, the rhizobia are not likely to spread in the soil, and so might not be available to spread to subsequent cohorts of the outplanted species. Therefore, inoculating subsequent crops in the nursery before outplanting on the same site is advisable.

Tripartite Symbiosis

Most plants that form partnerships with nitrogen-fixing bacteria also require mycorrhizal partners. When a nitrogen-fixing plant has effective partnerships with both nitrogen-fixing bacteria and mycorrhizal fungi, this is called "tripartite symbiosis" because three partners exist (a host plant and two microsymbionts) (figure 13.12). When working with both types of microsymbionts, simply apply each inoculant separately, as described in the sections of this chapter.

Several studies have shown that legumes may need to first form arbuscular mycorrhizae before they can form

Figure 13.12—*The* Gliricidia sepium *plants on the far left were inoculated with both rhizobia (R) and mycorrhizal fungi (M) and show tripartite symbiosis: a beneficial partnership among the plant host, rhizobia bacteria, and arbuscular mycorrhizal fungi. Photo by Kenneth W. Mudge*

rhizobia nodules. This may occur because nitrogen fixation is an energy-demanding process, and the plant's energy metabolism is highly phosphorus-dependent. In other words, a grower who applies only rhizobia inoculant may have difficulty getting good nodulation if the mycorrhizal partnership is not in place (or if adequate phosphorus is not available in the growing medium). The next section describes how to introduce mycorrhizal fungi to nursery crops—they often are incorporated in the growing medium before the rhizobia inoculant is applied.

Mycorrhizal Fungi

Unlike nitrogen-fixing bacteria, mycorrhizal fungi form partnerships with nearly all plant families and forest trees. "Myco" means "fungus" and "rhiza" means "root;" the word "mycorrhizae" means "fungus-roots." Most of the world's plants depend on their partnership with mycorrhizal fungi to grow and thrive. The host plant's roots provide a substrate for the fungi and supply food in the form of simple carbohydrates. In exchange, the mycorrhizal fungi offer the following benefits to the host plant:

- **Increased Water and Nutrient Uptake**—Mycorrhizal fungi help plants absorb mineral nutrients, especially nitrogen, phosphorus, and several micronutrients such as zinc and copper. The fungal hyphae extend out into the soil far beyond the host's roots, expanding the mineral- and water-absorbing surface area for the host plant. Researchers estimate that mycorrhizal fungus hyphae can explore volumes of soil hundreds to thousands of times greater than roots can alone.

- **Stress and Disease Protection**—Mycorrhizal fungi protect the plant host in several ways. With ectomycorrhizal fungi, for example, a fungus sheath (called a "mantle") completely covers fragile root tips and acts

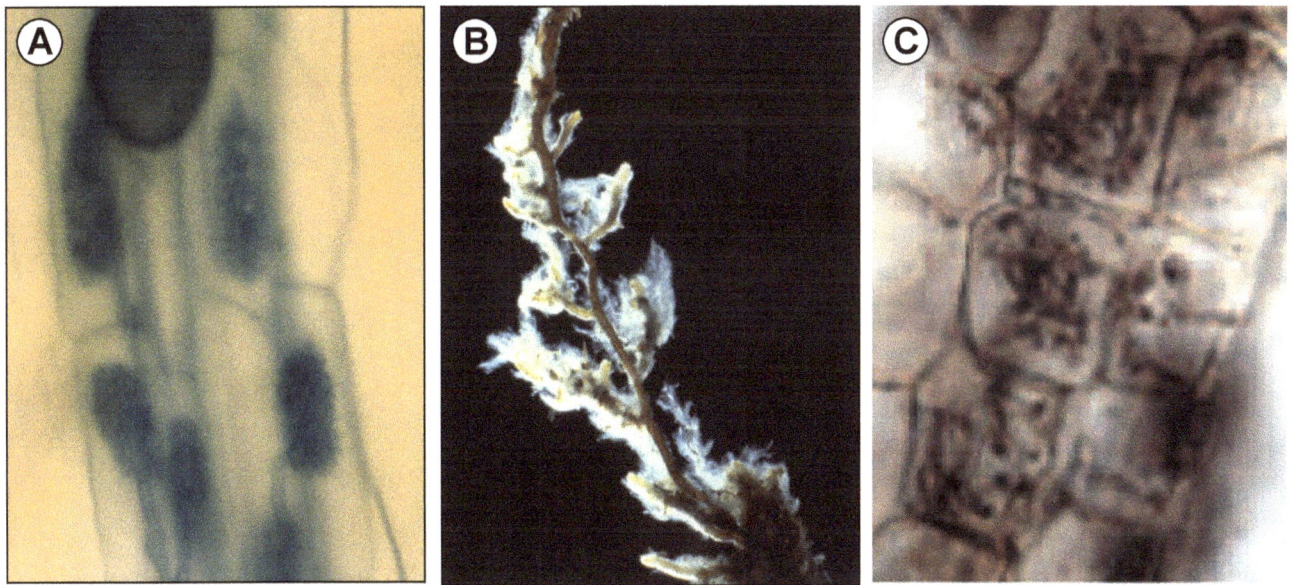

Figure 13.13—*The three types of mycorrhizal fungi. Arbuscular mycorrhizal (AM) fungi (A). Ectomycorrhizal (ECM) fungi (B)—the mantles of ECM may be visible to the unaided eye, although ECM on* Eucalyptus *can be inconspicuous. Ericoid mycorrhizal (ERM) fungi (C). Both AM and ERM can only be seen on plant roots with the aid of a microscope. Photos A and B by Michael A. Castellano, and photo C by Efren Cazares.*

as a physical barrier to dryness, pests, and toxic soil contaminants. Other mycorrhizal fungi may produce antibiotics, which provide chemical protection.

- **Increased Vigor and Growth**—Plants with mycorrhizal roots may have an improved hormone status, and they survive and grow better than noninoculated plants after they are planted out on a project site. Studies show that establishing a partnership with mycorrhizal fungi while the plants are in the nursery results in improved field growth (Habte and others 2001, Baker and others 2009).

The following three types of mycorrhizae are important to tropical native plant nurseries (table 13.2):

- **Arbuscular Mycorrhizae (AM)**—Formed by the most ancient and predominant type of mycorrhizal fungi. AM fungi are found on the roots of most tropical plants and many of the world's food crops (including rice, corn, and legumes), associating with more than 80 percent of the world's plant families (figure 13.13A).

- **Ectomycorrhizae (ECM)**—Partnerships with many temperate forest trees and a few abundant tropical trees including pines (*Pinus*), eucalypts (*Eucalyptus*), poplars (*Populus*), and dipterocarps (*Dipterocarpus*) (figure 13.13B).

- **Ericoid Mycorrhizae (ERM)**—Partnerships with plants in the heath or heather (Ericaceae) family, including the genera of blueberries, cranberries, azaleas, and rhododendrons (figure 13.13C).

Mycorrhizal fungi are not "one size fits all," but they often are "one size fits many." Also, one plant can partner simultaneously with several species of mycorrhizal fungi, and a plant may change partners over time as it grows and adapts to its environment (Amaranthus 2010).

Table 13.2—*Plants and their mycorrhizal partners. Adapted from Castellano and Molina (1990) and Wang and Qiu (2006).*

Mycorrhizal fungi	Plants
Arbuscular mycorrhizal (AM)	More than 80% of the world's plant families including most tropical trees, herbs, and ferns
Ectomycorrhizal (ECM)	Fewer than 10% of plant families, including the genera pine (*Pinus*), oak (*Quercus*), eucalyptus (*Eucalyptus*)
AM and ECM	Some *Allocasuarina, Acacia, Eucalyptus,* juniper (*Juniperus*), poplar (*Populus*), and willow (*Salix*)
Ericoid mycorrhizal (ERM)	Heather or heath family (Ericaceae in the broad sense, including the former Epacridaceae and Empetraceae), including blueberry (*Vaccinium*) and *Rhododendron* (including azaleas)

Because most plants are associated with a particular type of mycorrhizal fungus, however, different plant species have different fungal partners that must be matched appropriately to be effective (table 13.2).

Mycorrhizal fungi may be obtained either from commercial suppliers or from roots around a healthy host plant of the species being propagated. In all cases, mycorrhizal inoculum must physically contact living roots of the plant to colonize most effectively. Ways to acquire and successfully apply mycorrhizal fungi are explained in subsequent sections. Although the fungi are similar in how they function and in their benefits to host plants, they appear differently on roots. Also, each mycorrhizal fungi type has a unique application method that must be described separately. Management practices in the nursery are similar and will be discussed together at the end of this section.

Arbuscular Mycorrhizal (AM) Fungi

AM fungi are essential for most tropical trees and other plants and for many annual crops and grasses. AM fungi are not visible on plant roots to the unaided eye and must be observed under a microscope. The large spores of AM fungi are not easily disseminated by wind, unlike the wind-dispersed microscopic spores of ECM fungi.

Inoculant for AM fungi is sometimes collected from root systems of AM host plants or soil underneath them and incorporated into growing media. This method can work well because the fungi collected are likely to be adapted to prevailing site conditions (Janos and others 2001). Freshly collected and chopped mycorrhizal roots must be used within six days of collection or their efficacy will decline. This method is often discouraged, however, because of damage to plants and natural ecosystems, variable effectiveness, and the risk of introducing pests and pathogens along with the soil or roots. The two main sources of AM fungi inoculant for nurseries are "pot culture" made from a known fungus species, and commercially available cultures. Because AM spores are relatively large, it is critical to ensure that spores come in direct contact with the root systems. Spores will not pass easily through irrigation injectors or nozzles. Therefore, for all inoculant types, thorough incorporation into growing media is the best practice.

Pot Culture Inoculant

In pot culture inoculant, a specific AM fungus species is acquired either commercially or from a field site as a starter culture and then incorporated into a sterile growing medium. A host plant such as corn, sorghum, clover, or an herbaceous native plant, is grown in this substrate. As the host plant grows, the AM fungi multiply in the medium

Figure 13.14—In pot culture inoculant, a specific arbuscular mycorrhizal fungus species is acquired as a starter culture and added to a sterile growing medium with a fast-growing host plant (A). The shoots of host plants are later removed, and the substrate, now rich in roots, spores, and mycelium, is chopped up (B) and incorporated into the growing medium before containers are filled. Photos by Thomas D. Landis.

(figure 13.14). After the host plant roots have spread throughout the medium, their shoots are removed and the substrate, now rich in roots, spores, and mycelium, is chopped up and incorporated into fresh growing medium before containers are filled and seeds are sown or cuttings stuck. This technique is highly effective for propagating AM fungi in the nursery. For further details on how to use this method, consult the publications in the References section of this chapter (particularly Habte and Osorio 2001, Miyasaka and others 2003).

Commercial Inoculant Sources

Commercial sources of AM fungi inoculant are also available, usually containing several species or strains. Because AM fungus spores are fragile, they are usually mixed with a carrier such as vermiculite or calcined clay to aid in application. These products are thoroughly incorporated into the growing medium before filling containers.

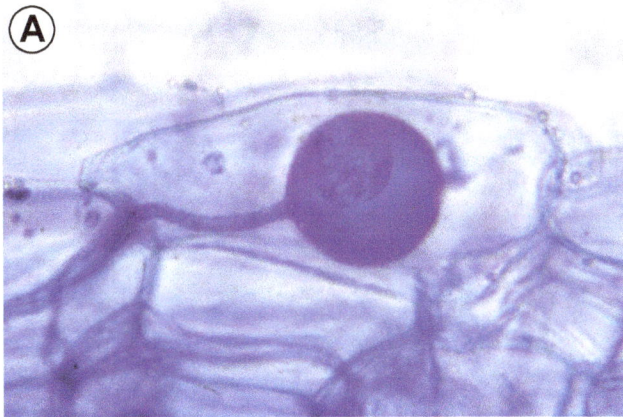

Figure 13.15—In this microscope photo (400 times magnification), a tropical tree root has been clarified and stained with a blue dye so that an AM fungus "vesicle" within the walls of a root cortical cell is clearly visible (A). Vesicles are places where AM fungi store excess energy-rich materials, such as lipids. Vesicles always are attached to AM fungus filament (a hypha), which distinguishes them from the spore-bearing structures of some root-parasitic fungi. Although AM fungi are visible only under a microscope, nursery workers may observe differences in plant growth of inoculated versus noninoculated plants. A mosaic pattern of nutrient deficiencies as shown by these mahogany (Swietenia *species) seedlings, may indicate that some plants have formed successful partnerships while others have not (B). Photo A by David P. Janos, and photo B by Tara Luna.*

Inoculation effectiveness has been shown to differ considerably between different products so it is wise to test before purchasing large quantities of a specific product. Laboratories can provide a live spore count per volume, which is the best measure of inoculum vigor.

Verifying the Effectiveness of AM Fungi Inoculation

To verify the effectiveness of AM fungi inoculation, roots must be stained and examined under a microscope (figure 13.15A). This verification can often be done through a soil scientist at a local agricultural extension office. After some practice, nursery staff may get a feel for when inoculation is successful, because noninoculated plants often grow more slowly and may have higher incidence of root rot issues. The plants also may exhibit signs of phosphorus deficiency (a frequent consequence of lack of mycorrhiza), indicated by purple coloration of leaves or other symptoms (figure 13.15B).

Ectomycorrhizal (ECM) Fungi

Many recognizable mushrooms are fruiting bodies of ECM fungi. These fruiting bodies are a small portion of the total organism; underground, the amount of fungus covering the short feeder roots of plants may be enormous. ECM fungi extend the volume of the feeding area of roots by many times and protectively coat the feeder roots. On some species, such as pines (*Pinus*), the mantles of ECM are visible on the roots of the host plant. For other species, such as many *Eucalyptus* ECM, the mantles can be inconspicuous. ECM are important to many temperate forest species, especially evergreens. In the tropics, far fewer plant species

partner with ECM fungi than with AM fungi. In Hawai'i, for example, no native ECM are known, although some strains may have been introduced along with introduced trees (Amaranthus 2010). ECM only affect a small percentage of tropical species, including pines, eucalypts, poplars, oaks, dipterocarps, and some legumes (table 13.3).

Four sources of ECM fungi inoculant have been used in nurseries. Nurse plants and soil spores have been used historically while spores and pure culture inoculant are usually recommended for nurseries.

Nurse Plants as Inoculum Sources

In the early days of trying to establish pines in the tropics where they were not native, "nurse" plants were sometimes used. Conspicuously vigorous mycorrhizal seedlings were transplanted to nursery beds at 3- to 6-ft (1- to 2-m) intervals and allowed to become established, maintaining the ECM fungi on their roots. Seeds were then sown or germinants transplanted around and between these mycorrhizal nurse plants. After becoming colonized by ECM fungi spreading from the nurse plants, the seedlings were transplanted to the outplanting site. Some plants were left in the beds to serve as nurse plants for the next crop of seedlings. Sometimes the spread of mycorrhizal fungi from the nurse seedlings was slow (roughly 2 ft per year), which suggested that some unfavorable soil property (such as high pH) should have been remedied. The mycorrhizal fungi usually spread fastest among seedlings in sterilized soil. This method was laborious, and, as with all bareroot crops, care had to be taken not to cause damage when lifting seedlings (Mikola 1973).

Table 13.3—*Tropical families and genera with ectomycorrhizal associations. Adapted from Brundrett (2009).*

Family	Genera
Gnetaceae	*Gnetum*
Pinaceae	*Cedrus, Keteleeria, Larix, Picea,* and *Pinus*
Nyctaginaceae	*Guapira, Neea,* and *Pisonia*
Polygonaceae	*Coccoloba*
Myrtaceae	*Allosyncarpia, Agonis, Angophora, Baeckea, Eucalyptus, Leptospermum, Melaleuca, Tristania,* and *Tristaniopsis*
Fabaceae: Caesalpinioideae	*Afzelia, Anthonotha, Aphanocalyx, Berlinia, Brachystegia, Cryptosepalum, Dicymbe, Didelotia, Eperua, Gilbertiodendron, Gleditsia, Intsia, Isoberlinia, Julbernardia, Microberlinia, Monopetalanthus, Paraberlinia, Paramacrolobium, Pellegriniodendron, Tetraberlinia,* and *Toubaouate*
Fabaceae: Papilionoideae	*Aldinia, Gastrolobium, Gompholobium, Jacksonia, Lonchocarpus, Mirbelia, Oxylobium,* and *Pericopsis*
Fabaceae: Mimosoideae	*Acacia* and *Calliandra*
Casuarinaceae	*Allocasuarina* and *Casuarina*
Fagaceae	*Castanea, Castanopsis, Fagus, Lithocarpus,* and *Quercus*
Phyllanthaceae (Euphorbiaceae)	*Uapaca* and *Poranthera*
Salicaceae	*Populus* and *Salix*
Rhamnaceae	*Cryptandra, Pomaderris, Spyridium,* and *Trymalium*
Dipterocarpaceae	*Anisoptera, Dipterocarpus, Hopea, Marquesia, Monotes, Shorea, Vateria, Vateriopsis,* and *Vatica*
Sarcolaenaceae	*Leptolaena, Sarcolaena,* and *Schizolaena*

Soils as Inoculum Sources

Topsoil, humus, or duff from beneath ECM fungi host trees has historically been used to inoculate nursery plants. This practice is more common in bareroot nurseries in temperate regions than in container nurseries. Because sterilization would kill these beneficial fungi, unsterilized soil and organic matter are incorporated into the growing medium, up to 10 percent by volume. Today, this practice is generally discouraged for ECM fungi because (1) large quantities of soil are required, which can make the process labor intensive and have a detrimental effect on the natural ecosystem, (2) the quality and quantity of spores may be highly variable, and (3) pathogens may be introduced along with the inoculant. If soil is used, inoculum should be collected from plant communities near the outplanting site. Small amounts should be collected from several different sites, then thoroughly mixed, and care should be taken not to damage the plants during soil collection.

Spores as Inoculum Sources

Nurseries can make their own ECM inoculum from spores. Collected from the fruiting bodies (figure 13.16) of mushrooms, puffballs, and especially truffles, these fruiting bodies, full of spores, are rinsed, sliced, and pulverized in a blender for several minutes. The resulting thick liquid is diluted with water and poured into the growing media of germinating seedlings or newly rooted cuttings. Plants are usually inoculated 6 to 12 weeks after sowing (figure 13.17). Two applications 2 to 3 weeks apart are recommended to ensure even inoculation.

Pure-Culture Inoculum

ECM fungi are available commercially as pure cultures, usually in a peat-based carrier (figure 13.18). The quality of commercial sources varies, however, so it is important to verify vigor by testing formation of mycorrhizae. Most commercial sources contain several different species of

Figure 13.16—*Fruiting bodies of ecto-mycorrhizal fungi. A puffball of* Pisolithus tinctorius, *showing the cavities where the spores are located (A). An* Amanita *from pine forest in Guatemala (B), and gilled ectomycorrhizal mushrooms and roots from dipterocarp forest in Malaysia (C). Photo A by Michelle M. Cram, and photos B and C by David P. Janos.*

Figure 13.17—*Inoculating tree seedlings with ectomycorrhizal fungi. Two applications 2 to 3 weeks apart are recommended to ensure even inoculation. Photo by Michael A. Castellano.*

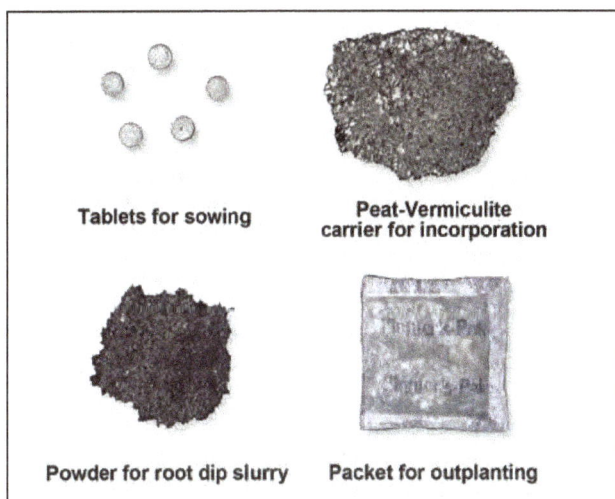

Figure 13.18—*Forms of commercial ectomycorrhizal inoculants available for nurseries. Photo by Thomas D. Landis.*

ECM fungi. Commercial inoculum can be purchased separately and mixed into the growing medium as per the instructions on the product and before filling containers. In some areas, bales of growing medium with inoculum already premixed may be purchased. It is important to inquire if selected strains to match site needs are available through suppliers.

Verifying the Effectiveness of ECM Fungi Inoculation

With practice, nursery staff can learn to recognize ECM fungi on the root systems of plants—they are fairly easy to see and often involve conspicuous morphological changes of the finest roots. During the hardening phase, short feeder roots need to be examined for a cottony white appearance on the root surface or a white or brightly colored mantle or sheath over the roots (figure 13.19A). Unlike pathogenic fungi, mycorrhizae never show signs of root decay. Sometimes, mushrooms or other fruiting bodies will appear in containers alongside their host plants (figure 13.19B). Although these structures are visible to the unaided eye, it is also recommended to send plant samples to a laboratory for verification. A local soil extension agent or university likely can assist with this process.

Figure 13.20—*A native Hawaiian Ericoid,* Vaccinium reticulatum, *'ōhelo, growing on a recent lava flow. Partnerships with ericoid mycorrhizal fungi enable these plants to survive and thrive in harsh conditions. Photo by Kim M. Wilkinson.*

Ericoid Mycorrhizal (ERM) Fungi

Plants that form partnerships with ERM fungi are able to grow in exceptionally nitrogen-poor soils and harsh conditions, including bogs, alpine meadows, tundra, and even in soils with high concentrations of certain toxic metals (figure 13.20). ERM fungi form partnerships in the plant order Ericales in the heath (Epacridaceae), crowberry (Empetraceae), and most of the rhododendron (Ericaceae) family (table 13.4). Similar to ECM fungi and AM fungi, ERM fungi must come in contact with the host plants roots to form partnerships. Ericoid mycorrhizal inoculant is available as commercial cultures or from soil near healthy host plants. The product or soil is mixed into nursery growing medium. The fungus forms a net over the narrow "hair roots" (the fine, ultimate rootlets of the plants that are only a few cells

Figure 13.19—*Nursery staff can learn to recognize the presence or absence of ectomycorrhizal fungi by examining plants. Cottony white ectomycorrhizae may be visible on roots of some species (A), fruiting bodies may be growing from containers (B). Photo A by William Sayward, and photo B by Michael A. Castellano.*

Table 13.4—*Genera known to associate with ericoid mycorrhizal fungi. Adapted from Read (1996) and Smith and Read (1997).*

Family	Genera
Ericaceae	*Acrotriche, Andersonia, Astroloma, Brachyloma, Cassiope, Calluna, Ceratiola, Conostephium, Corema, Cyathodes, Dracophyllum, Empetrum, Epacris, Erica, Gaultheria, Kalmia, Ledum, Leucopogon, Lissanthe, Lysinema, Melichrus, Monotoca, Needhamiella, Oligarrhena,* *Pentachondra, Richea, Rhododendron, Rupicola, Sphenotoma, Sprengelia, Styphelia, Trochocarpa, Vaccinium, Woollsia*

wide), infecting the outer cells. As with AM fungi, nutrients are shared through the membranes that form the boundary between the fungus and plant roots. Laboratory confirmation is recommended to verify that successful inoculation has taken place.

Management Considerations for Mycorrhizal Fungi

When using mycorrhizal inoculants for the first time, it is recommended to start small and evaluate a few techniques and sources. Compare some trays or benches with and without mycorrhizae to determine how management and scheduling need to be modified to culture mycorrhizal roots. In some cases, working with a manufactured product of known quality may be the easiest way to begin; the nurs-

ery can then expand into collecting and processing its own inoculant sources. Monitor the effectiveness of inoculation and keep records of crop development. See Chapter 20, Discovering Ways to Improve Nursery Practices and Plant Quality, to learn more about how to create some small trials and experiments.

Although mycorrhizal fungi are not very specialized, different strains of mycorrhizae are believed to perform differently for given site challenges. Some select or pure-culture inoculants may support high productivity in certain site conditions but may be less productive than native strains on other sites. For example, some strains may be more beneficial if lack of nutrients is the main challenge while others may be particularly helpful to their hosts in withstanding soil pathogens or even heavy metals. If possible, working with several strains for diversity in the field may be a good safeguard, especially because plants can partner with multiple strains simultaneously and can change partners if necessary to adapt to site conditions. The nursery can do a little research or work with a specialist to help with the following tasks:

- Select optimal mycorrhizal partners for the species and outplanting sites.
- Determine the most appropriate sources of inoculant and evaluate their effectiveness in the nursery.
- Design outplanting trials to evaluate plant vigor and survival and modify the inoculant sources if improvements are needed.

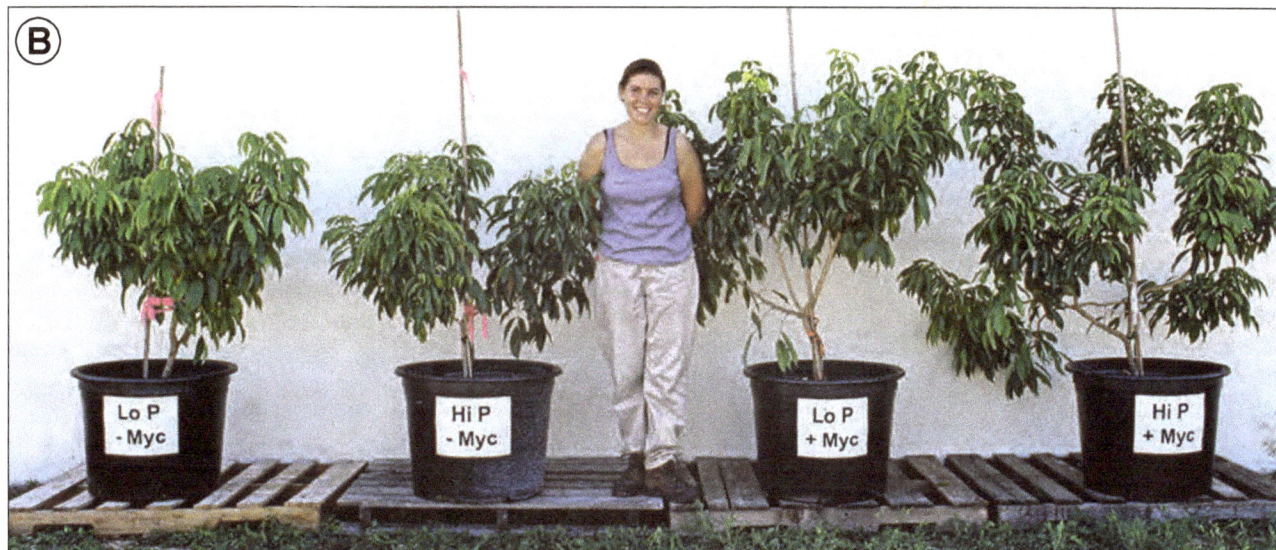

Figure 13.21—*Four-month-old guava seedlings* (Psidium guajava) *in the nursery in a low fertility (about 8 ppm available phosphorus) lowland tropical acid clay soil; the plant on the right has a mycorrhizal partnership in place while the plant on the left does not (A). Even with abundant phosphorus fertilization, lack of mycorrhizal fungi can slow plant growth. The photo shows lychee* (Litchi chinensis) *air layers grown for 16 months in 25 gal pots of a soil-free medium after cutting from the source trees (B). Although phosphorus fertilization did not affect growth, AM fungus inoculation with field-collected inoculant improved shoot growth by 39 percent (see Janos and others 2001). Photos by David P. Janos.*

Inoculation with mycorrhizal fungi affects plant growth (figure 13.21). Fertilization practices will need to be adjusted to support the formation of mycorrhizal partnerships in the nursery. An excessive amount of phosphorus inhibits formation of the partnership; therefore phosphorus must be reduced. Enough phosphorus must be present to keep the mycorrhizal fungi from competing with its host plant for the nutrient, however, and potentially becoming parasitic instead of symbiotic. The recommendation is to use "low but sufficient" levels of phosphorus to facilitate the partnership (Miyasaka and others 2003). In some cases, the overall quantity of fertilizer may need to be reduced by half or more because of the efficiency of nutrient uptake by mycorrhizal fungi. Fertilizer type and form is also important. If nitrogen is applied, ammonium-nitrate is better used by a wide variety of plants than nitrate-nitrogen alone (Castellano and Molina 1990). In general, controlled-release fertilizers may be better than liquid fertilizers for inoculated plants because they release small doses of nutrients gradually rather than sudden high doses periodically. Excessive or inadequate water will inhibit the presence of mycorrhizal fungi and the formation of the partnership, so watering schedules need to be modified accordingly. Nursery staff who are willing to be observant and flexible as the nursery embarks on the use of mycorrhizal fungi will be the best decision makers in terms of modifying fertilization and watering regimes to support the microsymbionts.

Other management adjustments may be necessary because of improved survival and growth. Improved survival percentages will affect estimates and oversow rates. Scheduling also may be affected; inoculated plants may be ready for outplanting sooner than noninoculated plants. Applications of certain fungicides are detrimental to mycorrhizal fungi; susceptibility varies by species and pesticide applications need to be assessed and adjusted.

Some plants form partnerships with both AM fungi and ECM fungi. These plants include some of the *Allocasuarina, Acacia, Eucalyptus, Juniperus,* and *Populus* species. In these cases, trials should be done to see which inoculant produces the best results in the nursery, and if those results persist after outplanting. For some species, additional inoculation with the second type of mycorrhiza (usually ECM fungi following AM fungi) may be necessary before outplanting.

Also, most plants that form partnerships with nitrogen-fixing bacteria also require mycorrhizal partners. For example, many leguminous trees partner with both rhizobia and AM fungi; in these cases, it may be beneficial to apply the AM fungi before the rhizobia (as discussed previously). Trees such as alders (*Alnus*) partner with both *Frankia* and ECM fungi. In these cases, inoculants can be applied separately to the same crop of plants.

Other Beneficial Microorganisms

In natural soil, communities of bacteria, fungi, algae, protozoa, and other microorganisms make nutrients available to plants, create channels for water and air, maintain soil structure, and cycle nutrients and organic matter. A healthy population of soil microorganisms helps to maintain ecological balance, preventing the onset of major problems from soil viruses or other pathogens. Realizing that soil is alive, and reducing or eliminating practices that may be harmful to soil microlife is important. As Aldo Leopold advised, "The first rule of intelligent tinkering is to keep all the parts." Using compost, mulch, and organic matter is important for soil life. Protecting soil from erosion and unnecessary disturbances, eliminating pollution from soluble fertilizers, and minimizing the use of fungicides, disinfectants, and other chemicals that may kill microlife are all key practices. Introductions of mycorrhizal fungi and nitrogen-fixing bacteria in the nursery can support the balance of beneficial soil microorganisms.

Acknowledgements

The authors thank the following people for sharing their assistance and expertise while this chapter was being developed:

Mike Amaranthus, Grants Pass, OR. Microbiologist; Adjunct Associate Professor, Oregon State University; President, Mycorrhizal Applications, Inc.

Mitiku Habte, Honolulu, HI. Professor of Soil Science, University of Hawai'i at Mānoa Department of Tropical Plant and Soil Sciences.

Harold Keyser, Kahului, HI. Maui County Administrator, University of Hawai'i College of Tropical Agriculture and Human Resources (CTAHR).

Jim Trappe, Corvallis, OR. Professor, Oregon State University, Department of Forest Science.

Kenneth Mudge, Ithaca, NY. Associate Professor, Cornell University Department of Horticulture.

References

Amaranthus, M. 2010. Personal communication. Grant's Pass, OR. Microbiologist; Adjunct Associate Professor, Oregon State University; President, Mycorrhizal Applications, Inc.

Baker, P.J.; Scowcroft, P.G.; Ewel, J.J. 2009. Koa (*Acacia koa*) ecology and silviculture. Gen. Tech. Rep. PSW-GTR-211. Albany, CA: U.S. Department of Agriculture, Forest Service, Pacific Southwest Research Station. 129 p.

Brown, L.; Johnson, J.W. 1996. Nitrogen and the hydrologic cycle. Ohio State University Extension Fact Sheet AEX-463-96.

Columbus, OH: Ohio State University, Food, Agricultural and Biological Engineering. http://ohioline.osu.edu/aex-fact/0463.html. (June 2012).

Brundrett, M.C. 2009. Mycorrhizal associations and other means of nutrition of vascular plants: understanding the global diversity of host plants by resolving conflicting information and developing reliable means of diagnosis. Plant and Soil. 320: 37–77.

Castellano, M.A.; Molina, R. 1990. Mycorrhizae. In: Landis, T.D.; Tinus, R.W.; McDonald, S.E.; Barnett, J.P.; The Container Tree Nursery Manual, Volume 5. Agriculture Handbook 674. Washington, DC: U.S. Department of Agriculture, Forest Service: 101-167.

Evans, J. 2002. Plantation forestry in the tropics. 2nd ed. New York: Oxford University Press Resources. 47 p.

Habte, M.; Miyasaka, S.C.; Matuyama, D.T. 2001. Arbuscular mycorrhizal fungi improve early forest tree establishment. In: Horst, W.J.; Schenk, M.K.; Burkert, A.; Classen, N., eds. Plant nutrition-food security and sustainabiity of agro-ecosystems. Dordrecht, Netherlands: Kluwer Academic Publishers. 644-645 p.

Habte, M.; Osorio, N.W. 2001. Arbuscular mycorrhizas: producing and applying arubscular mycorrhizal inoculum. Honolulu, HI: University of Hawai'i, College of Tropical Agriculture and Human. 47 p.

Janos, D.P.; Schroeder, M.S.; Schaffer, B.; Crane, J.H. 2001. Inoculation with arbuscular mycorrhizal fungi enhances growth of *Litchi chinensis* Sonn. trees after propagation by air-layering. Plant and Soil. 233: 85–94.

Keyser, H. 2002. Personal communication. Paia, HI: University of Hawai'i NifTAL Project.

Landis, T.D.; Tinus, R.W.; McDonald, S.E.; Barnett, J.P. 1989. The container tree nursery manual: volume 5, the biological component: nursery pests and mycorrhizae. Agriculture Handbook 674. Washington, DC: U.S. Department of Agriculture, Forest Service. 171 p.

Mikola, P. 1973. Application of mycorrhizal symbiosis in forestry practice. In: Marks, G.C.; Kozlowski, T.T., eds. Ectomycorrhizae: their ecology and physiology. New York and London: Academic Press: 444 p. Chapter 10.

Miyasaka, S.C.; Habte, M.; Friday, J.B.; Johnson, E.V. 2003. Manual on arbuscular mycorrhizal fungus production and inoculation techniques. Honolulu, HI: University of Hawai'i at Mānoa, College of Tropical Agriculture and Human Resources. 4 p.

Nitrogen Fixing Tree Association (NFTA). 1989. Why nitrogen fixing trees? NFTA 89-03: 1-2. Morrilton, AR: Forest, Farm and Community Tree Network (FACT Net), Winrock International. http://www.winrock.org/fnrm/factnet/factpub/FACTSH/WhyNFT.htm.

Read, D.J. 1996. The structure and function of the Ericoid mycorrhizal root. Annals of Botany. 77: 365–374.

Schmidt, L. 2000. Guide to handling of tropical and subtropical forest seed. Humlebaek, Denmark: Danida Forest Seed Centre. 511 p.

Schmidt, L. 2007. Tropical forest seed. Berlin, Germany: Springer-Verlag. 409 p.

Singleton, P.W.; Somasegaran, P.; Nakao, P.; Keyser, H.H.; Hoben, H.J.; Ferguson, P.I. 1990. Applied BNF technology: a practical guide for extension specialists. Module Number 3: Introduction to rhizobia. Honolulu, Hawai'i: University of Hawai'i-Mānoa, College of Tropical Agriculture and Human Resources. 13 p. http://www.ctahr.hawaii.edu/bnf/Downloads/Training/BNF%20technology/rhizobia.PDF. (April 2012).

Smith, S.E.; Read, D.J. 1997. Mycorrhizal symbiosis. 2nd ed. San Diego: Academic Press. 605 p.

Wall, L. 2000. The actinorhizal symbiosis. Journal of Plant Growth Regulation. 19: 167–182.

Wang, B.; Y.L. Qiu. 2006. Phylogenetic distribution and evolution of mycorrhizas in land plants. Mycorrhiza. 16: 299–363.

Wilkinson, K.M.; Elevitch, C.R. 2003. Growing koa: a Hawaiian legacy tree. Holualoa, HI: Permanent Agriculture Resources.

Additional Reading

Alexander, I.; Selosse, M.A. 2009. Mycorrhizas in tropical forests: a neglected research imperative. New Phytologist. 182: 14–16.

Brundrett, M.C. 2008. Mycorrhizal associations: the Web resource. http://mycorrhizas.info/info.html http://mycorrhizas.info/info.html. (February 2013).

Dawson, J.O. 2009. Ecology of Actinorhizal plants. In: Pawlowski, K., ed.; Newton, W.E. series ed. Nitrogen-fixing Actinorhizal symbioses. Dordrecht, The Netherlands: Springer: 199–227. Chapter 8.

Margulis, L.; Sagan, D. 1997. Microcosmos: four billion years of evolution from our microbial ancestors. Berkley, CA: University of California Press. 301 p.

Problem Prevention and Holistic Pest Management

14

Thomas D. Landis, Tara Luna, R. Kasten Dumroese, and Kim M. Wilkinson

As any experienced grower knows only too well, nursery management is a continuous process of solving problems. One recurring problem is pests. In the past, nursery managers waited for an insect or disease to appear and then sprayed some toxic chemical to wipe out the pest or disease. This approach, however, also wipes out natural predators of the pest, resulting in an expensive and repeating pesticide cycle. Instead of a knee-jerk reaction to a specific problem, "holistic" pest management is a series of interrelating processes that are incorporated into the entire spectrum of nursery culture. Holism is the theory that systems, and each part of a system, should be viewed as a whole and not as isolated parts. "Holistic," then, is an approach that looks at the big picture and considers all parts. Holistic pest management is an integrated and preventative approach that considers the overall health of the plant and the nursery environment to prevent problems and to manage them wisely if they arise. The holistic approach to nursery pest management involves a series of four interrelated practices, which ideally function together (Wescom 1999):

- **Problem Prevention Through Cultural Measures**—through good sanitation, proper scheduling, management of the nursery environment, and promotion of plant health.

- **Problem Detection and Diagnosis**—through monitoring, recordkeeping, and accurate problem identification.

- **Problem Management**—including, if necessary, timely and appropriate pest suppression measures and balance of pest populations with beneficial organisms and pest predators.

- **Ongoing Process Evaluation**—to learn from experience by assessment and improved effectiveness of pest management approaches.

Facing Page: *Beneficial insects are an important part of holistic pest management. The ladybugs (*Hippodamia *species [Coleoptera: Coccinellidae]) in this photo can be seen feeding upon the psyllid pest* Heteropsylla cubana *(Hemiptera: Psyllidae). Photo by J.B. Friday.*

Figure 14.1—*A collage of biotic nursery pests. Fungal pests include damping-off (A), Phytophthora root canker (B), fungal rust on ōʻhiʻa leaves (C), and Botrytis blight (D). Insect pests include aphids (E), fungus gnat larvae eating seeds (F) and roots (G), leaf miners (H), mealybugs on palm (I), and mites making leaf galls (J). Snails and slugs (K) can damage nursery plants. Plants such as weeds, liverworts, and algae (L, M) can smother small plants. Photos A through J by Thomas D. Landis, photo K by Brian F. Daley, photo L by R. Kasten Dumroese, and photo M by William Pink.*

Nursery Diseases and Pests

Nurseries have many potential pests, including fungi (figures 14.1A–14.1D), insects (figures 14.1E–14.1J), nematodes, snails, slugs (figure 14.1K) and even larger animals such as mice and deer. Other plant species, such as weeds and cryptogams (moss, algae, or liverworts) (figures 14.1L, 14.1M) can become pests when they compete with crop plants for growing space and light.

Plant disease can also be caused by abiotic (environmental) stresses, including heat (figures 14.2A, 14.2B), light (figure 14.2C), and too much or too little water (figures 14.2D, 14.2E). Sometimes, people are pests when they misuse chemicals such as applying too much lime (figure 14.2F) or fertilizer (figure 14.2G).

A useful concept to explain nursery pest problems is the "disease triangle," which illustrates the interrela-tionships among the pest, host, and environment (figure 14.3). All three factors are necessary to cause biotic disease. For example, a fungus or insect pest is able to survive inside the warm greenhouse environment and attack the host plant. Although many diseases may appear to involve only the host plant and the biological pest, environmental factors are always involved. Environmental stress may weaken the plant and predispose it to attack by the pest, or a particular environment may favor pest populations, enabling them to increase to harmful levels.

Abiotic disease can be visualized as a two-way relationship between the host plant and adverse environmental stress (figure 14.3). Abiotic diseases may develop suddenly as the result of a single injurious climatic incident, such as a heat wave or dust storm, or more gradually as a difficult-to-detect growth loss resulting from below-optimum environmental factors, such as a mineral nutrient deficiency.

Figure 14.2—*Abiotic disease can be caused by any excessive environmental stress, including heat injury to germinants (A), or sunscald of mature foliage (B). Exposing shade-loving plants, like these Norfolk Island pine, to full sunlight can damage their ability to photosynthesize (C). Irrigating too much can lead to high humidity and condensation (D), which predisposes plants to many bacterial and fungal pests. Too little irrigation causes wilting (E), which inhibits growth. Overliming of growing media (F), misapplication of pesticides, or improper fertilization (G) can cause chemical injuries. Photos by Thomas D. Landis.*

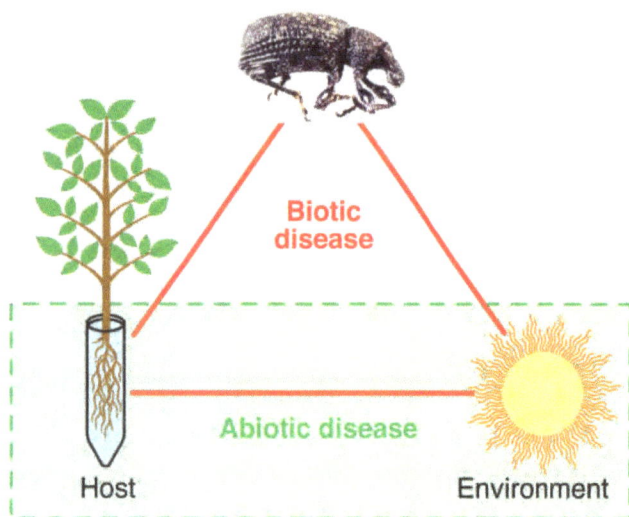

Figure 14.3—*The "disease triangle" illustrates the concept that a host, a pest, and a conducive environment are necessary to cause biotic disease. Abiotic disease occurs when environmental factors, like excessive moisture or heat, injure the host plant. Illustration adapted from Dumroese and others (2008).*

Problem Prevention Through Cultural Measures

Preventing problems is better than having to deal with them after symptoms occur. Prevention steps include maintaining good sanitation and hygiene in the nursery, proper crop scheduling to avoid diseases and health problems in holdover stock, and promoting plant health through good nursery management.

Good Sanitation

The most logical approach to disease management is to prevent diseases by excluding pests from the growing area. All diseases are much easier to prevent than to cure. Sanitation begins with nursery site selection and preparation.

A source of clean water for irrigation is one of the key considerations in site selection. Some water sources harbor damping-off fungi including *Pythium* and *Phytophthora* (Jaenicke 1999) and need to be avoided if possible. (Treating water may be an option; see Chapter 11, Water Quality and Irrigation.) A weed-free fabric groundcover or concrete floor under nursery benches can also be instrumental in preventing problems. In contrast, having bare soil under plants can allow soil pathogens to splash or blow onto nursery plants and can be a favorable environment for weeds. Weeds near or under benches may provide cover for insect pests including thrips, aphids, whiteflies, and weevils. Weeds can also be a source of pathogenic fungi, such as *Fusarium* (James 2012). Excluding seed-eating rodents and birds with screens or other barriers

can prevent these animals from becoming problems and also keeps out any diseases and pests they might bring in on their bodies. Vegetation adjacent to nurseries should be assessed to see how it might positively or negatively affect nursery plant health. For example, a nearby hedge consisting only of mahogany trees infested with the local mahogany shoot borer may increase the likelihood of these pests entering the nursery and affecting a crop of mahogany seedlings. Well-planned adjacent vegetation in hedgerows and windbreaks can provide refuge for beneficial organisms, however, including pollinators and pest predators such as ladybugs, predatory wasps, spiders, amphibians, and birds.

Pests generally enter the nursery growing area through the following modes:

- **Wind**—Airborne fungal spores, seeds, or insects can be introduced on the wind.

- **Water**—Fungus and cryptogam spores and weed seeds can be introduced through irrigation water.

- **Growing Media**—Most growers try to use growing media components that are free from pathogens. However, potentially harmful fungi can sometimes be isolated from some growing media components. When topsoil is used as the growing medium, or as part of a mix, it can carry a variety of insect, fungal, and weed pests to the nursery. See Chapter 6, Growing Media, for more information about the risks associated with using soil as the growing medium.

- **Containers**—Reusable containers may contain residual growing medium or plant roots that harbor potentially pathogenic fungal propagules, moss, or algae.

- **Surfaces in the Growing Area**—Floors, benches, and other surfaces in the growing area may harbor pests.

- **Propagation Materials**—Seeds, transplants, or cuttings are sometimes contaminated before they reach the nursery. Importing plants from other nurseries poses a very high risk of introducing new pests. If the plants have been imported from other islands, this poses a risk not only to the nursery but to the entire island ecosystem as well. Imported nursery stock has been the culprit for introducing several invasive pests and plants into island ecosystems.

- **Transported Pests**—Infested soil or other materials can be carried into the growing area on tools, equipment, or the shoes of workers or visitors.

- **Mobile Pests**—Insects, birds, and rodents can enter the growing area directly.

Checklist for Preventing Diseases and Pests With Good Sanitation

- Start with clean seeds. Seeds can be rinsed with a diluted bleach or hydrogen peroxide solution before stratification or sowing to help prevent seed and seedling diseases (see Chapter 9, Seed Germination and Sowing Options).

- Remove all plant debris from the nursery area before sowing each crop. Also, clean tables, aisles, sidewalls, and floors with a mild bleach or soap solution before sowing.

- Regularly and vigilantly remove all weeds growing under benches and within the crop.

- Use containers that have been cleaned (see Chapter 7, Containers).

- Heat-pasteurize (steam or solarization) any growing media ingredients that may contain pests or diseases. Use soil-free media if possible (see Chapter 6, Growing Media).

- Prevent algae from forming on the floors and benches by ensuring rapid drainage of excess irrigation water and by properly managing irrigation frequency (see Chapter 11, Water Quality and Irrigation). Algae and pools of water provide a breeding ground for fungus gnats and shore flies and the slick surfaces can be a safety hazard to nursery staff.

- Use hooks to keep the hose nozzles off the floor and disinfect planting tools after each use.

- Keep plants off the floor and out of contact with soil if feasible. Elevating plants on benches, with a fabric groundcover or concrete floor underneath, helps to reduce pest problems.

- Test nursery water for problems and treat if necessary.

- Use precaution if importing plant material from other nurseries, especially from other islands. Imported plant materials should be certified pest free. You will ideally use only local, native, or traditional plant materials in your nursery to minimize the risk of spreading insects, diseases, and invasive plants.

Proper Scheduling

Crop scheduling is an important component of holistic pest management. A typical tropical plant nursery will be growing a wide variety of plant sizes and species with different growth rates. For example, in Hawai'i, koa can be grown from seeds to shippable size in as little as 3.5 months, whereas native Hawaiian sandalwood seedlings take 1 year or longer to be large enough to ship. Slow-growing plant species should be started first so they have maximum time to grow. Species that grow very quickly should be scheduled later in the season so that they do not become "top heavy" (figure 14.4A) or rootbound (figure 14.4B). Plants that have grown too large for their containers are easily stressed and

Figure 14.4—Keeping nursery stock at the ideal size for their containers is a challenge with rapidly growing species, such as this Acacia koa, *which quickly become "top heavy" (A). Although it is harder to detect, roots may grow so fast that they become "rootbound" (B) and stressed, which leaves them susceptible to fungal root diseases. Tropical plants cannot be held over for too long without becoming unbalanced, so crop scheduling is critical (C). Photos by Thomas D. Landis.*

can harbor insects and other pests that can infect the rest of the crop. One of the most common problems in tropical nurseries is that most plants never stop growing and so it is challenging to keep crops from becoming too large for their containers (figure 14.4C). See Chapter 4, Crop Planning: Propagation Protocols, Schedules, and Records, for more information on crop scheduling.

If you are growing a new species and are unsure of the growth rate, contact other nurseries, and check the propagation protocols in the Native Plant Network (http://www.nativeplantnetwork.org).

Managing the Nursery Environment

An important aspect of preventing disease is to maintain environmental conditions (such as moisture, light, and ventilation) that are conducive for plant growth but that do not favor pests or have damaging environmental extremes. For example, root diseases are common in all types of nurseries worldwide, and are often brought on by environmental stresses. Swedish researchers studied the fungal pathogen *Cylindrocarpon destructans* in relation to root rot problems of pine seedlings in container nurseries. Suspected predisposing stress factors included excessive moisture, low light, and exposure to fungicides. They found that *C. destructans* typically invades dead or dying roots and then uses these sites as a base for invasion into healthy roots (Unestam and others 1989). Opportunistic pathogens, such as Fusarium, are more likely to cause disease when plants are under environmental stress (figure 14.5).

Marginal environmental conditions often favor insect pests. For example, fungus gnats become a problem only under wet conditions and especially in locations where algae, moss, and liverworts have been allowed to develop. Often, these conditions exist under nursery benches, where water can puddle and excess fertilizer promotes their growth. This

---

Water Can Be Harmful to Plant Health

Too much water on plants (figure 14.2D) encourages damping-off, root disease, fungus gnats, moss and liverwort growth, excessive leaching of mineral nutrients, potential groundwater contamination, and foliar diseases such as Botrytis blight (figure 14.1D), powdery mildew, and Rhizoctonia. Over-irrigation may cause plants to grow rapidly and spindly making them more susceptible to environmental stresses such as excessive heat, wind, or cold. Too little water on plants may cause damage to root systems through salt accumulation or desiccation, allowing entry points for root disease pests. Plants under severe moisture stress have lower resistance to pests and stresses associated with heat, humidity, and wind.

Proper irrigation management is one of the best ways to limit pest problems.

---

problem is particularly common where nursery floors are covered by a weed barrier or gravel. Switching to concrete floors can often cure a fungus gnat problem because concrete dries faster and is easier to keep clean.

Checklist for Preventing Diseases and Pests by Managing the Nursery Environment

- During sowing and the establishment phase of the crop, keep humidity levels and condensation problems low by venting the nursery area well. Do not overwater germinating seeds and seedlings. During the active growth stage, reduce humidity within the leaf canopy to prevent the development of many foliar diseases. Reducing humidity can be accomplished by improving air circulation by increasing distance between plants, increasing the frequency of ventilation, and pruning shoots as necessary.

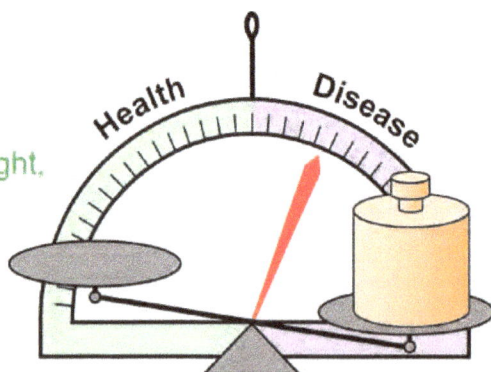

Good Management
Proper nutrition, sunlight, and water; good sanitation practices; appropriate growing media and container sizes

Stresses
Excessive or insufficient nutrition, sunlight, and water; poor sanitation practices; inappropriate growing media or container sizes

Figure 14.5—Many nursery diseases are caused by stresses, which predispose plants to attack by opportunistic pests. Illustration adapted from Dumroese and others (2008).

- Water only in the morning, never later in the day. Favorable environmental conditions for several fungal diseases include a film of moisture for 8 to 12 hours, high relative humidity, and warm temperatures. By watering early, rising daytime temperatures will cause water to evaporate from the leaf surfaces and reduce favorable conditions. (As an exception, Botrytis problems often occur when conditions are humid but temperatures are cool [James 2012].)

- To optimize healthy environmental conditions for different crops, use separate propagation structures for growing plants with different environmental and cultural requirements, or, if you have a single growing area, group plants with similar growing requirements together and take advantage of microenvironments within the nursery area. For example, north of the equator, the south side of the nursery is usually warmer and drier than the north or east section of the nursery. Plants requiring drier conditions will benefit from being grouped on the south and west sides of the nursery. Plants requiring cooler temperatures (such as high-elevation species) or those requiring more frequent irrigation can be grouped together on the north and east sides.

- Improve air circulation and reduce humidity and condensation with spacing between plants, using fans, and orienting to prevailing breezes to produce horizontal airflow.

Promotion of Plant Health

Healthy plants are more able to resist infection from pathogenic fungi and attack from insects and other pests and can also tolerate environmental stresses better. Much of this resistance can be attributed to physical characteristics such as a thick, waxy cuticle on the foliage, balanced shoot and root, and optimum mineral nutrient contents. Some healthy plants also produce chemicals such as tannins, which deter pests. Management of the nursery environment to ensure plants receive proper sunlight and water as described previously, as well as the steps of good sanitation and proper scheduling, is important for plant health. Appropriate nutrition, growing medium, and container size and type; use of beneficial microorganisms and other practices described in this manual are important for promoting plant health on all levels.

Plants must have a proper growing medium to be healthy. Good growing media provides physical support and aeration to the roots, and holds water and nutrients for the plant, as described in Chapter 6, Growing Media. Appropriate container selection is described in Chapter

7, Containers. Different species will require different containers types and sizes based on their growth characteristics and target specifications. Fertilization at the appropriate level to help plants grow in a healthy and balanced way is discussed in Chapter 12, Plant Nutrition and Fertilization. Excessive fertilization can make plants more susceptible to problems, including sucking insects and diseases. Consider eliminating nitrogen fertilization during germination because it encourages damping-off fungi (James 2012).

If plants do become sick or unhealthy, it is rarely, if ever, practical to try and "save" them. Remove dead and dying plants; dispose of them away from the nursery to prevent reinfection. Remove any plant debris in the containers or on the floor on a regular basis.

Problem Detection and Diagnosis

Even with good sanitation, crop planning, plant health, and management of the nursery environment, problems may appear. A holistic approach emphasizes detecting problems early through regular monitoring and recordkeeping so they can be addressed quickly and with minimal cost and effort. If a problem is detected, the time is taken to diagnose it accurately and determine its true source. With an accurate diagnosis, the problem can then be treated accordingly.

Monitoring and Recordkeeping

Regular monitoring or "scouting" is a critical part of the holistic approach. A daily walk-through of the nursery will reveal developing pest outbreaks or environmental problems that are conducive to pests while problems are still minor and easily corrected. In small nurseries, the grower or nursery manager should do the inspections, but, in larger facilities, one person should be designated as the pest scout. This person should have nursery experience and be familiar with all the plant species at all growth stages. It is essential to know what a healthy plant looks like before you can notice any problem. It is also essential to know what beneficial organisms look like (such as natural enemies of pests, mycorrhizal fungi growing on the roots, and so on). The person should also be inquisitive and have good observation skills. Often, irrigators serve as pest scouts because they are regularly in the nursery, checking whether plants need watering.

Crop monitors (figures 14.6A, 14.6B) need to carefully inspect each species being grown, record the environmental conditions in the growing area, and make other observations. It is important to establish a monitoring and recordkeeping system for all areas of the nursery, including any structures, rooting chambers, and outdoor

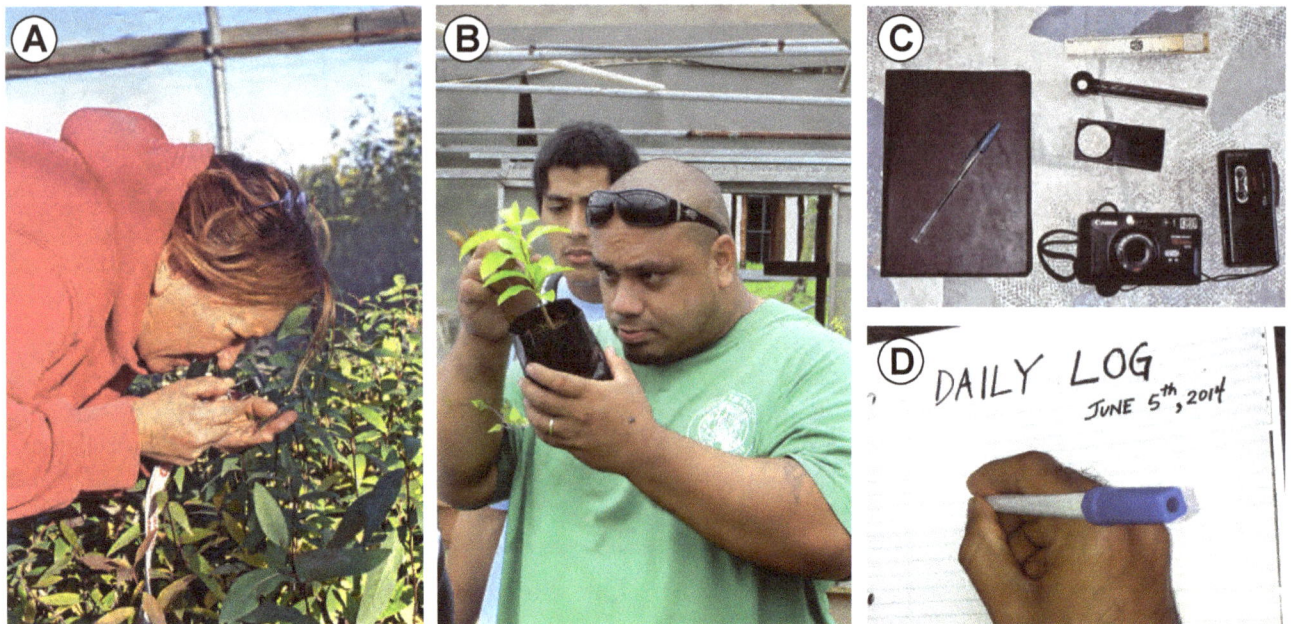

Figure 14.6—Regular pest monitoring or "scouting" is critical to identifying problems early (A). Pest scouts inspect the seedlings and the nursery environment (B). Pest scouts should carry a hand lens, notebook or recording device, and camera to identify and document problems (C). All potential problems need to be noted in the daily log (D) and reported to the nursery manager. Photo A by Tara Luna, photo B by Diane L. Haase, photo C by Thomas D. Landis, and photo D by Kim M. Wilkinson.

growing areas. These records are invaluable for avoiding future pest problems when planning the next crop. In addition to looking at crop plants, pest scouts should check all nursery equipment and should carry a 10X to 20X hand lens for close examination and a notebook or voice recorder to record observations. When a problem is noted, a camera with a closeup lens is an excellent way to document the problem (figure 14.6C). All observations should be recorded in a daily log (figure 14.6D), and any suspicious problems need to be immediately reported to the nursery manager. Inspections need to occur on a daily basis after sowing the crop and during the establishment phase, when plants are most susceptible to diseases such as damping-off. When problems are detected early, plants can be treated or isolated from the rest of the nursery or greenhouse crop.

Use yellow sticky cards (figure 14.7) to detect white flies, aphids, fungus gnats, and shore flies. Place one to four cards every 1,000 ft^2 (90 m^2) and space them evenly in a grid pattern, with extra cards placed near vents and doorways. Inspect these cards weekly to detect and monitor these pests. Record the information and replace the cards as needed. Use blue sticky cards, which are more attractive to thrips, around plants susceptible to this pest. Observing and recording pest predators can also be valuable: insect-eating birds, amphibians, spiders, predatory wasps, and other creatures that may be residing in or near the nursery.

Accurate Problem Identification

Nursery managers and pest scouts must be able to identify problems quickly and accurately before the problems can cause significant damage. Although biological pests such as fungi and insects are always present, abiotic stresses typically cause more problems. Disease diagnosis requires a certain degree of experience and training, and nursery workers need to be trained to quickly spot

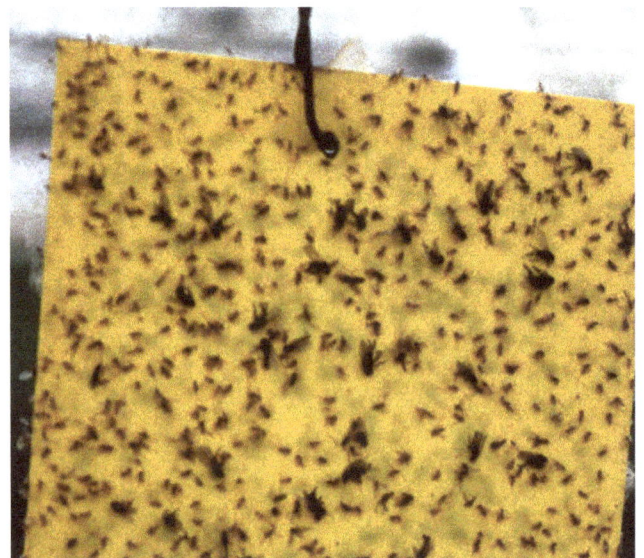

Figure 14.7—Yellow sticky cards are essential for monitoring the types and population levels of insects pests. Photo by Thomas D. Landis.

new problems and incidents of abiotic injury. Workers who are in the growing area daily have the best chance of detecting potential problems so they can be accurately identified and treated before they can intensify or spread.

A general characteristic of abiotic diseases is that the symptoms tend to show up very quickly (see textbox example). Problems caused by biotic agents generally take longer to develop, with decline occurring over time (James 2012). If abiotic damage has been eliminated as the cause of the problem, then a pest or disease must be diagnosed. Landis and others (1990) features identification keys (figure 14.8), and color photographs of many diseases, insect pests, and horticultural problems of conifer crops, but no single reference is available about diseases and pests of tropical plant species. Although pest scouts can make a tentative diagnosis of disease and pest problems, they need to confirm their conclusions with the nursery manager and a trained nursery pest specialist. Plants with undiagnosed symptoms may be sent whole to the nearby extension office or land-grant university for diagnosis and suggested followup.

Many diseases and insect pests damage a wide variety of host plants. For example, damping-off fungi (figure 14.1A) affect all species during germination and emergence and Phytophthora root rot (figure 14.1B) can infect larger plants. Other pests are host specific, however, and pest scouts must understand their basic biology and life cycle for accurate diagnosis. In tropical nurseries, it is very important for nursery growers to be aware of newly introduced diseases and the range of species that are affected by them. For example, 'ōhi'a rust is caused by a fungus (*Puccinia psidii*), which also infects guava, eucalyptus, and a range of native species in the Myrtle family. In Hawai'i, it has been found on introduced timber and ornamental species and native and endangered species of nīoi. It affects leaves and meristems, inhibiting growth and development and is especially severe on seedlings, cuttings, and saplings. The first symptoms are chlorotic specks, which after a few days become pustules containing uredia producing yellow masses of spores (figure 14.1C). Pustules can coalesce and parts of the plant can be completely covered with them. After about 2 to 3 weeks, pustules dry and become necrotic. The disease can cause deformation of leaves, heavy defoliation, dieback, stunted growth and eventual death. On fruits of guava, and other hosts in the Myrtle family, the lesions occur mostly on buds and young fruits that eventually rot as the rust matures. Understanding the life cycle of the pest is essential for accurate diagnosis and management. Some of the more common tropical plant pests and ways to monitor, diagnose, prevent, and, if necessary, treat them, are included in table 14.1.

Abiotic Factors as "The Usual Suspects"

I was growing a new crop of a mahogany species. The plants were fairly young with only four to six leaves each. They were growing slower than past crops, and some of the oldest leaves had brown leaf margins that I attributed to uneven watering. Otherwise the seedlings seemed fine. Because they were growing slowly, I thought I would help them along by applying a fertilizer. But a day or two after that, the seedlings were all wilting and the brown leaf margins were spreading into the leaves. With the leaf margin burning and the plants wilting and dying, I suspected root rot. I immediately sent some affected plants to the local land grant university extension service, with an urgent message. While I waited for the reply, I researched options for treating root rot, most of which involved safety gear and unattractive pesticides. The extension agent contacted me sooner than I had hoped, saying he had not completed his diagnosis but so far had detected dangerously high levels of salts in the growing medium; the plants were exhibiting signs of salt toxicity. As we talked, I remembered that I had used a batch of untested coir as one of my growing medium components for this crop. I had heard that coir can sometimes contain high levels of salts because of processing, but I had not taken the time to test this batch before planting. The seedlings had been struggling along in somewhat salty conditions (which explained the slower growth and burned leaf margins) and my fertilizer application added even more salts, pushing them over the edge into salt toxicity. With that, they could not take in enough water with their roots because of salts in the medium, and the chloride they were taking up was scorching their leaves. The extension agent suggested I flush out the salts from the growing medium. As soon as I got off the phone, I drenched the seedlings with clean water until water dripped out the bottom of the containers, and repeated again a few hours later. Almost overnight, the seedlings perked up. Some of the smallest had died and were a loss, but the remaining trees quickly grew new leaves and within a few weeks were in full health. I learned from this scare that abiotic factors need to be the first suspects when diagnosing plant problems. A quick check from an EC meter would have revealed the problem inexpensively in only a few minutes. I also learned that taking the time to ensure the basics, such as growing medium quality, are okay can save a lot of stress—for me and for the plants. — Kim Wilkinson

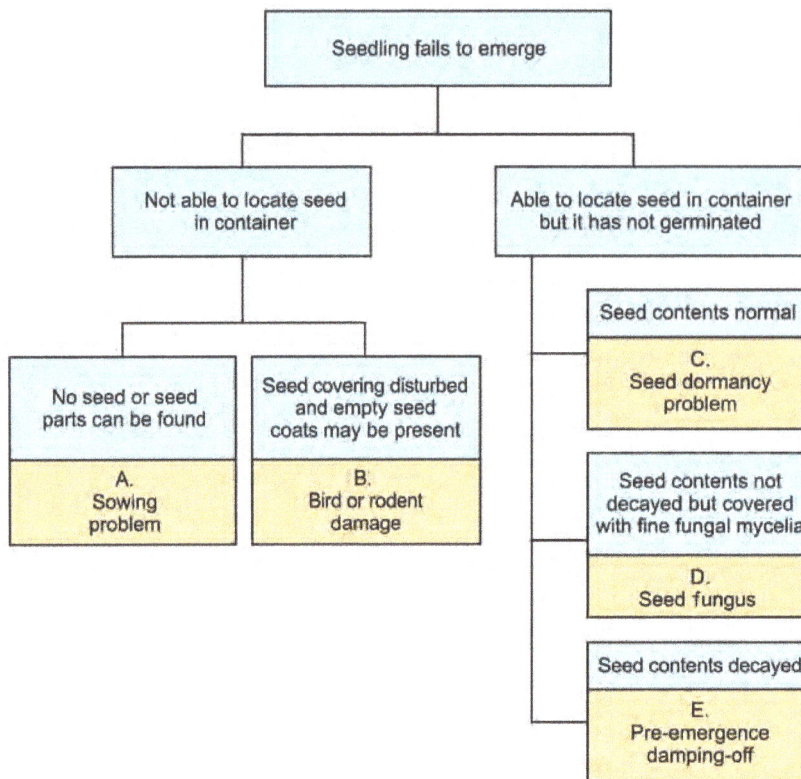

Figure 14.8—Pest identification keys are very useful in helping make the correct diagnosis of nursery pests. Illustration from Dumroese and others (2008).

Check with local regulations before ordering and introducing biological control organisms.

Problem Management

After a problem is accurately diagnosed, it must be evaluated to determine what, if any, management action is necessary. The first line of defense is always to assess and, if possible, improve pest prevention practices including good sanitation, physically excluding pests, proper crop scheduling, and promotion of optimal plant health through appropriate fertilization, irrigation, ventilation, and other care. If the problem persists, the holistic approach calls for assessing the effects of the pest or disease. In some cases, simply doing nothing may be the most cost-effective solution; plants can tolerate some damage and nature can be allowed to take its course (Mizell and Short 2009).

If action is taken, the goal is usually to reduce crop losses to acceptable levels, rather than to eradicate pests. A spectrum of management options is available, with treatments including—

- Modifying and managing the nursery environment.
- Culling affected seedlings.
- Mechanically removing pests (picking off, swatting, trapping—ensure staff are trained to know the difference between beneficial pest predators and actual pests).
- Using biological controls such as beneficial microorganisms and pest predators, diseases, or parasites (table 14.1).
- Using the least toxic pesticides available as a last resort to lower pest populations to a tolerable level (Wescom 1999).

Timely and Appropriate Pest Suppression Measures

Synthetic or natural pesticides should be considered only as a last resort after other environmental and horticultural control measures have been considered. Practicing good hygiene and sanitation, including using pathogen-free seeds, growing media, and containers, is critical. You can often reduce or even eliminate the use of pesticides by physically excluding pests with screens or barriers that can keep out pests large and small, from insects to rats to pigs (figure 14.9). If seedlings are affected by fungi, you can reduce the seedling's susceptibility by spacing out the plants and increasing air movement through the nursery area, and by watering appropriately and lowering the humidity around the plants (Wescom 1999).

Table 14.1—*Common pests of tropical plants and their symptoms, prevention, and treatment. Although a variety of pesticides are available for these diseases, only biological and organic control options are provided. Ideally, nursery staff will monitor daily for signs of these diseases.*

Type of pest	Signs and symptoms	Monitoring	Prevention	Biological control options
Fungi				
Botrytis blight (*Botrytis cinerea*)	Plants have leaf blights, stem cankers, gray mold. Mold is most noticeable on older foliage. Affected seedlings are usually in groups.	Concentrate monitoring where crop is closely spaced and air circulation is poor and at the base of plants. Look for dieback, stem cankers, and powdery gray mold on foliage.	Increase spacing between containers as crops grows larger. Water only in the morning or use subirrigation. Keep humidity low by increasing air flow. Surface sterilize greenhouse floors, walls, and benches between seedling crops.	Apply products containing *Trichoderma harzianum* or *Streptomyces griseoviridis* to foliage. When discovered, remove symptomatic seedlings from growing area.
Fusarium wilt (Example: *Fusarium oxysporum*)	Leaves cup downward or stems bend in a crook. In later stages, brown or red streaks can be seen on the leaves. Orange spores (sporodochia) may be on stem.	Look for downward bending leaves or "cupping" of leaf margins. Can be confused with water stress or root rot. Send sample to laboratory to confirm.	Use mesh benches to encourage airflow. Do not overwater crop. Keep humidity low. Sterilize reused containers between seedling crops. Use pathogen-free seeds and growing media.	Apply products containing *Trichoderma harzianum* or *Streptomyces griseoviridis* as a soil drench. Remove and isolate infected plants as soon as problem is detected.
Crown rots (Example: *Fusarium* species)	Plants are stunted, wilted, and off-color. Roots are discolored and turn brown or black. Main stem becomes weak and water soaked in appearance. Some affected seedlings may have orange-yellow spore structures [sporodochia] on main stem just above the ground line.	Monitor weekly for wilted, off-colored plants with discolored root systems. Pay attention to media that stays wet. Affected seedlings are usually concentrated in groups. Send samples to diagnostic laboratory to confirm pathogen identity.	Do not overwater crop. Increase spacing between containers as crop grows larger. Keep humidity low.	Apply products containing *Trichoderma harzianum*, *Trichoderma virens*, or *Streptomyces griseoviridis* as a drench. When discovered, remove symptomatic seedlings from growing area.
Root rots (Examples: species of *Fusarium*, *Pythium*, *Rhizoctonia*, *Phytophthora*, and *Cylindrocarpon*)	Seedlings are stunted, wilted, chlorotic, or necrotic and often occur in groups. Roots are discolored (dark brown or black) and decayed (epidermal tissues may be easily sloughed off). Main stems become weakened and water soaked. Some affected seedlings may have orange-yellow spore structures [sporodochia] on the main stem just above the ground line.	Monitor weekly for wilted, chlorotic, and necrotic seedlings with discolored and decayed roots. Problems can be especially severe in containers with prolonged wet growing media (poorly drained). Affected seedlings are usually concentrated in groups. Send samples to diagnostic laboratory to confirm pathogen identity.	Do not overwater crop. Increase spacing between containers as the crop grows larger. Keep humidity low. Sterilize re-used containers between seedling crops. Use pathogen-free seeds and growing media.	Apply *Trichoderma harzianum*, *Trichoderma virens*, or *Streptomyces griseoviridis* as a drench.
Damping-off (Examples: species of *Fusarium* and *Pythium*)	Seeds do not germinate or seedlings collapse at soil line just after emergence. Dark decayed spots appear on stems at soil line of emerged seedlings. Surviving plants may later develop crown or root rot.	Monitor new sowing daily during germination and establishment phases. Excavate seeds and cut to check for decay and discard infected containers immediately.	Cleanse seeds and growing area. Use sterile media and containers. Avoid over-sowing, crowding of seedlings, or planting seeds too deeply. Keep greenhouse and media temperatures warm during germination and establishment. Keep humidity low. Do not fertilize with nitrogen during seedling establishment phase.	Treat seed with running-water rinses for a minimum of 48 hours prior to sowing, or surface sterilize with bleach or hydrogen peroxide solutions (1:10). Apply products containing *Trichoderma harzianum* or *Trichoderma virens* as a drench at time of sowing.
Powdery mildew (Examples: species of *Blumeria*, *Podosphaera*, *Microsphaera*, and *Erysiphe*)	Plants may have white powdery fungal growth on upper or lower leaf surfaces. If severe, a white coating can be seen on foliage.	Monitor weekly. Inspect susceptible species. Look in areas near vents and greenhouse entrances or any location with a sharp change between day and night temperatures. Use a hand lens to see white, powdery threads and spores.	Place susceptible species where drastic changes in temperatures do not occur. Water only in the morning or use subirrigation. Keep humidity low. Increase spacing between containers as crop grows larger.	Remove infected leaves as soon as detected. Move infected plants to structure with more constant temperatures. Treat with Neem oil or horticultural oil. Try test tray first. Can also use sulfur powder as an organic preventative fungicide. Some plants are sensitive to sulfur injury so use lowest rate recommended. Do not apply within 2 weeks of an oil spray treatment.

Table 14.1—Continued

Type of pest	Signs and symptoms	Monitoring	Prevention	Biological control options
Rhizoctonia web blight (Example: *Rhizoctonia solani*)	Stems and leaves may collapse and turn to mush with fine, web-like fungal strands on the plant tissue and at soil line.	Monitor leafy herbaceous plants, especially where they are closely spaced. Look for cobweb-like growth that mats leaves. Send samples to diagnostic laboratory to confirm pathogen identity.	Sterilize containers between seedling crops. Use mesh benches to encourage airflow. Place susceptible crops near vents and fans. Increase spacing between containers as crop grows larger. Keep humidity low.	Apply products containing *Trichoderma harzianum* as a preventative.
Fungal rusts (Examples: species of *Gymnosporangium*, *Cronartium*, *Peridermium*, and *Melampsora*)	Rust brown spots or stripes may be seen on lower and upper leaf surface.	Monitor regularly and be sure to check undersides of foliage.	Group susceptible species where temperature and humidity can be easily controlled. Increase spacing between containers as the crop grows larger. Keep humidity low. May have to eliminate rust-alternate hosts if present in the vicinity of the nursery.	Isolate plants immediately.
Fungal leaf spots (Examples: species of *Alternaria*, *Septoria*, *Botryosphaeria*, *Taphrina*, *Rhytisma*, and *Phyllosticta*)	Alternaria leaf spots are usually brown or black with a yellow border. Septoria leaf spots are small gray to brown with a dark brown edge.	Monitor weekly for leaf spots. With a hand lens, look for small fungal fruiting bodies. Send samples to diagnostic laboratory to confirm pathogen identity.	Use mesh benches to encourage airflow. Keep nursery floor clean and free of pooled water. Water only in the morning or use subirrigation. Do not overwater crop. Keep humidity low. Increase spacing between containers as crop grows larger.	Periodically remove affected seedlings from growing areas. Apply products containing *Trichoderma harzianum* as a preventative. Remove infected leaves as soon as problem is detected. Isolate infected trays of plants from the rest of the crop.
Insects				
Sucking insects (Example: Aphids)	Plants have distorted new growth, sticky honeydew, and/or sooty mold.	Monitor twice weekly. Look on underside of leaves and on tips of new stems.	Don't overfertilize. Shoot prune vigorous tender growth as needed. Watch for outbreaks.	Use aphid midges, aphid parasites, or lady bugs. Apply insecticidal soap every 6 days. Pyrethrin-based products can also be effective as a contact insecticide.
Fungus gnats (Example: *Bradysia* species)	Seeds that do not germinate or plants with weak or stunted growth and root damage.	Monitor every other day, especially during germination and establishment phases. Look for tiny winged flies near growing media surface. Use yellow sticky cards to detect adults.	Keep nursery floor clean and free of pooled water and algae. Do not overwater crop. Use a good seed mulch.	Use yellow sticky cards to reduce adult population levels. Apply products containing *Bacillus thuringiensis* ssp. *israeliensis* every 7 days as a drench. Formulations of entomopathogenic or insecticidal nematodes in the genera *Steinemema* and *Heterorhabditis* are also effective.
Mealybugs	Plants may have white cottony residue. Sticky honeydew on leaves and sooty mold may develop.	Look for small, oval, soft-bodied insects covered with a white, wax-like layer on the underside of leaves.	Keep nursery environment clean. Increase spacing among plants. Practice good sanitation. Keep temperatures cool. Remove infected plants.	Apply *Cryptolaemus montrouzieri*. Use predatory beetles or parasitic wasps; pyrethrin insecticides are effective but must contact the pests. Spray with insecticidal soap or oil, or swab bugs with rubbing alcohol (limit alcohol contact with foliage).
Soft scales	Honeydew and sooty mold develop if scales are present.	Look for yellow brown to dark brown scale insects along veins and stems.	Provide plants with good growing conditions and proper care, especially irrigation, so they are more resistant to scale damage.	Use parasitic wasps, insecticidal soap, or pyrethrins. Prune infested branches or cull entire plant.
Spider mites	Plants may have light-yellow flecking of leaves, discolored foliage. Leaf drop and webbing occur during outbreaks and severe infestation.	Look on undersides of leaves, especially along veins. Use a hand lens to look for webbing, egg clusters, and red adult mites. Look in areas of that are hot and dry, near the heaters and vents.	Lower nursery temperatures and raise humidity levels, especially in the south and west edges of the nursery and near vents and furnaces.	Use predatory mites or predatory midges. Apply insecticidal soap every 6 days.

Table 14.1—Continued

Type of pest	Signs and symptoms	Monitoring	Prevention	Biological control options
Thrips	Plants may have distortion of new leaves, buds, and shoot tips. White scars on expanded leaves.	Use blue or yellow sticky cards placed just above canopy foliage for detection.	Increase container spacing on leafy crops as needed to detect problems early.	Use predatory mites, pirate bugs, lacewings, insecticidal soap, and pyrethrins.
White flies	Plants may have distorted new shoot and leaf growth.	Use yellow sticky cards to detect adults. Look for adults on the uppermost tender leaves. Immature larvae are found on the underside of leaves.	Inspect new plants coming into the greenhouse and reject infested plants. Create a "host-free" period in the growing area for 2 weeks to starve the flies. Practice good weed control in and around the nursery.	Use predatory beetles or whitefly parasites. Apply insecticidal soap every 7 days. Pyrethrin-based products can also be effective as a contact insecticide.
Stem or twig borers (Example: species of mahogany shoot borer, twig borers [*Xylosandrus compactus* and *Xyloborus* species])	Affected seedlings usually have main stem cankers that may cause stem breakage at point of insect activity. Cankered tissues are usually black and insect frass may be present.	Look for main stem cankers often associated with blackened tissues and frass from insect activity. Damage can be randomly spread throughout seedling growing areas.	Don't allow infested stands of tree hosts near nursery area. Avoid holding susceptible seedlings past readiness date.	Remove damaged seedlings when they are found.
Caterpillars	Foliage with chewing damage; moths may be visible around plants.	Inspect plants regularly. Look for fecal droppings, bites taken out of leaves, and webbing (tent caterpillars). Check in evening or at night; some species hide during day.	Install screens around greenhouse to keep moths out.	Apply products with *Bacillus thuringiensis* ssp. *kurstaki*, as needed. Pyrethrin-based products can also be effective as a contact insecticide.
Other biotic pests				
Bacterial diseases (Examples: species of *Pseudomonas*, *Xanthomonas*, and *Agrobacterium*)	Plants are stunted with swollen or misshapen leaves. Look for water-soaked leaf spots or angular lesions on the stems. May have gall-like growths on main stem at or just below the ground line.	Inspect new plants coming into nursery. Look for water-soaked, dark brown to black leaf spots on leaves and wilted stem tips. Confirm diagnosis with a laboratory.	Increase spacing between containers as crop grows larger. Water only in the morning or use subirrigation. Keep humidity low.	Remove infected leaves as soon as problem is detected. Isolate infected trays of plants from the rest of the crop.
Nematodes (Examples: species of *Xiphinema*, *Meloidogyne*, *Pratylenchus*, and *Radopholus similes*)	Affected seedlings will be stunted, with chlorotic or necrotic foliage; roots will be damaged with evidence of feeding [lesions] or galls.	Look for chlorotic and necrotic seedlings, often concentrated within groups. Roots will appear damaged or have galls.	Use soil-free media. Keep plants at least 3 feet off the ground on benches, with a groundcover or concrete floor underneath.	Prevent soil from entering nursery. Formulations of entomopathogenic or insecticidal nematodes in the genera *Steinemema* and *Heterorhabditis* are available as biological control agents.
Slugs	Plants may have chewed holes on leaves with smooth edges and slime that dries into silvery trails on foliage.	Look for chewed holes on leaves and trails of slime. Slugs hide under dense foliage and under containers and benches.	Keep plants on raised benches or pallets. Space containers as needed so that slugs can be detected easily.	Pick slugs off plants. Keep containers on benches. Use saucers filled with beer to attract slugs away from plants. Put down a piece of plywood or wet cardboard at night; slugs will gather underneath. Ducks will eats slugs.
Viruses	Look for mosaic patterns on foliage, leaf crinkle or distortion, streaking, chlorotic spots, and distinct yellowing of veins and stunted plants.	Monitor weekly. Inspect all incoming plants. Send samples to laboratory to confirm.	Usually not a problem with native plants; can be a problem on cultivated varieties, ornamentals, plants grown by tissue culture.	None. Remove and discard all infected plants immediately. Thoroughly clean area of nursery where infected plants were growing.

Figure 14.9—*Large-seeded species can be especially vulnerable to pests such as mice and birds after they are sown in containers. Measures such as caging newly seeded containers and young seedlings (A) or adding mesh or screen walls (B) can be used to exclude a variety of pests from insects to mammals. Photo A by Tara Luna, and photo B by Thomas D. Landis.*

In contrast, using a pesticide even once can put you on a treadmill of escalating use and collateral damage that can be difficult to escape. For example, if you have a rat problem, you can easily and cheaply poison the rats with a rat poison (rodenticide). The rats that ingest this poison will die over the next few days. The poison, however, may move through the food web to natural enemies of rats, including wild raptors and owls, and to domestic or feral cats and dogs. The few rats that survive the poisoning can reproduce much more quickly than their slower reproducing natural predators can. In other words, a time lag will occur between when the rat population recovers and when their predator populations recover. During this time lag, another infestation of rats can emerge, with numbers now unchecked by scarcer, slower recovering predator populations. A reinfestation may compel you to poison the rats again, setting the struggling predator population back even further, if not eliminating them locally. This cycle could be avoided by considering alternate measures, such as finding ways to prevent the rats from entering the nursery area in the first place. If full exclusion is not feasible, trapping the rats and killing them yourself can bring their population down to a tolerable level without poison, or you can adopt a skillful cat or two to do the rat-trapping and killing for you. These options are more labor-intensive in the short term, but can pay dividends in the long term by keeping natural checks and balances healthy. This example uses large animals such as rats, owls, and cats to illustrate a concept, but the same population dynamics apply with many insects. For example, aphids multiply more rapidly than the ladybug predators that can help keep aphid populations in check, as long as the ladybugs are not indirectly poisoned by the nursery manager's attempts to control the aphids (Hemenway 2009).

Most tropical plants can be grown without fungicides and insecticides. Because the nursery environment is so favorable for many pests, however, chemicals are sometimes used. If choosing to use chemicals, the important thing is to choose a pesticide that is least toxic, safest to use, targeted for the specific pest, short-lived in the environment, and will not contaminate the environment or reduce populations of pest predators (Mizell and Short 2009). The chemical must be registered for the pest and crop plant being treated and used as the label directs.

Many people believe that any natural or organic pesticide is always safe to use, but a number of registered botanical insecticides can be toxic to applicators or the environment. The relative toxicity rating for any chemical is known as the LD_{50}, which indicates the lethal dose that is required to kill 50 percent of a population of test animals. As can be seen in table 14.2, insecticides from natural sources can be as hazardous as chemical pesticides.

Still, if considering pesticides, we recommend that you always consider natural pesticides first because they tend to degrade faster than synthetic pesticides, which reduces their effect on nontarget organisms. Most natural pesticides are more likely to meet the holistic criteria of lower toxicity, pest-specific, short-lived, and least collateral damage compared with synthetic pesticides. The drawbacks of natural pesticides are that they must be applied more frequently because of their rapid degradation, commercial ones are often more expensive and may be more difficult to obtain, homemade ones may vary in efficacy and safety, and little data exist on their effectiveness and long-term toxicity.

Table 14.2—*Comparative safety of common botanical and synthetic insecticides. Adapted from Cloyd (2004).*

Insecticide	Class	Toxicity rating (oral LD$_{50}$ in mg/kg)	Label warning (danger is most toxic and caution is the least)
Nicotine	Botanical	50 to 60	Danger
Sevin	Synthetic	850	Warning or caution
Malathion	Synthetic	885 to 2,800	Caution
Pyrethrin	Botanical	1,200 to 1,500	Caution
Neem	Botanical	13,000	Caution

LD$_{50}$ = lethal dose to 50% of subjects.

Balancing Pest Populations With Beneficial Organisms and Pest Predators

Holistic management involves using beneficial fungi, insects, and other organisms to help prevent pest effects on crop plants (table 14.1). When these methods are used, it is important to maintain a healthy biological balance in the nursery.

Microsymbionts

As described in Chapter 13, Beneficial Microorganisms, microsymbionts such as mycorrhizal fungi, rhizobia, and *Frankia* have many benefits to the host plant, including protection against root pathogens. For example, rhizobia bacteria in nitrogen-fixing plants can help reduce or eliminate nitrogen fertilizer use for those crops, reducing risks of attracting sucking insects with overfertilized succulent foliage. A study of tropical hardwood nurseries in Haiti reported that "trees inoculated with the proper microsymbiont are more vigorous and have far fewer diseases or nutrient deficiency problems" (Josiah and Allen-Reid 1991: 56). Inoculants included manufactured rhizobia for nitrogen-fixing legumes, crude *Frankia* inoculants made from nodules for ironwood (*Casuarina* species), and locally gathered ectomycorrhizae for pines (Josiah and Allen-Reid 1991).

Biological Disease Control

Biological disease control uses beneficial or benign organisms to help protect nursery plants from diseases. Biological controls must also be registered for the crop, pathogen, and location where they will be used. Biologicals are generally designed for a particular plant patho-

system and may not have efficacy for others, although these products are sometimes advertised or applied as broad-spectrum use (James 2012). For example, biological fungicides are made of beneficial or nonharmful organisms applied to the growing medium to protect roots from certain pathogens (Francis 2009). Different types of biological fungicides have different ingredients and modes of action, some preventing pathogen infestations in crops by competing with or excluding pathogens, and others by producing antagonist, antifungal, or antibiotic substances to inhibit pathogens. Some of these products are certified for organic production, while others are patented, hybrid organisms with specific modes of action. Growers in tropical areas may wish to explore the concept of biological disease controls and see if locally appropriate, naturally occurring options for disease control are feasible to make or purchase. Introduction of new microorganisms is usually not appropriate or legal for island ecosystems. Also, effects on pathogens are generally much more subtle than chemical pesticides. A few examples of biological fungicides are included in table 14.1.

Ecosystem Balance

Only a few species of insects, bacteria, and fungi are harmful to plants. Most are harmless or beneficial, acting as pollinators, nutrient recyclers, food for birds and mammals, and pest predators (figure 14.10). The use of broad-spectrum chemical pesticides can be deadly to many harmless and beneficial organisms and to some of the wildlife that eat them. Furthermore, widespread herbicide use has enabled people to annihilate supposedly "useless" vegetation in hedges, gulches, edges, and fallow areas—destroying much of the food and shelter needed for diverse life forms. With the loss of ecological balance caused by these indiscriminant practices (Hemenway 2009), crop losses have been increasing. Reversing the loss of biodiversity and ecological balance on a local level is beneficial for nurseries and for the environment.

Practicing holistic pest management avoids harming beneficials with indiscriminant pesticide use. It is important that everyone who works in the nursery recognizes and protects benign and beneficial critters. Uninformed people may see a harmless spider and react by squishing it unless they understand how that spider might be helpful. Insect pest predators can include spiders, beetles, lacewings, wasps, Syrphid flies, pirate bugs, snakes, birds, toads, lizards, and more (Josiah and Allen-Reid 1991). In addition, parasitic insects exist, such as parasitic wasps and tachinid flies, that kill pests by laying eggs inside them (Hemenway 2009).

Figure 14.10—Sometimes called "the gardener's best friend," anoles (Anolis species) eat many pest insects including moths, locusts, and cockroaches. Photo by Brian F. Daley.

Nurseries may also protect and create habitat for beneficials and foster biodiversity, from soil organisms to insects, birds and, where appropriate, larger mammals. These "refuges" can include a simple patch of native flowers planted around the nursery's entrance sign, a border planting at the edge of the groundcover, a fallow area, windbreaks, hedgerows, or dedicated reforestation areas. For example, windbreaks have been found to harbor beneficial insects and birds that help to balance out populations of crop pests, reducing needs for pesticides (Stace 1995). Windbreaks on farmlands have been shown to harbor not only native wildlife, but also to foster native tree seedlings and ecosystem regeneration processes within the windbreak (Harvey 1999).

A key to planning refuge areas near the nursery is to consider what sorts of life forms you want to attract. Then, consider what they need for food and forage, safe travel corridors, reproductive habitat and nesting sites, and shelter from weather and predators. For example, native bees are important pollinators for native plants in many parts of the world, and their populations have been in decline. Different bees have different needs, but most native bees require a year-round supply of pollen and nectar from a diversity of native flowering plants. For shelter, native bees need a safe place to nest, usually in undisturbed ground, in hollow stems, or holes in trees (Vaughan and Black 2008).

The tips below can help to attract a diversity of benign and beneficial insects, animals, and other organisms to available areas including borders, hedges, windbreaks, and other refuge spots around the nursery (adapted from Wilkinson and Elevitch 2000):

- Learn about the intended species' needs for food, habitat, and other necessities. Plant the known food sources for target species. Native plant species are most likely to support native life, from soil fauna to birds. Some native wildlife may also have become accustomed to exotic species for food or habitat as well, however, and some naturalized exotic species may be important predators for exotic pests.

- Do not practice "clean culture." As long as it does not pose a safety problem, leave leaf litter and mulch, uncultivated soil, dead logs, and snags, which are important to many kinds of life from native bees to birds.

- Plant and protect a variety of species. Complex, multistoried plantings are more attractive to diverse animals than plantings of only a few species.

- Create a variety of habitats within the area. Tall trees, smaller shrubs, herbaceous plants, and standing dead snags provide important niches where different creatures can find their preferred shelter, food, and so forth.

- If possible, try to create corridors—connected areas where birds and insects can live or travel through safely. Ideally, the corridors will be contiguous, without large gaps. If the nursery is near a larger forest, park, or riparian area, creating a corridor between this area and the new planting may help species colonize the refuge area. Cooperation with neighbors may also help create larger and wider corridors.

Another recommendation is to ensure alternate hosts for certain pests are not grown near the nursery. For example, not all rust fungi have alternate hosts but those that do can be controlled by removal of these alternate hosts.

Diversity

Nursery areas can sometimes be devoted to a single plant species grown closely together—a potential buffet for the pests of that species. Studies in silviculture, agroforestry, and sustainable agriculture illustrate the benefits of mixed plantings for reducing pest problems. For example, in Southern Florida and the Caribbean, the mahogany shoot borer (*Hypsipyla grandella* [Lepidoptera: Pyralidae]) has a major effect on the survival and health of native West Indies mahogany seedlings and trees (figure 14.11). To reduce the likelihood of attack by mahogany shoot borers, researchers and growers are moving away from mahogany monocultures and into diversified plantings, with some success (Howard and Merida 2010). Reasons for the effec-

Figure 14.11—*The mahogany shoot borer* (Hypsipyla grandella) *has a major effect on the survival and health of native West Indies mahogany seedlings. Photos by Thomas D. Landis.*

tiveness of diversification range from not attracting large numbers of pests to providing habitat for greater biodiversity to balance out pest populations. Nursery growers who wish to diversify can mix plants of different species throughout the nursery instead of growing all the same species in one section (see story about "hiding" seedlings from rust in Chapter 20, Discovering Ways to Improve Nursery Practices and Plant Quality), although they will still want to group mixtures of species according to their growth stage and culturing needs. They can also diversify areas around the nursery as described in the previous section. Clients may also be interested in outplanting in diverse patterns instead of large monocultures.

Ongoing Process Evaluation

Assessment and Improved Effectiveness of Pest Management Approaches.

Take time to assess and learn from problem prevention and holistic pest management practices in your nursery. Evaluate the nursery's daily log seasonally and annually to assess the effectiveness of current practices. What is working well? Where is there room for improvement? How effective are the sanitation practices? Are any pest trends noticeable, such as a decrease in one type of pest but an

increase in another over time? Are any crops being grown that are so susceptible to pests that it may not be cost-effective to produce them anymore? Do any instances exist where some seedlings are unaffected by a pest while others are hit hard? If so, what is the difference? Has the presence of beneficial organisms and natural pest predators been documented? How can new staff be trained to help scout for pests, recognize beneficials, and diagnose problems in the nursery? Do any management practices exist that might warrant a small experiment in the nursery (see Chapter 20, Discovering Ways To Improve Nursery Practices and Plant Quality)? What lessons did you learn that you can share with other growers?

Taking time to observe and reflect on pest patterns and holistic management processes can make it easier year after year to prevent problems and manage them effectively if they arise.

Acknowledgment

The authors thank Robert L. James, retired plant pathologist, Forest Service for reviewing this chapter.

References

Cloyd, R.A. 2004. Natural instincts. American Nurseryman. 200: 38–41.

Dumroese, R.K.; Luna, T.; Landis, T.D. 2008. Nursery manual for native plants: volume 1, a guide for tribal nurseries. Agriculture Handbook 730. Washington, DC: U.S. Department of Agriculture, Forest Service. 302 p.

Francis, J. 2009. Biological disease control—grow your own. International Plant Propagators' Society, Combined Proceedings. 59: 292–295.

Harvey, C.A. 1999. The colonization of agricultural windbreaks by forest trees: effects of windbreak connectivity and remnant trees. Ecological Applications 10:1762-1773

Hemenway, T. 2009. Bringing in the bees, birds, and other helpful animals. Chapter 7 of Gaia's garden: a guide to home-scale permaculture. 2nd ed. White River Junction, VT: Chelsea Green Books: 150–172. Chapter 7.

Howard, F.W.; Merida, M.A. 2010. *Hypsipyla grandella*, the mahogany shoot borer. Featured Creatures (online publication of the University of Florida, Department of Entomology and Nematology). http://entnemdept.ufl.edu/creatures/trees/moths/mahogany_borer-english.htm (July 2013).

Jaenicke, H. 1999. Good tree nursery practices: practical guidelines for research nurseries. International Centre for Research in Agroforestry. Nairobi, Kenya: Majestic Printing Works. 93 p.

James, R. 2012. Personal communication. Vancouver, WA: Plant Disease Consulting Northwest.

Josiah, S.J.; Allen-Reid, D. 1991. Important nursery insects and diseases in Haiti and their management. Information Report BC-X-331. Victoria, B.C., Canada: Forestry Canada, Pacific Forestry Centre: 51–59.

Landis, T.D.; Tinus, R.W.; McDonald, S.E.; Barnett, J.P. 1990. The container tree nursery manual: volume 5, the biological component: nursery pests and mycorrhizae. Agriculture Handbook 674. Washington, DC: U.S. Department of Agriculture, Forest Service. 171 p.

Landis, T.D.; Tinus, R.W.; McDonald, S.E.; Barnett, J.P. 1989. The container tree nursery manual: volume 4, seedling nutrition and irrigation. Agriculture Handbook 674. Washington, DC: U.S. Department of Agriculture, Forest Service. 119 p.

Mizell, R.F., III; Short, D.E. 2009 (revised). Integrated pest management in the commercial ornamental nursery. IFAS Publication ENY-336, 2003, edis.ifas.ufl.edu/IG144. Gainesville, FL: University of Florida, Florida Cooperative Extension Service, Institute of Food and Agricultural Sciences.

Stace, P. 1995. Windbreak trees for economic biodiversity: a habitat for pests, predators, and crop pollinators. The Sixth Conference of the Australasian Council on Tree and Nut Crops, Lismore, NSW, Australia, 11–15 September 1995. Lismore, NSW, Australia: Australasian Council on Tree and Nut Crops. http://www.newcrops.uq.edu.au/acotanc/papers/stace.htm (July 2013).

Unestam, T.; Beyer-Ericson, L.; Strand, M. 1989. Involvement of *Cylindrocarpon destructans* in root death of *Pinus sylvestris* seedlings: pathogenic behaviour and predisposing factors. Scandinavian Journal of Forest Research. 4(4): 521–535.

Vaughan, M.; Black, S.H. 2008. Native pollinators: how to protect and enhance habitat for native bees. Native Plants Journal. 9: 80–91.

Wescom, R.W. 1999. Nursery manual for atoll environments. SPC/UNDP/AusAID/FAO Pacific Islands Forests and Trees Support Programme, RAS/97/330. Working Paper 9. 53 p.

Wilkinson, K.M.; Elevitch, C.R. 2000. Multipurpose windbreaks: design and species for Pacific Island agroforestry. Agroforestry Guides for Pacific Islands #4. Holualoa, HI: Permanent Agriculture Resources. http://www.agroforestry.net. (July 2011).

Additional Reading

Arentz, F. 1991. Forest nursery diseases in Papua New Guinea. Information Report BC-X-331. Victoria, BC, Canada: Forestry Canada, Pacific Forestry Centre. pp. 97-99.

de Guzman, E.D.; Militante, E.P.; Lucero, R. 1991. Forest nursery diseases and insects in the Philippines. Information Report BC-X-331. Victoria, BC, Canada: Forestry Canada, Pacific Forestry Centre. pp. 101-104.

Dumroese, R.K.; Wenny, D.L.; Quick, K.E. 1990. Reducing pesticide use without reducing yield. Tree Planters' Notes. 41(4): 28–32.

Lopez, R.A.; Duarte, A.; Guerra, C.; Cruz, H.; Triguero, N. 2002. Forest nursery pest management in Cuba. In: Dumroese, R.K.; Riley, L.E.; Landis, T.D., tech. coords. National proceedings: forest and conservation nursery associations—1999, 2000, and 2001. Proceedings RMRS-P-24. Fort Collins, CO: U.S. Department of Agriculture, Forest Service, Rocky Mountain Research Station: 213–218.

Mohanan, C. 2000a. Epidemiology and integrated management of web blight in bamboo nurseries in India. Proceedings of the 4th meeting of IUFRO Working Party 7.03.04—diseases and insects in forest nurseries. Research Paper 781. Vantaa, Finland: Finnish Forest Research Institute: 107–121.

Mohanan, C. 2000b. Introduction of rootrainer technology in forestry—impact on nursery disease management. Proceedings of the 4th meeting of IUFRO Working Party 7.03.04—diseases and insects in forest nurseries. Research Paper 781. Vantaa, Finland: Finnish Forest Research Institute: 39–47.

Thakur, M.L. 1993. Pest management in forest nurseries in arid and semiarid regions. In: Puri, S.; Khosla, P.K., eds. Nursery technology for agroforestry: applications in arid and semiarid regions. New York: International Science Publisher: 329–352.

Thornton, I. 1996. A holistic approach to pest management. Nursery Management and Production. 12(6): 47–49.

Hardening

15

Douglass F. Jacobs, Thomas D. Landis, and Kim M. Wilkinson

To promote survival and growth following outplanting, nursery stock must first undergo proper hardening. Hardening increases plant durability and resistance to stress by gradually acclimating plants to field conditions before outplanting. Without proper hardening, plants are likely to suffer from transplant shock, grow poorly, or die on the outplanting site. It is important to understand that native plant nurseries are different from ornamental nurseries in that most native plants planted in reforestation and restoration projects must endure an outplanting environment in which little or no aftercare is provided.

Hardening refers to practices during the nursery cycle that prepare plants for the stresses of handling, shipping, outplanting, and field establishment (Longman and Wilson 1998, Landis and others 1999). Plant hardiness primarily develops internally, although certain external characteristics such as thickening stems and reduced succulence in the foliage are indicators of hardiness. This process takes time and a common mistake of nursery growers is not to schedule adequate time to harden their crops.

To properly harden plants, it is important to consider the Target Plant Concept presented in Chapter 3, Defining the Target Plant, and crop planning presented in Chapter 4, Crop Planning: Propagation Protocols, Schedules, and Records. Using knowledge of the expected conditions of a given outplanting site, nursery cultivation may be adjusted to acclimatize plants for site conditions by promoting specific traits. For instance, on sites where drought is anticipated, a larger proportion of roots relative to shoots may be desirable to improve plant resistance to moisture stress. Based on the client's anticipated outplanting date, the propagation schedule can then be developed to include an appropriate hardening period in the nursery before plants are delivered to the client.

In this chapter, we illustrate the importance of proper hardiness in promoting plant performance following outplanting, discuss how hardiness changes through the nursery growing cycle, describe how plants may be conditioned to prepare them for the characteristics of a particular outplanting site, and suggest treatments that may be used in tropical plant nurseries to help promote hardiness.

Facing Page: *Well-hardened crops at Native Nursery on Maui. Photo by Diane L. Haase.*

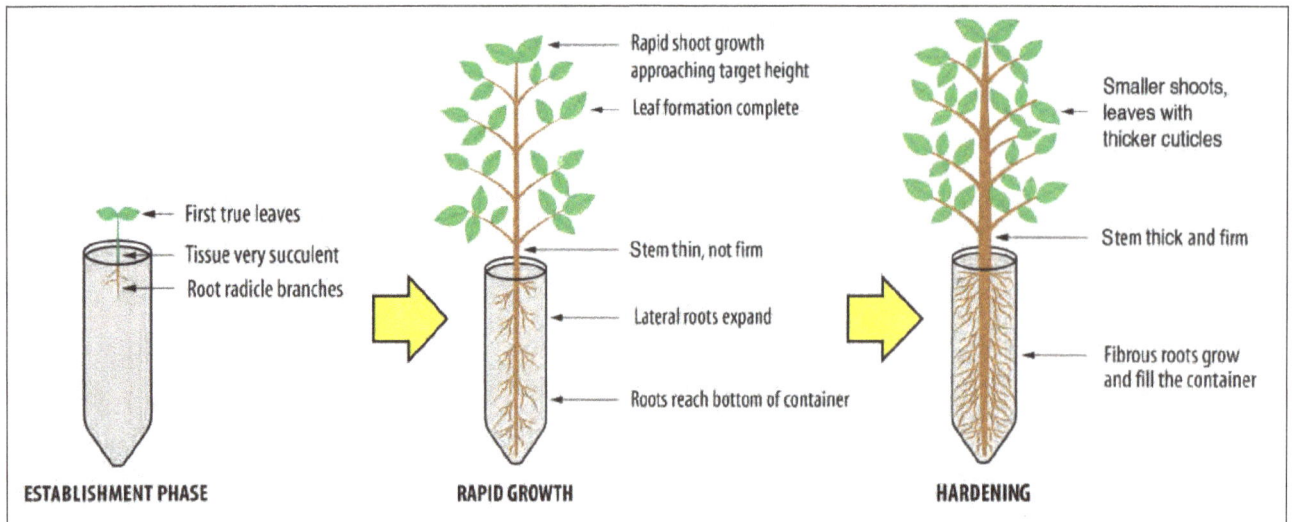

Figure 15.1—*Nursery plants go through three stages of growth: establishment, rapid growth, and hardening. The hardening phase is crucial to plant survival after outplanting, yet is too often neglected by nursery managers. Illustration adapted from Dumroese and others 2008.*

The Importance of Hardening

As described in Chapter 3, Defining the Target Plant, the success of nursery plants is not determined by how nice the plants look in the nursery, but rather by how well the plants survive and thrive after outplanting. As described in Chapter 4, Crop Planning: Propagation Protocols, Schedules, and Records, plants need to be cultured through three phases of growth: establishment, rapid growth, and hardening (figure 15.1). During the establishment and rapid growth phases, ideal conditions for development and growth are provided (figure 15.2A). These first two growth phases provide plants with optimal levels of all potentially limiting factors (water, light, nutrition, and so on) while minimizing environmental stresses. Plants should not go out to the field while they are still in their rapid growth phase; these plants look lush and healthy but are not prepared for the stresses of outplanting (figure 15.2B). The hardening phase of nursery culture is essential to acclimate plants to the stresses of handling and transport, and the conditions of the outplanting site.

All good growers will do their best to reduce stresses to plants when they leave the nursery, as described in Chapter 16, Harvesting and Shipping, and Chapter 17, Outplanting. Nevertheless, nursery plants will be exposed to a series of unavoidable stresses when it is time for them to leave the nursery. The harvesting process requires moving and handling plants, which creates potential for physical and internal damage. Following harvesting, nursery plants are transported to the outplanting site (figure 15.3). During transportation and handling at the site, plants are often exposed to unfavorable environmental conditions until

Figure 15.2—*Succulent shoot tissue (A) would be damaged by the stresses of handling, transport, and outplanting. Plants in their rapid growth phase look lush but are not prepared for the stresses of outplanting. The hardening phase creates a controlled amount of stress for plants, gradually acclimating them to the conditions of the outplanting site (B). Photo A by Douglass F. Jacobs, and photo B by J.B. Friday.*

being outplanted. For instance, a ride in the back of a truck, even when protected under a cover, will be bumpy and possibly hot. Sunny and windy conditions on the outplanting site can result in overheating or desiccation damage.

The hardening phase creates a controlled amount of stress for the plants while they are still in the nursery, helping the plants to survive the stresses of handling and shipping and acclimating them to the conditions of the outplanting site (figure 15.2B). Often, these conditions include full sun, low amounts of available nutrients, and limited soil moisture. After outplanting (figure 15.4), the plants may undergo a period of "transplant shock". This shock is primarily because of moisture stress and lasts until the roots are able to grow out into the surrounding soil to access water and nutrients, compete with other plants, resist insect and animal browse damage, and endure extreme temperatures.

Proper hardening takes time, and it is a common mistake to rush the process. This mistake often happens when growing more than one crop per season or when growers try to force a little extra height growth with crops that grow more slowly than expected. Improper hardening can also be an issue if the outplanting window was not properly defined, as described in Chapter 17, Outplanting. For example, for areas with a pronounced dry season, the late or early arrival of the wet season may complicate hardening schedules. Hardening requirements vary by species and outplanting sites, but for many tropical species, hardening phases of 4 to 12 weeks are common.

Objectives of the Hardening Phase

The objectives of the hardening phase will vary by species and outplanting environments. In general the objectives are to—

- Slow shoot growth.
- Encourage root and stem diameter growth (for good shoot-to-root balance).
- Acclimate to the outplanting environment.
- Condition to endure stress.
- Fortify for survival after outplanting.

Practices to reach these objectives may include—

- Introducing gradual, moderate moisture stress.
- Progressively exposing plants to sun equivalent to outplanting conditions (full sun in most cases, partial shade for understory plantings).
- Reducing fertilization rates and changing mineral nutrient ratios.
- Providing good airflow and wind exposure.
- Culturing for root health and proper shoot-to-root balance.

Figure 15.3—Hardening prepares nursery plants for a series of unavoidable stresses they will experience when it is time for them to leave the nursery. These stresses include handling and transportation, such as a ride in the trunk of a car. Photo by Thomas D. Landis.

Figure 15.4—Recently outplanted nursery stock must rapidly develop new roots that can grow out into the surrounding soil to access water and nutrients, compete with other plants, resist insect and animal browse damage, and endure extreme temperatures. Photo by Douglass F. Jacobs.

Figure 15.5—This native plant grew way too large for such a small and inappropriate container; it is unlikely that this tree would flourish if outplanted (A). These tall, spindly seedlings were grown close to one another and have been held too long (B). These seedlings are root-bound from being held too long (C). Photo A by J.B. Friday, photo B by Diane L. Haase, and photo C by Thomas D. Landis.

Shoot-to-Root Balance

Shoot-to-shoot balance is the ratio of shoot biomass to root biomass, not shoot length to root length. It is one important way to describe plant size and balance. Growing nursery plants to the appropriate size for a specific container size is critical. Plants grown too long in small containers or too close to one another become tall and spindly and do not have enough stem strength to resist physical stresses after outplanting (figures 15.5A, 15.5B). In addition, these "top-heavy" plants do not have enough roots to provide moisture to the foliage, so water stress can develop after outplanting. In tropical areas, top-heavy plants face the additional risk of storm-force winds and are susceptible to blow overs, particularly in the first few years after outplanting. Roots in containers that are too small often begin to spiral and become compacted (figure 15.5C). In these "rootbound" plants, most roots become woody and less effective in water uptake and, after outplanting, do not grow out from the compacted root mass to promote structural stability.

One key to developing a plant with a sturdy shoot and well-balanced root system is to select a container that is appropriate for the species and conditions on the outplanting site (figure 15.6). Plants should be moved from the shaded or protected areas in the nursery as soon as they have reached their target height. Experienced growers know that moving plants from a protected area of the nursery to an open compound is an easy and effective way to keep them in proper shoot-to-root balance. Managing light, nutrition, airflow, and other factors are also important, as described in the following sections.

Conditioning Plants for Outplanting

To induce plant hardiness and properly condition plants to resist stresses, nursery practices are gradually adjusted.

Figure 15.6—Some keys to developing a plant with a sturdy shoot and well-balanced root system are to select an appropriate size container; to move plants from protected areas to open compounds; and to otherwise manage light, nutrition, airflow, and water. Photo by Ronald Overton.

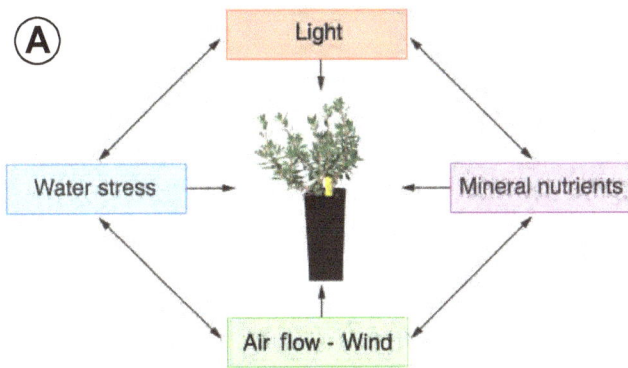

Figure 15.7—Nurseries manipulate environmental factors—light, nutrition, airflow, and water—to slow shoot growth and induce hardiness (A). At the Metropolitan Arboretum nursery for Parque Doña Inés in Puerto Rico, native palm seedlings are hardened on weed barrier cloth in full sun (B). The pots are mulched with locally available white stones to reduce weeds and water loss from evaporation. Illustration A by Jim Marin, and photo B by Brian F. Daley.

Figure 15.8—Reducing irrigation to induce a mild moisture stress helps harden crops (A). Severe water stress to the point that plants wilt (B) is harmful, however. Photos by Thomas D. Landis.

These adjustments must not be too severe, however, because overly stressed plants will actually be less hardy. To understand how nursery practices affect hardening, growers need to know the role that environmental conditions play in creating hardiness in plants. In the tropics, the main environmental factors that affect plant hardiness are light, water, and nutrition (figure 15.7). Wind, airflow, and other conditions also affect plant hardiness. When nursery plants have reached their optimum ("target") size, growers adjust shade/sunlight, water stress, fertility, airflow/wind, and physical factors such as root or shoot pruning to slow shoot growth and induce hardiness.

In determining how to properly condition plants for the intended outplanting site, it is important to consider the characteristics of the species and the outplanting site. For instance, is this a light-demanding species or a shade-loving species? Will plants be outplanted in an open field or underneath an existing canopy of trees? Will the site be prone to extended dry periods? Do other extreme site conditions exist such as high wind, poor soils, or salt spray? Understanding the character of the site is best accomplished by interacting closely with the client ordering the plants. These factors all reflect the main principles of Chapter 3, Defining the Target Plant, which suggest that the characteristics of nursery stock be matched to those of the intended outplanting site. Experience is the best teacher—experiment on a few plants and discover which hardening practices work best in your nursery circumstances and outplanting sites.

Water

Reducing irrigation duration or frequency creates a mild moisture stress, slows shoot growth, and helps condition nursery stock to withstand drier conditions on outplanting sites (figure 15.8A). This reduced water availability decreases the possibility of producing top-heavy plants and encourages the formation of smaller leaves with thicker cuticles that transpire less (lose less water) after outplanting. Smaller shoots are also less likely to be physically damaged during transplant.

Watering frequency needs to gradually be reduced to ensure that plants do not permanently wilt or experience severe water stress (figure 15.8B). Adjusting irrigation for hardening requires close observation and experience. The best way to quickly and accurately evaluate the water status of container plants is to weigh the growth container. See Chapter 11, Water Quality and Irrigation, for a discussion of irrigation monitoring with container weight.

After plants are hardened, they will still require a full watering before outplanting and will need good soil moisture availability at the outplanting site during their early establishment in the field. Many tropical areas have pronounced wet and dry seasons. Planting shock can often be minimized by outplanting after the onset of the rainy season, as described in Chapter 3, Defining the Target Plant, and Chapter 17, Outplanting.

Sunlight

The use of sunlight and shading as a conditioning treatment depends on the conditions on the outplanting site and the light needs of the species. Plants that will be planted into full sun conditions should receive minimal or no shading during nursery cultivation, especially during the hardening phase. If plants were started in a covered area (figure 15.9A), they need to be progressively exposed to a level of sunlight equivalent to the outplanting site (full sun in most cases, partial shade for understory plantings) (figure 15.9B). Growing plants in outdoor areas also exposes them to ambient temperatures.

Install shadecloth or move the crop to a shadehouse to reduce the amount of light a crop receives when it will be outplanted in understory or partial shade conditions. Shading is probably an overused treatment in nurseries, however, because most species (even those classified as shade tolerant) tend to grow best in full sunlight. In addition, many tropical plants often grow excessively in height ("stretch") under high shade, which may create a shoot-to-root imbalance. Nonetheless, if the species is shade loving and will be planted onto a site underneath an existing canopy, then shading may be a useful treatment.

Mineral Nutrition

Reducing or stopping fertilization along with reducing irrigation slows shoot growth and hardens plants. Among the mineral nutrients, nitrogen, particularly in the ammonium form, is the primary driver of shoot growth. During hardening, it can be helpful to reduce or stop nitrogen fertilization to induce a mild nutrient stress. (Note: the use of controlled-release fertilizers with long release periods can prevent or delay hardiness from developing.)

Some fertilizers have been specifically developed to aid in plant hardening, often containing a low-nitrogen–high-potassium formulation. Calcium nitrate is also a useful hardening fertilizer because it contains the nitrate form of nitrogen, which does not promote shoot growth. Calcium also helps develop strong cell walls and leaf waxes. Be sure not to use a similar product known as

Figure 15.9—Shade may be used during early phases of plant growth (A), but shade should be removed in the hardening phase to expose plants to a level of sunlight equivalent to the outplanting site (B). Photo A by Thomas D. Landis, and photo B by Diane L. Haase.

calcium ammonium nitrate because the ammonium can stimulate shoot growth.

Air and Wind

Increased distance between individual containers improves air circulation, allows more sunlight to reach lower leaves, encourages the development of shorter plants with larger stem diameter, and also promotes thickening of the leaf cuticle. Containers with individual, removable cells can be changed to every other slot to increase spacing within the trays during the hardening period (figure 15.10).

An interesting wind simulation treatment is known as "brushing." This practice came about after growers observed plants repeatedly handled during crop monitoring tended to develop greater stem diameter. The effect is replicated by gently moving a horizontal pole (such as a clean length of bamboo, or a light PVC pipe) through the crowns of the plants in both directions. Of course, this practice must be done gently, especially when the foliage is still succulent. Nurseries with traveling irrigation booms have mechanized the process by hanging a PVC pipe from the boom. A good time to brush plants is right after overhead irrigation because the rod also shakes excess water from the foliage and reduces the potential for foliar diseases such as Botrytis.

Root Culturing

A vigorous, fibrous root system distributed evenly throughout the container will rapidly proliferate after outplanting. Containers with vertical ribs facilitate healthy root structure by limiting root spiraling and are designed to promote air pruning at the drainage hole. Other root culturing features such as sideslit air pruning and copper pruning are effective, especially with vigorous rooted species. See Chapter 7, Containers, for more information on these features.

After plants are moved outdoors, it is important not to place the containers directly on the ground (figure 15.11). Instead, plants need to be placed on benches or pallets to facilitate air pruning of roots (figure 15.12). Otherwise, roots may grow directly into the ground, which will require the added task of root pruning during harvest. Root pruning immediately before outplanting can make the plants more vulnerable to pathogenic fungi and may delay quick root outgrowth after outplanting. If plants must be on the ground, placing groundcovers under them that are impenetrable to roots (such as fabrics treated with copper) can be helpful.

Shoot Pruning

Pruning shoots or "top pruning" is sometimes required if the top is too large for the root system. In general, the shoots of grasses, forbs, and some shrubs and trees can be pruned. However, many trees can be negatively affected by shoot pruning, so it is generally only recommended as a problem-solving technique for species known to be tolerant of pruning. Faster growing plants with a multi-stemmed form tend to tolerate shoot pruning whereas slower growing plants or species characterized by a single leading shoot tend not to tolerate shoot pruning. When working with new species, a small pruning trial is the best way to see how the species responds.

Figure 15.10—*Containers with individual, removable cells can be changed to every other slot to increase spacing within the trays during the hardening period. Photo by Diane L. Haase.*

Figure 15.11—*Plants grown in direct contact with soil (A) may grow into the ground (B). Photos by Douglass F. Jacobs.*

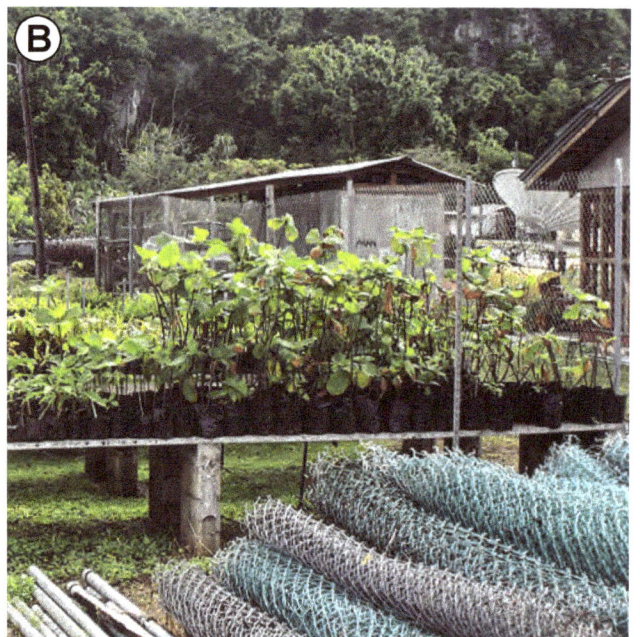

Figure 15.12—*Plants in a hardening area need to be placed on benches designed to facilitate air pruning and prevent roots from growing into the ground (A) such as the benches used in this nursery in Rota (B). Photos by Thomas D. Landis.*

For species that can tolerate shoot pruning, shoot pruning can help maintain a proper shoot-to-root balance and reduce water stress resulting from excessively high transpirational demand. Pruning also stimulates more stem and root growth. Pruning should be done just above the height of the smaller plants that have been overtopped (figure 15.13). This practice results in additional light for smaller plants and helps them reestablish a growth rate that is consistent with the rest of the crop.

It is critical that shoot pruning treatments not be too severe; a rule of thumb is never to remove more than one-third of the total shoot. Pruned plants should always be healthy and have enough stored energy to rapidly grow new tissue. The International Society of Arboriculture

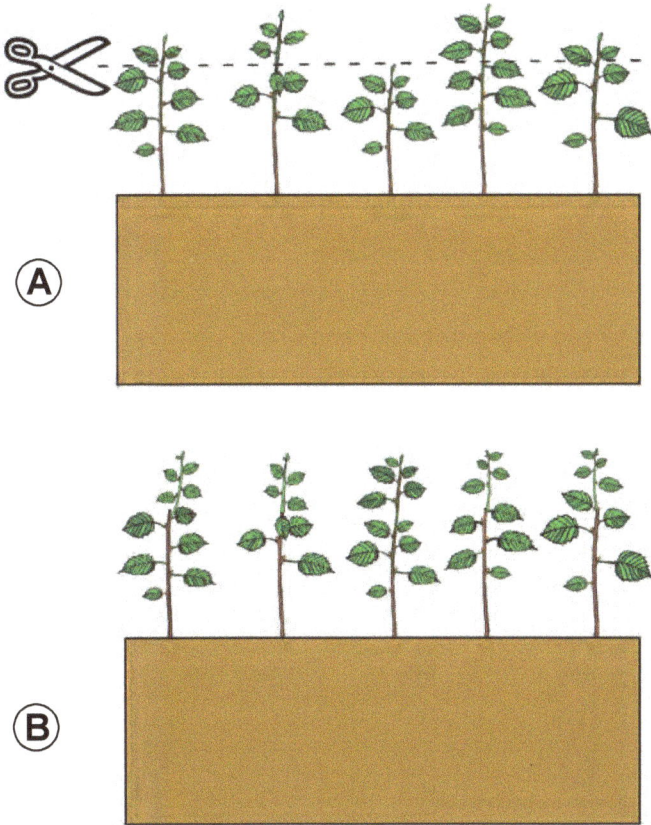

Figure 15.13—For species that can tolerate shoot pruning, the objective is to reduce the height of taller plants (A), thereby exposing smaller plants to more light and allowing them to "catch up" (B). Illustrations by Jim Marin.

(http://www.isa-arbor.com/) publishes extensively on when and how to best prune plants for improved plant health and form. It is best to prune succulent tissue because woody stem tissue has less regenerative ability.

Some growers have delivered "striplings" for outplanting, which are severely pruned saplings, sometimes with foliage also removed. The perceived advantage to striplings is they are easy to transport, harder to damage in shipping, and lose less water to transpiration immediately after planting. This extreme practice is not recommended because stripping plants of their foliage often results in mortality after outplanting.

References

Landis, T.D.; Tinus, R.W.; Barnett, J.P. 1999. The container tree nursery manual: volume 6, seedling propagation. Agriculture Handbook 674. Washington, DC: U.S. Department of Agriculture, Forest Service. 167 p.

Longman, K.A.; Wilson, R.H.F. 1998. Protecting growing trees: preparing young trees for planting. In: Longman, K.A. Growing good tropical trees for planting. London, United Kingdom: Commonwealth Science Council: 155–158.

Harvesting and Shipping

Diane L. Haase, Thomas D. Landis, and Tara Luna

16

Plants are ready for harvest and delivery to clients after they have reached target specifications (see Chapter 3, Defining the Target Plant) and have been properly hardened to withstand the stresses of handling and outplanting (see Chapter 15, Hardening). The "harvesting window" is the time period during which plants are at target size, maximum hardiness, and most tolerant to stress, that is, they are in the best condition for harvesting, shipping, and outplanting. The harvest window timing needs to be coordinated with the client's outplanting schedule to coincide with optimum conditions on the outplanting site.

Tropical plants do not achieve a deep dormancy condition and are therefore difficult to store and can be vulnerable to handling stresses. Plants need to be handled with utmost care at all times to minimize effects of temperature, moisture, or physical stresses. It is critical that plants be transported quickly and outplanted as soon as possible after leaving the nursery. This chapter describes proper scheduling, harvesting, handling, and shipping procedures for maintaining plant quality from the nursery to the field.

Facing Page: *A nursery staff member from the University of the Virgin Islands, Agriculture Experiment Station, delivers a healthy black olive (Bucida buceras) tree to a satisfied project partner. Photo by Brian F. Daley.*

Scheduling the Harvesting Window

In tropical nurseries, scheduling harvesting is based on the condition of both the plants and the outplanting site. Some tropical climates allow for a wide planting window so plants can be outplanted nearly year round if they are properly hardened and if soil moisture and temperature conditions at the planting site are favorable for survival and growth. Other tropical climates have pronounced dry seasons, monsoon seasons, or other times when planting windows are not open. Nurseries growing for projects with limited outplanting windows must schedule crop production carefully to ensure crops are not ready too early or too late (see Chapter 4, Crop Planning: Propagation Protocols, Schedules, and Records).

Site Conditions

For sites where a distinct dry season exists, scheduling harvesting according to the calendar along with experience of the nursery and field staff can be quite effective. In general, outplanting is most successful when planting is done just after the onset of the rainy season. The dates are selected based on past weather records and how well plants harvested on those dates have survived and grown after outplanting.

Figure 16.1—*Properly hardened tropical plants ready for harvest have lignified stems, well developed crowns, and healthy, leathery leaves. Photo by Diane L. Haase.*

Plant Characteristics

Growers use plant characteristics as indicators to help determine when plants are hardy enough to harvest and outplant. Hardened tropical seedlings have the following characteristics (Hall 2003) (figure 16.1):

- Firm, lignified stems, often brown in color.
- Sturdy, well developed crowns with leaves extending more than three-fourths of the length of the stem.
- Vigorous, compact, leathery leaves.

Client Communication

One challenging aspect of scheduling the harvesting window is coordinating with the client. Clients sometimes want their plants before the nursery has had adequate time for plants to achieve their target size and hardiness. More often, clients postpone the delivery dates, thereby increasing the likelihood of plants becoming rootbound or vulnerable to pests. Clear, frequent communication is essential to determine exactly when plants are needed for outplanting. It is crucial for the nursery staff to educate the client about the importance of timing and the consequences of hastening or delaying the harvesting window (reduced plant quality, reduced outplanting growth and survival, increased costs for hold over, and so on; see Chapter 18, Working With People, and Chapter 4, Crop Planning: Propagation Protocols, Schedules, and Records).

Grading Plants for Outplanting

Before being sent for outplanting, plants can be graded for size and quality according to established standards, outplanting objectives, or specifications agreed upon with the client. "Culls" are plants that do not meet the grading criteria or are damaged or deformed. Sometimes these criteria are adjusted during the grading process based on other cull and shipping factors that become apparent during the process. Typical grading criteria include size measurements such as shoot height and stem diameter at the root collar ("caliper") (figure 16.2). In addition, plants are inspected for root plug integrity, physical injury, or disease.

With single-cell containers in trays or racks, the typical grading process consists of removing each container from the rack, grading the plant within it, and then placing the container into either a "shippable" or "cull" rack. For polybag or larger containers, seedlings can be graded individually and sorted into separate areas based on size and quality. Plants that meet size and quality standards are considered shippable and are counted to establish an accurate inventory. The inventory of shippable plants can then be shared with the client. The nursery can also use the inventory as a

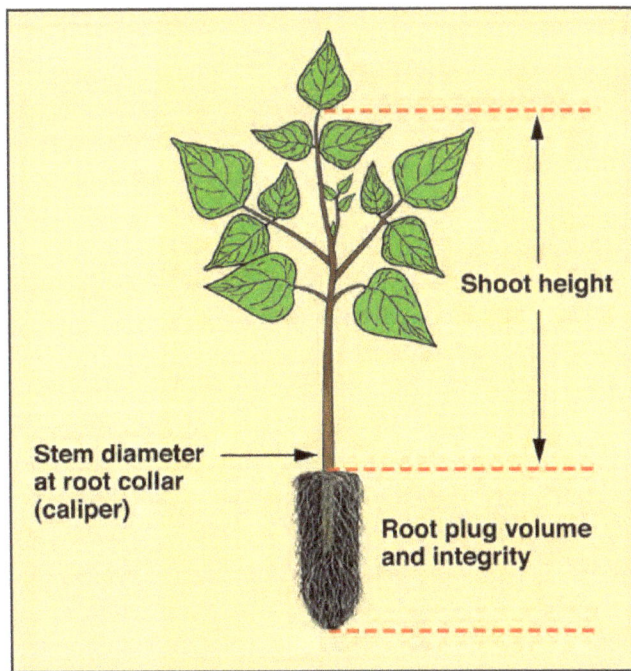

Figure 16.2—*Common grading standards include shoot height, stem diameter at the root collar ("caliper"), and root plug volume and integrity. Illustration by Jim Marin.*

record of plant sales and for planning future crops (see Chapter 4, Crop Planning: Propagation Protocols, Schedules, and Records).

Most nurseries grade their stock as part of the harvesting process while others ship ungraded stock to the outplanting site where they are graded immediately before outplanting.

Processing Cull Plants

Culls that are damaged or diseased are discarded or, better yet, incorporated into a compost pile (figure 16.3A). Composted culls can be reused as a soil amendment. For woody species, culls can be run through a hammer mill, tub grinder, or other machinery to hasten decomposition and speed-up the composting process (figure 16.3B). On a smaller scale the plants can simply be chopped with machetes or other hand tools. For some species, undersized but otherwise healthy plants can be held over for additional growth or transplanted into larger containers for future outplanting dates. This approach is common with cultivars that can be outplanted over a large geographic area or for threatened or endangered species where every plant is valuable.

Short-Term Storage

Plants destined for understory plantings or partially shaded sites can be held in a shadehouse (figure 16.4A) until they are shipped. Plants that have been hardened

Figure 16.3—*Culled seedlings, old growing media, and other greenhouse waste can composted (A). Woody materials and other green waste can be ground into smaller pieces by machinery to speed-up the composting process, as shown here at the nursery at Parque Doña Inés in San Juan, Puerto Rico (B). Photos by Brian F. Daley.*

Figure 16.4—*Tropical plants can be held in a shadehouse (A) or open area (B) until they are shipped. Photos by Diane L. Haase.*

for full-sun conditions can be held in an open compound (figure 16.4B) because they may lose their conditioning if stored too long in the shade. Both structures are typically equipped with a reliable water source, so irrigation and fertigation are possible (see Chapter 5, Propagation Environments).

Larger containers can be stored in wire racks to keep them upright (figure 16.5A) or on pallets (figure 16.5B) to stop roots from growing into the ground. To aid in drainage, prevent seedling roots from growing into the soil, and retard weeds, plants can be placed on a layer of pea-sized gravel covered with landscape fabric. Fabric impregnated with copper can also be purchased that chemically prunes roots as they emerge from the bottom of the containers (figure 16.6).

Figure 16.5—Racks or benches can be used to store large container stock (A) and pallets can be used to keep plants off the ground (B). Photos by Ronald Overton.

Packing

Tropical container seedlings are typically shipped in their containers. Seedlings in trays or racks can be shipped as is while seedlings in individual polybag containers or plastic pots can be placed in open-topped boxes or crates to minimize toppling and protect against mechanical injury (figure 16.7).

Because containers are expensive, nurseries may wish to remove plants from the containers at the time of packing. If seedlings are removed from containers, however, care must be taken to protect the root plug with plastic wrap or some other covering to prevent desiccation. As an alternative approach, nurseries may wish to charge a deposit or develop some other method to ensure containers are returned to the nursery for reuse.

Plants need to be packed for shipping in a manner that encourages air exchange and allows for possible irrigation on the outplanting site. Restricted airflow can trap the heat generated by plant respiration and result in damaging stresses. After the plants are graded and packed, the final step before shipping is to clearly mark each group of plants with the species, seedlot, number of plants, and other important information.

Shipping

When nursery stock is ready to outplant, it must be transported to the client or outplanting site. The most appropriate delivery method depends on the distance involved, the number of plants, and the hardiness of the stock. Most nursery stock in the tropics is delivered by truck or sometimes by boat. Nursery plants can be subjected to severe mechanical shocks during transport, especially on gravel or dirt roads,

Figure 16.6—Copper-treated fabrics are ideal for ground storage because they chemically prevent plant roots from growing into the ground. Photo courtesy of Stuewe and Sons, Inc.

Figure 16.7—*Plants need to be packed for shipping to minimize toppling and protect against mechanical injury. Photo A by Ronald Overton, and photo B by J.B. Friday.*

Figure 16.8—*Large container stock can be grown in special racks like these at the Forest Service J.H. Stone nursery in Central Point, Oregon (A). These plant can then be transported to the field in their nursery racks (B). Photos by Thomas D. Landis.*

and reducing speed will minimize potential injury (Stjernberg 1997). When shipped by boat, the plants need to be packed so that they do not come in contact with sea spray, which can severely damage foliage and roots, although the damage is usually not visible for several days later.

Containers in racks, pots, or polybags are usually placed carefully on the floor or stacked on metal or wooden shelves inside the delivery vehicle. Large container stock can be transported in the same racks used at the nursery (figure 16.8).

The risk of injury to nursery stock increases with the shipping distance. High temperature is the major risk factor during nursery stock transport. The temperature inside the truck, van, trailer, or cargo container needs to be moni-

tored during transit. Delivery vehicles should be aluminum or painted white to reflect sunlight and parked in the shade during stops and when they reach the outplanting site. An insulated truck liner can also be used to protect seedlings from heat (Anonymous 2006). Adding "blue ice" in the boxes of small shipments can help keep temperatures down although it could increase delivery costs. In some areas, refrigerated cargo containers are available; they are commonly used to transport produce but can be rented for transporting plants. Usually no need exists to turn on the refrigeration (it might cool the seedlings too much) because the containers are well-insulated and can keep plants cool and protected during transport even without the refrigeration on. Cargo containers can be left at the nursery and outplanting

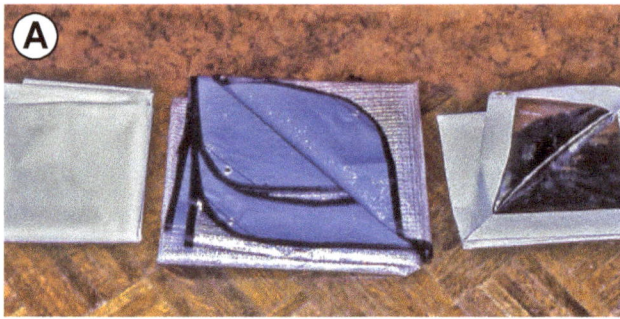

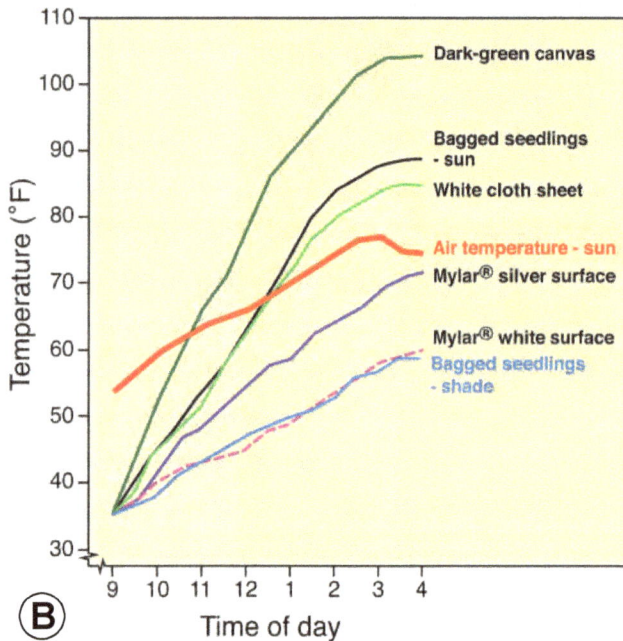

Figure 16.9—Special tarps protect nursery plants from direct exposure to sun and wind during shipping (A). Research has shown that reflective Mylar® tarps provide much better insulation than standard green canvas ones (B). Photo A by Thomas D. Landis, and illustration B modified from DeYoe and others (1986).

blocks) between racks, pots, and boxes can be used to reduce heat buildup and to prevent the load from shifting.

Handling

Nursery plants are in a period of high risk from the time they leave the protected environment of the nursery until they are outplanted. Proper care when handling nursery stock during this vulnerable time is critical to ensure that it has the best chance for survival and growth after outplanting. During handling and shipping, nursery stock may be exposed to many damaging stresses including desiccation, extreme temperatures, or mechanical injuries (table 16.1). This period incurs the greatest financial risk because nursery plants have reached their maximum value right before shipping (Paterson and others 2001). In fact, handling nursery stock is considered a more important factor affecting plant quality than the type of outplanting tool (Adams and Patterson 2004).

It is important to emphasize to everyone who will be handling nursery stock that nursery plants are alive and perishable, and so should be treated with utmost care at all times. It is a waste of time and money to produce or purchase high-quality plants only to have them die or grow poorly after outplanting as a result of unnecessary stresses.

Plants are best able to tolerate stress when they are not actively growing. Nonhardened, succulent plant tissue is much more vulnerable to stresses. Regular monitoring of plant condition, close supervision of nursery and field personnel, periodic testing of plant quality, and maintenance of detailed records are essential during shipping and handling.

Moisture Stress

Desiccation is the most common stress encountered during handling, shipping, transport, and planting, and can have a profound effect on survival and growth. When exposed for only 5 minutes, seedlings can exhibit increasing moisture loss with increasing air temperature and wind speed (figure 16.10). A comprehensive evaluation of the various types of stresses affecting plants during handling and outplanting (DeYoe 1986) revealed that desiccation of the root system was the most damaging factor and that direct sunlight and high temperatures were significant only as they increased moisture stress. Plant water potential influences every physiological process and at stressful levels can greatly reduce growth even if survival is unaffected. These damaging effects can persist for several seasons after outplanting. Roots are very vulnerable to desiccation because, unlike leaves and needles, they have no

site for a few days to allow time for loading and unloading but should be monitored for temperature and kept ventilated with a fan.

If open pickups must be used, then plants need to be protected from wind and sun damage by covering with a reflective tarp. A frame needs to be constructed to suspend the tarp above the seedlings so it does not crush the shoots or inhibit air circulation. Specially constructed Mylar® tarps with white outer and silver inner surfaces are available from reforestation supply companies (figure 16.9A). In operational trials, plants under such tarps were as cool as those stored in the shade (figure 16.9B). Dark colored tarps, such as army green canvas tarps, however, allow plants to heat to damaging levels and should never be used (DeYoe and others 1986).

Regardless of the vehicle used for shipping, air circulation created by spacers (such as wooden boards or foam

Table 16.1—*Nursery plants are subjected to a series of potential stresses from harvest through outplanting. Adapted from Landis and others (2010).*

Process	Potential for Stress			
	Temperature extremes	Desiccation	Mechanical injuries	Storage molds
Nursery storage	High	Low	None	Medium
Handling	Medium	Medium	High	None
Shipping	Medium	Low	High	None
Onsite storage	High	High	None	High
Outplanting	High	High	High	None

waxy coating or stomata to protect them from water loss. Fine root tips have greater moisture content than woody roots and are therefore most susceptible to desiccation; if fine roots appear dry, then they are probably already damaged or dead.

Roots of container plants are protected somewhat by the growing medium, which serves as a reservoir of water and nutrients. If the plug becomes too dry, however, desiccation damage can be severe. After roots have dried, subsequent growth reductions are inevitable, even when shoot water potential recovers (Balneaves and Menzies 1988). Moisture stress can be avoided by making sure plugs are kept moist (but not saturated) throughout their journey from nursery to outplanting. Container stock

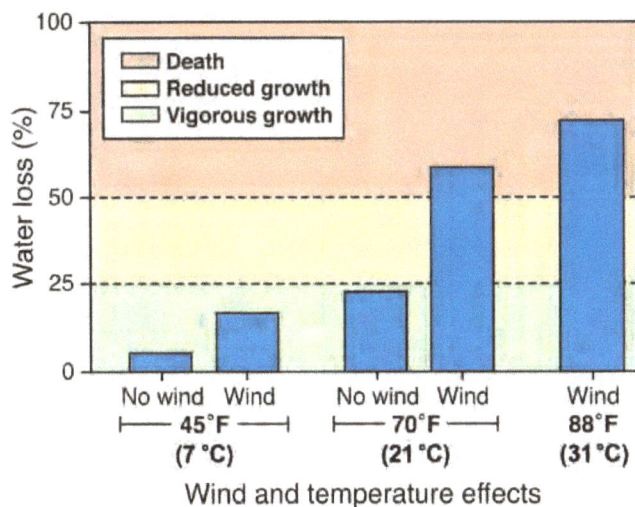

Figure 16.10—*When bareroot conifer nursery stock was exposed for 5 minutes, plant moisture loss increased with higher temperatures and wind until plant survival and growth were adversely affected. Adapted from Fancher and others (1986).*

should be irrigated 1 to 2 days before harvesting depending on weather conditions (Fancher and others 1986). This approach allows the plugs to drain to field capacity; saturated media is unhealthy for roots; it increases shipping and handling weight and increases the potential for mold development.

Temperature Stress

Either hot or cold temperature extremes can quickly reduce plant quality during handling and shipping. Exposure to warm temperatures can damage stock by causing moisture stress or heat stress. Plants are alive and respiring and when they are exposed to warm temperatures, their respiration adds heat to their environment; this condition is particularly serious when air circulation is inadequate. Maintaining good air circulation will minimize heat buildup because of plant respiration. Exposure to direct sunlight results in a rapid temperature increase and can quickly dry out plants. During outplanting, the nursery stock usually sits for short periods during packing, shipping, and staging. It is important to have any or all of these activities occur in the shade to reduce temperature stresses.

Physical Stresses

Rough handling can result in reduced plant performance after outplanting. Each person involved in the handling and shipping of nursery stock needs to receive training on how to minimize physical stresses. The potential for physical damage to nursery stock can come from dropping, crushing, vibrating, or simply rough handling. Studies have shown that the stress of dropping boxes of seedlings reduced root growth potential, decreased height growth, increased mortality, and increased fine-root electrolyte

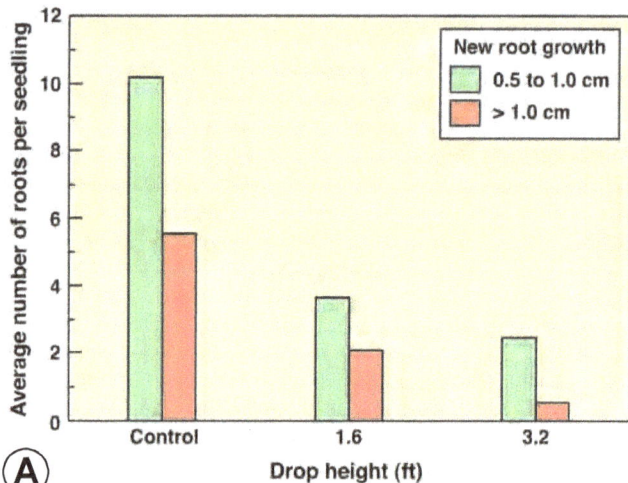

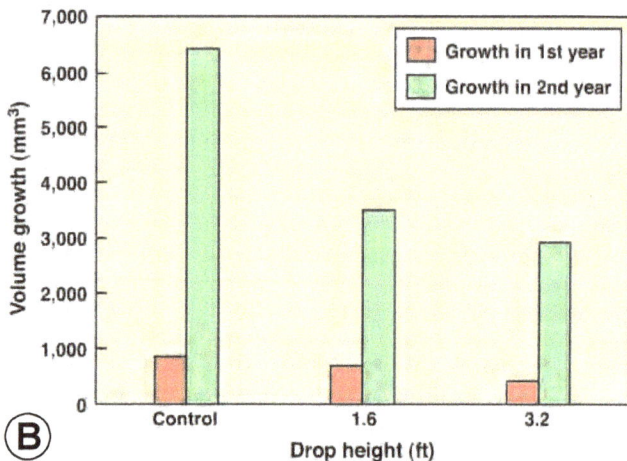

Figure 16.11—When bags of conifer seedlings were dropped from different heights, their ability to produce new roots (root growth capacity) was significantly reduced (A). This mechanical injury still affected plant growth 2 years after outplanting (B). Adapted from Stjernberg (1996). [Metric conversions: 1 in = 2.5 cm; 1 ft = 0.91 m]

leakage (Tabbush 1986, Sharpe and others 1990, McKay and others 1993). Stjernberg (1996) did a comprehensive evaluation of the physical stresses that nursery stock is subjected to during transport from the nursery to the outplanting site and found that white spruce seedlings produced fewer new roots as the distance the seedlings were dropped increased (figure 16.11A). Volume growth of these seedlings was still depressed 2 years after outplanting (figure 16.11B).

Accumulated Stresses

Nursery plants are at their maximum quality immediately before they are harvested at the nursery, but they then must pass through many hands before being outplanted. Outplanting success is dependent on maintaining plant quality by minimizing stress at each phase of the operation. As stress increases, the plant shifts energy from growth to damage repair. Physiological functions are damaged and survival and growth are reduced. These effects are exacerbated further when plants are outplanted on harsh sites. Extreme careless handling of planting stock usually manifests itself immediately after outplanting—plants die within days or weeks. Stressful injuries incurred between harvesting from the nursery and outplanting, however, may not always be evident until several weeks or months after planting. Symptoms include browning, chlorosis (yellowing), poor survival, or decreased growth.

It is useful to think of plant quality as a chain in which each link represents one of the events from harvesting at the nursery until planting at the outplanting site (figure 16.12). Because all types of abuse or exposure are cumulative, think of nursery plant quality as a checking account. Plants are at 100 percent of quality when they are at the nursery, and all stresses are withdrawals from the account (figure 16.13). Note

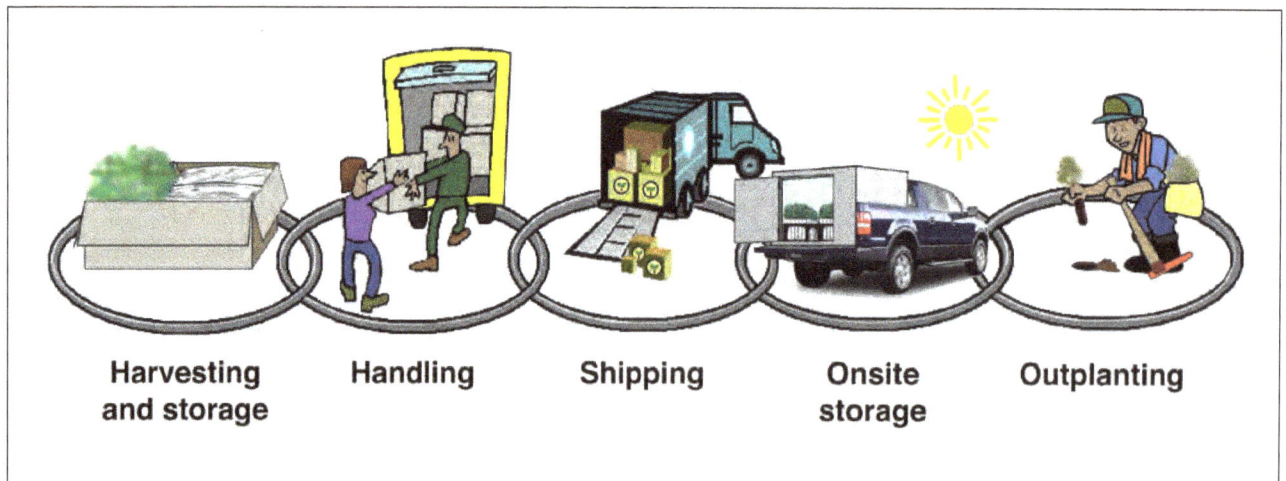

Figure 16.12—Nursery plants are subjected to a series of stresses from the time they are harvested to when they are outplanted. Each stage in the process represents a link in a chain, and overall plant quality is only as good as the weakest link. Illustration from Landis and others (2010).

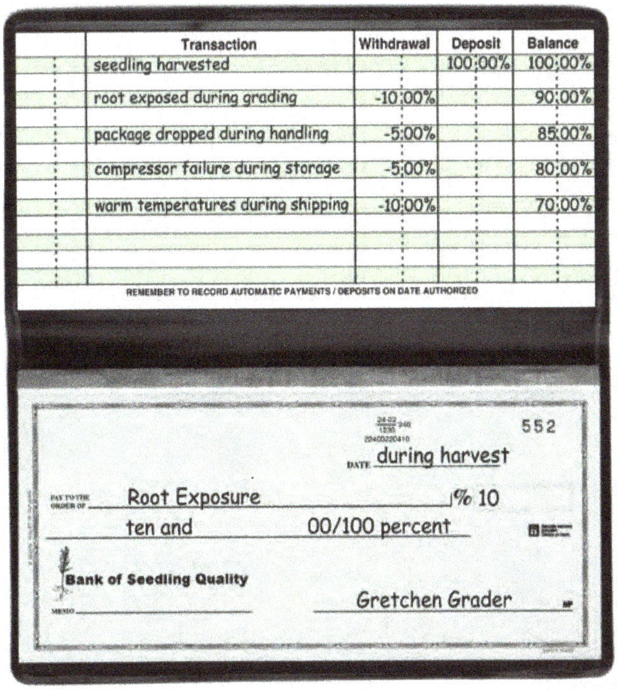

Transaction	Withdrawal	Deposit	Balance
seedling harvested		100;00%	100;00%
root exposed during grading	-10;00%		90;00%
package dropped during handling	-5;00%		85;00%
compressor failure during storage	-5;00%		80;00%
warm temperatures during shipping	-10;00%		70;00%

REMEMBER TO RECORD AUTOMATIC PAYMENTS / DEPOSITS ON DATE AUTHORIZED

552

DATE _during harvest_

PAY TO THE ORDER OF _Root Exposure_ |% 10

ten and 00/100 percent

Bank of Seedling Quality

MEMO _Gretchen Grader_

Figure 16.13—It is useful to think of nursery plant quality as a checking account in which all types of abuse or stress are withdrawals. Note that all stresses are cumulative and no deposits can be made—it is impossible to increase plant quality after nursery harvest. Illustration from Landis and others (2010).

that it is impossible to make a deposit; nothing can be done to increase plant quality after a plant leaves the nursery. Therefore, care must be taken during all the harvesting and shipping processes to help ensure outplanting success.

References

Adams, J.C.; Patterson, W.B. 2004. Comparison of planting bar and hoedad planted seedlings for survival and growth in a controlled environment. Connor, K.F., ed. Proceedings of the 12th Biennianl Southern Silvicultural Research Conference. GTR SRS-71. Asheville, NC: U.S. Department of Agriculture, Forest Service, Southern Research Station: 423–424.

Anonymous. 2006. Greenhouse on wheels: new shipping technology converts dry vans into nursery stock haulers. Digger. 50: 46–47.

Balneaves, J.M.; Menzies, M.I. 1988. Lifting and handling procedures at Edendale Nursery: effects on survival and growth of 1/0 Pinus radiata seedlings. New Zealand Journal of Forestry Science. 18: 132–134.

DeYoe, D. 1986. Guidelines for handling seeds and seedlings to ensure vigorous stock. Special Publication 13. Corvallis, OR: Oregon State University, Forest Research Laboratory. 24 p.

DeYoe, D.; Holbo, H.R.; Waddell, K. 1986. Seedling protection from heat stress between lifting and planting. Western Journal of Applied Forestry. 1(4): 124–126.

Dumroese, R.K.; Luna, T.; Landis, T.D. 2008. Nursery manual for native plants: volume 1, a guide for tribal nurseries. Agriculture Handbook 730. Washington, DC: U.S. Department of Agriculture, Forest Service. 302 p.

Fancher, G.A.; Mexal, J.G.; Fisher, J.T. 1986. Planting and handling conifer seedlings in New Mexico. New Mexico State University, Cooperative Extension Service (NMSU CES), Circ. 526. Las Cruces, New Mexico: NMSU CES. l0 p.

Hall, K.C. 2003. Manual on nursery practices. Kingston, Jamaica: Ministry of Agriculture, Forestry Department. 69 p.

Landis, T.D.; Dumroese, R.K.; Haase, D.L. 2010. The container tree nursery manual: volume 7, seedling processing, storage, and outplanting. Agriculture Handbook 674. Washington, DC: U.S. Department of Agriculture, Forest Service. 200 p.

McKay, H.M.; Gardiner, B.A.; Mason, W.L.; Nelson, D.G.; Hollingsworth, M.K. 1993. The gravitational forces generated by dropping plants and the response of Sitka spruce seedlings to dropping. Canadian Journal of Forest Research. 23: 2443–2451.

Paterson, J.; DeYoe, D.; Millson, S.; Galloway, R. 2001. The handling and planting of seedlings. In: Wagner, R.G.; Colombo, S.J., eds. Regenerating the Canadian forest principles and practice for Ontario. Markham, Ontario, Canada: Ontario Ministry of Natural Resources and Fitzhenry & Whiteside Ltd.: 325–341.

Sharpe, A.L.; Mason, W.L;, Howes, R.E.J. 1990. Early forest performance of roughly handled Sitka spruce and Douglas-fir of different plant types. Scottish Forestry. 44: 257–265.

Stjernberg, E.I. 1996. Seedling transportation: effect of mechanical shocks on seedling performance. Tech. Rep. TR-114. Pointe-Claire, Quebec, Canada: Forest Engineering Research Institute of Canada. 16 p.

Stjernberg, E.I. 1997. Mechanical shock during transportation: effects on seedling performance. New Forests. 13(103): 401–420.

Tabbush, P.M. 1986. Rough handling, soil temperature, and root development in outplanted Sitka spruce and Douglas-fir. Canadian Journal of Forest Research. 16: 1385–1388.

Outplanting

17

Diane L. Haase, Thomas D. Landis, and R. Kasten Dumroese

Survival and growth after outplanting are the ultimate tests of nursery plant quality. After the nursery plants are established in the field, they will provide many benefits to the environment by improving soil quality, enhancing biodiversity, inhibiting establishment of invasive plants, sequestering carbon, restoring native plant populations, providing windbreaks, creating wildlife habitat, and preventing soil erosion. In addition, established native and traditional plants can provide food, fuel, medicines, crafts, animal fodder, beautification, and many other benefits. Careful planning well in advance is important with attention to the eight steps of the Target Plant Concept. In addition, care with site preparation, onsite plant handling, selection of planting spots, proper planting techniques, support and protection of seedlings, and quality control during the outplanting process all help ensure the plants will have the best chance to survive. Long-term monitoring by the client and follow up with the nursery can help refine target plant requirements and improve future project successes.

Facing Page: *Native seedlings ready to be outplanted on a former pasture in Hawai'i. Photo by Douglass F. Jacobs.*

Review of the Target Plant Concept and Implications for Outplanting

Applying the target plant concept and proper crop scheduling are accomplished by working with clients to define the target plant for their outplanting site (Chapter 3, Defining the Target Plant, and Chapter 4, Crop Planning: Propagation Protocols, Schedules, and Records). The target plant is of the right species and genetic source; is of the appropriate size, age, and shape for its purpose; and is ready at the right time for outplanting with the best chance to thrive on the site. The eight steps for defining the target plant are—

Step 1—What are the outplanting objectives?

Step 2—What are the conditions of the outplanting site?

Step 3—What factors on the project site could limit success?

Step 4—How will limiting factors be mitigated?

Step 5—What species and genetic sources will meet project objectives?

Step 6—What types of plant material (stocktypes) are best suited to the project site and objectives?

Step 7—What are the best outplanting tools and techniques?

Step 8—What is the best time for outplanting?

Outplanting performance (survival and growth) depends on careful consideration of each step. To meet the project objectives (step 1), the plant material (steps 5 and 6) must be matched to the specific site conditions (steps 2 and 3). Furthermore, successful outplanting depends on optimum timing (step 8), site preparation (step 4), and proper planting techniques (step 7). A quick review of some of these key aspects of the target plant as it relates to the outplanting process follows.

The Outplanting Window

The outplanting window is defined as the period of time during which environmental conditions on the site are most favorable for survival and growth of outplanted nursery stock. Soil moisture is the primary determining factor, but other environmental or biological factors can also influence the outplanting window. On tropical sites that have wet and dry seasons, the outplanting window needs to be as soon as possible after reliable rains begin so that plants have sufficient time to develop established root systems before the dry season begins. Nursery stock is outplanted when soil moisture is high and evapotranspirational losses (from wind and sun) are low. Where a very short dry season exists, as is the case for the Caribbean side of much of Central America and in some of the wetter Caribbean islands, planting can be done throughout the year. To ensure that outplanting can commence at the optimum time, careful planning is crucial, alongside close coordination with the nursery (see Chapter 4, Crop Planning: Propagation Protocols, Schedules, and Records).

Limiting Site Conditions

It is critical to identify the outplanting site's environmental factors that may limit plant survival and growth. Temperature and moisture are usually the most limiting and are discussed in the following sections. Other site factors, such as aspect and soil type, must also be considered. Limiting conditions on each outplanting site must be evaluated well in advance of the actual outplanting to determine the optimum planting window.

Soil Moisture

Soil moisture plays a vital role in the uptake and translocation of nutrients and can have a significant influence on tropical plant survival and growth (Engelbrecht and Kursar 2003). Following outplanting, a root system must be able to take up sufficient water from the surrounding soil to meet the transpirational demands of the shoot. If soil moisture is inadequate, the newly planted seedling can become stressed, resulting in lower photosynthetic rates, reduced growth, and mortality.

Air Humidity and Wind Speed

Weather conditions at the time of outplanting have a direct effect on plant moisture stress. An increase in both air temperature and wind speed affect transpiration, especially when relative humidity is low. Relative humidity does not influence evapotranspiration rates as much as vapor pressure deficit, which is the difference between the amount of water the air can hold at a given temperature and the amount of water at saturation. Therefore, planting is best done during the early morning hours when air temperatures are cool and wind speeds are low. When weather is sunny, windy, or dry, it is necessary to take extra protective precautions to minimize plant stresses. In extreme cases, the planting operation may have to be suspended until conditions are more favorable for outplanting.

Site Aspect and Planting Sequence

Conditions can vary at different locations in the planting area, especially in mountainous terrain. Aspect, or direction of hill and mountain slopes to solar exposure, can have a strong influence on outplanting success. In the northern hemisphere, south- and west-facing aspects have a hotter, drier environment than north and east aspects while in the southern hemisphere north- and east-facing aspects have a hotter, drier environment than south and west aspects. Depending on the severity of moisture or temperature stress, shading of outplanted stock can help mitigate these stresses.

Temperature

In tropical regions, low temperatures are only an issue for mountainous planting sites and frost is rarely a consideration. Plants destined for these sites need to be adequately hardened off to minimize vulnerability to cold damage. High temperatures and solar loading are more frequently a serious concern during outplanting, especially in lowland sites. Ground temperatures in full sun are commonly much hotter than ambient temperature. Abandoned pastures and other forest restoration/rehabilitation sites are notorious for having extreme ground temperatures that can contribute to rapid soil moisture loss and even contraction and cracking of the soil. Sun scald or leaf burn on newly outplanted plants can result. Even if temperatures are high, simple cloud cover can dramatically reduce the plants' solar load and decrease ground temperatures.

Other Limiting Factors

Proper culturing of stock in the nursery can help overcome many other limiting site factors such as lack of beneficial microorganisms and low soil fertility. Other limiting site factors can be overcome by site preparation, outplanting methods, and maintenance practices, as described later in this chapter.

Species Selection

Choosing the plant species to be outplanted depends on the project objectives and needs to be tailored to meet the existing conditions at each outplanting site. If the primary objective is to restore the site to its natural condition, then selection of plant species indigenous to that area could be a logical choice. On degraded sites, such as abandoned pastures, however, climatic and edaphic conditions are highly altered and vastly different from conditions to which native species are adapted. In such cases, it is often more appropriate to plant species (noninvasive) that can withstand the extreme conditions. If the site will be managed for agroforestry, then species selection will be based on value for food or fodder production. For roadside plantings, trees must be able to handle difficult conditions and not produce messy flower or fruit that can interfere with cars or pedestrians.

The light requirements of a species are especially important to consider. Shade-intolerant species require full sunlight and tend to be "pioneer" species that can establish following disturbance. Shade-tolerant species can survive with less light and tend to grow slower than shade-intolerant species. In addition, some species are capable of fixing nitrogen from the atmosphere and can help mitigate poor soil conditions. These plant characteristics can be useful in deciding which species to use on a specific site. For instance, the use of a shade-intolerant, nitrogen-fixing pioneer species such as a noninvasive or native *Acacia* species may be ideal for "badlands," abandoned bauxite and phosphate mine sites, and pasture lands. After those are established and site conditions have improved, the site can be underplanted with native plant species. In some cases, an overstory of exotic trees is established. The canopy of these trees functions protectively over the underplanted native plant species (figure 17.1), thereby having a nurse effect (Feyera and others 2002).

Restoring abandoned pastures is common throughout the tropics. These pastures tend to be dominated by exotic, invasive species and have unique conditions that require special consideration when selecting species for outplanting. Pioneer species generally perform better when planted in former pastureland than mature forest species (Holl and Aide 2011; Hau and Corlett 2003) and using many species is preferable to using few (Van der Putten and others 2000). An additional planting at a later successional stage can be made to introduce a broader range of species to enhance diversity (Lamb and others 2005). Establishing fast-growing shrubs has also been shown to increase tree seedling survival (Holl 2002).

The project objectives will also dictate how many species to plant on a given site. A single species ("monoculture")

Figure 17.1—*Native plant species underplanted beneath a nonnative overstory on Guam badlands. The overstory helped to improve the soil, and serves as shelter for the native plants. Photo by Ronald Overton.*

may be desirable when growing crops or tree farms. The lack of diversity in a monoculture may make the site vulnerable to disease or insects, but the temporary overstory can stabilize the microclimate, provide a forest structure, and encourage regeneration (Lugo 1997). Multiple species may be chosen based on their ability to provide multiple benefits or to create a multistoried mixture of native trees and shrubs. For instance, a mixture of shrubs and trees can provide an ideal structure for a windbreak or shelterbelt (Upton and deGroot 2008).

For any species used on a site, it is important that they meet the target size specifications suited to the particular outplanting site conditions (see Chapter 3, Defining the Target Plant). For example, smaller plants with shallow root systems are best for poorly drained sites. Smaller plants also require less water than larger plants. On the other hand, larger plants can better compete with existing vegetation. In addition, the proper genetic source should be selected (see Chapter 8, Collecting, Processing, and Storing Seeds).

Site Preparation

Many tropical sites have become overgrown with invasive plants (figure 17.2) and cannot be restored successfully without intensive site preparation (referred to as "site prep") to achieve adequate control of competing vegetation. Exotic, invasive plants aggressively compete for nutrients, water, and sunlight and can severely suppress or devastate newly planted nursery plants. In some cases, exotic, invasive plants can also pose a severe fire risk.

Removing competing vegetation has several benefits (USDA 2002), which can combine to give outplanted nursery plants a competitive advantage over exotic, invasive plants. Competitive advantage is critical in tropical sites where weed development is rapid and persistent. Site preparation is labor intensive and costly, but can be well worth the effort. Lowery and others (1993) noted that growth and survival of planted trees on tropical sites can increase by as much as 50 and 90 percent, respectively, with early control of vegetative competition.

Site prep also makes the physical process of planting easier by reducing or managing some of the surface debris on the site. Some surface debris is a valuable site resource. For example, woody material can be chipped and used on site as mulch and fallen logs or standing stumps can provide favorable microsites for planting as described later in this chapter.

Site prep can be accomplished by mechanical or chemical means. It is important to remember that site prep is a form of disturbance and exotic, invasive plants are well adapted to successfully invade freshly disturbed sites. Therefore, timely replanting of sites where vegetation has been removed is important to prevent weeds from recolonizing the cleared area.

Scalping

Scalping is the removal of grasses, forbs, small shrubs, and organic debris ("duff") around planting holes (figure 17.3A). Scalping reduces weed competition and increases soil moisture availability. Removing organic debris around the planting hole also ensures that roots are in contact with mineral soil (figure 17.3B); nursery stock planted in organic matter or duff tend to dry rapidly and often die. Scalping is ineffective against larger, woody, deep-rooted plants.

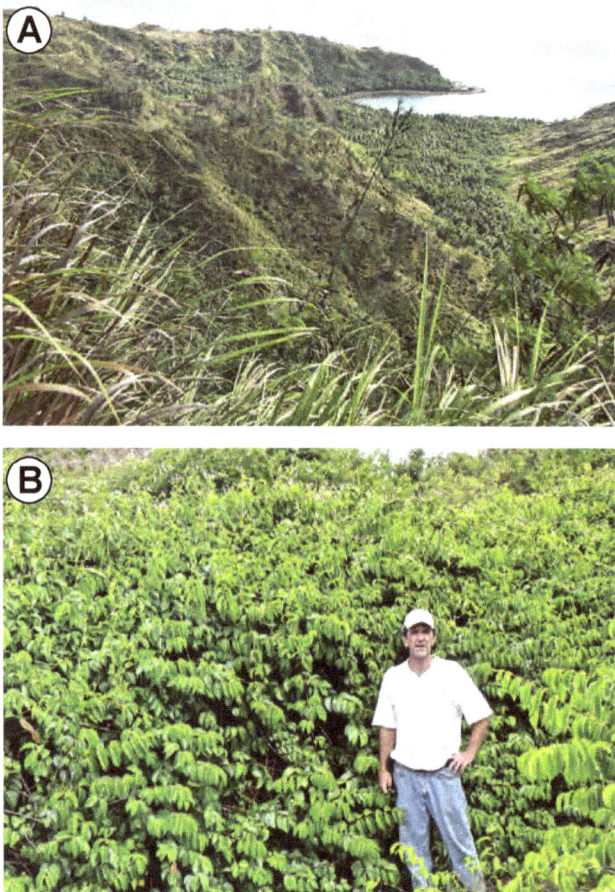

Figure 17.2—Existing vegetation on tropical sites often requires intensive site preparation to reduce competition with outplanted nursery stock. Shown: restoration site invaded with sword grass (Miscanthus floridulus) and tangantangan (Leucaena leucocephala) in Guam (A); an 8-ft-tall (2.4 m) wall of exotic, invasive rubber vine (Cryptostegia grandiflora) smothers all remaining woody plants in an abandoned pasture in coastal St. Croix, U.S. Virgin Islands (B). Photo A by Ronald Overton, and photo B by Brian F. Daley.

Figure 17.3—Scalping is the physical removal of plants and organic debris from around the planting hole (A). Scalping helps to control competing vegetation and ensures that plants are planted into mineral soil (B). Illustration A by Jim Marin, modified from Rose and Haase (2006), and photo B by J.B. Friday.

Physical Scalping

Scalping can be accomplished with planting tools such as a hoe or the side of a hoedad blade. With other planting implements, such as augers, another worker scalps beforehand. Planting contracts often contain specifications for the size and depth of scalping. For example, the Forest Service requires that all vegetation be removed from an area 12 to 24 in (30 to 60 cm) around the planting hole and 1 to 2 in (2 to 5 cm) in depth. On exposed sites, duff, litter, and decaying plant material should be placed back on the cleared surface after planting to serve as mulch (USDA 2002). In one study, increasing scalp size resulted in significant improvement in growth of planted conifer seedlings after 4 years (Rose and Rosner 2005).

Chemical Scalping (Herbicide Application)

Another site preparation option is to kill competing vegetation on the site with herbicides, especially around the planting holes,. Herbicide treatment is particularly effective against grasses and other herbaceous plants and is useful in tropical sites where plant growth is rapid (Ammondt and others 2013). A general-purpose herbicide such as glyphosate is effective against a broad spectrum of plant species. Herbicide application temporarily eliminates competition for water and also creates a mulch of dead organic matter that reduces surface evaporation. Vegetation control with herbicides has been shown to increase subsequent survival and growth of outplanted nursery stock. In a study with native tropical hardwoods in Costa Rica, tree diameter was significantly greater in plots treated with herbicide (Wightman and others 2001). An experiment evaluating three levels of vegetation control with chemical scalping significantly increased stem volume, basal diameter, and height of conifer seedlings on four of five sites with increasing area of weed control, and the magnitude of difference between treatments increased with time (Rose and Ketchum 2002). Although herbicide applications are effective in eradicating nonnative plants, they can also kill native plants so judicious and selective use is necessary.

The most appropriate herbicide application method depends on the type of project. For projects where the plants will be planted in rows, herbicides can be sprayed in rows by all-terrain vehicles (ATVs). For smaller projects, a person trained to select likely planting spots can apply herbicides with a backpack sprayer. Where the competing grasses and weeds are tall, they are first reduced mechanically, manually, or by burning before herbicides are applied to the emerging grasses and weeds. Herbicide application can be carefully timed to use the minimum amount possible for the maximum result. Never apply herbicide on the same day as planting and always follow the label instructions for application rates and time to reentry to the site after application. Quickly filling cleared areas with desirable plants is important to keep weeds from moving back in (figure 17.4).

Figure 17.4—Competing vegetation can be killed with herbicides before planting. Quickly filling cleared areas with desirable plants is important to keep weeds from moving back in. Photo by J.B. Friday.

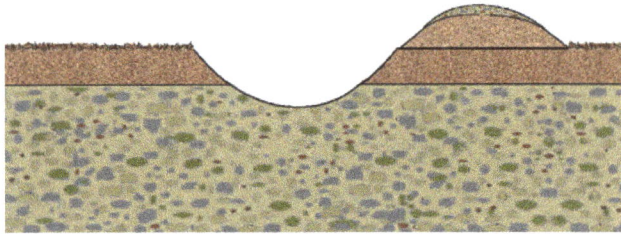

Figure 17.5—*On sites with heavy duff layers or in water-logged soils, mounding has proven to benefit plant survival and growth. Illustration from Landis and others (2010).*

Mounding

In some tropical sites, clay soils and organic matter combined with heavy rainfall can result in poor drainage and be an impediment to planted nursery stock. Mounding can be used to treat several potentially limiting factors: plant competition, poor soil aeration on wet sites, shallow soils, and nutrient deficiencies. Sutton (1993) provides a thorough discussion of mounding and how it has been used worldwide. For our purposes, we define mounding as the mechanical excavating and inverting of soil and sod to create planting spots that are higher than the existing terrain. With thick duff layers, the resulting mounds consist of a mineral soil cap over a double layer of humus (figure 17.5). The results of mounding have been generally favorable, at least in the short term. A study found that mounding was an effective alternative to herbicides for establishing pedunculate oaks (*Quercus robur*) on water-logged sites (Lof and others 2006). Mounding has been criticized from an aesthetic and ecological standpoint and can have a negative effect on other forest values such as recreation (Lof and others 2006). So, as with all site preparation treatments, mounding needs to be carefully evaluated on a site-by-site basis and compared with other site preparation options. It is generally only appropriate in areas where waterlogging and heavy rainfall are a problem.

Pit Planting (Zaï Holes)

In arid tropical soils, shallow planting pits can be prepared during the dry season (Kaboré and Reij 2004). The planting pit (zaï) dimensions vary according to soil type (8- to 16-in [20- to 40-cm] diameter and 4- to 8-in [10- to 20-cm] depth). The excavated soil is ridged around the pit to improve its water retention capacity and the pit is filled with composted organic matter. After the first rainfall, the pit is planted and covered with a layer of soil. The zaï functions to conserve water and reduce soil erosion.

Preparation of Severely Degraded Sites

Many tropical planting sites are established on degraded lands, such as abandoned pasture land, old agricultural fields, or mine land. On level, well-drained soils with heavy textures, mechanical site preparation using tractors with disc harrows can be used (Ladrach 1992). On low, wet sites, discing can help remove excess water and increase soil aeration. Subsoiling is effective for treating soils compacted from years of grazing or farming or on sites that have a natural hardpan.

On severely disturbed restoration sites, unusual site preparation to create suitable planting may be required. After the eruption of Mt. St. Helens in Washington State, the restoration of 150,000 acres (60,700 ha) of timberland posed some serious challenges (figure 17.6A). Experiments showed that seedlings must be planted in mineral soil to survive, which required digging through 1 to 2 ft (30 to 60

Figure 17.6—*Some restoration sites require special preparations before they can be planted. The blast zone of Mt. St. Helens in Washington State was covered with volcanic ash (A), which had to be dug away so that seedlings could be planted in mineral soil (B). Photos by Thomas D. Landis.*

cm) of volcanic ash at each planting spot (figure 17.6B).

In many cases, planting sites must undergo major stabilization before planting can occur. Because of their steep slopes and the erosive power of water, stream banks must be stabilized with bioengineering structures before they can be revegetated (figure 17.7A). Woody cuttings of many riparian species used in the structures will sprout (figure 17.7B) and provide rapid revegetation (Hoag and Landis 2001). With stabilization, careful planning, and planting quality stock, riparian areas can be restored (figure 17.7C).

In other conditions, the disturbance may be so severe that recovery has to take place in stages. For example, a strategy for addressing watershed restoration, biodiversity, invasive species, and wildfire problems in southern Guam involves a diversified landscape approach with objectives and prescriptions adapted to local site conditions which range from extremely eroded badlands to highly flammable, swordgrass-dominated grasslands. Steps include creating fuel breaks, planting nonnative *Acacia* trees to shade out sword grass and rehabilitate the soil, and ultimately planting native trees (Bell and others 2002).

Onsite Inspection, Storage, and Handling

Nursery Stock Inspection

As discussed in Chapter 16, Harvesting and Shipping, nursery plants are vulnerable to stresses from the time they are harvested at the nursery until they are outplanting. Therefore, it is a good idea to conduct a thorough inspection of nursery stock when it arrives at the outplanting site. The plants should appear green and healthy with full canopies and without signs of insect, disease, or other stresses. Nursery stock should not smell sour or sweet, which is evidence that it has been too warm or too wet. Root systems need to be moist but not saturated. The bark should not easily slough off and the tissue underneath should be creamy white, not brown or black. If white or gray mycelia (evidence of mold) are present, check the firmness of the tissue underneath. Soggy or water soaked tissue indicates serious decay and those plants need to be culled. Plants with superficial mycelia without corresponding decay need to be planted immediately. Fungal molds will not survive after exposure to ambient conditions on the site.

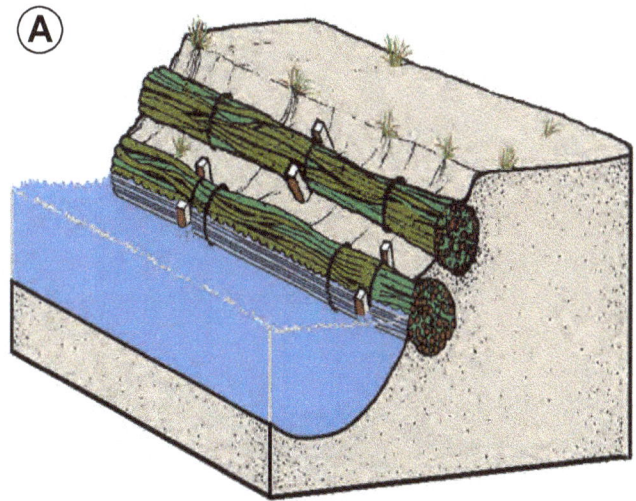

Figure 17.7—Stream banks often require bioengineering structures (A) for stabilization. When cuttings of certain species are used, they can sprout quickly (B). Careful planning and quality planting stock help ensure restoration success (C). Illustration A from Hoag and Landis (2001), illustration B from Steinfeld and others (2008), and photo C by Brian F. Daley.

Onsite Storage

Nursery stock need to be outplanted upon arrival to the project site. Therefore, it is always wise to plan ahead. Bring only as much stock as can be planted on a given day. Weather delays, distance, worker scheduling, poor communication, or other logistical issues can make it operationally impossible to complete planting in a single day, however, and therefore short-term onsite storage may be needed. The duration of onsite storage should last for only a day or two.

Whether for a couple hours or a couple days, overheating and desiccation are the major stresses that can occur during onsite storage. To dissipate heat and promote good air exchange, the plants need to be set upright and placed in a shady area as soon as they arrive on site. Plants should never be left in a closed vehicle. Trees and other natural shade are often absent on many restoration sites, but even when natural shade is available, it can be difficult to keep plants in the shade all day. Therefore, plan on erecting some type of artificial shade. Tarps or shadecloth suspended between poles is effective. Light-colored tarps are preferred. As shown in Figure 16.9B, dark-colored tarps absorb and reradiate solar heat (Emmingham and others 2002) and need to be suspended above the nursery stock for good air circulation.

Plant respiration and transpiration rates are a function of temperature, which is influenced by sunlight intensity. Therefore, check that root plugs are kept moist and plants are not under any moisture stress. Irrigating plants on the project site is not commonly done but can increase survival when site conditions may dry stock. So, the best onsite storage has access to a reliable water source.

On mountainous sites, the plants need to be covered to protect the roots from excessive cold if frost is anticipated during onsite storage.

Plant Handling

During the planting process, plants should always be handled with utmost care. Plants must be protected at all times from desiccation, temperature extremes, and physical damage. The same principles of careful handling described for harvesting and shipping (see Chapter 16, Harvesting and Shipping) need to be applied to the planting operation. Crews need to be instructed to never toss or drop plants. Research shows that dropping seedlings from various heights can result in growth reductions after planting (Sharpe and others 1990, McKay and others 1993). Larger plants need to be carried by the container or the rootball, never by their stems. Planters should never shake or beat

plants to remove excess growing medium. Each planter should carry only as many plants as can be planted in 1 or 2 hours. On larger reforestation and restoration projects, it is most efficient to use runners that carry batches of nursery stock from onsite storage to planters.

All planters need to be thoroughly trained in gentle handling and planting procedures. Even high-quality nursery stock will die if improperly outplanted. Training is particularly important with volunteers or other inexperienced planters. Many of these people lack the skill or strength necessary to properly plant on wildland sites. One option is to have an experienced planter create the planting holes just ahead of the volunteer crew, and let the volunteers place and tamp plants into position. This technique ensures that the experienced planter chooses the proper planting spot, creates the desired planting pattern, and makes certain that the planting hole is large and deep enough so that plants can be situated properly.

Selecting Planting Spots

Pattern and Spacing

The selected pattern and spacing of outplanted plants reflects the project objectives. Most planting projects specify a desired number of established plants per area (table 17.1). These density targets need to be considered general guidelines and should never override the selection of planting spots in biologically suitable areas. Trees grown for timber or fruit production are often planted with uniform spacing in rows (figure 17.8A). Trees planted for windbreaks are planted in staggered rows positioned perpendicular to the prevailing winds. Where ecological restoration is the objective, however, planting distribution and spacing will be more representative of natural vegetation patterns based on reference sites (see Chapter 3, Defining the Target Plant). For aesthetics and a more natural look, other projects may choose random outplanting of individual plants (figure 17.8B) or outplanting in random groups (figure 17.8C).

When planting with larger tree species, proper spacing is of utmost importance to minimize competition after the trees reach maturity. This spacing is generally achieved by assigning minimum distances between plants (table 17.1). It can be advantageous to plant at a higher density than the final target density to avoid the need to replant after some plants die. In fact, denser planting can promote plant growth by forming a thicket to protect against animals, wind, and competing vegetation and by promoting mycorrhizal development (Upton and deGroot 2008). If necessary, plants can be thinned out as they mature.

Microsites

Choosing the best planting spots is critical and more important than exact spacing. Planting in favorable microsites protects nursery stock and greatly improves the probability of survival. Examples of unfavorable planting spots include depressions with standing water, rocky spots, deep duff, and compacted soils. Plants shaded by a stump, log, or large rock tend to grow well, especially on hot, dry sites (figures 17.9A, 17.9B). High sunlight on plant foliage causes moisture stress and direct sunlight can cause ground temperatures lethal to the seedling. Planting around physical

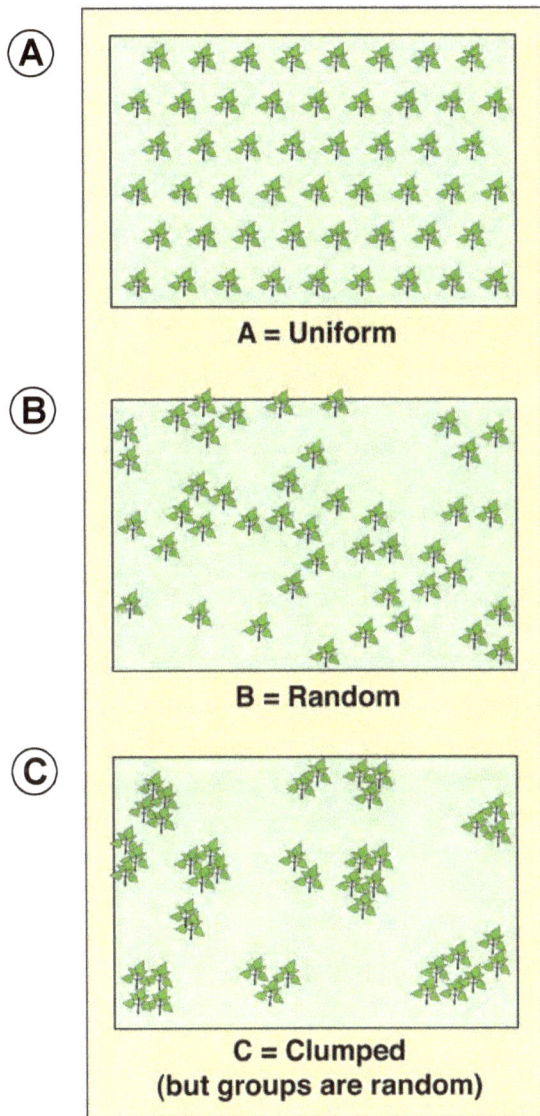

Figure 17.8—In addition to target plant specifications, the objectives of the outplanting project also affect planting patterns. If the objective is timber or agroforestry, then plants are often regularly spaced (A). Most restoration projects are spaced in a more random pattern to mimic natural conditions (B) or in a random clumped pattern where different species are planted in groups (C). Illustrations adapted from Landis and others (2010).

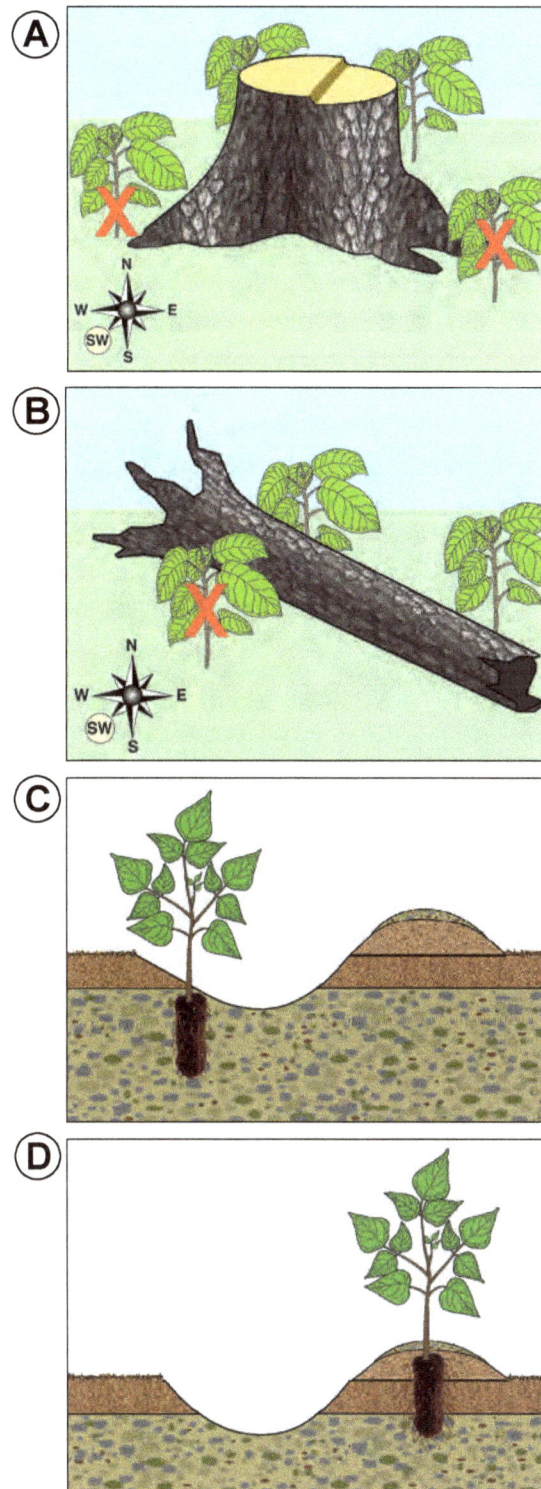

Figure 17.9—On sites with uneven terrain with physical obstructions, the best planting spots are in microsites in the shade of stumps (A) or other debris (B). Compass designations in A and B are for the northern hemisphere; planting orientation is the opposite for the southern hemisphere. Specific planting spots are also prescribed on sites that have been prepared by discing (C) or mounding (D). Illustrations A and B adapted from Rose and Haase (2006), and illustrations C and D adapted from Heiskanen and Viiri (2005).

Table 17.1—Plant spacing based on regular grids with resultant densities. Adapted from Cleary and others (1978).

Spacing (m)	Plants per hectare	Plants per acre	Spacing (ft)
6.4 by 6.4	247	100	20.9 by 20.9
14.8 by 14.8	494	200	4.5 by 4.5
3.7 by 3.7	741	300	12.0 by 12.0
3.2 by 3.2	988	400	10.4 by 10.4
2.8 by 2.8	1,236	500	9.3 by 9.3
2.6 by 2.6	1,483	600	8.5 by 8.5
2.4 by 2.4	1,730	700	7.9 by 7.9
2.2 by 2.2	1,977	800	7.4 by 7.4
2.1 by 2.1	2,224	900	7.0 by 7.0
2.0 by 2.0	2,471	1,000	6.6 by 6.6

obstructions also provides protection from animal damage. Where planting sites have been mechanically prepared with disc scarifiers, nursery stock need to be planted on the side of the hole in mineral soil (figure 17.9C). On mounds, the best planting spot is on the top (figure 17.9D).

Proper Planting Technique

Planting Hole

Good root-to-soil contact is necessary for nursery stock to become established on the site and be able to readily access water and mineral nutrients. The planting hole needs to be made deep enough so that, when filled, the soil is up to the plant's root collar. For container plants, the root plug needs to be completely covered with mineral soil (figure 17.10A). "J-rooting" and unnecessary exposure of the root plug are avoided when the planting hole is sufficiently deep (figure 17.10B), but the plant should not be planted too deep (figure 17.10C). Burying foliage should be avoided. According to Forest Service specifications, the minimum-size hole for container stock is 1 in (2.5 cm) deeper than the plug length, and at least 3 in (7 cm) wider than the plug at top of the hole and 1 in (2 cm) wider at bottom (USDA 2002). By making the hole larger than the root system, the planter can break up any compacted soil around the root system, thereby creating more favorable soil conditions for roots to grow.

The planters need to be instructed to plant at the correct depth and not to pull up on the plant to adjust depth or straightness. Plants should not be oriented more than 30 degrees from the vertical plane (figure 17.10D); this configuration seems obvious on level ground, but the steeper the slope, the more important this orientation becomes. Planting holes need to be backfilled with mineral soil without grass, sticks, or rocks (figure 17.10E). It is important to firmly tamp the soil around the root plug to remove air pockets (figure 17.10F), but refrain from stomping around plants to avoid excessive soil compaction or stem injury.

Planting Tools

Although the choice of the proper planting tool is important, experienced planters can achieve success with a variety of implements and may choose to use a combination of tools

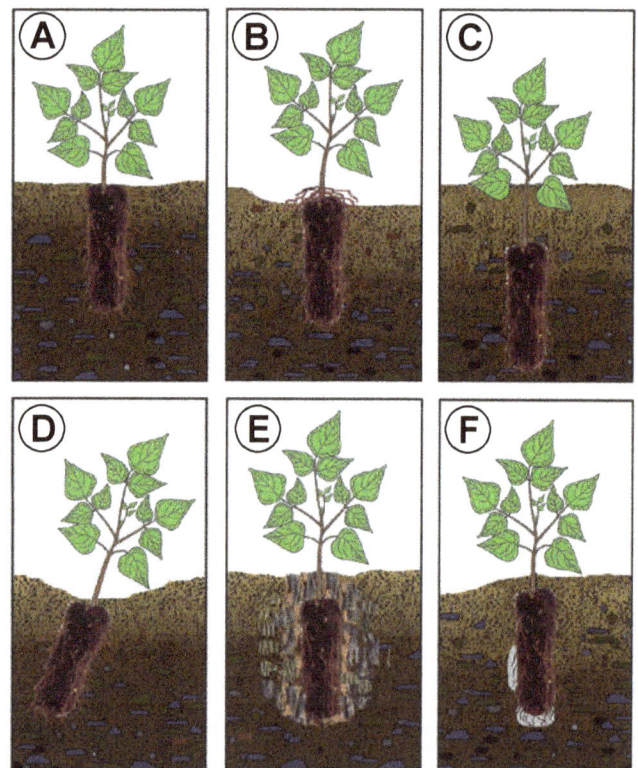

Figure 17.10—Nursery stock should be planted properly (A). Common problems include planting too shallow (B), planting too deep (C), not placing vertically (D), filling the hole with debris (E), or allowing air pockets around the roots (F). Adapted from Rose and Haase 2006.

depending on site conditions. Planting failures are often more attributable to improper technique or handling rather than choice of planting tool (Adams and Patterson 2004). Appropriate planting tools and techniques can mean the difference between a live or dead plant, and an on-budget or over-budget project (Kloetzel 2004). Hand-planting methods provide maximum flexibility in plant placement and distribution. A well-trained and experienced hand planter can surpass the planting quality and generally match the speed of many automated methods, especially over rough terrain. Hand planting is especially recommended for placing plants into microsites, and when planting a mixture of species or stock types. Motorized auger planting may be useful for larger stock sizes, especially on open, flat sites with deep soil and few rocks or roots.

Dibbles

Dibbles or dibble sticks were among the first tools used to plant small container stock, primarily because they are easy to use (figure 17.11A). Dibbles are custom-made probes that create a planting hole specific to one container type and size. Most designs have one or two metal foot pedals for forcing the point into the soil (figure 17.11B). After making the hole, the planter simply inserts the container plant and moves to the next hole. One drawback is the lack of loose soil to cover the top of the plug and prevent possible desiccation of the medium. Dibbles are most appropriate for lighter textured upland soils or alluvial bottomland soils in wetland restoration projects. Dibbles should be avoided on heavier textured clay soils because they can compact soil and form a glaze around the planting hole that can restrict root egress (figure 17.11C). Hollow dibbles are a recent modification that extract a core of soil and therefore reduce soil compaction (figure 17.11D). The hollow dibble heads are interchangeable to provide the correct dibble for different container sizes (Trent 1999). Commercially produced dibbles are available for specific container types and sizes, including Ray Leach Cone-tainer™ cells and several cavity sizes of Styrofoam® block containers (Kloetzel 2004). The 'o'o bar (Hawaiian name) or oso planting stick (Samoan name) is a traditional planting tool similar to a dibble stick and is useful for breaking through layers of lava to help tree roots reach mineral soil (figure 17.12).

Bars

Planting bars originated with bareroot stock, but this tool is also used for smaller container plants. Bars are typically cylindrical with a wedge-shaped blade welded on the tip, and side pedals to help force the blade into the soil. Like dibbles, planting bars require little experience or training. The bar is dropped and forced into the ground with the side pedals (figure 17.13A), and by working the bar back and forth the planting hole is formed. The nursery plant is vertically positioned along one cut face (figure 17.13B), and then the hole is closed by reinserting the bar into the soil on the opposite side of the planting hole and rocking the bar back and forth (figure 17.13C). The final step is to finish tamping any loose soil around the plant to remove any air pockets (figure 17.13D). Planting bars are often preferred for rocky soils but should not be used in heavier textured clays where they cause excessive compaction. They are also popular on reforestation sites with sandy soils. Planting bars are durable and simple to maintain, with only occasional blade sharpening required (Kloetzel 2004).

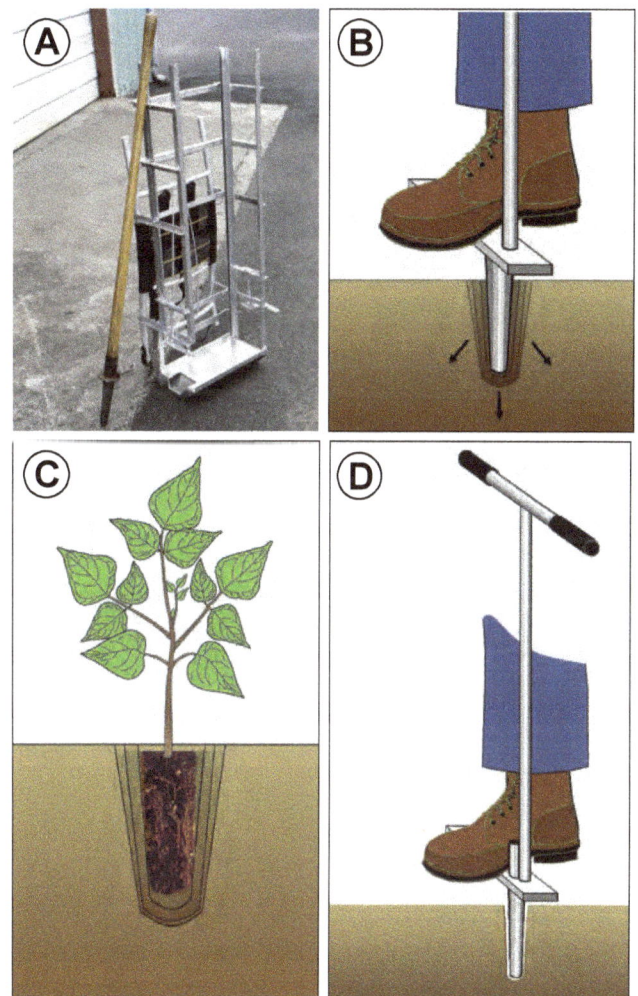

Figure 17.11—Dibbles are a useful tool for hand planting container nursery stock (A). Because they displace soil to form the planting hole (B), compaction can be severe enough to restrict root egress (C). Hollow dibbles are an improvement because they remove a core of soil to create a planting hole (D). Photo A by Thomas D. Landis, and illustrations B, C, and D by Steve Morrison, modified by Jim Marin.

Figure 17.12—'O'o bars or oso digging sticks are traditional planting tools useful for digging through lava to plant seedlings in mineral soil. Photo by Diane L. Haase.

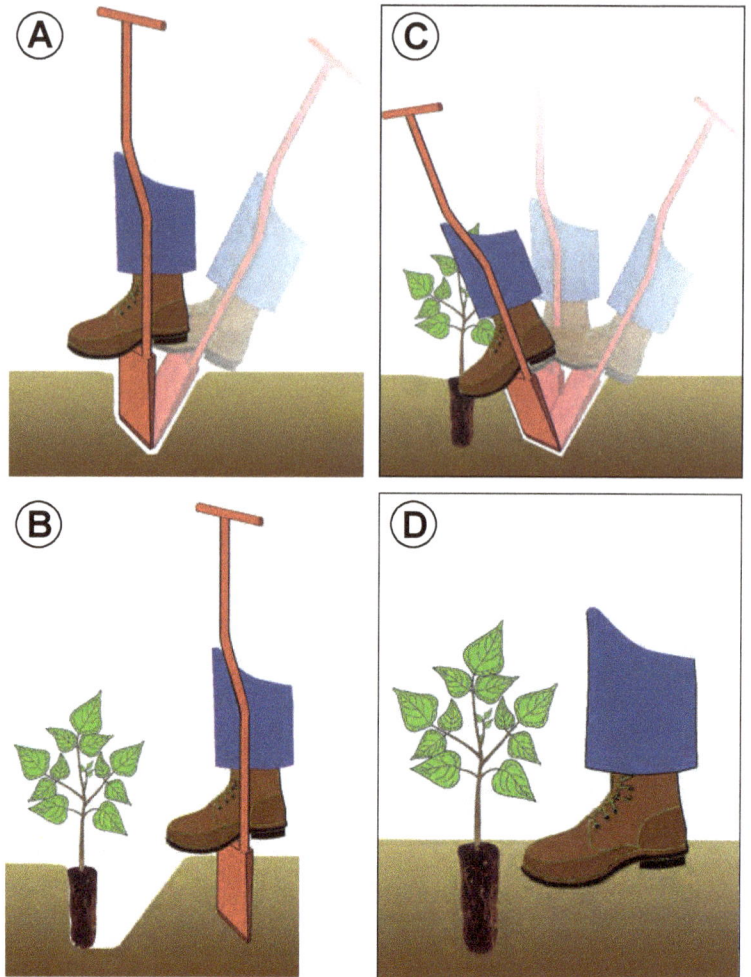

Figure 17.13—Bars are planting tools that create a planting hole by lateral movement (A). The plant is positioned along one side of the planting hole (B), and soil is backfilled by leverage from the other side (C). Soil should be gently compacted around the plant with hand or foot (D). Illustrations by Steve Morrison, modified by Jim Marin.

Hoedads

Hoedads are one of the more popular and versatile tools for outplanting reforestation and restoration stock. Brackets, holding the wooden handle to the desired blade, are typically brass for extra weight and penetration, or tin alloy ("Tinselite") for lighter applications. Brackets can be found in two blade angle configurations: 100° angle for applications on gently sloped or flat areas and 90° angle for steep ground planting. It is a good idea to purchase and keep handy spare blades, handles, and nuts and bolts with matching socket or box wrenches. Blades should also be regularly sharpened with a metal file or electric grinding wheel (Kloetzel 2004). Hoedads are particularly useful on steep sites, and on rocky and compacted sites. They are swung much like a pick, and it may take several swings to create a proper planting hole. With each swing, the planter lifts up and back with the butt of the handle to open the planting hole (figure 17.14A). After a proper hole is opened, the planter uses the tip of the hoedad to gently loosen soil on the sides of the planting hole to avoid any compaction effects. Then, the plant is inserted and positioned to the proper depth (figure 17.14B). While holding the plant, the planter uses the hoedad blade to backfill the soil around the plug (figure 17.14C). Finally, the planter gently tamps the soil around the plant (figure 17.14D) and moves to the next planting spot. If plant competition is a problem, or a planting basin is required, the back and side of the hoedad's blade is a useful scalping tool. Some compaction in the planting hole can occur from the backside of the hoedad's blade, but compaction is typically less than with other methods. Planting rates vary with container size, planter skill, and terrain. Kloetzel (2004) reported that beginning planters can install 20 plants per hour while

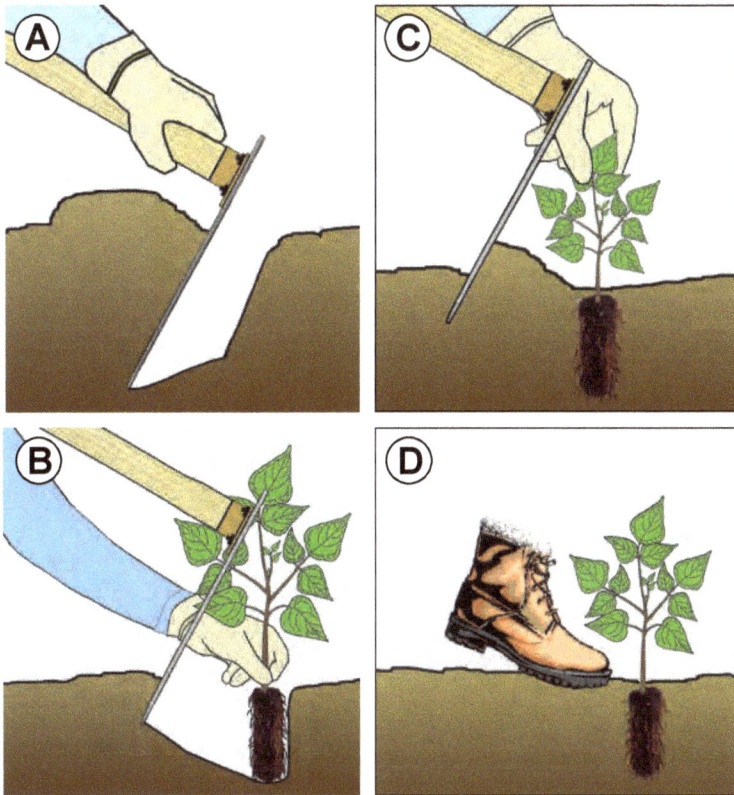

Figure 17.14—After several swings with the hoedad to create a deep enough planting hole (A), the plant is positioned and held (B) while backfilling with soil (C). The final step is to gently tamp the soil around the plant to remove any air pockets (D). Illustrations by Steve Morrison, modified by Jim Marin.

experienced planters may reach up to 100 plants per hour, and that on wetland planting projects with small stock and favorable soil conditions, production reached 240 plants per hour.

Shovels

Although standard garden tile spades can be used, professional planters use customized shovels with blades long enough to accommodate large containers (figure 17.15A). Wooden handles are standard but fiberglass models are lighter, and reinforced blades (figure 17.15B) can endure the vigorous prying action used to open planting holes (figure 17.15C). Although not as difficult to learn to use as hoedads, planters need to be trained to use tree-planting shovels efficiently. After the hole is excavated to the proper size and depth, the nursery plant is placed in the hole and held in a vertical position (figure 17.15D) while the planter backfills around the root plug (figure 17.15E). Soil amendments, fertilizers, and other such in-soil treatments are easily applied with planting shovels. When using planting shovels, keep some spare handles and footpads on hand, along with tools for installing parts and sharpening blades (Kloetzel 2004).

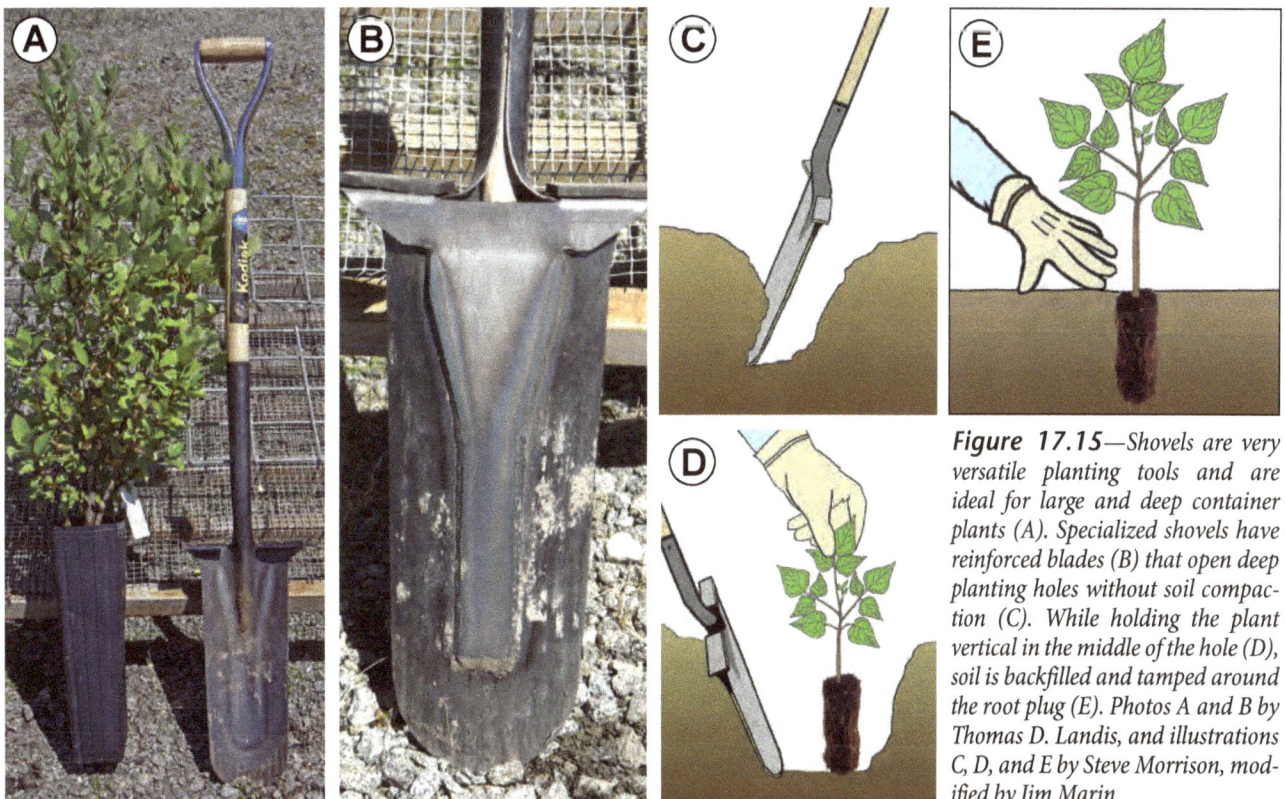

Figure 17.15—Shovels are very versatile planting tools and are ideal for large and deep container plants (A). Specialized shovels have reinforced blades (B) that open deep planting holes without soil compaction (C). While holding the plant vertical in the middle of the hole (D), soil is backfilled and tamped around the root plug (E). Photos A and B by Thomas D. Landis, and illustrations C, D, and E by Steve Morrison, modified by Jim Marin.

Mattocks

The mattock ("talacho") is a versatile tool used for digging and chopping (figure 17.16). It is especially useful for cutting through overstory tree roots when doing enrichment plantings under native tropical forests. In a comparison of three planting tools used for establishing tropical hardwood seedlings, no difference existed in seedling performance attributable to the type of tool but workers preferred the talacho because it was easy to use, it cut roots even better than a machete, and soil did not adhere to it as readily as on the other tools (Mexal and others 2005). Planting technique with a mattock is very similar to the hoedad (figures 17.14, 17.16) but the sharp axe-like end can be used to clear roots and other barriers.

Figure 17.16—*Mattocks (left) are versatile tools useful for digging and chopping through roots. They are similar to the hoedad (on the right) but have a sharp axe-like end for clearing roots and other barriers. Photo adapted from Forestry Suppliers, Inc., (2013) by Jim Marin.*

Mechanized Dibbles (Planting Tubes)

Mechanized dibbles create a planting hole by compressing soil to the sides and bottom with a pointed pair of hinged jaws. The jaws are switched open with a foot lever, and a container plant is dropped through the hollow stem tube into the hole (figure 17.17). The Pottiputki planting tube is the most popular brand and is available in several models with different tube diameters. In some models, the planting depth is adjustable, which would be necessary for stocktypes with longer plugs. One attractive benefit of planting tubes is less worker fatigue because the operator does not have to bend over. Planting tubes are popular in the Northeastern United States and Canada, although they are considered expensive to purchase and maintain. In one comparison, planting tubes were as effective as dibbles or planting bars (Jones and Alm 1989).

Motorized Augers

Power augers have been used in reforestation for decades and are becoming popular for restoration projects (figure 17.18A). Augers work best in deep soils without too many large rocks or roots, and are the best planting

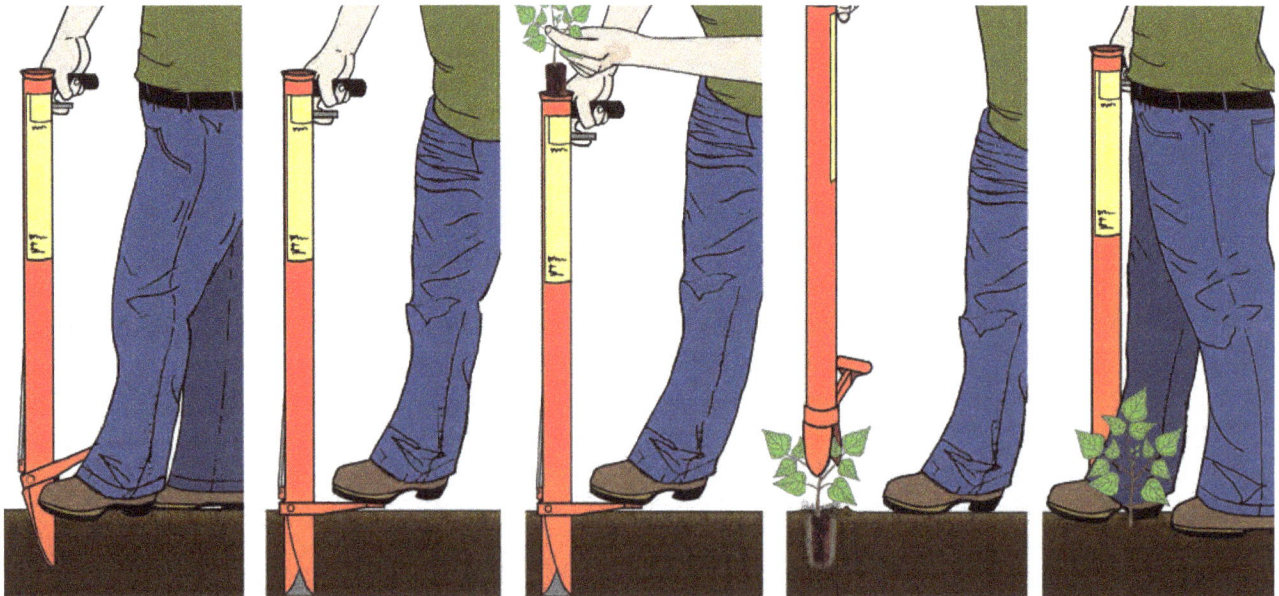

Figure 17.17—*Planting tubes have pointed jaws that open the planting hole. The plant is then dropped down into the hole through the hollow stem. Original illustration by Steve Morrison, and modified by Jim Marin.*

tool to use for larger, taller stocktypes. One concern has been compaction or glazing on the sides of augered holes that occurs under some soil conditions (Lowman 1999); this effect can be minimized by rocking the auger bit slightly. A gasoline-powered hand drill can be used with auger bits from 1 to 4 in (2.5 to 10.0 cm) diameter, and the reversible transmission helps when the bit becomes stuck (Trent 1999). Larger augers (10 to 16 in [25 to 40 cm] in diameter) mounted on a skid steer can also be used depending on soil type and terrain (figure 17.18B).

One benefit of auger planting projects is that the operator selects the location of planting spots and also controls the quality of the planting holes (figure 17.18C). One operator can drill enough holes for several planters to follow and plant the nursery stock (figure 17.18D). When scalping is required, the scalper will select the planting spots and create the scalp in advance of the auger operator. In some soil types, the operator will have to excavate extra mineral soil near each hole to ensure proper planting. When possible, it is best to rotate the auger operator to reduce fatigue.

Digging auger holes deeper than the depth of the container reduces compaction and can promote downward root growth. This approach leaves the planter to support the plant at the proper depth in the hole, while filling with soil from the bottom up (figures 17.8D, 17.8E). Soil settling can be a problem with auger planting so it is a good idea to mound soil around the base of the plant. A wide variety of augers are commercially available for rent or sale. When doing large-scale reforestation or restoration projects, it is more cost effective to purchase one. If you are inexperienced with their operation, however, it is a good idea to rent first to ensure that you have the correct machine for the project. Augers are high maintenance planting tools, so have an extra one handy, as well as extra parts and bits. Well-organized auger teams can reach production rates ranging from 30 to 70 plants per person/hour (Kloetzel 2004). In some parts of Hawai'i, the auger has become the ideal planting tool when volunteers or other nonprofessional planters are involved, because the planting rate is 2.5 times that of standard hand tools (Jeffrey and Horiuchi 2003).

Figure 17.18—*Augers are effective planting tools and are available in handheld (A) or tractor-mounted (B). One skilled operator can create planting holes (C) while other workers plant the stock and fill the holes by hand (D and E). Photo A by ©Jack Jeffrey Photography, photo B by Brian F. Daley, and illustrations C, D, and E by Steve Morrison, modified by Jim Marin.*

Worker Protection

Planting nursery stock can be strenuous. Encourage workers to wear hard hats, safety glasses, and sturdy footwear to protect them from sun, insects, and site hazards. If possible, workers need to rotate with each other for carrying, digging, planting, and other tasks. Workers need to have plenty of fluids available to drink and need to take adequate breaks to avoid exhaustion. The time and resources spent on worker protection will be offset by potential downtime and workers' compensation claims (Kloetzel 2004).

Treatments at the Time of Planting

In addition to site preparation to control competing vegetation on tropical reforestation or restoration sites, other treatments may be applied to plants at the time of outplanting to improve survival and growth. These solutions to potential limiting factors need to be identified during the site evaluation and planning process.

Dipping Roots

The seedling root system or container plug needs to be moist when it is placed in the planting hole. The practice of dipping plant roots in water or a clay slurry to protect them from desiccation during outplanting has been used for many years, especially for bareroot stock, and has proven beneficial on dry sites. Roots of nursery plants dry as they are exposed to the atmosphere during harvesting and handling and so it makes sense to rehydrate them or apply a coating to protect them. Simply dipping the root systems in a bucket of clean water to saturate them before outplanting is beneficial. Wetting some of the soil and using it to "muddy-in" the hole with wet soil and water also helps ensure that no air pockets exist around the plant's roots.

Many commercial root dips are available and most are hydrogels, which can absorb and retain many times their own weight in water. Little published research exists on hydrogels and the results are mixed (Landis and Haase 2012). In a trial with Eucalyptus root plugs dipped in a hydrogel slurry, significantly lower mortality rates emerged 5 months after outplanting compared with the controls. The author attributed this outcome to increased soil moisture or contact between the root plug and the field soil (Thomas 2008).

Water Catchment

When filling the planting hole, a small bund (embankment) can be made around the base of individual trees or blocks of trees to prevent runoff of rainwater and direct it to the roots (Upton and deGroot 2008). This method can be vital during the dry season when plants are becoming established. The raised bund can be made on the downhill side of the tree and a trench or small swale is made on the uphill side to encourage water to infiltrate into the root zone.

Protection From Animal Damage

Compared with wild plants, fertilized nursery stock has higher levels of mineral nutrients and is therefore preferred browse by many animals. In many tropical areas, introduced pigs, goats, cattle, sheep, horses, deer, and other animals severely damage or destroy plantings by grazing, browsing, rooting, and trampling (figure 17.19). If the outplanting area is known to have a problem with animal damage, then control measures will be necessary. Physical barriers installed immediately after planting such as netting, rigid mesh tubing, bud capping, and fencing can be helpful to protect plants long enough for them to grow large enough to resist animal damage. Most mesh tubes and netting are designed to biodegrade over time. Even still, periodic maintenance is usually required because shoots can get tangled in the mesh and deform the stem. After plants grow out of the netting or tube, they are again vulnerable to browsing damage.

Fencing is expensive but in areas with dense animal populations, exclusion via fencing is often the most effective method. In Hawai'i, an intensive restoration program to rebuild functional ecosystems in the Auwahi forest of Maui includes installation of a 7 ft (2 m) tall fence to exclude ungulates, application of a 1- to 2-percent concentration of

Figure 17.19—Animals can cause significant damage to outplanted nursery stock such as the browse damage on this seedling planted in Guam. Photo by Ronald Overton.

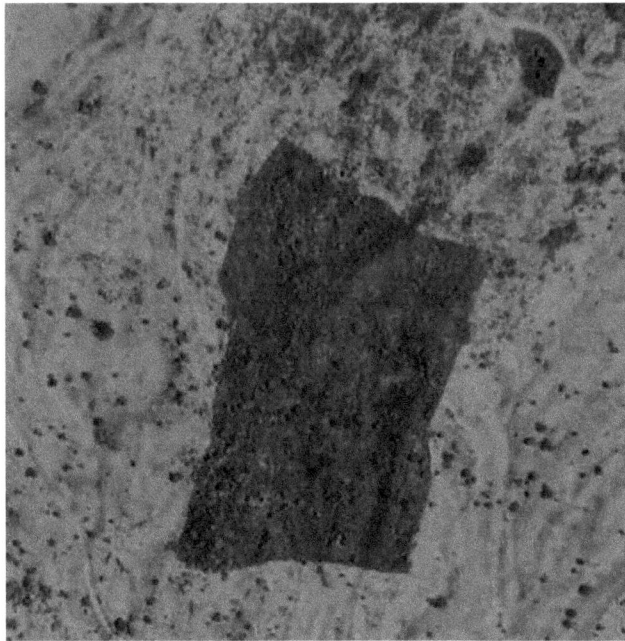

Figure 17.20—*This intensive restoration project by the Leeward Haleakala Watershed Restoration Partnership to rebuild functional ecosystems in the Auwahi forest of Maui includes fencing to exclude ungulates and can be seen by satellite imagery. Source: "Maui Restoration." 20°38.627' N 156° 20.519' W. Google Earth. March 20, 2011. Accessed March 2013.*

glyphosate to kill exotic grasses, outplant of quick-growing native shrubs, and public involvement (Medeiros and vonAllmen 2006). Within 10 years, the results were dramatic and could be seen in satellite photos (figure 17.20). Weller and others (2011) concluded that effective conservation of native tropical forests requires ungulate exclusion, removal of invasive exotic plant species, and proactive restoration programs for native species without natural sources of propagules. In some instances, "live fencing," made of species that grow densely and have thorns that will keep animals (and people) away from the newly planted nursery stock, can be used. This approach requires advanced planning, however, because it may take 2 to 3 years before the live fence is sufficiently developed.

Chemical repellents are another option to protect from animal damage. These repellents are less costly than physical barriers but their efficacy can be shorter lived. A variety of products are available that have an odor (often from predators) or taste that is repugnant to wildlife.

Fertilization

Mineral nutrition is a key component of plant performance after outplanting. Studies have shown a positive field response to fertilizer applied at the time of planting or incorporated into the growing medium of container seedlings (Haase and others 2006). Fertilizer efficacy, however, varies with site conditions (Rose and Ketchum 2002). On moisture-limited sites, fertilizer salts can build up to toxic levels resulting in a negative effect on survival and growth (Jacobs and others 2004). Before applying any fertilizer, it is crucial to consider the formulation, application rate, placement, solubility/release rate, and existing nutrient levels on the site.

Phosphorus is quite often deficient for tree growth in tropical soils. Boron can also be deficient in tropical soils, particularly in volcanic ash soils and soils of basaltic origin. Applications of these elements are routinely made at the time of planting and can produce dramatic growth responses on nutrient-deficient tropical soils (Ladrach 1992). Fertilizer responses are often not realized where high competition exists from surrounding vegetation. In plots treated with herbicide, fertilizer increased height and diameter of tropical hardwood seedlings in Costa Rica by 19 and 31 percent, respectively, but no response occurred from the fertilizer used in manually weeded plots (Wightman and others 2001). When soil pH is too high or too low, nutrient availability is reduced; combined applications of mulch, lime, and fertilizer to highly acidic soils in Palau resulted in dramatic growth responses of planted trees (Gavenda and Nemesek 2008, Dendy 2011).

Mulches

Mulching with organic or inorganic materials can reduce recurrence of vegetative competition for a longer duration than initial site preparation. Mulch mats made from materials such as plastic, fabric, sod, or paper are held in place with rocks, branches, or stakes. Mulching can also be accomplished with a thick layer of loose organic matter such as corncobs, coconut fiber, pine straw, sawdust, or bark chips (figure 17.21). In addition to inhibiting growth of competing vegetation, mulch insulates soil from temperature extremes, helps maintain soil moisture by reducing surface evaporation, and provides protection against soil erosion. Organic mulches also have the benefit of providing nutrients to the soil and improving soil structure as they decompose.

Although purchase and installation of mulch materials can be costly, mulches can significantly improve plant survival and growth on droughty sites. In a study to examine the effects of mulches on the survival and relative growth rate of three species in a degraded seasonally dry tropical forest, soil water content and sapling growth and survival were higher in plots mulched with polyethylene than in bare soil plots. Sapling survival under organic mulches (alfalfa straw and forest litter) were similar, and lowest in bare soil (Barajas-Guzmán and others 2006).

Figure 17.21—Mulching can reduce competing vegetation around the outplanted seedling. Photo by Ronald Overton.

Shelters

Tree shelters (figure 17.22A) can protect plants from animal damage and can limit the intensity of UV light and drying winds that cause damage by desiccation and sunscald. Engelmann spruce (*Picea engelmannii*) seedling survival after 11 growing seasons increased from 35 percent to 78 percent when shelters were installed (Jacobs 2011). Tree shelters are available in a variety of sizes and colors (allowing varying amounts of solar radiation to penetrate) and with or without venting. Selection of a specific shelter is based on

expected site conditions and the growth habit of the species. In a comparison of ventilated and nonventilated shelters, ventilation consistently reduced inside shelter temperatures by about 5 °F (2.7 °C) (Swistock and others 1999). Plants kept in tall, rigid shelters for a long period of time can become spindly (reduced stem diameter relative to height) and incapable of standing upright after shelter removal (Burger and others 1996). Management considerations for using tree shelters need to include the costs of purchase, assembly, installation, and annual maintenance. Nevertheless the increased cost may be offset by increased survival, thereby reducing the need to replant at a later date when competing vegetation is established.

Shelters can also be used to protect newly planted plants from frost at high elevations (figure 17.22B).

Shading

Ideally, an outplanting site provides adequate materials such as stumps, logs, rocks, or remnant vegetation to provide microsites for planting. It is sometimes useful, however, to install artificial shade to protect plants from damaging heat. Resistance to heat damage increases with plant size as the ability of the plant to shade itself increases. Shading only the basal portion of the stem can be as effective in preventing heat damage as shading the entire stem and some foliage, which can also reduce transpiration (Helgerson 1989). Artificial shade materials include cardboard, shingles, rigid shade cloth, or other

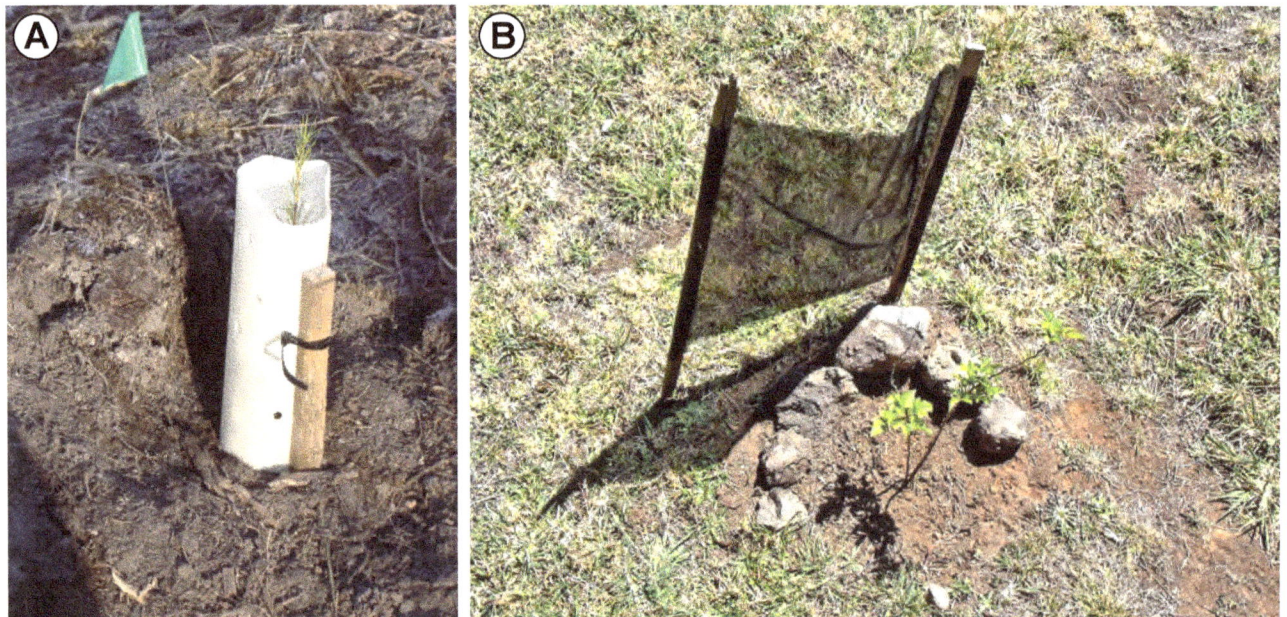

Figure 17.22—Tree shelters can provide favorable microsites to improve seedling growth and establishment on hot, dry sites (A). Frost shelters can be used to help decrease heat loss to the night sky and protect plants from frost at high elevations. At 6,500 ft (1,980 m), the Hakalau Forest National Wildlife Reserve on the Big Island of Hawai'i is high enough that frost can kill seedlings during the winter months; this frost shelter can help keep this 'akala (Rubus hawaiensis) seedling safe (B). Photo A by Diane L. Haase, and photo B by J.B. Friday.

materials and need to be installed on the "sun" side of the seedling (south or southwest side for sites north of the equator or north or northeast side for sites south of the equator).

Monitoring Planting Quality

The best way to determine if planting has been done correctly is to conduct an inspection during or immediately after planting. With contract planting jobs, these inspections certify whether the work meets specifications, and the results are used to calculate payment. A typical planting inspection consists of determination of the number and distribution of plants and examination of aboveground and belowground planting quality. These quality control checks during outplanting help ensure that each plant was installed properly and has the best chance of survival possible.

Determination of the Number and Spatial Distribution of Planted Plants

Plots are established to determine whether the correct number of plants was installed in a given area, whether good planting spots were selected, and whether plants were properly spaced. See Survey Types section later in this chapter for descriptions of plot establishment.

Aboveground Inspection

A representative sample of plants is examined to check the quality of the scalping, stem orientation, and planting depth. Planting depth is one of the most critical details to check and is usually specified in relation to top of the root plug or the root collar.

Belowground Inspection

A hole is dug with a planting shovel alongside the planted plant to check for proper root orientation, loose soil, air pockets, foreign material in the hole, and so on. Begin digging the hole far enough away from the main stem (10 in [25 cm]) so that the shovel does not disturb the roots. Then, gently clear soil away while digging toward the plug so that the plug can be inspected in the position it was planted. The plant's root system must be in a vertical plane and not twisted, compressed, or jammed and the hole should not contain large rocks, sticks, litter, or other foreign debris. Soil needs to be nearly as firm as the undisturbed surrounding soil with no air pockets. In auger plantings, be sure to check soil firmness near the bottom of the holes (USDA 2002).

Monitoring Outplanting Performance

Reforestation and restoration outplantings can be an expensive investment so it makes sense to conduct surveys to track outplanting success over time. An excellent guide on how to evaluate restoration plantings is available in chapter 12 of Steinfeld and others (2008). Quality control during or immediately after outplanting ensures plants are installed correctly. Longer term monitoring provides feedback to the nursery and the client, which can lead to improved seedling quality and increased outplanting success in subsequent projects.

When and What To Monitor

Plots of seedlings should be monitored for growth and survival during the first month or two after outplanting and again at the end of the first year. Growth can be measured as height growth and stem diameter growth (figure 17.23). Subsequent checks after 3- and 5-year periods will give a good indication of plant growth and survival rates. Survival can be expressed in percentages; if the client planted 100 trees, but after 2 months, 20 were dead, the survival is 80 percent at that point in time.

Some projects define measurable goals within specified time frames as part of their objectives. These goals are sometimes called "success criteria" or "desired future conditions." For example, a reforestation project might set a goal of 400 living trees per acre 2 years after outplanting. A native plant project might have a goal to reach a certain percentage of native groundcover or species composition within the first year after outplanting. Monitoring is then conducted to measure if these goals were achieved.

The client and the nursery manager then use this performance information to refine the target plant specifications for the next crop. The client may also alter his or her outplanting and management practices to achieve better survival and growth based on this information.

Survey Types

Two types of surveys, circular plots and stake rows, have traditionally been performed, and each has its own advantages.

Circular Plots

The traditional method to determine planting density is to measure 1/100 acre (40 m²) plots that are evenly distributed throughout the planting site. An adequate sample is about one plot per acre (2.5 plots per hectare),

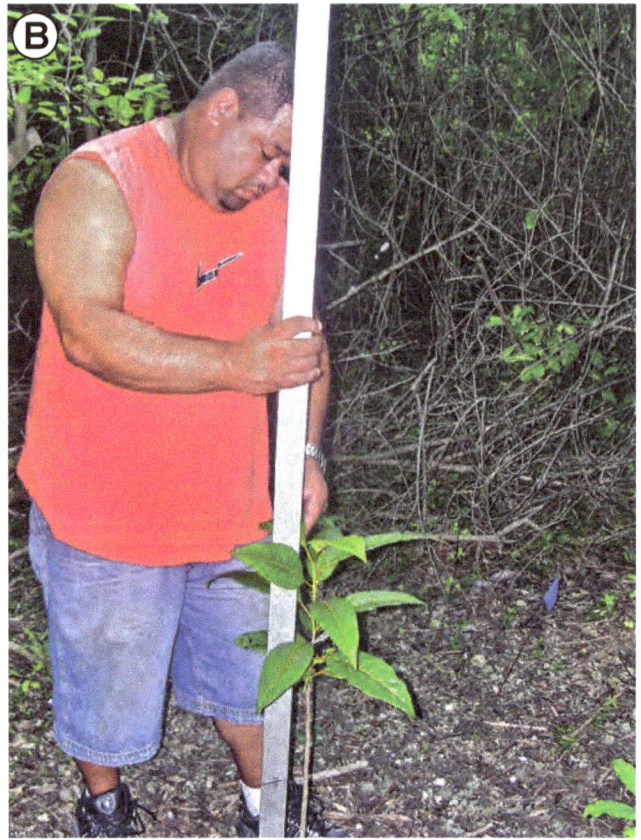

Figure 17.23—*Yard or meter sticks can be used to monitor height growth of planted trees as seen here with* Senna polyphylla *(A) and* Cordia rickseckeri *(B) in a forest enrichment project in the U.S. Virgin Islands. Photos by Brian F. Daley.*

with usually no more than 30 plots evenly distributed throughout the planted area. A 1/100 acre plot has a radius of approximately 12 ft (3.6 m), which is established with a center stake and a piece of string or twine cut to this length (Londo and Dicke 2006). All planted plants within the plot are counted, and their tops examined and measured. The root system of the plant closest to the center is excavated to evaluate planting technique. Record each plot separately on a survey form (figure 17.24) using the examination criteria shown in figure 17.10.

Stake Rows

Because it is hard to relocate plants on sites with rapid weed growth, 10-plant stake rows can be used to make plants easier to find in subsequent evaluations. One row plot consists of a starting point that can easily be relocated and 10 plants staked along a compass bearing. Height, diameter, and plant condition are recorded on the data form, along with average spacing between plants. Stake row data is typically used to determine survival, growth rates, and plants per area (Londo and Dicke 2006).

Sampling Design

Systematic, stratified sampling is often recommended because plots are located at standard predetermined distances and are therefore easy to establish and relocate. Stratification means that the entire population of plants in the outplanting area is subdivided into homogeneous units before sampling begins. First, strata of uniform conditions are identified, and then sample plots are located systematically within these areas (Pearce 1990). These strata could be based on species, nursery of origin, planting crew, or any other factor that could introduce serious variation. Machine-planted stock on abandoned farmland would have less variability because conditions are relatively uniform and planter-to-planter variation is not an issue. In contrast, considerable variability exists on hand-planted projects in mountainous terrain because of differences in aspect, soil, and planting technique.

Number of Plots

The number of plots to establish is generally a function of two factors: (1) available resources (time and money),

Plantation: ____________ Date Planted: ____________ Inspector: ____________

Plot Number: ____________ Date Inspected: ____________ Contract Number: ____________

Plant No.	Species Code	Height (cm)	Caliper (mm)	Condition Codes	Comments

Plant Condition Codes

1 = Poor planting spot
2 = Planted too deep
3 = Planted too shallow
4 = "J" root
5 = Poor compaction — Air pockets
6 = Foreign material in hole
7 = Not planted vertically
8 = Poor scalp
9 = Planted too close to another plant
10 = Other — Provide comments

Plot Map

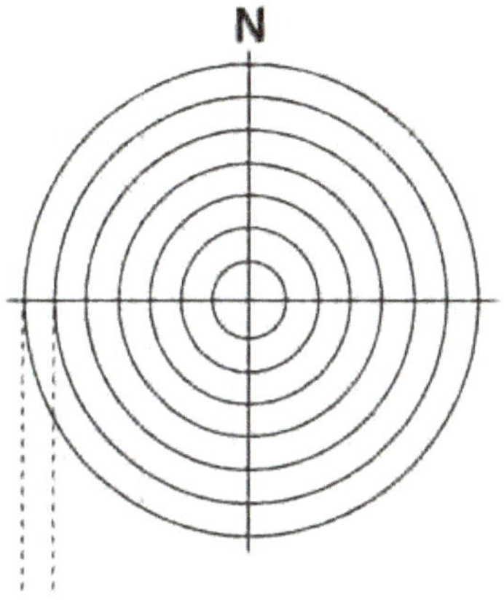

Scale = ____________

Figure 17.24—Using a standard survey form will ensure that the same information is collected at each plot. Figure by Jim Marin.

and (2) variability of the attributes that will be measured. In calculating an appropriate number of plots, statisticians are interested in some measure of variability, such as the standard deviation of plant heights in the outplanting. For example, if a quick check of plant heights shows great variability within the site to be sampled, then more plots should be added. On the other hand, if the heights appear to be very uniform, then fewer plots will be sufficient. If you want statistical significance, more complex calculations are available to compute appropriate number of plots using an estimate of the variability of the attribute and the degree of statistical accuracy desired (Stein 1992). Determining the number of plots based on variability is often a judgment call but, in most cases, a 1- to 2-percent sampling intensity is sufficient (Neumann and Landis 1995).

Post-Planting Maintenance

The most significant threat to success of planted seedlings on tropical sites is competing vegetation and animal damage. In addition to preventative measures performed by site preparation and treatments at the time of planting, post-planting treatments may be required to ensure the early growth and survival of seedlings.

Weed Control

Aggressive growth of grasses and weeds makes post-planting vegetation control an absolute necessity for the successful establishment of nursery plants on tropical project sites. Climbing vines can severely damage young trees and must be cut several times a year during the first years to keep them from shading, deforming, or even toppling young trees. Many field sites are infested with exotic grasses, such as the kikuyu grass (*Pennisetum clandestinum*) from Africa, which was introduced into many tropical areas a century ago and has effectively colonized expansive areas (figure 17.25). This grass has large roots, is a fierce competitor for soil moisture and nutrients, and is allelopathic (produces growth inhibitors to other

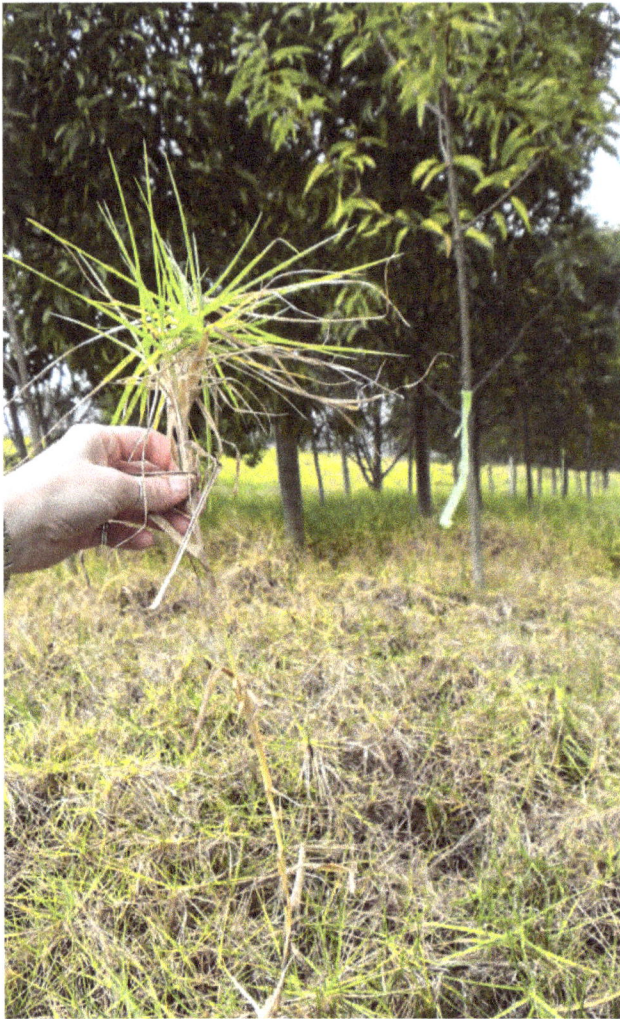

Figure 17.25—Kikuyu grass has formed a thick, dense cover across vast areas in Hawai'i and must be controlled to enable establishment and long-term growth and survival of desirable plant species. Photo by Diane L. Haase.

ing can be accomplished by mechanical or chemical means. Care must be taken not to damage the planted nursery stock, however. Intensive weed management and planting desired species eventually will increase the site's resistance to further weed invasion by favoring the growth and establishment of the desired species.

Animal Control

As with weed control, continued protection against animal damage after outplanting can be pivotal to ensuring the project's success. Periodic monitoring and maintenance needs to be done for installed mesh tubing to ensure that the plant is not tangled in the mesh and that it is still providing adequate protection; sometimes the tube can be slid upward as the plant grows for continued protection of the top. Fences need to be examined regularly and mended as needed for continued exclusion of animals.

Long-Term Followup: Refining Target Plant Specifications

Both the nursery manager and the client learn from the outplanting experiences and monitoring results. Checking in with clients for the first few years (or longer) after outplanting is valuable for improving nursery practices, outplanting techniques, and overall project successes. As described in Chapter 3, Defining the Target Plant, and Chapter 4, Crop Planning: Propagation Protocols, Schedules, and Records, the client and the nursery manager must work together from the outset to define target morphological and physiological specifications for the plants based on the assessment of site conditions, limiting factors, outplanting windows, and so on. Working together to assess what worked and what can be improved helps refine the target plant for similar conditions and improve results in the future. Chapter 18, Working With People, shows how to create clear agreements and responsibilities so the client and the nursery manager can enjoy an ongoing cooperative relationship. See Chapter 20, Discovering Ways to Improve Nursery Practices and Plant Quality, for more information on capturing lessons learned from clients and outplanting experiences.

vegetation). Tree growth is severely inhibited if this grass is not completely controlled around young trees. Herbicides have been found to be more effective than manual weed control because they kill the allelopathic roots as well as the tops (Ladrach 1992). In a planting of bluegum eucalyptus (*Eucalyptus globulus*) in Colombia, glyphosate was applied to kikuyu grass in a 3 ft (1 m) diameter along with hoed planting scalps at the time of planting and again 7 months later. After 2 years, tree volumes increased by more than 250 percent by the use of herbicide, compared with trees in plots where weeds were controlled by hoeing (Lambeth 1986).

Weed control during the first 2 years after planting helps the nursery stock to become established and controls the undesired species until they can be outcompeted or shaded out. As with site prep, weed maintenance after outplant-

References

Adams, J.C.; Patterson, W.B. 2004. Comparison of planting bar and hoedad planted seedlings for survival and growth in a controlled environment. In: Connor, K.F., ed. Proceedings of the 12th biennial southern silvicultural research conference. Gen. Tech. Rep. SRS-71. Asheville, NC: U.S. Department of Agriculture, Forest Service, Southern Research Station: 423–424.

Ammondt, S.A.; Litton, C.M.; Ellsworth, L.M.; Leary, J.K. 2013. Restoration of native plant communities in a Hawaiian dry lowland ecosystem dominated by the invasive grass Megathyrsus maximus. Applied Vegetation Science. 16: 29-39.

Barajas-Guzmán, A.E.; Campo, J.; Barradas, V.L. 2006. Soil water, nutrient availability and sapling survival under organic and polyethylene mulch in a seasonally dry tropical forest. Plant and Soil. 287: 347–357.

Bell, F.; Falanruw, M.; Lawrence, B.; Limtiaco, D.; Nelson, D. 2002. Draft vegetation strategy for southern Guam. Honolulu, HI: U.S. Department of Agriculture, Forest Service and Natural Resources Conservation Service; Government of Guam Division of Forestry. 11 p.

Burger, D.W.; Forister, G.W.; Kiehl, P.A. 1996. Height, caliper growth and biomass response of ten shade tree species to tree shelters. Journal of Agriculture. 22(4): 161–166.

Cleary, B.D.; Greaves, R.D.; Hermann, R.K. 1978. Regenerating Oregon's Forests. Corvallis, OR: Oregon State University Extension Service. 286 p.

Dendy, J. 2011. Low input methods of forest restoration and observations of native birds and flying foxes in savanna habitat in the Lake Ngardok Nature Reserve, Palau. MS Thesis, University of Hawai'i at Hilo.

Emmingham, W.H.; Cleary, B.C.; DeYoe, D.R. 2002. Seedling care and handling. In: Oregon State University Extension Service: The woodland workbook: forest protection. Corvallis, OR: Oregon State University Extension Service. 4p.

Engelbrecht, B.M.J.; Kursar, T.A. 2003. Comparative drought-resistance of seedlings of 28 species of co-occurring tropical woody plants. Oecologia. 136: 383–393.

Feyera, S.; Beck, E.; Lüttge, U. 2002. Exotic trees as nurse-trees for the regeneration of natural tropical forests. Trees. 16: 245–249.

Forestry Suppliers Inc. 2013. Forestry Suppliers website. http://www.forestry-suppliers.com/. (March 2013).

Gavenda B.; Nemesek J. 2008. Soil quality and land use changes on a humid tropical island-Palau. USDA Natural Resource Conservation Service, Pacific Islands Area, Mongmong, Guam, USA.

Haase, D.L.; Rose, R.W.; Trobaugh, J. 2006. Field performance of three stock sizes of Douglas-fir container seedlings grown with slow-release fertilizer in the nursery growing medium. New Forests. 31: 1–24.

Hau, B.C.H.; Corlett, R.T. 2003. Factors affecting the early survival and growth of native tree seedlings planted on a degraded hillside grassland in Hong Kong, China. Restoration Ecology. 11: 483–488.

Heiskanen, J.; Viiri, H. 2005. Effects of mounding on damage by the European pine weevil in planted Norway spruce seedlings. Northern Journal of Applied Forestry. 22(3): 154–161.

Helgerson, O.T. 1989. Heat damage in tree seedlings and its prevention. New Forests. 3: 333–358.

Hoag, J.C.; Landis, T.D. 2001. Riparian zone restoration: field requirements and nursery opportunities. Native Plants Journal. 2: 30–35.

Holl, K.D. 2002. Effect of shrubs on tree seedling establishment in an abandoned tropical pasture. Journal of Ecology. 90: 179–187.

Holl, K.D.; Aide, T.M. 2011. When and where to actively restore ecosystems? Forest Ecology and Management. 261(10): 1558–1563.

Jacobs, D.F. 2011. Reforestation of a salvage-logged high-elevation clearcut: Engelmann spruce seedling response to tree shelters after eleven growing seasons. Western Journal of Applied Forestry. 26:53-56.

Jacobs, D.F.; Rose, R.; Haase, D.L.; Alzugaray, P.O. 2004. Fertilization at planting inhibits root system development and drought avoidance of Douglas-fir (Pseudotsuga menziesii) seedlings. Annals of Forest Science. 61: 643–651.

Jeffrey, J.; Horiuchi, B. 2003. Tree planting at Hakalau National Wildlife Refuge—the right tool for the right stock type. Native Plants Journal. 4: 30–31.

Jones, B.; Alm, A.A. 1989. Comparison of planting tools for containerized seedlings: two-year results. Tree Planters' Notes. 40): 22–24.

Kaboré, D.; Reij, C. 2004. The emergence and spreading of an improved traditional soil and water conservation practice in Burkina Faso. Paper 114. IFPRI. Washington, DC: International Food Policy Research Institute, Environment and Production Technology Division. 43 p.

Kloetzel, S. 2004. Revegetation and restoration planting tools: an in-the-field perspective. Native Plants Journal. 5: 34–42.

Ladrach, W.E. 1992. Plantation establishment techniques in tropical America. Tree Planters' Notes. 43: 125–132.

Lamb, D.; Erskine, D.P.; Parrotta, A.J. 2005. Restoration of degraded tropical forest landscapes. Science. 310: 1628–1632.

Lambeth, C.C. 1986. Grass control with the herbicide Roundup increases yield of *Eucalyptus globulus* in Salinas. Res. Rep. 108. Cali, Colombia: Carton de Colombia, S.A. 5 p.

Landis, T.D.; Dumroese, R.K.; Haase, D.L. 2010. The container tree nursery manual: volume 7, seedling processing, storage, and outplanting. Agriculture Handbook 674. Washington, DC: U.S. Department of Agriculture, Forest Service. 200 p.

Landis, T.D.; Haase, D.L. 2012. Applications of hydrogels in the nursery and during outplanting. In: Haase, D.L.; Pinto, J.R.; Riley, L.E., tech coords. National proceedings: forest and conservation nursery associations—2011. Proceedings RMRS-P-68. Fort Collins, CO: U.S. Department of Agriculture, Forest Service, Rocky Mountain Research Station. 53–58.

Lof, M.; Rydberg, D.; Bolte, A. 2006. Mounding site preparation for forest restoration: survival and short term growth response in *Quercus robur* L. seedlings. Forest Ecology and Management. 232: 19–25.

Londo, A.J.; Dicke, S.G. 2006. Measuring survival and planting quality in new pine plantations. Tech. Bull. SREF-FM-001. Athens, GA: University of Georgia, Southern Regional Extension Forestry. 5 p.

Lowery, R.F.; Lambeth, C.C.; Endo, M.; Kane, M. 1993. Vegetation management in tropical forest plantations. Canadian Journal of Forest Research. 23: 2006–2014.

Lowman, B. 1999. Tree planting equipment. In: Alden J., ed. Stocking standards and reforestation methods for Alaska. Misc. Pub. 99-8. Fairbanks, AK: University of Alaska Fairbanks, Agricultural and Forestry Experiment Station: 74–77.

Lugo, A.E. 1997. The apparent paradox of reestablishing species richness on degraded lands with tree monocultures. Forest Ecology and Management. 99: 9–19.

McKay, H.M.; Gardiner, B.A.; Mason, W.L.; Nelson, D.G.; Hollingsworth, M.K. 1993. The gravitational forces generated by dropping plants and the response of Sitka spruce seedlings to dropping. Canadian Journal of Forestry Research. 23: 2443–2451.

Medeiros, A.C.; vonAllmen, E. 2006. Restoration of native Hawaiian dryland forest at Auwahi, Maui. Fact Sheet 2006–3035. Reston, VA: U.S. Department of the Interior, U.S. Geological Survey. 4 p.

Mexal, J.G.; Negreros-Castillo, P.; Rangel, R.A.C.; Moreno, R. 2005. Evaluation of seedling quality and planting tools for successful establishment of tropical hardwoods. International Plant Propagators Society, Combined Proceedings. 55: 524–530.

Neumann, R.W.; Landis, T.D. 1995. Benefits and techniques for evaluating outplanting success. In: Landis, T.D.; Cregg, B., tech. coords. National proceedings, forest and conservation nursery associations. Gen. Tech. Rep. PNW-GTR-365. Portland, OR: U.S. Department of Agriculture, Forest Service, Pacific Northwest Research Station: 36–43.

Pearce, C. 1990. Monitoring regeneration programs. In: Lavender, D.P.; Parish, R.; Johnson, C.M.; Montgomery, G.; Vyse, A.; Willis, R.A.; Winston, D. Regenerating British Columbia's forests. Vancouver, BC, Canada: University of British Columbia Press: 98–116.

Rose, R.; Haase, D.L. 2006. Guide to reforestation in Oregon. Corvallis, OR: Oregon State University, College of Forestry. 48 p.

Rose, R.; Ketchum, J.S. 2002. Interaction of vegetation control and fertilization on conifer species across the Pacific Northwest. Canadian Journal of Forest Research. 32: 136–152.

Rose, R.; Rosner, L.S. 2005. Eighth-year response of Douglas-fir seedlings to area of weed control and herbaceous versus woody weed control. Annals of Forest Science 62: 481-492.

Sharpe, A.L.; Mason, W.L.; Howes, R.E.J. 1990. Early forest performance of roughly handled Sitka spruce and Douglas-fir of different plant types. Scottish Forestry. 44: 257–265.

Stein, W.I. 1992. Regeneration surveys and evaluation. In: Hobbs, S.D.; Tesch, S.D.; Owston, P.W.; Stewart, R.E.; Tappeiner, J.C.; Wells, G.E., eds. Reforestation practices in southwestern Oregon and northern California. Corvallis, OR: Oregon State University, Forest Research Laboratory: 346–382.

Steinfeld, D.E.; Riley, S.A.; Wilkinson, K.M.; Landis, T.D.; Riley, L.E. 2008. Roadside revegetation: an integrated approach to establishing native plants. Vancouver, WA: U.S. Department of Transportation, Federal Highway Administration. 413 p.

Sutton, R.F. 1993. Mounding site preparation: a review of European and North American experience. New Forests. 7: 151–192.

Swistock, B.R.; Mecum, K.A.; Sharpe, W.E. 1999. Summer temperatures inside ventilated and unventilated brown plastic treeshelters in Pennsylvania. Northern Journal of Applied Forestry. 16: 7–10.

Thomas, D.S. 2008. Hydrogel applied to the root plug of subtropical eucalypt seedlings halves transplant death following planting. Forest Ecology and Management. 255: 1305–1314.

Trent, A. 1999. Improved tree-planting tools. Timber Tech Tips 9924-2316-MTDC. Missoula, MT: U.S. Department of Agriculture, Forest Service, Technology and Development Program. 6 p.

Upton, D.; de Groot, P. 2008. Planting and establishment of tropical trees. Propagation and Planting Manuals. Vol. 5. London, United Kingdom: Commonwealth Secretariat. 142 p.

U.S. Department of Agriculture (USDA). 2002. Silvicultural practices handbook (2409.17): chapter 2—reforestation. Missoula, MT: U.S. Department of Agriculture, Forest Service. 106 p.

Van der Putten, W.H.; Mortimer, S.R.; Hedlund, K.; Van Dijk, C.; Brown, V.K.; Leps, J.; Rodriguez-Barrueco, C.; Roy, J.; Len, T.A.D.; Gormsen, D.; Korthals, G.W.; Lavorel, S.; Regina, I.S.;

Smilauer, P. 2000. Plant species diversity as a driver of early succession in abandoned fields: a multi-site approach. Oecologia. 124: 91–99.

Weller, S.G.; Cabin, R.J.; Lorence, D.H.; Perlman, S.; Wood, K.; Flynn, T.; Sakai, A.K. 2011. Alien plant invasions, introduced ungulates, and alternative states in a mesic forest in Hawaii. Restoration Ecology. 19: 671–680.

Wightman, K.E.; Shear, T.; Goldfarb, B.; Haggar, J. 2001. Nursery and field establishment techniques to improve seedling growth of three Costa Rican hardwoods. New Forests. 22: 75–96.

Working With People

18

Kim M. Wilkinson

The ability to produce healthy, vibrant plants is an art, a science, and a learned skill. Success, however, depends not only on your ability to produce quality plants, but also on your ability to work effectively with people. This chapter provides an overview of skillfully managing relationships with diverse groups of people including staff, clients, and the community (figure 18.1).

Figure 18.1—Managing a nursery includes working with the community and relating with the public. Friends of Hakalau Forest National Wildlife Refuge raised funds to install this new water tank to support the greenhouse work at the refuge. Volunteers from the Hawai'i Nature Center installed the sign. The greenhouse propagates some of the rarest plants in the world for outplanting on the Refuge. Photo by Dick Wass, Friends of Hakalau Forest National Wildlife Refuge.

Facing Page: *U.S. Virgin Islands Department of Agriculture nursery on St. Croix. This nursery grows both native tree species and fruit and vegetable plants for urban and community forestry. Photo by Ronald Overton.*

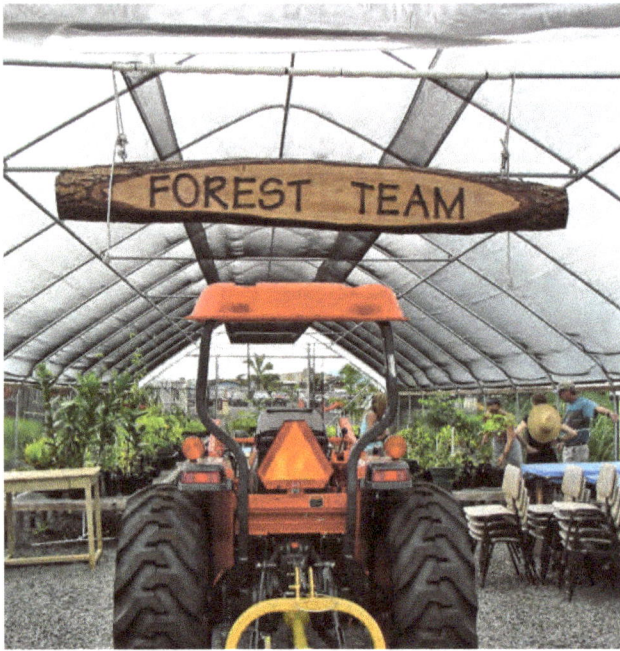

Figure 18.2—*Regular reconnection with the nursery's vision serves as a guide and a reminder. This "Forest Team" sign reminds everyone the nursery is about more than the trees. Photo by Douglass F. Jacobs.*

Interact Based on the Nursery Vision and Objectives

Nurseries are founded on a vision, as described in Chapter 2, Planning a Tropical Nursery. The vision involves a sense of how the human communities and local ecosystems could be in the future as a result of the efforts put forth by the nursery today and is a key part of relating with other people. Regular attention to the vision can help to motivate staff (including yourself), keep management on track, attract and retain good clients, relate with other growers and researchers, engage with the public, and garner support from the community at large. In daily interactions with staff, clients, and the community, regular reconnection with the vision serves as a guide and a reminder of what needs to be done and why. Keep your nursery's vision, objectives, and mission statement in a visible place and refer to them when working with people (figure 18.2).

Working With Yourself

Personalities and management styles vary widely among effective nursery managers. Some general characteristics, however, are important to good nursery management. A clear understanding of and commitment to the vision are essential along with practical management attributes.

Consider cultivating the following attributes in yourself:

• Keen observation skills.

• A flexible management style (scheduling must be adaptable to the shifting needs of living, growing plants).

• An ability to "think like a plant" (managing plants effectively is an art as well as a science; someone who has a "feel" for the crops will likely do better as a manager than someone who approaches crops strictly from a technical perspective).

• A sense of responsibility for plants in the nursery.

• A creative approach to working with land managers, staff, and other people.

• Enthusiasm for promoting a culture of learning and sharing within the nursery and with the larger community.

A small nursery usually has one person, the manager, who takes care of everything. Even so, it is essential to have at least one backup person who also understands crop status, knows basic things that need to be done, and knows how to do these things. The backup person can keep the nursery running and the plants alive and healthy in case the primary person becomes unavailable. In a larger nursery, the manager oversees the same tasks but delegates many of them to employees. Many individuals contribute their task to the process, but nursery management cannot be conducted "by committee." All nurseries, large or small, ultimately need one person, the manager, to take responsibility for the crop (figure 18.3).

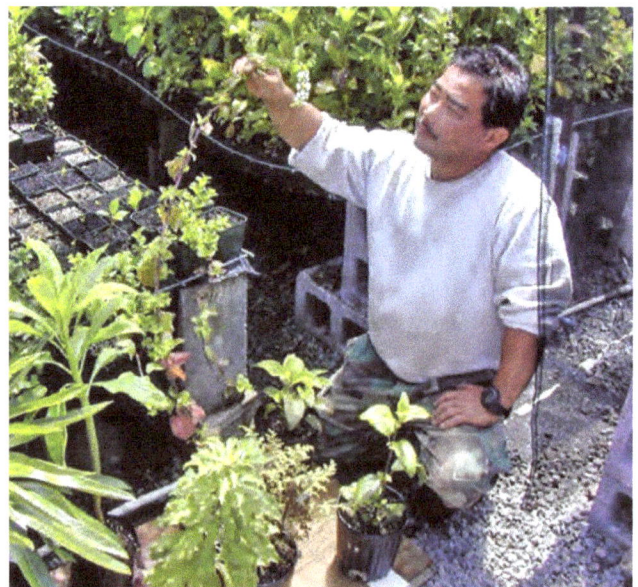

Figure 18.3—*Keen observation skills and the ability to "think like a plant" are key attributes of an effective nursery manager. Photo by Thomas D. Landis.*

Working With Nursery Staff

As the manager, you should help each employee connect with the nursery's vision. When everyone shares and is knowingly working towards the vision, each day will be a meaningful day, even when filled with tedious tasks such as pulling weeds. Sharing the nursery's mission and overall goals fosters a greater sense of purpose among staff thereby elevating morale and avoiding "it-is-just-a-job" attitudes (figure 18.4).

Staff need to be trained to observe the crops, detect problems, and understand and carry out their direct responsibilities. Some education in horticulture is helpful to enable employees to "think like a plant" and they can be encouraged to stay curious and learn more about the plants and their production. Safety training is essential.

Clear communication is core to great employee relations. Your daily communication with staff will be to assign roles, tasks, and goals. You should encourage dialogue and be open to feedback from employees about how they think they can work more efficiently. You should also provide feedback to staff so they can optimize the value of their work. Brief, weekly meetings are valuable for linking the day-to-day tasks with the nursery's vision. Meetings can be scheduled on Monday morning to assess plans and prioritize activities for the week and again at the end of the week to evaluate progress and identify potential activities for the coming week. Connecting to the vision at the beginning and end of the week sets the tone for current and future work.

Figure 18.5—It is important to develop an organizational culture within the nursery that facilitates learning and collaborating. Nursery staff in Yap work together to test the irrigation system. Photo by George Hernández.

Creating a Learning Organization

Learning takes place on an individual level and also within the nursery as an organization. If a nursery is to grow and adapt, it is necessary to develop an organizational culture that facilitates learning and collaboration (figure 18.5).

Adaptive learning within an organization depends on a willingness to accept new information and ideas, to build bridges and make connections among other sources of knowledge, and to occasionally revisit and question fundamental assumptions, even if doing so may mean changing "the way things have always been done." Table 18.1 summarizes some ways that organizations may or may not be set up for adaptive learning. Creating a nursery culture that facilitates, rather than hinders, learning and adaptation is important.

Figure 18.4—Each person who works at the nursery may choose to state in his or her own words his or her vision for his or her work and how it links to the nursery's mission and objectives. Then, even on days when the task is pulling weeds all day, it is still a meaningful day. Photo by Susan Charnley.

Table 18.1—How organizations treat information. Adapted from Westrum (1994).

Pathological organization	Bureaucratic organization	Learning organization
Do not want to know	May not find out	Actively seek information
Messengers are shot	Messengers are listened to	Messengers are trained
Responsibility is shirked	Responsibility is compartmentalized	Responsibility is shared
Bridging is discouraged	Bridging is allowed but neglected	Bridging is rewarded
Failure is punished or covered up	Organization is just and merciful	Inquiry and redirection
New ideas are crushed	New ideas present problems	New ideas are welcomed

Discovering

Daily observation and recordkeeping, maintaining plant development records, and updating propagation protocols are the foundation for understanding how crops grow and develop in your nursery environment. Making discoveries through simple experimentation is often a key aspect of successful nursery management. Monthly or seasonal staff meetings are useful for determine some of the most pressing questions facing the nursery. These questions will shape priorities for trials. For example, at the beginning stages of nursery development when production levels are low, the nursery may decide to try different container types to determine the best ones for the crops to be grown at the nursery, or to experiment with different seed treatment techniques for a new species. Later in nursery development, other pressing questions may arise such as: What problems are recurring that might be preventable? What could improve efficiency? What could improve crop quality? The nursery might decide to test seed sources and assess their performance in the nursery and the field to refine target plant objectives. Ways to design, execute, and assess these experiments are detailed in Chapter 20, Discovering Ways to Improve Nursery Practices and Plant Quality.

Training

Training and ongoing education is of great value to you and your staff. The more that everyone understands his or her work and the effects of his or her activities, the more he or she will be able to relate to the crop and improve plant quality and nursery efficiency. Attending training sessions and conferences and reading pertinent publications are important investments in the nursery's adaptability and growth (figure 18.6). Visiting other nurseries and reciprocating by hosting other growers at your nursery is an important part of cultivating supportive, informative, sharing relationships (figure 18.7) and are a wonderful opportunity to gain a broader perspective.

Working With Clients

Nurseries take many different forms: retail, wholesale, research, nonprofit, community-based, or some combination thereof. Clients may be farmers, forest planters, conservation area managers, schools, landscapers, nonprofit organizations, gardeners, or government agencies. With increasing awareness of the importance of quality plants well-matched for conditions on the outplanting site, more clients seek nurseries that can provide those kinds of plants. Working with clients involves understanding their target plant needs, contracting, ongoing communications, and following-up after outplanting to see how the plants performed in the field.

Defining Target Plant Needs

As discussed in Chapter 3, Defining the Target Plant, nursery managers and land managers ideally engage in an ongoing discussion about project objectives, reevaluate successes and failures observed on the outplanting site, and subsequently redefine the target plant to improve future plant quality in the nursery and on the outplanting site.

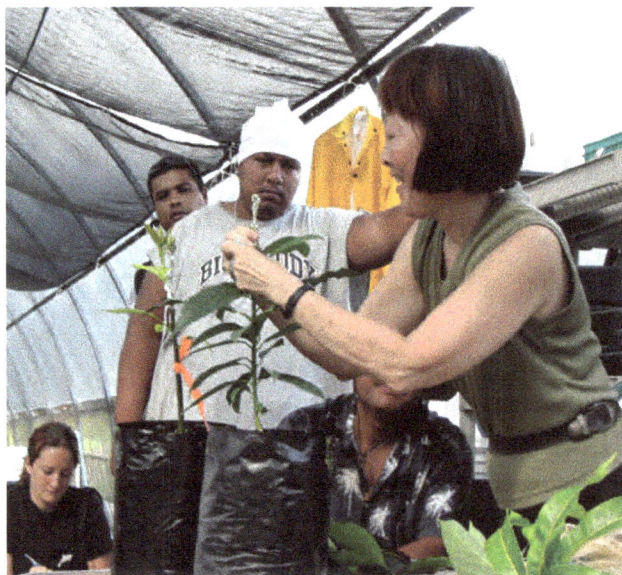

Figure 18.6—Training and ongoing education is of great value to you and your staff. Here, nursery workers gathered for a training to learn about grafting techniques in Volcanoes National Park, on the Big Island of Hawai'i. Photo by Kim M. Wilkinson.

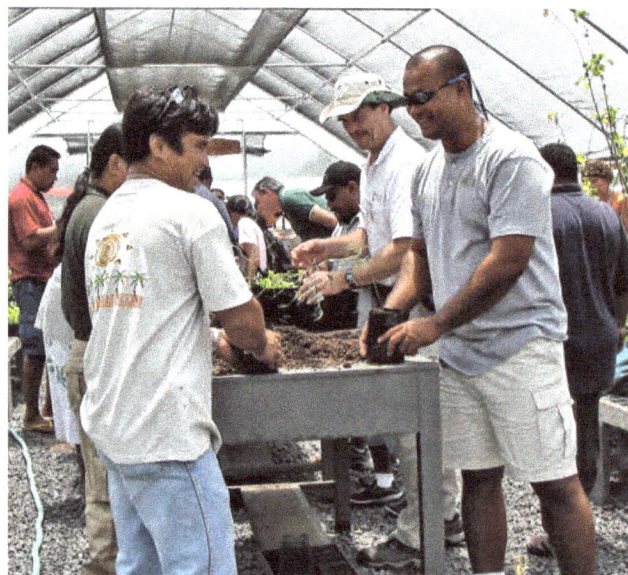

Figure 18.7—Hosting visits to your nursery and attending events at other nurseries is a great way to cultivate information exchange and supportive relationships. Photo by Kim M. Wilkinson.

1. Outplanting Objectives

2. Site Conditions

3. Limiting Factors

4. Mitigating Measures for Limiting Factors

5. Species and Genetic Sources

6. Stocktype

7. Outplanting Tools and Techniques

8. Outplanting Window

Figure 18.8—The process of defining target plant materials is an essential tool for specifying what the nursery will grow for the client. Illustration adapted from Landis (2011) by Jim Marin.

For new nurseries, clients, or projects, a good starting point for the Target Plant Concept dialog is to consider past experiences on similar sites and determine the target plant needs for the project. For complex, large, or specialized projects, another professional may need to assess the site and create a plan including appropriate species selection, spacing, and other target plant needs. Examples include government-supported projects that warrant a Forest Stewardship Plan, a Conservation Plan (such as the USDA Natural Resources Conservation Service might do for soil conservation or riparian restoration), a Habitat Improvement Plan, or commercial Farm Plans. If a new client might require this level of assistance, steer the client to the appropriate agency or professional and invite him or her to order from you when his or her plan is ready and the target plant material requirements are defined. Sometimes, agencies may have general plant recommendations, such as appropriate windbreak species, requiring you and the client to fill in the remaining "blanks" for the target plant, or sometimes you and the client may simply need to determine outplanting window and local genetics. The example from Chapter 4, Crop Planning: Propagation Protocols, Schedules, and Records, of a client and nursery working together is revisited here (see textbox) with more emphasis on how the communication process works.

Working With Noncontracted Clients

Nurseries that grow on contract may also grow additional seedlings or have overstock to sell to potential customers that need plants immediately. If the seedlings are genetically appropriate for their site, these customers may wish to purchase them for their project. A potential customer occasionally may have the notion that your nursery can provide "cheap, all-purpose, ready-made, grow-anywhere plants"—we know that does not exist. In this circumstance, it is your job to help them learn; by requiring the target plant information you are supporting the success of their project, which reflects favorably on your nursery. Not everyone can be your client, and that is okay. If you are having trouble getting a potential client to think through his or her project and define his or her target plant needs, be friendly but firm and give the client a way to come back: "Our nursery takes pride in providing high-quality plant materials suitable for client's needs. I would be happy to help you with your plants after you have determined your target plant needs for your outplanting site."

Working With Contracted Clients

Communication about plant targets is easier when clients order plants on contract. Many nurseries grow most of their native and traditional plants to order on contract, which ensures that plants are matched to specific project objectives and outplanting sites. This approach is the opposite of speculative growing, where nurseries produce plants based on estimates of future demand. Contract growing involves producing plants to a client's target specifications (figures 18.8, 18.9). The ecological and economic benefits of this approach are plentiful—clients benefit by getting exactly the plants they need when they need them, nurseries benefit by minimizing waste and maximizing time and resources propagating only plants that will be used, and plants and the environment benefit from greater success in survival, growth, and establishment of locally appropriate species. For conservation work and habitat improvement, growing locally adapted, genetically appropriate plant materials on

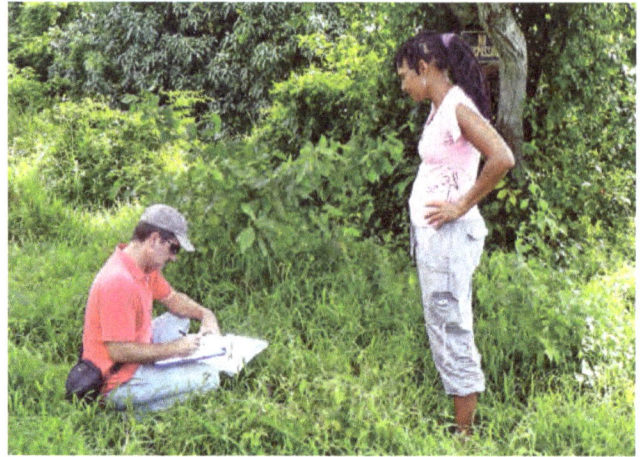

Figure 18.9—*The nursery manager and the land manager meet at the outplanting site to define target plant specifications for the project. Photo by Brian F. Daley.*

have only one contact person for that client. This one-on-one arrangement precludes many potential misunderstandings, streamlines time and energy spent on communication, and helps develop long-term relationships and trust. For contract growing, create a clear agreement in writing. In some circumstances, such as growing for neighbors or close community members, a written agreement may seem overly formal; however, it can be invaluable for creating clear expectations, enhancing communication, demonstrating your professionalism, and making the entire process a smooth one for everyone concerned. Often your client will be new to purchasing plants by contract and will be relieved you have a protocol in place to ensure everything goes smoothly, and the client's investment is protected. Both the client and the nursery representatives need to sign the agreement, and each need to keep a signed copy.

The terms of the agreement must include the following—

- Description of the plant materials to be provided (such as species, genetics, container type, plant size).

- Anticipated schedule.

- Quantity of plants to be provided.

- Price per unit and the total price for the order.

- Any additional fees that may apply, such as delivery charges and refundable container deposits.

- When and how payment will be made.

Crop production may vary from year to year. If possible, when the order is placed, agree on a window of time for plant delivery that spans a few weeks rather than setting an exact date. Based on crop development, the exact date for delivery can be determined closer to the tentative delivery date.

contract helps maximize benefits to pollinators and other wildlife. When ordering plants on contract, clients need to give the nursery sufficient time to produce them to specification for outplanting at the correct time.

If the client is a family or an organization with several members, ask the client to assign one sole contact person for the order with the nursery. This person should be your contact from the time of drafting and signing the contract through to delivery of the plants. In turn, the nursery should

The sample contract in the textbox below is for demonstration purposes only. Contracts at your nursery should be tailored to meet your and your client's needs. It is best to consult with a legal expert to ensure the contract protects your nursery and conforms to local legal statutes.

Ongoing Communications With Clients

Clients appreciate staying informed about their crop's progress. Sending e-mail updates (including digital photos), having periodic phone conversations, or inviting clients to visit their crop at the nursery is vital to keeping them involved and committed to the schedule (figure 18.10).

Sample Contract With Green's Tree Nursery

This agreement, entered into this ___7th___ (day) of ___March___ (month), ___2014___ (year), by and between **Green's Tree Nursery** and ___Upland Ranch and Forest___ (hereinafter referred to as "Client") witnesses as follows:

Whereas Green's Tree Nursery is organized to provide plant materials for outplanting; whereas Client is interested in purchasing plant materials from Green's Tree Nursery, it is agreed between the parties as follows:

I. Plant Materials Provided by Green's Tree Nursery

In time for the planting window ___December 10–20___ Green's Tree Nursery will provide ___500 koa (Acacia koa)___ seedlings of the following specifications:

- Species—koa (Acacia koa).

- Genetic source—Seeds sourced from minimum 50 parent trees of good form (large, straight-boled) from koa forest neighboring Upland Ranch.

- Size and description—Containers: Ray Leach "Stubby" cells; Seedling size: 15 to 30 cm tall, minimum stem diameter 3.5 mm; Roots: firm and nodulating with rhizobia, inoculated with mycorrhizal fungi (AMF).

- Price—$3.50 per seedling.

II. Fees

Client agrees to pay Green's Tree Nursery ___$1,750___ for the ___500___ plants listed above. Payment shall be made in the following way: an initial fee of ___$875___ (50% of the total for plant materials) is required to begin propagation, with the balance of ___$875___ to be paid before dispatch of the plant materials. Other fees, such as container deposits (10 cents per "Stubby" cell) and shipping/delivery charges (TBD based on carrier) if applicable, will be billed separately and are also to be paid in full before dispatch of the plant materials.

If any payment as per the above schedule remains overdue for more than 60 days, Client acknowledges that Green's Tree Nursery may take legal action to collect the overdue amount. In such event, Client will be responsible for all reasonable litigation expenses incurred by Green's Tree Nursery, including, but not limited to, court costs and attorney fees.

III. General Conditions

Green's Tree Nursery agrees to use its best efforts to provide the plant materials listed in Section I above.

Client understands and acknowledges that Green's Tree Nursery shall in no way bear liability for results produced in use of plant materials. Green's Tree Nursery's maximum liability is limited in amount to the amount paid by Client to Green's Tree Nursery for the purchase of the plant materials under all circumstances and regardless of the nature, cause, or extent of any loss.

In the event that Client cancels the order for plant materials in whole or in part, Client agrees to pay the balance due for the full amount for plant materials as listed in Section I.

Green's Tree Nursery reserves the right to prorate or cancel any order, in whole or in part, because of natural disaster, disease, casualty, or other circumstances beyond our control. In the event that Green's Tree Nursery is unable to provide the plant materials listed in Section I above by ___December 20___, the initial fee paid by Client may be applied to another purchase, credited to a future order, or refunded, as requested by Client. In any other event, the initial fee is nonrefundable and the entire balance is due.

Continued on next page

Client agrees that all plant materials ordered must be dispatched (picked up, shipped, or delivered) within 30 days of notification of readiness as determined by Green's Tree Nursery. Plant materials not dispatched within 30 days are subject to a storage fee of $0.05 cents per plant per day; plant materials not claimed within 45 days of notification of readiness are forfeited.

IV. Conclusion

This agreement, executed in duplicate, sets forth the entire contract between the parties and may be canceled, modified, or amended only by a written instrument executed by each of the parties thereto.

This agreement shall be construed as a contract under the laws of___Hawai'i___ (name of State or territory and country).

Witness the hands and seals of the parties hereto, each duly authorized, the day and year first written above.

_____

Maria Planter   Date
Upland Ranch and Forest

_____

Gloria Green   Date
Green's Tree Nursery

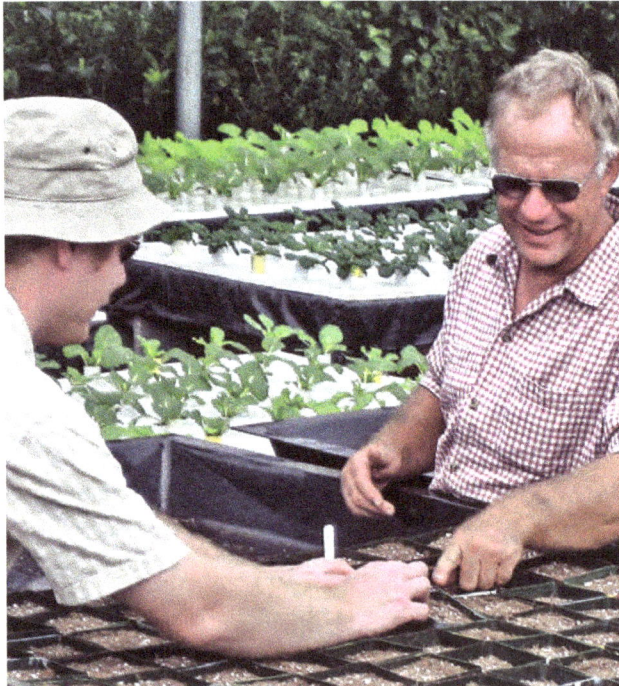

Figure 18.10—Clients often enjoy staying informed about their crop's progress. Sending e-mail updates with photos or inviting clients to visit their crop helps keep clients in the loop. Photo by Douglass F. Jacobs.

Sample Client Update

Re: Update on your order for 500 koa (Acacia koa)

Date: November 10

Dear Maria,

I hope this note finds you well. I'm writing to let you know your 500 koa seedlings are doing great—we moved them into the final hardening stage of production last week, so they are getting toughened up for outplanting. We are right on schedule. Let's arrange a pickup date for some time between December 10 and December 15. I think you said you have a van to transport them? If not, let me know, and we will find a safe transport solution. Please write or call back to confirm that you got this message, when you get a chance. I look forward to hearing from you.

—Gloria, Manager, Green's Tree Nursery

Staff should remember that tremendous effort and expense go into planning a project and preparing land for outplanting. Acquiring plants is a central part of this process but may be a small percentage of the total project cost. Nursery staff should do everything in their power to meet set schedules. If any problems or delays are anticipated with the crop, clients must be updated immediately so they can modify their plans accordingly.

Educating Clients About Shipping, Handling, and Outplanting

As described in Chapter 16, Harvesting and Shipping, plants are vulnerable to damaging stresses during the transition from the nursery to the outplanting site. Some nurseries take charge of shipping and handling, others leave it to the client to pick up and transport their plants. In most cases, clients will do their own outplanting. Many clients will be knowledgeable about plants and treat them properly to ensure success after leaving the nursery. Other clients, however, may compromise their plants' quality by stressing them during transport, delaying planting by weeks without watering, or planting improperly. Everyone loses when these problems occur: the client is unhappy (and may blame the nursery), the nursery's hard work to cultivate the plants is wasted, the plants do not survive or thrive, and the environment does not benefit from the presence of the plants. These problems can be avoided by educating clients in advance so they know how to properly transport, store, and outplant their new plants (figure 18.11).

Well before the delivery date for plants, provide clients with information to help them properly plan for the best shipping, handling, storage, and outplanting practices after they receive their plants. For example, you could send them copies of Chapter 16, Harvesting and Shipping, and Chapter 17, Outplanting, from this manual, or you could create a checklist of "do's" and "don'ts" based on those chapters and your own experiences. These educational materials will also help clients communicate best practices to everyone who will work with the plants after they leave the nursery.

Following Up With Clients

The success of the nursery, the clients, and the plants in the field are interrelated. After an order is complete, you need to have a system in place whereby clients can provide feedback. Sometimes nursery managers are reluctant to follow up because they are concerned that they will be blamed for losses or problems. With a good contract in place (as described previously), however, the limits of the nursery's responsibility are clearly defined.

Often, success of reforestation and restoration projects is monitored after outplanting by tracking survival or other important characteristics, as described in Chapter 17, Outplanting. Clients may also keep track of specific problems affecting plant survival and growth in the field (pests, grazing animals, drought, and so on). This information, whether formal or observational, should be shared with the nursery.

Figure 18.11—*Educate clients in advance so they know how to properly transport, store, and outplant their new plants. Photo by Brian F. Daley.*

Figure 18.12—Hosting workshops or field days helps educate the community about the nursery's mission and plant materials being produced, such as this group of university students learning about reforesting Hawaiian dryland native species. Photo by Yvonne Yarber Carter.

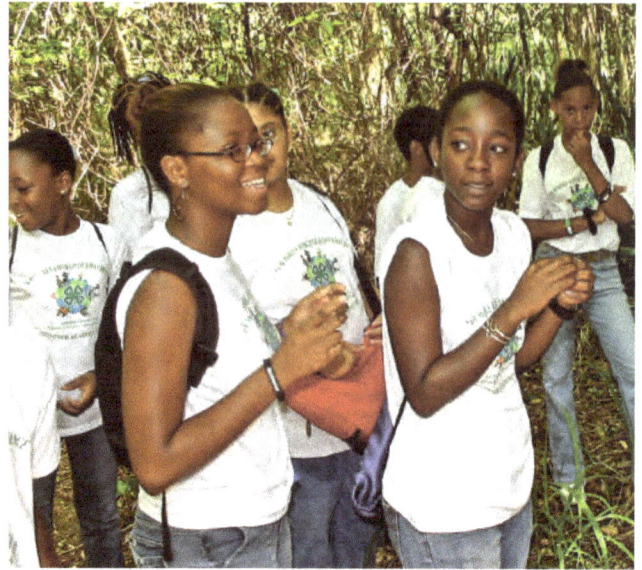

Figure 18.13—Discussing the role of native plants in the local forest ecology is an engaging way to involve youth groups. Shown are members of the St. Croix, Virgin Islands 4-H club hiking on a trail that leads to a forest restoration site where native trees were planted. Photo by Brian F. Daley.

This field information is important for learning and improving nursery practices and is a key part of customer relations. Although some failures and problems are inevitable, you will also get an opportunity to see successes, which will add to your satisfaction with your work. Ideally the nursery contact person can visit the outplanting site and check on the progress of the plants over time. Observations can then be used to improve target plant specifications for that outplanting environment.

Working With the Community

Community education and outreach are important activities for many tropical plant nurseries. The perpetuation of native and culturally important plants is often a part of the nursery's mission, but the best efforts are lost if the community is not ready, willing, or able to use plants the nursery will produce. Hosting tours, workshops, or field days, writing educational materials, articles, or blogs, and attending local fairs, farmer's markets, or trade shows can all help educate the community about the nursery's mission and availability of plant materials being produced. People who might one day plant species from your nursery would benefit from learning interesting details about the plants, such as their interactions with pollinators or their traditional medicinal properties, as well as some of the more practical aspects of working with the plants, such as how to plant a tree or the importance of locally adapted seed sources (figure 18.12).

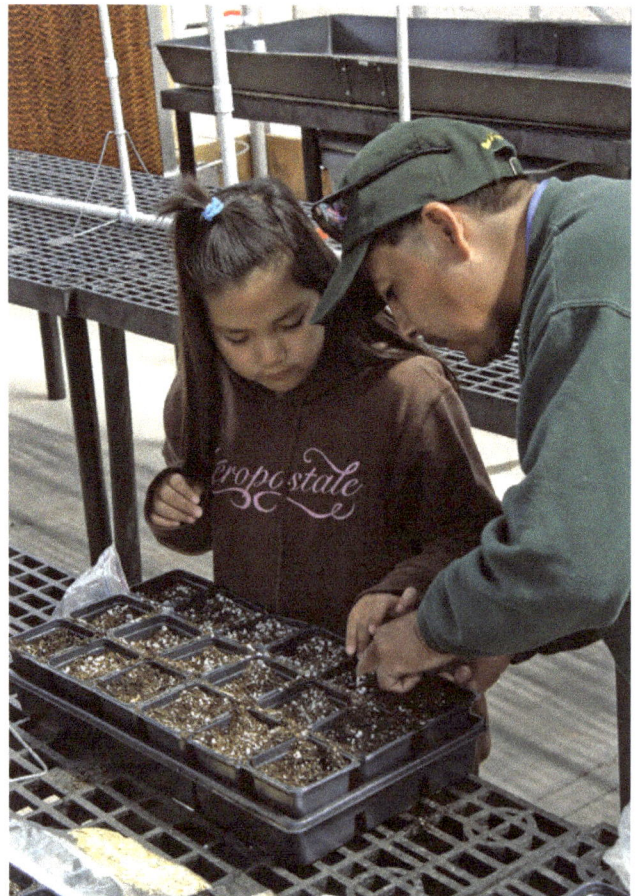

Figure 18.14—Sharing knowledge of local plants and their uses with future generations is a goal shared by many native plant nurseries. Photo by Thomas D. Landis.

Many tropical plant nurseries work with school groups and environmental or cultural education activities, such as ecohikes and forest restoration site visits (figure 18.13). Connecting with living, growing plants can be a wonderful activity for both youth and adults and a meaningful way to pass traditional and scientific knowledge about plant species, especially their uses and benefits, to younger generations (figure 18.14). These activities can also increase the community's desire to plant and care for plants from the nursery.

References

Landis, T. D. 2011. The Target Plant Concept—a history and brief overview. In: Riley, L.E., Haase, D.L. and Pinto, J.R.tech coords. National proceedings: forest and conservation nursery associations—2010. Proceedings RMRS-P-65. Fort Collins, CO: US Department of Agriculture, Forest Service, Rocky Mountain Research Station, Proceedings: 61-66.

Westrum, R. 1994. An organizational perspective: designing recovery teams from the inside out. In: Clark, T.W.; Reading, R.P.; Clark, A.L., eds. Endangered species recovery: finding the lessons, improving the process. Washington, DC: Island Press: 327–349.

Nursery Management

Kim M. Wilkinson and Thomas D. Landis

19

Tropical nursery management includes all aspects of growing plants through all their growth phases as described in Chapter 4, Crop Planning: Propagation Protocols, Schedules, and Records. Management involves an understanding of practical, scientific, technical, interpersonal, and economic aspects of the nursery. Nursery management includes ordering materials and supplies, maintaining facilities, scheduling activities, keeping horticultural and financial records, and much more (figure 19.1). This chapter outlines some essential elements of the day-to-day and year-to-year aspects of managing the nursery.

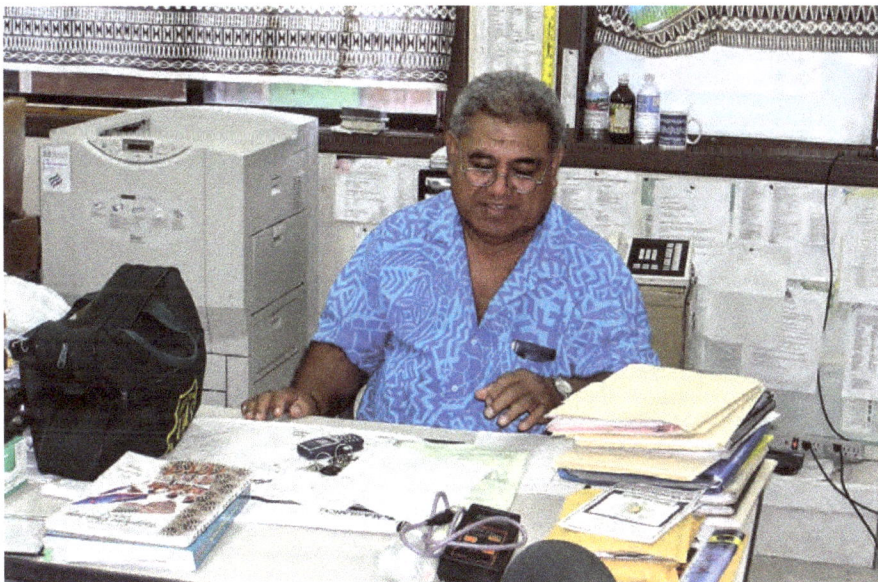

Figure 19.1—Nursery management includes not only growing plants, but keeping horticultural and financial records, managing supplies, planning activities (as shown here in American Samoa), and much more. Keeping good records is essential to keeping production on track. Photo by Ronald Overton.

Facing Page: *Planning space and facilities is an important part of nursery management. Pictured here, staff at the main nursery on Palau hook up new irrigation lines. Photo by George Hernández.*

Figure 19.2—*Organized management oversees the growth of the plants and the growth of the nursery itself. A nursery manager discusses constructing seedling benches in an area with morning sunlight in the U.S. Virgin Islands. Photo by Brian F. Daley.*

Figure 19.3—*Periodic educational activities help the nursery staff to expand their knowledge and skills towards achieving the nursery's mission. Here, nursery professionals meet for a workshop in American Samoa. Photo courtesy of Diane L. Haase.*

Identifying Nursery Tasks

A checklist can help provide an overview of the interrelated tasks involved in managing a nursery. The example checklist in the textbox on the following page can be modified and customized to describe your nursery's daily, weekly, monthly, and seasonal tasks.

Only a few required tasks must happen each day; these tasks are the essential activities that keep the crops alive and healthy and the nursery functioning on a daily basis. These tasks include watering, keeping daily records, and monitoring crops as they go through the establishment, rapid growth, and hardening phases. Other tasks need to be done less frequently but are as important. Good planning and oversight will ensure that all nursery tasks are prioritized and scheduled accordingly.

Planning and Scheduling

Schedule an overview and planning session on a weekly basis to assess immediate needs, periodic tasks, and long-term goals. This assessment provides an opportunity to prioritize tasks for the coming week and month (figure 19.2). The needs of the plants, environmental conditions, and many other factors require flexibility and responsiveness in management style. Crops usually do not respond well to a rigid schedule and may perform differently in different years, which is why weekly assessment and planning is so important. Attempts to make rigid schedules (such as "weed every Tuesday") are often far less effective than regular planning to tailor tasks to the observed needs and conditions of the crop.

The observation skills of the nursery manager and staff are the greatest assets to effective planning. Taking time on a weekly basis to review the daily log, plant development record, and other observations will help with prioritizing the work to be done. Observations in the nursery can answer many questions: What growth phase is the crop in: establishment, rapid growth, or hardening? Is it on schedule? What needs to be done next: transplanting, moving to a new structure, altering fertilization rates? Are we observing anything that might indicate a potential problem, such as the presence of a potential pest? When do we next update clients on the crop's progress? Is it time to sow a new crop? These observations aid the nursery manager to plan and schedule important activities and to assign roles, tasks, and deadlines to the appropriate staff members.

Some proactive planning should also occur, focusing beyond what is most urgent. Keeping the nursery's vision and objectives as a focus during meetings can help maintain a broader view for nursery activities. Planning should include activities that are important to the nursery's larger mission beyond the day-to-day details such as public relations or educational activities (figure 19.3). Updating plant protocols and working to improve plant quality with some simple experiments are also valuable activities that should be included in the nursery's schedule.

Nursey Management Checklist

Planning and Scheduling (weekly, monthly, yearly)

- Make a list of what needs to be done based on daily observations, daily logs, and crop development records.
- Establish propagation protocols.
- Create and update crop-growing schedules and facilities schedules.
- Prioritize and delegate tasks.
- Follow up to ensure tasks were done.
- Refine nursery vision and objectives annually; anticipate new crops to grow, changes in production, infrastructure improvements or expansion, and other planning for the future.

Routine Tasks (daily)

- Irrigate
- Crop culturing (for example, weed or pest control, fertilizing).
- Monitor and observe the crops.

Recordkeeping

- Record observations and actions in daily journal or log (daily).
- Make notes in the plant development records for each crop (daily or weekly).
- Update and revise plant protocols (at end of each crop).
- Conduct crop inventory assessment (ongoing).

Crop-Phase Production Tasks

- Establishment tasks (for example, making growing media, sowing seeds, inoculating with microsymbionts).
- Rapid growth phase tasks (for example, fertilizing, monitoring).
- Hardening phase tasks (for example, changing fertilization and light regimes).
- Update clients about crop development.
- Harvesting, packing and shipping tasks.

Seasonal Cleanup

- Purge or transplant holdover stock.
- Clean floors, tables, tools, equipment, and so on.
- Clean and sterilize containers.
- Check and repair equipment, tools, and infrastructure such as irrigation lines.

Financial Management

- Determine expenses, including labor, time and supplies needed to produce crops, and overhead costs (for example, utilities).
- Determine estimated income.
- Create and manage an annual budget based on anticipated income and expenses.
- Administer contracts.
- Inventory supplies for production and maintenance (for example, growing media, fertilizers, containers and trays, irrigation parts) and order as needed.
- Estimate future costs and income and adjust budget accordingly.

Problem Solving and Troubleshooting

- Identify and analyze problems as they arise.
- Know who to call for help (for example, another grower, a soil scientist, a pest expert, an irrigation specialist) and contact them as needed.
- Develop and test hypotheses to solve the problem.
- Implement a solution.

Cultivating Good Relationships with Staff, Clients, and the Community

- Provide staff education and training.
- Connect staff with nursery vision and objectives.
- Give and receive feedback and input (observations and improvement suggestions).
- Plan meetings, safety awareness, and so on.
- Develop target plant specifications with clients.
- Educate clients about key issues for handling, outplanting, and care.
- Visit outplanting sites and clients to check up on survival and growth; follow up with clients to discuss field performance of plants, revisions of target plant criteria, and future needs.
- Offer public education and outreach.

Learning and Sharing

- Attend training events and conferences.
- Learn from other nurseries; host and attend field days and visits.
- Read published literature (for example, *Native Plants Journal*).
- Explore ways to improve crop production and plant quality.

Figure 19.4—*Daily activities include the essentials of keeping the plants alive and healthy, including watering (A), weeding (B), and timely transplanting (C). Photo A in Yap by Tara Luna, photo B in Tanzania by Ronald Overton, and photo C in U.S. Virgin Islands by Brian F. Daley.*

Daily Tasks and Observations

Daily activities include the essentials of keeping the plants alive and healthy such as irrigating, weeding, monitoring, fertilizing, and pest management (figure 19.4). Daily observation of the crop is essential for good nursery management and an important way to determine their needs.

The manager or a designated "crop monitor" needs to observe the crop every day (figure 19.5). This task can be done once daily as a formal practice separate from other tasks. Measurements occasionally will be taken to evaluate the crops progress or to quantify environmental conditions. The person monitoring the crop needs to understand what "normal" is for that crop and for the nursery environment and be highly sensitive to any deviations from that norm (figure 19.6).

Experience and daily observations can identify potential problems long before they become emergencies.

Observations may include the following (Landis 1984)—

- **Appearance**—Inspect the crop visually to see if plant size and shoot-to-root ratio are proper for the stage of growth. Look for signs of nutrition or disease problems on the roots and foliage. Inspect closely for insect pests. Examine roots to see if beneficial microsymbionts are visible.

- **Smells**—Some problems, such as gray mold, may be discernible to the experienced grower by its odor. Overheating motors, broken fans, composting troubles, and other potential problems can also be detected by the sense of smell.

- **Noises**—Listen for unusual sounds in the nursery such as an engine running unsteadily or water running when it should not be.

- **Feel**—Pay attention to the temperature and humidity in the nursery. Feel the growing medium to determine if it is at the proper moisture level.

Figure 19.5—A manager or a designated "crop monitor" should observe the crop every day. Photo at Volcanoes National Park, on the Big Island of Hawai'i, by Brian F. Daley.

Figure 19.6—Making regular observations of the crop and staying alert and aware are key to avoiding problems. Photo by Tara Luna.

Although one designated crop monitor is responsible for this task, all staff need to understand that observation and being alert and aware are key to precluding problems. The manager should welcome and encourage staff to share their observations and contribute to the daily log; this practice builds observation skills and greater crop awareness.

Recordkeeping

As described in Chapter 4, Crop Planning: Propagation Protocols, Schedules, and Records, keeping good records is essential to keeping production on track and precluding serious problems (figure 19.7). Nursery recordkeeping includes the following—

- **A Daily Log**—can be as simple as writing the day's date and jotting down some notes in a notebook about observations and activities at the end of each day. Make a habit of entering something in the log each day, even if the observations seem unimportant at the time.

- **Plant Development Records**—for each crop should be kept in an easily accessible place and a few notes should be jotted down as changes occur with the crop.

- **Propagation Protocols**—show how to produce each kind of crop successfully in your nursery. The protocols provide guidance for each new crop in developing the production plan and listing needed facilities and supplies and should be regularly updated and revised.

- **Inventory Assessment**—should include all plants in the nursery by bench or structure number, current

developmental stage of each crop, and details of delivery (target requirements, outplanting site, name of client, seed source, and anticipated delivery date).

As the nursery grows in size and complexity, entering records into a computer will make the information easier to track. Every day creates small amounts of vital information that will contribute immeasurably to improving nursery management and productivity over time (figures 19.8, 19.9).

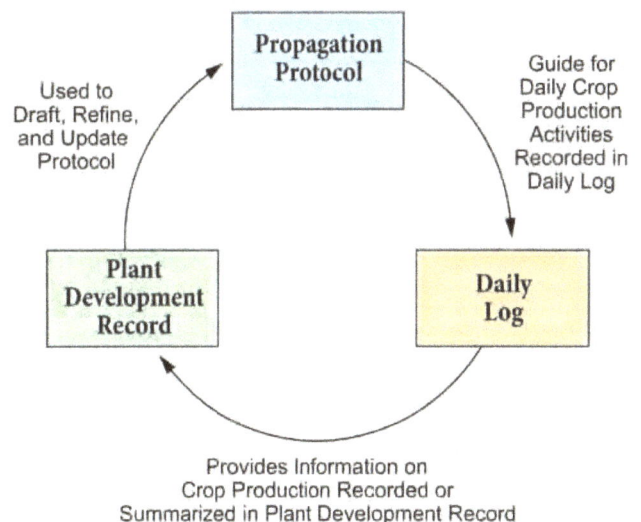

Figure 19.7—The daily log, the plant development record, and the propagation protocol are the foundation of nursery recordkeeping and are used to support plant production and inform nursery management. Illustration adapted from Dumroese and others (2008) by Jim Marin.

Figure 19.8—Recordkeeping tools should be easily accessible at the manager's workstation; make a habit of entering something in it each day. Photo by Kim M. Wilkinson.

Figure 19.9—The timing of nursery tasks, such as transplanting, should be recorded in the daily log and the plant development log. These records will help you keep the current crop on track and will help you plan, budget, and schedule for future crops. Photo by Kim M. Wilkinson.

This information is invaluable for many aspects of nursery management, including the following—

- Budgeting funds.
- Estimating schedules to produce future crops.
- Determining what labor-saving equipment might give the most benefit for the cost.
- Analyzing nursery expenses.
- Improving profits or production.
- Replicating successful crops.

Crop Planning and Production Tasks

The details of planning crops are discussed in Chapter 4, Crop Planning: Propagation Protocols, Schedules, and Records. Management needs during the crop production include—

- Understanding the three growth phases crops go through (establishment, rapid growth, and hardening) and the distinct requirements for each phase.
- Making growing schedules for crop production from seed procurement through outplanting and detailing changes as the growing cycle progresses (figure 19.10).
- Listing space, labor, equipment, and supplies required to support the crop during the three stages of growth.

The work to produce a crop consists of managing the plants through each phase of development so that plants receive what they need and are as strong and healthy as possible for outplanting. After a schedule has been made

showing what plants need to be sown and by when, the tasks of preparing growing media, filling containers, and sowing can be scheduled. In the establishment phase, plants begin to germinate, and thinning, transplanting, and inoculation with beneficial microorganisms will take place. As the plants move from the germinant phase to the rapid growth phase and later the hardening phase, their needs will change.

For some nurseries, plants will be physically moved from a germination or rooting area to a more open environment (figure 19.11). For other nurseries, climate control (such as removing shadecloth) might have the same effect. Fertiliza-

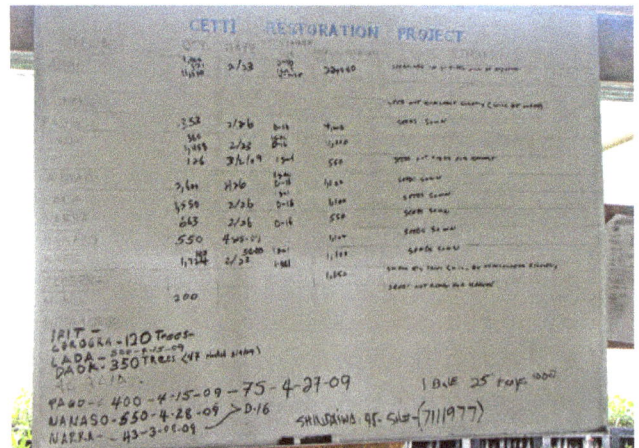

Figure 19.10—The work to produce a crop consists of managing activities and resources through each phase of crop development. This whiteboard at the Guam Division of Forestry and Soil Resources nursery lists crops being grown for the Cetti Bay restoration project including how many plants are needed (species and container types) and the current status of the crops. Photo by Ronald Overton.

Figure 19.11—Plants are moved from one structure to another as they go through their three phases of growth. Good planning and management maintains open paths and an easy flow of work between structures. Photo by Tara Luna.

tion and watering regimes are changed for each of the three phases. When the crop is ready, it will be harvested and shipped, as described in Chapter 16, Harvesting and Shipping.

To keep up with production, planning for space and facilities is important. The manager also needs to have the necessary materials on hand when they are needed (figure 19.12). These materials include supplies for production such as seeds, growing media, containers, and so forth. For nurseries in remote areas, obtaining supplies may require ordering months ahead of the time when they are needed. In these cases, extras of essential items need to be kept on hand. If spare parts are used for repairs, they need to be replaced right away.

Seasonal Cleanup and Maintenance

Time is usually available between crops or at the end of each season for some "deep cleaning" and maintenance. Cleanliness is essential to avoid disease problems and to maintain a professional, appealing image for the nursery. A clean environment builds customer confidence and staff morale. Perform the following tasks every 2 to 6 months:

- Dispose of any holdover stock.
- Clean and hose down the floors and tables (applying dilute bleach or other cleanser if no plants are present).
- Clean and sterilize containers (see Chapter 7, Containers).
- Flush out irrigation system and run a cup test (see Chapter 11, Water Quality and Irrigation).
- Conduct equipment checks and make any repairs.
- Replace roof plastic, if necessary.

Financial Management

Good financial management is necessary for the nursery is to thrive in the long term. The daily journal and other records should include the amount of labor spent on various activities, money spent for materials, and overhead costs such as rent and utilities. These costs can be used to estimate the cost of each crop, thereby enabling the manager to accurately budget time and funds. This information also is essential for determining what the nursery must charge for various plant materials sold. Learning more about basic business planning through publications and local learning opportunities can be very helpful for making wise financial choices.

Figure 19.12—Management involves planning the timing of essential production tasks and ensuring that all the necessary supplies are available. Shown here: checking a seed supply in Hawai'i (A), filling bags with growing medium made from composted coffee cherries in East Timor (B), and assembling a drip irrigation system on Yap (C). Photo A by Kim M. Wilkinson, photo B by J.B. Friday, and photo C by George Hernández.

In keeping financial records, be sure to note the following factors:

- Size of stock and growing space needed to produce it.

- Time to grow.

- Labor (in person-hours) required through all phases.

- Materials required and their cost (for example, seeds, containers, growing media).

- Need for custom culture (for example, special containers, extra labor).

- Overhead costs (for example, utilities).

- Cost inflation over time.

- Typical losses (percentage of crop discarded).

- Price charged when the crop left the nursery.

Problem Solving

Good management, staff training, monitoring, and planning will generally preclude emergency situations in the nursery. Even the best manager, however, cannot avoid problems entirely. Some problems, such as difficulties with the irrigation system, appear suddenly and must be handled instantly. Others require a longer term approach. With experience, troubleshooting problems may become easier. Do not be reluctant to reach out to colleagues, other nursery managers, or other professionals. Everyone has problems once in a while, and we can all help each other learn more about plants as we share our experiences.

The problem should next be classified into some sort of order, separating problems into three types based on the amount of information available (Landis 1984, Van Gundy 1980):

- **Type I problems** are well structured. These are the routine problems that occur daily. Their main characteristic is that all the information needed to solve them is already available. Problems in this category have probably occurred before and can usually be solved by standard procedures. Expertise for solving these problems can normally be found at the nursery, so outside help is not required.

- **Type II problems** are semistructured. This is an intermediate category—some information about the problem is available, but some degree of uncertainty also exists. These problems may have occurred before but something about them makes them different. Existing techniques must be adapted to solve this type of problem, and some expert help may be needed. The final solution is probably a combination of standard and newly developed methods.

- Type III problems are poorly structured. Their distinguishing characteristic is that little or no information is available about them. These are the problems never encountered before; therefore, expert help should be sought and the information needed to solve these problems generated through the problem-solving process. Solutions to poorly structured problems usually have to be custom made and require creative problem-solving techniques.

Type 1 problems are usually solved with standard operating procedures, whereas Types II and III require more creative steps.

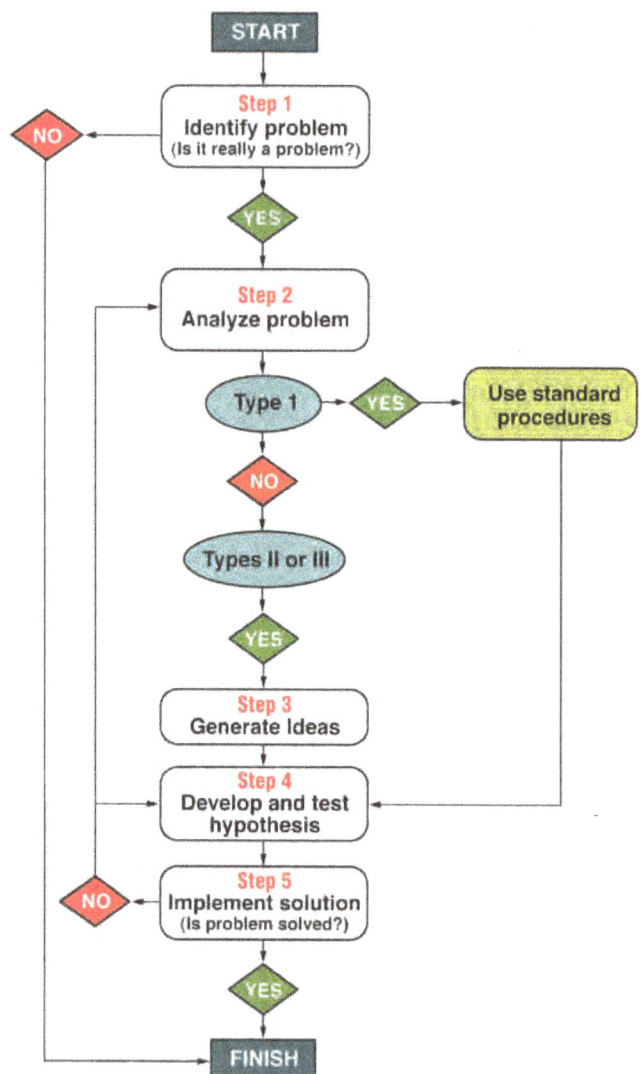

Figure 19.13—*A problem-solving matrix. Illustration adapted from Landis (1984) by Jim Marin.*

This five-step systematic approach can be helpful when approaching long-term challenges (figure 19.13; Landis 1984):

- **Identify the Problem**—Is it really a problem? What seems to be wrong?

- **Analyze the Problem**—What happened exactly? When did it start?

- **Generate Ideas**—Identify potential sources of the problem. Consult literature, other nurseries, staff members, or outside sources of help such as extension agents or specialists.

- **Develop and Test Hypotheses**—At some point, a conclusion about the source of the problem must be decided and acted upon.

- **Implement a Solution**—Decide on a way to solve the problem. Observe the results. If the problem is not solved, start again with step 2.

References

Dumroese, R.K.; Luna, T.; Landis, T.D. 2008. Nursery manual for native plants: volume 1, a guide for tribal nurseries. Agriculture Handbook 730. Washington, DC: U.S. Department of Agriculture, Forest Service. 302 p.

Landis, T.D. 1984. Problem solving in forest-tree nursery with emphasis on site problems. In: Duryea, M.S.; Landis, T.D., eds. Forest nursery manual production of bareroot seedlings. The Hague, The Netherlands: Martinus Nijhoff/Dr. W. Junk Publishers: 307–314.

Van Gundy, A. B. 1981. Techniques of structured problem solving. Van Nostrand Reinhold, New York. 301 p.

Discovering Ways To Improve Nursery Practices and Plant Quality

20

Kim M. Wilkinson and Diane L. Haase

Working with plants is a process of discovery. Being curious and aware, paying close attention, and staying open and adaptive are important practices. Books and people can help us learn about plants in the nursery, but the very best teachers are the plants themselves. "Research" is simply tracking what is happening, asking questions about what is causing it to happen, and seeking answers. In other words, research is something most growers already do. Astronomer Carl Sagan (1996) said, "Every time we exercise self-criticism, every time we test our ideas against the outside world, we are doing science." Scientific research is simply "the testing (systematic, controlled, empirical, and critical investigation) of ideas (hypothetical propositions about presumed relations among natural phenomena) generated by intuition" (Dumroese and Wenny 2003). If research is done well, the process can yield useful, accurate information. The purpose of this chapter is to provide information about how to design easy trials and experiments to discover useful, meaningful ways to improve crop production and quality.

Some people may be lucky enough to have an elder or mentor pressing them to explore and discover more. Carrying out research, asking questions, and keeping records are ways to self-mentor. Using a systematic approach supports making accurate observations so that discoveries otherwise missed can be made and shared. It is widely acknowledged that working with plants is an art as well as a science: observation, senses, emotions, empathy, and intuition play important roles. When a question arises that is important to answer, it is time to consider conducting a trial or experiment. Growers often work with plants for which minimal literature or outside information is available. Nursery research may be subjective or objective, simple or complex. Learning how to effectively carry out experiments to evaluate new plant production techniques is essential to discovering relevant and applicable practices.

Managing a nursery in the tropics is a profession where you will learn as much or more from your own direct experience than you will learn from readings, classes, and other formal teaching. Some learning comes from experiments; but some comes from experience and reflection. A few tips for reflective practice as a way to continually learn and adapt are provided at the end of this chapter.

Facing Page: A germination experiment. Photo by Brian F. Daley.

The Importance of Trying New Things in the Nursery

Often, the tendency is to take the path of least resistance and use known or established nursery production techniques. The first propagation technique that was tried and that produced an adequate plant may have become the established protocol. The technique, however, may be more costly or inefficient than alternate methods, and may not produce the best quality plant for the outplanting site. A few modifications could improve production, plant quality, and, ultimately, plant survival and growth after outplanting. Simple experiments enable the nursery to try out new techniques, ideas, and problem-solving strategies (figure 20.1).

The tasks of keeping up with day-to-day nursery management may feel like more than enough to fill your schedule, and time for experimentation may seem a low priority. In truth, however, most growers already engage in investigations on a regular basis. Experimentation happens every time a new idea is tested, a question leads to alternative strategies, or a problem is analyzed and solved. Taking a little care to be systematic and follow a few guidelines will dramatically increase the benefits of these activities and will provide greater confidence in the conclusions you draw from them.

Simple experiments can be carried out simultaneously with filling an order for plants. For example, in most cases, the nursery can produce plants using an established protocol and also grow some additional plants for research at the same time. One variable can be altered for the experimental plants, such as using a different seed treatment, a modified growing medium, a new type of container, or a different mycorrhizal inoculant. Your results for the experimental group can then be compared against those for the established protocol. In this way, each new crop represents an opportunity to try something new on a small scale. The discoveries can greatly improve production efficiency and seedling quality over time. Because of these potential benefits, it is worth putting a little effort into experimenting and trying new things.

The Value of Experimenting

Today's best methods for raising native plants came from growers like you learning through experimentation, then sharing what they learned. For example, Kerin E. Lilleeng-Rosenberger describes her process: [in 1989] "I was hired and put in charge of the new native Hawaiian plant nursery…I was provided with a variety of native seeds, but had neither instructions nor reference guides to follow; the majority of these plants had never been grown in cultivation before… For more than ten years, I experimented with different potting mixes, seeds, and cutting treatments, along with many other types of plant materials. I kept detailed records, which helped identify what had contributed to the successful results. Eventually, the knowledge I had gathered filled fourteen notebooks." Her book, *Growing Hawai'i's Native Plants*, shares what she learned.

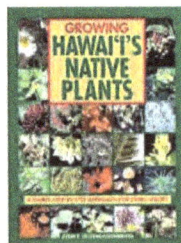

(Lilleeng-Rosenberger 2005)

Figure 20.1—*Simple experiments and trials, such as this fertilization trial, can teach us a lot about how to grow plants. Photo by R. Kasten Dumroese.*

Conducting simple experiments and trials in the nursery can accomplish the following—

- Produce better plants.

- Speed up production.

- Save money, labor, seeds, and other materials.

- Improve outplanting survival and performance.

- Refine target plant criteria for outplanting sites.

- Contribute to greater knowledge of the plants.

Making Observations and Keeping Records

A foundation for improving plant health and quality is a good understanding of current production practices and how plants respond to them. The following three basic types of records, as discussed in Chapter 4, Crop Planning: Propagation Protocols, Schedules, and Records, are the foundation of good nursery recordkeeping (figure 20.2):

1. A daily log of general conditions and activities.

2. Development records for each crop that are filled out as the plants develop.

3. Propagation protocols that describe from start to finish how the plants are currently grown.

Additional records may also be enjoyable and valuable, such as an informal, personal journal that documents reflections in growing plants or a photo diary.

These records prevent the nursery from wasting time repeating strategies that do not work while providing a plan to help duplicate successful crops. This information also establishes how crops normally perform and can be used to recognize problems or gauge the effect of alternative production methods. Perhaps most important, keeping data and cultural records in a written format creates information that can be passed on to future nursery staff or others in the community. Without these records, valuable information (perhaps gleaned from a lifetime of nursery work) may be lost, and the new grower will have to start over. Knowing in a measurable way what is "normal" helps the nursery experiment with modifications that can improve crops and productivity over time.

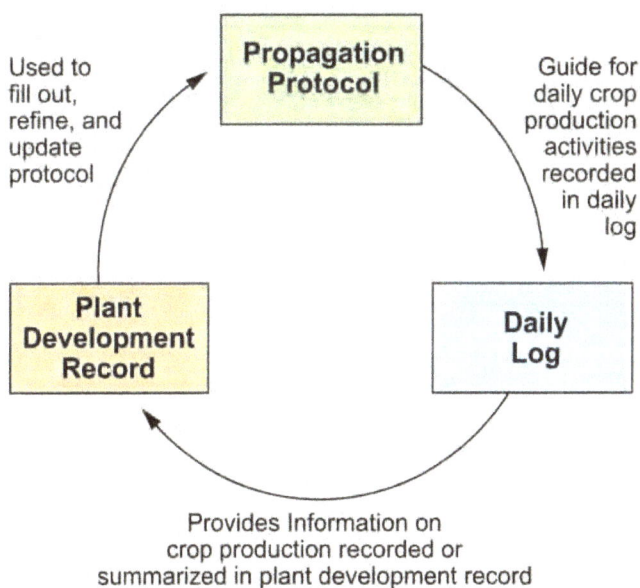

Figure 20.2—*The nursery's daily log, plant development record, and propagation protocol are the three basic kinds of records that form the foundation for learning. Illustration adapted from Dumroese and others (2008) by Jim Marin.*

Solving Problems Through Collaboration and Questioning Assumptions

In our small research nursery, we had poor results growing the Virgin Islands native tree *Clusia rosea* (in some places known as the "autograph tree"). We kept having low germination rates. I shared this experience with my friend who is the local nursery owner at Cruzan Gardens. He offered to give the seeds a try. When he reported a nearly 100-percent germination, I knew he found "the trick." What had he done differently?

The tiny seeds of *Clusia rosea* are embedded in the flesh of a succulent fruit and often are eaten by bats. My standard protocol for all tree species at the time included removing all fruit and flesh from seeds before germination. My friend, however, found this method too time consuming and simply spread the seeds, still embedded in their fruit pulp, into trays of potting mix, as if he were spreading jam on toast! It turns out that my method was dessicating the tiny seeds that are not normally exposed to air.

Naturally, we revised our protocol to keep the seeds in their pulp during germination, and we were able to get great germination results, too. I learned from this experience to share my challenges with other growers and to question my assumptions.

—Brian F. Daley, U.S. Virgin Islands

We grow an important Hawaiian endemic tree, the ʻōhiʻa tree. This tree is a foundation of many Hawaiian native ecosystems. A problem we had is ʻōhiʻa rust (figure 20.3). ʻŌhiʻa rust is easily spread by the wind, and our nursery in Kamuela, on the north tip of the Island of Hawaiʻi, is always windy.

The disease would get so bad at our nursery that our mortality rate was quite high. So we started observing the ʻōhiʻa plants in different locations around the nursery. Although not fully scientific in our methods, we noticed some things that caused us to rethink the plant locations throughout our nursery.

Basically we found that—

- Plants in our greenhouse were very susceptible to the rust disease (which may be because the wind slows down and "circles" in the greenhouse because only one side of the building is open, causing the wind to blow the rust spores gently around in a circular pattern over all the plants in the greenhouse).

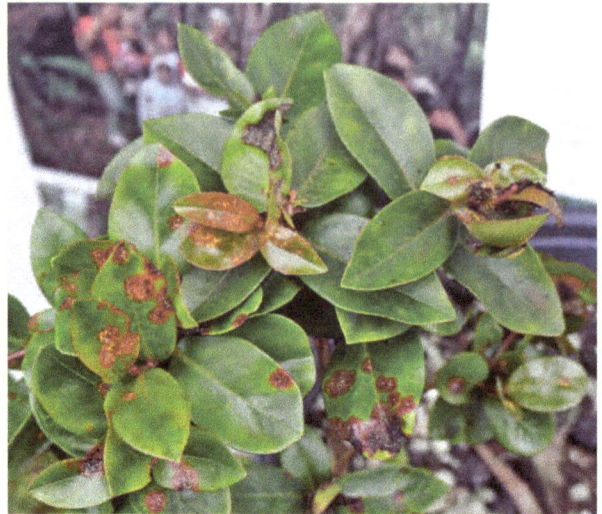

Figure 20.3—ʻŌhiʻa rust, shown here on an ʻōhiʻa leaf, is a disease spread by wind. Observations of wind patterns and experiments with plant locations helped staff at the State Tree Nursery in Kamuela, Hawaiʻi, to minimize losses. Photo by J.B. Friday.

- Plants outside exposed directly to the wind (such as on the windward side of a table or pallet) seemed as susceptible as the plants in the greenhouse.

- ʻŌhiʻa seedlings located outside on the leeward side of larger plants were relatively rust free. The larger plants may cause a disruption in the wind pattern, pushing the rust up and away from the smaller plants behind them.

After we observed these three things, we adjusted the locations of our ʻōhiʻa seedlings so they would be protected from the wind, essentially hidden from the rust. It did not totally eliminate the problem, but we experience far lower mortality rates and fewer diseased plants. We can tolerate the amount of loss now. We have tried this approach with limited success with other diseases and problems such as moving plants susceptible to mildew or powdery mold to be surrounded by plants that do not seem nearly as susceptible. So far, however, nothing has been quite as dramatic or successful as "hiding" our ʻōhiʻa seedlings from the ʻōhiʻa rust.

—Jacob Witcraft, Nursery Forester, State Tree Nursery, Kamuela, Hawaiʻi

Step 1: Developing Ideas for Nursery Experiments

Ideas for experiments may come from many places, including the following—

- A casual observation the nursery wishes to verify.

- A pressing question that seems to recur in the daily log or journal.

- An informal trial in which a difference is observed.

- A need to improve something (for example, percentage of germination).

- A need to change practices or materials (for example, the rise in cost of a potting media ingredient requiring use of substitutes).

- A desire to work with a new species.

- A desire to try out a new technique or idea.

Because staff time is limited, ideas for experiments will likely be prioritized in terms of their potential positive effect and importance to production. Nevertheless, it is good to keep a list of any potential experiments or trials that you or other staff believe would be beneficial and keep these ideas on hand to try as time allows. As described earlier, some experiments may be easy and quick to carry out and can be done efficiently as part of crop production.

Many topics lend themselves well to experimentation, including the following—

- Developing seed treatments and germination techniques.
- Testing culturing options for new species or seed sources.
- Researching microsymbiont sources or application methods.
- Altering watering regimes.
- Trying new container types.
- Trying new blends or materials in potting media.
- Changing an aspect of management, such as timing for moving crops from one phase to another.

Step 2: Gathering Information

After you have an idea of what you want to investigate, some background research is in order. Check your existing plant development records, plant protocol, and daily log to review what has happened and has been tried in the past, reflecting on your experiences and observations. Information can also be gathered from nursery staff, specialists, extension agents, and associates from other nurseries. Look up the subject in journals, books, and electronic sources of information. This background research can help narrow the focus of the experiment to a question that can be answered.

Step 3: Specifying a Question and Creating the Hypothesis

The question must be limited in scope, pertaining to only one aspect of production. It would not work to focus on multiple variables at the same time. For example, if more than one aspect of the seed treatment process (such as, season harvested, collection and processing method, sowing times and methods, and medium used during the germination phase) were modified at the same time, how would you know which modification caused a difference?

The hypothesis is the proposed answer to the focused question.

Step 4: Designing the Experiment

A good study design to answer a specific question and test the hypothesis starts with careful selection of the treatments to be evaluated (the independent variable) and the

Example: Step 1—An Idea for an Experiment

A native species consistently has less than a 25-percent germination after sowing. In addition, germination is sporadic, taking place over 4 weeks. These results occur despite good seed sterilization and handling practices. A seed test sent to a laboratory indicated that a higher percentage of the seeds are viable. The nursery wishes to increase the percentage germination. The first step is to look at the options for experimentation. What could be contributing to the low germination for this species in your nursery? And what could increase germination?

Example: Step 2—Gathering Information

An Internet search, along with a review of this manual's Chapter 8, Collecting, Processing, and Storing Seeds, indicates that when viable seeds fail to germinate, the seeds may be dormant and, therefore, may require a treatment to break dormancy. A bit of reading into the natural history of this species reveals that its seeds are often passed through the digestive system of birds, which can be a form of scarification, breaking natural dormancy. According to publications and other nursery growers consulted, several closely related species have a hard seedcoat that is usually scarified before planting. A search on the Native Plant Network (http://www.nativeplantnetwork.org/) may not find your exact species, but it shows that several growers have had success with a few related species when using mechanical scarification.

Example: Step 3—Specifying the Question and Creating the Hypothesis

From your information gathering, it appears that lack of scarification may be causing the poor germination of your species. The question that the experiment will address is now formulated: How does scarifying the seeds of this species affect its germination? The hypothesis might be, "Mechanical scarification of the seeds by hand nicking the seedcoat with a small nail clipper will result in improved germination." If time allows, it may be desirable to pose more than one treatment to answer the same question. Perhaps a second treatment to be tested separately for this example would be, "Hot water scarification for 20 seconds will result in improved germination."

response to be measured (the dependent variables). From there, the experimental design can be decided. The "Three R's" of designing a good experiment are Replication, Randomization, and Representation and are described in the following sections. Even the simplest study design needs to include these important elements to minimize the risk of generating incorrect or meaningless data. The components of the study including the question, hypothesis, plant material, treatments, and experimental design should all be written into a study plan. The study plan needs to read like a recipe so that you know what, why, when, where, and how to conduct your study.

Independent Variable
(Treatments)

The independent variable is the one factor purposely changed for the sake of the experiment. It is the factor that is expected to create a response. A factor could be seed source, seed treatment method, growing medium, irrigation frequency, fertilizer rate, and so on. But, only one needs to be used as the independent variable in a simple nursery trial; all other factors must stay the same. This approach enables you to isolate whether or not changes in that factor result in a desired response. The independent variable can be modified one or more ways (treatments) and compared with an unmodified treatment (the control).

The Control

An essential aspect of experimenting is to have a control treatment. For experiments in plant production, the con-

trol treatment is simply the way the nursery usually does things according to established protocols. The performance of control plants grown in the usual way will be compared with the performance of plants grown in the modified way. All plants in the experiment need to be started at the same time and kept in the same areas of the nursery to eliminate further variation among them, thereby isolating effects of the independent variable (figure 20.4).

Dependent Variables

The dependent variables are the variables being observed or measured. These are the variables that are hypothesized to be influenced by the independent variable. Although many variables can be affected by specific treatments, you will want to decide ahead of time which dependent variables are most important to measure. For instance, fertilizer rate can change foliar nutrients, growth, survival, media chemistry, and so on. However, you will want to focus on the variable(s) that address your experimental question and hypothesis.

Figure 20.4—Seed scarification and stratification requirements are often discovered through experimentation and trials. Careful labeling of the control and each treatment is essential. Photo by Tara Luna.

Figure 20.5—Replications need not be large scale but should consist of at least 30 plants per treatment (including the control). Photo by Brian F. Daley.

Replication

Research is largely about isolating the independent variable and eliminating the possibility that any other factors could be contributing to observed differences in the dependent variables. Replication is an essential aspect of this process (figure 20.5). Without replication, you cannot confidently conclude that your findings are repeatable. If too few plants are used in the experiment, any differences observed among treatments may simply be a coincidence. For this reason, it is valuable to have as many plants as is reasonable included in the experiment.

Variability in the nursery environment can profoundly affect experiments. For example, two benches may differ in the amount of irrigation or light received. Because of environmental variability, it is best to place plants from all treatments (including the controls) right next to each other, on the same bench or even in the same tray. (Of course, this placement is not possible if the objective of your experiment is to compare different growing environments; in that case, the plants will have to be located separately.) Every effort needs to be made to keep all conditions the same except the one being studied. Otherwise, you might find differences among treatments that are not actually caused by the treatment.

Replications can be individual plants or can be a group (block) of several plants (for example, a tray of seedlings). When blocking, place each of the replications in different parts of the nursery if possible. That way, if the same relative treatment differences are observed within each of the blocks, in spite of variations around the nursery, you can have greater confidence that the results are not a fluke. Each block needs to consist of a similar number of plants from every treatment (including the control). For example, a block might consist of 10 control plants, 10 treatment-1 plants, and 10 treatment-2 plants for a total of 30 plants in each block.

A few tips for having good replication include the following—

- Have at least 30 to 40 plants total per treatment (including the control)

- When blocking, use a minimum of 4 blocks and include at least 10 plants from each treatment in each block.

- For each replication, situate all treatments (including the control) adjacent to each other to reduce variation in microclimate.

- If possible, place replications in three or four different locations within the nursery.

- Because each growing season is different, the experiment may be repeated one or two times on subsequent batches of plants to confirm results.

Representation

Another important aspect of experimental design is to make sure the plant materials and treatments used in the experiment are representative of the same plant materials and treatments to which you plan to apply your results. For example, if you want to learn about the effect of fertilizer on seedlings grown in a particular sized container, then you do not want to do your study on seedlings grown in smaller or larger containers.

Randomization

It is important to randomly select the plants to be included in the study from the pool of representative plants (or seeds). It is also important to randomly assign treatments to each replication (plant or group of plants as described previously). Randomization prevents any systematic or personal bias from being introduced into the study and skewing the results; for example, using only the largest seedlings for one of the treatments would lead to the incorrect conclusion that that treatment made the seedlings grow more. Many ways exist to randomize. For example, you can roll a die or draw from a deck of cards to determine which numbered tray of seedlings to use in a study or you can draw slips of paper out of a bag with treatment names: control, treatment 1, and so on.

Step 5: Conducting the Experiment

If you feel unsure about the validity of the proposed elements of an experiment, find an ally in the local university or agricultural extension system to discuss your plan briefly. This investment of time is wise and ensures that the research successfully addresses the question posed.

After the hypothesis is posed and the treatments and experimental design determined, it is time to plan when and how to carry out the experiment. Unless the problem addressed is urgent (that is, interferes with production), it may be most economical to wait until you have an order for the species you wish to investigate. A group of plants from those grown according to the usual protocol will be designated as the control treatment. Extra plants can be planted at the same time from the same seed source and on the same day, with only the independent variable manipulated.

A few tips for starting and carrying out the experiment include the following—

- Have one person in charge of setting up the experiment, making observations, and collecting all data.

Example: Step 5—Conducting the Experiment

The experiment on seed scarification will be carried out simultaneously with growing an order of plants for that species. Do not expect to be able to use any of the seeds from the experiment (the new method may increase, decrease, or have no effect on germination percentages). So, the procedures to produce the correct number of seedlings to meet the order need to be carried out as described in your usual protocol for that species. If an order for 100 plants of the species with the usual expected 25-percent germination is received, according to the established protocol, the nursery will need to sow about 450 seeds to compensate for the low germination and other losses. A portion of those seeds (100) are designated to be part of the experiment as the control. At the same time, 100 additional seeds from the same seedlot would be scarified using mechanical scarification and 100 seeds would be subjected to the hot water treatment according to the experimental design. The four experimental seed trays (replications) and the group of 25 seeds of each treatment within each tray are clearly marked. All seeds will be treated identically otherwise. Because germination usually takes place sporadically over a 4-week period to achieve a 25-percent germination, the experiment will run 4 weeks.

Having one person in charge helps eliminate unnecessary variations in the data.

- If special materials are needed for the experiment (for example, a different microbial inoculant, a new seed source, a special growing medium ingredient), be sure to have them on hand before the experiment starts.

- Mark treatments (including the control) clearly with durable, easy-to-read labels. Nothing is worse than discovering a group of plants performing outstandingly but with no record of what was done differently.

- Do not count on experimental treatments to produce marketable plants. Use established protocols to meet client requirements. Plants devoted to research need to be above the count required for the order. If the experimental subjects turn out to be of high quality and saleable, that will be a side benefit. If growing on contract, the client may be interested in accepting research plants and to continue the trial in the field. Agreements need to be clarified in advance regarding experimental plants.

- Take careful notes and keep a journal documenting every step of the experiment as it is carried out. Changes may occur rapidly and go unnoticed if care is not taken to record them. Sometimes the independent variable will affect one brief but important stage of plant development. Keep data organized, ideally entered into a computer spreadsheet soon after taking measurements and observations.

- Be prepared to carry out the experiment more than once.

Step 6: Making Observations and Collecting Data

When gathering data, keep the process as simple and straightforward as possible, and reduce risks of nonappli-

---

Example: Step 6—Observations and Data Collection

Each of the three seed treatments in the four seed trays (replications) in the experiment is monitored daily for 4 weeks and the number of germinants recorded. (If the emergents are to be transplanted into larger containers before the end of the experiment, it is critical to ensure the counts are accurate before transplanting. Germinants from each treatment are transplanted in separate trays and carefully marked, even in their new containers.) The percent and rate of germination are calculated from the collected data.

---

cable or meaningless results. For example, the wet weight of live plants will vary considerably depending on irrigation and time of day; therefore, weighing live plants does not usually generate meaningful data for experiments. For small experiments, have only one person take measurements and gather hard data (such as plant height or stem diameter) to reduce variations in the way data are collected. For larger experiments, however, it may be necessary for several people to collect data. If several people will be collecting data, make sure each person is trained to measure using the same procedures. In these cases, it is a good idea for the different people to take data on all treatments, including the control, to cancel out bias in data collection (instead of having one person collect all the data for the control and a different person collecting the data for the experimental plants).

Data collection for the experiment needs to focus on the dependent variable for that experiment. Other data and observations, if available, however, may be collected as well if time allows. Even if they are not quantified, observations about the appearance and vitality of plants can be especially useful for many experiments. Taking several photos of the experiment is another way to document your findings.

Remember, by doing this type of work, you are gaining expertise; your observations are meaningful.

The best timing for data collection varies depending on what is being studied. Although any period of rapid change for the crop can be a useful time to gather data, in general, the most meaningful results tend to be gathered—

- During germination (as in the example in this chapter).
- At the beginning and end of the rapid growth phase.
- At the end of the hardening phase (just before shipping).
- After outplanting (usually after the first 3 to 12 months in the field, up to 5 years).

Stick to simple measurements and observations that are meaningful and relevant to your study. Depending on the subject of your experiment, your data collection may include one (or sometimes more) of the measurements described below.

Germination Rate and Percentages

A percentage of germination can be determined by comparing the total number of seeds planted versus the number of healthy germinants that emerge for each seed treatment.

Figure 20.6—Stem diameter measurements are usually taken just above the medium line or on the stem (A). Height can be measured from the medium surface to the top of the growing point on the stem (not the top of the leaf) (B). Photos by Tara Luna.

Germination rate is also important to monitor: sometimes the percentage of germination will ultimately be the same but one treatment may result in uniform and rapid germination while another treatment may be uneven or delayed. Daily or weekly measurements will capture differences in germination rate.

Plant Height and Stem Diameter

These measurements are useful to compare changes in plant development among the treatments and to previous crops described in the plant development records and propagation protocol. Stem diameter measurements are often taken about 0.25 in (0.5 cm) above the medium (figure 20.6A). Height can be measured from the growing medium surface to the top of the growing point on the stem (not the top of the leaf) (figure 20.6B).

Shoot-to-Root Ratios

Shoot-to-root ratios are taken only periodically and usually only as small samples, because these measurements destroy the plants sampled. They are based on oven-dry weight. Carefully remove any medium from the roots and dry the plant samples for 72 hours at 150 °F (66 °C). A convenient way to handle plants is to put them into paper lunch bags labeled by treatment and then place them into a drying oven. After the plants are dry, cut the sample at the place where the stem meets the roots (the root collar; often a change of color occurs here) and weigh the shoots and roots separately to calculate the ratio.

Plant Survival and Vigor

Plants can be subjectively rated at the beginning and end of each of the growth phases using a numeric rating system,

---

Experiments Provide Opportunities To
Learn More and Improve Nursery Practices

Figure 20.7 illustrates an innovative trial that resulted in a modest improvement in seed germination.

Figure 20.7—*The small seeds of* Guazuma ulmifolia, *native to Puerto Rico and the U.S. Virgin Islands, are embedded in a hard, sweet smelling woody capsule (A). In a preliminary trial, standard treatments and a control treatment all resulted in less than 2 percent germination. Treatment with a mild acid solution caused each seed to produce a clear protective gel around itself, but the seeds still did not germinate. It was hypothesized that the seeds may benefit from passing through an animal's digestive tract. Students at the University of the Virgin Islands weighed fruit, calculated seed numbers, and mixed the fruit in with feed for sheep in pens (B). Students then collected the sheep feces from the pens daily, removed debris with screens (C), soaked the sheep pellets in water and transferred the material to germination trays (D). Germination rates were higher than the control, but variable, and averaged 20 percent. Although the students did not completely solve the problem, they obtained images of the seeds' development stages, and improved the original germination rate from 2 to 20 percent. Photos by Brian F. Daley.*

such as 0 to 5. Clear guidelines must be developed for the numerical scale to give a consistent relative estimate of plant vigor. For example, 0 = dead; 1 = no vigor, plant appears on verge of death; 2 = poor and slow growth; 3 = some growth, some vigor; 4 = plant looking vigorous; 5 = plant appears to be thriving and very vigorous.

Insect and Disease Analysis

The start and end of the rapid growth phase and the end of the hardening phase are good times to inspect for pests and disease. Some types of diseases, such as root rots, are easy to quantify and you can know what percent of your crop you lose to the disease. For other types of pests and diseases, the damage may be more subtle and you may only make qualitative observations. Samples of pests or diseases can be sent to the local agricultural extension office for identification, if necessary.

Outplanting Survival and Growth

Field performance after outplanting can also be evaluated by measuring height, stem diameter, survival, vigor, or other measures of interest (for example, amount of animal damage). See Chapter 17, Outplanting for details about ways to monitor performance after outplanting.

Step 7: Assessing, Recording, and Sharing Results

Keeping detailed records is a key part of successful experimentation. Entering observations and measurements into a computer or project journal is a very good practice (figure 20.8). A simple tabular format is fine for most types of data and makes capturing and assessing the data easier.

While only one person is recording the data, others may contribute to subjective evaluations. Also, the person in charge of the research project may solicit the observations of other staff members and enter these observations in the journal as well.

Some experiments may focus on only one phase of growth, such as the germination phase. Many others will follow plants through all phases. Regardless, when the final phase is complete, it is important to assess the data and observations collected. Data must be organized to be interpreted. In many cases, data can be graphed to visually show differences among the controls. Any results should be shared with other staff and entered into the records. If the experiment focused on producing one species, the results need to be entered into the protocol notes for that species, even if no difference was observed. If a difference was observed, and one or more of the treatments resulted in better germination, survival, or quality than the

Figure 20.8—Keeping good records is a key part of successful experimentation. Photo by Tara Luna.

control, the experiment needs to be repeated at least once or twice more to verify the results. In the interim, however, the new production technique can tentatively become the new protocol. If, after a few repetitions, the same results are found, the new technique can be adopted as the official protocol.

If no difference was observed, or if the control treatment performed the best, that is still very valuable information. Keep good records in the plant protocol notes of what was tried, even if it failed. Otherwise, someone might think to try it again, wasting time, resources, and energy. In addition, noting ideas for future experiments is an important part of concluding the experiment.

Consider sharing your experimental results at nursery meetings, by submitting short papers to professional publications such as *Native Plants Journal*, or by uploading the information into the Native Plant Network (http://www.nativeplantnetwork.org).

Requesting Assistance When Needed

The ability to carry out your own experiments as described in this chapter is an empowering tool for improving plant growth, quality, and survival in your nursery. Experimenting can also help save you and your clients money and time over the years. Sometimes, however, an idea arises for a much-needed experiment that is beyond the scope of what you are comfortable exploring by yourself. Perhaps the idea is too complex, costly, or time-consuming or requires more intensive statistical analyses. If you believe your idea would benefit you and other growers like you, discuss the problem you are facing and the ideas for possible solutions with an extension specialist or someone at your local university. Often, researchers are interested in conducting research to help native plant growers

The final count of germinants from each replication of the control treatment is counted, and 26 out of 100 seeds germinated (table 20.1). For the seeds that were mechanically scarified, 79 of the 100 seeds germinated (79 percent) but there were no germinants for seeds treated with hot water at the end of the 4 weeks (table 20.1). A graph can be drawn to show cumulative germination on each day for each treatment (figure 20.9). For control seeds, cumulative germination increased at a constant rate throughout the 4 weeks of the trial and it appeared germination would continue to occur although the experiment had concluded. For seeds that were mechanically scarified, however, the graph indicates that most of the germinants emerged 3 to 8 days after sowing, with germination rates tapering off after the eighth day. This small trial showed that mechanical scarification yielded higher germination percentages and faster germination rates than the control. Although some variation existed from block to block, the differences among treatments within each block were similar indicating that the treatment results were not an isolated, chance event. As a result, the germination protocol for this species can be revised to include mechanical scarification as the seed treatment method.

The hot water treatment will also be noted in the protocol notes. Although a closely related species is known to respond well to hot water, the 20-sec treatment in 200 °F (93 °C) water on these seeds resulted in a 0-percent germination. It is likely that the 20-sec exposure was too long for this species—perhaps this species is smaller seeded than the related species described in the other protocol. A shorter time in the same temperature water or a lower water temperature could be tested to see if those treatments scarify the seeds effectively without harming them. A future experiment could include only 10 sec in 200 °F (93 °C) water or 20 sec in 170 °F (77 °C) water. If a large order for this species is received in the future, scarification will be very labor-intensive to do mechanically by hand. The notes about the hot water option, what did not work and what might work, will be a key piece of information for future discoveries.

In addition to the nursery's records, the manager publishes the experimental findings on the Native Plant Network (http://www.nativeplantnetwork.org) to help other growers who are learning to produce this species.

Table 20.1—Example experiment results.

Treatment	Seeds treated	Germinated
Control		
Block 1	25	8
Block 2	25	6
Block 3	25	5
Block 4	25	7
Total	100	26 (26%)
Mechanical nick		
Block 1	25	22
Block 2	25	19
Block 3	25	16
Block 4	25	21
Total	100	79 (79%)
Hot water		
Block 1	25	0
Block 2	25	0
Block 3	25	0
Block 4	25	0
Total	100	0 (0%)

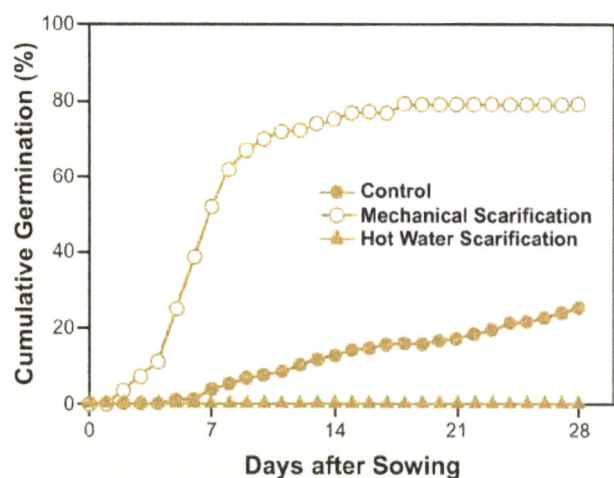

Figure 20.9—After the final germination count, a graph can be drawn from the table to show cumulative germination on each day. Illustration by Jim Marin.

Figure 20.10—*If an idea for an experiment is beyond the scope of what you are comfortable exploring yourself, get in touch with an extension agent or researcher. A nursery manager discussed the drawbacks of overhead irrigation of broad-leaved tropical plants—for example, these mahogany seedlings in Palau (A)—with a Forest Service nursery specialist. The specialist communicated the issue to researchers, who took up the challenge of testing and developing subirrigation systems for tropical nurseries (B). Photo A by Tara Luna and photo B by Douglass F. Jacobs.*

and may be glad to receive suggestions from a practitioner about what would be a useful study. For example, the sub-irrigation techniques for tropical plants described in Chapter 11, Water Quality and Irrigation, came about after a nursery manager discussed the challenges and drawbacks of overhead irrigation of broad-leaved tropical plants with a Forest Service nursery specialist. The grower suggested that it would be useful to have a way to water plants from below instead of from above to improve water-use efficiency for tropical nurseries. The nursery specialist was aware of subirrigation practices, but not of applications for tropical seedlings, and so he passed the idea along to researchers at Purdue University and in the Forest Service. The researchers developed and tested some uses of sub-

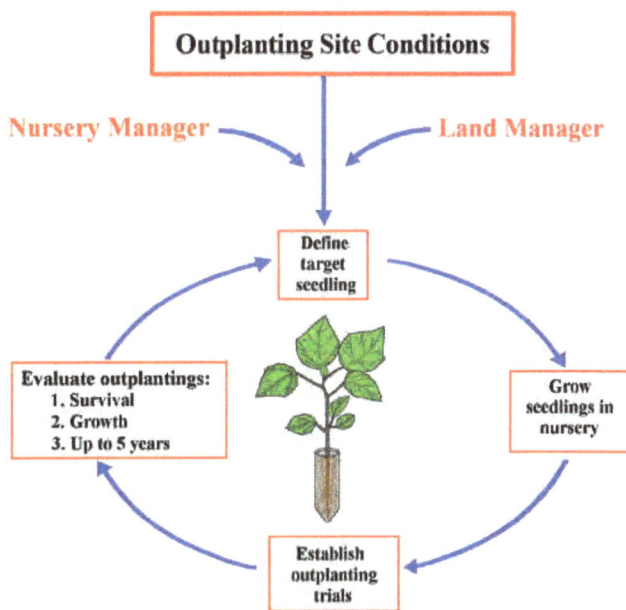

Figure 20.11—*Field testing and refining the target plant criteria for various sites and objectives is an important part of nursery management. Illustration by Jim Marin.*

irrigation with tropical tree seedlings (figure 20.10). The methods are promising and are being shared at nursery and native plant conferences and in publications (Dumroese and others 2007). This type of cooperation between practitioners and researchers benefits growers and researchers and their nursery plants. Because many researchers work to serve the public interest, make sure you mention how the study would be helpful not only for your nursery, but also for other growers of native plants.

Field Testing To Refine the Target Plant

Beyond experiments to improve nursery production, field testing, and improving the target plant criteria for various sites and objectives is an important part of nursery management. This testing was described in Chapter 3, Defining the Target Plant. At the beginning of a planting project, the land manager and the nursery manager agree on certain target morphological and physiological specifications for the plants the nursery will grow. These specifications are based on the eight-step assessment of site conditions, limiting factors, outplanting windows, and so on. After this prototype target plant is grown in the nursery, it is outplanted and monitored for survival and growth to assess its suitability for the site conditions. Both the nursery manager and the land manager learn from field monitoring (figure 20.11).

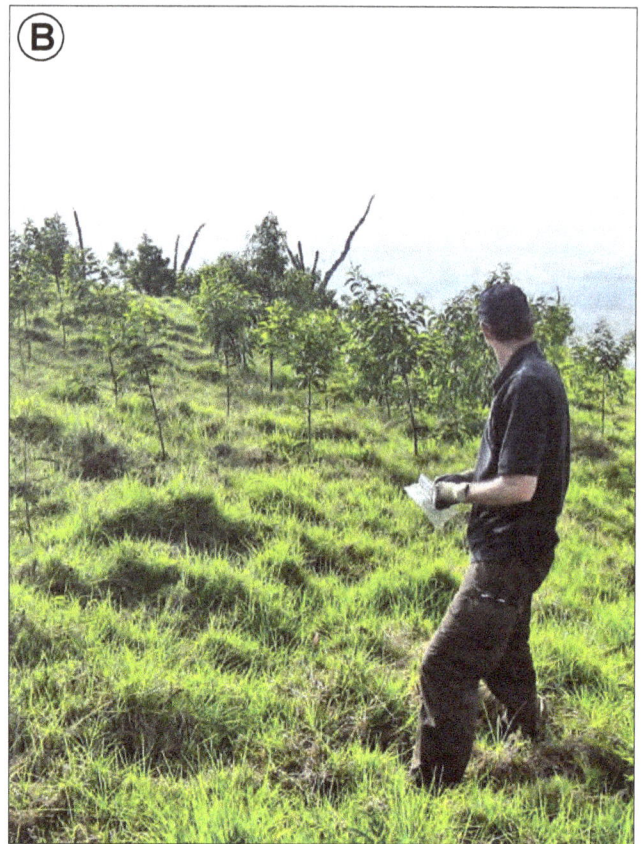

Figure 20.12—*The most useful measurements and observations after outplanting include plant growth rates (A,* Cedrela odorata *in Costa Rica) and survival (B,* Acacia koa *in Hawai'i). Photos by Douglass F. Jacobs.*

Plots need to be monitored during the first month or two after outplanting and again at the end of the first year for initial survival (figure 20.12). Subsequent checks after 3 and 5 years will give a good indication of plant growth and survival rates. The client and the nursery manager then use this performance information to refine the target plant specifications for the next crop. The client may also alter their outplanting practices to achieve better survival and growth based on this information.

Beyond Experiments: Learning Through Reflective Practice

Managing a nursery is a profession in which you will learn as much or more from your own experience as you will learn from books, classes, and other formal teaching. In addition, managing a nursery is both an art and a science. Much of this book has been about the science. This chapter's focus has been on learning from, and experimenting with, plants. Some types of learning, however, cannot come from controlled experiments; some learning comes from experience and reflection. The social, economic, and ecological context in which your nursery operates will change and shift over the years; your own motivations,

values, and strategies will also evolve as you grow personally and professionally. Making room in your schedule to reflect on larger experiences, observations, and questions allows you to learn from and adapt to these inner and outer changes; this is called "Reflective Practice" (Schön 1983).

Reflective practice is gaining use within many professions where learning from direct experience is as important as formal learning; the educational and medical professions are two examples (Wikipedia 2011). Reflective practice is valuable for nursery management and other environmental professions, providing time and space to question and refine beliefs, values, strategies, and practices and to reflect on the changes happening locally and globally. Reflective time enables the practitioner to improve results and to align work more fully over time with personal values and interests.

The question of how to continually learn from experience is an important one for nursery managers. Reading on the subject of reflective practice or taking a training can help you cultivate a reflective practice. The most important thing is to simply be aware of the value of reflection and make time to reflect regularly. Setting aside even 1 hour per week or month for uninterrupted reflection time can be invaluable. Taking this time can actually save time in the

With the different hats I wear at the nursery and in my community, I am busy. But I know the time I take to sit and reflect has helped me to adapt to the changing needs of the land and people on this island. Here are some ways I have adapted over the years:

I noticed that when many people came to visit the nursery, they wished to connect with the serene environment and the forest nearby, to simply enjoy the land and see native plants growing. I'm probably not the only nursery manager in the tropics who's had people come to visit and want to stay all day! I also enjoy sharing with my visitors. So, the question I contemplated was, how to share this environment yet still make a living? After a while, I found my solution. Right on the nursery grounds, I set up a retreat cottage for overnight stays, stocking it with all the creature comforts including local Kona coffee, plus field guides about our native birds and forests. I also began to offer guided forest walks to guests. This cottage has been a source of side income and given me a chance to share with visitors a deeper experience of the forest and the native plants growing in the nursery.

Most local restoration efforts 20 years ago, including mine, focused on our upland and cloud forests. Somehow we as a society were blind to the critical value of our endangered tropical dryland ecosystems. As the importance of dryland forests came on our radar, I did my research and learned ways to help restore these forests and to grow their plants. I now provide endemic dryland species including mamane, ulei, naio, lama, aweoweo, and many others that were not available commercially a decade ago. I also took on coordinating the Native Hawaiian Seed Bank Cooperative to help protect these and other native species by saving seed. This shift has been a good match between society's changing priorities, my conservation interests, and the needs of the land.

Although my passion is growing plants, I've long been concerned about helping the native wildlife that depend on these plants. I have taken time over the years to sit in observation in the local forests and watch the ways plants and birds associate with each other. I know birds that eat the manono with dark purple fruit, pilo with orange fruit, akala, the Hawaiian raspberry (figure 20.13A), and naio with white fruit. Observing the birds taught me to prioritize learning to grow their important habitat plants in my nursery. The observation and reflection also helps me to better understand processes and interactions in a diverse and healthy forest, to better mimic them in restoration of disturbed lands.

I don't know what the future will bring. But I know as I take time to reflect, learn, and stay aware of what is going on around me as well as within, my nursery will be able to evolve with the changing times.

—Jill Wagner, Forestry Consultant, Kailua Kona, HI
Owner, Future Forests Nursery, LLC
Coordinator, Hawai'i Island Native Seed Bank Cooperative

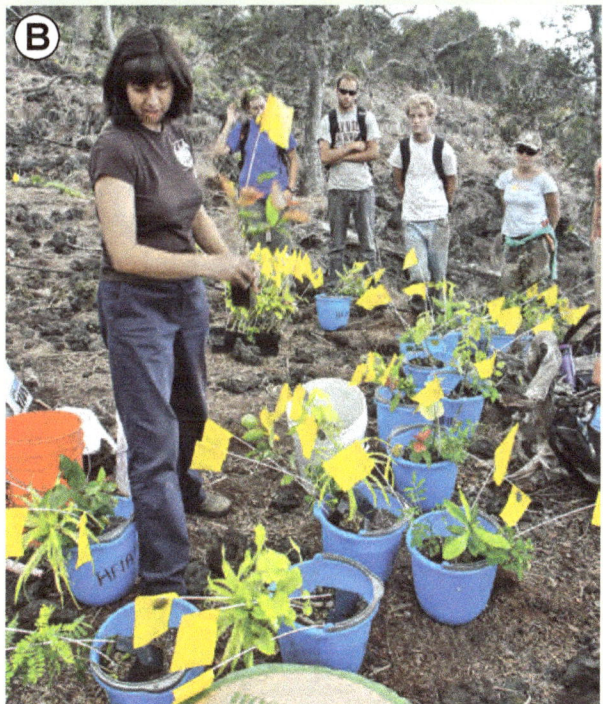

Figure 20.13—Ripe fruits of 'akala, the native Hawaiian raspberry (Rubus hawaiensis), observed to be an important food source for native birds (A). Jill Wagner at a dryland forest outplanting site (B). Photo A by J.B. Friday, and photo B by Yvonne Yarber Carter.

long run by raising awareness of inefficiencies and helping prioritize where to focus energy and resources. Examples of reflective practices include—

- Keeping a journal and reviewing it from time to time.
- Revisiting your nursery's vision statement, guiding principles, roles, and goals.
- Interacting with clients a few years after planting to follow up on the experience.
- Contemplating your own practices and beliefs, the results you are currently achieving, and your own dreams or ideas.
- Considering the changing community needs and public concerns, and how these criteria may align with your own values and the nursery's vision.
- Sitting and observing interactions in healthy ecosystems similar to the ecosystems you work to restore, and making notes of what you learned.
- Reviewing photos of your plants, projects, and nursery operations and reflecting on your thoughts and feelings.
- Taking time after a meeting or conference to sum up what you learned and what it might mean for you and your work.
- Sharing your insights with colleagues or friends.

Whether your nursery is large or small, for-profit, nonprofit, or public, reflective practice will help you continually learn, adapt, and evolve.

References

Dumroese, R.K.; Jacobs, D.F.; Davis, A.S.; Landis, T.D. 2007. An introduction to subirrigation in forest and conservation nurseries and some preliminary results of demonstrations. In: Riley, L.E.; Dumroese, R.K.; Landis, T.D., tech. coords. 2007. National proceedings: forest and conservation nursery associations—2006. Proc. RMRS-P-50. Fort Collins, CO: U.S. Department of Agriculture, Forest Service, Rocky Mountain Research Station: 20-26.

Dumroese, R.K.; Wenny, D.L. 2003. Installing a practical research project and interpreting research results. Tree Planters' Notes. 50(1): 18–22.

Dumroese, R.K.; Luna, T.; Landis, T.D. 2008. Nursery manual for native plants: volume 1, a guide for tribal nurseries. Agriculture Handbook 730. Washington, DC: U.S. Department of Agriculture, Forest Service. 302 p.

Lilleeng-Rosenberger, K.E. 2005. Growing Hawai'i's native plants: a simple step-by-step approach for every species. Honolulu: Mutual Publishing. 420 p.

Sagan, C. 1996. The demon-haunted world: science as a candle in the dark. New York: Ballantine Books: 480 p.

Schön D. 1983. The reflective practitioner: how professionals think in action. New York: Basic Books.

Wikipedia. 2011. Reflective practice. http://en.wikipedia.org/wiki/Reflective_practice. (November 2011).

Additional Reading

Landis, T.D.; Tinus, R.W.; McDonald, S.E.; Barnett, J.P. 1994. The container tree nursery manual: volume 1, nursery planning, development, and management. Agriculture Handbook 674. Washington, DC: U.S. Department of Agriculture, Forest Service. 188 p.

White, T. L. 1984. Designing nursery experiments. In Duryea, M.L.; Landis T.D. (eds.). 1984. Forest nursery manual: production of bareroot seedlings. Martinus Nijhoff/Dr W. Junk Publishers. The Hague/Boston/Lancaster, for Forest Research Laboratory. Corvallis: Oregon State University: 291-306.

www.ingramcontent.com/pod-product-compliance
Lightning Source LLC
Chambersburg PA
CBHW042337030426
42335CB00030B/3379